D1483633

1968: The World Transformed

1968: The World Transformed presents a global perspective on the tumultuous events of the most crucial year in the era of the Cold War. By interpreting 1968 as a transnational phenomenon, authors from Europe and the United States explain why the crises of 1968 erupted almost simultaneously throughout the world. Together, the eighteen chapters provide an interdisciplinary and comparative approach to the rise and fall of protest movements worldwide. The book represents an effort to integrate international relations, the role of the media, and the cross-cultural exchange of people and ideas into the history of 1968. That year emerges as a global phenomenon because of the linkages between domestic and international affairs, the powerful influence of the media, the networks of communication among activists, and the shared opposition to the domestic and international status quo in the name of freedom and self-determination.

Carole Fink is a professor of history at the Ohio State University in Columbus.

Philipp Gassert is a research fellow at the German Historical Institute in Washington, D.C.

Detlef Junker is a professor of history at the University of Heidelberg and the director of the German Historical Institute in Washington, D.C.

PUBLICATIONS OF THE GERMAN HISTORICAL INSTITUTE
WASHINGTON, D.C.

Edited by Detlef Junker
with the assistance of Daniel S. Mattern

1968: The World Transformed

THE GERMAN HISTORICAL INSTITUTE, WASHINGTON, D.C.

The German Historical Institute is a center for advanced study and research whose purpose is to provide a permanent basis for scholarly cooperation among historians from the Federal Republic of Germany and the United States. The Institute conducts, promotes, and supports research into both American and German political, social, economic, and cultural history, into transatlantic migration, especially in the nineteenth and twentieth centuries, and into the history of international relations, with special emphasis on the roles played by the United States and Germany.

Recent books in the series

Peter Graf Kielmansegg, Horst Mewes, and Elisabeth Glaser-Schmidt, editors, *Hannah Arendt and Leo Strauss: German Emigrés and American Political Thought After World War II*

Dirk Hoerder and Jörg Nagler, editors, *People in Transit: German Migrations in Comparative Perspective, 1820–1930*

R. Po-chia Hsia and Hartmut Lehmann, editors, *In and Out of the Ghetto: Jewish-Gentile Relations in Late Medieval and Early Modern Germany*

Sibylle Quack, editor, *Between Sorrow and Strength: Women Refugees of the Nazi Period*

Mitchell G. Ash and Alfons Söllner, editors, *Forced Migration and Scientific Change: Emigré German-Speaking Scientists and Scholars After 1933*

Manfred Berg and Geoffrey Cocks, editors, *Medicine and Modernity: Public Health and Medical Care in Nineteenth- and Twentieth-Century Germany*

Stig Förster and Jörg Nagler, editors, *On the Road to Total War: The American Civil War and the German Wars of Unification, 1861–1871*

Norbert Finzsch and Robert Jütte, editors, *Institutions of Confinement: Hospitals, Asylums, and Prisons in Western Europe and North America, 1500–1950*

David E. Barclay and Elisabeth Glaser-Schmidt, editors, *Transatlantic Images and Perceptions: Germany and America Since 1776*

Norbert Finzsch and Dietmar Schirmer, editors, *Identity and Intolerance: Nationalism, Racism, and Xenophobia in Germany and the United States*

Susan Strasser, Charles McGovern, and Matthias Judt, editors, *Getting and Spending: European and American Consumer Societies in the Twentieth Century*

Manfred F. Boemeke, Gerald D. Feldman, and Elisabeth Glaser, editors, *The Treaty of Versailles: A Reassessment After 75 Years*

1968: The World Transformed

Edited by
CAROLE FINK, PHILIPP GASSERT, *and* DETLEF JUNKER

GERMAN HISTORICAL INSTITUTE

Washington, D.C.

and

 **CAMBRIDGE**
UNIVERSITY PRESS

PUBLISHED BY THE PRESS SYNDICATE OF THE UNIVERSITY OF CAMBRIDGE
The Pitt Building, Trumpington Street, Cambridge CB2 1RP, United Kingdom

CAMBRIDGE UNIVERSITY PRESS
The Edinburgh Building, Cambridge CB2 2RU, UK   http://www.cup.cam.ac.uk
40 West 20th Street, New York, NY 10011-4211, USA   http://www.cup.org
10 Stamford Road, Oakleigh, Melbourne 3166, Australia

First published 1998

Printed in the United States of America

Typeset in Bembo 11/13 pt. in QuarkXPress [BB]

A catalog record for this book is available from the British Library.

Library of Congress Cataloging-in-Publication Data
1968 : the world transformed / edited by Carole Fink, Philipp Gassert,
and Detlef Junker.
p. cm. – (Publications of the German Historical Institute)
Papers from a conference organized by the German Historical
Institute.
Includes index.
ISBN 0-521-64141-1 (hardcover : alk. paper). – ISBN 0-521-64637-5
(pbk. : alk. paper)
1. World politics – 1965–1975 – Congresses.   I. Fink, Carole, 1940–
. II. Gassert, Philipp.   III. Junker, Detlef.   IV. German
Historical Institute (Washington, D.C.)   V. Series.
D839.2.A17   1998
909.82 – dc21   98-23253

ISBN 0-521-64141-1 hardback
ISBN 0-521-64637-5 paperback

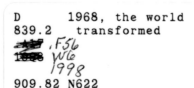

Contents

Preface

This book grew out of a conference organized by the German Historical Institute (GHI) on May 23–5, 1996, in Berlin. For three days, thirty-five scholars from nine countries became *acht-und-sechziger* (sixty-eighters), not on the streets and barricades but in lively debate over the events and significance of the momentous year 1968. This book consists of revised versions of many of the original papers as well as entirely new essays that complement our overall theme. I thank all of the authors and also those who participated in the conference but whose work could not be included here. I am grateful to Carl-Ludwig Holtfrerich (Free University Berlin), Luisa Passerini (European University Institute, Florence), Keith A. Reader (University of Newcastle), and Dieter Rucht (Wissenschaftszentrum Berlin) for chairing the various sessions and for guiding us through spirited discussions.

In Berlin, the Wissenschaftszentrum afforded a comfortable setting for three days of intensive debate. I thank Friedhelm Neidhardt, the center's director, and his dedicated staff – Birgit Hahn, Britta Heinrich, Ilse Kischlat, Dietmar Kremser, and Burckhard Wiebe – for hosting the conference and helping with its organization. Dieter Senoner of the mayor's office kindly welcomed us to Berlin at a reception at the Rotes Rathaus. Anneke de Rudder, who took us on a "1968 Walking Tour" through the German capital, gave us the opportunity to visit the key sites of that historic year.

At the GHI, I thank Bärbel Bernhardt, Christa Brown, Dieter Schneider, and Bärbel Thomas – all of whom were involved in the organization before, during, and after the conference. Pamela Abraham tracked down the copyrights for the illustrations and assisted in assembling the manuscript. Daniel S. Mattern, the series editor at the Institute, deserves a special note of appreciation for guiding us through the difficult process of publishing this collection and for preparing a readable, clear, and concise manuscript. Frank Smith, the executive editor for social sciences at Cambridge University Press, took great interest in this project from the beginning and helped bring about its final shape. Further, I thank the two anonymous readers for their very useful critical evaluations of the manuscript.

Finally, I thank my two coeditors. Carole Fink provided the original plan, which she presented to me at another GHI conference, in Berkeley, California, in May 1994. In subsequent discussions, we discovered that "1968" is a particularly well-suited topic for understanding the intellectual challenges that increasing global interdependence poses to historians of the twentieth century. We were later joined by Philipp Gassert, who worked with us to organize the conference and edit the book. I shall miss these last three and a half years of spirited collaboration among three very engaged historians.

The topic of this book dovetails nicely with the efforts of the GHI in Washington to promote comparative research. In fact, most of the four to five international conferences the Institute organizes annually are based on this perspective, comparing events, ideas, and structures in the United States and Europe. At times we have even taken a global perspective, with *1968: The World Transformed* being a case in point. In this age of globalization, historians should also become global players – at least mentally.

Washington, D.C.   DETLEF JUNKER
April 1998

Contributors

Manfred Berg is an associate professor of history at the John F. Kennedy Institute, Free University of Berlin.

Alan Brinkley is a professor of history at Columbia University.

Arif Dirlik is a professor of history at Duke University.

Jerzy Eisler is the director of the Ecole Polonaise in Paris.

Carole Fink is a professor of history at the Ohio State University.

Philipp Gassert is a research fellow at the German Historical Institute, Washington, D.C.

Ingrid Gilcher-Holtey is a professor of history at the University of Bielefeld.

George C. Herring is a professor of history at the University of Kentucky, Lexington.

Stuart J. Hilwig is a doctoral candidate in history at the Ohio State University.

Gerd-Rainer Horn is an associate professor of history at Western Oregon University.

Konrad H. Jarausch is a professor of history at the University of North Carolina at Chapel Hill.

Detlef Junker is the director of the German Historical Institute, Washington, D.C.

Mark Kramer is the director of the Cold War Studies Program at the Davis Center for Russian Studies at Harvard University.

Diane B. Kunz is an associate professor of history at Yale University.

Claus Leggewie is a visiting professor at New York University.

Bernhard Maleck teaches at the Institute for European Studies, Berlin.

Eva Maleck-Lewy is the scholarly director of the Women's Academy for Arts and Sciences, Berlin.

Harold Marcuse is an assistant professor of history at the University of California at Santa Barbara.

Gottfried Niedhart is a professor of history at the University of Mannheim.

Chester J. Pach Jr. is a professor of history at Ohio University.

Nancy Bernkopf Tucker is a professor of history at Georgetown University.

Lawrence S. Wittner is a professor of history at the State University of New York at Albany.

Introduction

CAROLE FINK, PHILIPP GASSERT, AND DETLEF JUNKER

Nineteen sixty-eight, the year of global crisis halfway between the end of World War II and the end of the Cold War, has yet to establish a solid position in contemporary history – either in the recollections of the participants or in the interpretations of two generations of scholars. The memories of witnesses to the events of this *annus mirabilis* are still fragmentary and colored by partisanship, personal injury and defeat, or nostalgia for a heroic time, whereas historians have barely begun to treat "1968" as a coherent historical phenomenon.

The events of 1968 happened within national contexts yet took place across the globe – from Berkeley to Berlin, Bangkok to Buenos Aires, Cairo to Cape Town, Paris to Tokyo. In addition, many contemporaries – particularly students and intellectuals – believed that their actions were linked to a global revolt against capitalism, imperialism, and colonialism that spanned the First, Second, and Third Worlds. People everywhere recognized and responded to photographs, films, tales, and written accounts that spread around the world by word of mouth, in newspapers, or over radio and television, depicting wars and civil wars, strikes and protests, student demonstrations, and police repression.

Although no organized international movement existed in 1968, there were many informal links of sympathy and support among the hundreds of protest movements that sprang up around the world. Yet despite the widespread contemporary belief that the year was one of global crisis, scholars studying this year have focused more on its national than on its international elements. There are relatively few comparative studies of the rise and fall of protest movements from a regional or global perspective[1] and scarcely

---

1 Gianni Statera, *Death of a Utopia: The Development and Decline of Student Movements in Europe* (Oxford, 1975); Cyrill Levitt, *Children of Privilege: Student Revolt in the Sixties: A Study of Student Movements in Canada, the United States, and West Germany* (Toronto, 1984); George Katsiaficas, *The Imagination of the*

I

any comprehensive accounts of 1968 as a global phenomenon.[2] To date, no work has incorporated the ruptures in world politics within a systematic analysis of the events of 1968.

Until recently, 1968 has largely been the domain of social and cultural historians. In this book, the editors and contributors have tried to integrate international relations, the role of the media, the cross-cultural exchange of peoples, and the history of ideas into a wide-ranging examination of that tumultuous year. By interpreting 1968 as a global or transnational phenomenon, we propose to explain the simultaneity of the crises that erupted throughout the world. By stressing the international dimension, we hope to stimulate further comparative research on the global history of 1968.[3]

This book represents a collaborative effort by an international group of historians. It presents diverse perspectives on 1968, including some that dispute each other and even challenge our major theses. In this introduction, we suggest four theses that underscore the significance of international and transnational developments.

First, the events of 1968 unfolded at a crucial phase in the Cold War. The long bipolar rivalry between the two superpowers had created a peculiar linkage between domestic and international affairs, between social and cultural developments, on the one hand, and world politics, on the other. As a result of the complex set of relationships that existed in the international system, fundamental shifts on the local, national, or global level resonated with and grew out of each other.

Second, 1968 was a global phenomenon because the mass media – television and the press in the First World, radio and film in the Second and Third Worlds – exerted a powerful influence and became instruments of social movements worldwide. The media created transnational and inter-

New Left: A Global Analysis of 1968 (Boston, 1987); Ronald Fraser, *1968: A Student Generation in Revolt* (New York, 1988); Peppino Ortoleva, *Saggio sui movimenti del 1968 in Europa e in America* (Rome, 1988); Philip G. Altbach, ed., *Student Political Activism: An International Reference Handbook* (New York, 1989); Seymour Martin Lipset, *Rebellion in the University,* with a new introduction by the author (New Brunswick, N.J., 1993); Ingo Juchler, *Die Studentenbewegungen in den Vereinigten Staaten und der Bundesrepublik Deutschland der sechziger Jahre: Eine Untersuchung hinsichtlich ihrer Beeinflussung durch Befreiungsbewegungen und -theorien aus der Dritten Welt* (Berlin, 1996).

2 David Caute, *The Year of the Barricades: A Journey Through 1968* (New York, 1988); Robert V. Daniels, *Year of the Heroic Guerrilla: World Revolution and Counterrevolution in 1968* (New York, 1988); Etienne Francois, *1968 – ein europäisches Jahr* (Leipzig, 1997).

3 *Historical* comparisons of the movements of 1968 are still very rare. Most comparative studies take a social scientist approach; see Friedhelm Neidhart and Dieter Rucht, "The Analysis of Social Movements: The State of the Art and Some Perspectives of Further Research," in Dieter Rucht, ed., *Research on Social Movements: The State of the Art in Western Europe and the USA* (Boulder, Colo., 1991), 421–64.

cultural linkages, giving the "1968ers" the impression that they were part of a united political front.

Third, activists throughout the world operated as part of formal and informal networks of communication and collaboration. Thus, 1968 was a global phenomenon because of the actual and perceived cooperation among protest movements in different countries.

Fourth, 1968 was a global phenomenon because the protagonists believed in a common cause: They struggled in opposition to the domestic and international status quo in East and West as well as in North and South, and in support of freedom, justice, and self-determination. In the Communist world, they fought against authoritarian governments and for liberal democracy; in the West, they fought against social repression, hierarchical structures, the tyranny of consumption, for personal emancipation and "true" participatory democracy.

WORLD POLITICS AND THE WORLD ECONOMY

Nineteen sixty-eight was a major watershed in the history of the Cold War, marking the climax of a period of confrontation and the beginning of the era of détente. "Tet" and "Prague" forced both superpowers and their allies to weigh the consequences of American and Soviet imperialism, to examine the framework of the postwar order, to rethink their own national interests, and to renew efforts to strengthen international stability.

With the double shocks of Tet and the United States's mounting financial problems, the Johnson administration was compelled to face the realities of imperial overstretch and the huge costs of its global foreign policy. The validity of the two sacred maxims of America's Cold War diplomacy, the Truman Doctrine and the domino theory, were called into question. Since 1947, the first had provided justification for intervention against communist threats; and the second, harking back to the "lessons of Munich" that aggressors must be stopped early on and on all fronts, became a rigid formula that presumed military force to be the only option.[4]

As George C. Herring has written, it was the founding fathers of containment policy – Acheson, Clifford, Harriman, Nitze, and others – who tried during the crisis of March 1968 to convince Lyndon B. Johnson to

---

4 Melvyn P. Leffler, *A Preponderance of Power: National Security, the Truman Administration, and the Cold War* (Stanford, Calif., 1992); Frank Ninkovich, *Modernity and Power: A History of the Domino Theory in the Twentieth Century* (Chicago, 1994).

alter his policy on Vietnam. Arguing against the hawks and the military, which wanted to commit more troops, they urged the president to withdraw gradually from Vietnam and concentrate on America's strategic interests in Europe, Japan, the Middle East, and Latin America.[5] This realpolitik critique of the Manichaean Cold War perspective provided the basis for Richard Nixon's concept of American diplomacy. Faced with an unwinnable war, Nixon and his foreign policy advisor, Henry Kissinger, proceeded to revise the dogmas of containment policy and bipolarism.[6] In order to establish a more stable international order and reduce America's burdens, they forged a "triangular diplomacy" that aimed to create a new multipolar structure that would include the Soviet Union, China, Japan, and Europe.[7]

In 1968 Johnson still lacked the will and the imagination to break with containment policy because he feared becoming the "new Chamberlain." When the "wise men" of the Cold War changed their minds about the war in Southeast Asia, he protested bitterly that "the establishment bastards have bailed out."[8] As he had done throughout his long political career, Johnson sought a middle ground between hawks and doves. As a concession to the hawks, he slightly raised the number of troops in Vietnam, and as a concession to the doves and the general public, he ordered a partial halt to air attacks over North Vietnam and prepared new peace initiatives. Hoping to mollify domestic opinion, Johnson withdrew as a candidate for a second term. Thus, the massive, if ultimately unsuccessful, Tet Offensive by the combined North Vietnamese and Vietcong, coupled with the economic shocks that shook the United States in March 1968, not only aroused public opinion and instigated a major debate over strategy but also prepared the way for a fundamental reevaluation of America's role in the Cold War.[9]

At the same time as the domino theory was losing its plausibility and moral legitimacy in Vietnam, the Soviet Union ordered the tanks and troops of the Warsaw Pact into Prague, Czechoslovakia, in August 1968. Acting

---

5 See the essay by George C. Herring (Chapter 1) in this book.
6 Raymond L. Garthoff, *Détente and Confrontation: American-Soviet Relations from Nixon to Reagan* (Washington, D.C., 1985), 25–36; Robert D. Schulzinger, *Henry Kissinger: Doctor of Diplomacy* (New York, 1989); Richard C. Thornton, *The Nixon-Kissinger Years: The Reshaping of America's Foreign Policy* (New York, 1989); Joan Hoff, *Nixon Reconsidered* (New York, 1994), 147–207.
7 On the new "triangular diplomacy," which was by and large grounded in Kissinger's view of nineteenth-century history, see Henry Kissinger, *Diplomacy* (New York, 1994), 703–32.
8 See Herring's chapter, 44.
9 Robert D. Schulzinger, "'It's Easy to Win a War on Paper': The United States and Vietnam, 1961–1968," in Diane B. Kunz, ed., *The Diplomacy of the Crucial Decade: American Foreign Relations During the 1960s* (New York, 1994), 183–218; Warren I. Cohen and Nancy Bernkopf Tucker, eds., *Lyndon Johnson Confronts the World: American Foreign Policy, 1963–1968* (Cambridge, 1994).

on its own domino theory, the politburo in Moscow and its Eastern European allies were increasingly concerned over the possible spread of an "anti-socialist bacillus" into Poland, the German Democratic Republic (GDR), Hungary, and the other Eastern European states as well as into Ukraine, Moldavia, Georgia, the Baltic states, and perhaps even into Russia itself. Brezhnev suspected that the students and intellectuals of the Soviet Union would form the counterrevolutionary vanguard.[10]

Moscow also feared that some of the more independent members of the Warsaw Pact were on the verge of establishing closer ties with the West, particularly with "revanchist-capitalist" West Germany. Moreover, there was the danger that a weakened Czechoslovak army, less controlled by the Soviet Union, would be incapable of guarding a sensitive stretch of the Iron Curtain and might even endanger the planned stationing of Soviet nuclear weapons on Czechoslovak soil. As Mark Kramer makes clear in his chapter, the Prague Spring threatened to create a "spillover" effect involving the vital interests of the Soviet Union and the future of socialism. With the invasion of Czechoslovakia and the proclamation of the Brezhnev Doctrine, the Soviet Union cemented the status quo in Eastern Europe without solving – and to some extent even exacerbating – its security and economic problems. Thus, like the United States, it was now prepared for a shift in its foreign policy, replacing its hard-line stance toward the United States and its allies with steps that would lead to détente.[11]

Perhaps the most striking example of the interconnectedness in world politics and of the links between foreign and domestic policy in 1968 was China's reaction to both Tet and Prague. One month after Mao Zedong ordered his Red Guards to reduce the chaos of the "Great Proletarian Cultural Revolution," which had already claimed millions of casualties, he expressed shock at the invasion of Czechoslovakia and at the subsequent proclamation of the Brezhnev Doctrine. The leadership in Beijing feared that their country's weakness might encourage Moscow to apply its new doctrine by sending Soviet troops into the contested northern border areas, making nuclear threats, and generally threatening China's independence and international status. According to Nancy Bernkopf Tucker, it was the invasion of Czechoslovakia that convinced Mao to back away from the Cultural Revolution.[12]

10 See the essay by Mark Kramer (Chapter 4) in this book; Wladimir K. Wolkow, "Sowjetische Parteiherrschaft und Prager Frühling 1968," *Aus Politik und Zeitgeschichte,* B36, Aug. 28, 1992, 11–17.
11 Garthoff, *Détente and Confrontation,* 36–53.
12 See the essay by Nancy Bernkopf Tucker (Chapter 6) in this book. On Sino-Soviet Relations in the aftermath of Prague, see also Garthoff, *Détente and Confrontation,* 200–13.

At the same time, the Chinese leadership began its search for a powerful diplomatic ally, the enemy of its enemy so to speak, following "the ancient tradition of using barbarians to control barbarians."[13] In the bipolar world of superpowers, there was only one barbarian capable of neutralizing the Soviet threat and easing Beijing's concerns over the security of its northern frontier: the United States of America. Although the U.S.-Chinese confrontation in Vietnam might have hindered this rapprochement, the scaling down of American involvement after Tet was duly registered in Beijing. Thus, China's invitation to the United States in November 1968 to resume talks in Warsaw marked the beginning of a significant change in its diplomacy, culminating in Nixon's sensational journey of 1972, the first visit of an American president to China, indeed to Communist China.[14]

The invasion of Czechoslovakia also had important strategic consequences in the heart of Europe, especially for the Federal Republic of Germany. The Germans, other Europeans, and the Chinese – as well as the Russians – were astonished by the extraordinarily mild reaction of the United States to this naked display of Soviet power. Indeed, when Soviet Ambassador Anatoly Dobrynin personally delivered the news to President Johnson, he was relieved to discover that Johnson's chief concern was the danger to his scheduled summit meeting with Brezhnev, which had been planned to coincide with his departure from office. Apparently Johnson never considered using American troops for a "rollback" in East-Central Europe.[15]

Nineteen sixty-eight confirmed once again what the world had learned during the East German uprising in 1953, the risings in Poland and Hungary in 1956, and the building of the Berlin Wall in 1961, namely, that the United States was unprepared and unwilling to risk a world war, or even a nuclear war, to assail the Iron Curtain. Indeed, after the dual crises over Berlin and Cuba between 1958 and 1962, the United States increasingly defined its strategic interests in terms of accepting the status quo in Europe and pursuing arms control agreements with the Soviet Union. Shortly before the invasion of Czechoslovakia both superpowers, together with Britain, had signed what was perhaps the most important status quo agreement of the Cold War. In the Nonproliferation Treaty of July 1, 1968, these three countries had attempted to secure their nuclear monopoly and

---

13 See Tucker's chapter, 202.
14 On Nixon's carefully staged journey to China and the secret negotiations since 1968, see Walter Isaacson, *Kissinger: A Biography* (New York, 1992), 333–54; Garthoff, *Détente and Confrontation,* 213–40; Hoff, *Nixon Reconsidered,* 187–91.
15 Anatoly Dobrynin, *In Confidence: Moscow's Ambassador to America's Six Cold War Presidents, 1962–1986* (New York, 1995), 180ff.

prevent the uncontrolled proliferation of atomic weapons in order to create a rational system of deterrence. For example, the three powers were united in opposition to granting West Germany access to nuclear weapons.[16]

According to Gottfried Niedhart, the United States' tacit acceptance of the Soviet invasion convinced the Bonn government that the question of German unification had vanished from the agenda of world politics, a sacrifice for the benefit of European security and harmony between the two superpowers.[17] If the invasion of Czechoslovakia strengthened West Germany's resolve to revise the strategic orientation of its diplomacy, it also enabled the Soviet Union to embark on substantive talks with Bonn. The kernel of the Federal Republic's new Ostpolitik, which by 1972 produced a series of major treaties, was a subtle dialectic that even Kissinger did not completely understand. West Germany's diplomacy toward Eastern Europe followed the model Gustav Stresemann had successfully applied to Western Europe in the 1920s, that is, to undermine the status quo over the long term one had to acquiesce in the short term.[18] By acknowledging existing realities, the Federal Republic was able to establish itself as one of the leading forces of détente; at the same time, it also bound the Soviet Union to a relationship that might eventually lead to German unification.[19] Moreover, Ostpolitik not only enhanced the flexibility of West Germany's diplomacy toward East and West but also gave Bonn a small measure of independence vis-à-vis the United States and its other NATO allies.[20] Thus, although the world political events of 1968 appeared to reinforce the rigid structure of the Cold War, they also prepared the basis for its end two decades later.

With regard to the world economy, 1968 signaled the close of the postwar economic era. Although economic trends and cycles cannot be linked directly to politics, certain political decisions that were made between 1968

16 Wolfram F. Hanrieder, *Germany, America, Europe: Forty Years of German Foreign Policy* (New Haven, Conn., 1989), 91–5; Matthias Künzel, *Bonn und die Bombe: Deutsche Atomwaffenpolitik von Adenauer bis Brandt* (Frankfurt am Main, 1992).
17 See the essay by Gottfried Niedhart (Chapter 5) in this book.
18 On Stresemann's foreign policy see Marshall Lee and Wolfgang Michalka, *German Foreign Policy, 1917–1933: Continuity or Break?* (Leamington Spa, 1987), 73–85; Manfred Berg, *Gustav Stresemann und die Vereinigten Staaten von Amerika: Weltwirtschaftliche Verflechtung und Revisionspolitik 1907–1929* (Baden-Baden, 1990); Christian Baechler, *Gustav Stresemann (1878–1929): De l'impérialisme à la sécurité collective* (Strasbourg, 1996), 469–902.
19 As Egon Bahr, Federal Chancellor Willy Brandt's foreign policy advisor, wrote in a memorandum on October 1, 1968, "The Soviet goal is to legalize the status quo. Our goal is to overcome it. It is a real conflict of interest." Quoted by Niedhart in Chapter 5 of this volume; on Brandt's and Bahr's foreign policy, see also Andreas Vogtmeier, *Egon Bahr und die deutsche Frage: Zur Entwicklung der sozialdemokratischen Ost- und Deutschlandpolitik vom Kriegsende bis zur Vereinigung* (Bonn, 1996).
20 Hanrieder, *Germany, America, Europe*, 195–219; Timothy Garton Ash, *In Europe's Name: Germany and the Divided Continent* (London, 1993); Frank Ninkovich, *Germany and the United States: The Transformation of the German Question Since 1945,* rev. ed. (New York, 1995), 136–43.

and 1973–4 undoubtedly precipitated the end of the unparalleled growth of the post–World War II period. It was not possible to explore fully these issues in greater detail in this book, but it should be noted that within the crucial half decade between 1968 and 1973 the first visible signs of a major change in the world economy became apparent. After the Six-Day War of 1967, the oil-producing countries seized the initiative from the powerful multinational corporations in defense of their own national economic and political interests.[21] The oil-price shocks of 1973–4 marked the end of a quarter century of growth and the "easy affluence" to which Western societies had become accustomed.[22]

The economic turbulence of 1968 represented a major challenge to America's dominant position in the world economy. In 1968 the world saw "the most serious economic crisis since the Great Depression."[23] As Diane B. Kunz notes, President Johnson had committed the United States to costly domestic and military expenditures without raising adequate revenue through taxation. Through the international capital markets, America's European and Asian allies paid for Washington's mounting budget deficits. The results – rising prices, a weakened dollar, and chronic trade and payments imbalances – threatened the stability of the international exchange and currency system that had existed since 1945.[24]

America's growing weakness had become manifest as early as the summer of 1967, when Washington asked Bonn not to exchange its dollar reserves for gold.[25] Although the United States remained Western Europe's military shield against the Soviet Union, it could not prolong its beggar-thy-neighbor economic policies, which French President Charles de Gaulle had already challenged. The dramatic gold crisis of March 1968, coupled with the Tet Offensive, forced the United States to devise temporary alterations that ultimately led to the end of the Bretton Woods system.[26] It was

21 Daniel Yergin, *The Prize: The Epic Quest for Oil, Money, and Power* (New York, 1991); Jens Hohensee, *Der erste Ölpreisschock 1973/74: Die politischen und gesellschaftlichen Auswirkungen der arabischen Erdölpolitik auf die Bundesrepublik Deutschland und Westeuropa* (Stuttgart, 1996).
22 Hermann van der Wee, *Prosperity and Upheaval: The War Economy, 1945–1980* (London, 1987); Robert M. Collins, "Growth Liberalism in the Sixties: Great Societies at Home and Grand Designs Abroad," in David Farber, ed., *The Sixties: From Memory to History* (Chapel Hill, N.C., 1994), 11–44; see also the essays by Diane B. Kunz (Chapter 3) and Alan Brinkley (Chapter 7) in this book.
23 Robert M. Collins, "The Economic Crisis of 1968 and the Waning of the 'American Century'" *American Historical Review* 101, no. 2 (April 1996): 396.
24 See Kunz's chapter; Carl-Ludwig Holtfrerich and Hans-Otto Schötz, *Vom Weltgläubiger zum Weltschuldner: Erklärungsansätze zur historischen Entwicklung und Struktur der internationalen Vermögensposition der USA* (Frankfurt am Main, 1988).
25 On this so-called Blessing-Brief, see Diane B. Kunz, *Butter and Guns: America's Cold War Economic Diplomacy* (New York, 1997), 173–4.
26 Kunz, *Butter and Guns,* 192–222.

no coincidence that President Nixon in 1969 curtailed the grand project epitomizing the optimism of the early 1960s, namely, the Apollo space program, after public and congressional support for the immensely costly manned space program had waned and after the rivalry between the super-powers had given way to a more cooperative approach.[27]

Ironically, the Soviet Union reaped few benefits from these convulsions in the world economy. Since the early 1960s it had been forced to purchase the compliance of its allies – and their populations' grudging acquiescence – by a "goulash communism" that substituted consumer benefits for a personal and national freedom. After 1968, Moscow finally had to bury its hopes of equaling or surpassing the West. The invasion of Czechoslovakia further strained the economic and military resources of the Soviet empire and would ultimately contribute to its collapse.[28] Thus, the global economic upheaval begun in 1968 reduced both superpowers' room for maneuver and reinforced the trend toward cooperation, bridge-building, and détente.[29] After Tet and Prague, the two Cold War empires moved closer together out of mutual need to scale down their huge commitments while maintaining control over their respective allies. This had the paradoxical result of encour-aging new forms of independence among the latter and of enabling the for-mer vanquished countries, particularly Germany and Japan, to emerge as new global economic players in their own right.[30]

THE ROLE OF THE MEDIA

In 1968, the crises in the institutions of military, political, and financial power and the growing opposition movement in the streets, factories, and universities was covered by a media with an almost global reach. The events of Tet and Prague, Chicago and Tokyo, as well as the images of Ho Chi Minh and Dubček, Lyndon Johnson and Charles de Gaulle elicited instant recognition and immediate responses by people in places far and near. The protest movements adopted and transformed these icons in and through

---

27 Walter A. McDougall, . . . *the Heavens and the Earth: A Political History of the Space Age* (New York, 1985), 421–3.
28 See Valerie Bunce, "The Empire Strikes Back: The Transformation of the Eastern Bloc from a Soviet Asset to a Soviet Liability," *International Organization* 39 (1984–5): 1–46; Randall W. Stone, *Satellites and Commissars: Strategy and Conflict in the Politics of Soviet-Bloc Trade* (Princeton, N.J., 1996). See also the chapter by Kramer.
29 Keith L. Nelson, *The Making of Détente: Soviet-American Relations in the Shadow of Vietnam* (Balti-more, 1995).
30 See Lothar Kettenacker, *Germany Since 1945* (Oxford, 1997); Paul John Baily, *Postwar Japan: 1945 to the Present* (Oxford, 1996).

their chants and posters. Even when the students' demands addressed issues specific to their own country, they were expressed and disseminated through global means of communication.[31]

In Western countries, the media, traditionally pillars of the establishment, became powerful instruments of protest movements. The participants, with their graffiti and slogans, their strikes and boycotts, their sit-ins and teach-ins, their marches and demonstrations, their happenings and audacious antics, relied on the media to reinforce and spread their messages. As Konrad H. Jarausch points out, the mythic events and collective memories of 1968 were often the joint creation of sensationalist media and manipulative demonstrators, which used each other for self-enhancement.[32]

In the West, the dominant medium in 1968 was television. This was particularly true for the United States, which during the 1960s had become a "televisual society."[33] Eddie Adams's photograph of the execution of a Vietcong suspect by the police chief of Saigon, reproduced millions of times in newspapers and on television, became a major factor in undermining the shaky domestic consensus on the Vietnam War.[34] In Asia, the American army and its South Vietnamese ally were engaged in a slow and painful, but in the end successful, military counteroffensive against the North Vietnamese. At home, however, the widely disseminated photographs of Tet undermined Johnson's policies and, ultimately, his presidency. Lyndon B. Johnson, the most powerful figure in the world, who had amassed some of his fortune in the media, utterly miscalculated their power. This despite the fact that Johnson had been the guiding political spirit behind the Apollo program, one of America's greatest technological and public-relations triumphs. Johnson, who in his optimistic press announcements of 1967 had prematurely raised expectations of "victory," lost control of the media debate in 1968.[35] The result of the coverage of Tet was not simply a change in U.S. public opinion and a renewed intensity of the anti–Vietnam War demonstrations. By remaining an almost passive

31 Todd Gitlin, *The Whole World Is Watching: Mass Media in the Making and Unmaking of the New Left* (Berkeley, Calif., 1980); Rüdiger Schmitt-Beck, "Über die Bedeutung der Massenmedien für soziale Bewegungen," *Kölner Zeitschrift für Soziologie und Sozialpsychologie* 42 (1992): 642–62.
32 See the essays by Konrad H. Jarausch (Chapter 18) and Stuart J. Hilwig (Chapter 12) in this book.
33 Chester J. Pach Jr., "And That's the Way It Was: The Vietnam War on the Network Nightly News," in Farber, ed., *The Sixties*, 92.
34 See the reproduction of this photograph in the essay by Chester J. Pach Jr. (Chapter 2) in this book; Robert Hamilton, "Image and Context: The Production and Reproduction of the *The Execution of a VC Suspect* by Eddie Adams," in Jeffrey Walsh and James Aulich, eds., *Vietnam Images: War and Representation* (New York, 1989), 171–83.
35 On the debate over the role of the media in Vietnam, see the introduction to Marc Jason Gilbert and William Head, *The Tet Offensive* (Westport, Conn., 1996).

observer of the news from Vietnam that it seemed unable to refute, the White House conveyed an aura of indecision and powerlessness.[36]

The dramatic visual images of the war in Vietnam transformed political opinion in the United States and abroad. Large segments of the American public became convinced that the war could not be won without a huge commitment of troops and money. Furthermore, Tet had a "most dramatic political and inspirational impact on the student world everywhere," as Ronald Fraser concludes in his oral history of 1968.[37] Supported by student activists, the antiwar candidate Eugene McCarthy came close to defeating the president in the New Hampshire Democratic primary; shortly afterward Johnson withdrew from the campaign to concentrate all his resources on pursuing peace in Vietnam.[38] Across the Atlantic, the photographs of Tet dramatically changed people's perceptions of the war and tarnished the once shining image of the United States. One British student remembered that "the [Tet] Offensive completely destroyed the political image and confidence of the U.S. It was a shattering blow for the U.S. globally." A radical German heard echoes of 1917: "There next to the American embassy in Saigon the battle was raging from house to house, [and the] NLF's flag was flying over Hue. . . . There was no doubt – the world revolution was dawning."[39]

The media provided the indispensable forum for protest. In August 1968, during the Democratic National Convention in Chicago, the presence of cameras and reporters turned a demonstration, which had almost failed because of a disappointingly low turnout, into an event of historical significance. Keenly aware of their mass audience, the protesters chanted, "The whole world is watching!" while they battled the Chicago police. Jerry Rubin, one of their leaders, later admitted how they exploited the situation: "We wanted exactly what happened. . . . We wanted to show that America wasn't a democracy. . . . The message of the week was of an America ruled by force. This was a big victory." The authorities, on their part, blamed the media for creating the sort of publicity that inevitably transformed a skirmish into a highly charged and symbolic event.[40] The widely

36 See the chapters by Herring, Pach, and Brinkley; see also Herbert Y. Schandler's thorough account in *The Unmaking of a President: Lyndon Johnson and Vietnam* (Princeton, N.J., 1977).
37 Fraser, *1968,* 176.
38 See Brinkley's chapter; Milton Viorst, *Fire in the Streets: America in the 1960s* (New York, 1979), 414–20; Todd Gitlin, *The Sixties: Years of Hope, Days of Rage,* rev. ed. (New York, 1993), 300–1; David Farber, *The Age of Great Dreams: America in the 1960s* (New York, 1994), 212–16.
39 Fraser, *1968,* 176–7.
40 Rubin is quoted in Brinkley's chapter. For more on Chicago, see David Farber, *Chicago '68* (Chicago, 1988), 250–1; on the instrumentalization of the media by Italian students, see Hilwig's

reported disorders in Chicago, together with the other incidents of urban rioting, accelerated the "unraveling of liberal America" and provided Nixon and the Republican Party with the political symbolism they could exploit in the presidential election of 1968.[41]

It is significant that some student protesters recognized and criticized the media's strong ties to the establishment. As Stuart J. Hilwig writes, by attacking the media the students were protesting the weakening of democracy by "a manipulative press supporting politically myopic regimes."[42] The conflicts between the Springer publishing empire and West German students as well as between the mainstream press and Italian students represented a larger debate over the instruments of power and the limits of personal and political freedom in two relatively new and prosperous, but still unsettled, democracies. In Italy, students expressed their frustration with the bureaucratic and hierarchic university regime and an "undemocratic society" by fighting its most visible mouthpiece, the popular press. For West German students, the Springer press symbolized everything that was wrong with their society: the inadequate engagement with the Nazi past, the authoritarianism and lack of democracy, and the pervasive influence of anticommunism.[43]

In most of Eastern Europe and in the Third World the media played a markedly different role than in the West. Whereas members of Western societies "could literally watch" the unfolding of worldwide events, in communist and Third World societies news was mostly obtained from sometimes heavily censored radio and newspapers reports or through informal networks.[44] In many places, "the news belonged to the government."[45] In Poland, for example, the student revolt of March 1968 was barely covered by the mass media. Unlike their American and Western European counterparts whose demands were widely disseminated, Polish students had to struggle against "lies, misinformation, [and] defamation" as well as silence. Jerzy Eisler reminds us that "whereas student leaders in the West became mass heroes, as popular as film or rock stars, their Polish counterparts were

---

chapter; on Germany, see Tilman Fichter and Siegward Lönnendonker, *Kleine Geschichte des SDS: Der sozialistische deutsche Studentenbund von 1946 bis zur Selbstauflösung* (Berlin, 1977), 103.

41 See the essays by Brinkley and Manfred Berg (Chapter 15) in this book; Jonathan Rieder, "The Rise of the 'Silent Majority,'" in Steve Fraser and Gary Gerstle, eds., *The Rise and Fall of the New Deal Order, 1930–1980* (Princeton, N.J., 1989), 243–68; David Farber, "The Silent Majority and Talk About Revolution," in Farber, ed., *The Sixties,* 291–316.

42 See Hilwig's chapter.

43 See the essays by Harold Marcuse (Chapter 16) and Claus Leggewie (Chapter 10) in this book; Mary Fulbrook, *The Divided Nation: A History of Germany, 1918–1990* (Oxford, 1991), 278–86.

44 See the essay by Arif Dirlik (Chapter 11) in this book.

45 See the essay by Jerzy Eisler (Chapter 8) in this book.

imprisoned."[46] Excessive press exposure, particularly in Western journals, could even create adverse results in communist countries. Two Polish students who had provided information to a reporter for *Le Monde* about the protests at Warsaw University were expelled and imprisoned.[47]

In the absence of a free press, alternative news channels sprouted up throughout Eastern Europe. In Ukraine, the crisis over Czechoslovakia spread by word of mouth.[48] In Poland, protest posters appeared on city walls, and leaflets were distributed in public places.[49] The underground radio was an essential element in the Czechoslovak resistance against the Warsaw Pact invasion.[50] Citizens of the GDR tuned in to Western broadcasts and to the German-language Czechoslovak Radio; East German youngsters attended "illegal gatherings," dissidents distributed leaflets, and churches organized lectures and discussions.[51]

After the invasion of Czechoslovakia spontaneous protests broke out in Moscow, Sofia, and Budapest. Throughout the Soviet Union, intellectuals refused to attend official meetings called to manifest support of the Warsaw Pact's intervention. Workers and students in East Germany refused to sign official statements that endorsed the invasion.[52] Wherever the media was stifled or repressed, citizens grew increasingly resentful, cynical, and ingenious in constructing alternative forms of communication that reduced their isolation from the rest of the world. Thus, during the "silent 1970s" in the Soviet bloc there was a steady stream of nonviolent, human rights activism that depended on the typewriter together with the virtually unblockable messages of Western broadcasts.

THE NETWORKS OF REBELLION

Although many scholars acknowledge that the local and national protest movements of 1968 took place within a context of a global rebellion, little has been written about the concrete forms of cooperation and the exchange of ideas among the protagonists. Historians are now beginning to investigate the roots and nature of these international networks, which derived from the anticolonial, feminist, pacifist, and civil rights movements of the early and mid twentieth century.[53]

---

46 Ibid. 47 Ibid. 48 See Kramer's chapter. 49 See Eisler's chapter.
50 Daniels, *Year of the Heroic Guerrilla,* 190–1.
51 Mary Fulbrook, "Popular Discontent and Political Activism in the GDR," *Contemporary European History* 3 (1993): 272–4.
52 Ibid.; see the essays by Kramer and Lawrence S. Wittner (Chapter 17) in this book.
53 Juchler, *Studentenbewegungen;* Fraser, *1968.*

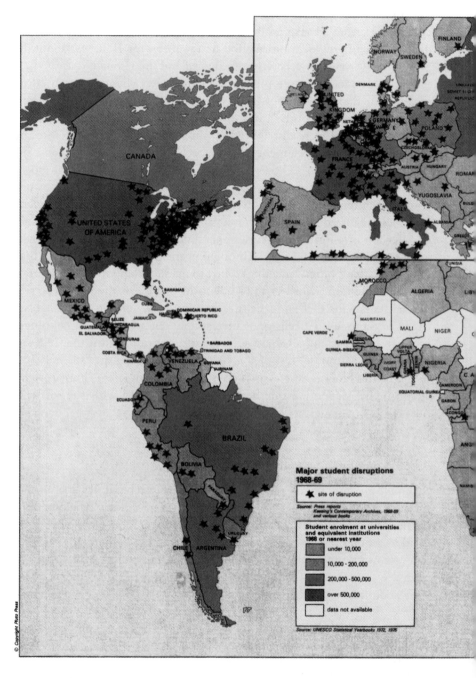

Figure I.1. The Student Sixties. Reproduced with permission from Michael Kidron and Ronald Segal, *The State of the World Atlas,* 1st ed. (London, 1981).

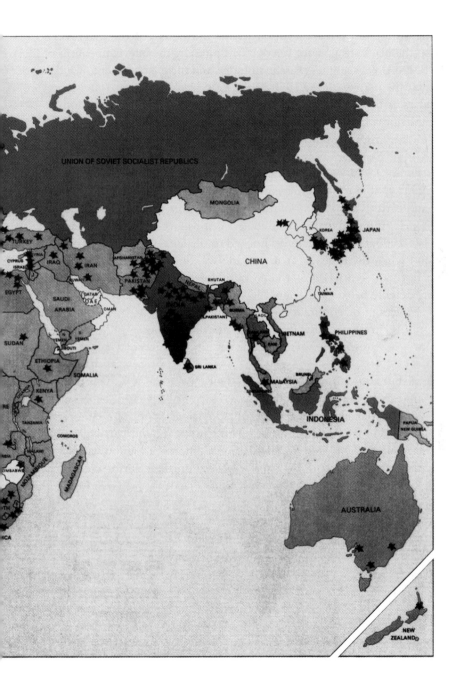

Perhaps the most powerful supranational movement of the 1960s centered on the black struggle for freedom. Inspired by the internationalism of W. E. B. Du Bois, Gandhi's crusade in India, and the establishment of independent African states in the 1950s and 1960s, black Americans envisioned themselves as being part of a global movement for rights and freedom at home and abroad.[54] The civil rights movement in Northern Ireland in the 1960s took its inspiration from Martin Luther King Jr.'s nonviolent marches in the United States.

As Lawrence S. Wittner shows, another important precursor of the 1968 movement was the campaign against the atomic bomb, which by the late 1950s and early 1960s had mobilized global support, even across the Cold War divide.[55] It is true that the antinuclear campaign temporarily dissipated in the late 1960s, when its activists flocked to the anti–Vietnam War movement and when the urgency of its crusade was diminished by the Atmospheric Test Ban Treaty (1963), the Nonproliferation Treaty (1968), and the budding détente between the superpowers. Nevertheless, there was a considerable measure of continuity – of personnel and organization, rhetoric and symbols, strategy and tactics – with the international protest movements of 1968 against the Vietnam War and the invasion of Czechoslovakia.[56]

Part of, but also separate from, the student movement was the reemerging feminist movement that created its own forms of international cooperation. As Eva Maleck-Lewy and Bernhard Maleck write, the American women's movement was an inspiration to European, and particularly to West German, women. Despite their national differences, feminists created a transatlantic and international network based on their personal contacts and the influence of major texts, such as Betty Friedan's *The Feminine Mystique* and Simone de Beauvoir's earlier classic, *The Second Sex*.[57] Indeed, three of the most important feminist works of the years 1968–9, Ti-Grace Atkinson's *Amazon Odyssey,* Shulamith Firestone's *Dialectic of Sex,* and Kate Millett's *Sexual Politics,* were all dedicated to de Beauvoir.[58]

54 See Berg's chapter; James Forman, *The Making of Black Revolutionaries,* 2d ed. (Seattle, 1990), 480–90.
55 See Wittner's chapter.
56 Richard Taylor, *Against the Bomb: The British Peace Movement, 1958–1965* (Oxford, 1988); Lothar Rolke, *Protestbewegungen in der Bundesrepublik: Eine analytische Sozialgeschichte des politischen Widerspruchs* (Opladen, 1987), 226–38; see also the references to nuclear disarmament in the Port Huron statement: James Miller, *Democracy Is in the Streets: From Port Huron to the Siege of Chicago* (New York, 1987), 346ff., 355ff.
57 See the essay by Eva Maleck-Lewy and Bernhard Maleck (Chapter 14) in this book.
58 Betty Friedan, *The Feminine Mystique* (New York, 1963); Simone de Beauvoir, *Le deuxième sexe* (Paris, 1949), translated as *The Second Sex* (New York, 1953); Shulamith Firestone, *The Dialectic of*

By the 1960s, the primary impetus to establishing global cooperation among Western and Third World students was their struggle against the Vietnam War. Young people throughout the world joined in a "front against U.S. capitalism and imperialism." Their hero was the Argentine guerrilla leader Che Guevara who, until his death in October 1967, had called for international solidarity and whose writings were translated into several languages and widely disseminated among leftist students.[59] Western Europeans avidly embraced their American fellow students. At their antiwar rally in February 1966, groups from West Germany, Austria, France, Sweden, Norway, Italy, and the Netherlands declared their solidarity with American student protesters.[60] In October 1967, the march on the Pentagon was echoed by closely coordinated solidarity demonstrations against the American military installations in West Berlin and by antiwar rallies in Amsterdam, London, Oslo, Paris, Rome, and Tokyo.

Throughout the world, antiwar protests stimulated the growth and expansion of student movements. In Paris, the attack on the American Express building by left-wing commandos may have precipitated the student uprisings in May.[61] In Britain, groups that had originally organized over issues of college discipline were transformed into a mass movement against the Vietnam War, peaking in 1968 with two massive demonstrations, in March and in October, in which more than one hundred thousand people are estimated to have participated.[62] The war in Vietnam, which contributed significantly to Japan's economic growth, also seriously strained U.S.-Japanese relations and produced militant antiwar demonstrations by Japanese students.[63] There is evidence from Belgium, Italy, the Netherlands, the Philippines, Thailand, and Sweden that opposition to the American engagement in Vietnam stimulated the growth of radical student movements. In Latin America, many protesters followed Che Guevara's slogan, "Create Two, Three, Many Vietnams."[64] In Zambia as in much of southern Africa, American involvement in the civil war in Angola created an additional stimulus for student radicalism.[65]

Sex: The Case for Feminist Revolution (New York, 1969); Kate Millett, *Sexual Politics* (London, 1970); Ti-Grace Atkinson, *Amazon Odyssey* (New York, 1974). We thank Rosi Braidotti, Utrecht, for bringing this point to our attention.

59 Gitlin, *The Sixties*, 246; Juchler, *Studentenbewegungen*, 145; Jon Lee Anderson, *Che Guevara: A Revolutionary Life* (New York, 1997).
60 Juchler, *Studentenbewegungen*, 120.
61 Keith A. Reader, with Khursheed Wadia, *The May 1968 Events in France: Reproductions and Interpretations* (New York, 1993), 8.
62 Katsiaficas, *Imagination of the New Left*, 56.
63 Henry D. Smith, *Japan's First Student Radicals* (Cambridge, 1972); Thomas Havens, *Fire Across the Sea: The Vietnam War and Japan* (Princeton, N.J., 1987).
64 Katsiaficas, *Imagination of the New Left*, 48.   65 Altbach, *Student Political Activism*, 49.

The actual extent of cooperation between these protest movements has not been thoroughly explored and merits investigation. For example, the extremely close ties between American and West German protesters formed a striking parallel with their governments' Cold War collaboration, which had promoted extensive faculty and student exchanges. Important figures of the German Socialist Students' League (Sozialistischer Deutscher Studentenbund or SDS) had become acquainted with the American New Left as a result of their studies in the United States in the early 1960s. One of them, Michael Vester, who developed ties with American activists such as Tom Hayden, even contributed to the legendary 1962 conference at which the Port Huron statement was drafted.[66] After their return to West Germany, they helped to organize the growing protest against the American war in Vietnam, which culminated in February 1968, when the German SDS convened a Vietnam Congress that attracted more than six thousand participants from Europe, Turkey, and the United States.[67] Based on the urging of radical Italian and French delegates and of American deserters, the SDS devised a plan to storm the U.S. Army's McNear Barracks in Berlin to provoke a mutiny of U.S. soldiers.[68] In turn, the radicalization of the students at Columbia University took place in April 1968 after the American Students for a Democratic Society (SDS) responded to the attempt to assassinate the German SDS leader Rudi Dutschke with protest demonstrations against Springer offices in Rockefeller Center in New York.[69]

The "export" of the Paris May, which proved to be particularly contagious, is perhaps the most striking example of the global nature of 1968. As in earlier times – 1789, 1830, and 1848 – the general strike of the workers and students in the French capital set an example that led to solidarity demonstrations all over the world. The gains made in Paris convinced protesters in other countries that it was possible to make similar demands elsewhere, leading to the exchange of ideas and methods of revolution across national borders.[70]

As in the past, Paris provided both the model for dissent and a cautionary lesson for the authorities. In Italy, the battles between the students and

66 Doug McAdam and Dieter Rucht, "The Cross National Diffusion of Movement Ideas," *Annals of the American Association of Political and Social Science* 528 (July 1993): 70.
67 See the interview with Karl-Dietrich Wolff, quoted in Juchler, *Studentenbewegungen,* 260 n. 10.
68 Ulrich Chaussy, *Die drei Leben des Rudi Dutschke: Eine Biographie* (Darmstadt, 1983), 209–10.
69 Columbia University, Oral History Research Office, Student Movements of the 1960s, the Reminiscences of Jeff Jones, interview with Ronald Grele, New York, Oct. 24, 1984, 49. Quoted in Juchler, *Studentenbewegungen,* 289; Fraser, *1968,* 195.
70 See Charles Tilly, *European Revolutions, 1492–1992* (Oxford, 1993), 14; international cycles of protest in historical comparative perspective are thoroughly analyzed in Sidney Tarrow, *Power in Movement: Social Movements, Collective Action, and Politics* (New York, 1994), 153–69.

the police reached their climax in June 1968. In Belgium, on the other hand, officials decided not to call the police after students occupied the administrative offices of the Free University of Brussels.[71] In Istanbul, where external events had an even greater impact than elsewhere, students occupied their campus at the same time as the takeover of the Sorbonne.[72] In Berkeley and Belgrade, Berlin and Buenos Aires, protest demonstrations supported the workers and students of France. In Spain and Uruguay, students and workers, following the "French example," attempted general strikes of their own.[73] English students, impressed with the French May and the successes of the SDS, decided to create a revolutionary organization of their own.[74]

The personal contacts and exchanges of 1968 bridged the Cold War frontier. Václav Havel, the Czech writer and future president, who was in New York City in May and June 1968, witnessed the protests and occupations at Columbia University.[75] That summer, when numerous Czech and Slovak students used their newly won freedom to travel to the West, many were still abroad when the Soviets invaded, including 1,500 who were stranded in Britain. At the World Youth Festival in July and August in Bulgaria there was a remarkable collaboration between Czechoslovak and Yugoslav students as well as among West German, British, and Dutch students. Protesting the control by the official Communist youth organization over the festival, this multinational group organized its own teach-ins and even sparred with the Bulgarian police.[76]

The young Polish intellectuals called the "commandos" who disrupted meetings of the party's official youth organization became legendary in French anarchist and Trotskyite circles. One of their pamphlets, the "Open Letter to the Party," written in 1965, became one of the most widely circulated texts among Sorbonne students in May 1968.[77] West Germany's most famous revolutionary, Rudi Dutschke, himself a refugee from the GDR, traveled to Prague in late 1968 to attend the Christian peace conference, which attracted youth from Eastern and Western Europe. In his lecture at the Charles University, Dutschke reminded the large Czech audience, many of whom were attracted by the model of Western democracy, that he rejected representative government and Stalinism because both led

---

71 See Hilwig's chapter; Caute, *Year of the Barricades,* 108.
72 Ahmet Samim, "The Left," in Irvin C. Schick and Ertugrul Ahmet Tonak, eds., *Turkey in Transition: New Perspectives* (New York, 1987), 157.
73 Katsiaficas, *The Imagination,* 3.   74 Fraser, *1968,* 273.
75 Paul Berman, *A Tale of Two Utopias: The Political Journey of the Generation of 1968* (New York, 1996), 233.
76 Caute, *Year of the Barricades,* 197.   77 See Eisler's chapter, 242.

to the depoliticization of the masses. According to Dutschke, the Prague Spring had kindled the hope of creating a "producers' democracy" leading to a true "democratic self-organization of the masses."[78]

Students in Western countries, although sharing few of the experiences, premises, or goals of their Eastern counterparts, nevertheless followed developments in Czechoslovakia with concern and sympathy. In the West, the experiment of a "socialism with a human face" was seen by many as an attractive "third way" between bourgeois democracy and the "real existing socialism" of the Warsaw Pact countries.[79] Although we know far less about the reactions of students in communist countries, it is clear that their governments' fear and castigation of the Prague Spring did not stifle their interest in Dubček's bold experiment.[80] As the news that Soviet tanks were rolling into Prague reached West Germany, SDS students were still producing and distributing leaflets in support of a reformed communism.[81] In Moscow's Red Square, a young physics instructor named Pavel Litvinov and a handful of adherents briefly distributed protest leaflets before being arrested and then imprisoned.[82]

Although global and interconnected, the movements of 1968 were also highly disparate in their nature and impact.[83] As some of the contributors to this book argue, each protest movement must be understood within its specific national context.[84] The American civil rights struggle, for example, was frequently clad in internationalist rhetoric of a "worldwide struggle being waged by the poor and oppressed against imperialism," yet it grew out of the distinctive history of the United States.[85] The German and Italian student movements cannot be understood without placing them in the historical context of their countries' slow, painful efforts to create new democratic polities and to come to terms with their fascist pasts.[86] Any meaning-

---

78 Chaussy, *Dutschke,* 224–8.
79 A counterexample, however, were Italian students, who preferred Mao and Che to Dubček; see Hilwig's chapter.
80 See Eisler's chapter; Fulbrook, "Popular Discontent."
81 Oskar Negt, *Achtundzechzig: Politische Intellektuelle and die Macht* (Göttingen, 1995), 328.
82 See Wittner's chapter.
83 See Anthony Oberschall, *Social Movements: Ideologies, Interests and Identities* (New Brunswick, N.J., 1993), 301–23; Sidney Tarrow's *Democracy and Disorder: Protest and Politics in Italy, 1965–1975* (Oxford, 1989), 3, although he is interested in international "cycles of protests," stresses the fact that "unless we place the movements of the late 1960s within their national and historical contexts, we shall not be able to judge either their newness, their breadth, or their impact on democracy."
84 See the chapters by Berg, Dirlik, Eisler, and Hilwig.
85 See the chapters by Berg and Brinkley.
86 See the chapters by Hilwig, Leggewie, and Marcuse; Robert G. Moeller, "War Stories: The Search for a Usable Past in the Federal Republic of Germany," *American Historical Review* 101 (1996): 1034–5; Norbert Frei, *Vergangenheitspolitik: Die Anfänge der Bundesrepublik und die NS-Vergangenheit*

ful analysis of the upheavals of 1968 in Czechoslovakia and Poland must take into account the long history of foreign domination of these two countries.

Nevertheless, we must recognize that although political action in 1968 was based on different assumptions, traditions, and historical experiences, the similarity in the values, actions, and mobilization strategies gave a universal dimension to 1968. As Ingrid Gilcher-Holtey writes, the protest movements all confronted the establishment with counter power and counter publicity that negated traditional structures of authority and challenged the basic assumptions of the postwar order.[87]

GLOBALISM OF FREEDOM

The last, and perhaps most striking, element of global 1968 was the widespread belief among contemporaries that they were taking part in a worldwide struggle against the existing order in East and West, and in North and South. The year witnessed an explosion of revolutionary student movements and two major challenges – Tet and Prague – to the hegemonial claims of the two superpowers. It also represented a fundamental critique of the ideological premises of the Cold War in the name of three principles: freedom, justice, and self-determination.

Although these principles were understood differently throughout the world, they nevertheless represented more than a superficial application of the same terms to totally different circumstances. From the perspective of the participants, the struggles for individual and collective rights and for self-determination provided a solid and unifying thread that linked them to the imagined community of a world revolution of 1968.

Anecdotal evidence suggests that the protesters saw themselves in the same global fight against colonialism and imperialism, against exploitative capitalism and repressive communism. In East Germany, for example, there were demands for "Freedom for Vietnam – Freedom for Czechoslovakia."[88] Before a court in Paris, the student leader of Nanterre, the young German exchange student Daniel Cohn-Bendit, identified himself as "Kuroń-Modzelewski," the names of the two leading Polish dissidents.[89] And after the French Communist leader, Georges Marchais, denounced Cohn-

---

(Munich, 1996); Jeffrey Herf, *Divided Memory: The Nazi Past in the Two Germanys* (Cambridge, Mass., 1997).
87 See the essay by Ingrid Gilcher-Holtey (Chapter 9) in this book.
88 Fulbrook, "Popular Discontent," 273.   89 See Eisler's chapter.

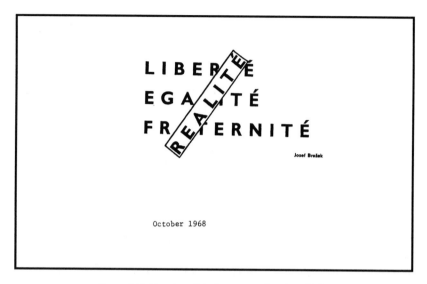

Figure I.2. Czech political cartoon, October 1968.

Bendit as a "German anarchist," at least fifty thousand demonstrators responded with chants and banners proclaiming, "We are all German Jews."[90]

In Eastern Europe, the demonstrators fought for the basic human and political rights — freedom of speech, the press, assembly, and religion — as well as the fundamental personal and property rights already firmly established in Western Europe and North America. Saturated by official tirades against American and Israeli imperialism, they protested not against the war in Vietnam but against Soviet repression and the local communist regimes they regarded as illegitimate and arbitrary.

Cultural expression had long performed a national and political function in Eastern Europe. Jerzy Eisler states that it was no accident that the rebellious behavior in Poland in March 1968 was provoked by the government's decision to ban performances of the nineteenth-century drama *Dziady* (The Forefathers) by the beloved writer Adam Mickiewicz, whose strong anti-Russian passages had aroused audiences and alarmed the authorities. In its quick and brutal reaction to the demonstrations, the Gomułka government gave proof of its solidarity with those Warsaw Pact hard-liners in favor of crushing of the Prague Spring.

90 *L'Humanité,* May 3, 1968; June 17, 1968; May 17, 1969; see also Katsiaficas, *Imagination of the New Left,* 104.

Despite Dubček's repeated assurances to his communist allies, the unfolding of the Prague Spring revealed the impossibility of combining internal liberalization with loyalty to the Warsaw Pact system.[91] As the free press in Czechoslovakia grew increasingly hostile to Moscow and demanded even more independence, and as protesters in Warsaw began calling for Poland's own Dubček, the governing elites in Moscow and the other Eastern European capitals perceived a threat to the Soviet bloc and to their own monopoly of power.[92]

The protest movements in Eastern Europe, particularly in Czechoslovakia and Poland, were in some respects similar to their Western counterparts. The dissenters were mostly young, well educated, and from privileged backgrounds.[93] As in France and Italy, the Czechoslovak students were joined by a growing number of workers. The workers' council movements, which gained momentum after the Soviet invasion, behaved similarly to their Western counterparts by moving from purely economic to political demands, namely, free elections and elementary civil rights.[94]

Despite their differences, many of the dissenters in Eastern and Western Europe shared a common hope that a third way might be created between communism and capitalism. Nevertheless, the students and intellectuals in socialist countries remained distrustful of the "dreams of the New Left" in the West, and the New Left suspected their Eastern European comrades of tacitly promoting the "counterrevolution." Although the ideas of Eastern European intellectuals in 1968 have never been sufficiently analyzed, it seems clear that figures such as Václav Havel and Adam Michnik had probably not yet become adherents of Western-style democracy.[95]

In Western Europe, the struggle against the status quo was also fought in the name of freedom, democracy, and self-determination. In contrast to the fight against political repression in Eastern Europe, the protests in the West were aimed at expanding personal emancipation and grassroots democracy. A generation of twenty- and thirty-year-olds that had grown up in peace and relative prosperity and in the belief that freedom and wealth brought personal fulfillment had come to recognize that Western societies were incomplete democracies that had failed to live up to their self-

---

91 See Kramer's chapter.
92 See Lutz Priess, Václav Kural, Manfred Wilke, *Die SED und der "Prager Frühling" 1968: Politik gegen einen "Sozialismus mit menschlichem Anlitz"* (Berlin, 1996).
93 Daniel, *Year of the Heroic Guerrilla,* 202–3; Caute, *Year of the Barricades,* 200–2.
94 See the essay by Gerd-Rainer Horn (Chapter 13) in this book; Tomalek Pavel [pseudonym], *Czechoslovakia, 1968–70: The Worker-Student Alliance* (Boston, 1971). Polish workers were less attracted to the student movement; see Neal Ascherson, *The Polish August* (Harmondsworth, 1981), 94–95.
95 Berman, *Tale of Two Utopias,* 224–30; Roger Garaudy, *Le Grand Tournant du Socialisme* (Paris, 1969).

proclaimed ideals.[96] What began as student protests against the bureaucratic and hierarchical structures of their universities and their governments' attempts to limit access to higher education grew into an attempt to expand the boundaries of liberal democracy to include a whole range of positive social, economic, and human rights.[97]

Student activists in Western Europe and the United States combined anticapitalism with a fundamental critique of the parliamentary system. They claimed that the principles of representative democracy were "mere formalities" in contrast with the "true will" of the people. Ultimately, the political naiveté of many sixty-eighters, their obsession with unfettered, radical democracy and self-expression, and their demands for an absolute moral purity led to dogmatic factionalism and atomization. Whereas most sixty-eighters began their long march through the institutions, others continued to try to meliorate society by peaceful protest. There was also the small but highly visible group in some Western countries that turned to terrorism as a means of destroying the "structural violence" of the "authoritarian state." These well-publicized excesses had a powerful impact on the larger society and provoked the political and cultural backlash of the 1970s and 1980s.[98]

Although the political legacy of 1968 is still contested, there is little doubt that the upheavals of the 1960s transformed Western societies, at least culturally.[99] This was most striking within the Left itself. The New Left, distinguishing itself from the "Old Left," not only changed the style of left-wing politics but also shifted its concern away from the exploitation of workers by capitalists.[100] The works of André Gorz, Alain Touraine, and Serge Mallet maintained that the revolutionary spirit no longer resided in the proletariat but in a "new working class" of well-educated technicians,

---

96 See the chapters by Brinkley, Hilwig, Leggewie, and Marcuse; on the "generation paradigm," see Fraser, *1968;* Berman, *Tale of Two Utopias;* Heinz Bude, *Das Altern einer Generation: Die Jahrgänge 1938 bis 1948* (Frankfurt am Main, 1995); Luisa Passerini, *Autobiography of a Generation: Italy 1968,* trans. Lisa Erberg (Hanover, N.H., 1996).

97 This is, of course, the central grievance of the authors of the famous Port Huron statement, the most important manifesto of the early American student movement. See Miller, *Democracy;* Tom Hayden, *Reunion: A Memoir* (New York, 1988), 77ff.

98 On the splintering of the American and German student movements and early terrorism, see Juchler, *Studentenbewegungen;* on various backlashes see the chapters by Berg, Brinkley, Hilwig, Jarausch, and Leggewie; some of the anti-New Left literature is summarized in Barbara Ehrenreich, "Legacies of the 1960s: New Rights and New Lefts," in Barbara L. Tischler, ed., *Sights on the Sixties* (New Brunswick, N.J., 1992), 227–34.

99 Steven Macedo, ed., *Reassessing the Sixties: Debating the Political and Cultural Legacy* (New York, 1997).

100 On the New Left, see Maurice Issermann, *If I Had a Hammer: The Death of the Old Left and the Birth of the New Left* (New York, 1987); Katsiaficas, *Imagination;* Ingrid Gilcher-Holtey, *"Die Phantasie an die Macht": Mai 68 in Frankreich* (Frankfurt am Main, 1995), 44–104; Andrei S. Markovits and Philip S. Gorski, *The German Left: Red, Green, and Beyond* (New York, 1993).

skilled workers, middle managers, intellectuals, and students. This spirit
was also spreading to other groups at the margins of Western society and to
non-Western peoples.[101] By invoking the early Marx, the insights of psychoanalysis and existentialism, feminism and anticolonialism, the New Left
made a broad, sweeping critique of the growing alienation that had developed within the advanced industrial societies. The solution required not
only a social, political, and international revolution but also a complete
change in the conditions of human existence, from modes of work to
forms of private behavior, from relations between the sexes to the structure
of the family.[102] The New Left also hoped that a transformation in the cultural realm, the replacement of formal, monolithic structures with alternative and oppositional subcultures that exuded spontaneity and wit, egalitarianism and critical perspectives, would accelerate the transformation of
national and international politics.[103]

The New Left thus raised issues that had never been central to the theoretical debates among Marxists. This was undoubtedly the result of its
experiences and perceptions during the years since 1945, a world of huge
disparities between rich and poor, power and powerlessness, violent
struggles and spiritualist movements. With the fading of the Marxist
and Soviet models, the heroic factory worker and peasant had been replaced
by the heroic Third World freedom fighter. According to the precepts
of its ideological leader, Herbert Marcuse, the New Left linked the anti-
imperialist struggles of the Third World with its own efforts to loosen the
bonds of tradition and hierarchy, prejudice and discrimination in their own
societies.[104]

According to the youthful protesters, the difference between the communist and "free" worlds had been eradicated by the Vietnam War, which
they regarded as the climax of a century of Western imperialism in Asia
and Africa. America's official mission, to defend the freedom, democracy,
and self-determination of the South Vietnamese people against the threat
of a communist dictatorship, had been debunked. The Saigon regime was
not a democracy, and a large majority of its people did not support America's mission. Moreover, the United States had become the accomplice to

101 Alain Touraine, *Le Communisme Utopique: Le Mouvement de Mai 68* (Paris, 1968); see also Horn's chapter.
102 See Leggewie's chapter; on gender, see Alice Echols, "'Nothing Distant About It': Women's Lib-eration and Sixties Radicalism," in Farber, ed., *The Sixties,* 149–74; *Reader, May 1968 Events in France,* 148–66; see also Maleck-Lewy and Maleck's chapter.
103 Passerini, *Autobiography,* 125–55.
104 Ingo Juchler, *Rebellische Subjektivität und Internationalismus: Der Einfluss Herbert Marcuses und der nationalen Befreiungsbewegungen in der sog. Dritten Welt auf die Studentenbewegungen in der BRD* (Mar-burg, 1989).

brutal human rights violations, the Loan execution and the My Lai massacre.[105] Thus, the conduct of the war belied the myth of Western innocence and exposed the "structural violence" of the Western democracies.
At the same time, the Vietnam War and the Six-Day War caused the youthful protesters of 1968 to reflect on the Holocaust as not merely a distant
atrocity but a vital concern for the present.[106]

In North America and Europe, the New Left was inspired by the successful national liberation movements in Algeria (1954–62), Cuba
(1956–9), and the Congo (1959–65) as well as on the long anticolonial
struggle in Vietnam. These battles all refuted the classic Western and Marxist formulation of the First World as center and revolutionary model for
the Third World periphery. Now the revolutionary ideals and activism
seemed to be coming from the periphery. Thus, the Tet Offensive, the
struggle between a peasant people and the world's mightiest military force,
was an overwhelming stimulus to Western protest movements.[107]

This emphasis on the periphery was highlighted by the fact that the
European and North American protesters were inspired by Latin American guerrilla movements and, above all, by the Chinese Cultural Revolution, which created a "spiritual homeland for a generation which could no
longer believe in the USSR."[108] As Arif Dirlik stresses in his chapter, the
Cultural Revolution and the Sino-Soviet split brought China "into the
center of world radicalism." In countries such as the Philippines and Peru as
well as in Western Europe and North America, Mao became one of the
heroes of 1968. More than the socialist reformers of the Prague Spring,
Mao provided an alternative revolutionary paradigm that promised to avoid
the "uncontrolled consumerism of advanced capitalist societies and the
bureaucratism of Soviet-style socialism," which, for all of their differences,
seemed to generate oppression, exploitation, and alienation instead of
"democratically distributed happiness."[109]

---

105 Benjamin R. Barber, "The Importance of Remembering: The Vietnam Legacy's Challenge to
American Democracy," in D. Michael Shafer, ed., *The Legacy: The Vietnam War in the American Imagination* (Boston, 1990), 3–8; Barbara L. Tischler, "Promise and Paradox: The 1960s and American
Optimism," in ibid., 30–53.
106 See the chapters by Marcuse and Leggewie.
107 Consequently, two contemporary American observers dedicated their survey of the worldwide
student movement "to the Vietnamese people." See Barbara and John Ehrenreich, *Long March,
Short Spring: The Student Uprising at Home and Abroad* (New York, 1969), 5.
108 Lumley, *States of Emergency,* 120; see A. Belden Fields, *Trotskyism and Maoism: Theory and Practice in
France and the United States* (New York, 1988); Winfried Schlaffke and Franz Schneider, "Maois-
mus: Kulturrevolution – Späte Einsichten," in Franz Schneider, ed., *Dienstjubiläum einer Revolte:
"1968" und 25 Jahre* (Munich, 1993), 80–96; Arif Dirlik, Paul Healy, and Nick Knight, eds., *Critical Perspectives on Mao Zedong's Thought* (Atlantic Heights, N.J., 1997).
109 See Dirlik's chapter, 299.

One of the greatest ironies of 1968 is that many in the New Left in industrialized countries, despite their preoccupation with liberation movements in the Third World, were in many respects victims of Eurocentric projections that prevented them from understanding the fundamental distinctions between West and East, North and South. All over Europe and the United States in 1968 placards displayed the revolutionary trio, Mao Zedong, Ho Chi Minh, and Che Guevara, who became linked with the ideals of Western youth, yet it was overlooked that there were basic differences between movements at the "core" and the "periphery."

Third World supporters in the West barely understood that their role models were "worlds apart" from each other not only in terms of geography but also in ideological and political terms. Among the masses of European and American protesters who wore Mao hats and brandished his "Little Red Book," few grasped the actual conditions in Communist China. As Tucker writes, they knew little about the horrendous sacrifice of human life during the Cultural Revolution or the fact that it represented the consolidation of power by a ruling elite that had incited Chinese youth to strike down its real and imagined enemies.[110] Few Western radicals could comprehend the extent of the brutal repression of freedom, legality, and self-determination in Eastern Europe, despite the shock and outrage they produced. Neither could they fully grasp the longings of students and workers in Asia, Africa, and Latin America, where liberation from poverty and local authoritarianism was as important as liberation from capitalism and imperialism.

For a brief moment in 1968, a "third way" seemed to have been a possibility, that is, a new national and international orientation traversing the boundaries of the Cold War, transcending capitalism and communism, encompassing the West as well as the non-Western world. In 1968, as historian Eric Hobsbawm has written, "the writing appeared on the wall." As a testing ground for a "new world order," 1968 prefigured the great transformation of 1989–90. In the short run, the Soviet Union had vanquished the Czechoslovak challenge; but in the long run, the communist world proved rigid and fragile, ultimately discrediting the idea of a socialist third way. In the capitalist world, 1968 seemed to mark the "end of the feast," but the West proved more resilient in its responses to the social, economic, and political challenges it faced.[111]

110 See Tucker's chapter.
111 The two quotes are from Eric Hobsbawm, "1968: A Retrospect," *Marxism Today* 22 (May 1978): 136.

PART ONE

Tet and Prague

The Bipolar System in Crisis

I

Tet and the Crisis of Hegemony

GEORGE C. HERRING

The Tet Offensive of 1968 has long been recognized as a turning point in the Vietnam War, leading to Lyndon B. Johnson's decision to reduce the bombing of North Vietnam, open peace negotiations with Hanoi, and, most dramatically, take himself out of the upcoming presidential race. Tet 1968 was also significant in another way. It marked the first time in the post–World War II era when the United States came face to face with the limits of its power, or, to borrow Paul M. Kennedy's phrase, the reality of "imperial overstretch." The North Vietnamese offensive occurred at the same time as the *Pueblo* crisis in Korea and a major economic crisis in Western Europe, Great Britain, and the United States. The shock of these simultaneous crises led some U.S. policymakers and leaders of the foreign policy elite to conclude that the nation was overextended and to propose adjustments. Johnson eventually muddled through this crisis of hegemony without resolving or even addressing in any substantive way the fundamental issues raised by it. But in doing so he laid the foundation for détente and the Nixon doctrine, the major adjustments to America's changed position instituted by his successor.

I

The crisis of 1968 originated in the circumstances and nature of LBJ's July 1965 decisions for war in Vietnam. In committing the United States to prevent North Vietnam and the National Liberation Front (NLF) from overrunning its client state in South Vietnam, the president juggled a variety of conflicting pressures. He had been at the center of the political bloodletting that had followed the fall of China in 1949, and he was certain that the "loss" of South Vietnam would produce an even more explosive upheaval, a "mean and destructive debate," he later commented, "that would shatter

my Presidency, kill my administration, and damage our democracy."[1]
Deeply committed to his Great Society program of domestic reforms, he
feared that if he faltered in Vietnam, southern conservatives, angered by his
commitment to racial equality, would turn on him with a vengeance. "If I
don't go in now and they show later that I should have," he predicted,
"they'll . . . push Vietnam up my ass every time."[2] Aware at the same time
of the dangers posed to his beloved domestic programs by expenditures for
the war, he refused to mobilize the reserves, as his military advisers urged,
and hid from the nation the depth of his commitment in Vietnam and the
potential costs.

   Johnson and his advisers also sought to parry conflicting international
pressures. In the aftermath of the Cuban missile crisis and the Sino-Soviet
split, the Soviet Union appeared in a conciliatory phase, and some Americans entertained long-range hopes for "détente." But no one could be certain the Russians had abandoned their expansionist goals. Competition
with China, it was reasoned, might increase their aggressiveness, and in a
strife-torn world the Soviets could be drawn into local conflicts against
their will. Whatever the Soviet intent, most Americans agreed that an
aggressive and militant China had assumed leadership of the forces of world
revolution. American officials thus continued to believe that the way they
responded to "Communist provocations" in Vietnam would have "profound
consequences everywhere."[3] To contain China, discourage Soviet tendencies toward adventurism, and uphold the credibility of U.S. commitments,
the administration concluded that it must maintain a strong global defense
posture and stand firm in Vietnam.

   At least with regard to the USSR, the United States also pursued a conciliatory line. Americans hoped to use the Sino-Soviet split to improve
relations with the Soviet Union and reduce the danger of nuclear war. In a
study commissioned by Johnson himself on the eve of war in Vietnam, the
Central Intelligence Agency (CIA) warned that escalation might inflame
Cold War tensions. The administration sought to counter this danger by
putting precise limits on the war and by avoiding provocation to the Soviet
Union and China. While expanding the war, it also kept the door open to
the presumably more conciliatory Soviets to broker a settlement in Vietnam, explored the possibility of negotiations with Moscow on arms con-

---

1 Quoted in Doris Kearns, *Lyndon Johnson and the American Dream* (New York, 1976), 252.
2 Quoted in Brian VanDeMark, *Into the Quagmire: Lyndon Johnson and the Escalation of the Vietnam War*
   (New York, 1991), xv, 60.
3 Quoted in George C. Herring, *America's Longest War: The United States and Vietnam, 1950–1975,* 3d
   ed. (New York, 1996), 129.

trol and other outstanding issues, and attempted to build bridges to the Soviet Union and Eastern Europe through expanded trade and cultural contacts.[4]

By the end of 1967, Johnson's delicate strategy was in tatters. The United States steadily escalated the bombing of North Vietnam, committed more than 500,000 soldiers to the war, and mounted extensive search and destroy operations against North Vietnamese and NLF forces, but it could not force an elusive and resilient enemy to quit or negotiate on its terms. In the meantime, the dissent against the war that had begun in the United States on a small scale in the spring of 1965 mounted to a fever pitch, culminating in October 1967 with a large and dramatic protest march on the Pentagon. Accompanying the rise of dissent – and perhaps more important – was rising public frustration and weariness with a war that incurred growing costs in blood and treasure and seemed to produce no more than a stalemate.

At least in part because of Vietnam, the Johnson administration's hopes for détente with the Soviet Union went unrealized. American escalation of the war posed difficult choices for Moscow and, as the CIA had predicted, vastly complicated superpower relations. Whether the Soviets wished to help the United States end the war remains unclear, but their ability to do so was limited. Expansion of the war forced them in the interest of ideological solidarity to dramatically increase their aid to North Vietnam. They could not go too far to accommodate the United States without risking their leadership of the communist world. In any event, they could not impose their will on North Vietnam. A divided Soviet leadership, still uncertain of its future course, responded angrily to escalation of the war and warily to U.S. overtures for détente. On the other side, the Johnson administration's growing absorption in Vietnam sharply limited its ability to deal with other issues, and it encountered difficulties in terms of domestic politics trying to fight communists in Asia but make peace with them in Europe. An increasingly rebellious Congress denied the president a major weapon of détente by refusing to approve most-favored-nation status for the Soviet Union and its allies while they supplied North Vietnam. The two sides opened preliminary discussions on arms control but accomplished little else, and the outbreak of war in the Middle East in 1967 sparked increasing tensions in superpower relations.[5]

4 VanDeMark, *Into the Quagmire,* 181–2; Frank Costigliola, "Lyndon B. Johnson, Germany, and the 'End of the Cold War,'" in Warren I. Cohen and Nancy Bernkopf Tucker, eds., *Lyndon Johnson Confronts the World* (New York, 1994), 193–8.
5 Costigliola, "End of the Cold War," 207–8; Vladislav M. Zubok, "Unwrapping the Enigma: What

At a time of renewed uncertainty in the Cold War, Vietnam put enormous strain on America's ability to meet its global defense commitments. The Defense Department had calculated that the United States should be prepared to fight two and one-half wars: one against Soviet forces in Europe, one against China in Asia, and one in a smaller theater with a second- or third-level adversary. By 1967, the "half-war" in Vietnam was consuming a great portion of America's available defense forces. Johnson's adamant refusal to mobilize the reserves meant that almost all combat-ready units had been committed to Vietnam. Forces in Europe were stripped of experienced men to meet needs in Vietnam, and those remaining in the United States consisted of little more than a "training establishment." There was not a National Guard unit "that could fight its way out of a paper bag," one frustrated officer complained.[6]

A crisis in the Western alliance, in part triggered by America's commitment in Vietnam, further strained U.S. military capabilities. As the economic burden of Western defense increased and the Soviet threat in Europe appeared to ease, America's North Atlantic Treaty Organization (NATO) allies increasingly went their own way. Asserting French independence from the United States, President Charles de Gaulle withdrew seventy thousand troops from NATO and cut off funds for NATO operations. In early 1967, an economically beleaguered Great Britain announced plans to reduce its overseas forces by one-third and warned that it would have to remove all its troops from Europe unless West Germany assumed the entire foreign exchange cost. West Germany in turn threatened to curtail the purchases of U.S. equipment that had helped to offset American military expenditures. The European moves provoked angry demands in Congress to withdraw U.S. forces from Europe.

A crisis was averted when the Germans agreed to procure U.S. and British goods on a reduced scale, and the United States and Britain agreed to "redeploy" troops from Germany to home territories, keeping them under NATO command and ready to redeploy if needed. But these makeshift arrangements did not solve the problem. Britain announced further cutbacks in July, and West Germany indicated it would reduce its forces to 400,000 instead of building them to 508,000 as originally planned. By late 1967, the "NATO shield appeared to be disintegrating under the com-

Was Behind the Soviet Challenge in the 1960s?" in Diane B. Kunz, ed., *The Diplomacy of the Crucial Decade* (New York, 1994), 167–70; Anatoly Dobrynin, *In Confidence: Moscow's Ambassador to America's Six Cold War Presidents* (New York, 1966), 135–6, 143.

6 Hanson Baldwin, "U.S. Forces Spread Thin," *New York Times,* Feb. 21, 1966.

bined influence of nationalism, political complacency, and mounting financial pressures."[7]

Growing economic problems in the Western nations, both cause and effect of the crisis in NATO, added another ominous dimension. Expenditures for Vietnam imposed a burden of as much as $3.6 billion a year on an already overheated U.S. economy, stoking a rising inflation and contributing to a balance of payments deficit of $1.4 billion in 1966. These forces combined to weaken the dollar in international money markets and place the world monetary structure in jeopardy. A financial crisis in Britain, leading to devaluation of the pound and the gold crisis of late 1967, caused further problems, including huge American losses from the gold pool.[8]

The war had grave domestic consequences for the United States. Riots in the ghettos of the nation's cities produced heightened racial tensions. The Great Society was all but dead, the victim, as LBJ had feared, of spending for Vietnam. To meet the growing costs of guns and butter, the president in 1967 belatedly and reluctantly proposed a 10 percent surtax, but congressional foes such as the powerful Wilbur Mills, chairman of the House Ways and Means Committee, refused to approve an increase in taxes without drastic cuts in domestic spending.[9]

By late 1967, an increasingly bitter debate on Vietnam had expanded into a much more fundamental debate on the United States's foreign and military policy. "Politically, militarily, and economically, . . . the country is moving into trouble," wrote Democratic Senator Stuart Symington of Missouri. Symington was especially concerned with the impact of Vietnam on the nation's overall defense posture, fearing that inadequate conventional forces would leave the United States no option, in a confrontation with the Soviet Union, but to "start throwing nuclear weapons from tubes and silos."[10]

Frustrated by the stalemate in Vietnam and alarmed by the weakening of the nation's defense capabilities, the Joint Chiefs of Staff (JCS) and congressional "hawks" urged Johnson to take drastic measures to win the war

---

7 Richard B. Stebbins, *The United States in World Affairs: 1967* (New York, 1968), 197–206.
8 Burton I. Kaufman, "Foreign Aid and the Balance-of-Payments Problem: Vietnam and Johnson's Foreign Economic Policy," in Robert A. Divine, ed., *The Johnson Years*, vol. 2: *Vietnam, the Environment, and Sciences* (Lawrence, Kan., 1987), 88–95; Diane B. Kunz, "Cold War Dollar Diplomacy: The Other Side of Containment," in Kunz, ed., *Crucial Decade*, 99–105; see also Diane B. Kunz's chapter in this book.
9 Donald F. Kettl, "The Economic Education of Lyndon Johnson: Guns, Butter, and Taxes," in Divine, ed., *Johnson Years*, 2:67–8.
10 Symington to General J. P. McConnell, Aug. 8, 1967, J. P. McConnell Collection, U.S. Air Force Historical Research Center, Maxwell Air Base, Ala.

and meet the nation's other commitments. Repeating proposals they had made since 1965, the JCS pressed for declaration of a national emergency, mobilization of the reserves, stepped-up bombing attacks against North Vietnam, a major increase in ground forces, and ground operations against North Vietnamese sanctuaries in Cambodia and Laos.[11]

On the other side, "doves" saw America's growing military and economic problems as obvious signs of overcommitment. The United States had fallen victim to the "arrogance of power," according to Arkansas Senator J. William Fulbright, and was "showing signs of that fatal presumption, that overextension of power and mission which brought ruin to ancient Athens, to Napoleonic France and to Nazi Germany."[12] Some doves began to speak candidly of terminating the war in Vietnam. In July 1967, Fulbright introduced a "national commitments resolution," declaring that the only valid commitments were those in which Congress had participated through a treaty or some other kind of formal authorization. A strange collection of hawks and doves steadfastly opposed U.S. involvement in crises in the Middle East and the Congo and proposed drastic cuts in foreign aid.

Taking a middle ground that focused on Vietnam without confronting the larger issues, a group of "establishment" figures meeting in Bermuda in late 1967 under the auspices of the Carnegie Endowment proposed that the United States shift from its costly search and destroy strategy to a less expensive "clear and hold" strategy. Presumably, such an approach could stabilize the war at a politically and economically acceptable level and save South Vietnam without surrender or a wider war.[13] Some of Johnson's top advisers, including a now thoroughly disillusioned Secretary of Defense Robert McNamara, proposed stopping the bombing, changing the ground strategy, and shifting to an incipient form of what would later be called Vietnamization. The idea, of course, was to reduce the cost in blood and treasure and thereby salvage the commitment in Vietnam and America's deteriorating global position.[14]

Whipsawed between hawk and dove, still clinging desperately to a steadily shrinking center, Lyndon Johnson dealt with these challenges in

---

11 The JCS proposals and Johnson's response are covered in detail in George C. Herring, *LBJ and Vietnam: A Different Kind of War* (Austin, Tex., 1994), 51–7.

12 Quoted in Thomas Powers, *The War at Home* (Boston, 1984), 118.

13 "Carnegie Endowment Proposals," Dec. 5, 1967, Matthew B. Ridgway papers, U.S. Army Military History Institute, Carlisle Barracks, Pa., box 34a.

14 See especially McNamara Draft Presidential Memorandum, Nov. 1, 1967, Lyndon Baines Johnson papers, National Security File, Country File: Vietnam, box 75, Lyndon Baines Johnson Library, Austin, Tex.

what had become characteristic fashion. By late 1967, the president was a man at war with himself. Frustrated by the self-imposed restraints on military action, he ached to "pour steel" on his adversaries in Hanoi and pound them into submission. Weary of the struggle, he anticipated on another occasion his March 31, 1968, decision, wondering aloud about the effect on the war if he decided not to run for reelection. Still, he refused to act decisively. As throughout his career, he sought to patch together a consensus among divergent viewpoints rather than confront the issues head-on. He dismissed as "pure bunk" the notion that the United States was overextended. At the same time, he rejected the military's proposals to expand the war, approving only a token increase in ground troops and several new bombing targets. He also rejected dove proposals to stop the bombing, put a ceiling on ground forces, alter the ground strategy, and seek a negotiated settlement. He proposed a number of stopgap measures to ease the growing balance of payments deficit. To deal with domestic dissent, he mounted in the fall of 1967 a large-scale, multifaceted public relations campaign to rally support, hoping thereby to solidify the home front until the war could be won.[15]

II

A series of traumatic events in early 1968 brought forth full-blown the crisis of hegemony. Military challenges in Korea and Vietnam and chaos on the London gold market posed, as no event had before, the question of overextension of American power. Again, hawks urged resolving the crisis by mobilizing to win in Vietnam. On the other side, leading establishment figures pressed for scaling back or even ending the war as a means of salvaging America's global position.

The crisis of 1968 began with near-simultaneous military challenges in Korea and Vietnam. On January 23, North Korea seized the U.S. intelligence ship *Pueblo* in the Sea of Japan, imprisoning the officers and crew. A week later, the North Vietnamese launched their biggest offensive of the war. Striking at Tet, the beginning of the lunar new year and the most festive of Vietnamese holidays, they shifted their military operations from the countryside to the urban areas, attacking 5 of the 6 major cities, 36 of 44 provincial capitals, 64 district capitals, and 50 hamlets. In Saigon, the center of American power, they hit Tan Son Nhut airport, the presidential palace, the headquarters of the South Vietnamese general staff, and, most

---

15 Tom Johnson notes on meetings, Oct. 2 and 4, 1967, Johnson papers, Tom Johnson notes on meetings, box 1. For LBJ's nondecisions of later in 1967, see Herring, *LBJ and Vietnam,* 57–62.

dramatically, the U.S. embassy. In Hué, the former imperial capital, seventy-five hundred North Vietnamese and NLF soldiers stormed and eventually took control of the ancient Citadel, once the seat of the emperors of Annam.

The two crises left Washington in a state of shock. The administration continued to deny that the United States was overextended and immediately called up fourteen thousand reservists to strengthen its position in South Korea. Although caught off guard in Vietnam, U.S. forces rallied and, along with South Vietnamese units, repulsed the initial assaults and inflicted huge losses on the enemy. Still, the suddenness and magnitude of the attacks created a crisis atmosphere. An "air of gloom" hung over White House discussions, presidential adviser General Maxwell Taylor later recalled, and JCS chairman General Earle Wheeler likened the mood to that after the First Battle of Bull Run. Speechwriter Harry McPherson called February 1968 the "most dismaying month I ever remembered in the White House."[16]

The longer-range prospects appeared grave. Administration officials speculated that what had happened in Korea was not an isolated incident but part of a concerted Communist effort to open a "second front" to divert U.S. attention from Vietnam and perhaps prevent South Korea from sending additional forces to Vietnam. The United States feared a second round of attacks in Vietnam, and intelligence reports warned of possible flare-ups in Berlin and the Middle East. Speaking to congressional leaders on January 31, the president speculated that the Communists had launched "one large determined offensive . . . to put them back in the ball game." Their hope, he added, was to make the American people conclude: "We can't do that. Maybe we ought to come home."[17]

Facing possible crises across the globe, the administration had few forces at its disposal. The "half-war" in Vietnam consumed ten of its twenty-three divisions. Units in Korea and Europe had been stripped of officers and men with critical skills to support those in Vietnam. The Marine Corps was already unable to sustain its Vietnam operations. The 82d Airborne Division was the only combat-ready army division in the United States, and two of its brigades had been depleted to fill a third brigade for deployment to Vietnam. Wheeler warned that to send the 82d Airborne to Viet-

16 Earle G. Wheeler and Harry McPherson oral history interviews, Johnson Library.
17 Notes on NSC meeting, Jan. 24, 1968, Johnson papers, Tom Johnson notes on meetings, box 2, and notes on meeting with congressional leaders, Jan. 31, 1968, Johnson papers, meeting notes file, box 2.

nam would leave the United States with "no readily deployable strategic reserve." The president himself worried that committing it to Vietnam would leave no forces to quell possible disturbances at home.[18]

The Joint Chiefs of Staff attempted to use the crisis atmosphere provoked by the *Pueblo* seizure and the Tet Offensive to secure what they had sought since 1965 – mobilization of the reserves. In the immediate aftermath of Tet, the JCS recommended that the 82d Airborne Division and a Marine division be readied for possible deployment to Vietnam, warning that this could not be accomplished without the call-up of at least 120,000 reservists. When the president, in a fashion that by this time had become standard operating procedure, agreed to deploy a brigade of the 82d Airborne and a Marine regiment, the JCS went a step further. After a trip to Vietnam and intensive discussions with General William C. Westmoreland, Wheeler conceived a series of measures ostensibly to deal with the emergency in Vietnam but in fact to rebuild the nation's depleted force structure. One hundred and eight thousand men would be deployed by May and earmarked for Vietnam. An additional ninety-seven thousand would be deployed by the end of the year and designated as a strategic reserve in the United States. Painting a grim picture of the situation in Vietnam – even hinting ominously that the two northern provinces of South Vietnam might have to be abandoned – and carefully concealing his larger goal of reconstituting a depleted strategic reserve, Wheeler warned that without these deployments the United States could suffer irreparable reverses.[19]

Wheeler's report shocked a government already in a state of alarm. The sheer magnitude of the request stunned civilian officials. In terms of policy choices, it posed a harsh dilemma. The general suggested that denial of his request could result in military defeat or at least in the war continuing indefinitely. McNamara estimated, on the other hand, that acceptance of the proposals would require an additional four hundred thousand men on active duty at a cost of $10 billion. This would impose heavy demands on the American people in an election year, when public anxiety about Vietnam was already pronounced. Long since disenchanted with the war and in the last tortuous days of his tenure, the secretary of defense questioned whether 206,000 men could break the stalemate in Vietnam. The North

18 Herbert Y. Schandler, *Lyndon Johnson and Vietnam: The Unmaking of a President* (Princeton, N.J., 1983), 100, 109; notes on president's meeting with the Joint Chiefs of Staff, Feb. 9, 1968, Johnson papers, Tom Johnson notes on meetings, box 2.

19 Wheeler report, Feb. 27, 1968, excerpted in Neil Sheehan et al., *The Pentagon Papers as Published by the New York Times* (New York, 1971), 615–21; Tom Johnson notes on meeting, Feb. 28, 1968, Johnson papers, Tom Johnson notes on meetings, box 2.

Vietnamese, as in the past, would simply match the American escalation. Not inclined to make a hasty decision on such a grave issue, the president turned the problem over to his new secretary of defense, Clark Clifford, with the grim instruction "Give me the lesser of evils."[20]

While the troop request was under consideration, a new "gold crisis" set off further alarm signals in Washington. In March, pressure on the dollar began to mount again, and by the end of the first week gold purchases reached a new high. On March 9, Britain announced plans to withdraw all troops east of Suez by the end of 1971, placing added defense burdens on the United States and more pressure on the dollar. The next day, the *New York Times* leaked word of the military's request for additional troops. These events combined to generate a growing lack of confidence in the U.S. economy and provoke wild speculation in gold. On March 14 alone, the United States lost $372 million in gold trading. At Washington's urging, the London gold market was closed.[21]

The troop request was increasingly linked to the nation's economic problems. Even before the gold crisis, Johnson's budget director, Charles Zwick, estimated that increases in spending for Vietnam might take the defense budget above $100 billion. Secretary of the Treasury Henry Fowler warned that adoption of Westmoreland's proposals would cost $2.5 billion in 1968 and $10 billion in 1969, adding $500 million to the balance of payments deficit. They would require cuts in domestic programs of up to $3 billion and a major tax increase at a time when the 1967 tax proposal was still hung up in Congress. Fowler even suggested a temporary freeze on wages, salaries, and prices to deal with the likely inflationary pressures.[22] Wheeler warned Westmoreland that the monetary crisis impinged directly and "heavily" on attitudes toward the increased expenditures required for a reserve call-up and additional deployments to Vietnam. The combination of the monetary crisis and proposals for troop deployments, he went on, placed the government in "as difficult a situation as I have seen in the past five years." Together with the "gloom and doom" generated by Tet, they significantly affected support for the war.[23] "The gold crisis has dampened

20 Clark Clifford with Richard Holbrooke, *Counsel to the President: A Memoir* (New York, 1991), 484–5.
21 Paul Joseph, *Cracks in the Empire: State Politics in the Vietnam War* (Boston, 1981), 262–4.
22 Zwick to LBJ, Mar. 2, 1968, Clark Clifford papers, Lyndon Baines Johnson Library, box 1; Fowler memorandum, "Economic and Financial Problems and Measures," Mar. 3, 1968, Clifford papers, box 1.
23 Wheeler cable to Westmoreland, Mar. 16, 1968, Backchannel messages, Westmoreland/CBS files, Federal Records Center, Suitland, Md., box 23.

expansionist ideas," former Secretary of State Dean Acheson wrote a friend. "The town is in an atmosphere of crisis."[24]

In this context, leading organs of business opinion began to question the nation's ability to finance the war at existing or higher levels. A February 1968 *Fortune* editorial blamed the war for the nation's financial difficulties. The *Wall Street Journal* editorialized that the administration was "duty bound to recognize that no battle and no war is worth any price, no matter how ruinous." Vietnam made clear, *Business Week* added, that "even the mighty U.S. lacks the means to fight anywhere, anytime and prevail." It called for a policy of de-escalation in Vietnam and fiscal restraint at home, editorializing that "somehow the United States is going to have to bring its international commitments in line with its resources – military, economical and political. Of these, the political resource, in other words the price the people of the United States are willing to pay to keep order in the world – may be the most crucial."[25] Clifford reported a "tremendous erosion of support" among the nation's business elite. These men felt the United States was in a "hopeless bog," he added, and the idea of "going deeper into the bog" struck them as "mad."[26]

Simultaneously, some leading establishment figures, including, most importantly, some of the major architects of America's Cold War policies, concluded that the war was doing irreparable damage to the nation's overall security position and pressed for basic changes in policy. Longtime adviser to presidents and Soviet expert W. Averell Harriman had for years been uneasy with U.S. policy in Vietnam and had especially feared that it was obstructing progress toward détente with the Soviet Union. Unwilling to challenge the president directly for fear of squandering his influence, he had worked assiduously – and unsuccessfully – to find a way out. Tet provided an opportunity to press his point.[27]

Harriman helped persuade the ultimate Cold Warrior and former Secretary of State Acheson that Vietnam was a dangerous diversion from Europe and that, as Acheson put it, "Our Leader ought to be concerned

24 Acheson to John Cowles, Mar. 14, 1968, Dean G. Acheson papers, Yale University Library, box 7. Secretary of the Treasury Fowler later described Mar. 14, 1968, as "the most hectic day of my life." See Fowler oral history interview, Johnson Library.

25 Quoted in Joseph, *Cracks in the Empire,* 193–5; see also James N. Tilson, "Rally 'Round the President: United States Business Journal Opinion During the Vietnam Era," M.A. thesis, University of Kentucky, 1991, 52–63.

26 Memorandum of conversation with Clifford, Mar. 20, 1968, Arthur Krock papers, Princeton University Library; Clark Clifford, "A Viet Nam Reappraisal," *Foreign Affairs* 47 (1969): 613.

27 Rudy Abramson, *The Life of W. Averell Harriman: Spanning the Century, 1891–1986* (New York, 1992), 655–60.

with areas that count." A towering figure, Acheson had been instrumental in the creation of the containment policy, and he was deeply committed to NATO. As a personal adviser to LBJ, he had served as a sort of "de facto assistant secretary for Europe" from 1965 to 1967 and had watched with growing alarm the administration's absorption in Vietnam and the breakdown of the European alliance. Originally a hawk on Vietnam – in 1965 he had instructed Johnson to stop whining and get on with the war – he had eventually concluded that Vietnam was draining American resources and diverting it from what should be its top priorities, and he joined Harriman in working for a change in policy.[28]

Deputy Secretary of Defense Paul Nitze, author of National Security Council document 68, the Truman administration's blueprint for global containment, reached similar conclusions. As early as 1965, then Secretary of the Navy Nitze had concluded that the cost of success would be enormous, if indeed it could be attained, and doubted that the gain would be worth the cost. Like other establishment "dissidents," he had remained in office, dutifully implementing policies he did not like, but Tet confirmed his skepticism. Vietnam was causing "enormous difficulties" in terms of American policies in Europe and elsewhere and was eroding public support for an "outward looking foreign policy."[29] The time had come, he felt, for a review of Vietnam policy in the context of America's global strategy. He set out to convert Clifford to that view, in staff meetings arguing with him "until I was hoarse."[30]

Eventually he succeeded. Reputed to be a Vietnam hawk when he took office, Clifford had vigorously backed the bombing of North Vietnam and opposed bombing pauses in 1965 and 1966. But he had also privately opposed the commitment of ground troops in 1965, and a trip through Southeast Asia in 1967 in search of additional troops from allied countries had raised further doubts in his mind. Nitze's arguments and Clifford's intensive discussions with the military after Tet confirmed and deepened his skepticism. In conversations he later described as "often confused and emotional," he pressed the JCS to tell him what would be required to succeed in Vietnam. To his dismay, they would offer no assurance that 206,000 additional soldiers could end the war, and they could not estimate how many more would be required. "I was appalled," he later wrote. "Nothing had prepared me for the weakness of the military's case." Clifford gradually

28 Douglas Brinkley, *Dean Acheson: The Cold War Years, 1953–1971* (New Haven, Conn., 1992), 248–57.
29 Schandler, *Unmaking of a President,* 125.
30 Paul H. Nitze, *From Hiroshima to Glasnost: At the Center of Decision* (New York, 1989), 258–9, 274–6.

moved from a skeptical hawk to a closet dove to leader of a cabal seeking to move the president toward disengagement.[31]

Along with Acheson, Clifford took the lead in working for a change in policy. He mobilized a group of "conspirators" within the government to resist Westmoreland's proposals for additional troops and expansion of the war and to work for de-escalation and peace negotiations. Acheson had worked his way into the White House inner circle, and he increasingly used his influence to promote a change in policy. He met with Johnson on March 14, the day of the crisis on the London gold market, and proposed, among other things, a time limit for getting South Vietnam to be self-sufficient, after which the United States would seek disengagement. In a long memorandum of March 26, he warned the president that the gold crisis and concern with America's "broader interests in Europe" required a "decision now to disengage within a limited time."[32]

The former secretary of state also widely disseminated within the government an editorial by Wallace Carroll, a former *New York Times* correspondent and then publisher of a Winston-Salem, North Carolina, newspaper. Entitled "Vietnam Quo Vadis," the editorial observed that absorption with the war in Vietnam had caused the nation to lose sight of its ideals. Americans needed to stand back and get their priorities straight. The vital strategic areas were Western Europe, Japan, the Middle East, Latin America, "and only then Southeast Asia." Commending the editorial to Johnson, presidential speechwriter and Clifford coconspirator Harry McPherson noted that it was "the most cogent case I have read for getting out soon – in order to cut our losses elsewhere in the world."[33]

Most important, Acheson arranged for the so-called Wise Men to meet with the president on March 26 and 27. This group of senior establishment figures – the men who had midwifed the birth of American postwar internationalism and, with Acheson, had been "present at the creation" of global containment – had been formed in 1964 to give respectability and credibility to Johnson's foreign policy and thereafter had met with him sporadically. In November 1967, they had generally endorsed his policies. This time, to his dismay, they pressed for change. After extensive briefings arranged by Clifford, a majority of the group urged immediate steps toward de-escalation. The United States could "no longer do the job we set out to

31 Clifford, *Counsel to the President,* 493–4.
32 Acheson memorandum of meeting with the president, Mar. 14, 1968; Acheson memorandum, Mar. 26, 1968, Acheson papers.
33 For Acheson's handling of the Carroll editorial, see Walter Isaacson and Evan Thomas, *The Wise Men: Six Friends and the World They Made* (New York, 1986), 696–7. Key parts of the editorial are reproduced in Joseph, *Cracks in the Empire,* 270.

do in the time we have left," Acheson observed, "and we must begin to . . . disengage."[34] The Wise Men's meetings of March 26–7 represented a sort of "high-water mark of U.S. hegemony," Walter Isaacson and Evan Thomas have observed.[35] "The establishment bastards have bailed out," a dispirited Johnson is said to have remarked.[36]

III

Perhaps not surprisingly, the crisis of hegemony was "resolved" in a manner both inconclusive and anticlimactic. Governments rarely deal with complex issues of state head-on, of course, and democratic governments representing pluralistic societies may be least capable of doing so. Lyndon Johnson's entire political career had been built on reconciling conflicting interests, and his leadership style stressed finding consensus among disparate groups. The Johnson administration thus improvised short-term expedients to ease the gold crisis without addressing the larger economic issues that had sparked it, and after months of gridlock the White House managed to extract from Congress a compromise tax bill. Similarly, the president concocted a makeshift strategy that defused the Vietnam crisis without resolving the fundamental issues, maneuvering skillfully between hawks and doves, quieting fears at home by de-escalating while, incongruously, continuing to entertain hopes of eventual victory. Indeed, to the end of his term, LBJ clung desperately, almost pathetically, to hopes of a peace settlement in Vietnam and an eleventh-hour summit with Soviet leaders to end the Cold War, but the Soviet invasion of Czechoslovakia in August 1968, South Vietnamese obstruction of a last-minute deal, and the election of Richard Nixon shattered his dreams.

The gold crisis did not lend itself to delay. Shortly after the closing of the London gold market on March 14, bankers representing the Western industrialized nations met in Washington to find solutions. There they developed a two-tiered system to stabilize the cost of gold, an official market where monetary authorities could buy and sell at $35 an ounce and a commodity market where the price would fluctuate according to supply and demand. At a monetary conference in Stockholm later in March, allied finance ministers approved the establishment in the International Monetary Fund of Special Drawing Reserves (SDR), credit that could be extended

34 Summary of notes, Mar. 26, 1968, Johnson papers, meeting notes file, box 2.
35 Isaacson and Thomas, *Wise Men,* 699.
36 Quoted in Roger Morris, *An Uncertain Greatness: Henry Kissinger and American Foreign Policy* (New York, 1977), 44.

to member nations according to their IMF quotas, as a further means of stabilizing the dollar.[37]

A tax bill would not come so easily. Throughout the spring and summer of 1968, the White House and Congress remained deadlocked over the particulars of a tax increase. The president was resigned to the measure but determined to salvage as much as possible of his domestic programs. On several occasions, he even tossed out such "radical new ideas" as pulling troops out of Vietnam to make possible budget cuts. To sway recalcitrant congressmen, he spoke privately of an economic crisis as grave as 1931 and warned of possible "disaster." "We are fiddling while Rome burns," he admonished congressional leaders in late April.[38] When the intransigent Wilbur Mills still refused to budge, administration strategists sidestepped him, attaching the tax measure to another house bill. The maneuver forced Mills into line, and in June Congress approved a 10 percent surtax, with $6 billion in immediate spending cuts and a later cut of $8 billion, $11 billion less than Mills had wanted.[39]

LBJ hailed the spring of 1968 as a "historic turning point" in international efforts to stabilize the world economy, but it was considerably less. The steps taken eased the immediate crisis, to be sure, and made possible a measure of stabilization, but they did not address the larger balance of payments issues that had triggered the crisis. Abandonment of the gold pool represented a significant retreat on the part of the United States from its long-standing commitment to the Bretton Woods system created after World War II to stabilize the world economy. The gold crisis in fact revealed how weak the international monetary system had become, dependent on a shaky U.S. dollar that in turn rested precariously on a huge and growing balance of payments deficit. The tax bill also helped, but in terms of larger economic issues it also was too little too late, and Congress rejected other administration proposals to deal with the balance of payments. The administration's unwillingness to address problems raised by spending for the war contributed to major long-term economic difficulties. "By this time," Donald Kettl has concluded, "the seeds of fundamental economic instability had been planted," leading to a decade of what came to be called stagflation.[40]

---

37 Kunz, "Cold War Dollar Diplomacy," 106–7; Kaufman, "Foreign Aid and the Balance of Payments," 96–7; see Kunz's chapter in this book.
38 Tom Johnson notes on meeting, Apr. 23, 1968, Johnson papers, Tom Johnson notes on meetings, box 2.
39 Kettl, "Economic Education," 70–1.
40 Ibid., 71–4; see Kunz's chapter in this book.

Whatever their long-term shortcomings, Johnson's measures in the spring and summer of 1968 did ease the sense of crisis that had gripped the nation in March. Along with the president's March 31 initiatives on Vietnam, the economic measures gave a breathing spell and a shot of optimism to a shaken nation, and the stock market enjoyed a brief upward surge. The same organs of business opinion that had spouted gloom and doom in February and March indulged in a bit of optimism in the late spring. "The problems underlying the past month's bombshells certainly haven't been solved yet," *Fortune* opined in May 1968, "but for the short run, at least, the result has been to return the business outlook to the status quo ante Tet."[41]

As with the economy, LBJ's major Vietnam decisions of March 1968 eased the nation's concern and diverted its attention without addressing the fundamental issues. The president rejected out of hand military proposals to mobilize the reserves and expand the war. He ached to strike back at Hanoi, and he continued to fret about a possible revolt among the hawks. But he had steadfastly opposed such measures since July 1965, and his decisions of March 1968 represented adherence to long-held principles. He was keenly aware of the dangers of drastic escalation, and the gold crisis brought home to him even more painfully the economic costs of an expanded war. In any event, the military situation in Vietnam improved markedly in March as the full extent of enemy losses became clear. Without any real danger of an American defeat, Wheeler's proposals appeared excessive and unnecessary. The president thus approved only a token increase of 13,500 soldiers, even fewer than Clifford's task force had recommended.[42]

To stifle potential military criticism, he called in Generals Wheeler and Creighton Abrams for a remarkable session on March 26. Obviously torn with emotion and playing on the sympathies of his top military advisers, an embattled commander-in-chief explained his decisions in terms of the powerful pressures he faced and the personal cost he would pay: an "abominable" fiscal situation, panic and demoralization in the country, near-universal opposition in the press, and his own "overwhelming disapproval" in the polls. "I will go down the drain," he gloomily concluded.[43]

Responding to the mood of the nation and the entreaties of Clifford and the doves, LBJ also made major peace moves. In a dramatic speech on March 31, after nearly a month of intensive deliberations, he announced a partial bombing halt, offered a new proposal for negotiations, and, to the shock of even close friends, removed himself from the presidential race.

41 Quoted in Tilson, "Business Journal Opinion," 74–5.
42 Herring, *LBJ and Vietnam,* 160–1.
43 Tom Johnson notes on meetings, Mar. 26, Johnson papers, Tom Johnson notes on meetings, box 2.

Such moves, he reasoned, would cost little militarily and might quiet the home front. They might neutralize the doves without inciting the hawks, and they would ease the nation's fears and buy time to stabilize the situation in Vietnam.[44]

As dramatic as they were, Johnson's proposals of March 31 did not get at the fundamental issues raised by the war. He appears never to have seriously considered the proposal of Nitze and other Cold Warriors to reevaluate Vietnam in the context of the nation's global commitments. In effect, rejection of the troop request spared him the necessity of doing so. Although he recalled General Westmoreland to Washington to serve as Army chief of staff, he did not encourage or even permit a reassessment of the general's costly search and destroy strategy. The fact that his bitter rivals Senators Robert F. and Edward Kennedy had proposed such a move must have made it politically and personally unpalatable to him. Privately, he conceded the utility of reassessing policies from time to time, but, he explained to his advisers, he did not want to be holding a "seminar" on strategy "back here while our house is on fire." A review of strategy, he also rationalized, might "create doubt" by indicating that "we are doubtful."[45]

Most important, he did not commit himself to disengagement along the lines advocated by Harriman, Acheson, Nitze, and the Wise Men. To the surprise of some of his advisers, the North Vietnamese responded positively to his March 31 overture, and LBJ subsequently agreed to negotiations in Paris, but from the outset he took a tough line. Success in the battles of Tet reinforced the convictions of some U.S. officials that an independent, noncommunist South Vietnam could be salvaged from the rubble of war, and the president's post-Tet decisions appear contrived to attain that result. By stepping up ground operations against an already battered enemy, expanding bombing of staging areas and supply lines below the twentieth parallel and in Laos, and shifting greater responsibility to the South Vietnamese, the United States might yet snatch victory from the jaws of stalemate.[46]

Like earlier decisions, the March 31 moves derived from wishful thinking. Militarily, the means were scaled back without modification of the ends, and it is impossible in retrospect to see how U.S. officials hoped to achieve with the application of less force aims that had thus far eluded them. The United States had taken over the war in 1965 because of poor

44 *Public Papers of Lyndon B. Johnson, 1968–1969*, 2 vols. (Washington, D.C., 1970), 1: 469–76.
45 Tom Johnson notes on meetings, Mar. 4, 6, 11, 12, 19, 1968, Johnson papers, Tom Johnson notes on meetings, box 2.
46 Herring, *LBJ and Vietnam*, 161–4.

performance by the South Vietnamese, and the concept of Vietnamization was equally dubious. Negotiations were certainly desirable from a domestic political viewpoint, but in the absence of a clear-cut military advantage on the side of the United States and because it was not prepared to make concessions, they could not be expected to achieve anything. And the mere fact of negotiations might soften U.S. resolve and limit the administration's ability to prosecute the war.

Throughout the remainder of Johnson's term, he and his advisers fought bitterly over the war. The stakes were high, the participants exhausted, nerves frayed. Clifford remembered 1968 as the most difficult year of his life, a year, he said, that seemed to last five years. Secretary of State Dean Rusk recalled only a "blur" and claimed to have survived on a daily regimen of aspirin, Scotch, and cigarettes. Personal attacks ascended to unprecedented levels. "The pressure grew so intense that at times I felt that the government itself might come apart at the seams," Clifford later remembered. "There was, for a brief time, something approaching paralysis, and a sense of events spiraling out of control of the nation's leaders."[47]

On one side were Rusk, national security adviser Walt Rostow, and the military. Certain that the enemy had suffered a smashing defeat at Tet and that in negotiations the United States would hold the upper hand, they sought to maintain maximum military pressure in Vietnam and hold the line in negotiations. If the home front could be stabilized and the United States could improve its military position, the North Vietnamese would have to make major concessions. On the other side, Clifford and Harriman, the chief Paris negotiator, continued to seek disengagement. They had long since concluded that Vietnam was crippling America's global position. Through what Clifford called a "winching down" process, they promoted mutual de-escalation and eventual disengagement through negotiations, even at the expense of South Vietnam.[48]

Through much of the rest of the year, Johnson wavered between the two positions. He had always hated conflict in his official family, and he was distressed with the bitter infighting of 1968. He too was exhausted from four years of war. Torn between wanting to be rid of Vietnam and fear of losing, he veered erratically between a hard and soft line. He refused

47 W. Averell Harriman memorandum, "General Review of the Last Six Months," Dec. 10, 1968, W. Averell Harriman papers, Manuscript Division, Library of Congress, Washington, D.C., box 521; Dean Rusk, as told to Richard Rusk, *As I Saw It* (New York, 1990), 417; Clifford, *Counsel to the President*, 476.

48 Tom Johnson notes on meetings, Apr. 6, 8, 1968, Johnson papers, Tom Johnson notes on meetings, box 3; Rostow to LBJ, Apr. 3, 1968, Johnson papers, National Security file, Rostow files, box 6; Clifford, *Counsel to the President*, 534–6.

to reescalate the air war. Responding to the urgent appeals of his advisers, he approved a total bombing halt in October 1968 as a way of getting the Paris negotiations off dead center. But he refused to make the sort of political concessions that would have been required to effect a settlement, and when the South Vietnamese obstructed the negotiation process he refused to dump them. He continued to wage the war aggressively, expanding the bombing of supply lines in Laos and ground operations in Vietnam. Follow the enemy in "relentless pursuit," he instructed Abrams late in the year. "Don't give them a moment's rest. Let them feel the weight of everything you've got."[49]

To the end, LBJ appears to have persuaded himself that he might yet achieve the goal of an independent, non-Communist South Vietnam he had set in 1965. In fact, his refusal to commit to either escalation or disengagement ensured that he would pass on to his successor a stalemated war and a deadlocked negotiation process.

Nor did the administration in its last months address the larger Cold War issues highlighted by the crisis of 1968. The events of March prompted several proposals for fundamental change. Alarmed by the nation's deteriorating economic position, Treasury Secretary Fowler pressed for a full-scale reassessment of U.S. commitments in Europe. In an effort to force the Western allies to bear a greater share of the burden of their own defense, Senator Symington and Senate Majority Leader Mike Mansfield proposed drastic reductions in U.S. forces in Europe.

Throughout the remainder of Johnson's term, his administration continued along lines staked out earlier. To a high degree, of course, the president and his advisers remained preoccupied by Vietnam, and other issues received less attention. The U.S. Cold War policies had been fixed for years, moreover, and it was difficult for weary and beleaguered officials even to contemplate change in their waning months in power. In terms of Europe and the Cold War, the United States thus continued along the two-track approach set earlier.

The Johnson administration used every means at its disposal to maintain NATO strength against assaults at home and from abroad. Resisting European efforts to secure cheaper defense by placing greater reliance on nuclear weapons, U.S. officials continued to stress the essentiality of conventional forces to deter or respond to possible Soviet military challenges. The stabilization of forces in Vietnam helped prevent further weakening of forces in

---

49 Tom Johnson notes on meeting, Oct. 14, 1968, Johnson papers, Tom Johnson notes on meetings, box 4; Lewis Sorley, *General Creighton Abrams and the Army of His Times* (New York, 1992), 253.

Europe. To hold NATO strength at existing levels and prevent worsening of the balance of payments deficit, the administration sought to check further German force reductions and to hold the Germans to the level of off-set purchases agreed upon earlier. At home, Johnson and his advisers steadfastly opposed the Symington-Mansfield proposals. Not wishing to negotiate with the Soviets from a position of weakness or to "throw in the towel as I go out," the president intervened personally to block a measure that in the summer of 1968 seemed likely to pass.[50]

At the same time, the United States pressed forward with détente. Throughout the summer of 1968, Harriman kept in close touch with Soviet diplomats in Paris, seeking to promote détente through the Vietnam negotiations and use Soviet influence to end the war. The president by this time was deeply committed to arms control negotiations with Moscow, as a means of easing the threat of nuclear war, redeeming an administration tainted by Vietnam, and leaving his own mark on history. The United States seemed to achieve a major breakthrough in May when the Soviets indicated a readiness to begin negotiations on a treaty to limit strategic arms, and a Kosygin-Johnson summit was set for Leningrad in September. On July 1, the two nations and Great Britain signed a Nuclear Nonproliferation Treaty.[51]

The Soviet invasion of Czechoslovakia in August 1968 doomed détente and settled European issues for the remainder of Johnson's term. As tensions mounted during the anxious "Prague Spring" of 1968, American officials naively calculated that the Soviets would not do anything to jeopardize détente.[52] The invasion thus came as a rude shock. "The Cold War is not over," Johnson ruefully conceded, and General Wheeler privately denounced what he labeled a "personal insult" to the United States. For a time, there was fear that Moscow might also move against Rumania or even Yugoslavia, opening the possibility of a much more dangerous conflict.

Still eager to negotiate with the USSR, the administration responded in an embarrassingly mild manner, making no more than perfunctory protests and token retaliatory moves. The president and his advisers saw no choice except to cancel the impending summit, but they kept the door open for negotiations after a respectable interval. Indeed, until he left office, LBJ

---

50 Tom Johnson notes on meeting, June 25, 1968, Johnson papers, Tom Johnson notes on meetings, box 4; Thomas Schwartz, "Victories and Defeats in the Long Twilight Struggle: The United States and Western Europe in the 1960s," in Kunz, ed., *Crucial Decade,* 140–1.

51 Robert A. Divine, "Lyndon Johnson and Strategic Arms Limitation," in Robert A. Divine, ed., *The Johnson Years: LBJ at Home and Abroad* (Lawrence, Kan., 1994), 269–70.

52 For the background of the Soviet decision, see Mark Kramer's chapter in this book.

clung desperately, even pathetically, to hopes of a last-minute summit while at the same time demanding from the Soviets prior assurances of positive results on such complex issues as arms control. Moscow was understandably wary of such arrangements, and President-elect Richard Nixon let it be known that he would not honor the results of an eleventh-hour summit. Johnson's efforts to ease Cold War tensions thus came to naught. U.S. acquiescence in the invasion of Czechoslovakia reinforced Western acceptance of the Soviet sphere of influence in Eastern Europe and ended bridge-building except through Moscow.[53]

The United States did use the Soviet invasion of Czechoslovakia to keep in line recalcitrant European allies and critics at home. From the administration standpoint, the Soviet move mercifully diverted world attention from American intervention in Vietnam. At home, support for the Symington-Mansfield proposals dropped sharply, easing at least for the moment any threat of major cutbacks in U.S. forces in Europe. The invasion of Czechoslovakia also sent "shivers" through Western Europe, in the words of Ambassador to NATO Harlan Cleveland. For the first time, the Germans seemed fully to appreciate the danger and possible consequences of nuclear war. In the wake of the Soviet action, West Germany came closer to accepting the U.S. emphasis on conventional defense. The West Germans immediately agreed to increase their military budget and upgrade the readiness of their forces. U.S. officials moved quickly and with some success in the wake of the crisis to get NATO to effect qualitative improvements in its units and speed up its capacity to mobilize.[54]

The dramatic events of 1968 created circumstances that in time produced a major reversal in U.S. relations with China, but these changes came too late for the Johnson administration to act upon. Annoyed by Hanoi's independence, preoccupied with its own domestic problems, and increasingly alarmed with the Soviet threat, China became frustrated with its role in Vietnam. Thus when the Vietnamese ignored Chinese objections and agreed to negotiate in Paris, Beijing withdrew its troops from Vietnam. Along with Johnson's decisions not to escalate the war, this removed Vietnam as a major obstruction to Sino-American rapprochement. More important, the Soviet invasion of Czechoslovakia deeply alarmed the Chinese, provoking some officials to look toward repairing relations with

53 Divine, "Lyndon Johnson and Strategic Arms Limitation," 269–70; record of National Security Council meeting, Sept. 14, 1968, Johnson papers, NSC meeting file; Tom Johnson notes on meetings, Nov. 26, 1968, Johnson papers, Tom Johnson notes on meetings, box 4; see Kramer's chapter in this book; Dobrynin, *In Confidence,* 184–7.
54 Lawrence Kaplan, "The U.S. and NATO in the Johnson Years," in Divine, ed., *LBJ at Home and Abroad,* 137; Tom Johnson notes on meetings, Oct. 14, 1968, Johnson papers, Tom Johnson notes on meetings, box 4.

the United States as a means of containing a more dangerous enemy. Perceiving the subtle shifts in Chinese attitudes and policies, U.S. officials responded positively in late 1968 to faint signals from Beijing. These events occurred in the waning days of the Johnson administration, however, and did not produce substantive results.[55]

IV

Historian Gabriel Kolko pinpoints the 1968 Tet Offensive as the highwater mark of U.S. hegemony, that crucial turning point where Americans experienced a "long-postponed confrontation with reality."[56] To some extent, as noted here, he is right. In the frenzied aftermath of Tet and the gold crisis, key members of the business community, the foreign policy elite, and top Johnson administration officials concluded that the cost of the commitment in Vietnam exceeded any possible gain. They thus advocated scaling back or even liquidating the war to salvage America's deteriorating global position and defend more vital interests elsewhere. The president grudgingly responded, stopping the process of escalation, cutting back the bombing, making a new move for negotiations, and, most important symbolically, removing himself from the presidential race.

Turning points and watersheds are rarely so sharply demarcated, however, and 1968 brought at best a partial "revolution" in U.S. foreign policy. If the gloomy days of March 1968 evoked from many Americans a sense of limits on the nation's power, the subsequent easing of the economic and military crises calmed fears and removed any immediate compulsion to conduct a full-scale reassessment or make major adjustments. The United States did not reexamine its policies on Vietnam, Europe, or East Asia or alter its goals in any fundamental way. Old habits and modes of thinking die hard, and especially in the case of Vietnam, the president incongruously and inexplicably deluded himself into believing that he could do more with less, clinging to the end of his tenure to hopes that he might yet achieve a negotiated settlement without making major concessions or abandoning American goals. It would take the trauma of 1975 and the emergence of the so-called Vietnam syndrome to complete the process of education begun in 1968.[57]

55 See Nancy Bernkopf Tucker's chapter in this book; Arthur Waldron, "From Nonexistent to Almost Normal: U.S.-China Relations in the 1960s," in Kunz, ed., *Crucial Decade,* 241–2.
56 Gabriel Kolko, *Anatomy of a War* (New York, 1986), 334.
57 Richard A. Melanson, *American Foreign Policy Since the Vietnam War: The Search for Consensus from Nixon to Clinton* (New York, 1996), 17–37.

The modest changes introduced by the Johnson administration in its last days did have long-range importance. The cautious and ultimately unsuccessful effort to alter relations with the Soviet Union through what came to be called détente and the hints of a change in relations with China provided a foundation for the polestars of Richard Nixon's foreign policy, a means of reducing the costs of containment through easing Cold War tensions. Johnson's March 1968 initiatives on Vietnam were difficult, if not impossible, to reverse and foreshadowed ultimate U.S. withdrawal. Shifting a greater burden of the war to the Vietnamese heralded the Nixon policy of Vietnamization. It was also the basis for what would be called the Nixon Doctrine, a means of avoiding future Vietnams by providing allies economic and military assistance but leaving to them primary responsibility for their own defense. In a broader sense, the Johnson administration's refusal in Vietnam to pay any price, bear any burden, as John F. Kennedy had pledged in 1961, implicitly conceded the limits it refused to acknowledge explicitly, and at least started the United States in a different direction.

2

Tet on TV

U.S. Nightly News Reporting and
Presidential Policy Making

CHESTER J. PACH JR.

Clad in a bush jacket and standing amid Saigon's ruins of war, America's most respected television journalist, Walter Cronkite, began the most famous assessment of the Tet Offensive. Cronkite, the anchor of the *CBS Evening News*, spent a week in Vietnam in mid-February 1968 and expressed his conclusions in a half-hour special on February 27. Reporting from "a burned and blasted and weary land," Cronkite made himself the surrogate for millions of perplexed American viewers who were trying to figure out how the North Vietnamese and the National Liberation Front (NLF) could have launched their most powerful and ambitious offensive of the war at a time when President Lyndon B. Johnson and many of his top advisers had repeatedly insisted that the United States was making tremendous progress in Vietnam.[1]

Even after talking to high-level U.S. and Vietnamese officials, visiting refugee centers, and observing the fighting, Cronkite could only say in answer to the question of who had prevailed, "I'm not sure. The Vietcong did not win by a knockout, but neither did we." The enemy fell short of inciting a massive uprising of South Vietnamese against their government, but they succeeded in destroying the illusion of security that existed in the cities and in setting back pacification in the countryside. Once a supporter

The author thanks Mary Jane Kelley, Bruce Steiner, Marvin Fletcher, William Frederick, and John Lewis Gaddis for their support; Richard Immerman, Randall Woods, Walter Hixson, and Robert Buzzanco for comments on earlier versions of this chapter; D. J. Clinton for research assistance; Steve Roca for help at National Archives II, College Park, Maryland; and Mike Parrish for assistance at the Lyndon Baines Johnson Library, Austin, Texas.
1 "Who, What, When, Where, Why: Report from Vietnam by Walter Cronkite," CBS, Feb. 27, 1968, A596, Museum of Television and Radio, New York, N.Y.

of the U.S. war effort, Cronkite returned from Vietnam doubtful that victory was possible. "Past performance," he observed, "gives no confidence that the Vietnamese government can cope with its problems," now exacerbated by 470,000 more refugees. Nor did he believe any longer in the hopeful predictions of U.S. officials who found "silver linings" in "the darkest clouds." "To say that we are closer to victory today is to believe, in the face of the evidence, the optimists who have been wrong in the past. To suggest that we are on the edge of defeat is to yield to unreasonable pessimism. To say that we are mired in stalemate seems the only realistic, yet unsatisfactory conclusion." Since the enemy could match any U.S. escalation, the only solution now was disengagement and negotiation, "not as victors but as honorable people who lived up to their pledge to defend democracy and did the best they could."[2]

On the same day as Cronkite's special broadcast, a remarkably similar assessment of the Tet Offensive came from a very different observer, General Earle G. Wheeler, the chair of the U.S. Joint Chiefs of Staff. After surveying the situation in Vietnam at Johnson's direction, Wheeler reported to the president that the enemy attacks had all too often come frighteningly close to success.[3] "In short, it was a very near thing," he concluded. Like Cronkite, Wheeler asserted that the North Vietnamese and Vietcong had failed to achieve their maximum objective of fomenting a general uprising. Yet he also thought that they had dealt the people of South Vietnam "a psychological blow, particularly in the urban areas where the feeling of security had been strong." They had, in addition, severely damaged rural pacification efforts. The enemy had "the will and capability to continue" to attack, even after suffering enormous losses, and Wheeler warned of additional "reverses." He agreed with Cronkite that the government of South Vietnam functioned "at greatly reduced effectiveness" at a time when it faced monumental new problems of reconstruction and resettlement of refugees.[4]

Yet the general, unlike Cronkite, "saw opportunities as well as dangers" in these bleak circumstances. Exploiting them, however, came at a high price. Wheeler endorsed a request – one he had helped to inspire – from General William C. Westmoreland, the commander of U.S. forces in South Vietnam, for an additional 206,000 troops. This enormous infusion of

---

2 Ibid.; CBS News. *Vietnam Perspective: CBS News Special Report; Analysis by Walter Cronkite* (New York, 1965), xi–xii; Don Oberdorfer, *Tet!: The Turning Point of the Vietnam War* (New York, 1971), 246–51.

3 Although Wheeler made public comments about his trip, this summary of his findings comes from his top secret report to Johnson.

4 *The Pentagon Papers as Published by the New York Times* (New York, 1971), 596–7, 615–21.

strength, he believed, would enable the United States and its South Vietnamese allies to defeat the enemy offensive and "regain the initiative" in the war.[5]

Wheeler's report was alarming, since it acknowledged that the Tet Offensive had been a hard blow to the U.S. war effort and it proposed massive escalation. But Cronkite's assessment sent "shock waves . . . through [the] government."[6] A public declaration rather than a top-secret memorandum, Cronkite's "Report from Vietnam" reached an audience of nine million viewers and stirred considerable public comment.[7] Even more important was the effect of Cronkite's broadcast on the president. "If I've lost Cronkite, I've lost middle America," Johnson despaired.[8] So, too, had he lost the establishment as represented by the Wise Men, elder statesmen who told Johnson that the time had come to disengage from Vietnam. "We have no support for the war," the beleaguered president complained.[9] Facing an "unbearable" situation, Johnson took dramatic action.[10] In a nationally televised address on March 31, he announced a partial bombing halt of North Vietnam, called for negotiations, and declared that he would not seek another term as president.[11]

Johnson, who often equated criticism with disloyalty, was bitter about television coverage of the Tet Offensive. As he wrote in his memoirs, "there was a great deal of emotional and exaggerated reporting of the Tet Offensive in our press and on television. The media seemed to be in competition as to who could provide the most lurid and depressing accounts." The "daily barrage of bleakness and near panic" made the public think "that we must have suffered a defeat."[12] Other analysts have echoed Johnson's words, criticizing television for reporting that was sensational, distorted, or just plain wrong.[13]

5 Ibid.

6 William Small, *To Kill a Messenger: Television News and the Real World* (New York, 1970), 123.

7 Oberdorfer, *Tet!,* 250.

8 Phillip B. Davidson, *Vietnam at War: The History, 1946–1975* (New York, 1991), 486.

9 Richard H. Immerman, "'A Time in the Tide of Men's Affairs': Lyndon Johnson and Vietnam," in Warren I. Cohen and Nancy Bernkopf Tucker, eds., *Lyndon Johnson Confronts the World: American Foreign Policy, 1963–1968* (New York, 1994), 79.

10 Doris Kearns, *Lyndon Johnson and the American Dream* (New York, 1976), 343.

11 *Public Papers of the Presidents of the United States: Lyndon B. Johnson, 1968–69,* 2 vols. (Washington, D.C., 1970), 1:469–76.

12 Lyndon Baines Johnson, *The Vantage Point: Perspectives on the Presidency, 1963–1969* (New York, 1971), 384. See also *Public Papers,* 1:483–6.

13 Peter Braestrup, *Big Story: How the American Press and Television Reported and Interpreted the Crisis of Tet 1968 in Vietnam and Washington,* 2 vols. (Boulder, Colo., 1977); Robert Elegant, "How to Lose a War," *Encounter* 57 (Aug. 1981): 73–90; Davidson, *Vietnam at War,* 484–92; W. W. Rostow, *The Diffusion of Power: An Essay in Recent History* (New York, 1972), 518–20; William Colby, *Lost Victory: A Firsthand Account of America's Sixteen-Year Involvement in Vietnam* (New York, 1989), 232–4; Dave Richard Palmer, *Summons of the Trumpet: U.S.-Vietnam in Perspective* (San Rafael, Calif., 1978), 191.

Television did not determine the outcome of the Tet Offensive, as Johnson and other like-minded critics have alleged. Yet TV news coverage during early 1968 did shape official thinking and public attitudes, perhaps more than at any other time during the Vietnam War. Television presented Tet as a crisis, as it should have, and carried film reports whose vividness and immediacy exceeded previous coverage of the war. Television's weaknesses were also highly visible – a preoccupation with conventional military operations, a narrow focus on Americans that relegated the South Vietnamese to a minor role, and a penchant for visually dramatic stories. Yet despite these limitations, TV news coverage challenged official assurances of progress in the war and helped viewers make sense of a crisis that the Johnson administration was unable to explain. Television reporting of Tet reflected – and surely intensified – the sense of shock, anguish, and uncertainty that Americans felt in early 1968, whether they watched the nightly news in their living rooms or in the Oval Office.

Before the Tet Offensive, television news coverage, on balance, suggested that the war was going well for U.S. forces in Vietnam. Television's war was combat, especially fighting that involved American soldiers, marines, or pilots. "Cameras. That's all I see wherever I look," one American complained. "Sometimes I'm not sure whether I'm a soldier or an extra in a bad movie."[14] Network correspondents usually reported that U.S. troops prevailed on the battlefield because of their sophisticated technology, punishing firepower, or effective leadership. The weekly casualty figures, a Thursday evening ritual, seemed to measure the progress toward victory. Correspondents and anchors – Peter Jennings and then Bob Young on ABC, Walter Cronkite on CBS, Chet Huntley and David Brinkley on NBC – concentrated their reporting on a series of military encounters in the highlands, jungles, or rice paddies whose connection to a coherent strategy was uncertain but that nonetheless seemed to be leading toward victory.[15]

Despite the emphasis on combat, television showed little of the horrors of battle. The North Vietnamese and Vietcong were elusive fighters; they relied heavily on booby traps, mines, and snipers. U.S. troops often complained that they could not find the enemy, and television cameras had the same problem. Yet even if camera operators happened to film heavy action, the most graphic scenes usually did not make the final cut. "I had a very

---

14 Walter LaFeber, "Johnson, Vietnam, and Tocqueville," in Cohen and Tucker, eds., *Lyndon Johnson Confronts the World,* 51.

15 Chester J. Pach Jr., "And That's the Way It Was: The Vietnam War on the Network Nightly News," in David Farber, ed., *The Sixties: From Memory to History* (Chapel Hill, N.C., 1994), 94–101.

high 'queasy quotient,'" said the producer of the *CBS Evening News*. "That is to say that there was a limit to how much blood and gore we could put on a broadcast that was seen at dinnertime for most American households."[16] Scenes of mangled bodies may have impressed viewers out of all proportion to their number, especially at a time of rapid increase in the percentage of households with color TV.[17] "Mud and blood were indistinguishable in black and white," historian Erik Barnouw has written. "In color, blood was blood."[18] But blood was rare. As critic Michael Arlen has observed, television's war consisted "mainly of scenes of helicopters landing, tall grasses blowing in the helicopter wind, American soldiers fanning out across a hillside on foot, rifles at the ready, with now and then (on the soundtrack) a far-off ping or two, and now and then (as the visual grand finale) a column of dark, billowing smoke a half mile away, invariably described as a burning Vietcong ammo dump."[19]

The Johnson administration mounted a major public relations effort to influence media coverage of the war. U.S. military authorities did not censor the news, as they had during World War II and the Korean War, since they feared that such restrictions would not work in Vietnam. Instead, U.S. public affairs officials in Saigon tried to cultivate reporters by offering transportation to battle areas, interviews with commanders, and daily news briefings.[20]

In Washington, the public relations effort was even more ambitious, and Lyndon Johnson was at its center. As historian David Culbert has noted, Johnson was "obsessed" with mass media, had "an inordinate concern with his own image," and made significant efforts to influence news coverage of his administration's policies.[21] Johnson would tell reporters, "I'm the only president you've got," implying that favorable news coverage was a patriotic duty. Cooperation would produce exclusive interviews and abundant information. "Play[ing] it the other way," however, would mean losing White House sources of news except routine press handouts.[22]

16 David Farber, *The Age of Great Dreams: America in the 1960s* (New York, 1994), 154–5.
17 Cobbett Steinberg, *TV Facts* (New York, 1985), 87.
18 Erik Barnouw, *Tube of Plenty: The Evolution of American Television*, 2d ed. (New York, 1990), 401.
19 Michael J. Arlen, "The Air: The Falklands, Vietnam, and Our Collective Memory," *New Yorker*, Aug. 16, 1982, 73; Pach, "And That's the Way It Was," 94–5, 106.
20 Pach, "And That's the Way It Was," 92; William M. Hammond, *Public Affairs: The Military and the Media, 1962–1968* (Washington, D.C., 1988), 135–48, 193–5.
21 David Culbert, "Johnson and the Media," in Robert A. Divine, ed., *The Johnson Years*, vol. 1: *Foreign Policy, the Great Society, and the White House* (Lawrence, Kan., 1987), 214.
22 Kathleen J. Turner, *Lyndon Johnson's Dual War: Vietnam and the Press* (Chicago, 1985), 32, 44–5; Robert Dallek, "Lyndon Johnson and Vietnam," *Diplomatic History* 20 (spring 1996): 156–9; Pach, "And That's the Way It Was," 92.

The administration's media offensive produced mixed results. TV journalists did not dispute the president's decision to send U.S. fighting forces to Vietnam or his commitment to the containment of communism. Yet such support was less the product of administration pressures or inducements than of widespread acceptance of the fundamentals of U.S. policy at the beginning of the Vietnam War. However, news reports from Vietnam in 1966–7, while on balance still favorable, questioned the effectiveness of the U.S. war effort more frequently and pointedly. Popular support for Johnson's war policies also slipped, and in January 1967 public opinion for the first time turned against the administration's handling of the situation in Vietnam. By the fall of 1967, the war had become so unpopular and Johnson so beset by critics – both hawks and doves – that his presidency was imperiled.[23] "I am in deep trouble," Johnson admitted, but he added that "there has never been a major war when there hasn't been major trouble at home."[24]

To recoup the losses in the polls, the administration launched a "Progress Campaign," an elaborate attempt to show that the United States was achieving its goals in Vietnam. To counter the pessimistic reports of stalemate that allegedly dominated the news media, Walt W. Rostow, Johnson's special assistant for national security affairs, asked Westmoreland and Ellsworth Bunker, the U.S. ambassador in Saigon, in September 1967 to "search urgently for occasions to present sound evidence of progress in Vietnam. . . . [The] President's judgment is that this is at [the] present stage a critically important dimension of fighting the war."[25] Rostow chaired an interagency committee that accelerated the flow of upbeat reports from government agencies and leaked them to the news media. Top administration officials reinforced these efforts with optimistic pronouncements about the war. Westmoreland and Bunker traveled to Washington in November for a series of high-level meetings, photo opportunities, and public appearances. "We have reached an important point when the end comes into view," Westmoreland declared in his summary of the war effort at the National Press Club.[26] Johnson echoed these judgments. "We are making progress," he told a White House news conference. "We are pleased with the results

23 According to Roper public opinion polls, those who disapproved of Johnson's Vietnam policies outnumbered those who approved for the first time in January 1967. The percentages were: approve, 38; disapprove, 43; no opinion, 19. Burns W. Roper, "What Public Opinion Polls Said," in Braestrup, *Big Story,* 1:700; Pach, "And That's the Way It Was," 105–6.
24 Notes of the president's meeting with educators from Cambridge, Massachusetts, colleges and universities, Sept. 26, 1967. Tom Johnson's notes of Meetings, Lyndon Baines Johnson Library, Austin, Texas (hereafter LBJ Library).
25 Larry Berman, *Lyndon Johnson's War: The Road to Stalemate in Vietnam* (New York, 1989), 84–5.
26 Stanley Karnow, *Vietnam: A History* (New York, 1983), 514.

that we are getting. . . . [Our armed forces] are going to bring us an honorable peace."[27] Progress was even the theme of the New Year's Eve party
at the U.S. Embassy in Saigon, which invited guests to "come see the light
at the end of the tunnel."[28]

The Progress Campaign reclaimed some public support for the war.
Opinion surveys revealed in November 1967 that 51 percent of the public
believed the United States and its allies were making progress in Vietnam,
compared to 33 percent who thought they were standing still and only 8
percent who concluded they were losing ground. Polls also showed a surge
in approval for the administration's Vietnam policies at the end of 1967. Yet
the war was only less unpopular, since Johnson's critics still outnumbered
supporters 47 to 39 percent in January 1968 (as compared to 54 to 32 percent in August 1967).[29]

Selling the war increased the dangers to Johnson's already battered credibility. Throughout 1967 journalists complained about the gap between
Johnson's rhetoric and the realities of the war.[30] The Progress Campaign
nevertheless relied on exaggeration, manipulation, and distortion. The
imperative of showing progress in the war, for example, also influenced
intelligence estimates. Westmoreland informed reporters in late November
that enemy strength had declined to less than 250,000. This figure, however, excluded 120,000 militia and clandestine forces that the Central Intelligence Agency thought should be counted. As one CIA official explained,
"any higher figure would not be sufficiently optimistic and would generate
[an] unacceptable level of criticism from the press."[31] Bureaucratic artifice
and public relations expedients did not persuade Secretary of Defense
Robert S. McNamara, who reached the harsh conclusion that victory was
impossible. McNamara submitted his dissenting views to the president, and
that memorandum "raised the tension" between them "to the breaking
point." At the end of November, Johnson announced that McNamara
would soon leave the cabinet to become director of the World Bank.[32]
Rather than reconsidering its objectives or its strategy in Vietnam, the

27 Oberdorfer, *Tet!*, 99–103; *Public Papers of the Presidents of the United States, Lyndon B. Johnson, 1967*, 2 vols. (Washington, D.C., 1968), 2:1048–9; Culbert, "Johnson and the Media," 233.
28 David Halberstam, *The Best and the Brightest* (New York, 1972), 647.
29 Roper, "What Public Opinion Polls Said," in Braestrup, *Big Story*, 1:695, 700.
30 On the credibility gap, see Turner, *Lyndon Johnson's Dual War*, 141, 176–7, 200–3; Ronald Steel, *Walter Lippmann and the American Century* (Boston, 1980), 575–8.
31 Berman, *Lyndon Johnson's War*, 82–83. On the controversy over estimating enemy strength, see Hammond, *Public Affairs*, 325–7; James J. Wirtz, *The Tet Offensive: Intelligence Failure in War* (Ithaca, N.Y., 1991), 158–62; John Prados, *The Hidden History of the Vietnam War* (Chicago, 1995), 121–8; and Ronnie E. Ford, *Tet 1968: Understanding the Surprise* (London, 1995), 171–7.
32 Robert S. McNamara, *In Retrospect: The Tragedy and Lessons of Vietnam* (New York, 1995), 306–13.

administration pressed ahead with its Progress Campaign, raising public expectations that success was just around the corner. Bad news from Vietnam would now not simply be hard to explain, but might be a fatal blow to the credibility of the administration's war policies.

The Progress Campaign was still going on when the Tet Offensive began on January 30, 1968. Suddenly war engulfed South Vietnam. From the Demilitarized Zone to the Mekong Delta, infantry battalions and commando forces, guerrillas and terrorists launched startling, ferocious, coordinated attacks. Within twenty-four hours, more than eighty thousand North Vietnamese and Vietcong soldiers struck at more than 150 locations, including thirty-six of forty-four provincial capitals and five of the six largest cities. Brazenly, they attacked in places that had previously been invulnerable or immune to the fighting – the U.S. embassy in Saigon, the South Vietnamese presidential palace, Westmoreland's headquarters at Tan Son Nhut air base, and the residential streets of Saigon. Mortars, rockets, and small arms fire overwhelmed the celebratory Tet firecrackers. For millions of South Vietnamese, the festive lunar new year holiday turned into a nightmare.[33]

"Was Tet a surprise?" asked historian John Prados, an authority on U.S. intelligence. "Yes and no," he answered. For months U.S. intelligence officials had picked up indications of North Vietnamese plans for a major offensive. Westmoreland, who insisted that the way to win the war was to fight big battles that could grind down enemy strength, interpreted this intelligence according to his preconceptions. He thought that the main enemy effort would occur at Khe Sanh, a remote outpost in the north fortified by U.S. marines. Expecting the North Vietnamese commander, General Vo Nguyen Giap, to try to win another decisive battle as he had in 1954 against the French at Dienbienphu, Westmoreland shifted troops to the northern provinces and canceled the thirty-six–hour Tet cease-fire in that area. At most, he expected an increase in terrorism around Saigon to divert attention from Khe Sanh, but he made no special preparations to deal with it. The Tet Offensive jolted U.S. and South Vietnamese forces. They recovered quickly, however, and in most cases repelled the attacks in a few hours or a few days. Yet the scope, intensity, and timing of the Tet Offensive astonished high U.S. officials. "I was there at Westy's elbow," recalled

---

33 George C. Herring, *America's Longest War: The United States and Vietnam, 1950–1975,* 2d ed. (New York, 1986), 189; George Donelson Moss, *Vietnam: An American Ordeal,* 2d ed. (Englewood Cliffs, N.J., 1994), 254; Larry Berman, "The Tet Offensive," in Marc Jason Gilbert and William Head, eds., *The Tet Offensive* (Westport, Conn., 1996), 21.

Ambassador Robert Komer, the head of U.S. pacification efforts. "Boy was it a surprise, lemme tell you!"[34]

The evening news programs reflected Westmoreland's view of enemy intentions and devoted considerable attention to the fighting at Khe Sanh during the last ten days of January. "For weeks," Chet Huntley noted on Monday, January 22, "United States military sources have been predicting a new North Vietnamese offensive south of the Demilitarized Zone. Well, it began over the weekend." In a film interview, Westmoreland said he expected that the North Vietnamese would try for a spectacular victory before the Tet truce. NBC reported two days later that the U.S. military command believed that the offensive against Khe Sanh might be the biggest of the war. Ron Nessen observed that the fighting at Khe Sanh was fierce, a judgment confirmed the following evening on CBS when Cronkite noted that correspondent Igor Ogonesof had suffered a shrapnel wound while waiting to film at the besieged marine outpost.[35] CBS and NBC both carried scenes of the marines, grimly joking about the similarity to Dienbienphu, digging in to withstand the pounding from heavy artillery as far as seventeen miles away in North Vietnam and the mortar and rocket fire from the surrounding hills "swarming" with enemy troops. "Whatever result is written into history," Nessen concluded, "it will be written in blood."[36]

The buildup around Khe Sanh became even more ominous after the North Korean capture on January 23 of the U.S. intelligence ship *Pueblo*. The Johnson administration's supporters and critics insisted that this seizure was related to the war, even though there still is no evidence thirty years later to sustain that conclusion. J. William Fulbright (D-Ark.), the chair of the Senate Foreign Relations Committee, argued, for example, that U.S. preoccupation with Vietnam emboldened North Korea. Senator Richard Russell (D-Ga.) advanced the more popular interpretation that the North Koreans timed their action to assist the North Vietnamese. "All of these

34 Prados, *Hidden History of the Vietnam War,* 129–40; Prados, "The Warning That Left Something to Chance: Intelligence at Tet," in Gilbert and Head, eds., *Tet Offensive,* 143–63; Larry Cable, "Don't Bother Me with the Facts; I've Made Up My Mind: The Tet Offensive in the Context of Intelligence and U.S. Strategy," in Gilbert and Head, eds., *Tet Offensive,* 176–9; Ford, *Tet 1968,* 192–4; William C. Westmoreland, *A Soldier Reports* (Garden City, N.Y., 1976), 145–53.

35 Comments by Huntley and interview with Westmoreland by Tuckner, Jan. 22, 1968, NBC; report by Webster, Jan. 22, 1968, CBS; comments by Brinkley and report by Nessen, Jan. 24, 1968, NBC; and comments by Cronkite, Jan. 25, 1968, CBS, all in A131, Weekly News Summary, Assistant Secretary of Defense for Public Affairs, Record Group 330, National Archives, College Park, Maryland (hereafter DOD Weekly News Summary).

36 Reports by Nessen, Jan. 26 and 29, 1968, NBC, and Ogonesof, Jan. 26, 1968, CBS, both in A132, DOD Weekly News Summary.

moves, it now seems, are coordinated," ABC's John Scali reported from the
State Department. "And there may be more to come because the Communists don't act in isolation in this part of the world."[37]

The spectacular Tet assault on the U.S. embassy in Saigon and the simultaneous wave of coordinated attacks quickly replaced Khe Sanh as the big
story from Vietnam on the nightly news. Wire service dispatches of the
fighting reached New York far in advance of film reports, which had to be
flown to Tokyo for satellite transmission. NBC carried the first news of the
Saigon attacks when Huntley informed viewers on January 30 – inaccu-
rately, as it turned out – that twenty suicide commandos were holding part
of the embassy's first floor. The next evening, Huntley declared in evocative language that the embassy grounds had been "cleansed" of Vietcong
after a seven-hour fight, but that none had "penetrated" the building
proper.[38] Live via satellite from Tokyo, Jack Perkins narrated film of the
battle at the embassy. It had arrived just ten minutes prior to airtime, and it
was "raw, . . . unedited, . . . just as it happened." Perhaps better than a pol-
ished report, the film captured the tense, frantic atmosphere in the embassy
compound, as military police crouched to avoid sniper fire and advanced
on the infiltrators. "We have not seen it before either," Perkins reminded
viewers, and it was as close to live coverage of the war as was possible in
1968.[39]

During the next few days, the networks carried a flurry of stories that
showed South Vietnam under "hard, desperate, communist attack."[40] Damaged U.S. aircraft littered the air base at Danang, where the Vietcong took
the war into the city for the first time. South Vietnamese troops were so
busy trying to expel a North Vietnamese regiment from Ban Me Thuot,
NBC's Wilson Hall said, that they had not even counted the dead. At Nam
O, terrified civilians rushed from their homes to escape the deadly cross-
fire.[41] Saigon was "a city besieged," where fires and air strikes sent columns
of smoke into the air.[42] Correspondents emphasized the unprecedented,

37 Reports by Scali, Jan. 23, 1968, ABC; and by Marvin Kalb, Jan. 23, 1968, CBS, both in A131,
   ibid.
38 For a provocative discussion of the implications of such language, see Frank Costigliola, "The
   Nuclear Family: Tropes of Gender and Pathology in the Western Alliance," *Diplomatic History* 21
   (spring 1997): 163–83.
39 Comments by Huntley, Jan. 30 and 31, 1968, NBC; and report by Perkins, Jan. 31, 1968, NBC,
   both in A132, DOD Weekly News Summary.
40 Comment by Brinkley, Feb. 1, 1968, NBC, A132, ibid.
41 Reports by Syvertsen, Jan. 30, 1968, CBS, A132; Hall, Feb. 2, 1968, NBC, A133; Nessen, Feb. 1,
   1968, NBC, A132; and Syvertsen, Feb. 1, 1968, CBS, A132, all in ibid.
42 Report by Peterson, Feb. 2, 1968, ABC, A133, ibid.

Figure 2.1. Execution of a suspected Vietcong officer by General Nguyen Ngoc Loan, the chief of the South Vietnamese National Police, February 1, 1968. Reproduced by permission of AP/World Wide Photos.

astonishing, and frightening sights of Saigon – tanks in the streets, fighter aircraft hitting targets in residential neighborhoods, refugees who had come to the city to escape the war fleeing once again, corpses stacked on sidewalks. The normal routines of the city had come to a halt; only the coffin makers were open for business, ABC reported.[43]

"Rough justice on a Saigon street," is how John Chancellor described the most spectacular image of the Tet Offensive and, indeed, the entire war – the summary execution of a suspected Vietcong officer by General Nguyen Ngoc Loan, the chief of the South Vietnamese National Police (see Figure 2.1). Chancellor made this comment on the *Huntley-Brinkley Report,* as he summarized the sharp fighting that had brought "the charmed life of the city of Saigon . . . to a bloody end." The last in a series of photographs that accompanied Chancellor's narration showed Loan pointing his revolver at

43 Reports by Tuckner, Feb. 1, 1968, NBC, and Webster, Feb. 1, 1968, CBS, both in A132, ibid.; report by Webster, Feb. 2, 1968, CBS; and anchor comments, Feb. 2, 1968, ABC, both in A133, ibid.

the victim, whose face twisted in death. This stunning picture, which won a Pulitzer Prize for Associated Press photographer Eddie Adams, appeared prominently in almost every major U.S. newspaper.[44]

The next evening, February 2, both NBC and ABC carried film reports of the execution. Both began with scenes of fighting around the An Quang pagoda, headquarters of a Vietcong commando unit. As NBC's Howard Tuckner explained, "government troops were ordered to get as much revenge as possible." The exchange of fire at times almost drowned out Tuckner's stark narrative. Terrified civilians huddled together, since "no one was above suspicion." Others fled, although the bullets had wounded a score of them, including one who lay with his back to the camera, bleeding from his side. The NBC and ABC films then showed South Vietnamese marines leading away a prisoner, clad in a plaid shirt and shorts, hands bound behind him. "He was roughed up badly but refused to talk," Tuckner said. General Loan "was waiting for him." The NBC film ended with Loan pulling the trigger and the Vietcong officer collapsing. The screen then went black. ABC cut to the Adams photograph at the moment of death, since their camera operator stopped filming just before Loan fired. The ABC report concluded with South Vietnamese soldiers throwing the corpse onto a truck.[45]

Why would network news programs carry such gruesome footage? Surely it was not because of the importance of the dead Vietcong soldier. The victim had no name on U.S. television. ABC called him a "Vietcong terrorist"; NBC identified him as "the commander of the Vietcong commando unit" headquartered at the An Quang pagoda. Nor was it because television journalists wanted to criticize the brutality of Saigon justice or emphasize the horrors of Tet or the Vietnam War. Neither Tuckner, nor Roger Peterson, who narrated the ABC film, depicted Loan as anything more than a symbol of South Vietnamese anger and frustration during Tet. Instead, the NBC news staff considered their report newsworthy because it contained exclusive footage with startling visual images of a remarkable act by a high South Vietnamese official. "CBS and ABC were there but we are the only ones who have film on the execution," exclaimed the chief of NBC's Saigon bureau. For Robert Northshield, the executive producer of the *Huntley-Brinkley Report* and a combat veteran of World War II, the film

44 Report by Chancellor, Feb. 1, 1968, NBC, A132, ibid.; George A. Bailey and Lawrence W. Lichty, "Rough Justice on a Saigon Street: A Gatekeeper Study of NBC's Tet Execution Film," *Journalism Quarterly* 49 (summer 1972): 221–5; Hammond, *Public Affairs,* 350; Pach, "And That's the Way It Was," 108–9.
45 Reports by Tuckner, NBC, Feb. 2, 1968, and Peterson, Feb. 2, 1968, ABC; and anchor comments, Feb. 2, 1968, ABC, all in DOD Weekly News Summary.

was "too rough," so he trimmed a segment that showed blood gushing from the head of the executed man.[46]

Although twenty million viewers watched Loan mete out rough justice on NBC, the film had much less impact than the Adams picture. It was rebroadcast only a few times, perhaps because it was so horrifying, surely because endless replays were neither as feasible nor as common as they would become by the time of the *Challenger* explosion, the demonstrations in Tiananmen Square, or the Rodney King beating. The Adams picture, however, became one of the most reproduced images in history, appearing in books as well as magazines and newspapers. More widely circulated and more accessible, the photograph became a convenient symbol that both critics of the war and advocates of stern retribution against an unscrupulous enemy could invoke to sustain their positions.[47]

The nightly news programs showed other harrowing images during the first days of the Tet Offensive. Among the most unsettling were scenes of correspondents themselves suffering wounds as the violence erased familiar distinctions between observer and participant. On the same evening, viewers saw George Syvertsen's report from Nam O abruptly stop when the CBS camera operator fell injured and ABC's Andrew Pearson carried a stricken sound technician to safety during the fighting near the South Vietnamese presidential palace.[48] A week later, Tuckner became the story as he covered the street fighting in the Saigon suburb of Cholon. "There's blood on my pants, and I guess I'm hit," Tuckner exclaimed after a piece of shrapnel slammed into his leg. An eerie stream of consciousness monologue followed as a medic dressed his wounds. "Well, this is [sic] the streets of Saigon, and that's where the war is now. . . . I guess it could have been much worse. And anybody who told you that they don't think about these things is a damn liar. This is one of the lucky ones."[49]

Not so lucky were the anguished, afflicted, and uprooted South Vietnamese civilians. Night after night TV news programs showed the human toll of the fearful urban battles of Tet. The Vietcong had brought the war to Saigon with a vengeance, George Syvertsen declared in his report on the civilian victims of the fighting in the run-down area known as the "Chessboard." The film showed the residents lugging their possessions, as Syvertsen cataloged their miseries – destroyed homes, soaring food prices, cur-

---

46 Pach, "And That's the Way It Was," 108–9; Bailey and Lichty, "Rough Justice on a Saigon Street," 223–9, 238; Braestrup, *Big Story*, 1:460–5; Oberdorfer, *Tet!*, 170.
47 Bailey and Lichty, "Rough Justice on a Saigon Street," 227–8; Hammond, *Public Affairs*, 352–3.
48 Report by Syvertsen, Feb. 1, 1968, CBS; and report by Pearson, Feb. 1, 1968, ABC, both in A132, DOD Weekly News Summary.
49 Report by Tuckner, Feb. 9, 1968, NBC, A133, ibid.

fews that prevented them from earning a living.[50] Tuckner divided the responsibility for the plight of the civilians at My Tho in the Mekong Delta. The Vietcong used them as human shields; South Vietnamese troops overreacted and fired at them; U.S. planes devastated their neighborhoods. All of the local physicians were on holiday when the shooting began, and many of the fifteen hundred wounded civilians could not receive adequate treatment – or any at all. The report ended with the widow of a South Vietnamese soldier sobbing in the background.[51] "Some of the things you see are incredible," declared ABC's Roger Grimsby as he inspected Saigon's overflowing hospitals. There was no medicine or staff in one children's ward. Grim scenes of maimed civilians in other medical facilities, Syvertsen concluded, were the "real tragedy of the fighting."[52]

Top U.S. officials, even though privately worried, tried to put the best face on the jarring news from Vietnam. Johnson's first reaction to the Tet attacks was: "This could be very bad." But two days later, he called White House correspondents into the Cabinet Room and read a statement in which he insisted that the Tet Offensive was no surprise and that the enemy had failed to spark a popular uprising against the government of South Vietnam. While cautioning that the situation was fluid, he said he saw no reason to change his opinion that the United States was still winning the war.[53] "There may have been a sergeant asleep with a beer in his hand and his zipper open, or a man in a jeep with a woman in his lap," Johnson told reporters in the off-the-record meeting. But overall, he maintained, allied troops had been ready for the communist offensive.[54]

In Saigon, U.S. civilian and military authorities were similarly upbeat. After returning to the battered U.S. embassy in an armored personnel carrier, Bunker prematurely proclaimed that Saigon was secure. Westmoreland first dismissed the action in Saigon as diversionary, a sideshow to the main event at Khe Sanh. He then emphasized the enormous costs that the North Vietnamese and the Vietcong absorbed for transitory gains – an estimated fifteen thousand casualties and four thousand prisoners in the first week of fighting alone. ABC and NBC noted that the general sent a con-

---

50 Report by Syvertsen, Feb. 6, 1968, CBS, A133, ibid.
51 Report by Tuckner, Feb. 6, 1968, NBC, A133, ibid.
52 Reports by Grimsby, Feb. 5, 1968, ABC; and Syvertsen, Feb. 8, 1968, CBS; and comment by Cronkite, Feb. 5, 1968, CBS; all in A133, ibid. See also reports by Webster, Feb. 2, 1968, CBS; Anderton, Feb. 2, 1968, ABC; and Cioffi, Feb. 5, 1968, ABC, all in A133, ibid.
53 *Public Papers,* 2:155–61; notes of the president's foreign affairs luncheon, Jan. 30, 1968, Tom Johnson's notes of meetings, LBJ Library.
54 Oberdorfer, *Tet!,* 162–3, 168–9.

gratulatory message to U.S. troops for inflicting losses so heavy that they may have shortened the war.[55]

This optimistic rhetoric inspired little public confidence. Anger, frustration, and belligerence characterized the U.S. public's immediate reaction to the Tet Offensive. Those who favored stronger action in Vietnam rose to 61 percent, while those who wanted to reduce the U.S. military effort fell to 23 percent.[56] These self-proclaimed hawks may have "rallied round the flag" but not behind the president, as disapproval of Johnson's handling of the war increased from 47 to 53 percent between January and early February.[57] By a small margin – 45 to 43 percent – the public thought it had been a mistake to commit U.S. troops to combat.[58] The polls, in short, showed that official assurances had failed to ease popular bewilderment and discontent.

Television news coverage of Tet challenged the Johnson administration's assertions of progress in Vietnam. Anchors sometimes took issue with official interpretations of the fighting. Huntley, who had a reputation as a supporter of the war, declared that even if the attacks in Saigon were diversionary, as Westmoreland believed, they were still highly destructive. Brinkley, who advocated disengagement, was more acerbic. Even though Westmoreland emphasized the frightful enemy casualties, the general, Brinkley noted, "did not say it [the Tet Offensive] was not effective." In a commentary on ABC on February 1, Joseph C. Harsch criticized the administration's spin doctors. "What government officials say in private bears little resemblance to the highly orchestrated public good cheer," he bluntly declared. The enemy had mounted the biggest and boldest offensive of the war, "the exact opposite of what American leaders have for months been leading us to expect." Robert Schakne of CBS offered a similar assessment a week after the fighting began. "All those comfortable, offi-

55 Report by Perkins and comments by Huntley, Jan. 31, 1968, NBC, A132; comments by Huntley, NBC, Feb. 1, 1968, A132; report by Schakne, Feb. 5, 1968, CBS, A133; comments by Huntley, Feb. 6, 1968, A133; and comments by Young, Feb. 6, 1968, ABC, all in DOD Weekly News Summary; Prados, "The Warning That Left Something to Chance," 161.
56 Between January and early February 1968, those who considered themselves "hawks" increased from 56 to 61 percent, "doves" declined from 27 to 23 percent, and those with no opinion dropped slightly from 17 to 16 percent. Roper, "What Public Opinion Polls Said," in Braestrup, *Big Story*, 681.
57 In January and early February 1968, "hawks" became much more sharply critical of Johnson's war policies. In January, 50 percent approved, 40 percent disapproved, and 10 percent had no opinion. A month later, 41 percent approved, 52 percent disapproved, and 7 percent had no opinion. Comparable percentages for doves were 20, 70, and 10 in January and 22, 68, and 10 in February. Ibid., 697.
58 Ibid., 679; John E. Mueller, *War, Presidents, and Public Opinion* (New York, 1973), 106–8.

cial assumptions about steady progress in the war turned out to be wrong," he asserted. "For Americans in South Vietnam, the world turned upside down in the past week," Schakne concluded. "Our troubles may just be beginning."[59]

Reports of tough, persistent fighting after the first wave of attacks seemed to confirm Schakne's prediction. The Vietcong fought stubbornly in and around Saigon, frustrating U.S. and South Vietnamese soldiers who could not blast them out with heavy firepower but instead had to clear them house by house. The fighting was slow and dangerous, and TV news repeatedly showed U.S. forces braving fire from snipers who were "everywhere and nowhere." No part of Saigon was safe, Lou Cioffi told viewers of the *ABC Evening News* on February 6. Cronkite stated two days later that only three of the city's nine districts were secure. TV journalists suggested that Saigon would probably not again experience its pre-Tet tranquility even after the current guerrilla attacks subsided. As ABC's Bill Brannigan explained, the guards along the city's perimeter seemed more interested in extortion than security. Ho Chi Minh, Brannigan speculated, could probably get within fifty yards of Westmoreland's headquarters by paying a bribe of two or three dollars.[60]

The attacks on the periphery of Saigon in late February emphasized Saigon's continuing vulnerability. A major target was Tan Son Nhut airport, where more planes took off and landed than at any other location in the world. The grounds contained Westmoreland's headquarters and forty thousand soldiers, so it was a large and tempting target, as NBC's Wilson Hall noted. The Vietcong began a "war of nerves" against Tan Son Nhut, Douglas Kiker told viewers of the *Huntley-Brinkley Report* on February 19. Rockets and mortars crashed into the airport's chapel and public information building, as well as a barracks where Kiker stood. Morale, not property, was the target, Kiker said, but Peter Kalischer's interviews with some of the wounded that aired that same night on the *CBS Evening News* revealed that the victims were hurt but unshaken. Kalischer expressed frustration over the inability to locate the rocket sites and mortar tubes at "the very doorstep of Saigon." Hall explained that the residents in nearby villages did not report enemy action, and there would never be enough troops

59 Comments by Huntley, Jan. 31, 1968, NBC; comments by Huntley, Feb. 1, 1968, NBC; commentary by Harsch, Feb. 1, 1968, ABC, all in A132, DOD Weekly News Summary; report by Schakne, Feb. 5, 1968, CBS, A133, ibid.; Peter Stoler, *The War Against the Press: Politics, Pressure and Intimidation in the 80s* (New York, 1986), 67–8; Small, *To Kill a Messenger*, 124.
60 Reports by Syvertsen, Feb. 6, 1968, CBS; Cioffi, Feb. 6, 1968, ABC; North, Feb. 7, 1968, ABC; and comments by Cronkite, Feb. 8, 1968, all in A133, DOD Weekly News Summary; reports by Glennon, Feb. 15, 1968, CBS; and Brannigan, Feb. 15, 1968, ABC, both in A134, ibid.

for the continuous patrolling necessary to keep Tan Son Nhut free from hostile fire.[61]

TV journalists provided conflicting information about whether the attacks at Tan Son Nhut and elsewhere in the last half of February and early March constituted a second – or even third – wave of the Tet Offensive. Whatever the difficulties of distinguishing distinct waves of enemy attacks, television news programs indicated that horrendous casualties had not destroyed North Vietnamese or Vietcong capacity for formidable and ambitious military initiatives. They also suggested that the enemy had the initiative, a judgment that General Wheeler secretly confirmed in his report to Johnson.[62]

The fighting at Hué also showed enemy boldness and tenacity. Throughout February U.S. marines and South Vietnamese soldiers tried to dislodge North Vietnamese and Vietcong regulars from the Citadel, a walled fortress where Vietnamese emperors once lived. The concentration of forces, prolonged and savage fighting, as well as dramatic scenes of courage and determination commanded the attention of TV journalists. So did the juxtaposition of brutality and destruction with the traditions and cultural significance of this former imperial capital.[63]

In "battered, bloody Hué," the battle proceeded "inch by inch."[64] The first scenes of the fighting, which aired on CBS on February 2 in a report by Jeff Gralnick, showed marines advancing slowly against enemy forces that "could take and hold almost any area they chose." Gralnick said individual bravery was "not uncommon," as the film showed a marine in the line of fire dragging a wounded comrade to safety. Don Webster echoed this judgment five days later, as he explained that the marines were now winning the battle of Hué on sheer courage. Several correspondents compared the fighting in Hué to World War II action, associations that evoked memories of heroism. "It reminds this correspondent from World War II a little bit of the battle of Bastogne," Cronkite remarked nostalgically in a film report that he sent back from Hué during his tour of South Vietnam. The culmination occurred a few days later at the Citadel, whose inner

61 Comments by Huntley and report by Kiker, Feb. 19, 1968, NBC; report by Kalischer, Feb. 19, 1968, CBS; report by Hall, Feb. 22, 1968, NBC, all in A135, ibid.; comments by Young, Feb. 23, 1968, ABC; Reasoner, Feb. 23, 1968, CBS; and Huntley, Feb. 23, 1968, NBC, all in A136, ibid.
62 Report by Schakne, Feb. 5, 1968, CBS; and comments by Huntley, Feb. 6, 1968, NBC, both in A133, DOD Weekly News Summary; comments by Huntley, Feb. 19, 1968, NBC, and report by Kiker, Feb. 21, 1968, NBC, both in A135, ibid.; comments by Huntley, NBC, and by Cronkite, CBS, Mar. 4, 1968, both in A137, ibid.
63 Report by Laurence, Feb. 5, 1968, A133, ibid.
64 Ibid.; comments by Young, Feb. 15, 1958, ABC, A134, ibid.

sanctum was the Palace of Perfect Peace, ABC's Bob Young noted ironically. The last two hundred yards, though, were the toughest, CBS's John
Laurence observed.[65]

The costs of the struggle for Hué were enormous, although in some
ways not as great as suggested by TV journalists. "Death is literally just
around the corner," ABC's Sam Jaffe observed, and Laurence illustrated
that point by noting that only twenty of the eight hundred members of
First Battalion, Fifth Marines, emerged from Hué's fierce street fighting
unharmed. Yet these descriptions of Hué's lethality may have misled viewers, since only 142 U.S. marines died in Hué.[66] There was no doubt, however, that civilians suffered grievously. More perished than soldiers, and
three-fourths of the survivors were homeless, NBC's David Burrington
learned as he walked through the rubble. Food prices had soared 400 percent in the past month, but rice was more precious than other staples and
sold only on the black market. Especially troubling was the looting, much
of it by South Vietnamese soldiers. Residents of Hué protested, pointing
out that the North Vietnamese had not stolen from them. A few days later,
ABC's Edgar Needham found signs of hope – cleanup efforts and the opening of a new market. Hué was devastated, but like a phoenix it was rising
from the ashes, according to Needham.[67]

Khe Sanh commanded even more attention than Hué on the nightly
news. At the base at Khe Sanh six thousand U.S. marines were held under
siege by some twenty thousand of the enemy in the nearby hills. Here, too,
life was perilous and trying, as marines dug in to protect against the shelling
and confronted the uncertainties of growing isolation, brought on by enemy
guns and bad weather that made aerial resupply ever more risky and unre-
liable. Here, finally, was where the "full fury" of the Tet Offensive was supposed to occur, the one place where a decisive battle might take place,
judgments based on Westmoreland's and Johnson's reckoning. Johnson
demanded of the Joint Chiefs, David Brinkley remarked, that history not
repeat itself, that Khe Sanh not become another Dienbienphu. General
Wheeler explained to the president and the public the reasons for fortifying
Khe Sanh – it anchored the western defenses of South Vietnam, and its loss
would leave coastal cities vulnerable. Wheeler expressed confidence in
Westmoreland's judgment and the marines' resiliency. But as the North

65 Comments by Huntley, Feb. 5, 1968, NBC, A133, ibid.; reports by Cronkite, Feb. 19, 1968,
    A135, CBS; Jaffe, Feb. 21, 1968, ABC; and Laurence, Feb. 21, 1968, CBS, all in A135, ibid.
66 Reports by Jaffe, Feb. 21, 1968, ABC; and Laurence, Feb. 21, 1968, both in A135, ibid.; Allan R.
    Millett, *Semper Fidelis: The History of the United States Marine Corps* (New York, 1980), 593–4.
67 Reports by Glennon, Feb. 26, 1968, NBC; and Burrington, Feb. 28, 1968, ABC, both in A136,
    DOD Weekly New Summary; report by Needham, Mar. 4, 1968, ABC, A137, ibid.

Vietnamese moved in closer, TV journalists could not help wondering, along with the public and the marines themselves, what would happen.[68] Here, in short, was a story with drama, human interest, remarkable images, and large significance, characteristics that ensured extensive coverage in a visual medium that combined information and entertainment and that emphasized theatrical reporting.[69]

The waiting at Khe Sanh produced conflicting assessments of North Vietnamese intentions. Colonel David Lownds, the marine commander, told reporters that he had to prepare for "the worst possible contingency" to protect his troops, but that he fully expected an all-out assault. While Lownds was confident that his garrison could repel a major attack, CBS's Murray Fromson emphasized that the North Vietnamese held the initiative and that they would determine the fate of Khe Sanh. In a second report, Fromson took issue with Lownds's – and Westmoreland's – interpretation of North Vietnamese intentions. "It may be the biggest battle of the war," Fromson said of Khe Sanh, "or it may be the biggest bust." The enemy, he asserted, might be quite happy to pin down the marines in a static defense of a remote location of doubtful importance. NBC's Paul Cunningham, who had just returned from Vietnam, reached similar conclusions a few days later. Instead of an all-out attack, the North Vietnamese, he suggested, might be content with continuing the shelling, inflicting heavy casualties, and weakening U.S. resolve.[70]

While everybody waited to see what would happen, television news programs carried dramatic stories of persistence and survival at Khe Sanh. The accuracy of North Vietnamese guns made close air support and aerial supply missions extremely risky. ABC's Bill Downs reported about Major William Loftus, whose plane crashed outside the marine base and who parachuted into contested territory. A helicopter rescued Loftus, bringing about, Downs explained, what the marines call "a very hairy happy ending." Other reports showed marines eating, writing letters, or getting haircuts, moments of respite during life under siege.[71] The most frightening story concerned Russ Bensley, a CBS producer who was hit by shrapnel on

---

68 Peter Brush, "The Battle of Khe Sanh, 1968," in Gilbert and Head, eds., *Tet Offensive,* 192–5; 203–5; comments by Brinkley, Feb. 5, 1968, NBC, A133, DOD Weekly News Summary; comments by Young, Feb. 19, 1968, ABC, A135, ibid.
69 On the nature of television news reporting, see Pach, "And That's the Way It Was," 101.
70 Reports by Fromson, Feb. 14, 1968, CBS, A134, DOD Weekly News Summary; report by Fromson, Feb. 16, 1968, CBS; interview with Lownds, Feb. 19, 1968, ABC; and report by Cunningham, Feb. 21, 1968, NBC, all in A135, ibid.
71 Reports by Duncan, Feb. 23, 1968, ABC; North, Feb. 23, 1968, ABC; and Downs, Feb. 26, 1968, ABC, all in A136, ibid.

Khe Sanh's runway when enemy gunners opened up on a supply plane that was about to take off. Lying in his hospital bed, Bensley told correspondent Don Webster that a visit to Vietnam could change an individual's perspective on the war. "But I rather suspect that being here is the worst place on earth to try to make moral and political judgments about the war in Vietnam," he reflected. Transferred to a Danang hospital, Bensley suffered more serious wounds during a rocket attack. Vietnam, Webster concluded, was "a much more dangerous place than ever before."[72]

The high point of the coverage of Khe Sanh occurred in mid-March, on the anniversary of the beginning of the siege of Dienbienphu. The marines were on special alert, even holding stethoscopes to the ground, Bob Young told viewers, to listen for telltale sounds that the enemy's elaborate network of subterranean tunnels had penetrated the perimeter of their base. To mark the occasion, CBS showed film of the French defeat and an interview with journalist François Sully who covered the earlier battle and whose first reaction to Khe Sanh was "Oh my God! Dienbienphu over again."[73] Yet the climactic assault never came, and Khe Sanh ended with more of a whimper than a bang. The three major networks reported on "Pegasus," an operation that opened a land route to Khe Sanh in mid-April. Television news, however, provided no explanation of why the big battle that Westmoreland expected and desired did not occur or whether General Giap had intended to take Khe Sanh or divert U.S. attention from the other Tet attacks, questions that still are controversial and difficult to answer.[74]

As the Tet attacks receded or diminished in intensity, television journalists tried to assess their significance. Often they did so by providing vignettes, stories that in microcosm illustrated, in their view, the larger consequences of the Tet Offensive. NBC's Douglas Kiker, for example, asserted that what happened in Ban Me Thuot was "more or less the same thing" as the situation in forty other South Vietnamese towns and cities. In this supposedly secure location in the Central Highlands, the Vietcong fought fiercely for five days. The battle killed or wounded five hundred civilians, created twenty thousand refugees, destroyed every municipal building, and weak-

72 Report by Webster, Mar. 4, 1968, CBS, A137, ibid.
73 Comments by Young, Mar. 12, 1968, ABC; and comments by Cronkite and interview with Sully, Mar. 12, 1968, CBS, A138, ibid.
74 Reports by Watson, Apr. 3, 1968, ABC; Gralnick, Apr. 3, 1968, CBS; and Hall, Apr. 3, 1968, NBC, all in A141, ibid.; report by Quint, Apr. 5, 1968, CBS, A142, ibid. On North Vietnamese intentions, see Brush, "The Battle of Khe Sanh," 195–210. For general works on Khe Sanh, see John Prados and Ray W. Stubbe, *Valley of Decision: The Siege of Khe Sanh* (Boston, 1991); and Robert Pisor, *The End of the Line: The Siege of Khe Sanh* (New York, 1982).

ened popular morale. The people of Ban Me Thuot were now caught between, on the one hand, the Vietcong, which remained active and ruthless, and, on the other, a corrupt Saigon regime and its U.S. sponsors, "who came here to win their hearts and minds and ended up contributing to the destruction." In Phong Dinh province in the Mekong delta, NBC's Garrick Utley also found ruins and refugees. The Vietcong had the initiative, and pacification had ceased. Life was returning to normal, Utley asserted, but it was not the same. Farther south at Ca Mau, Bert Quint learned that the enemy held the upper hand, and the most pressing problem was where to bury the dead. The Tet Offensive, in short, had negated earlier U.S. and South Vietnamese gains and made the task of recouping these losses difficult, if not impossible.[75]

So, too, had the Tet Offensive exposed the weaknesses of the South Vietnamese government. The heroic portrayal of U.S. marines at Khe Sanh and Hué contrasted sharply with many assessments of South Vietnamese performance during the crisis. After the fighting ceased in Hué, Young reported that U.S. advisers complained that municipal officials were "leaderless and gutless." The province chief hid in civilian clothes for a week, and the thousand South Vietnamese troops who were on leave in the city stayed in refugee camps rather than join the fighting. "Why are their Vietnamese – the Communists – so good," asked one U.S. advisor, "and our Vietnamese frequently so bad?" Corruption flourished among South Vietnamese officialdom, several journalists emphasized. Brinkley remarked that recent U.S. Senate investigations had uncovered extensive misuse of American assistance. As soon as the aid reached South Vietnamese soil, "the stealing begins, and it never stops." ABC's Bill Brannigan insisted that U.S. officials spent more time battling a corrupt and uncooperative South Vietnamese bureaucracy than trying to win people's hearts and minds. "It is no wonder," he concluded, "that the peasants, largely, continue their neutrality and just try to stay alive." Record U.S. combat deaths – over 500 per week – called attention to "Saigon cowboys," eighteen- and nineteen-year-old males, too young to be drafted, who sometimes made their living through the graft arising from U.S. aid programs.[76] Under pressure from the Johnson administration, the government of President Nguyen Van Thieu announced an expansion of the armed forces, a lowering of the

75 Report by Kiker, Feb. 22, 1968, A135, DOD Weekly News Summary; reports by Utley, Mar. 5, 1968, NBC; and Quint, Mar. 7, 1968, CBS, both in A137, ibid.
76 Comments by Young, Feb. 27, 1968, ABC, A136, ibid.; comments by Brinkley, Mar. 6, 1968, NBC; report by Brannigan, ABC; and comments by Young, Mar. 7, 1968, ABC, both in A137, ibid.

draft age, a crackdown on official corruption, and a program of emergency austerity that included the closure of nightclubs and dance halls.[77] Still, television reporting left the impression that the South Vietnamese lacked sufficient commitment to the war effort.

Perhaps most important, TV journalists maintained that the Tet Offensive had widened the Johnson administration's credibility gap. The dispute between Westmoreland's headquarters and the CIA over estimating enemy strength became public in late February. Dan Rather, the CBS White House correspondent, described the CIA assessments as "much bleaker" than the public statements of high administration officials. Joseph C. Harsch, the ABC commentator, charged that Johnson accepted the lower estimates of enemy strength because they were more politically convenient. The gulf between the administration's assurances of progress and the harsh realities of the Tet Offensive had placed the president's credibility, according to ABC's Frank Reynolds, "under heavy fire."[78]

These themes – the damage to the pacification programs, the inefficiencies of the South Vietnamese government, the problems with credibility – all came together in Cronkite's "Report from Vietnam." As he toured the war zones and rode in a helicopter that carried the bodies of twelve marines who had died at Hué, Cronkite recalled becoming increasingly skeptical of official assertions that more troops would make it possible to "finish the job" in South Vietnam. "There was no way that this war could be justified any longer – a war whose purpose had never been adequately explained to the American people," Cronkite recollected. He recognized that the final, "editorial" section of his special broadcast, however "clearly labeled," was "a radical departure from our normal practice." Still, he did not hesitate. He did not learn for several months of Johnson's despairing reaction. "I think it is possible that the President shared my opinion, and that, in effect, I had confirmed it for him," Cronkite speculated. "He probably had as much difficulty as I had in accepting the military command's continued optimism in the face of the Tet setback."[79]

There may be some truth to Cronkite's conjecture. Johnson clearly was unwilling to approve Westmoreland's request for 206,000 more troops. Less

77 Comments by Young, Feb. 28, 1968, ABC; and Cronkite, Feb. 28, 1968, both in A136, ibid.; comments by Young and report by Brannigan, Mar. 6, 1968, ABC, A137, ibid.; comments by Cronkite, Mar. 15, 1968, CBS, A139, ibid.; report by Syvertsen, Apr. 2, 1968, CBS, A141, ibid.; comments by Young, Apr. 9, 1968, ABC; and report by Gralnick, Apr. 10, 1968, both in A142, ibid.

78 Report by Rather, Feb. 23, 1968, CBS, A136, ibid.; commentary by Harsch, Mar. 19, 1968, ABC; and report by Reynolds, Mar. 21, 1968, both in A139, ibid.

79 Walter Cronkite, *A Reporter's Life* (New York, 1996), 354–8.

than a year earlier, the president rejected a similar recommendation. "When we add divisions, can't the enemy add divisions?" he asked Westmoreland. "If so, where does it all end?"[80] In February 1968, there were additional reasons to demur – divided advisers, strong public opposition to the war, the additional cost to the defense budget at a time when the administration was experiencing severe financial difficulties. "Give me the lesser of evils," Johnson asked Clark Clifford, the new secretary of defense, who took charge of reviewing Westmoreland's troop request.[81]

Adding to the president's gloom was the plummeting public support for his administration's handling of the war.[82] By late February, polls showed that only 32 percent of Americans endorsed Johnson's war policies. Those who thought the United States was making progress in the war had plunged from 51 to 32 percent. And for the first time, a majority – just over 50 percent – thought it had been a mistake to send U.S. troops to Vietnam.[83] Public relations had been a critical part of Johnson's management of the war effort since the commitment of U.S. combat forces in 1965 and especially since the beginning of the Progress Campaign in autumn 1967. But after the optimistic assertions in early February, the efforts to reassure the public sputtered and collapsed. The Tet Offensive punctured the illusion of progress in Vietnam, and the administration had no effective response. "The pressure grew so intense that at times I felt the government itself might come apart at the seams," Clifford recalled years later. "There was, for a brief time, something approaching paralysis, and a sense of events spiraling out of the control of the nation's leaders."[84] Johnson never approved the request for massive reinforcements, but neither did he reject it. His clearest decision when he finally addressed the nation on March 31 was to acknowledge that his presidency was the latest casualty of the Vietnam War.[85]

"It was the first time in American history that a war had been declared over by an anchorman," David Halberstam wrote of Cronkite's "Report from Vietnam."[86] The war, of course, did not end until seven years after Cronkite's special broadcast. But the greater problem with Halberstam's

80 Berman, *Lyndon Johnson's War,* 35.
81 Clark Clifford, *Counsel to the President: A Memoir* (New York, 1991), 486; Immerman, "'A Time in the Tide of Men's Affairs,'" 67–71.
82 Melvin Small, *Johnson, Nixon, and the Doves* (New Brunswick, N.J., 1988), 128, 132.
83 Roper, "What Public Opinion Polls Said," in Braestrup, *Big Story,* 693, 695, 698–9.
84 Clifford, *Counsel to the President,* 476.
85 *Public Papers,* 1:469–76. For a full discussion of the president's decisions, see George C. Herring's chapter in this book.
86 David Halberstam, *The Powers That Be* (New York, 1979), 716.

assertion is that it attributes too much power to television journalists. Cronkite's advocacy of disengagement did have a significant effect on Johnson, but only because it confirmed the dissatisfaction with the administration's policies that was so evident in the polls or visible in the halls of Congress and in the streets. In a discussion with his top advisors, Johnson noted the "dramatic shift in public opinion on the war." Secretary of State Dean Rusk thought that change occurred because "the element of hope had been taken away by the Tet Offensive. People don't think there is likely to be an end."[87] Yet the early drafts of Johnson's speech to the nation called on the American people to meet the challenge of the Tet Offensive and see it through.[88] It was not until a month after Cronkite's special broadcast, when he heard the devastating conclusion of the Wise Men – "we can no longer do the job we set out to do in the time we have left and we must begin to take steps to disengage" – that Johnson decided to announce a peace initiative. "Everybody is recommending surrender," he lamented, even people "whom I had always regarded as staunch and unflappable."[89]

It is also easy to exaggerate the power of television news to shape public attitudes. By the late 1960s, almost 95 percent of American homes had television, and about half of the public relied on television as their primary source of news. Nielsen surveys showed that about 10 million homes tuned in each night in early 1968 to both the *Huntley-Brinkley Report* and the *CBS Evening News.*[90] Yet television is a medium that people watch intermittently – between answering the telephone and checking on the evening meal in the kitchen – and inattentively – with an eye on the newspaper or the two-year-old child about to tumble down the stairs. People also have trouble remembering the stories that they have seen, even immediately after the news program.[91] The only poll that tried to determine the effects of television viewing on popular attitudes toward the Vietnam War occurred in the summer of 1967. Eighty-three percent of the respondents said that television coverage made them "feel more like . . . backing up the boys fighting in Vietnam." The response, however, may have reflected patriotic support for U.S. troops as much as the effects of TV coverage.[92] Tele-

87 Ronald H. Spector, *After Tet: The Bloodiest Year in Vietnam* (New York, 1993), 19.
88 Clifford, *Counsel to the President,* 550.
89 Immerman, "A Time in the Tide of Men's Affairs," 78–9.   90 Oberdorfer, *Tet!,* 159–60.
91 Steinberg, *TV Facts,* 86; Jane Feuer, "The Concept of Live Television: Ontology as Ideology," in
     Regarding Television: Critical Approaches – An Anthology (Frederick, Md., 1983), 15; Daniel C. Hallin,
     The "Uncensored War": The Media and Vietnam (Berkeley, Calif., 1989), 106–7.
92 Mueller, *War, Presidents, and Public Opinion,* 167.

vision news, in short, often does not command public attention. And when it does, its effects are almost impossible to determine with precision.[93]

Even if it is difficult to know exactly how television shaped public attitudes, Johnson and other critics have insisted that the network news programs provided viewers with misleading information during the Tet crisis. The most influential advocate of this interpretation was Peter Braestrup, a Vietnam reporter for the *Washington Post* and the author of an encyclopedic study of media coverage of the Tet Offensive. "Rarely has contemporary crisis-journalism turned out, in retrospect, to have veered so widely from reality," Braestrup concluded. "Essentially, the dominant themes of the words and film from Vietnam . . . added up to a portrait of defeat for the allies. Historians, on the other hand, have concluded that the Tet offensive resulted in a severe military-political setback for Hanoi in the South." This supposed failure, according to Braestrup, arose not from ideological bias or antiwar sentiment, but the sudden eruption of the Tet Offensive, which overwhelmed reporters and led to mistakes. The routines of television news, which emphasized clear, dramatic story lines, encouraged oversimplification and a lack of analysis that perpetuated errors. "The result," Braestrup insisted, "was that the media tended to leave the shock and confusion of early February . . . as the final impression of Tet."[94]

Television journalists provided a more complex assessment of the Tet Offensive than Braestrup described. Cronkite stated categorically that "first and simplest the Vietcong suffered a military defeat" in a film report he filed from Saigon.[95] Yet Cronkite, as well as many of his colleagues, did not evaluate the Tet Offensive only on the basis of the body count or territory seized and held. Reporting from Hué on February 2, Jeff Gralnick quoted a U.S. intelligence officer who said that if the enemy's goal was "political gain rather than a military victory, an attack on Hué – to take and hold it for even six to twelve hours – would be a tremendous triumph. And that they have done." Correspondents like Gralnick recognized the political and psychological dimensions of the Tet attacks, and their stories called attention to the harm done to pacification programs, the shortcomings of the Saigon government, and the surprise and bewilderment that affected both government leaders and South Vietnamese peasants.[96]

93 Chester J. Pach Jr., "Clinton, the Media, and Foreign Policy," paper presented at the New Zealand Institute for International Affairs, Dunedin Branch, Apr. 20, 1995.
94 Braestrup, *Big Story,* 1:705–9, 714.
95 Report by Cronkite, Feb. 14, 1968, CBS, A134, DOD Weekly News Summary.
96 Report by Gralnick, Feb. 2, 1968, CBS, A133, ibid.

Top U.S. political and military officials privately assessed the Tet Offensive in remarkably similar terms. "From a realistic point of view, we must accept the fact that the enemy has dealt the G[overnment of] V[ietnam] a severe blow," Westmoreland cabled Wheeler. "He has brought the war to the towns and cities and has inflicted damage and casualties on the population." General Edward Lansdale, a special assistant to Ambassador Bunker, believed that the enemy attacks had "destroyed all faith in the effectiveness" of the Saigon government, pushed popular morale "dangerously low," and left the countryside "vulnerable to further VC exploitation." Wheeler advised the president that the Joint Chiefs "feel that we have taken several hard knocks. The situation can get worse." Several months later, General Creighton Abrams, Westmoreland's successor, confirmed the accuracy of this warning. Counterinsurgency, he reported, was at a "virtual halt," provincial capitals were "marginally safe," but the "situation was subject to further deterioration." In the final analysis, enemy objectives "were primarily psychological and political," Westmoreland informed Washington. According to historian Robert Buzzanco, the reporting from Saigon throughout the Tet crisis revealed "that the enemy criteria for success – undermining the southern government and military, prompting popular discontent, and destabilizing American policy – had indeed been accomplished throughout" South Vietnam.[97] Wheeler's top-secret report to the president and Cronkite's special broadcast illustrated the broad agreement between official and journalistic evaluations of Tet.

Despite Braestrup's contention, there is no consensus among historians that Tet represented a defeat for the North Vietnamese and Vietcong. Those who apply the criteria of conventional warfare – gaining control of territory, inflicting greater losses on the adversary – insist that Tet was a disaster for the North Vietnamese and Vietcong.[98] Those who concentrate on the political and psychological dimensions of insurgency warfare make very different judgments. One who does, Andrew F. Krepinevich Jr., maintains that "Tet was a victory for Hanoi."[99] The most thorough analysis of the warfare in 1968 after Tet concludes that neither side achieved victory. "The battles of 1968 were decisive . . . because they were so indecisive," argues historian Ronald H. Spector. "Despite the drama of the Tet attacks, . . . the Vietnam War remained what it had been and would remain until 1973: a stalemate." Spector's analysis, in short, confirms the "realistic, yet unsatis-

---

97 Robert Buzzanco, *Masters of War: Military Dissent and Politics in the Vietnam Era* (New York, 1996), 311–37.
98 See, e.g., Palmer, *Summons of the Trumpet,* 199–200; and Westmoreland, *A Soldier Reports,* 331–4.
99 Andrew F. Krepinevich Jr., *The Army and Vietnam* (Baltimore, 1986), 250.

factory conclusion" about the deadlock in Vietnam that Cronkite reached in 1968.[100] The critical difference, though, is that stalemate was nothing new, but a characteristic of the war that some observers first recognized during the Tet Offensive.

TV journalists, then, did not get the big story of Tet wrong. Their reports were perceptive and informative. They were also unsettling, both for viewers who had become accustomed to the misleading optimism of the Progress Campaign and for top government officials, who recognized the damage to their credibility. Television news coverage of the Tet Offensive affected public policy and influenced popular attitudes – changing minds, confirming prejudices, sowing controversy. The war on TV had become part of the war at home.

100 Spector, *After Tet,* 313; "Who, What, When, Where, Why."

3

The American Economic
Consequences of 1968

DIANE B. KUNZ

Nineteen sixty-eight was the most explosive year of the Cold War. From Columbia University to the barricades of Paris to the Democratic national convention in Chicago, student protests triggered violent reactions against authority. The "Prague spring," the liberalizing of Communist rule in Czechoslovakia begun by Alexander Dubček at the beginning of the year, ended tragically as Soviet tanks rushed into Czechoslovakia in August. For the Johnson administration 1968 was a year of unmitigated disaster. Hopes of a Soviet-American summit died in the Prague tragedy. It became apparent that the light at the end of the Vietnam tunnel would always elude Lyndon B. Johnson. The American international financial position came under the most severe attack since 1933. Given the continued American reluctance to adopt a wartime economy, the president could only square the foreign and domestic economic circle by drastically eroding Washington's international financial commitments.[1]

Johnson wanted to have it all – and almost did. That the United States could fight a three-front war against the Soviets in Europe and the Chinese in Asia, and the Communists in Vietnam while expanding the economic pie at home is a tribute to the strength of the American economy (see Figure 3.1). It also demonstrates the benefits of being the reserve currency country, as French President Charles de Gaulle pointed out: "What they [the United States] owe those countries they pay, at least in part, in dollars that they themselves can issue as they wish, instead of paying them totally

---

1 The timing of the 1968 gold crisis, the arcane nature of financial issues, and the general neglect of economic issues by diplomatic and political historians have led to the slighting of the financial side of the crises of 1968. Robert Collins's recent article is a welcome exception. See his "The Economic Crisis of 1968 and the Waning of the 'American Century,'" *American Historical Review* 101, no. 2 (Apr. 1996): 396–422. See also Anthony Compagna, *The Economic Consequences of the Vietnam War* (New York, 1991).

**"THERE'S MONEY ENOUGH TO SUPPORT BOTH
OF YOU – NOW, DOESN'T THAT MAKE
YOU FEEL BETTER?"**

Figure 3.1. Cartoon of LBJ, from *The Washington Post,* Aug. 1, 1967. Reproduced by permission of Herblock Cartoons.

in gold, which has a real value, and which one can possess only if one has earned it."

But even de Gaulle understood that he could not survive without the United States: by providing economic systemic stability as well as international security, Washington made the good life possible for its allies, as well as for itself. And in this era of mass democracy, a consensus in favor of continuing a war, hot or cold, that was not a response to unprovoked attack could be nurtured only with heavy doses of individual consumption.

The 1960s were the apotheosis of the post–World War II economic miracle. Throughout the Western economic system national economies boomed, providing benefits spread through all strata of societies. Depression and war babies, now grown up, lost their economic fears as their children imbibed the good life. Economists enjoyed their highest level of prestige – it became accepted wisdom that economic growth was there for the creating. Indeed the political events of 1968 could only have happened in an atmosphere where expanding economies were taken for granted. Yet three years later the American government, which had created the Bretton Woods system, destroyed it. The combination of an unhinged economic order and oil shocks set in motion the worst economic slump since the Great Depression. The easy prosperity of the first half of the Cold War was over. In its ashes lay the reflexive New Deal assumptions that had provided a sound safety net for hundreds of millions of people as well as a means of social mobility for a whole generation.

The Bretton Woods agreements creating the International Monetary Fund and the World Bank had set out the parameters for a re-created global economy. Central to the new system was the commitment of the United States to supply gold to foreign governments and central banks at $35 per ounce. This undertaking, easy enough when the United States owned one-third of all monetary gold, returned the capitalist world to the interwar gold/exchange system with one difference – the United States had agreed to be the lender of last resort. The Soviet decision in 1945 not to join the IMF left the United States in sole command of the free-market economy. The catastrophic European economic performance in 1946–7 demonstrated the insufficiency of the Bretton Woods system: it could fuel a working locomotive but could not jump-start the stalled international economic engine. With the Cold War fast becoming a reality the American government authorized the Marshall Plan to help Western European nations regain their economic health. The process was not complete until 1958 when the European Monetary Agreement signified a return to monetary convertibility and freely exchanged currencies.

Immediately the Bretton Woods framework began to crack. Its basis lay in the agreement of the United States to fuel the system with new reserves of dollars and gold while simultaneously safeguarding the system's integrity by limiting the amount of dollars in circulation. Yale economist Robert Triffin identified this contradiction (thereafter known as the "Triffin Dilemma") in 1958. The reality of the problem became evident the next year as gold started flowing out of the United States and into foreign hands. How to increase liquidity without undermining the strength of the dollar occupied central bankers for the next decade.

The push and pull factors on the capitalist international economy proved numerous. The ongoing American military commitment spawned by the requirements of the Cold War constantly drained American international accounts as did U.S. support of free trade. As European economies rapidly expanded, they made ever greater demands on the system. Foreign companies, looking for cheap financing, used American capital markets while booming foreign markets drew American companies to invest offshore.

President John F. Kennedy pledged during his campaign that "if elected President I shall not devalue the dollar from the present rate. Rather, I shall defend the present value and its soundness." Under his leadership the American government after 1961 engineered a series of systemic backstops designed to shore up the Bretton Woods order.[2] At the same time the Kennedy administration actively monitored American expenditures abroad while eagerly seeking burden-sharing agreements with foreign allies to cover the cost of American military expenditures overseas.

Kennedy's devotion to "sound money" and orthodox principles of finance had been imbibed at his father's knee. Nothing is known of Sam Johnson's views on the gold standard, but Lyndon Johnson, who became president on November 22, 1963, demonstrated little interest in foreign economic policy. His heart lay in domestic politics. Johnson sought to enlarge the American dream and make it accessible to the poorer echelons of society. Yet as important as was the War on Poverty, Johnson always understood that his popularity rested on pleasing the middle class. They were the chief beneficiaries of the Great Society. The swath of legislation passed from 1964 through 1966, combined with rapid economic growth, enabled an enlarged sector of American society to enjoy the good life. American youth, especially college students, were the products and chief beneficiaries of what became known as the Age of Affluence.

They were not alone. The growth of Western European social security states had sparked an enormous growth in the numbers of college students ready to take advantage of the economic growth their societies had produced. No longer the province of the rich, a university education, provided by governments free of charge, was now open to all who qualified. These students – a new leisure class – spent their free time emulating the United States while lambasting American administrations, which safeguarded their security.

Western European leaders were far more cognizant of the interrelated economic and security dynamics that powered the international economic system. British governments faithfully served NATO and followed the American lead economically while West German leaders offset an ever greater percentage of the foreign exchange cost of the Anglo-American defense of West Germany. But French President Charles de Gaulle took a different tack. Realizing that the United States would not cede dominance of the international payments system, he declared war against the gold exchange system in February 1965. Other nations had to pay a price for

2 Robert V. Roosa, *The Dollar and World Liquidity* (New York, 1976), appendix 2, "A Statement by Senator John F. Kennedy on the Balance of Payments," Oct. 31, 1960, 268.

payments deficits – if they lost reserves, the market would force them to raise interest rates, cut their deficits, obtain support credits, or devalue. De Gaulle resented the fact that no such constraints operated against the United States.[3] Encouraged by French economist and gold bug Jacques Rueff, de Gaulle began a crusade to eliminate the dollar's reserve currency status.[4]

As part of de Gaulle's campaign, France now balked at the idea of creating a new form of monetary reserves. The French government had been a prime mover behind this way to solve the liquidity problem, but once Washington jumped on the bandwagon, French officials did an about-face. The French proposals had been at least partly designed to redistribute power in the international system and limit the freedom of the United States, as the reserve currency country, to print money with few international constraints. When the United States joined the reserve increase bandwagon, it did so on the condition that the distribution of new assets be made in the same ratio as IMF quotas. Such a calculation would allow the United States to maintain its dominance of the system.

De Gaulle and the French minister of finance and economic affairs Valéry Giscard d'Estaing now advocated a true gold standard that would make gold the only reserve against which currency could be issued. At the annual meetings of the Bretton Woods institutions in September 1965, Giscard chastised reserve currency countries (in other words, the United States and Great Britain) for their free ride on the backs of other OECD countries. Because of the trading and reserve position of dollars and sterling, these currencies stayed in demand notwithstanding the fiscal and monetary policies followed by Washington and London. In so doing, said Giscard, the United States, his main target, might "expose the world community which bears no responsibility therein, to a crisis which would be all the more serious as it would be sudden and unpredictable."[5]

The basic problem throughout the 1960s remained Europe's love/hate relationship with America's balance of payments deficits. European nations, particularly France, complained about these deficits. They worried that the increasing amount of American dollars in international circulation compared to America's gold reserves would force the United States to end dollar convertibility. In such a case the billions of dollars in foreign government treasuries would drastically decline in value. At the same time,

3 Library of Congress, Averell W. Harriman papers, box 454, President de Gaulle's Press Conference on Feb. 4, 1965.
4 Ibid.
5 John F. Kennedy Library (hereafter JFKL), Walter Heller papers, box 46, statement by the Hon. Valéry Giscard d'Estaing, Sept. 29, 1965.

European officials could not push the United States too far. The easiest way for the United States to end its balance of payments deficits was to eliminate or significantly decrease the American defense commitment to Europe. Alternatively, the United States could jettison the Kennedy-Johnson push for greater free trade and erect tariff barriers that would keep more foreign goods out of the United States. Both these steps jeopardized Europe's interests at least as much as they threatened those of the United States. But American officials attempting to walk this tightrope found themselves increasingly distracted by a far bigger problem.

VIETNAM

The Vietnam War sucked the life from the Johnson presidency. The president understood that this conflict in Southeast Asia would strangle his domestic agenda, yet he could not bring himself to take bold action to end it. During his years as Senate majority leader, Johnson had been a team player, loyally supporting the Eisenhower administration's policy of containment. As soon as Johnson became president he had to confront the Vietnam issue. President Kennedy and his team had just blessed a military coup in South Vietnam in which Vietnamese generals deposed and murdered President Ngo Dien Diem and his brother Ngo Dien Nhu. Johnson approved a broader commitment to the war but postponed its full Americanization until 1965. Beginning in February of that year with the president's decision to authorize U.S. bombing of North Vietnam and combat troops in South Vietnam, the American military presence rapidly exploded. Yet Johnson refused to ask Congress for a declaration of war, instead relying on the Tonkin Gulf congressional resolution, passed in August 1964. By 1968, "40 percent of the nation's combat ready divisions, half of the tactical air power and a third of the nation's naval strength were at war in Vietnam."[6]

Trying to minimize casualties with technology, Washington relied heavily on the B-52 raids; but with every sortie costing $30,000 in bombs, the war wreaked havoc on U.S. defense estimates. In the fiscal years 1966 to 1968, the percentage of American gross domestic product devoted to military spending jumped from 7.9 percent to 9.7 percent (see Table 3.1). As a result, the federal budget went into deficit (see Table 3.2). Now revealed weekly in grisly body count statistics reeled off by U.S. military spokesmen, casualties mounted without appreciable progress. By the end of 1967

6 John Morton Blum, *Years of Discord: American Politics and Society, 1961–1974* (New York, 1989), 249.

Table 3.1. *National defense outlays, 1960–94*
(billions of constant 1987 dollars)

Year	Defense outlay: percentage of federal outlay	Percentage of gross domestic product
1960	52.2	9.5
1965	42.8	7.5
1966	43.2	7.9
1967	45.4	9.0
1968	46.0	9.7
1969	44.9	8.9
1970	41.8	8.3
1971	37.5	7.5
1972	34.3	6.9
1973	31.2	5.7
1974	29.5	5.7
1975	26.0	5.7
1976	24.1	5.3
1977	23.2	5.0
1978	23.8	5.1
1979	22.8	4.8
1980	22.7	5.1
1981	23.2	5.3
1982	24.9	5.9
1983	26.0	6.3
1984	26.7	6.2
1985	26.7	6.4
1986	27.6	6.5
1987	28.1	6.3
1988	27.3	6.0
1989	26.6	5.9
1990	23.9	5.5
1991	20.6	4.8
1992	21.6	5.0
1993	20.7	4.6
1994, est.	18.9	4.2

Source: National Defense Outlays and Veterans Benefits: 1960–94 (Washington, D.C., 1994), 352.

almost a half-million American troops were in Vietnam; nine thousand American soldiers died on the battlefield that year.[7] Domestic dissent over the war grew in tandem with the American commitment. Campus "teach-

7 On the Vietnam War, see George C. Herring, *America's Longest War*, 2d ed. (New York, 1986); Stanley Karnow, *Vietnam: A History – The First Complete Account of Vietnam at War* (New York, 1983); Gabriel Kolko, *The Anatomy of a War: Vietnam, the United States, and the Modern Historical Experience*

Table 3.2. *U.S. federal
budget deficit, 1965–8*

Year	Deficit
1965	$1.6 billion
1966	$3.8 billion
1967	$8.7 billion
1968	$25.2 billion

Source: Historical Abstract of the United States.

ins" began in 1965. The next year Senator J. William Fulbright, chairman of the Senate Foreign Relations Committee, began hearings on the American role in Vietnam. Johnson had become a virtual prisoner in the White House, afraid to venture out for fear that he would be greeted with chants of "Hey, hey, LBJ, how many kids did you kill today?"

This price might have been tolerable had the United States commitment brought victory. American commander General William Westmoreland remained unfailingly optimistic, reporting to the president that his strategy of attrition and escalating enemy body counts would soon produce results. But on January 31, 1968, the beginning of the Vietnamese lunar new year festival of Tet, the Vietcong (the communist guerrilla forces in South Vietnam) together with North Vietnamese soldiers struck throughout South Vietnam. They penetrated the American embassy compound in Saigon, seized the ancient city of Hué and wreaked havoc on claims that the American war effort had been successful. When America's most trusted broadcaster, Walter Cronkite, went to Saigon, his doubts reflected the nation's disillusionment. Westmoreland's reassurance that American and ARVN (Army of the Republic of Vietnam) troops had recaptured all disputed territory was futile – the Tet Offensive irretrievably damaged the American public's support for the war. Doves, those who wanted to extricate the United States from Vietnam, and hawks, those who wanted to increase the military presence, could agree on one thing: the Johnson policy, which avoided both extremes, was doomed.[8]

(New York, 1994) and *Vietnam: Anatomy of a Peace* (New York, 1997); Robert D. Schulzinger, " 'It's Easy to Win a War on Paper': The United States and Vietnam, 1961–1968," in Diane B. Kunz, ed., *The Diplomacy of the Crucial Decade: American Foreign Relations During the Nineteen Sixties* (New York, 1994), and *A Time for War: The United States and the Vietnam War, 1941–1975* (New York, 1997); Marilyn B. Young, *The Vietnam Wars, 1945–1990* (New York, 1991).
8 On the Tet Offensive, see George C. Herring's chapter in this book; on the impact of television, see Chester J. Pach Jr.'s chapter in this book.

Contributing to Johnson's decision, reached in March, to refuse any more troop requests was the effect of the Tet Offensive on foreign confidence in the dollar. Already in 1966 financial columnist Eliot Janeway had pointed out that the Vietnam War had created a financial windfall for France. Because of Vietnam's former position in the French colonial empire, American dollars fueling the war effort often ended up in French banks. Janeway estimated in 1966 that "of the nearly $600 million outflow in Viet Nam, nearly half goes right back to France as ammunition for her war against the dollar." Ultimately the de Gaulle government presented these dollars to Washington, seeking gold in return.[9] By 1968 the continuing American war effort had destabilized the American domestic economic system as well.

Now the military urged the president to raise the American stakes even higher. Westmoreland importuned the president to order another 206,000 men to be sent to Vietnam and to issue a reserve call-up of 400,000 soldiers, measures that together would cost $15 billion. The president required the secretaries of defense and state, in their analysis of the military's request, to consider not only the budget problems inherent in such an enlarged troop commitment but "what problems would we confront with respect to [the] balance of payments."[10] In his explanation of his decision to deny the military's request, Johnson on March 26 said that an increase in the number of American troops in Vietnam "would hurt the dollar and gold." Having allowed defense expenditures to climb markedly over the past three years without new taxes or general expense reductions, the president could no longer avoid the bottom line. Johnson had abandoned Kennedy's pledge to pay any price, bear any burden in defense of the "free world."[11]

JOHNSON'S CHOSEN WAR

Johnson's heart lay in domestic policy, particularly the Great Society social programs that he initiated beginning in 1964. His tragedy and the country's lay in the fact that the Vietnam War had swallowed up his presidency. Johnson, who had grown up poor in an impoverished region of the United States, was a child of Franklin Roosevelt's New Deal. As Johnson wrote in his memoirs, "My entire life, from boyhood on, had helped me recognize the work that needed to be done in America. My view of leadership had

9 *Washington Star,* Jan. 13, 1966 (courtesy of Robert D. Schulzinger).
10 Lyndon Baines Johnson Library (hereafter LBJL), National Security File/National Security Council, box 49, Johnson to secretaries of state and defense, Feb. 28, 1968.
11 LBJL, Tom Johnson meeting notes, box 1, Mar. 26, 1968 (courtesy of Robert D. Schulzinger).

always been an activist one."[12] Johnson was one of the most skilled politicians of his generation. Now fate had given him his chance to implement his dreams.

Johnson made Kennedy-era ideas reality. Marrying his political ability to the legislative malleability sparked by Kennedy's death, Johnson achieved passage of the giant Kennedy tax cut in February 1964. The final legislation reduced personal rates by an average of 21 percent over two years and clipped corporate levies down to 48 percent.[13] By slashing the federal budget to just under $100 billion he also robbed Republicans of the "sound economy" issue. In the short term the optimistic predictions made by Walter Heller, chairman of the Council of Economic Advisors (CEA), proved accurate. By September 1965 the tax cut had generated a $25 billion increase in gross national product and pushed the federal budget again into surplus. Unemployment fell to the historic low of 4.5 percent. Moreover, at the end of 1965 the American economy had achieved an annual growth rate of 5.3 percent – far from the average of 2.5 percent during the Eisenhower years.[14] The government-induced policy of wage-price moderation kept inflation in check as well – the rise in consumer prices for the years 1960–5 averaged 1.3 percent annually.[15] These were the great years of American prosperity.

Moreover, the economic statistics for 1964 followed exactly the predictions made by the CEA. The prestige of the economics profession had never been higher.[16] There was one hidden problem, however. Although it went unnoticed at the time, the 1960s would mark the end of a steady twenty-five-year period of working- and middle-class gains. American resources combined with war-driven (both World War II and the Cold War) needs engineered rising prosperity for almost all sectors of society. During the period from 1945 to 1970, income distribution remained stable with all classes sharing in the steady growth of American GNP. In fact, the largest relative gains went to the working and poorer classes. Job security

12 Lyndon Baines Johnson, *The Vantage Point: Perspectives of the Presidency, 1963–1969* (New York, 1971), 71, passim. See also Blum, *Years of Discord;* Robert Dallek, *Lone Star Rising: Lyndon Johnson and His Times, 1908–1960* (New York, 1991); Robert A. Divine, ed., *The Johnson Years;* 3 vols. (Lawrence, Kans., 1987); Kunz, *Diplomacy of the Crucial Decade.*
13 Johnson had failed to follow the Kennedy administration attempt to marry tax reduction with tax reform. See Blum, *Years of Discord,* 61–3; Raburn McFetridge Williams, *The Politics of Boom and Bust in Twentieth Century America: A Macroeconomic History* (Minneapolis, 1994), 329.
14 Blum, *Years of Discord,* 144; William Chafe, *The Unfinished Journey: America Since World War II* (New York, 1986), 193.
15 Stuart Bruchey, *The Wealth of the Nation: An Economic History of the United States* (New York, 1988), 193.
16 Allen J. Matusow, *The Unraveling of America: A History of Liberalism in the 1960s* (New York, 1984), 57–60.

was an accepted fact.[17] Highly skilled manufacturing workers in heavy industry were able to buy their own houses and have two cars in their garages. Their children went to college. And then, just when these students of the 1960s began to question the premises of the affluent society, its economic basis began to erode.

While Johnson was never willing to ask Congress for a declaration of war against North Vietnam, in his first state of the union address he declared "an unconditional war on poverty." Buoyed a year later by his landslide victory, Johnson convinced Congress during the 1965–6 session to pass legislation creating Medicare, multilevel federal aid to education, a model cities program, Operation Headstart, rent supplements, federal aid to mass transit, and a new housing act – not to mention the Voting Rights Act of 1965.[18] The number of families living in poverty declined from 40 million in 1959 to 25 million in 1968. Black family income particularly increased.[19]

Unfortunately, 1965 also marked the beginning of an onslaught of Vietnam-related expenditures. While in the fiscal year 1965 (July 1964–June 30, 1965), fighting in Southeast Asia had been budgeted at $100 million, at the end of the fiscal year the administration injected an additional $700 million to fight the escalating war. This was only the beginning: the president's August 1965 and January 1966 requests for Vietnam-related spending totaled $14 billion. Prudent economics dictated that Johnson seek a tax increase from Congress. Such an increase would not have overburdened American taxpayers – by 1966 the average of state and local taxation in the United States stood at 28 percent as compared to an average of 33.5 percent in Britain, West Germany, Italy, and France. But afraid of the domestic cuts legislative enemies would attempt to extract and fearful of the public reaction at sacrificing for a war whose popularity was never established, Johnson delayed requesting a tax increase until January 1967. Then he sought a 6 percent income tax surcharge but quickly withdrew the request when the economy appeared to slow down.[20]

The domestic economic costs of the Vietnam War were paid in the coin of inflation. Whereas CEA members had feared that 1965 might bring an economic slowdown necessitating another tax cut, by December 1965 it became clear that the economy was dangerously close to "full employment." Once unemployment drops below 4 percent, too many employers

---

17 *Historical Statistics of the United States: Colonial Times to 1970* (Washington, D.C., 1970), 293; *New York Times,* Jan. 7, 1996, review by Robert Kuttner.
18 Chafe, *Unfinished Journey,* 235.   19 Ibid., 242.
20 *Historical Statistics of the United States* (Washington, D.C., 1975), 1116; Geoffrey Hodgson, *America in Our Time: From World War II to Nixon – What Happened and Why* (New York, 1976), 245–51.

chase too few workers. In order to capture them, managers bid up wages and then raise prices, unleashing inflation. A wage-price spiral begins as workers, faced with a higher cost of living, demand wage rises. Already in 1966 inflation, although only at 3.4 percent, sufficiently frightened Americans that they ranked it third among the nation's problems, behind only the Vietnam War and race relations.[21] The president, fearing that any economic discussions would be politically damaging, had also avoided the customary wartime economic measure of wage and price controls.

The CEA had thought that a tax increase might be needed in 1966. As it turned out, a previously scheduled rise in Social Security taxes combined with a credit crunch (an increase in interest rates mandated by the Federal Reserve Board) caused the economy to slow down. Inflation rose only 2.7 percent, not the predicted 4 percent. The first half of 1967 even saw a minirecession. Having been wrong about every economic prediction during the past two years, the CEA was unprepared for the rapid economic reheating that began in July 1967. One month later Johnson sent Congress a special message predicting that the Vietnam-induced deficit could start a "spiral of ruinous inflation" and asking for a temporary 10 percent income tax surcharge. In so doing he was following Keynesian economic advice: tax cuts were for a slow economy what a tax increase was to a rapidly overheating one. Unfortunately, Wilbur Mills, chairman of the House Ways and Means Committee, intended to exact a quid pro quo – no tax increase without significant cuts in domestic spending. Mills's committee voted on October 3 to hold up the tax bill until the administration proposed acceptable spending cuts. The administration could not budge him, even though defense costs continued their rapid escalation.[22]

The eventual price was worse than Johnson could have imagined. Mills's agenda never changed: "We are going to have to find some way to bring about reductions on the spending side to coincide . . . with increases in revenues if we are to . . . get any acceptance by the American people of a tax increase." The bargaining had started at $2 billion; by June 1968 when Congress finally passed the tax increase, Johnson had been forced to agree to domestic spending cuts three times as large.[23] Even so legislators might not have passed the bill had the most serious American foreign financial crisis since the Great Depression not scared them into it. In

21 David Calleo, *The Imperious Economy* (Cambridge, 1982), 26–7; Matusow, *Unraveling of America,* 155.
22 Matusow, *Unraveling of America,* 155–71.
23 Hodgson, *America in Our Time,* 250–1; Johnson, *Vantage Point,* 451–60; Matusow, *Unraveling of America,* 171.

short, a brief Golden Age was wrecked by Vietnam and an overheated economy.

Johnson was doubly obsessed with his troops in Southeast Asia and his economy at home. This double vision obscured the continuing problems of the Triffin dilemma and the international exchanges already apparent at the beginning of the decade. Eventually, the mutual problems of Vietnam guns and inflated butter would bring about the destruction of the original Bretton Woods order.

AMERICAN GOLD RUSH

The British sterling crisis, which culminated in the devaluation of the pound on November 20, 1967, had exacerbated the American financial balancing act. As soon as the British decision became public, foreign gold purchases accelerated rapidly. These acquisitions were handled on the London gold market. The gold pool, which had been founded in late 1960 by the United States and its Western European allies, supplied the gold that the market then furnished to buyers. The pool's purpose was to secure an orderly flow of gold to the market, thereby ensuring that the price of gold remained at $35 an ounce. Its accounts broke even in 1961 and 1962: the amount of gold bought equaled the amount sold. During the next two years the demand for gold lessened so that the gold pool actually increased its gold holdings. In 1965 it broke even again, but during 1966 and 1967 the gold pool lost money, requiring its members to supply gold in $50 million increments during 1967. France dropped out after the first installment, and the United States took over its share of the joint commitment, which meant that of every $50 million of new gold required by the market, the United States put up about $30 million. Uncertainty in the world financial system, fears about American inflation, sterling-induced panic, new industrial demands on gold, and the ending of formerly sizable Russian gold sales all contributed to the heavy market activity. During October 1967 the gold pool lost $71 million; in the week from November 20 through November 27 it lost the unprecedented sum of $641 million. Investors, betting that the United States would have to abandon its gold policy, hastened to buy gold at the old price. Johnson's public statement that "I reaffirm unequivocally the commitment of the United States to buy and sell gold at the existing price of $35 per ounce" proved insufficient to reassure the market – the London gold rush continued.[24]

---

24 LBJL, Francis Bator papers, box 32, Fowler to the president, Nov. 13, 1967; N/N, box 53, memorandum of conversation (draft), Nov. 24, 1967, communiqué dated Nov. 26, 1967, WHCF-Fi,

Working together with virtually all of its allies, the United States sought to short-circuit the panic. Federal Reserve Board Chairman William Mc-Chesney Martin strongly urged that the United States continue to support the gold pool – American reserves should be used in the same way as a bank puts its money on the line during a run. As long as the operation remained multilateral, Johnson gave his blessing, even though estimated losses for the gold pool now stood at $3 billion. The gold pool members met in Frankfurt during the weekend of November 25. They agreed to continue the support operation and issued a public statement informing the market of their commitment.[25] Only France stayed aloof. Indeed, the de Gaulle government chose the first day of the gold rush, November 21, to reveal publicly its earlier decision to pull out of the gold pool, thereby exacerbating the week's drain.[26] Then the market began to stabilize, with the drain ceasing in the first week of December. The administration hoped that the run on gold might prove to be a temporary reaction to the sterling crisis. But the market remained uneasy; the gold pool could not sustain heavy losses indefinitely. Worse still, as the month progressed various European allies weakened in their support of the gold pool while American officials realized that the size of the U.S. balance of payments deficit might start the run anew. As a result, the administration decided "to move decisively to change the present climate and prospects and create conditions under which we can negotiate and move toward an improvement in the international monetary system." On Christmas Day, Treasury Secretary Henry Fowler told Johnson that after taking account of every available accounting gimmick, the balance of payments deficit for 1967 would be in the neighborhood of $3.5 to $4.0 billion. American fears about the domino effect of the British devaluation had not been exaggerated. Had the British decided to tough it out, Fowler calculated that the deficit would have been between $2.5 and $2.75 billion or about one-third lower.[27] As publication of these figures could begin another gold rush, administration officials cobbled together an achievable package of measures designed to staunch the hemorrhage of dollars to Europe.

While Fowler devised the proposals, the president reserved the right to veto any suggestions. Burned by various battles with legislators during 1967, Johnson wanted to avoid congressional action as far as possible.

box 9, memorandum for the president, Nov. 27, 1967; Administration History – State Department, B. Strengthening the International Monetary System.
25 In so doing, the pool members were following the advice given by Walter Bagehot in his classic *Lombard Street:* in a financial crisis, supply the market with all it needs, at a price.
26 LBJL, N/N Histories, box 53, "The Gold Crisis," 24.
27 LBJL, N/N, box 53, "The Gold Crisis," 4; N/N, box 54, Fowler to the president, Dec. 25, 1967. The direct quote is from Fowler.

Because the president's authority over economic questions was so sweeping in the Cold War period, this goal was attainable. In fact, Johnson now only wanted Congress to pass the income tax surcharge, an extra levy of 10 percent of the amount of income tax otherwise owed. Such a tax increase would lower the balance of payments deficit because it would leave consumers with less disposable income to spend on imports and foreign travel.

The president also insisted on avoiding unilateral protectionist measures. In this belief he reflected the pain and suffering of the past year's trade negotiations. Under the 1962 Trade Expansion Act (TEA) the United States had opened negotiations under GATT auspices with its trading partners to lower international tariffs. Three years after the so-called Kennedy round of negotiations began, with only three and a half months to go before congressional authority for negotiations ran out, diplomats reached an impasse.[28] Finally, on May 16, the Johnson administration had announced that it could accept the agreement, balancing concessions from the European Community against a failure to obtain the agreements that it had sought from Japan. What made the administration take half a loaf was the widespread belief that "the central issue transcended the matter of tariff levels." To disregard the multilateral negotiations would be to drive a stake in the Bretton Woods system and would have "risked a return to the damaging nationalistic trading practices of the 1930s."[29] The seriousness of the December crisis was not enough to convince Johnson to jettison the GATT agreements. Instead, at a meeting with senior advisors and key congressional leaders held at the LBJ ranch on December 29, Johnson announced that he would send a high-level mission to Europe and the Far East to sound out the allies on the possibility of cooperative action and to discuss their reaction to a possible U.S. border tax on imports. He would not risk a unilateral strike against free trade.

Johnson unveiled his balance of payments reduction program on New Year's Day. Sounding like Kennedy at his most conservative, he exhorted the American people to remember that the strength of the dollar depended on the American balance of payments position and the strength of the free world monetary system rested on the strength of the dollar. He called on Congress to pass the income tax surcharge, which he had introduced the previous year, and laid out a more effective voluntary wage-price restraint

---

28 The open issues were the treatment of an "American Selling Price" system of customs valuation for certain products, notably chemicals, the World Grains agreement, and the allocation of trade-offs between industrial and agricultural considerations. See LBJL, N/N, box 52, "The Kennedy Round Crisis," 1.

29 LBJL, N/N, box 52, "The Kennedy Round Crisis," 1–11.

program. These were old ideas. What was new was Johnson's mandatory program to restrain direct business investment abroad and to require business to repatriate foreign earnings to the United States.[30] The president ordered the Federal Reserve Board to tighten its restraints on foreign lending by banks and requested individuals to postpone for two years all nonessential travel outside the western hemisphere. (The White House continued to debate using an executive order to limit travelers' expenditures to $300 per person per trip. The outcry that would have resulted made it politically unpalatable.)[31] The administration would search for another $500 million in savings in balance of payments costs for American troops overseas. Congress would be asked to authorize an intensified five-year program to boost American sales abroad and to increase the lending authority of the Export-Import Bank. At the same time the administration intended to increase the flow of foreign investment and travel dollars to the United States (see Table 3.3).[32]

One notable omission from Johnson's program was a request to Congress to remove the gold cover from the dollar. Former Secretary of the Treasury C. Douglas Dillon's advice, given in 1963, summed up the administration's explanation for ducking this duty: any congressional debate would injure foreign confidence in the dollar. By 1967 the gold cover restriction had become steadily more suffocating. At the end of 1966, American gold holdings available to back the gold pool, for foreign payments and any other uses ("free gold"), amounted to only $3 billion.[33] In October 1967 officials estimated that free gold stocks would decline to $2.350 billion at the end of 1967 and $1.7 billion at the end of the following year.[34] The dwindling amount of free gold clearly alarmed foreign dollar holders; removing the gold cover provision might bolster the dollar on world markets.

30 Johnson used existing banking laws. On the crisis, see LBJL, Administration History – Treasury, Chapter IX, Balance of Payments.
31 LBJL, Anthony M. Solomon papers, box 22, Contingent Draft, Executive order no. _____, Governing Foreign Travel Expenditures by American Tourists. Jan. 22, 1968.
32 The savings of the Johnson package broke down as follows:

Savings		
Direct Investment Controls	$1,000	million
Foreign Lending Controls	$500	million
Travel Abroad Savings	$500	million
Government Expenditures Abroad	$500	million
Total	$2,500	million

Source: LBJL, N/N, box 54, statement by the president on the balance of payments, Jan. 1, 1968; The Balance of Payments Program of New Year's Day, 1968.
33 The calculation was total American gold stocks less 25 percent of American dollars in circulation equaled free gold.
34 JFKL, Presidential Office File, box 90, Dillon to the president, Feb. 11, 1963; LBJL, Bator-Chron, box 1, "The November-December Presidential Agenda: Foreign Economic Policy," Oct. 6, 1965; Fowler papers, box 83, Nicholas A. Rey to the secretary, Oct. 6, 1967.

Table 3.3. *U.S. foreign assets versus liabilities*
(billions of U.S. dollars), 1960–72

Year	Total assets	External liabilities	Balance
1960	24.6688	21.03	3.6388
1961	25.6029	22.93	2.6729
1962	24.5404	24.26	0.2894
1963	25.843	26.4	−0.557
1964	28.9124	29.35	−0.4376
1965	27.7	29.36	−1.86
1966	26.9117	31.02	−4.1083
1967	27.3602	35.66	−8.2998
1968	27.9889	38.47	−10.4801
1969	29.8936	45.9	−16.0064
1970	28.3569	46.95	−18.5931
1971	29.2546	67.8	−38.5454
1972	33.5803	82.87	−49.2897

Source: IFS tape series #DIL, DIAN, D5, and D6. Adapted from Paul Volcker and
Toyoo Gyothen, *Changing Fortunes: The World's Money Supply and the Threat to American Leadership* (New York, 1992), 366.

Johnson did not bite this bullet on New Year's Day because he believed that the battle for the tax surcharge was enough of a challenge. The Vietnam-induced budget deficit and the balance of payments deficit were related: the former weakened foreign confidence in the dollar, thereby exacerbating the latter, to which the Vietnam War had already significantly contributed. Lowering the budget deficit by increasing taxes would also curb the American appetite for foreign imports. While the American balance of trade still produced a surplus in 1968, the excess of American exports over American imports had declined drastically during the decade. As a result a positive balance of trade no longer significantly offset the balance of payments deficit. A tax increase would also dampen American inflation that had the effect of pricing American goods out of foreign markets.

The campaign for the president's fiscal program had begun in November. It was a difficult sell. As Johnson observed in his memoirs, "Somehow, I never got these dangers across to the public or the Congress." Immediately after learning about the British devaluation, the president urged the congressional leadership to pass his tax increase. He reemphasized the need for the tax increase in his New Year's Day message and in his state of the union address. But legislative leaders, up for reelection in November, remained recalcitrant. Knowing the price for a tax increase would come

out of the hide of his domestic programs, Johnson decided against requesting any money for the social welfare agenda, which the Kerner Commission report had strongly urged. This blue-ribbon panel had been appointed
in the wake of the riots that had swept ghetto areas of northern cities from
1964 to 1967. Led by former Illinois governor Otto Kerner, the commission presented a searing report to the president in early 1968, predicting
that if major steps were not taken immediately, the United States would
soon become two nations, one black and one white. Now a combination
of domestic and foreign economic factors had constricted the Johnson
administration's options.[35]

Although business leaders resented the controls on foreign investment
and reinvestment, the new balance of payments package initially garnered
support. Unfortunately, it rapidly became clear that the New Year's Day
proposals were insufficient. Responding to market pressures Johnson, in his
state of the union message delivered on January 17, finally asked for the
removal of the gold cover restriction. He had almost no choice. The gold
rush of November and December 1967 had rendered the calculations of
October 1967 absurdly optimistic. The Treasury stock of gold at the end of
1967 stood at $11.984 billion (a loss of $1.175 billion for the year; see
Table 3.4). As a result the Treasury possessed less than $2 billion of free
gold. This calculation persuaded the president that it was better to risk a
congressional debate on the gold cover restriction than to approach the 25
percent limit and let the mandatory provisions kick in.[36]

Congress began debating the gold cover bill in mid-February. One of
the most politically troublesome amendments from the floor was a suggestion that the French government be required to repay its First World War
debts to the United States before it could obtain any more gold from American stocks. In 1932 the French government had defaulted on its war debts
to the United States. As the loans had never been officially canceled, the
French government still owed billions of dollars to the United States. For
his part New Jersey Representative James Howard suggested in January that
Congress pass legislation imposing heavy duties on goods carried on American ships flying under foreign flags, which he argued would help the balance of payments.[37] During February legislators also discussed border taxes

---

35 Johnson, *The Vantage Point*, 450–1.
36 This amount did not include an American government gold obligation of $1 billion to the IMF.
   LBJL, Fowler papers, box 83, T. P. Nelson to the secretary, Jan. 2, 1968, box 32, "Proposed Removal
   of 25% Gold Cover for Federal Reserve Notes," Jan. 18, 1968.
37 LBJL, N/N, box 53, Barefoot Sanders to the president, Feb. 16, 1968; Sanders to Marvin Watson,
   Feb. 21, 1968.

Table 3.4. *American gold
stocks,* 1957–73

Year	Gold
1957	22.857
1958	20.582
1959	19.507
1960	17.804
1961	16.947
1962	16.057
1963	15.596
1964	15.471
1965	14.065
1966	13.235
1967	12.065
1968	10.892
1969	11.859
1970	11.072
1971	10.206
1972	10.487
1973	11.652

Source: IFS tape series #DIL DIAN,
D5, and D6. Adapted from Volcker
and Gyothen, *Changing Fortunes,* 366.

on imports. Congressional sentiment favoring troop withdrawals from Europe grew noticeably.[38]

Concurrently American officials fanned out abroad to increase foreign confidence in dollars. They also had a second mission – getting help from American allies. The case of Israel's dollar accounts illustrates the way external factors adversely impact a reserve country's balance of payments position while also showing the leverage a superpower possesses over those who rely on its protection. The June 1967 Six-Day War had given Israeli fund raising in the United States a special resonance. As a result, dollars flowed into Israel, raising Israeli reserves from $622 million before the war to $776 million on August 31. At the end of November they stood at $721 million. This amount was significant enough for Fowler to write Governor David Horowitz of the Bank of Israel to discuss the situation; Johnson per-

38 LBJL, meeting notes, box 2, notes on the president's meeting with the leadership, Nov. 18, 1967, notes on the president's meeting with bipartisan leadership, Nov. 20, 1967; WHCF, Fo, box 34, Ackeley to the president, "Responses to Your Balance of Payments Program," Jan. 6, 1968.

sonally raised the problem with Israeli Prime Minister Levi Eshkol during their meeting in January 1968.

As the Six-Day War had transformed the United States into Israel's key ally, the Israeli government had no choice but to pitch in and help. The Bank of Israel therefore invested $50 million in Eximbank securities, placed $5 million in long-term deposits with American commercial banks, and purchased $3 million of American government obligations. All of these purchases and investments went toward an Israeli pledge of $75 million of new investments in the United States by the end of the first quarter of 1968 and a $200 million total package "at the earliest possible date." These investments paid interest to the Israeli government, and for Washington their virtue was clear – they kept dollars in the United States. No longer a drain on the U.S. balance of payments, these deposits now became capital investments in the United States, an entirely different and beneficial book-keeping entry.[39]

Other allies contributed as well. Canada, which depended on American capital markets for the financing of its industrial and governmental needs, had long enjoyed an exemption from American legislation restricting foreign access to American capital markets. In exchange for this preferential treatment, the Canadian government pledged to prevent any third country or third-country citizen from using Canada as a conduit to violate the U.S. balance of payments restrictions. Ottawa also promised to invest virtually its entire dollar holdings in U.S. government securities. Japan pledged to assemble a package worth $350 million designed to improve the American balance of payments position as well as to remove specific quantitative restrictions on imports from the United States.[40]

The administration even explored eccentric solutions to the gold short-age. In mid-February Fowler gave forty-five minutes to Alexander Sachs, who proposed to use atomic technology to increase gold production. The Treasury Department, taking its cue from Congress, researched the validity of long-defaulted World War I debt obligations to the United States not only of France but also from Belgium, Italy, and Britain. Whereas the American claims remained legally valid, the sums would not be soon forth-coming. Moreover, even to broach the subject would increase the tension within the Western alliance.[41]

39 LBJL, Fowler papers, box 7, *New York Times,* Jan. 12, 1968, Horowitz to Fowler, Feb. 27, 1968.
40 LBJL, Bator papers – Chron, box 1, memorandum for the president, Feb. 9, 1965, Bundy to the president, Feb. 9, 1965; Fowler papers, box 4, Treasury Department Release, Mar. 7, 1968, Solomon papers, box 20, president's evening reading, Jan. 30, 1968.
41 LBJL, Fowler papers, box 88, Nelson to the secretary, Feb. 15, 1968, Fowler to Sachs, Feb. 14, 1968; Fowler papers, box 38, Fred B. Smith to the secretary, Feb. 19, 1968.

One option the administration rejected was raising the price of gold. This act would have lessened some of the pressure on the gold pool but at a politically unacceptable price: it would cause a devaluation of the dollar and could only be obtained with congressional permission. While the Bretton Woods architects had considered periodic devaluations to be a permanent part of the financial scene, any devaluation had come to be seen as an admission of fiscal or political failure. The price of gold had also come to have great symbolic importance. Just as enshrining $35 per ounce as the international gold price had increased the American power and influence in 1944, changing the equation would advertise abroad the diminution of U.S. standing. Early 1968 did not seem a propitious moment for any confession of weakness.

At the end of February, the gold market, which had remained quiescent since the New Year, became frantic. During the first week of March, the gold pool lost $395 million as a whole and $179 million on the last day of the week, the second largest daily loss on record. As usual this financial crisis had multiple causes. Congressional hearings on the president's proposals had brought forth suggestions that the United States halt all gold transactions. In particular, influential Senator Jacob Javits of New York advocated ceasing American sales of gold and suspending the gold pool. The continued weakness in sterling increased the demand for gold as former members of the Sterling Area, now all but defunct, rushed into gold. The growing talk of inevitable changes in the international monetary structure sapped faith in the current system. These doubts were reinforced by clear evidence at the end of February that both the tax increase and the gold cover legislation were in great trouble. The endgame of financial crises often comes down to a question of confidence. Once the market loses confidence, panic begins. Had Johnson been able to get his package passed in January and February, a crisis could have been avoided. But valuable time had been lost. Now the administration had to face the international and domestic consequences.[42]

THE GOLD CRISIS

The crisis came to a head on March 14. On that date the president's senior advisors informed him that "we can't go on, hoping that something will

---

42 LBJL, N/N, box 53, Fowler to the president, Mar. 4, 1968, "The Gold Crisis," 7; Fowler papers, box 82, Javits Press Release, Mar. 6, 1968; WHCO-CF, box 50, Arthur Okun to the president, Mar. 9, 1968.

turn up." Administration officials believed that Congress had inflamed an already volatile situation – Fowler described "the attitude on the Hill as one of the almost anarchistic willingness to pull the temple around their ears on the grounds that our budgetary expenditures are out of control." As Europeans lost faith in the administration's ability to obtain its tax increase, gold losses became untenable. During the week ending March 15, the gold pool lost $769 million with the loss on Thursday, March 14, hitting a new record of $374 million, equivalent to over a hundred tons of gold. At the same time, sterling came under intense pressure.

Contingency plans for just such a crisis had been made in February. Four options had been debated: (1) putting all American gold stocks on the line, (2) shutting the "gold window" completely and ending American governmental sales of gold, (3) establishing a more strictly controlled London private market for gold, which key countries would subsidize, and (4) ending the gold pool and letting the market alone determine the price of gold for private transactions. Johnson administration officials chose the last option. It would preserve the form of Bretton Woods while reducing American responsibility for the substance. Selecting this road required no congressional action and would draw less public attention than any of the other alternatives. What it did require was significant cooperation from Washington's allies. Other nations would have to promise not to buy gold for official purposes from the private market. There also remained the risk that if the private market price for gold rose substantially above $35 per ounce, foreign governments would be unable to resist the temptation to ask the United States to convert their dollars into gold. But the administration retained major leverage over its allies: American allies feared the consequences if the Bretton Woods system broke down and the United States remained the only country capable of holding it together.[43]

Now the American government summoned central bankers from gold pool countries to meet in Washington over the weekend of March 16–17. On Thursday night the British government agreed to close the gold market the next day. In cables sent abroad Johnson raised the specter of the 1931 financial collapse and the Great Depression. The foreign bankers had no idea what Washington had in mind – British Chancellor of the Exchequer Roy Jenkins speculated that the administration intended to abrogate the dollar's fixed value. In the end, the crisis proved less memorable, the solutions less drastic. Following the Johnson administration's blueprint, the

---

43 LBJL, N/N, box 53, "The Gold Crisis," 9–10.

conferees agreed to disband the gold pool. The central bankers agreed to bifurcate the gold market into two separate parts. The private market would be completely independent of government control, and the United States would end its promise to supply that market with gold at the price of $35 per ounce. Supply and demand, not government intervention, would determine the price of privately traded gold.

The United States would continue to buy and sell gold at the price of $35 per ounce to monetary authorities. Each government agreed not to purchase gold from the United States and then sell the gold on the private market. Foreign emissaries also pledged to work together to maintain the Bretton Woods order. Available international support monies for Britain rose to $4 billion, and the United States increased its ability to borrow foreign currencies (swap limits) by $2.275 billion to a total of $9.355 billion. Contrary to administration hopes, no agreement could be reached on an immediate activation of Special Drawing Rights (SDRs). The administration quickly solicited Japanese approval of the new rules and accepted a public French "we told you so" stoically.[44]

The administration had taken the least draconian of the options available. It had avoided the difficult domestic ramifications of raising the price of gold and devaluing the dollar, and it had rejected closing the gold window. Yet the chosen solution had further eaten away at the foundations of the Bretton Woods system. In March 1967 the United States had secured a pledge from West Germany that eroded Washington's Bretton Woods obligations: the *Blessing Brief* embodied the Bundesbank's agreement not to exchange dollars at the U.S. Treasury for gold.[45] Now the Johnson administration had eliminated an even larger part of the American promise made two decades earlier. That Washington had taken this step in consultation with its allies limited some of the damage to the international system. But within a multilateral framework the administration had foisted a unilateral decision on its allies. For neither the first nor the last time, other members of the Western alliance showed themselves willing to accept American decisions – the price of rejecting them was too high.

44 LBJL, WHCF-Fi, box 9, Rostow to the president, Mar. 14 and 15, 1968; WHCF-Co, box 50, Okun to the president, Mar. 16, 1968; N/N, box 53, "Outline of Data for Contingency Planning," Feb. 1968, E. V. Rostow, "Next Steps in International Monetary Policy," Mar. 13, 1968, SD to Bonn, no. 130816, Mar. 15, 1968, Rostow to the president, Mar. 14 and 15, 1968, London to SD, no. 7293, Mar. 15, 1968, Solomon to Edward Fried, Mar. 16, 1968; Fowler papers, box 39, rough translation of Debré statement, Agence France Presse, Mar. 15, 1968; Fowler papers, box 88, SD to Tokyo, Mar. 17, 1968.
45 See Diane B. Kunz, "Cold War Dollar Diplomacy," in Kunz, ed., *Diplomacy of the Crucial Decade*.

The solidarity of Western governments proved admirable – only France proved unwilling to subscribe publicly to the Washington Communiqué of March 17 and the Stockholm Agreement of the G-10 countries, which later in the month ratified the decisions reached at Washington.[46] Yet gratified as the administration was, officials understood that both the international monetary system and the United States had been granted a respite, not a permanent solution. Now Washington needed to turn its attention to activating SDRs, correcting the American balance of payments problem, and obtaining the tax increase.[47]

In the meantime, speculators who had struck blood twice in six months, first with the British sterling devaluation and now over the gold crisis, turned their attention to France. Concerns over the franc's potential overvaluation together with the effects of domestic political turmoil in May 1968 had made the franc an attractive target. The Johnson administration, rather than chortling at this twist of fate, hoped that the franc's parity could be maintained, not out of charity, but because of the disruptive effects on the international system. In November, a revaluation of the franc (downward) and the mark (upward) seemed likely. These issues came to a head during the Bonn G-10 meeting of November 22, 1968. German Finance Minister Franz Joseph Strauss, fearing its effects on exports, vociferously objected to a German revaluation, while German Chancellor Kurt Kiesinger had pledged himself to keep the current mark parity.

German stubbornness came in for much criticism and direct pressure. Britain, still nursing its wounds from the 1967 devaluation, threatened to withdraw its troops from Germany if there was no revaluation. But the German cabinet remained torn between revaluers and diehards. In these circumstances de Gaulle also stuck to his position. Ironically, having criticized the British attachment to the strength of sterling as an indicator of national power and prestige, the general had caught the same gold bug. Rather than devalue, the French government resorted to the same package of exchange controls, export incentives, and wage and price guidelines that Britain and the United States had previously utilized.[48]

46 LBJL, CEA box 2, memorandum for the president, Mar. 30, 1968.
47 LBJL, N/N box 53, "Round-up of Official Reactions to the March 17 Communiqué," Okun to the president, Mar. 23, 1968.
48 LBJL, National Security Council Meetings, box 2, summary notes of 594th NSC meeting, Nov. 25, 2968; NSF-Co, box 173–4, de Gaulle Text, Nov. 24, 1968, Paris to SD, no. 8484, Nov. 25, 1968, memorandum of conversation, Nov. 25, 1968; WHCF-Co, box 8, memorandum for the files, July 26, 1968; WHCF-Co, box 80, memorandum for the president, Nov. 23, 1968; Harold James, *International Monetary Cooperation Since Bretton Woods* (Washington, D.C., 1996), 195–7.

The Johnson administration's last attempt at international financial policy concerned South Africa. As the world's leading producer of gold, South
Africa had a vested interest in seeing the price of gold increase. Leading
central bank governors, meeting in October 1968, could not reach an
agreement with South Africa over the price of newly mined gold.[49] As
they prepared to leave office, Johnson officials could point to an improving
balance of payments picture. Foreign capital had been flooding into the
United States while the income tax surcharge had at last been enacted in
late June. The question of the gold price came up during the presidential
campaign. Candidate Richard M. Nixon, in a reprise of John F. Kennedy's
promise eight years earlier, said he saw "no need for a change in the price
of gold" if he were elected president.[50] Time would tell if he would emu-
late his former rival's record.

BALANCE SHEET

The dramas of 1968 illustrated the inextricability of foreign and domestic
economic policy and the reverberating effects of economic policy on military decision making. Johnson sought war and peace together with international financial stability. That he could aim so high shows the strength of
the American position. Only the United States had the economic power
and military force to accomplish a balancing act of this magnitude. The
American dominance of the Bretton Woods system bolstered the American position. Because the United States remained the linchpin of the Western international financial order, other nations ultimately had no choice
but to support American decisions. The pivotal position of the United
States within the Western financial order partly explains the quick acceptance of American decisions during the gold crisis of 1968. No other
nation could or would take on the burden of running the international
financial order.

But the Bretton Woods system – mark 1968 – was a weaker creature
than the original version. In 1944 the United States had committed to
stand irrevocably behind the new international order. Now Washington,
having extracted a promise from West Germany not to ask for gold in
exchange for U.S. dollars, limited its obligations to official transactions
only. The private market would be left to its own devices. The world's cen-

49 LBJL, Fowler papers, box 85, statement for the press, Oct. 4, 1968.
50 *Wall Street Journal,* Oct. 25, 1968.

tral bankers had decided to channel steadily growing international infla-
tionary pressures into the gold market and away from the foreign exchange
market. They hoped that the private gold market would relieve pressure on
official transactions. Instead it exerted further pressure on currency levels,
adding impetus to the continuing crisis in the international system that
would explode three years later.

Ultimately what the decisions of March 1968 bought was time – time
that could have been used to ameliorate the underlying strains on the Bretton Woods system. As the key currency country the United States had the
ball of international cooperation. But Richard Nixon was not a team player.
He preferred to destroy what was left of the original Bretton Woods system
rather than work with Western Europe and Japan to fix it. He gambled that
the United States could retain the benefits of the old system without the
burdens. Nixon was right because the United States remained the key military player as well as the pivot of the international financial order.

Lessening tensions between Washington and Moscow in 1966–7 had
not rendered NATO obsolete. The United States was the most important
member of the alliance; in the final analysis its nuclear umbrella and conventional forces shielded Europeans from the Soviet Union and Warsaw
Pact forces. An incorrect American public perception of an unfair financial responsibility for NATO had led to strident calls for the United States
to reduce its military commitments in Europe. West Germany had already
raised its contribution to the United States and Britain. Neither German
leaders nor any other member of the NATO combined forces wanted to
push the United States out of Europe. Because failing to cooperate with
American financial policies might have triggered an American departure or
emasculation of its commitment to NATO, the security equation provided
additional impetus for financial cooperation. The men who made the decisions of March 1968 also remained haunted by the collapse of the international financial order and the Great Depression that had followed. Johnson
himself believed that a failure to pass his tax legislation could have brought
on "an uncontrollable world monetary crisis of 1931 proportions and consequences."[51] Remembering the price of autarchy a generation earlier,
politicians compromised in order to maintain international financial cooperation.

Johnson found achieving his domestic goals far more difficult than

51 Johnson, *Vantage Point*, 451.

obtaining international acquiescence. For political reasons he had delayed seeking a tax increase until it was far too late. Once he made his request, intertwined foreign policy and domestic roadblocks delayed passage of his legislation. Johnson, famous for his congressional leadership, ironically found it much easier to have his way with foreign leaders than with Democratic legislators. One explanation for Johnson's reluctance to fund the Vietnam War openly was his belief that Americans would not sacrifice their standard of living for this particular conflict. Perhaps the president should have realized that if he could not sell the funding of the war to the American people, the United States should not have been fighting in Vietnam.

The president's decision to delay the day of reckoning for as long as possible bequeathed to the American people the worst of all worlds. Inflation had begun eating away at the American economy. The consumer price index rose less than 2 percent in 1963, 1964, and 1965. It went up almost 3 percent in 1966, more than 3 percent the next year, and more than 4 percent in 1968.[52] Inflation represents a tax on those least able to afford it. At the same time it destroys confidence in the economy and in the future. Because the surge in prices was not matched by a growth in American productivity, American manufacturers' lead over their foreign competitors seriously eroded, both within the United States and abroad. The pie was shrinking, leaving Americans with less to divide at a time when internal dislocation had already frayed social cohesion.

In company with their peers abroad, protesting Americans did not realize that 1968 marked an end of an era. The prevalent assumption of the 1960s was that the affluent ye shall always have with you. Accepting the miraculous postwar economic growth as the norm, students (the chief beneficiaries of the improved world order) looked outward from their own concerns. They felt free to protest segregation and the war in Vietnam because they assumed that their economic future was ensured. The downward trajectory of international economic growth illustrated in Figure 3.2 made a mockery of that belief.

The political ramifications were soon clear: the politics of plenty became the politics of parsimony. As the pie shrunk, the automatic support for New Deal safety nets disappeared. The year 1968 rang down the curtain on share the wealth economics. By the end of the 1970s state socialism was on

52 Hodgson, *America in Our Time*, 253.

I. Real Gross Domestic Product

United States

G-4 (France, West Germany, Japan and
the United Kingdom

II. Inflation

United States

G-4

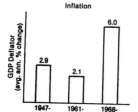

Figure 3.2. International Economic Performance. From Henry Nau, *The Myth of America's Decline: Leading the World Economy into the 1990s* (New York, 1990), pp. 134–5.

the defensive; ten years later it was on its deathbed. Victory in the Cold War contributed to this denouement. Equally important was the steady importance of consumption politics. Baby boomers had been weaned on a diet of steady consumption. They were willing to extend these rights to others, if their portion was ensured, but would not sacrifice their share in order to assure others of a decent portion.

4

The Czechoslovak Crisis and the Brezhnev Doctrine

MARK KRAMER

Until the late 1980s, the Soviet Union's determination to preserve Communism in East-Central Europe was not in doubt. When Communist regimes in Eastern Europe came under violent threat in the 1950s – in East Germany in 1953 and in Hungary in 1956 – Soviet troops intervened to subdue those challenges. A very different problem arose in 1968, when Czechoslovakia embarked on a dramatic, but entirely peaceful, attempt to change both the internal complexion of Communism and many of the basic structures of Soviet–Eastern European relations. This eight-month-long experiment, widely known as the "Prague Spring," came to a decisive end in August 1968 when hundreds of thousands of Soviet and Warsaw Pact soldiers invaded Czechoslovakia.

Neither the Soviet Union nor Czechoslovakia exists any longer, but the legacy of the Prague Spring and the Soviet invasion is still being felt. The reforms that took place in Czechoslovakia in 1968 under the leadership of Alexander Dubček offered the first opportunity for an Eastern European Communist regime to earn genuine popular support. Moscow's unwillingness to tolerate those reforms ensured that, from then on, stability in the Eastern bloc could be preserved only by the threat of another Soviet invasion. That threat sufficed to hold the bloc together for more than twenty years, even when tested by severe crises like the one in Poland in 1980–1. But soon after Mikhail Gorbachev became head of the Soviet Communist Party (CPSU) and was no longer willing to use military force in Eastern Europe, the whole Soviet bloc collapsed. Because of the legacy of 1968, all Eastern European regimes lacked the legitimacy they would have needed to sustain themselves without Soviet military backing. The invasion of Czechoslovakia saved Soviet-style Communism in Eastern Europe temporarily, but it helped guarantee the system's ultimate demise.

This chapter draws on newly declassified materials and memoirs to provide a reassessment of the 1968 crisis and shows how the confrontation with Czechoslovakia fitted into Soviet policy toward Eastern Europe. The chapter discusses first the context of the 1968 crisis, highlighting trends in Soviet policy in the late 1950s and 1960s. It then turns to the Prague Spring itself, explaining why the bold changes in Czechoslovakia provoked such a harsh reaction in Moscow. Finally, the chapter explores the consequences of the invasion, focusing in particular on the promulgation of the "Brezhnev Doctrine," which set the tone for Soviet–Eastern European relations for the next twenty-one years.

CONTEXT OF THE 1968 CRISIS

Between 1956, when Soviet troops crushed a popular uprising in Hungary, and 1968, when the Prague Spring began, Soviet–Eastern European relations underwent several notable changes. Some developments facilitated greater Soviet control over Eastern Europe and better cohesion among the Warsaw Pact states, but many other factors tended to weaken Soviet control and to create fissures within the Eastern bloc.

Sources of Cohesion

In the early 1960s, the Soviet Union sought to reinvigorate the Council for Mutual Economic Assistance (CMEA), which had been largely dormant since it was created by Joseph Stalin in 1949. The Soviet leader at the time, Nikita Khrushchev, hoped to use CMEA as a means of formally integrating the Soviet and Eastern European economies.[1] The "Basic Principles of Socialist Economic Integration," announced by Khrushchev with much fanfare in 1961, did not yield many results in the end, but the Soviet Union was able to exploit its economic preponderance to promote bilateral integration with each of the CMEA member-states, especially in trade relations. The unusually large proportion of foreign trade that Eastern European countries conducted with the Soviet Union and with other CMEA members rose to nearly 70 percent in the 1960s, except in the case of Romania.[2] This trend did not bring the supranational integration that

1 Jozef M. van Brabant, *Socialist Economic Integration: Contemporary Economic Problems in Eastern Europe* (New York, 1980), chap. 1; Alan H. Smith, *The Planned Economies of Eastern Europe* (London, 1983), 174–202; Michael Kaser, *COMECON: Integration Problems of the Planned Economies* (Oxford, 1967).
2 J. T. Crawford and John Haberstroh, "Survey of Economic Policy Issues in Eastern Europe: Technology, Trade, and the Consumer," in U.S. Congress, Joint Economic Committee, *Reorientation and*

Soviet leaders had envisaged, but it did ensure that Eastern European states remained crucially dependent on the Soviet economy, particularly for energy supplies.

The Soviet Union also fostered greater intrabloc cohesion in the military sphere, a policy reflected in the newly emerging concept of "coalition warfare." That approach, as described in a classified report by Soviet military planners in the mid-1960s, called for a rapid, massive offensive against NATO by a combination of Soviet and Eastern European forces using both nuclear and conventional weaponry:

> The defense strategy of the socialist countries must focus on seizing the most important regions and lines, and on absolutely preventing an incursion by the adversary's forces into the territory of the socialist countries. The strategy will be based on nuclear strikes in conjunction with the use of conventional firepower and mobile operations by combined forces, and also on the wide-scale use of obstruction.[3]

This new emphasis on joint military operations was accompanied by programs to ensure that Eastern European troops could perform effectively alongside Soviet forces. All Eastern European armies were significantly modernized and expanded in the early and mid-1960s; renewed efforts were made to promote the interoperability and standardization of Warsaw Pact armaments; and joint Soviet–Eastern European military exercises were initiated in October 1961.[4] As a result, the Warsaw Pact, which had been little more than a paper organization for several years after it was founded in 1955, finally started to acquire a few of the trappings of a real alliance.

The increased vigor of the Pact helped shore up the Soviet Union's position in Eastern Europe not only because the Soviet-dominated structures of the alliance were preserved, but also because more of the financial costs

Commercial Relations of the Economies of Eastern Europe: A Compendium of Papers, 93d Cong., 2d Sess., 1974, 41.

3 "Razvitie voennogo iskusstva v usloviyakh vedeniya raketno-yadernoi voiny po sovremennym predstavleniyam," report no. 24762s (Top Secret) from Col.-General P. Ivashutin, chief of the Soviet General Staff's Main Intelligence Directorate, to Marshal M. V. Zakharov, head of the General Staff Military Academy, Aug. 28, 1964, in Tsentral'nyi arkhiv Ministerstva oborony, Moscow, D. 158, L. 400. Preparations to carry out this type of strategy could be discerned in Pact exercises even in the late 1970s; see, e.g., "Referat des Stellvertreters des Ministers und Chefs der Landstreitkräfte zur Auswertung der Kommandostabsübung JUG-78," Apr. 18, 1978, in Militärisches Zwischenarchiv (hereafter MZA), Potsdam, VA-Strausberg/29371, pt. 1. For an early public enunciation of the new concept, see Marshal A. A. Grechko, "Patrioticheskii i internatsional'nyi dolg Vooruzhenykh sil SSSR," *Krasnaya zvezda* (Moscow), Oct. 6, 1961, 3.

4 V. V. Semin et al., *Voenno-politicheskoe sotrudnichestvo sotsialisticheskikh stran* (Moscow, 1988), 72–4, 185–201, and 231–43. Secret accounts of many of these exercises, prepared by officers in the East German National People's Army, can be found in the MZA.

of "defending the socialist commonwealth" could be passed off onto Eastern European governments. Wartime control of allied forces was retained by the Soviet High Command, and even in peacetime the Pact's joint military exercises were infrequently – and then only symbolically – under the command of Eastern European generals. Moreover, all the top posts in the Pact's Joint Command were still reserved exclusively for Soviet officers.[5]

Soviet hegemony in the Warsaw Pact was further strengthened in the early to mid-1960s by a number of top-secret agreements providing for the deployment of Soviet tactical nuclear warheads and nuclear-capable delivery vehicles on the territory of East Germany, Poland, Czechoslovakia, and Hungary.[6] The agreements were described as coming "within the framework of the Warsaw Pact," but all nuclear warheads were under strict Soviet control, and the dual-capable delivery vehicles that the Eastern European countries possessed would have come under direct Soviet command if they had ever been equipped with nuclear warheads during a crisis. Moreover, the thousands of tactical nuclear weapons deployed by Soviet forces on Eastern European territory were not subject to any sort of "dual-key" arrangement along the lines that NATO established in the mid-1960s to give the Western European governments an effective veto over the use of American tactical nuclear weapons. Whenever Warsaw Pact exercises included combat techniques for nuclear warfare (as they routinely did from early 1962), all decisions on whether to "go nuclear" were reserved exclusively for Soviet political leaders and military commanders.[7] Despite efforts by Romania and one or two other East-bloc governments in the 1960s to establish some form of nuclear "sharing" within the Warsaw Pact, Eastern European states were never given any say in the use of the alliance's "joint" nuclear arsenal.[8]

The growth of Soviet *strategic* nuclear power in the late 1950s and 1960s also helped strengthen Moscow's sphere of influence in Eastern Europe.

5 Mark Kramer, "Civil-Military Relations in the Warsaw Pact: The East European Component," *International Affairs* 61, no. 1 (winter 1985): 55–6.
6 "O przedsiewzieciu majacym na celu podwyższenie gotowosci bojowej wojska," Feb. 25, 1967, in Centralne Archiwum Wojskowe, Warszawa, F. 6, Kor. 234; "Dogovor mezhdu pravitel'stvami SSSR i ChSSR o merakh povysheniya boegotovnosti raketnykh voisk," Dec. 15, 1965, in Vojenský Historický Archiv (VHA), Praha, Fond (F.) Sekretariat Ministra Narodní Obrany (MNO), Svazek (Sv.) 16, Archivná jednotka (A.j.) 152; "Hungary: USSR Nuclear Weapons Formerly Stored in Country," translated in U.S. Joint Publications Research Service, *Nuclear Proliferation*, JPRS-TND-91-007, May 20, 1991, 14–16; and a series of agreements covering sixteen sites in East Germany, in MZA, VA-Strausberg/29555/box 155.
7 Bundesministerium für Verteidigung, *Militärische Planungen des Warschauer Paktes in Zentraleuropa* (Bonn, Jan. 1992), 3.
8 The nuclear "sharing" debate within the Warsaw Pact is covered in Mark Kramer, "Warsaw Pact Nuclear Operations and the 'Lessons' of the Cuban Missile Crisis," *Cold War International History Project Bulletin*, nos. 8–9 (winter 1996–7): 348–57.

Even at the time of the Hungarian revolution in 1956, when the Soviet Union's only means of delivering a nuclear attack against the continental United States was a limited number of long-range bombers, U.S. intelligence officials warned the president that any steps aimed at "preparing for military intervention" in Hungary "would materially increase the risk of general war," including the possibility of a nuclear exchange.[9] With the advent of Sputnik in October 1957 and the USSR's subsequent deployments of intercontinental ballistic missiles (ICBMs), as well as the expansion of the Soviet heavy bomber force, the Soviet Union by the early to mid-1960s clearly had the capacity to wreak untold destruction upon the U.S. homeland.[10] Although Soviet strategic nuclear forces at the time still lagged somewhat behind those of the United States, the important thing, as was shown by President John F. Kennedy's overwhelming desire to avoid a nuclear exchange during the 1962 Cuban missile crisis, was that Soviet ICBMs could now inflict "unacceptable damage" on the United States.[11] This new capability reinforced the pattern that emerged as early as 1953, when the threat of Soviet nuclear or conventional retaliation against Western Europe helped deter NATO from coming to the defense of East German workers. The much more dire consequences from any potential nuclear confrontation with the Soviet Union by the early to mid-1960s led U.S. Secretary of State Dean Rusk to acknowledge that "our capacity to influence events and trends within the Communist world is very limited. But it is our policy to do what we can."[12] Notions of "rollback" and "liberation" had been fanciful even in the 1950s, but they were all the more irrelevant by the mid- to late 1960s.

In the political sphere, as with the drive for economic integration and closer military relations, the Soviet Union accorded high priority to the goal of increased Soviet–Eastern European cohesion after 1956. That goal also was firmly supported by Eastern European leaders who had come to be key figures in the 1960s, notably Władysław Gomułka of Poland and Walter Ulbricht of East Germany. Soviet backing for Ulbricht during the

9 "Probable Developments in East Europe and Implications for Soviet Policy," Special National Intelligence Estimate SNIE 12-2-56 (Secret), Oct. 30, 1956, in FRUS/1955-1957/Volume XXV (Eastern Europe), 335.

10 U.S. Central Intelligence Agency, "Main Trends in Soviet Military Policy," National Intelligence Estimate no. 11-4-65 (Secret – Controlled Dissem), Apr. 14, 1965, 5–6 ("Changes in the Strategic Relationship"); reproduced in U.S. Central Intelligence Agency, *Estimates on Soviet Military Power, 1954 to 1984: A Selection* (Washington, D.C., Dec. 1994), 191–214.

11 Raymond L. Garthoff, *Reflections on the Cuban Missile Crisis,* rev. ed. (Washington, D.C., 1989), 78–95.

12 "Why We Treat Communist Countries Differently: Address by Secretary Rusk," *Department of State Bulletin* 50, no. 1290 (Mar. 16, 1964): 393.

severe crises of the late 1950s and early 1960s, when deepening economic strains and a large-scale exodus of East Germans to the Federal Republic of Germany (FRG) had raised doubts about the very existence of the German Democratic Republic (GDR), was crucial for the preservation of East Germany's front-line role in the Warsaw Pact. In particular, Khrushchev's decision to permit the building of the Berlin Wall in August 1961 halted the efflux of refugees from the GDR, staved off a further deterioration of the East German economy, and allowed the Socialist Unity Party (Sozialistische Einheitspartei or SED) to reassert tight control over the country.[13]

Soviet relations with Poland and East Germany remained a top priority in Moscow after Leonid Brezhnev replaced Khrushchev in October 1964. Brezhnev's chief foreign policy advisor in the 1960s, Andrei Aleksandrov-Agentov, recalled that the Soviet leader "greatly admired and respected" Gomułka and Ulbricht, and that Brezhnev, in turn, "acquired vast authority among the leaders of the other socialist states."[14] As both Ulbricht and Gomułka encountered new political challenges in the latter part of the 1960s, they looked increasingly to Moscow for support against their domestic rivals, a trend that gave the Soviet Union even greater influence in Poland and East Germany. (This became painfully evident when Brezhnev withdrew his backing for Gomułka and Ulbricht at the beginning of the 1970s, and both were quickly ousted.)

The Soviet Union's position in Eastern Europe was further enhanced by a highly publicized conference in Moscow in November 1960, which brought together officials from eighty-one of the world's Communist parties and reaffirmed the "universally recognized vanguard role" of the CPSU in the international Communist movement.[15] Eastern European party leaders worked closely with Soviet officials at the conference to ensure that the participants would support Moscow's calls for increased "unity" and "solidarity" in the "stand against imperialism." Much the same was true of a subsequent all-European conference of Communist parties, held in Karlovy Vary in April 1967. Although this meeting came a few years after Leonid Brezhnev had replaced Khrushchev, it was notable mainly for its continuity in emphasizing the Soviet Union's preeminent role in European Communism.

13 A valuable firsthand Soviet account of this whole episode can be found in the recent memoir by Yulii Kvitsinskii, *Vor dem Sturm: Erinnerungen eines Diplomaten* (Munich, 1993), 187–261.

14 *Ot Kollontai do Gorbacheva: Vospominaniya diplomata, sovetnika A. A. Gromyko, pomoshchnika L. I. Brezhneva, Yu. V. Andropova, K. U. Chernenko, i M. S. Gorbacheva* (Moscow, 1994), 135–44.

15 A CPSU plenum was convened in January 1961 to assess the results of the November 1960 conference; the transcript of the plenum and its associated documents were recently declassified. See "Plenum TsK KPSS 10–18 yanvarya 1961 g.," in Tsentr khraneniya sovremennoi dokumentatsii (TsKhSD), Moscow, Fond (F.) 2, Opis' (Op.) 1, Delo (D.) 495.

Sources of Friction

Despite these signs of greater Soviet–Eastern European cohesion, most developments between 1956 and 1968 pointed not toward an increase of Soviet control in Eastern Europe, but toward a loosening of that control. In part, this trend reflected the growing heterogeneity of Eastern European societies and the effects of Khrushchev's attempts to resume the de-Stalinization campaign at the 22d CPSU Congress in 1961, but it also was due to the schism in world Communism that had been opened by the Sino-Soviet conflict. A bitter split between the two leading Communist powers, stemming in part from genuine policy and ideological differences and in part from a personal clash between Khrushchev and Mao Zedong, developed behind the scenes in the late 1950s.[16] The dispute intensified in June 1959 when the Soviet Union abruptly terminated its secret nuclear weapons cooperation agreement with China (although this action was not in time to prevent the Chinese from building their own nuclear weapons just five years later). Khrushchev's highly publicized visit to the United States in September 1959 further antagonized the Chinese, and a last-ditch meeting between Khrushchev and Mao in Beijing right after Khrushchev's tour of the United States failed to resolve any of the issues dividing the two sides.[17] From then on, Sino-Soviet relations steadily deteriorated. In June 1960 all Eastern European Communist leaders learned of the rift, as Soviet and Chinese officials attending the Romanian Communist Party's congress traded polemics and recriminations. Over the next several months, as news of the conflict spread throughout the world, Khrushchev and Mao made a few additional attempts to reconcile their differences, but the split, if anything, grew even wider. Hopes of restoring a semblance of unity in the international Communist movement quickly faded, as the Soviet Union and China vied with one another for the backing of foreign Communist parties.

The spillover from the Sino-Soviet conflict into Eastern Europe was evident almost immediately. In late 1960 and early 1961 the Albanian leader, Enver Hoxha, sparked a crisis with the Soviet Union by openly aligning his

---

16 On the sources of the Beijing-Moscow dispute, see Mark Kramer, "Sino-Soviet Relations on the Eve of the Split," *Cold War International History Bulletin,* nos. 6–7 (winter 1995–6): 170–85.

17 For a transcript of these talks, see "Zapis' besedy N. S. Khrushcheva 2 oktyabrya 1959 g. v Pekine." Osobaya papka (Strictly Secret), Oct. 2, 1959, in Arkhiv Prezidenta Rossiiskoi Federatsii (APRF), Moscow, F. 54, Op. 1, D. 331, Listy (L1.) 1–33. Equally valuable is the detailed trip report by an influential Soviet Politburo member, Mikhail Suslov, shortly after he and the other members of the delegation returned to Moscow: "O poezdke Sovetskoi partiino-pravitel'stvennoi delegatsii v Kitaiskuyu Narodnuyu Respubliku," Osobaya papka (Eyes Only), Dec. 18, 1959, in TsKhSD, F. 2, Op. 1, D. 415, L1. 56–91.

country with China, a precedent that caused alarm in Moscow.[18] Quite apart from the symbolic implications of Hoxha's move, Khrushchev had always regarded Albania as a key member of the Warsaw Pact because of "its superb strategic location on the Mediterranean Sea."[19] The rift with Yugoslavia in 1948 had eliminated the only other possible outlet for the Soviet navy in the region. To ensure that Albania could serve as a full-fledged "military base on the Mediterranean Sea for all the socialist countries," the Soviet Union had been providing extensive equipment and training to the Albanian army and navy. In particular, the Albanian navy had received a fleet of twelve modern attack submarines, which initially were under Soviet control but were gradually being transferred to Albanian jurisdiction. Khrushchev believed that the submarines would allow Albania to pose a "serious threat to the operations of the NATO military bloc on the Mediterranean Sea," and thus he was dismayed to find that Soviet efforts to establish a naval bulwark on the Mediterranean might all have been for naught.[20]

As soon as the rift with Albania emerged, the Soviet Union imposed strict economic sanctions, withdrew all Soviet technicians and military advisers, took back eight of the twelve submarines, dismantled Soviet naval facilities at the Albanian port of Vlona, and engaged in bitter polemical exchanges with the Albanian leadership. Khrushchev also ordered Soviet warships to conduct maneuvers along the Albanian coast, and he secretly encouraged pro-Moscow rivals of Hoxha to carry out a coup.[21] The coup attempt was rebuffed, and the other means of coercion proved insufficient to get rid of Hoxha or to bring about a change of policy. In December 1961, Khrushchev broke diplomatic relations with Albania and excluded it from both the Warsaw Pact and CMEA. However, he was unwilling to undertake a full-scale invasion to bring Albania back within the Soviet orbit, not least because of logistical problems and the likelihood of con-

---

18 Valuable documentation on the Soviet-Albanian rift is available in *Albania Challenges Khrushchev Revisionism* (New York, 1976), a compilation put out by the Albanian government which includes full transcripts of meetings between senior Soviet and Albanian officials in 1960 as well as cables and other messages between Enver Hoxha and the Albanian participants in the meetings. The documents have been determined to be authentic and unaltered. A somewhat expanded edition of the collection is available in French: *La grande divergence 1960* (Paris, 1976). Key insights also can be gained by reading the surprisingly compatible accounts in Hoxha's and Khrushchev's memoirs: Nikita S. Khrushchev, *Vospominaniya N. S. Khrushcheva*, 5 vols. (typescript, Moscow, 1966–70), vol. 4: *Vzaimootnosheniya s sotsialisticheskimi stranami*, "Abaniya," 1109–31; and Hoxha, *The Artful Albanian: The Memoirs of Enver Hoxha*, ed. Jon Halliday (London, 1986), 224–47. For an early but still useful overview of the crisis, along with a handy collection of public statements and press articles, see William E. Griffith, *Albania and the Sino-Soviet Rift* (Cambridge, Mass., 1963).
19 Khrushchev, *Vzaimootnosheniya s sotsialisticheskimi stranami*, 1116.
20 Ibid., 1117.   21 Ibid.

fronting stiff armed resistance. The "loss" of Albania, although trivial compared to the earlier split with Yugoslavia and the deepening rift with China,
marked the second time since 1945 that the Soviet sphere of influence in
Eastern Europe had been breached.

To make matters worse, Soviet leaders soon discovered that China was
secretly attempting to induce other Eastern European countries to follow
Albania's lead. At a closed CPSU Central Committee plenum in December 1963, the top Soviet official responsible for intrabloc relations, Yurii
Andropov (who became head of the KGB in 1967), noted that the Chinese had been focusing their efforts on Poland, Hungary, and East Germany: "The Chinese leaders are carrying out a policy of crude sabotage in
relation to Poland, Hungary, and the GDR. Characteristic of this is the
fact that in September of this year, during conversations with a Hungarian
official in China, Politburo member Chu De declared that China would
welcome it if the Hungarian comrades diverged from the CPSU's line.
But, Chu De threatened, if you remain on the side of the revisionists, we
will have to take a stance against you."[22] China's efforts with these three
countries bore little fruit in the end, but Soviet leaders obviously could not
be sure of that at the time. The very fact that China was seeking to foment
discord within the Soviet bloc was enough to spark consternation in
Moscow.

Soviet concerns about the effect of the Sino-Soviet split were piqued
still further when Romania began to embrace foreign and domestic policies in the 1960s that were at times sharply at odds with the Soviet Union's
own policies. Initially, the Romanian quest for autonomy was inspired by
Khrushchev's attempts in 1961 to mandate a supranational economic integration program for CMEA, which would have relegated Romania to being
little more than a supplier of agricultural goods and raw materials for the
more industrialized Communist countries. In response, the Romanian government began shifting much of its foreign trade away from CMEA and, in
April 1964, issued a stinging rejection of Khrushchev's scheme.[23] From
then on, the reorientation of Romanian foreign trade gathered pace. By
the late 1960s, Romania's trade with other CMEA countries as a proportion of its total foreign trade had dropped from 70 to just 45 percent.[24]

22 "Materialy k protokolu No. 6 zasedaniya Plenuma TsK KPSS: O deyatel'nosti Prezidiuma TsK
KPSS po ukrepleniyu edinstva kommunisticheskogo dvizheniya, postanovlenie Sekretariata TsK
KPSS ob izdanii tekstov vystuplenii na Plenume TsK Ponmareva B. N., Androva Yu. V., i Il'icheva
L. F., rechi sekretarei TsK KPSS Ponomareva, Andropova, Il'icheva, i Khrushcheva N.S.," Dec.
9–13, 1963 (Top Secret), in TsKhSD, F. 2, Op. 1, D. 665, L. 30.

23 Romanian Press Agency (Agerpres), *Statement on the Stand of the Romanian Workers' Party Concerning
Problems of the World Communist and Working Class Movement* (Bucharest, 1964), 5–50.

24 Crawford and Haberstroh, "Survey of Economic Policy Issues in Eastern Europe," 41.

Before long, Romania's defiance extended from economic matters into foreign policy and military activities as well. Romania staked out a conspicuously neutral position in the Sino-Soviet dispute, refusing to endorse Moscow's polemics or to join in other steps aimed at isolating Beijing. Romania also became the lone Eastern European country to establish diplomatic ties with West Germany, a step that infuriated the East German leadership. In addition, the Romanians refused to attend the Karlovy Vary conference and maintained full diplomatic relations with Israel after the other Warsaw Pact countries had severed all ties in the wake of the Middle East war in June 1967.

More important, Romania adopted an independent military doctrine of "Total People's War for the Defense of the Homeland," as well as a national military command structure entirely separate from that of the Warsaw Pact.[25] Several years earlier, in 1958, the Romanian government had requested and obtained the withdrawal of all Soviet troops from Romania, but in the 1960s the new Romanian leader, Nicolae Ceauşescu, went much further by prohibiting joint Warsaw Pact maneuvers on Romanian territory and sending only token forces to participate in allied exercises elsewhere. Ceauşescu also stopped sending Romanian army officers to Soviet military academies for training and began openly challenging Soviet domination of the Warsaw Pact military command structures. When the Soviet-Romanian treaty of friendship and cooperation came up for renewal in 1967–8, Ceauşescu insisted that provisions be added to ensure that Romanian troops would be used only against "imperialist" countries, not against other socialist states. (Ceauşescu was thinking of China when he first proposed these amendments, but the provisions ended up being just as relevant to operations against Czechoslovakia.) Soviet leaders strongly resisted Ceauşescu's demands, but ultimately gave in.[26] Although Romania had never been a crucial member of the Warsaw Pact, Ceauşescu's growing recalcitrance on military affairs and foreign policy posed serious complications for the cohesion of the alliance.

Developments outside the Communist bloc also contributed to the loosening of Soviet control in Eastern Europe. The perceived threat of German aggression, which for so long had unified the Warsaw Pact governments, had gradually diminished. In the mid-1960s, West Germany had

---

25 Alexander Alexiev, *Romania and the Warsaw Pact: The Defense Policy of a Reluctant Ally* (Santa Monica, Calif., Jan. 1979).
26 The new treaty was finally concluded in July 1970, more than two-and-a-half years later than planned. See "Dogovor o druzhbe, sotrudnichestve i vzaimnoi pomoshchi," *Pravda* (Moscow), July 8, 1970, 2.

launched its Ostpolitik campaign to increase economic and political contacts in Eastern Europe, a campaign whose potentially disruptive impact on the Soviet bloc was well recognized in Moscow.[27] As early as 1956, senior officials in the CPSU Central Committee apparatus had expressed strong misgivings about the effect that conciliatory overtures from the FRG might have on Poland and Czechoslovakia. They warned that if circumstances went too far, Poland "would no longer be interested in hosting Soviet troops" and both Czechoslovakia and Poland might "pursue neutrality."[28] That notion seemed far-fetched at the time, no matter how much West German policy might change, but by the mid- to late 1960s, as the FRG's Ostpolitik gathered pace, those earlier warnings seemed all too plausible.

Soviet policy in Eastern Europe also was increasingly constrained by the improvement in U.S.–Soviet relations following the Cuban missile crisis, as symbolized by the signing of the Limited Nuclear Test Ban Treaty in August 1963. The incipient superpower détente raised hopes in Moscow that strategic nuclear arms control agreements and increased economic ties would be forthcoming. Such prospects gave the Soviet leadership an incentive to proceed cautiously in Eastern Europe before taking actions that would undermine the détente and provoke Western retaliation (although the escalating U.S. military involvement in Vietnam presumably had the opposite effect). The advent of a more cooperative U.S.–Soviet relationship even spawned fears in Europe, both West and East, that the superpowers might eventually seek a form of condominium. This concern was especially acute in East Germany, where Ulbricht constantly worried that the Soviet Union might cut a deal over his head, but similar anxieties were present in almost all Eastern European countries.

THE PRAGUE SPRING AND THE SOVIET RESPONSE

Amid these conflicting trends in Soviet–Eastern European relations, the events of 1968 unfolded in Czechoslovakia. In early January 1968, Alexander Dubček was chosen to replace the increasingly unpopular first secretary of the Czechoslovak Communist Party (KSČ), Antonín Novotný, who

---

27 On the genesis and conduct of Ostpolitik, see William E. Griffith, *The Ostpolitik of the Federal Republic of Germany* (Cambridge, Mass., 1978); Peter Bender, *Neue Ostpolitik* (Munich, 1986); and the chapter in this book by Gottfried Niedhart.

28 "Raschety i plany pravyashchikh krugov po germanskomu voprosu v svyazi s sobytiyami v Pol'she i Vengrii," memorandum no. 23055 (Top Secret), from the CPSU Information Committee to the CPSU Presidium, Nov. 29, 1956, in Arkhiv Vneshnei Politiki Rossiiskoi Federatsii (AVPRF), F. 595, Op. 77, D. 789, L1. 437–42.

had held the post since 1953. Within weeks of taking office, the new KSČ
leader embarked on a broad program of economic reform. Although
Dubček remained a loyal Communist to the end, the program that he set in
motion soon generated pressures for far-reaching political liberalization.
The sweeping reforms that ensued during the Prague Spring brought a
comprehensive revival of political, economic, and cultural life in Czechoslovakia.[29] When press censorship was effectively ended in early 1968, lively
discussions of political and social affairs began appearing in Czechoslovak
newspapers and journals. Unofficial political "clubs" sprang up all around
Czechoslovakia, and numerous commentators advocated the reestablish-
ment of non-Communist political parties from the pre-1948 era. The rehabilitation of victims of the show trials and repressions of the early 1950s,
which had begun very tentatively in the early 1960s, was sharply accelerated in the spring of 1968, and lengthy articles appeared condemning the
"crimes" of the early Communist period. A wide array of other political
reforms, which only a year earlier would have been inconceivable, were
swiftly implemented as the Prague Spring continued, giving rise to calls for
even bolder steps.

Because Czechoslovakia only recently had seemed to be one of the most
orthodox members of the socialist bloc, the measures adopted in 1968
quickly provoked anxiety in Moscow about the potential ramifications. As
early as January 18, less than two weeks after Dubček had taken office, the
Soviet Politburo discussed events in Czechoslovakia and received a detailed
briefing from the Soviet ambassador in Prague, Stepan Chervonenko. The
ambassador described Dubček as "unquestionably an honorable and faithful
man and a staunch friend of the Soviet Union," but Chervonenko warned
that the KSČ leadership overall was still "weak and divided," and that
Dubček was "vacillating."[30] The Soviet Politburo decided to increase bilat-

29 Of the many works dealing with the events of 1968, see in particular H. Gordon Skilling, *Czechoslovakia's Interrupted Revolution* (Princeton, N.J., 1976), which remains the best and most compre-
hensive treatment. Other books worth consulting about internal events in Czechoslovakia include
Galia Golan, *The Czechoslovak Reform Movement: Communism in Crisis, 1962–1968* (New York,
1971); Galia Golan, *Reform Rule in Czechoslovakia: The Dubček Era, 1968–1969* (New York, 1973);
Vladimír Horský, *Prag 1968: Systemveränderung und Systemverteidigung* (Stuttgart, 1975); Vladimír V.
Kusin, *The Intellectual Origins of the Prague Spring* (New York, 1971); Vladimír V. Kusin, *Political
Grouping in the Czechoslovak Reform Movement* (London, 1972); Jiří Kosta, "The Czechoslovak Economic Reform of the 1960s," in Norman Stone and Eduard Strouhal, eds., *Czechoslovakia: Crossroads and Crises, 1918–88* (New York, 1989), 231–52; and Eugen Löbl and Leopold Grünwald, *Die
intellektuelle Revolution: Hintergründe und Auswirkungen des "Prager Frühlings"* (Düsseldorf, 1969). See
also a recent collection of essays by Czech scholars: Václav Kural et al., eds., *Československo roku
1968* (Prague, 1993), vol. 1 (*Obrodný proces*) and vol. 2 (*Počátky normalizace*).
30 "Rabochaya zapis' zasedaniya Politbyuro TsK KPSS ot 18 yanvarya 1968 g.," Jan. 18, 1968 (Top
Secret), in APRF, F. 3, Op. 45, D. 99, Ll. 37–9. For similar concerns, see "Zapis' besed s zam. zav.
mezhdunarodnogo otdela TsK KPCh tov. M. Millerom v fevrale 1968 goda," cable no. 211 (Top
Secret), Mar. 5, 1968, from I. I. Udal'tsov, minister-counselor at the Soviet embassy in Czechoslo-

eral and multilateral contacts with Dubček and to keep a close watch on future developments in Czechoslovakia. In line with this decision, the KSČ leader was invited to Moscow for consultations at the end of January, and a top-level Soviet delegation reciprocated the visit a few weeks later. Moreover, Brezhnev kept in frequent touch with Dubček by telephone and through a series of confidential letters.[31]

Initially, Brezhnev and his colleagues expressed their concerns to Dubček in a low-key manner, and Dubček did his best to accommodate those concerns. Although Dubček supported wide-ranging political reforms, he also tried to preclude developments that would be perceived as hostile by his Warsaw Pact neighbors. Dubček continued, albeit often unsuccessfully, to admonish the press and other groups not to question the legitimacy of Czechoslovakia's alliances or the "leading role" of the KSČ, and he sought to dissuade intellectuals and dissenters from taking steps that would be tantamount to the formation of a full-fledged political opposition. To this end, Dubček publicly affirmed that the KSČ would not tolerate a revival of "certain nonsocialist modes . . . under the guise of democracy and rehabilitation," an obvious reference to the "clubs" and nascent political parties that had emerged.[32] The KSČ leader hewed to this basic line even as the Prague Spring took on a life of its own and moved gradually beyond the Communist Party's control.

Dubček's desire to prevent any impetuous actions was soon complicated by the tortuous sequence of events that led to the removal of his predecessor, Novotný, from the presidency (a post Novotný had retained after being ousted from the top party job). In late February 1968, General Jan Šejna, the chief of the party committee in the Czechoslovak Ministry of Defense, defected to the United States shortly before he was to be arrested on charges of corruption.[33] Rumors spread that Šejna and General Miroslav Mamula, the head of the KSČ Central Committee's Eighth Department overseeing the armed forces and internal security apparatus, had tried to use the Czechoslovak military in December 1967 and early January 1968 to keep Novotný in power, apparently at Novotný's request. Although details of

vakia, to M. A. Suslov, K. V. Rusakov, and A. A. Gromyko, in TsKhSD, F. 5, Op. 60, D. 299, Ll. 27–33; and "Otdel TsK KPSS," Mar. 18, 1968, memorandum (Secret) from V. Moskovskii to M. A. Suslov, in TsKhSD, F. 5, Op. 60, D. 25, Ll. 12–14.

31 The most important of these letters were declassified and published in Czech in 1991; see "Dokumenty: Dopisy L. Brežněva A. Dubčekovi v roce 1968," *Historie a vojenství* (Prague), no. 1 (Jan.–Feb. 1991): 141–58.

32 *K otázkam obrodného procesu KSČ: Vybrané projevy 1. tajemníka ÚV KSČA. Dubčeka* (Bratislava, 1968), 31–58.

33 The official KSČ report on the affair is in "Proč utekl Jan Šejna: Výsledky setřeni projednaný vládou," *Rudé právo* (Prague), June 12, 1968, 1–2.

the "Šejna affair" remained murky even after an official investigation was completed, what came out was damaging enough to inspire newspapers throughout Czechoslovakia to publish bitter criticism of Novotný and his supporters.

Confronted by these revelations and attacks, hard-line officials in key positions came under increasing pressure to resign. In the space of ten days, from March 5 to 14, many were forced out and replaced by prominent reform-minded officials. Jiří Hendrych was removed as KSČ secretary for ideology; Michal Chudík resigned as head of the Slovak National Council; Jan Kudrna was dismissed as Interior Minister; and Jan Bartuška was removed as procurator general. The ouster of Kudrna and Bartuška on March 14 was particularly significant because they had controlled the country's internal security apparatus and had maintained intimate links with the Soviet KGB. The new interior minister, Josef Pavel, not only was a leading proponent of reform, but was also wary of the KGB's intentions vis-à-vis Czechoslovakia – a position that infuriated Moscow. Over the next several months, Soviet leaders repeatedly demanded that Pavel be removed.

The shakeup in Czechoslovakia's internal security network was especially worrisome for Moscow because it came on the heels of major changes in the Czechoslovak People's Army (ČLA), which, like the ČSSR Interior Ministry, had traditionally been a crucial vehicle for Soviet influence in Czechoslovakia, both directly and indirectly. In late February a reform-minded officer, General Václav Prchlík, took over as head of the KSČ Central Committee State Administrative Department (the Eighth Department) after Mamula was forced out; and another reform-minded officer of Slovak origin, General Egyd Pepich, was appointed head of the ČLA's Main Political Directorate, the post Prchlík had vacated. Soon thereafter, a number of other senior officers were dismissed, and in early April the longtime defense minister under Novotný, Army-General Bohumír Lomský, was replaced by a Slovak officer with close ties to Dubček, General Martin Dzúr.[34]

The turnover of high-ranking personnel in the KSČ, the ČSSR Interior Ministry, and the Czechoslovak armed forces sparked ever greater anxiety in Moscow that traditional channels of Soviet influence in Czechoslovakia were being eroded and undermined by the Prague Spring.[35] At a CPSU Politburo meeting on March 15, the head of the KGB, Yurii

34 On Dzúr's earlier ties with Dubček, see memorandum no. 8468 (Top Secret) from Army-General A. Epishev, chief of the Main Political Directorate of the Soviet Armed Forces, to K. F. Katushev, CPSU Secretary, Oct. 23, 1968, in TsKhSD, F. 5, Op. 60, D. 311, Ll. 111–12.
35 See Dubček's intriguing comments on this point in *Hope Dies Last: The Autobiography of Alexander Dubček,* trans. and ed. Jiří Hochman (New York, 1993), 139, 146.

Andropov, who had served as ambassador in Budapest during the 1956 revolution, claimed that events in Czechoslovakia "are very reminiscent of what happened in Hungary." Brezhnev concurred, adding that "our earlier hopes for Dubček have not been borne out."[36] Brezhnev phoned Dubček during the session to emphasize how seriously the CPSU leadership viewed the situation in Czechoslovakia, and the two officials agreed that Dubček would meet soon with the Hungarian leader, János Kádár. Brezhnev expected that the Dubček-Kádár meeting would pave the way for a direct Soviet-Czechoslovak conclave.

Nevertheless, the phone call seemed to make less of an impact than Brezhnev had hoped. Over the next week, events in Prague continued to gather pace, culminating in the downfall of Novotný himself. On March 14, the same day that Kudrna and Bartuška were dismissed from the Interior Ministry, an announcement was made of the suicide of a deputy defense minister, General Vladimír Janko, following reports of his collaboration with Šejna in December and January on behalf of Novotný.[37] The outpouring of criticism that ensued in the Czechoslovak press led to further calls for Novotný's resignation, and the volume of those demands increased following disclosures that Novotný's son had been a friend of Šejna, and that Šejna's rapid advance in the army had been attributable solely to Novotný's largesse rather than to any professional qualifications. Under intense pressure, Novotný stepped down from the presidency on March 21 for "reasons of ill health."

If Novotný's forced departure had been an isolated event, it might not have stirred great unease in Moscow; but amid the flurry of other personnel changes in late February and March, as well as many changes that followed Novotný's resignation, the ouster of the president seemed to confirm that orthodox Communists in Czechoslovakia were in danger of being removed from the scene altogether. On the day that Novotný resigned, the Soviet Politburo met to discuss the latest developments in Czechoslovakia.[38] Brezhnev expressed dismay that events were "moving in an anticommunist direction" and that so many "good and sincere friends of the Soviet Union" had been forced to step down. He also noted that the situation in Czechoslovakia was beginning to spark ferment among Soviet "intellectuals and students as well as in certain regions" of the country, notably

36 "Rabochaya zapis' zasedaniya Politbyuro TsK KPSS ot 15 marta 1968 g.," Mar. 15, 1968 (Top Secret), in APRF, F. 3, Op. 45, D. 99, Ll. 123–4.
37 "Informace o samovražde gen. Vl. JANKA," Mar. 14, 1968 (Top Secret), in VHA, F. Sekretariat MNO, Operační správa Generálního štabu (GŠ/OS) čs. armády, 154/277.
38 "Rabochaya zapis' zasedaniya Politbyuro TsK KPSS ot 21 marta 1968 g.," Mar. 21, 1968 (Top Secret), in APRF, F. 3, Op. 45, D. 99, Ll. 147–58.

Ukraine. Brezhnev's misgivings were echoed by other Politburo members, including Prime Minister Aleksei Kosygin, who insisted that the Czechoslovak authorities were "preparing to do what was done in Hungary." The Ukrainian party leader, Petro Shelest, confirmed that events in Czechoslovakia were having adverse repercussions in Ukraine – repercussions that, in his view, meant the crisis would determine "not only the fate of socialism in one of the socialist countries, but the fate of the whole socialist camp." Aleksandr Shelepin and Mikhail Solomentsev spoke in similarly ominous tones about the effect of the Prague Spring on Soviet students and intellectuals. They joined Shelest in recommending that the Soviet Union be prepared, if necessary, to resort to "extreme measures," including "military action." Their recommendation was strongly endorsed by Andropov, who argued that "we must adopt concrete military measures" as soon as possible.

Soviet concerns were piqued still further by what happened in the wake of Novotný's removal. The process of selecting a replacement initially took the form of a "nomination campaign" in which the names of several outspoken advocates of reform were put forward. Although the eventual successor, Ludvík Svoboda, was a moderate with close ties to Brezhnev dating back to World War II and was chosen in the usual way – first by a KSČ Central Committee plenum and then by the National Assembly – the abrupt removal of Novotný and the unorthodox nomination procedures before Svoboda's election seemed to betoken a new way of selecting top elites that would loosen the KSČ's control and all but exclude Soviet influence.

Thus, even though the Soviet Union had never been deeply committed to Novotný (as was evidenced by Brezhnev's unwillingness to prevent Novotný's removal in December 1967), the unusual manner of replacing the president aroused concerns among Soviet officials that control of events was slipping away in Czechoslovakia.[39] Brezhnev was particularly upset about Dubček's failure even to consult with Moscow before Novotný was forced to resign. Although it may well be that Brezhnev would have approved the dismissal, it was the procedure rather than the result that provoked the Soviet leader's anger. After all, if Dubček would not consult with his Soviet counterparts about the fate of such a prominent figure as Novotný, that seemed to bode ill for dozens of other pro-Soviet officials in Czechoslovakia who were leery of reform and who were being ousted

---

39 See, e.g., the letter from Brezhnev to Dubček, Mar. 16, 1968, in Statní ústřední archiv (SÚA), Praha, Archiv Ústředního výboru Komunistické strany Československa (Arch. ÚV KSČ), F. 07/15, Zahr. kor. č. 787.

both from KSČ posts and from the military command and internal security network. Novotný's removal thus appeared, in Soviet eyes, to be a harbinger of a much wider purge that would eventually do away with all traces of Soviet influence in Czechoslovakia. A dangerous rift between Moscow and Prague was steadily emerging.

Reactions Within the Warsaw Pact

The growing unease in Moscow was reinforced by the much harsher complaints expressed in other East-bloc capitals, especially Warsaw and East Berlin. From the outset the Polish leader, Władysław Gomułka, and the East German leader, Walter Ulbricht, were determined to counter "inimical, antisocialist influences" along their borders. The two men feared that events in Czechoslovakia would prove "contagious" and threaten political instability in their own countries. As early as mid-January, when a high-level Soviet delegation led by Brezhnev paid an unofficial visit to Poland and the GDR, both Gomułka and Ulbricht expressed disquiet to their Soviet counterparts about recent developments in Czechoslovakia.[40] Gomułka reiterated his concerns in a private conversation with Dubček a few weeks later in the Moravian city of Ostrava, warning that "if things go badly with you [in Czechoslovakia], we in Poland, too, will find hostile elements rising against us."[41] In subsequent weeks, Gomułka's and Ulbricht's views of the Czechoslovak reform program took on an increasingly alarmist edge; and before long, both Eastern European leaders were calling, with ever greater urgency, for direct intervention by the Warsaw Pact to halt the Prague Spring.

Gomułka's fears that the "antisocialist" tendencies in Czechoslovakia would spread into Poland were heightened during the first few weeks of March, when students held riots and demonstrations on the streets of Warsaw and many other Polish cities, carrying signs in support of Dubček and proclaiming "Polska czeka na swego Dubczeka" (Poland is awaiting its own Dubček).[42] Although the Polish authorities violently quelled the student

---

40 See the materials pertaining to these discussions in Archiwum Akt Nowych (AAN) Warszawa, Archiwum Komitetu Centralnego Polskiej Zjednoczonej Partii Robotniczej (Arch. KC PZPR), Paczka (P.) 32, Tom (T.) 114.

41 "Protokół z rozmowy Pierwszego Sekretarza KC PZPR tow. Władysława Gomułki z Pierwszym Sekretarzem KC KPCz tow. Aleksandrem Dubczekem," Feb. 7, 1968 (Secret), in AAN, Arch. KC PZPR, P. 193, T. 24, Dok. 3.

42 On the effect of the turmoil in Poland, see the chapter in this book by Jerzy Eisler as well as Eisler's earlier study, *Marzec '68: Geneza – przebieg – konsekwencje* (Warsaw, 1991), which includes an extensive bibliography along with detailed analysis. See also the comments by one of Gomułka's chief rivals and his eventual successor, Edward Gierek, in Janusz Rolicki, ed., *Edward Gierek: Przerwana dekada* (Warsaw, 1990), 46–8. The unrest in Poland posed a dilemma for Soviet officials, who ini-

protests, the episode convinced Gomułka that events in Czechoslovakia, if allowed to proceed, would have an "increasingly detrimental effect on Poland."[43] The Polish leader became the first Soviet-bloc official to attack the Czechoslovak reforms publicly when, in a speech before party employees on March 19, he averred that "imperialist reaction and enemies of socialism" were active in Czechoslovakia.[44] By that point Gomułka's hostility to the Prague Spring had increased still further as a result of the challenge he was encountering from a group of ultranationalist "Partisan" officials who supported the hard-line Polish Internal Affairs Minister, Mieczysław Moczar. Eventually, Gomułka was able to thwart their efforts, but he was greatly weakened in the process.[45] To help shore up his position, the Polish leader soon resorted to even greater repression at home, including a sustained anti-Semitic campaign; and he became more dependent than ever on the Soviet Union, as he looked to Moscow for political backing against his rivals in Warsaw. Consequently, Gomułka's aversion to any possible "spillover" from Czechoslovakia intensified.

Ulbricht's reaction to the events in Czechoslovakia was similar to Gomułka's in two respects: first, the SED leader was worried about a potential "spillover" of the Prague Spring into East Germany; and second, Ulbricht's stance vis-à-vis Czechoslovakia was shaped in part by challenges and pressure he faced at home – in this case from his erstwhile protégé, Erich Honecker.[46] To guard against any possible "contagion" from the Prague Spring, the East German authorities prohibited the sale of certain

tially were unsure what, if anything, they should say about the riots. The director-general of the Soviet TASS news agency, Sergei Lapin, felt the need to contact the CPSU CC Politburo for permission just to publish in *Pravda* and *Izvestiya* a brief dispatch from the official Polish Press Agency. Brezhnev personally approved the request. See Lapin's secret memorandum of Mar. 11, 1968, in TsKhSD, F. 5, Op. 60, D. 25, L. 3. A notation in Brezhnev's handwriting at the bottom says "tov. Brezhnev L. I. soglasen" ("Comrade L. I. Brezhnev agrees").

43 "Dopeše sovetského velvyšlancě ve Varsave do Moskvy o názorech W. Gomułky na situaci v Československu," from A. Aristov, Soviet ambassador in Warsaw, to the CPSU Secretariat, Apr. 16, 1968 (Top Secret), in Ústav pro soudobé dějiny, Sbírka Komise vlády ČSFR pro analyzu udalosti let 1967–1970 (ÚSD-SK), Z/S – MID No. 2. See also "Wystąpenie Władysława Gomułki na naradzie Pierwszych Sekretarzy KW PZPR," Mar. 26, 1968 (Top Secret), in AAN, Arch. KC PZPR, P. 298, T. 1, Dok. 3.

44 "Umacniajmy jedność narodu w budownictwie socjalistycznej Ojczyzny: Przemówienie Władysława Gomułki na spotkaniu z aktywem warszawskim," *Żołnierz Wolności* (Warsaw), Mar. 20, 1968, 3–4. The full speech was republished in *Pravda* (Moscow) on Mar. 22, 1968, 3–4.

45 On the way the Moczar Affair affected Gomułka's response to the events in Czechoslovakia, see *Edward Gierek: Przerwana dekada*, 42–3, 47–50, 60–3, 88–9, and 92–3. Another firsthand account of the Moczar Affair, from a very different perspective, is by Franciszek Szlachcic, "Ze wspomnien Ministra Spraw Wewnętrznych," *Życie literackie* (Warsaw), no. 10, Mar. 6, 1988, 4–5. Szlachcic was a deputy Internal Affairs Minister in 1968 and a close friend of Moczar.

46 Heinz Lippmann, *Honecker: Porträt eines Nachfolgers* (Cologne, 1971), 204–6. See also Gerhard Naumann and Eckhard Trumpler, *Von Ulbricht zu Honecker: 1970 – ein Krisenjahr der DDR* (Berlin, 1990).

Czechoslovak publications in the GDR, ceased issuing visas for tourists wishing to travel to Czechoslovakia, curtailed scientific and cultural exchanges, and imposed restrictions on broadcasts from Czechoslovakia. As time went on, the East German government all but sealed off its border with the ČSSR. All these measures were similar to steps implemented in Poland.[47]

In one key respect, however, Ulbricht's motives during the crisis differed from those of Gomułka. The prospect of a rapprochement between Czechoslovakia and West Germany was clearly at the forefront of the East German leader's concerns.[48] After Romania had unilaterally established diplomatic relations with the FRG in early 1967, the rest of the Warsaw Pact states had resolved, at a special meeting in Karlovy Vary, not to do the same until the West German government met a number of stringent conditions. Ulbricht was worried, however, that some of the Pact leaders might eventually deviate from the Karlovy Vary agreement. He hoped that by opposing the reforms in Czechoslovakia, he could forestall any change in Prague's policy toward Bonn and exploit the events to head off a Soviet decision to seek closer relations with the FRG.[49] Even the slightest hint that Czechoslovakia was considering an opening to West Germany provoked belligerent accusations from Ulbricht.

The Prague Spring and the Soviet Politburo

The concerns expressed by Polish and East German leaders, combined with the disquiet that senior officials in Moscow were beginning to feel, induced the Soviet Politburo to give high priority to the "Czechoslovak question."[50] From mid-March 1968 on, the issue was constantly at the top of the Politburo's agenda. Brezhnev consulted and worked closely with his colleagues on all aspects of the crisis, ensuring that responsibility for the outcome would be borne collectively. Unlike in December 1967, when Brezhnev resorted to "personal diplomacy" during his sudden visit to Prague, the growing "threat" in Czechoslovakia by the spring of 1968 gave him an incentive to share as much of the burden as possible with the rest of the

---

47 Lutz Priess, Václav Kural, and Manfred Wilke, *Die SED und der "Prager Frühling" 1968: Politik gegen einen Sozialismus mit menschlichem Antlitz* (Berlin, 1996).

48 Among many studies of this topic, one of the best is still Adolf Müller and Bedrich Utitz, *Deutschland und die Tschechoslowakei: Zwei Nachbarvolker auf dem Weg zur Verständigung* (Freudenstadt, 1972).

49 See Ulbricht's handwritten notes to this effect in Stiftung Archiv der Parteien und Massenorganisationen der DDR im Bundesarchiv (SAPMDB), Zentrales Parteiarchiv der SED (ZPA), Berlin, IV 2/201/778.

50 Aleksandrov-Agentov, *Ot Kollontai do Gorbacheva*, 147–9.

Politburo and Secretariat. In particular, he ensured that his two top colleagues (and potential rivals), Aleksei Kosygin and Nikolai Podgornyi, were
prominently involved in all key decisions and negotiations, linking them in
an informal troika (with Brezhnev) that represented – and often acted on
behalf of – the full Politburo. Much the same was true of Brezhnev's
reliance on two other senior Politburo members: Mikhail Suslov, the top
official on ideological matters, and Petro Shelest, whose responsibilities in
Ukraine did not prevent him from playing a major role during the crisis.

At the same time, Brezhnev was careful not to get bogged down by
lower-level bureaucratic maneuvering. Throughout the crisis the CPSU
Politburo, led by Brezhnev, exercised tight control over Soviet policy. The
Politburo eventually set up a high-level "commission on the Czechoslovak
question," which kept a daily watch on events in Czechoslovakia, but this
body was no more than an organ of the Politburo and was directly account-
able to Brezhnev. (Six of the nine members of the commission, including
Podgornyi and Suslov, were on the Politburo, and the other three had been
taking an active part in the Politburo's deliberations.)[51] The commission's
findings and recommendations were regularly brought before the full Politburo for consideration. Brezhnev himself carefully guided the proceedings
and took chief responsibility for bilateral contacts with Dubček.

Contrary to assertions made by some Western analysts, the CPSU Politburo and Secretariat depended relatively little on lower-level party and state
agencies in their dealings with Czechoslovakia. Most of the time, the information flow during the crisis was from the top down (that is, the Politburo
ordered lower-level officials what to think and do), and all media outlets
were kept rigidly under the Politburo's control.[52] From at least early March
on, all significant articles about Czechoslovakia had to be cleared directly
with top officials, and often with Brezhnev himself.[53] A formal directive to
this effect was issued in early June. Moreover, the Politburo transmitted frequent "informational reports" about the crisis to lower-level party and state

51 "Rabochaya zapis' zasedaniya Politbyuro TsK KPSS ot 23 maya 1968," May 23, 1968 (Top Secret),
    in APRF, F. 3, Op. 45, L. 262. The nine members of the commission were Nikolai Podgornyi,
    Mikhail Suslov, Arvids Pel'she, Aleksandr Shelepin, Kirill Mazurov, Konstantin Rusakov, Yurii
    Andropov, Andrei Gromyko, and Aleksei Epishev.
52 Evidence about the top-down flow of information, based on newly declassified materials, is pro-
    vided in Mark Kramer, *Crisis in Czechoslovakia, 1968: The Prague Spring and the Soviet Invasion* (New
    York, forthcoming). This new information undercuts much of the utility of the "bureaucratic pol-
    itics" framework employed by Jirí Valenta in *Soviet Intervention in Czechoslovakia, 1968: Anatomy of a
    Decision*, rev. ed. (Baltimore, 1991). Further doubts about Valenta's approach are raised in Mark
    Kramer, "The CPSU International Department: Comments and Observations," in Sergei Grigoriev
    et al., *The International Department of the CPSU Central Committee* (Cambridge, Mass., 1995), 109–11.
53 See, e.g., the reference to a brief official news release about the unrest in Poland, which had to be
    cleared with Brezhnev, in note 42 to this chapter.

organizations, which were required to disseminate the Politburo's findings to all employees and party members.[54] Brezhnev and his colleagues used the CPSU CC Organizational-Party Work Department as an oversight mechanism to ensure that dissemination of the reports was carried out in strict accordance with the Politburo's wishes. Preparation of the reports was valuable both in forcing the Politburo to arrive at a common position and in preventing any divergences at lower levels from the top leadership's policies.

New Reforms and New Reactions

Despite the growing external pressure, senior Czechoslovak officials continued to advocate far-reaching political reform, particularly freedom of the press, on the grounds that uninhibited debate was the only way to ensure that the Communist Party would retain its dominant position in Czechoslovak society. In keeping with this notion, Dubček encouraged a lively and wide-ranging exchange of views within the KSČ about the future course of social, political, and economic liberalization. These discussions culminated in the adoption of a comprehensive "Action Program" at a plenary session of the KSČ Central Committee in early April, a document that became the symbolic blueprint for the last several months of the Prague Spring.[55]

The decision to adopt a sweeping reform program was accompanied by the removal or demotion of many prominent antireformist officials in the KSČ and the Czechoslovak government (almost all of whom had spent considerable time in the Soviet Union) and the replacement of numerous regional and local party secretaries left over from the Novotný era. The combination of these developments greatly expedited the pace of reform

54 See, e.g., "Informatsiya TsK KPSS o sobytiyakh v Chekhoslovakii" (Top Secret), Mar. 23, 1968, covered in TsKhSD, F. 5, Op. 60, D. 10, Ll. 1–12; "Informatsiya TsK KPSS po vazhneishim voprosam vneshnei politiki i polozheniya v otdel'nykh sotsialisticheskikh stranakh" (Top Secret) and "Informatsiya TsK KPSS o polozhenii v Chekhoslovakii i o nekotorykh vneshnepoliticheskikh shagakh rumynskogo rukovodstva" (Top Secret), June 18, 1968, covered in TsKhSD, F. 5, Op. 60, D. 1, Ll. 92–9 and D. 10, Ll. 15–26; "O sobytiyakh v Chekhoslovakii" (Top Secret), July 8, 1968, covered in TsKhSD, F. 5, Op. 60, D. 10, Ll. 27–50; "Informatsiya o vstreche v Chierne-nad-Tissoi i soveshchanii v Bratislave" (Top Secret), Aug. 4, 1968, covered in TsKhSD, F. 5, Op. 60, D. 24, Ll. 127–35; "TsK KPSS," memorandum no. P1513 (Secret), Sept. 30, 1968, from I. Shvets, deputy head of sector in the CPSU CC Department for Party-Organizational Work, in TsKhSD, F. 5, Op. 60, D. 10, L. 97; "O polozhenii v Chekhoslovakii" (Top Secret), Feb. 7, 1969, covered in TsKhSD, F. 5, Op. 61, D. 21, Ll. 79–111; "O sobytiyakh v Chekhoslovakii" (Top Secret), Feb. 12, 1968, covered in TsKhSD, F. 5, Op. 61, D. 21, Ll. 161–85. See also "TsK KPSS," memorandum no. 14194 (Top Secret), May 27, 1968, from V. Stepakov, K. Rusakov, and V. Zagladin, in TsKhSD, F. 5, Op. 60, D. 19, Ll. 109, 133–6.
55 "Akční program Komunistické strany Československa," *Rudé právo* (Prague), Apr. 10, 1968, 1–6.

in Czechoslovakia in April and May. Procedures for the rehabilitation of victims of past injustices were drafted and implemented, as were measures that effectively restored freedom of religion. Under the theory that the government was to become responsible to the National Assembly (that is, the parliament) rather than to the party, the powers of the Assembly were enhanced. A new government was organized with Oldřich Černík at its head, and the National Assembly met to begin considering legislation on its own. These reforms were somewhat offset by the KSČ's attempts to prohibit the return of the Social Democratic Party and the formation of any other independent political parties, but the pace of reform still greatly exceeded that of all earlier efforts. The country was responding enthusiastically to the KSČ leadership's calls for democratization, and popular support for both the party and the action program grew rapidly.

Yet at the same time that the Action Program and personnel changes were generating excitement and anticipation in Czechoslovakia, they were causing even deeper misgivings in Moscow and other Warsaw Pact capitals. Initially, the Soviet leadership's response to the Action Program was relatively muted (and excerpts from the Program were even published in the main CPSU daily, *Pravda,* on April 12), but by early May the Soviet Politburo, as Brezhnev remarked to his colleagues, was "united in the view that [the Action Program] is a harmful program, which is paving the way for the restoration of capitalism in Czechoslovakia."[56] Of particular concern to Soviet officials were the free-wheeling political discussions in the Czechoslovak media and the continued removal of hard-line opponents of the Prague Spring. Earlier, at a Warsaw Pact meeting in Dresden on March 23, the assembled leaders had rebuked Dubček for allowing "the press, radio, and television to slip away from the party's control" and for dismissing many "loyal and seasoned cadres, who have proven their mettle in years of struggle."[57] Events over the next several weeks had greatly reinforced these concerns. At a bilateral Soviet-Czechoslovak meeting in Moscow in early May, Soviet leaders repeated all their earlier complaints and raised a host of new allegations, leaving the Czechoslovak delegation almost speechless.[58]

---

56 "Rabochaya zapis' zasedaniya Politbyuro TsK KPSS ot 6 maya 1968," May 6, 1968 (Top Secret), in APRF, F. 3, Op. 45, D. 99, L. 202.

57 "Protokoll der Treffen der Ersten Sekretäre der kommunistischen Parteien Bulgariens, der ČSSR, der DDR, Polens, der Sowjetunion und Ungarns," Mar. 23, 1968 (Top Secret), in SAPMDB, ZPA, IV 2/201/778.

58 "Zapis' peregovorov s delegatsiei ChSSR, 4 maya 1968 goda," 4 May 1968 (Top Secret) in APRF, F. 3, Op. 91, D. 100, Ll. 1–148.

The growing impatience in Moscow was just as evident two days later, when the Soviet Politburo convened to discuss how events in Czechoslovakia might develop in the wake of the bilateral meeting.[59] Brezhnev claimed that the Czechoslovak media were "endangering socialist gains and the role of the Communist Party in Czechoslovakia," and he accused Dubček of having "decapitated the party" by releasing so many "honest and committed Communists." All participants in the session expressed their determination to "preserve socialism in Czechoslovakia" by any means necessary. They approved a number of steps to bring greater pressure to bear on the KSČ leadership and designated Petro Shelest to serve as a clandestine liaison with the hard-line forces in Czechoslovakia led by Vasil Bil'ak, Alois Indra, and Drahomír Kolder. Brezhnev acknowledged that the buildup of military and political pressure on Czechoslovakia would "evoke protests in the bourgeois and Czechoslovak media," but he added, "Well, so what? This won't be the first time it's happened. . . . And besides, after this everyone will know it's not worth fooling around with us."[60]

As the rift with Czechoslovakia widened in the spring of 1968, the CPSU Politburo authorized Soviet defense minister Marshal Andrei Grechko to begin preparing Soviet forces in Eastern Europe for a large-scale military contingency.[61] This marked the initial step in planning for Operation "Danube" (the eventual code name of the invasion). On May 6, the Soviet Defense Council, a political-military body headed by Brezhnev, considered further "concrete plans about our practical measures" for Czechoslovakia. The Defense Council's recommendations, including the dispatch of a high-level Soviet military delegation to Czechoslovakia in mid-May and the use of large-scale military exercises on Czechoslovak territory in late May and June to exert political pressure and carry out logistical preparations, were then considered and approved by the CPSU Politburo.[62] Brezhnev and his colleagues also took a number of important political steps to ensure that members of the CPSU Central Committee and other lower-ranking party officials would be ready for a vigorous stance against Czechoslovakia.[63] These steps were useful both in reaffirming the general thrust of Soviet policy and in giving Central Committee members a sense of involvement in policy making.

59 "Rabochaya zapis' zasedaniya Politbyuro TsK KPSS ot 6 maya 1968," Ll. 200–20.
60 Ibid., L. 218.
61 Directive no. MO/GOU/1/87567 (Top Secret – Eyes Only), Apr. 5, 1968, to Col.-General K. I. Provalov, in Magyar Honvédség Központi Irattára (MHKI), Budapest, 5/12/16.
62 "Rabochaya zapis' zasedaniya Politbyuro TsK KPSS ot 6 maya 1968," Ll. 208, 216–19.
63 For an extended discussion of these steps, see Kramer, *Crisis in Czechoslovakia, 1968.*

Within the Soviet Politburo itself, however, there was not yet full agreement about the best course to pursue. For the time being, Brezhnev was
unwilling to embrace a clear-cut position, and he permitted and indeed
encouraged other members of the Politburo to express their own opinions
about particular matters.[64] The diary of one of the senior Politburo members at the time, Petro Shelest, reveals that as late as the summer of 1968,
the differing approaches of Brezhnev, Aleksei Kosygin, Nikolai Podgornyi,
Mikhail Suslov, and others "prevented the Politburo from uniting firmly on
how to deal with the question of Czechoslovakia."[65] Newly released transcripts of the Politburo's deliberations amply corroborate Shelest's point.
The transcripts show that some members, such as Andropov, Podgornyi,
and Shelest, were consistent proponents of military intervention, whereas
others, particularly Suslov, were far more circumspect. The transcripts also
show that a substantial number, including Kosygin, Aleksandr Shelepin,
and Pyotr Demichev, fluctuated markedly during the crisis, at times favoring "extreme measures" (that is, military action) and at other times seeking
a political solution.

Nevertheless, even when top-ranking Soviet officials disagreed with one
another, their disagreements were mainly over tactics rather than strategic
considerations or fundamental goals. All the members of the Soviet Politburo agreed that the reform process in Czechoslovakia was endangering the
"gains of socialism" and the "common interests of world socialism." By the
late spring of 1968, most of them sensed that drastic action would be necessary to curtail the Prague Spring. Although some still hoped that
Czechoslovak leaders themselves would be willing to crack down, many
had begun to suspect that it was no longer possible to count on a purely
"internal" solution.

The time constraints that Soviet leaders believed they were facing
increased precipitously in June and July, as it became evident that reformist
delegates were going to dominate the KSČ's Fourteenth Congress in September. From Moscow's perspective, this trend posed the danger that antireformist, pro-Moscow officials (that is, "healthy forces") who were still in
place would be removed en masse by the Congress, setting Czechoslovakia
on a "nonsocialist" course. To forestall that prospect, Soviet leaders sharply
stepped up their pressure on Dubček, urging him to move expeditiously in
combating "antisocialist" and "counterrevolutionary" elements. In particular, they urged the KSČ first secretary to reimpose tight restraints on the

---

64 Aleksandrov-Agentov, *Ot Kollontai do Gorbacheva*, 147–9. See also P. E. Shelest, . . . *Da ne sudimy
      budete: Dnevnikovye zapisi, vospominaniya chlena Politbyuro TsK KPSS* (Moscow, 1995), 320–1.
65 Shelest, . . . *Da ne sudimy budete*, 321.

press. These demands, however, left Dubček in an unenviable position. Freedom of the press was the bedrock of the Prague Spring, symbolizing all the recent changes in Czechoslovakia. A crackdown would signal at least a temporary end to liberalization and would be politically disastrous.[66] Furthermore, the greater the pressure the Soviet Union exerted on Dubček, the more he believed that his best defense was to show that widespread popular support existed for both the KSČ and the reform program. Maintaining a free press, in his view, was the only viable way to achieve this objective, but it also created a problem: The freedom necessary to ensure press support for the regime was frequently used by journalists and public commentators to attack the Soviet Union and other Warsaw Pact member-states.

Hence, Dubček's leeway for maneuver became more and more attenuated. Throughout the spring and summer of 1968 he sought to persuade the press to halt its criticism of the Soviet Union and the party's leading role in Czechoslovak life, but his efforts met with little success.[67] The task of restraining the media was made all the more difficult by the growing number and severity of public attacks from the other Warsaw Pact countries, which spurred the Czechoslovak press to respond in kind and exacerbated the already tense atmosphere. Angered by the attempts of Soviet, East German, and Polish leaders to intimidate the reformers in Prague, many Czechoslovak journalists and intellectuals called for bold measures to guarantee the permanence of the latest reforms. These demands heightened Soviet concerns and led to further obloquy in the Soviet press against the Prague Spring, which in turn caused the Czechoslovak media to become even more outspoken.[68] The situation, to say the least, was an uncomfortable one for Dubček, but there were few steps he could take to rectify the situation short of reimposing censorship, which he was unwilling to do.

Soviet Concerns About Czechoslovakia's Foreign Alignment

In part because Dubček was unable to mollify Soviet displeasure over the press and other internal changes, he strove to reassure Moscow about the

---

66 On this point, see *Hope Dies Last,* 161–3.
67 "Soudruh Alexander Dubček: Hodnoceni současné situace, zpráva o činnosti orgánů ÚV, další taktický postup strany, příprava sjezdu KSČ," *Rudé právo* (Prague), June 2, 1968, 2.
68 See, e.g., "Po návštěve delegácie ČSSR v Moskvě," dispatch by ČTK correspondent Ján Riško, May 12, 1968, in SÚA, Arch. ÚV KSČ, F. 07/15.

firmness of Czechoslovakia's commitment to the Warsaw Pact and the "socialist commonwealth."[69] Looking back to the events of 1956 in Hungary, Dubček and other Czechoslovak officials had concluded that by upholding Czechoslovakia's membership in the Warsaw Pact and maintaining party control over the reform process, they could carry out far-reaching domestic changes without provoking Soviet military intervention.[70] Their judgment in this instance was probably erroneous even in the case of Hungary, inasmuch as the first Soviet intervention in 1956 and the decision to intervene a second time actually predated Hungary's withdrawal from the Warsaw Pact.[71] Whether valid or not, however, the "lesson" that KSČ officials drew from the 1956 crisis – that internal reform would be tolerated so long as membership in the Warsaw Pact and CMEA was never questioned – induced them to make frequent references to the "unbreakable" friendship and alliance between the Soviet Union and Czechoslovakia.[72] As domestic liberalization gathered pace, Dubček was particularly careful to issue repeated expressions of solidarity with Moscow and to pledge that Soviet interests would be safeguarded under all circumstances. He also emphasized that Czechoslovakia would uphold all its "external" obligations to the Warsaw Pact, including its role as a leading military supplier to key Third World countries such as North Vietnam.[73]

Despite these assurances, the rapid sequence of events since January had stirred doubts in Moscow about the integrity of Czechoslovakia's long-term commitment to the Warsaw Pact. Soviet leaders were alarmed by the "hostile" and "anti-Soviet" forces in Prague, and they suspected that the KSČ would be increasingly amenable to calls, from both within and outside the party, for policies favoring national over "internationalist" interests. Before long, some in Moscow came to fear that a major shift in Czechoslovak foreign policy – perhaps even a shift toward neutrality (à la Yugoslavia) or alignment with the West – could no longer be ruled out. Soviet foreign minister Andrei Gromyko warned the CPSU Politburo in early May that

---

69 See the comments of Czechoslovak Foreign Minister Jiří Hájek in 1968 in *Dix ans après: Prague 1968–1978* (Paris, 1978), 110–15, 163–4, 172–9.

70 See Dubček's comments on this matter in *Hope Dies Last,* 178–9.

71 "Vypiska iz protokola No. 49 zasedaniya Prezidiuma TsK ot 31 oktyabrya 1956 g.: O polozhenii v Vengrii," No. P49/VI (Strictly Secret), Oct. 31, 1956, in APRF, F. 3, Op. 64, D. 484, L. 41.

72 See, e.g., "Projev soudruha Alexandra Dubčeka," *Rudé právo* (Prague), Apr. 25, 1968, 1–2.

73 "Zapis' besedy s ministrom inostrannykh del NR Bolgarii tov. I. Bashevym," July 11, 1968 (Secret), from A. M. Puzanov, Soviet ambassador in Bulgaria, to the CPSU Secretariat, in TsKhSD, F. 5, Op. 60, D. 278, Ll. 78–82. Because of the Johnson administration's preoccupation with the Vietnam War, Czechoslovakia's continued role as a supplier of military equipment to North Vietnam inhibited U.S. support for the Prague Spring. See, e.g., "Notes on Emergency Meeting of the National Security Council," Aug. 20, 1968 (Secret), in National Security Council box no. 3, Tom Johnson's notes of meetings, Aug. 20, 1968, Lyndon Baines Johnson National Library.

"in the best scenario," the "burgeoning counterrevolution" in Czechoslovakia would soon "mean a second Romania, and this will be enough for the complete collapse of the Warsaw Pact."[74] Even those who did not believe that a radical change would take place immediately were concerned that the Prague Spring would induce a steady reorientation of Czechoslovakia's loyalties in Europe, especially if pro-reform elements in the KSČ gained an ever stronger hold.

Soviet perceptions of this matter were not entirely fanciful. Although Dubček himself never contemplated any far-reaching innovations in foreign policy, the press and non-Communist organizations in Czechoslovakia by mid-1968 had begun alluding to the need for "independence" from Moscow.[75] That theme also was being propounded by a growing number of researchers at the KSČ's specialized institutes on international affairs, as well as by a few more senior party officials. At the KSČ Central Committee plenum in late May, Kolder found it necessary to excoriate those who "allege that [Czechoslovakia's] orientation toward the Soviet Union has depreciated our international position and forced us to uphold and defend interests alien to us."[76] In retrospect, it may seem extremely unlikely that Czechoslovakia would have attempted a full-scale shift away from the Warsaw Pact in 1968, but at the time Soviet leaders could not afford to dismiss any possibility. The Prague Spring already had brought so many dramatic changes in Czechoslovakia's internal politics that there was no telling what might eventually become of the country's "socialist internationalist" stance on foreign policy.

The seeming plausibility and urgency of these concerns were magnified by signs of turmoil within the Czechoslovak People's Army. The ouster of many hard-line Communist (and pro-Soviet) military officers and National Defense Ministry personnel in the spring of 1968 allowed the reform movement to extend far into the ČLA. A lively debate arose in Czechoslovakia, both publicly and privately, about the possibility of sharply reducing military spending and transferring resources to the civilian economy. Implicit in any such move would be a diminution of the country's military obligations to the Warsaw Pact. Further controversy about Czechoslovakia's role in the Warsaw Pact arose in mid-May when twenty-one officers from the Klement Gottwald Military-Political Academy released a "memorandum"

---

74 "Rabochaya zapis' zasedaniya Polityuro TsK KPSS ot 6 maya 1968 g.," L. 211.

75 Skilling, *Czechoslovakia's Interrupted Revolution*, 617–58. See also Golan, *Reform Rule in Czechoslovakia*, 200–11.

76 "Z diskuse na plenu ÚV KSČ ve dnech 29. května – 1. června 1968," *Rudé právo* (Prague), June 7, 1968, 3.

which, although not advocating withdrawal from the Pact, strongly criticized existing alliance structures and proposed numerous reforms both in
the alliance and in Czechoslovak policy.[77] The implementation of these
measures would have resulted in a markedly different Soviet–Eastern European military relationship. The Gottwald Memorandum received overwhelming support within the Czechoslovak armed forces, and many of the
document's proposals were included in drafts prepared by the National
Defense Ministry for consideration at the KSČ's upcoming Fourteenth
Congress.

Combined with the ongoing personnel changes and the debates over
military spending, the Gottwald Memorandum sparked fresh apprehension
in Moscow about the future of Czechoslovakia's contribution to the Warsaw Pact. Detailed reports from the Soviet defense ministry and KGB,
which were sent regularly to the CPSU leadership, offered a gloomy view
of the "military-political standing and combat readiness of the Czechoslovak armed forces."[78] In a briefing to the CPSU Politburo on May 23, Marshal Grechko claimed that the Czechoslovak army was "rapidly deteriorating" and was "no longer capable of defending the border with the FRG."[79]
A few weeks later, Soviet military officials warned Brezhnev that if the
number of "ČLA officers who favor 'democratic reforms in the army'"
continued to grow, it would accelerate the "grave decline in the Czechoslovak army's combat capability."[80] Brezhnev, in turn, urged the KSČ leadership to realize that "when your army is being weakened, this is not and
cannot be a purely internal matter. We count on your [army's] strength,
just as you rely on the might of the Soviet Union."[81]

Far from abating, however, Soviet concerns intensified in mid-July when
the views expressed in the Gottwald Memorandum were openly endorsed
and substantially amplified at a press conference by General Prchlík, the
head of the powerful State-Administrative Department of the KSČ Central
Committee.[82] Prchlík chided the Soviet Union and other Warsaw Pact
countries for having "arbitrarily stationed their units on [Czechoslovak]

---

77 The memorandum was not published until several weeks later, in *Lidová armáda* (Prague), July 2,
1968, 1–2.
78 See, e.g., the voluminous reports and memoranda in TsKhSD, F. 5, Op. 60, Dd. 232, 243, and 309.
79 "Rabochaya zapis' zasedaniya Politbyuro TsK KPSS ot 23 maya 1968 g.," 23 May 1968 (Top Secret),
in APRF, F. 3, Op. 45, D. 99, Ll. 260–2.
80 Comments recorded in Shelest, . . . *Da ne sudimy budete,* 325.
81 "Zapis' peregovorov s delegatsiei ChSSR 4 maya 1968 goda," L. 144.
82 "Vystoupení generála V. Prchlíka na tiskové konferenci," *Obrana lidu* (Prague), July 16, 1968, 1–2.
For a typical Soviet response, see "Komu ugozhdaet general V. Prkhlik," *Krasnaya zvezda* (Moscow),
July 23, 1968, 2.

territory" (a reference to joint military exercises that had been prolonged since the end of June without Czechoslovakia's consent). He called for the "formulation of a Czechoslovak military doctrine" that would be distinct from Warsaw Pact doctrine. Prchlík also maintained that "qualitative changes" were needed in the alliance to bring about "genuine equality among the individual members." Under existing arrangements, he argued, the Pact's military organs were dominated "by marshals, generals, and lower-ranking officers of the Soviet Army," while representatives of Eastern European armed forces "hold no responsibilities at all nor have a hand in making decisions."

Prchlík's assessment of the need for major reforms in the Warsaw Pact was largely in accord with what many Eastern European officials had been saying in private for some time, and most of his recommendations had already been proposed by Romanian leaders. Nevertheless, Prchlík's willingness to raise the issue in such a blunt manner at a time of heightened tension was extraordinary. The news conference deeply antagonized Soviet leaders and army officers, who charged that Prchlík had "distorted the essence" of the Warsaw Pact, "defamed the Soviet military command," and "improperly divulged vital secrets about the deployment of the Joint Armed Forces."[83] Soviet responses to the news conference were particularly strident because of long-standing concerns about Prchlík. Since early May, reports had been filtering into Moscow that Prchlík was intent on drafting contingency plans to resist a Soviet invasion. His proposals had been rejected immediately both by Dubček and by Defense Minister Martin Dzúr, and no such preparations were actually carried out; but the disclosures of Prchlík's involvement – as the leading KSČ official responsible for military affairs – had generated alarm in Moscow. Soviet officials assumed that as time went on, there was a greater chance that the Czechoslovak armed forces would prepare an active resistance.[84] Coupled with the changes that had already taken place in the Czechoslovak military establishment, such a prospect aroused deep anxiety in Moscow about the impact of the Prague Spring on Czechoslovakia's military alignment. Memories of the heavy

---

83 "Pervomu sekretaryu KPCh, t. Aleksandru Dubcheku" (Top Secret) from Marshal I. Yakubovskii, commander-in-chief of the Warsaw Pact, July 18, 1968; in SUA, Arch. UV KSČ, F. 07/15.
84 "Interview with Jiří Pelikán: The Struggle for Socialism in Czechoslovakia," *New Left Review*, no. 71 (Jan.–Feb. 1972): 27. Pelikán was a member of the KSČ Central Committee, head of the state television service, and chairman of the Foreign Relations Committee of the National Assembly as of August 1968. On Prchlík's role, see also John Erickson, "International and Strategic Implications of the Czechoslovak Reform Movement," in Vladimir V. Kusin, ed., *The Czechoslovak Reform Movement, 1968* (Santa Barbara, Calif., 1973), 26.

losses that the Soviet Army experienced when confronted by armed resistance in Hungary in 1956 were still vivid for many of the Soviet officers
who were preparing the 1968 invasion.[85]

Soviet leaders demanded that Prchlík be removed from his post in the
KSČ Central Committee apparatus, but their demands were only partly
fulfilled. The State-Administrative Department that Prchlík had directed,
which had been a notorious organ of repression under Novotný, was simply abolished on July 25, as had been promised all along in the KSČ's Action
Program. Prchlík was then reassigned to other military duties (as commander of one of Czechoslovakia's military districts) rather than being fired
ignominiously. Soviet leaders were dismayed to learn that the general would
still be in an influential position. Indeed, in his new capacity, Prchlík was
even able to continue working on a draft report on the "external and internal security of the Czechoslovak state," which had been prepared under his
auspices in late July.[86] The report was to serve as the basis for the military
and national security policies adopted by the KSČ Congress in September.
The draft was never published, but a copy of it was leaked to the Soviet
embassy in Prague by "confidential sources" and was then promptly transmitted to high-ranking officials in Moscow, who could see for themselves
that the uproar following the news conference had in no way caused
Prchlík to back away from his positions. On the contrary, the draft report
went even further in recommending sweeping changes in Czechoslovakia's
approach to defense and national security. The report claimed that
the country's military policy was still based on "erroneous and obsolete
ideological-political premises of the Stalinist era," and it insisted that
Czechoslovakia must formulate "its own national military doctrine" and
seek "an equal role in the common decisions of the alliance," rather than
"just passively accepting those decisions." It also urged Czechoslovak leaders to reject "unrealistic and dangerous scenarios," especially scenarios
involving nuclear exchanges, which had always dominated the Warsaw
Pact's military planning.

---

85 See, e.g., the recent memoir by one of the top Soviet officers involved in the invasion, Lieut.-
     General S. M. Zolotov, "Shli na pomoshch' druz'yam," *Voenno-istoricheskii zhurnal*, no. 4 (Apr.
     1994): 15–24.
86 The Czech document, entitled "Problems with the Policy of Safeguarding the Internal and Exter-
     nal Security of the State, Their Status at Present, and the Basic Ways of Resolving Them," may be
     found in TsKhSD, F. 5, Op. 60, D. 310, Ll. 121–53, along with a cover memorandum (marked Top
     Secret) from the Soviet ambassador in Czechoslovakia, Stepan Chervonenko, to Defense Minister
     Andrei Grechko, Foreign Minister Andrei Gromyko, and the two most senior CPSU officials who
     were handling the crisis on a day-to-day basis, Konstantin Katushev and Konstantin Rusakov. Cher-
     vonenko noted that the author of the draft was the "infamous General Prchlík."

This last point brought to the fore the most sensitive military issue of all during the 1968 crisis: the role of Soviet nuclear weapons in Czechoslovakia. It is now known that the Soviet Union and Czechoslovakia secretly concluded two agreements in the early 1960s entitling the Soviet Army to deploy nuclear-armed weapons on Czechoslovak territory during an emergency.[87] In 1965 the two countries signed a more far-reaching agreement authorizing the Soviet Union to store nuclear warheads permanently at three sites in western Czechoslovakia under strict Soviet control.[88] Construction of the sites and deployment of the warheads were due to be completed by 1967, but last-minute delays meant that the facilities had not yet entered service when the Prague Spring began. It is clear, therefore, that Soviet anxiety in 1968 about the security of Czechoslovakia's borders and about the spread of reformist influences within the Czechoslovak army was tied, in no small part, to concerns about the proposed nuclear weapons sites in Czechoslovakia.[89] Those concerns were exacerbated still further when Soviet officials came across the report drafted by Prchlík and his colleagues. The document stated that any war in Europe involving nuclear weapons would be "purely senseless" and would "bring about the total physical destruction of the ČSSR." The document insisted that Czechoslovak military policy must be aimed first and foremost at ensuring the "continued existence and sovereignty" of the state. This line of argument implied that a military doctrine appropriate for Czechoslovakia would have to be based on the eschewal of nuclear weapons and nuclear warfare. Not only would such a doctrine have been incompatible with basic tenets of the Warsaw Pact's own military doctrine at the time; it also would have cast doubt on the status of proposed sites in Czechoslovakia for Soviet nuclear warheads.

Soviet Concerns About a "Spillover"

Even if no questions had emerged about Czechoslovakia's *foreign* orientation, Soviet leaders believed that the country's *internal* changes were themselves a grave threat to the cohesion of the Communist bloc. If the Prague Spring, with its tolerance of dissent, elimination of censorship, democratization of the Communist Party, and wide-ranging economic reforms, were

87 "Dohoda ČSSR-ZSSR o vzájemných dodávkach výzbroje a voj. techniky v rr. 1963–1965," Mar. 1963 (Top Secret), in VHA, F. Sekretariat MNO, A.j. 26, 2.

88 See note 6 to this chapter.

89 On this point, see Mark Kramer, "The Prague Spring and the Soviet Invasion: New Interpretations," *Cold War International History Bulletin*, no. 3 (fall 1993): 9–12.

to "infect" other Warsaw Pact countries, including the Soviet Union, it might well precipitate the collapse of the socialist camp. The threat of a spillover into Poland and East Germany had been of concern for some time, particularly after the outbreaks of unrest in Warsaw in early March. Gomułka repeatedly warned the Soviet leadership that "reactionary centers operated and inspired by foreign intelligence services" were seeking to extend their "subversive activities" beyond Czechoslovakia.[90] His complaints took on a more urgent tone after Czechoslovak students held large rallies in May to condemn political repression and anti-Semitism in Poland.[91] Brezhnev followed up on these complaints by admonishing Dubček to cease "interfering in [Poland's] internal affairs."[92] Like Gomułka, Ulbricht wanted to forestall any "contagion" from Czechoslovakia by swiftly and decisively resolving the crisis. Following a multilateral conference in Moscow in early May, he stayed "on vacation" in the Soviet Union for nearly three weeks as an official guest of the CPSU Central Committee.[93] During that time he had ample opportunity to convey further warnings to the Soviet authorities about events in Czechoslovakia. (Ulbricht also did his best to derail the tentative progress in Soviet–West German relations.) The repeated East German and Polish denunciations of the Prague Spring could not help but take their toll.

Even more worrisome from Moscow's standpoint was the prospect of a spillover into the Soviet Union itself. Soviet leaders had been on edge about this matter because of the resurgence of Soviet dissident groups and intellectuals in 1967 and early 1968. The authorities responded with vigorous repression and show trials, but events in Czechoslovakia seemed to give new impetus to the Soviet dissident movement. Leading proponents of democratic change such as Andrei Sakharov publicly hailed the Prague Spring and called on the Soviet leadership to halt its pressure against Czechoslovakia.[94] The elimination of censorship in Czechoslovakia enabled dissident Soviet writers to get their work published in Czechoslovak periodicals, in much the same way that Aleksandr Solzhenitsyn had sent a let-

90 "Zapis wystąpień na spotkaniu pierwszych sekretarszy KC: Bulgarii, NRD, Węgier, Polski i ZSRR w Moskwie, 8 maja 1968 r.," May 8, 1968 (Top Secret), in AAN, Arch. KC PZPR, P. 193, T. 24, D. 4.
91 "Zapis' besedy v TsK KPSS s rukovoditelyami bratskikh partii Bolgarii, Vengrii, Germanii, Pol'shi," May 8, 1968 (Top Secret), in ÚSD-SK, Z/S 3, Ll. 151–71; and "Depeše sovětského velvyslance ve Varšavě předsedovi rady ministrů SSSR A. N. Kosyginovi," May 22, 1968 (Top Secret), from A. Aristov, Soviet ambassador in Warsaw, to Soviet Prime Minister Aleksei Kosygin, in ÚSD-SK, Z/S – MID No. 5, Ll. 179–80.
92 "Zapis' peregovorov s delegatsiei ChSSR 4 maya 1968 goda," L. 136.
93 "Tovarishch Val'ter Ul'brikht na otdykhe v SSSR," *Krasnaya zvezda* (Moscow), May 11, 1968, 1.
94 Andrei Sakharov, *Vospominaniya* (New York, 1990), 371–89.

ter to the Czechoslovak Writers' Congress in June 1967 denouncing official censorship in the Soviet Union.[95] By the same token, activists involved in the underground press (samizdat) in the USSR began translating and disseminating a wide range of materials from Czechoslovakia. Soviet leaders tried to suppress these activities by adopting further harsh measures, but they sensed that a crackdown would be futile so long as publications and broadcasts from Czechoslovakia continued to enter the Soviet Union. Brezhnev emphasized this point to the KSČ leadership during bilateral talks in early May: "Your newspapers are read also by Soviet citizens and your radio broadcasts attract listeners in our country as well, which means that all this propaganda affects us just as much as it does you."[96]

Soviet concerns about a spillover from Czechoslovakia intensified as reports streamed into Moscow about disaffection among Soviet youth and growing ferment in several of the union republics, notably Ukraine, Moldavia, Georgia, and the Baltic states. Brezhnev and his colleagues learned from KGB sources that a surprising number of Soviet college students were sympathetic to the Prague Spring, including "some [who] are contemplating the possibility of replicating the Czechoslovak experience in our own country."[97] With the fiftieth anniversary of the Soviet Komsomol (Communist Youth League) due to be celebrated in 1968, Soviet officials were dismayed to find that a growing number of young people were being enticed by "false slogans about the 'liberalization' of socialism, which are being promoted by counterrevolutionaries."[98] The spate of revelations about the effects of the Prague Spring on Soviet youth spurred the Soviet Politburo to order the CPSU CC Propaganda Department to adopt special measures that would prevent "right-wing opportunism from overtaking the youth movement, as happened earlier in Czechoslovakia and Poland."[99]

Equally disconcerting from Moscow's perspective were the growing signs that events in Czechoslovakia had emboldened Ukrainian intellectuals and nationalist elements. Newly declassified materials, including Soviet Politburo transcripts, the diaries of the Ukrainian leader Petro Shelest, and

95 *IV. Sjezd Svazu československých spisovatelů (Protokol): Praha, 27.–29. června 1967* (Prague, 1968), 131–62.
96 "Zapis' peregovorov s delegatsiei ChSSR 4 maya 1968 goda," L. 138.
97 "Studenchestva i sobytiya v Chekhoslovakii," report transmitted by KGB chairman Yu. V. Andropov to the CPSU Secretariat, Nov. 5, 1968 (Top Secret), in TsKhSD, F. 5, Op. 60, D. 48, Ll. 120–53. See also the comments by Brezhnev, Aleksandr Shelepin, and Mikhail Solomentsev in "Rabochaya zapis' zasedaniya Politbyuro TsK KPSS ot 21 marta 1968 goda," Ll. 147–58.
98 "Zamechaniya k dokumentu 'Pod rukovodstvom Kommunisticheskoi partii po leninskomu puti: K 50-letiyu Vsesoyuznogo Leninskogo Kommunisticheskogo Soyuza Molodezhi 1918–1968 g.g.,'" Directive (Top Secret) from the CPSU Politburo to the CPSU CC Propaganda Department, Sept. 1968, in TsKhSD, F. 5, Op. 60, D. 23, Ll. 77–9.
99 Ibid., L. 79.

dozens of reports and memoranda now stored in the Ukrainian national archive, not only confirm Grey Hodnett's and Peter Potichnyj's earlier conclusion that "there was an important linkage between the situation in the Ukraine and the developments in Czechoslovkia," but also demonstrate that Soviet leaders themselves clearly believed the two situations were linked.[100] On numerous occasions, Shelest complained to Brezhnev that events in Czechoslovakia were "causing unsavory phenomena here in Ukraine as well."[101] The situation, he noted, was especially bad in Ukraine's "western provinces, where the inhabitants receive information directly from their neighbors across the border" and "watch both Czechoslovak and Western radio and television." Shelest reported that vigorous steps had to be taken to curb the "distribution of political and nationalist leaflets" and to prevent the circulation within Ukraine of newspapers published by the Ukrainian community in Czechoslovakia. During bilateral negotiations with KSČ leaders in late July, Shelest accused them of approving "the publication of counterrevolutionary tracts which are then sent through special channels into Ukraine."[102] Because Shelest was a full CPSU Politburo member and the leader of a key republic bordering on Czechoslovakia, his views during the crisis were bound to have a major effect on Soviet decision making.

The reports from Ukraine seemed even more worrisome after the Soviet Politburo learned that "support for the KSČ's course toward so-called liberalization" was also evident in Moldavia, Georgia, and the Baltic states.[103] Brezhnev and his colleagues were especially dismayed that periodicals, newspapers, letters, and other materials casting a positive light on the Prague Spring were "pouring in" from Czechoslovakia. At the Politburo's behest, party officials in the outlying Soviet republics undertook "comprehensive measures aimed at further increasing political work among the population."[104] Five Politburo members — Andrei Kirilenko, Aleksandr Shelepin,

100 See, e.g., "TsK KPSS," memorandum no. 15782, 1/51 (Secret), June 11, 1968, from P. Shelest, first secretary of the Ukrainian Communist Party, to the CPSU Secretariat, in TsKhSD, Op. 60, D. 1, Ll. 86–90. See also "Zapis' peregovorov s delegatsiei ChSSR 4 maya 1968 goda," Ll. 141. The quoted passage is from Grey Hodnett and Peter J. Potichnyj, *The Ukraine and the Czechoslovak Crisis,* Occasional Paper no. 6 (Canberra, 1970), 2.

101 Shelest, . . . *Da ne sudimy budete,* 303, 309, 319, 354, 376, 378. Quotations in the remainder of this paragraph are from Shelest's diary.

102 See also "Záznám jednání předsednictva ÚV KSČ a ÚV KSSS v Čierné n. T., 29. 7–1.8.1968," Aug. 1, 1968 (Top Secret), in SÚA, Arch. ÚV KSČ, F. 07/15, Sv. 12, A.j. 274, Ll. 311, 313.

103 See, e.g., "TsK KPSS: Informatsiya," cable no. 22132 (Secret), Aug. 1, 1968, from Yurii Mel'kov, 2d Secretary of the Moldavian Communist Party, to the CPSU Secretariat, in TsKhSD, F. 5, Op. 60, D. 2, L. 30; and "TsK KPSS," cable no. 13995 (Top Secret), May 23, 1968, from V. Mzhavanadze, Ist Secretary of the Georgian Communist Party, to the CPSU Secretariat, in TsKhSD, F. 5, Op. 60, D. 22, Ll. 5–9.

104 Ibid.

Arvids Pel'she, Pyotr Demichev, and Yurii Andropov – were designated to oversee these measures and to recommend other ways of "eliminating pernicious ideological and bourgeois nationalist phenomena."[105] Although it is questionable whether the burgeoning unrest in the USSR's western republics would ever have eluded the authorities' control, the threat of a spillover from Czechoslovakia by mid-1968 was fast becoming a reality in the Soviet Union.

All these concerns – political, ideological, and military – gradually fused into a widely shared perception in Moscow that events in Czechoslovakia were spinning out of control. The sense of impending danger, or of "spontaneity" and "unlimited decentralization" as a Soviet Politburo member, Viktor Grishin, put it, eventually colored Soviet views of the whole Prague Spring. It was this cumulative impact of events, rather than any single development, that seems to have convinced Brezhnev and his colleagues that internal changes in Czechoslovakia were threatening vital Soviet interests. The necessity of countering that threat was no longer in doubt by mid-1968; the only question remaining for Soviet leaders was not whether – but when – an external military solution would be required.

Soviet–Warsaw Pact Coercive Diplomacy

By July and early August, the Soviet Union was applying relentless pressure on the Czechoslovak authorities to reverse the liberalization program. The Soviet campaign was supported throughout by Poland, East Germany, Bulgaria, and antireformist members of the KSČ Presidium. Brezhnev used a variety of bilateral channels to urge Czechoslovak officials to combat "antisocialist" and "counterrevolutionary" elements; and he even approached a few of Dubček's reformist colleagues surreptitiously in the hope of finding a suitable replacement who would be willing to implement a crackdown.[106] In addition, a series of conclaves of Warsaw Pact leaders – in Dresden in March, Moscow in May, Warsaw in mid-July, and Bratislava in early August – generated increasingly harsh criticism and threats of joint

---

105 "Rabochaya zapis' zasedaniya Politbyuro TsK KPSS ot 3 marta 1968 g.," Ll. 93–5.
106 See the interview with Josef Smrkovský in "Nedokončený rozhovor," *Listy: Časopis československé socialistické opozice* (Rome) 4, no. 2 (Mar. 1975): 17; and the interview with Oldřich Černík in "Bumerang 'Prazhskoi vesnoi,'" *Izvestiya* (Moscow), Aug. 21, 1990, 5. Both Smrkovský and Černík were members of the KSČ Presidium in 1968. Smrkovský was also president of the National Assembly and a leading architect of the Prague Spring; Černík was the Czechoslovak prime minister. Shelest records an incident in his diary (. . . *Da ne sudimy budete,* 380) that suggests the overtures may have found a receptive audience in Smrkovský, but no further corroboration of this incident has emerged.

action to "defend the gains of socialism" in Czechoslovakia.[107] An additional meeting was held secretly in Moscow on August 18, two days before the invasion. Brezhnev seemed to prefer the leverage that these multilateral conferences afforded him, particularly because East German and Polish leaders had staked out such vehement positions against the Prague Spring from the outset.

Dubček was present at the Dresden conference, but he was not invited to (or even notified of) the Moscow conference in May, and he chose not to attend the meeting in Warsaw. The Warsaw meeting, on July 14–15, proved to be a turning point in many respects. It marked the first time that Hungarian officials, including Kádár, joined with their East German, Polish, and Bulgarian counterparts in expressing profound doubts about the ability of the Czechoslovak authorities to regain control of events. Kádár even pledged, in a conversation with Brezhnev, that "if a military occupation of Czechoslovakia becomes necessary, [Hungary] will take part without reservation."[108] The Warsaw meeting also marked the first time that Soviet officials who had earlier adopted a "wait-and-see" attitude began roundly condemning the Prague Spring and calling for "extreme measures." Far more than at previous gatherings of Warsaw Pact leaders in 1968, the option of military intervention loomed prominently throughout the deliberations in Warsaw.

The tone for the Warsaw meeting was set at a preliminary Soviet-Polish discussion on the eve of the formal talks.[109] Gomułka insisted that Brezhnev was being "deceived" and "hoodwinked" by Dubček, and he urged the Soviet leader to be "guided by principles, resoluteness, and honor," rather than by "emotions." Gomułka expressed concern that "up to now [the

---

107 Transcripts of the first three meetings are now available from the East German, Czechoslovak/Polish, and Polish archives, respectively. See "Protokoll der Treffen der Ersten Sekretäre der kommunistischen Parteien Bulgariens, der ČSSR, der DDR, Polens, der Sowjetunion und Ungarns," Mar. 23, 1968 (Top Secret), in SAPMDB, ZPA, IV 2/201/778; "Stenografický záznam schůzky 'pětky' k československé situaci 8. května 1968," May 8, 1968, in SÚA, Archiv ÚV KSČ, F. 07/15; and "Protokół ze spotkania przywódców partii i rządów krajów socjalistycznych – Bulgarii, NRD, Polski, Węgier i ZSRR – w Warszawie, 14–15 lipca 1968 r.," copy no. 5 (Top Secret), July 14–15, 1968, in AAN, Arch. KC PZPR, P. 193, T. 24, Dok. 4. Many other newly released documents and firsthand accounts shed further light on these meetings; see in particular the lengthy interview with János Kádár in "Yanosh Kadar o 'prazhskoi vesne,'" *Kommunist* (Moscow), no. 7 (May 1990): 96–103, which covers all three meetings, especially those in Dresden and Warsaw.

108 "Rabochaya zapis' zasedaniya Politbyuro TsK KPSS ot 3 iyulya 1968 g.," July 3, 1968 (Top Secret) in APRF, F. 3, Op. 45, L. 367.

109 This preliminary meeting was not included in the Polish transcript of the talks, but it was recorded in detail in Shelest's diary. See . . . *Da ne sudimy budete*, 330–1. Later, when Brezhnev informed the CPSU Central Committee about the proceedings of the Warsaw meeting, he chose not to mention the preliminary talks. See his lengthy speech in "Plenum TsK KPSS 17 iyulya 1968 g.," July 17, 1968 (Top Secret), in TsKhSD, F. 2, Op. 3, D. 323, Ll. 2–38.

Soviet leadership] has not raised the question of sending troops to Czechoslovakia." He insisted that a military solution had become unavoidable because of Moscow's earlier cunctations. Anything less than an invasion, Gomułka warned, would be an "empty gesture."

At the formal meeting the next day, Gomułka was more restrained, but he argued in his lengthy opening speech that the KSČ was "abandoning Marxism-Leninism" and that developments in Czechoslovakia were "endangering the whole socialist commonwealth."[110] Moreover, during a break in the talks, which was not recorded in the formal Polish transcript, Gomułka again charged that Soviet leaders were being "hoodwinked" by Dubček, and he repeated his demand that "troops be sent to Czechoslovakia."[111] Ulbricht and the Bulgarian leader, Todor Zhivkov, joined Gomułka in his hard-line stance. Zhivkov, in particular, openly called for joint military intervention to "restore the dictatorship of the proletariat" in Czechoslovakia: "There is only one appropriate way out – through resolute assistance to Czechoslovakia from our parties and the states of the Warsaw Pact. At present, we cannot rely on internal forces in Czechoslovakia. . . . Only by relying on the armed forces of the Warsaw Pact can we change the situation."[112] This appeal, for the time being, was not endorsed by the Soviet delegates, but Brezhnev's keynote speech confirmed that nonmilitary options were indeed nearly gone. Although the Soviet leader still wanted to pursue a political solution, he emphasized that the "Five" would have to look to the KSČ's "healthy forces" rather than to Dubček.[113] Brezhnev had not yet given up all hope of working with Dubček, but he clearly sensed that the KSČ leader would be unwilling to comply with key Soviet demands, especially about personnel changes and the press.

At Brezhnev's suggestion, the participants in the meeting agreed to send Dubček a joint letter denouncing the Prague Spring and calling for urgent remedial steps. The Warsaw Letter, as it quickly became known, was little more than an ultimatum, specifying a long series of measures that were "necessary to block the path of counterrevolution."[114] The Warsaw Letter provoked official and public consternation in Czechoslovakia, but Dubček and his supporters did not yet realize how dire the situation had become.

---

110 "Protokół ze spotkania przywódców partii i rządów krajów socjalistycznych," Ll. 4, 7.
111 This break was recorded in Shelest, . . . *Da ne sudimy budete,* 340–1.
112 "Protokół ze spotkania przywódców partii i rządów krajów socjalistycznych," L. 29. Shelest notes that in informal conversations with Zhivkov right before and after the Bulgarian leader's speech, Zhivkov had urged Brezhnev to be "more decisive," adding that "the sooner troops are sent, the better." See . . . *Da ne sudimy budete,* 338–9.
113 "Protokół ze spotkania przywódców partii i rządów krajów socjalistycznych," Ll. 30–42.
114 "Tsentral'nomu Komitetu Kommunisticheskoi Partii Chekhoslovakii," *Pravda* (Moscow), July 18, 1968, 1.

They were unaware, for example, that on July 19, four days after the Warsaw meeting, the CPSU Politburo began to consider "extreme measures" to replace the political leadership in Czechoslovakia. At this session and a follow-up meeting on July 22, the Politburo adopted a dual-track policy of (1) proceeding with all the steps needed to send troops into Czechoslovakia, while (2) making one final attempt at negotiations.[115] These two tracks were reaffirmed at an expanded meeting of the Politburo on July 26–7. On the one hand, the members unanimously "approved the [military] plans laid out by A. A. Grechko" and "authorized Cde. Grechko to take measures to carry out those plans in an expeditious manner."[116] On the other hand, they devised a negotiating strategy for bilateral talks that were due to begin on July 29 in the small border town of Čierná nad Tisou. These talks were seen as the only remaining opportunity to resolve the crisis by peaceful means.

To ensure that the first track (that is, the military option) could be implemented successfully, the Politburo sought greater assurance that "healthy forces" (that is, pro-Soviet hard-liners) in Czechoslovakia would be able to establish a viable regime. Earlier on, many Soviet officials had expressed deep skepticism about the prospects of relying on the "healthy forces."[117] A consensus emerged at the Politburo's July 19 meeting that the Soviet Union must obtain a formal document from the "healthy forces" that would credibly commit them to act once Soviet troops moved in. To this end, Brezhnev phoned Shelest on July 20 and instructed him to leave immediately for a clandestine meeting with Vasil Bil'ak, one of the leaders of the KSČ's antireformist group.[118] With assistance from Kádár and other Hungarian officials, Shelest linked up with Bil'ak late that night on a remote island in Hungary's Lake Balaton. He explained to Bil'ak the importance of receiving a formal "letter of invitation" from the KSČ hard-liners, which would provide a "guarantee of a bolder and more organized struggle against the rightists." Bil'ak promised that he would transmit such a letter to Shelest in the near future. Having secured that pledge, Shelest flew to Moscow where he met with Brezhnev on July 21 to inform him of the results. The next day, Shelest briefed the full Politburo.

115 "Rabochaya zapis' zasedaniya Politbyuro TsK KPSS ot 19 iyulya 1968 g.," July 19, 1968 (Top Secret), and "Rabochaya zapis' zasedaniya Politbyuro TsK KPSS ot 22 iyulya 1968 g.," July 22, 1968 (Top Secret), in APRF, F. 3, Op. 45, D. 99, Ll. 417–26 and 427–34, respectively.

116 "Rabochaya zapis' zasedaniya Politbyuro TsK KPSS ot 26/27 iyulya 1968 g.," July 27, 1968 (Top Secret), in APRF, F. 3, Op. 45, D. 99, Ll. 437–8.

117 See, e.g., the comments of Podgornyi, Demichev, and Kosygin in "Rabochaya zapis' zasedaniya Politbyuro TsK KPSS ot 16 maya 1968 g.," May 16, 1968 (Top Secret), in APRF, F. 3, Op. 45, D. 99, Ll. 237–41.

118 This entire episode was unknown until Shelest's diary became available in 1995; see . . . *Da sudimy ne budete*, 345–52.

With hopes buoyed by Shelest's secret liaison with Bil'ak, Soviet leaders traveled on July 28 to Čierná nad Tisou. They were ready, if necessary, to break off the talks after the first day and return to Moscow for an emergency meeting on July 30 with Polish, East German, Bulgarian, and Hungarian officials.[119] When the preliminary sessions ended on July 29, however, the Soviet participants decided it was worth staying to try to forge some sort of agreement. Although the talks produced mainly acrimony and recriminations, a fragile compromise emerged on the third and fourth days, which imposed ill-defined obligations on the Czechoslovak leadership and called for a follow-up meeting in Bratislava among all the Warsaw Pact countries (other than Romania). Some press reports claimed that a full-fledged "breakthrough" had been achieved at Čierná, but it soon became clear just how ephemeral this breakthrough was. As Brezhnev boarded the train on August 1 to return to Moscow, he bade farewell to the KSČ delegation with the following words: "You gave us a promise, and we are confident you will fight to carry it out. For our part, we want to affirm that we are prepared to give you unlimited help in this effort. . . . If our plan is thwarted, it will be very difficult to convene another meeting. I say this with full responsibility. We will then have to come to your assistance instead."[120] Although Brezhnev undoubtedly assumed that Dubček and other senior Czechoslovak officials shared his understanding of the "obligations" and "promises" they had taken on at Čierná, no such common understanding actually existed. In the absence of a written set of specific pledges, the two sides left the meeting with very different conceptions of what they had agreed to.[121] Despite the hopes that both parties attached to the upcoming Bratislava conference, the gulf between the KSČ and CPSU was rapidly becoming irreconcilable, and Brezhnev's vow to "give unlimited help" to the "healthy forces" in Czechoslovakia loomed ever larger.

The multilateral meeting in Bratislava was held on August 3, just two days after the Čierná negotiations ended. At the close of the daylong meeting, Dubček agreed to sign a joint declaration that included ominous references to "the common international duty of all socialist countries to support, strengthen, and defend the gains of socialism."[122] This phrase was

---

119 "Pamyatka dlya konfidentsial'nykh besed," July 1968 (Top Secret), memorandum for the CPSU Politburo, in APRF, F. 3, Op. 91, D. 99, Ll. 12–13. See also the intriguing passages in Shelest's memoirs, . . . *Da ne sudimy budete,* 367.
120 "Záznam jednání přesednictva ÚV KSČ a ÚV KSSS v Čierné n. T., 29.7.–1.8.1968," L. 349.
121 See, e.g., "Informace z jednání v Č. n. Tisou," Aug. 1, 1968 (Top Secret), in VHA, F. Sekretariat MNO, 1968–1969, 161/282 and 162/283.
122 "Zayavlenie kommunisticheskikh i rabochikh partii sotsialisticheskikh stran," *Pravda* (Moscow), Aug. 4, 1968, 1 (emphasis added).

cited repeatedly after August 1968 as a justification for the invasion. More important than the declaration, however, was the opportunity that the Bratislava conference gave to the antireformist members of the KSČ Presidium, led by Bil'ak. Aided by the KGB station chief in Bratislava, Bil'ak was finally able to transmit to Shelest the promised letter "requesting" Soviet military intervention.[123] Shelest promptly conveyed the document to Brezhnev, who expressed deep gratitude. Contrary to what has often been thought, the "letter of invitation" was not intended to provide a legal basis for Soviet military action in 1968. Shelest had assured Bil'ak from the very start that the letter would be kept secret and that the names of the signatories would not be released. Those assurances would have made no sense if the letter had been sought as a legal pretext. Instead, Soviet leaders viewed the document as a way of credibly committing the signatories to seize power when allied military units entered Czechoslovakia. With the letter in hand, the Soviet Union had much greater "freedom of action" (to use Shelest's phrase) during the crucial two-and-a-half weeks after the Bratislava conference.[124]

The pressure generated by the bilateral and multilateral meetings in July and early August was reinforced by large-scale exercises and maneuvers that Soviet military units were conducting with other Warsaw Pact armies. The joint exercises had begun in late March, and from then on the Soviet Union and its allies had engaged in almost daily troop movements in or around Czechoslovakia.[125] By late July and August, the joint maneuvers were designed not only to intimidate the KSČ leadership, but also to lay the groundwork for an invasion. The Soviet press devoted unusually prominent coverage to all these maneuvers in tones reminiscent of war reports, thus accentuating the psychological pressure on the Czechoslovak government.[126] Even then, however, Soviet power proved of little efficacy, as all

123 It seems likely that more than one "letter of invitation" was handed over. The version released by the Russian government in 1992 and published in "Kdo pozval okupační vojska: Dokumenty s razítkem nikdy neotvírat vydaly svědectví," *Hospodářské noviny* (Prague), July 17, 1992, 1–2, contains five signatures: Bil'ak, Alois Indra, Oldřich Švestka, Antonín Kapek, and Drahomír Kolder. However, Shelest's detailed account of this episode (in . . . *Da ne sudimy budete,* 383–5) refers to a letter with eleven, not five, signatures. The six additional signatories mentioned by Shelest are Emil Rigo, Jan Piller, František Barbírek, Lubomír Štrougal, Josef Lenárt, and Karel Hoffmann. In his memoirs, Bil'ak acknowledged that he had passed on a letter urging the Soviet Army to lend "fraternal assistance," but he does not mention the number of signatories. See *Paměti Vasila Bil'aka: Unikátní svědectví ze zákulisí KSČ,* 2 vols. (Prague, 1991), 2:88.
124 . . . *Da ne sudimy budete,* 385.
125 For a brief summary of the ten exercises conducted in 1968, see Jeffrey Simon, *Warsaw Pact Forces: Problems of Command and Control* (Boulder, Colo., 1985), 44–50.
126 See, e.g., "Ucheniya organov tyla," *Krasnaya zvezda* (Moscow), July 24, 1968, 1; the daily reports in *Krasnaya zvezda* (Moscow) entitled "Iz raiona uchenii organov tyla"; "Ucheniya 'Nebesnyi shchit'," *Krasnaya zvezda* (Moscow), July 25, 1968, 1; "Chasovye neba Rodiny," *Krasnaya zvezda* (Moscow), July 26, 1968, 1; "Na ucheniyakh 'Nebesnyi shchit': Ispytanieboem," *Krasnaya zvezda*

manner of troop movements, thinly veiled threats, and political and economic coercion failed to deflect the KSČ from its course. Dubček in fact seemed to benefit domestically the stronger the pressure from his Warsaw Pact allies became.

The Invasion

As the crisis intensified in late July and August, the high-level debate in Moscow gradually produced a consensus. After the Warsaw meeting, a few key members of the Soviet Politburo had still hoped to avoid military action; but after the Čierná and Bratislava conferences, sentiment in favor of military intervention steadily grew. The Politburo had tentatively decided at its meetings on July 22 and 26–7 to proceed with a full-scale invasion sometime in mid- to late August if the situation in Czechoslovakia did not fundamentally change. The receipt of the long-awaited "letter of invitation," coupled with Dubček's failure to carry out the "obligations" he had supposedly undertaken at Čierná and Bratislava, reinforced the decision to intervene. By the time the Soviet Politburo met in an expanded session on August 6 to review the Čierná and Bratislava negotiations, there was virtually no hope left that military action could be averted. Although a few participants in the session voiced reservations about the potential costs of an invasion – especially if, as Marshal Grechko warned, the incoming troops were to encounter armed resistance – the Politburo reached a consensus on August 6 to proceed with full-scale military intervention unless the Czechoslovak authorities took immediate, drastic steps to comply with Soviet demands. No specific timetable was set, but Soviet leaders realized that an invasion would have to occur sometime before the KSČ's Extraordinary Fourteenth Congress in September and, preferably, before the Slovak Party Congress in the last week of August. This consensus did not yet signify an irrevocable decision to invade, but it did mean that the Soviet leadership was on the verge of giving up hope that "anything more can be expected" of Dubček.[127]

In the meantime, the Soviet High Command was completing the extensive logistical and technical preparations needed for a full-scale invasion.[128]

(Moscow), July 30, 1968, 1; "Nadezhnyi shchit Rodiny: K itogam uchenii Voisk PVO strany," *Krasnaya zvezda* (Moscow), Aug. 1, 1968, 1; "Ukreplenie boegotovnosti – nasha glavnaya zadacha," *Krasnaya zvezda* (Moscow), Aug. 13, 1968, 1; and the daily reports in *Krasnaya zvezda* (Moscow) entitled "Iz raiona sovmestnykh uchenii voisk svyazi."

127 "Rabochaya zapis' zasedaniya Politbyuro TsK KPSS ot 6 avgusta 1968 g.," Aug. 6, 1968 (Top Secret), in APRF, F. 3, Op. 45, D. 99, L. 462.

128 On these preparations, see "Záznam z jednání sovětských generálů Tutarinova, Provalova a Maruščaka s náčelníkem generálního štábu MLA generálem Csémi o připravé operace 'Dunaj,' "

The largest of the Warsaw Pact maneuvers in early August were preceded by a mass call-up of Soviet and Eastern European reservists, the requisitioning of civilian vehicles and equipment, and the stockpiling of fuel, ammunition, communications gear, spare parts, and medical supplies. In Ukraine alone, more than seven thousand civilian vehicles were reassigned to the army.[129] Soviet commanders also diverted Czechoslovak supplies of fuel and ammunition to East Germany – ostensibly for new Warsaw Pact "exercises" but actually to obviate any possibility of Czechoslovak armed resistance. Much the same was done with Czechoslovak troops and equipment, which were unexpectedly transported for "maneuvers" to bases in southwestern Bohemia, far away from any planned invasion routes. Even if the ČLA had been determined to put up large-scale armed resistance against Soviet troops – and only a few officers like General Prchlík had even proposed such a thing, much less carried out the necessary preparations – the Soviet deception campaign and the size of the invading force effectively eliminated any options of this sort.

Even as the tentative date for an invasion approached, Brezhnev seemed to hold out a very faint hope that Dubček might yet reverse course. The Soviet leader was on vacation in the Crimea during the second week of August, but he kept in close touch with Dubček by phone throughout that time. Brezhnev also maintained contact with Dubček via the Soviet ambassador, Stepan Chervonenko. In a phone conversation on August 9, Brezhnev emphasized how "very serious" the situation had become and urged Dubček to act immediately in accord with "the conditions we jointly approved and agreed on at Čierná and Tisou."[130] But in a follow-up conversation four days later, Brezhnev was far more aggressive and belligerent, accusing Dubček of "outright deceit" and of "blatantly sabotaging the agreements reached at Čierná and Bratislava."[131] The Soviet leader warned that "an entirely new situation has emerged" that was "forcing [the Soviet Union] to consider new independent measures that would defend both the KSČ and the cause of socialism in Czechoslovakia."

To make matters worse, some of Dubček's remarks during the second conversation, especially his insistence that Soviet leaders should "adopt

July 27, 1968 (Top Secret), in ÚSD-SK, Materials of J. Pataki, NHKI, 5/12/11; "Depeše čs. titulářů z Berlina, Varšavy a Budapešti z 29. 7.–1. 8. 1968 o pohybu vojsk kolem hranic Československa," July–Aug. 1968, in Archiv Min. zahr. veci, Depeše nos. 7103, 7187, 7259, and 7269/1968; "Setkání ministrů obrany," *Mladá fronta* (Prague), Aug. 17, 1968, 2; "Grečko v Polsku," *Rudé právo* (Prague), Aug. 18, 1968, 2; and "Cvičeni v Mad'arsku," *Mladá fronta* (Prague), Aug. 17, 1968, 2.
129 Shelest, . . . *Da ne sudimy budete,* 353.
130 "Telefonický rozhovor L. Brežněva s A. Dubčekem, 9.8.1968," Aug. 9, 1968 (Top Secret), in ÚSD-SK, Z/S 8.
131 "Rozgovor tovarishcha L. I. Brezhneva s tovarishchom A. S. Dubchekom," Aug. 13, 1968 (Top Secret), in APRF, F. 3, Op. 91, D. 120, Ll. 1–18.

whatever measures you believe are necessary," may have been construed by Brezhnev as a tacit green light for military intervention.[132] Brezhnev warned Dubček that the Soviet Politburo would "indeed be adopting the measures we believe are appropriate," and he noted that "such measures would be easier for us to adopt if you and your comrades would more openly say that these are the measures you're expecting of us." Dubček's response to this warning – to wit, that "we [in Prague] are able to resolve all these matters on our own, but if you believe it is necessary for you to adopt certain measures, then by all means go ahead" – must have seemed to Brezhnev like a further hint that Dubček would acquiesce, if only grudgingly, in Soviet military action. Clearly, this was not the impression that Dubček wanted to convey, but a miscommunication in such circumstances would hardly be unusual. The phone call on August 13 may have made the situation worse, not only by reinforcing Brezhnev's belief that Dubček would not "fulfill his obligations" if left to his own devices but also by prompting Brezhnev to conclude that Dubček and perhaps other top KSČ officials had now resigned themselves to the prospect of Soviet military intervention.

Soon after this latest phone conversation, Brezhnev sent an urgent cable to Chervonenko ordering him to meet with Dubček as soon as possible to reemphasize Moscow's concerns.[133] Chervonenko did so that same evening, but his efforts were also of no avail. The failure of these different contacts seems to have been what finally led Brezhnev to conclude that "nothing more can be expected from the current KSČ Central Committee Presidium" and that a military solution could no longer be avoided.[134] From then on, the dynamic of the whole situation changed. Although Brezhnev was still in the Crimea, he had been conferring directly with other senior members of the CPSU Politburo and Secretariat, most of whom were vacationing nearby.[135] Ad hoc sessions of the Politburo were convened on August 13, 14, and 15 to discuss appropriate responses. The participants acknowledged that a military solution "would be fraught with complications," but they all agreed that a failure to act "would lead to civil war in Czechoslovakia and the loss of it as a socialist country."[136] On August 14, Brezhnev

---

132 Ibid.
133 "Vypiska iz protokola No. 94 zasedaniya Politibyuro TsK KPSS 13 avgusta 1968 g.," No. P94/101 (Top Secret), in APRF, Prot. No. 38.
134 "Vystoupení J. Kádára na zasedání ÚV MSDS a rady ministrů 23.8.1968 k maďarsko-sovětskému jednání v Jaltě, 12.–15.8.1968," in ÚSD-SK, Z/M 19.
135 Declassified documents reveal that Brezhnev met several times in the Crimea with Aleksei Kosygin, Nikolai Podgornyi, Petro Shelest, Mikhail Suslov, Aleksandr Shelepin, Arvids Pel'she, Kirill Mazurov, Gennadii Voronov, Viktor Grishin, Dinmukhamed Kunaev, Pyotr Masherov, Sharaf Rashidov, Vladimir Shcherbitskii, and Konstantin Katushev.
136 For very similar firsthand accounts, see Shelest, . . . *Da ne sudimy budete*, 390. Evidently, no full transcript of the sessions was compiled.

authorized a resumption of harsh press attacks on the Prague Spring, putting an end to the lull that had followed the Čierná and Bratislava conferences.[137] The Soviet leader also sent a stern letter to Dubček dated August 13 on behalf of the full CPSU Politburo, and he followed it up three days later with a personal letter (which itself was approved by the Politburo).[138] Both letters stressed the urgency of the situation and warned of dire consequences unless immediate changes were made. It is questionable, however, whether anything Dubček could have done at this point would have been enough to forestall the invasion.

On August 16, a formal session of the CPSU Politburo was convened in Moscow at Brezhnev's behest, even though he and his colleagues had not yet returned. The session was chaired by Andrei Kirilenko, one of Brezhnev's closest aides, who presented the latest assessments from the CPSU general secretary and from the Politburo's commission on Czechoslovakia.[139] By this point, the debate was effectively over. On August 17, with all the top leaders back in Moscow, the Politburo reconvened and voted unanimously to "provide assistance and support to the Communist Party and people of Czechoslovakia through the use of [the Soviet] armed forces."[140]

The following day, Brezhnev informed his East German, Polish, Bulgarian, and Hungarian counterparts of the decision at a hastily convened meeting in Moscow.[141] Similar briefings were held in Moscow on August 19 for the members of the CPSU Central Committee and the heads of union-republic, oblast, and city party organizations. When the briefings on August 19 were over, the CPSU Politburo convened for several hours to review the military-political aspects of the upcoming operation.[142] Detailed presentations by Grechko and the chief of the Soviet General Staff, Marshal Matvei Zakharov, provided grounds for optimism about the military side of Operation Danube (the code name for the invasion), but questions about

---

137 See, e.g., Yurii Zhukov, "Podstrekateli," *Pravda* (Moscow), Aug. 16, 1968, 4.
138 The letters are stored in SÚA, Arch. ÚV KSČ, F. 02/1 (Aug. 13) and SÚA, Arch. ÚV KSČ, F. 07/15, Zahr. kor. No. 822, respectively. The text of the second letter is also available in "Co psál Brežněv Dubčekovi: Hovoří dosud neuveřejněné dokumenty," *Rudé právo* (Prague), May 14, 1990, 1–2.
139 "Rabochaya zapis' zasedaniya Politbyuro TsK KPSS ot 16 avgusta 1968 g.," Aug. 16, 1968 (Top Secret), in APRF, F. 3, Op. 45, D. 99, Ll. 469–71.
140 "K voprosu o polozhenii v Chekhoslovakii: Vypiska iz protokola No. 95 zasedaniya Politbyuro TsK ot 17 avgusta 1968 g.," No. P95/1 (Top Secret), Aug. 17, 1968, in APRF, Prot. No. 38.
141 "Stenogramma Soveshchaniya predstavitelei kommunisticheskikh i rabochikh partii i pravitel'stv NRB, VNR, GDR, PNR i SSSR po voprosu o polozhenii v Chekhoslovakii," Aug. 18, 1968 (Top Secret), in APRF, F.3, Op. 91, D. 128, Ll. 2–40.
142 "Rabochaya zapis' zasedaniya Politbyuro TsK KPSS ot 19 avgusta 1968 g.," Aug. 19, 1968 (Top Secret), in APRF, F. 3, Op. 45, D. 99, Ll. 474–82.

the political side received less scrutiny. Although Brezhnev expressed confidence that Bil'ak's group would carry out their plan, at least a few members of the CPSU Politburo were doubtful about what would happen "after our troops enter Czechoslovakia."[143]

With the zero hour set for midnight on the night of August 20–1, Soviet leaders remained in close contact with their Eastern European counterparts. Unlike in 1956, when Soviet troops intervened in Hungary unilaterally, Brezhnev was determined to give the invasion in 1968 a multilateral appearance. Some 70,000 to 80,000 soldiers from Poland, Bulgaria, Hungary, and East Germany ended up taking part. In reality, though, Operation Danube could hardly be regarded as a "joint" undertaking. Soviet paratroopers and KGB special operations forces spearheaded the invasion, and a total of some 350,000 to 400,000 Soviet soldiers eventually moved into Czechoslovakia, roughly five times the number of Eastern European forces. Moreover, the invasion was under the direct control of the Soviet High Command at all times, rather than being left under the command of Warsaw Pact officers as originally planned.[144] Until August 17 the commander-in-chief of the Warsaw Pact's Joint Armed Forces, Marshal Ivan Yakubovskii, had been designated to oversee Operation Danube, but the Soviet Politburo accepted defense minister Grechko's recommendation that command of all forces be transferred to Army-General Ivan Pavlovskii, the commander-in-chief of Soviet ground forces. Some CPSU officials were concerned that this last-minute change might prove disruptive, but it ended up having almost no discernible effect on the conduct of the operation.

When the first Soviet troops crossed the border, Marshal Grechko phoned the Czechoslovak national defense minister, General Dzúr, to warn him that if ČLA units fired "even a single shot" in resistance, the Soviet army would "crush the resistance mercilessly." He also warned that Dzúr himself would "be strung up from a telephone pole and shot."[145] Dzúr heeded the warning by ordering all Czechoslovak troops to remain in their barracks indefinitely, to avoid the use of weapons for any purpose, and to offer "all necessary assistance to the Soviet forces."[146] A similar directive was issued by the ČSSR president and commander-in-chief, Ludvík Svoboda, after he was informed of the invasion – in more cordial terms – by

---

143 Comments recorded in Shelest, . . . *Da ne sudimy budete,* 393.

144 See the interview with the supreme commander of the invasion, Army-General Ivan Pavlovskii, in "Eto bylo v Prage," *Izvestiya* (Moscow), Aug. 19, 1968, 5.

145 Cited in Shelest, . . . *Da ne sudimy budete,* 393–4. See also the interview with Shelest in Leonid Shinkarev, "Avgustovskoe bezumie: K 25-letiyu vvoda voisk v Chekhoslovakiyu," *Izvestiya* (Moscow), Aug. 21, 1993, 10, and the recollections of Pavlovskii in "Eto bylo v Prage," 5.

146 "Obdobie od 21.srpna do konca roku 1968," from a report by ČSSR national defense minister General Martin Dzúr, June 9, 1970, in SÚA, Arch. ÚV KSČ, File for G. Husák.

the Soviet ambassador in Prague, Stepan Chervonenko, shortly before midnight.[147] Neither Dzúr nor Svoboda welcomed the invasion, but both believed that armed resistance would merely lead to widespread, futile bloodshed. The KSČ Presidium and the Czechoslovak government also promptly instructed the ČLA and People's Militia not to put up active opposition, and the Soviet commander of the invasion, General Pavlovskii, issued a prepared statement in the name of the Soviet High Command urging the ČLA to remain inactive.[148] As a result of all these appeals, the incoming Soviet and allied troops encountered no armed resistance at all.

Within hours, the Soviet-led units had seized control of Czechoslovakia's transportation and communications networks and had surrounded all the main party and state buildings in Prague and other cities. Soviet troops then began methodically occupying key sites and setting up new communications and broadcasting facilities. In the early morning hours of August 21, Soviet commandos from the elite Taman division, accompanied by KGB troops and Czechoslovak State Security forces, entered the KSČ Central Committee headquarters and arrested Dubček and the other reformers on the Czechoslovak Presidium. Prime Minister Černík had been arrested earlier at his office in the Government Ministers' building.[149]

By the time the KSČ leaders were carted off, all of Czechoslovakia was under Soviet military control. The Prague Spring, and its promise of "socialism with a human face," had come to an end.

Soviet Political Miscalculations

As decisive as the military results of Operation Danube may have been, they seemed rather hollow when the invasion failed to achieve its immediate political aims.[150] The Soviet Union's chief political objective on August 20–1 was to facilitate a rapid transition to a pro-Moscow "revolutionary

147 See the "extremely urgent" (vne ocheredi) cable from Chervonenko to the CPSU Politburo, Aug. 21, 1968, in ÚSD-SK, Z/S – MID, nos. 37 and 39.
148 "Prohlášení předsednictva ÚV KSČ z 21.8.1968," *Práce* (Prague), Aug. 21, 1968 (2d ed.), 1. For Pavlovskii's statement, see "Obrashchenie Chekhoslovatskoi narodnoi armii," in AVPRF, F. 059, Op. 58, Papka (P.) 127, D. 586, Ll. 33–5.
149 For firsthand accounts, see "Nedokončený rozhovor: Mluví Josef Smrkovský," *Listy: Časopis československé socialistické opozice* (Rome) 4, no. 2 (Mar. 1975): 16–18; Zdeněk Mlynář, *Nachtfrost: Erfahrungen auf dem Weg vom realen zum menschlichen Sozialismus* (Cologne, 1978), 181–7; František August and David Rees, *Red Star over Prague* (London, 1984), 134–42; Dubček, *Hope Dies Last,* 182–4; and Historický ústav ČSAV, *Sedm pražských dnů, 21.–27. srpen 1968: Dokumentace* (Prague, Sept. 1968), 53–8. On Černík's arrest, see the firsthand account by Otomar Boček, chairman of the Supreme Court, delivered to the 14th Congress in Vysočaný, in Jiří Pelikán, ed., *Tanky proti sjezdu: Protokol a dokumenty XIV. sjezdu KSČ* (Vienna, 1970), 66–8.
150 The military operation itself, it should be noted, was not wholly flawless. See Leo Heiman, "Soviet Invasion Weaknesses," *Military Review* 49, no. 8 (Aug. 1969): 38–45.

government." That objective failed to materialize when the "healthy forces" in Czechoslovakia were unable to gain majority support on the KSČ Presidium.[151] The resulting confusion was well described in an emergency cable to Moscow from Kirill Mazurov, a Soviet Politburo member who had been sent to Czechoslovakia to monitor and help direct Operation Danube. Mazurov reported that the KSČ hard-liners had "gone a bit haywire" and "lost their nerve when Soviet military units were slightly late in arriving" at the KSČ Central Committee headquarters.[152] Over the next several hours, the KSČ Presidium's statement condemning the invasion, which passed by a 7 to 4 vote, was broadcast repeatedly over radio and television and was published on the front page of *Rudé právo* on August 21. These developments, according to Mazurov, caused even greater disarray and panic among the "healthy forces," who were "unable to recover from the shock."[153]

Despite this setback, Soviet leaders were reluctant to abandon their initial plan, apparently because they had neglected to devise any fallback options. It is surprising, even in retrospect, that they would have committed themselves so heavily to such a dubious strategy without having devised a viable alternative. No doubt, this was due in part to the skewed nature of the information flowing into the Soviet Politburo from embassy officials in Prague, from KGB sources, and from Czechoslovak hard-liners, all of whom assured the Soviet authorities in August that "healthy forces in the KSČ Presidium have finally consolidated themselves and closed their ranks so that they are now a majority."[154] Soviet leaders genuinely expected that the invasion would earn widespread official and popular support (or at least acquiescence) once the "right-wing opportunists" in the KSČ had been removed and the initial shock of the invasion had worn off. Although martial law was to be imposed in certain parts of Czechoslovakia on August 21, that was regarded as a temporary and selective measure that could be lifted as soon as a "revolutionary government" was in place and the "antisocialist" and "counterrevolutionary" forces had been neutralized.[155] The lack of any attempt by the invading troops to take over the functions of the

151 "Prohlášení předsednictva ÚV KSČ z 21.8.1968," 1.
152 "Shifrtelegramma," Aug. 21, 1968 (Top Secret), in AVPRF, F. 059, Op. 58, P. 124, D. 574, Ll. 184–6. For Mazurov's retrospective account of his role in the invasion, see "Eto bylo v Prage," 5.
153 Ibid.
154 "Shifrtelegramma," Aug. 7, 1968 (Top Secret), from S. V. Chervonenko, Soviet ambassador in Czechoslovakia, to the CPSU Politburo, in AVPRF, F. 059, Op. 58, P. 124, D. 573, Ll. 183–5. For further relevant citations from the former Soviet archives, see Kramer, "The Prague Spring and the Soviet Invasion of Czechoslovakia," 6–8, 13, 54. See also Zdeněk Mlynář, *Československý pokus o reformu, 1968: Analyza jeho teorie a praxe* (Cologne, 1975), 232–3.
155 "Rozkaz správcu posádky číslo 1, Trenčín, 21. augusta 1968: Správca posádky Sovietskej armády podplukovník ŠMAŤKO," in ÚSD-SK, A, from I. Šimovček. See also Historický ústav, *Sedm pražských dnů*, 123, 278–81, 324–5.

ČSSR government or parliament, the very limited scale of the initial Soviet propaganda effort inside the country, and the meager quantity of provisions brought in by Soviet troops (because they assumed they would soon be resupplied by a friendly Czechoslovak government) all confirm that Soviet leaders were expecting a swift transition to a pro-Moscow regime.[156]

Only after repeated efforts to set up a post-invasion government had decisively collapsed and the invasion had met with universal opposition in Czechoslovakia – both publicly and officially – did Soviet leaders get an inkling of what the real situation in Czechoslovakia was.[157] An internal Soviet Politburo analysis of the invasion conceded that "75 to 90 percent of the [Czechoslovak] population . . . regard the entry of Soviet troops as an act of occupation."[158] While acknowledging this point, Brezhnev and his colleagues were loath to admit that they had fundamentally misread the political situation. Instead, they ascribed the fiasco solely to the "cowardly behavior" of the "healthy forces" and the "lack of active propaganda work" by Soviet units.[159]

Faced with massive popular and official resistance in Czechoslovakia, the Soviet Politburo decided to open negotiations on August 23 with Dubček and other top KSČ officials who had been arrested on the morning of the 21st. After four days of talks, the two sides agreed to sign the Moscow Protocol, which forced the reversal of several elements of the Prague Spring, but also ensured the reinstatement of most of the leading reformers, including Dubček. Brezhnev's willingness to accept the return of key Czechoslovak officials did not go over well with some of his colleagues on the Politburo and with hard-line leaders in Eastern Europe. At a Warsaw Pact conclave on August 24, Gomułka insisted that Soviet and Eastern European troops should be "ordered to combat the counterrevolution" and take

---

156 See "TsK KPSS," memorandum no. 24996 (Top Secret), Sept. 6, 1968, from Aleksandr Yakovlev, deputy head of the CPSU CC Propaganda Department, and Enver Mamedov, deputy head of Soviet television and radio, to the CPSU Politburo, in TsKhSD, F. 5, Op. 60, D. 19, Ll. 200–6; and "Nekotorye zamechaniya po voprosu podgotovki voenno-politicheskoi aktsii 21 avgusta 1968 g.," Nov. 16, 1968 (Special Dossier/Strictly Secret), in TsKhSD, F. 5 "OP," Op. 6, D. 776, Ll. 128–44.

157 "Shifrtelegramma," Aug. 21, 1968 (Top Secret), from Kirill Mazurov to the CPSU Politburo, in AVPRF, F. 059, Op. 58, P. 124, D. 574, Ll. 184–6.

158 "Nekotorye zamechaniya po voprosu podgotovki voenno-politicheskoi aktsii 21 avgusta 1968 g.," L. 137.

159 The first quotation is from "Záznam ze schůzek varšavské pětky v Moskvě ve dnech 24.–27.8.1968," Aug. 1968 (Top Secret), in USD-SK, Z/M 21; and the second quotation is from "Nekotorye zamechaniya po voprosu podgotovki voenno-politicheskoi aktsii 21 avgusta 1968 g.," L. 129. This was also the view put forth by Eastern European leaders of the "Warsaw Five." See, e.g., Gomułka's secret speech on August 29 to the PZPR Central Committee, reproduced in "Gomułka o inwazji na Czechosłowację w sierpniu '68: Myśmy ich zaskoczyli akcją wojskową," *Polityka* (Warsaw), no. 35 (Aug. 29, 1992): 13.

"whatever steps are necessary" to "prevent rightists and counterrevolutionaries from regaining power."[160] In his view, "the situation in Hungary [in 1956] was better than in Czechoslovakia today." Gomułka's complaints were echoed by Ulbricht, who declared that "if Dubček and Černík are going to be back in the leadership, what was the point of sending in troops in the first place?"[161] The KSČ reformers, according to Ulbricht, "deceived us at Čierná and Bratislava" and "will deceive us again." Both he and Gomułka joined Todor Zhivkov in demanding the imposition of a "military dictatorship" in Czechoslovakia. Andropov, Shelest, Podgornyi, and a few other Soviet officials endorsed their views during a meeting of the CPSU Politburo the following day.[162] Andropov proposed that a "revolutionary workers' and peasants' government" be installed in Prague, which would carry out mass arrests and repression. This suggestion was backed by another candidate Politburo member and CPSU secretary, Dmitrii Ustinov, who emphasized that "we must give a free hand to our troops."

Brezhnev, Kosygin, and other officials rejected these calls for a much more vigorous (and presumably bloodier) military crackdown. Although Brezhnev was prepared, in extremis, to impose direct military rule in Czechoslovakia for as long as necessary, he and most of his colleagues clearly were hoping to come up with a more palatable solution first. The task of finding such a solution was seriously complicated, however, by the collapse of Moscow's initial political aims. The reinstatement of Dubček's government after the KSČ hard-liners failed to set up a collaborationist regime enabled the reform program in Czechoslovakia to survive for some time. During the last few months of 1968, substantial leeway for economic and political reform continued, and the long-promised federalization of the country was implemented on schedule. For a while, moreover, many of the top reformers held onto their posts, despite constant pressure from the Soviet Union. These developments underscored the limits of what Soviet military power could accomplish in the absence of a viable political strategy.

CONSEQUENCES OF THE INVASION

Soon after the invasion, the Soviet Politburo concluded that the only way to prevent a resurgence of "counterrevolutionary and antisocialist forces" in

---

160 "Záznam ze schůzek varšavské pětky v Moskvě ve dnech 24.–27.8.1968," L. 3.
161 Ibid., L. 5.
162 "Rabochaya zapis' zasedaniya Politbyuro TsK KPSS ot 25 avgusta 1968 g.," Aug. 25, 1968 (Top Secret), in APRF, F. 3, Op. 45, D. 99, Ll. 484–91.

Czechoslovakia was to secure a formal bilateral treaty providing for a "temporary" Soviet troop presence. Soviet leaders publicly justified their decision to pursue a status-of-forces treaty in purely military terms (as being necessary to counter "West German militarism and revanchism"). But the transcripts from CPSU Politburo sessions and from a secret Warsaw Pact conference in September 1968 leave no doubt that Moscow's dominant motivation for seeking the agreement was to obtain greater leverage over Czechoslovakia's internal politics.[163] On October 16, 1968, a bilateral "Treaty on the Temporary Presence of Soviet Forces in Czechoslovakia" was signed with much fanfare, thus codifying what amounted to a permanent Soviet troop presence.[164] Czechoslovak leaders privately acknowledged that the document would "impose definite limits on the exercise of Czechoslovak state sovereignty," and that Soviet "troops will have a certain influence [on Czechoslovakia's internal affairs] by the very fact of their presence."[165] The extent of Soviet influence, however, turned out to be far greater and more lasting than most KSČ officials had anticipated.

Although the main purpose of the status-of-forces treaty was political – that is, it was intended to facilitate Soviet control over future political developments in Czechoslovakia – the military implications of the document were by no means insignificant. The establishment of a Central Group of Soviet Forces on Czechoslovak territory, numbering some five divisions (or roughly seventy thousand to eighty thousand soldiers), strengthened the Soviet Union's ability to launch a rapid offensive against Western Europe. A top-secret report by a senior CPSU official in December 1968 noted that the deployments had created "an entirely new situation in Europe because Soviet forces will now be able to confront NATO all along the East-West divide, from the Baltic Sea to Bohemia."[166] The creation of the Central Group of Forces thus provided a crucial link between the Soviet Union's Northern Group of Forces in Poland, its Southern Group of Forces in

---

163 "Stenografický záznam schůzky varšavské pětky v Moskvě z 27.9.1968 k situaci v Československu," Sept. 27, 1968 (Top Secret), in ÚSD-SK, Z/S 13.

164 "Dogovor mezhdu pravitel'stvom Soyuza Sovetskikh Sotsialisticheskikh Respublik i pravitel'stvom Chekhoslovatskoi Sotsialisticheskoi Respubliki ob usloviyakh vremennogo prebyvaniya Sovetskikh voisk na territorii Chekhoslovatskoi Sotsialisticheskoi Respubliki," *Pravda* (Moscow), Oct. 19, 1968, 1.

165 "K otázke Dohody mezi vládou Svazu sovětských socialistických republik a vládou Československé socialistické republiky o podmínkách dočasného pobytu sovětských vojsk na území Československé socialistické republiky," Oct. 1968 (Top Secret), from the KSČ Central Committee Ideological Department, to the KSČ Presidium, in TsKhSD, F. 5, Op. 60, D. 19, Ll. 259–82.

166 Memorandum no. 23923 (Top Secret) from L. Tolokonnikov to K. V. Rusakov, Dec. 18, 1968, in TsKhSD, F. 5, Op. 60, D. 311, Ll. 155–70.

Hungary, and the Group of Soviet Forces in Germany (which was later renamed the Western Group of Forces). The deployment of a Central Group of Forces also ensured that three long-planned storage sites for Soviet tactical nuclear warheads in Czechoslovakia could be safely completed and brought on line, thereby filling a key gap in Soviet nuclear preparations.[167] For the Soviet army, the achievement of its long-standing goal of obtaining a permanent military presence in Czechoslovakia was at least as important as the political leverage that the status-of-forces treaty afforded.

In that sense, the treaty helped offset other military results of the invasion that were not so favorable. The growth of reformist sentiment in the Czechoslovak People's Army during the 1968 crisis had undermined Soviet confidence in the reliability of the ČLA, which is why no troops from the Czechoslovak army were given any role in Operation Danube (in contrast to selected units of the Czechoslovak State Security forces, who helped arrest KSČ leaders).[168] The invasion itself was devastating to the morale of Czechoslovak soldiers, who were confined to their barracks for several days beginning on the night of August 20–1.[169] The morale of the ČLA was dealt a further blow when the incoming Soviet and Eastern European troops began systematically disarming Czechoslovak soldiers, a process that continued long after it was clear that the ČLA would put up no resistance.[170] Moreover, the combat capability of the ČLA was severely eroded by the massive transfer of bases and facilities to Soviet units in October 1968 and by the subsequent purges of the Czechoslovak officer corps. The trauma of the invasion and post-invasion period was so great that Czechoslovakia's role in Warsaw Pact strategy ultimately collapsed for many years.[171] The

---

167 For further discussion of this matter, see Kramer, "The Prague Spring and the Soviet Invasion of Czechoslovakia," 9–12.

168 It is worth noting, however, that neither the State Security nor the People's Militia was wholly immune to the "winds of reform." See, e.g., "O deyatel'nosti kontrrevolyutsionnogo podpol'ya v Chekhoslovakii," Oct. 13, 1968 (Special Dossier/Top Secret), from KGB Chairman Y.V. Andropov to the CPSU Secretariat, in TsKhSD, F. 4, Op. 21, D. 32, Ll. 99–157.

169 "Rozkaz generála Provalova, velitele jižní skupiny intervenčních vojsk v odzbrojeníjednotek ČSLA," Aug. 26, 1968, in ÚSD-SK, N – VHA; and "Zpráva náčelníka generálního štábu ČSLA generála Rusova a náčelníka Hlavnípolitické zprávy generála Bedřicha na schůzi předsednictva Narodního shromáždění," Aug. 26, 1968, in ÚSD-SK, O – Arch. Narodního Shromáždění.

170 See the items adduced in the previous footnote as well as "Zápis ze zasedání Vojenské rady MNO ČSSR," Aug. 26, 1968, in ÚSD-SK, N –VHA, File MNO-Vojenská Rada.

171 J. Paulik, *Československá armáda po srpnu 1968* (Prague, 1992), 40–72. Soviet officials were aware of this possibility at the time; see, e.g., memorandum no. 23923 (Top Secret) from L. Tolokonnikov to K. V. Rusakov, head of the CPSU CC Department for intrabloc relations, Dec. 18, 1968, in TsKhSD, F. 5, Op. 60, D. 311, Ll. 164–70; "O deyatel'nosti kontrrevolyutsionnogo podpol'ya v Chekhoslovakii," Ll. 132–7; and "O politiko-moral'nom sostoyanii i boesposobnosti Chekhoslovatskoi Narodnoi Armii," Feb. 1969 (Top Secret), in TsKhSD, F. 5, Op. 61, D. 367, Ll. 37–45. See also the Soviet defense ministry's follow-up reports in TsKhSD, F. 5, Op. 61, D. 289.

once impressive Czechoslovak ground and air forces, numbering some 230,000 troops, 2,700 main battle tanks, 3,000 armored personnel carriers, and 600 combat aircraft in 1968, became a glaring weak point in the Warsaw Pact's Northern Tier. Czechoslovak divisions were no longer expected to fill the main axis of advance running from Plzeň to Coblenz.

A further casualty of the invasion was the hope that Soviet leaders once had of giving much greater emphasis to "coalition warfare." The events of 1968 made clear that in the end the Soviet Union would have to rely predominantly on its own forces in Europe. Soviet confidence in Eastern European militaries was shaken not only by the turmoil in the KSČ, but also by the performance of the Polish, Hungarian, Bulgarian, and East German soldiers who took part in the invasion. The total number of Eastern European troops involved was small (only about one-fifth the number of Soviet troops), and they engaged in no fighting. Their contribution was almost entirely symbolic. Thus, the invasion provided no test of the combat prowess of the four Eastern European armies. The most it could show was whether soldiers from those armies were able to offer limited support when they encountered no armed resistance. Judged even by that very modest standard, the results were less than satisfactory. Signs of demoralization and disaffection cropped up among Polish soldiers stationed in northern Moravia and among Hungarian troops deployed in southern Slovakia, a region inhabited predominantly by ethnic Hungarians.[172] Similarly, the morale of East German communications and logistical troops (the only East German units that actually took part in the invasion) declined when Czech protesters repeatedly accused them of serving as a "new Gestapo."[173]

---

172 On the general question of Eastern European troop morale during and after the invasion, see memorandum no. 2613y-Ts (Top Secret) from S. Tsvigun, deputy chairman of the KGB, to the CPSU Secretariat, Nov. 19, 1968, in TsKhSD, F. 5, Op. 60, D. 311, Ll. 139–42. See also document no. 145. On the problems with Polish troops, see Lech Kowalski, *Kryptonim "Dunaj": Udział wojsk polskich w interwencji zbrojnej w Czechosłowacji w 1968 roku* (Warsaw, 1992), 180–91; and George Gomori, "Hungarian and Polish Attitudes on Czechoslovakia, 1968," in E. J. Czerwinski and Jaroslaw Piekalkiewicz, eds., *The Soviet Invasion of Czechoslovakia: Its Effects on Eastern Europe* (New York, 1972), 109. The problems among Hungarian troops are discussed at length in "Uznesenie Maďarskej revolučnej robotnicko-roľnickej vlády: 'O stiahnutí maďarských vojsk rozmiestnených v Československu,'" Sept. 16, 1968, in Archiv Komisia vlády Slovenskej Republiky pre analýzu historických udalostí z rokov 1967–1970, F. Generálny konzulát MLR, A.j. 2, 224–5.

173 Thomas M. Forster, *Die NVA – Kernstück der Landesverteidigung der DDR,* 5th ed. (Cologne, 1979), 93. For further details on the role of the GDR's Nationale Volksarmee (NVA), see two recent publications by Rüdiger Wenzke: *Prager Frühling – Prager Herbst: Zur Intervention der Warschauer-Pakt-Streitkräfte in der ČSSR 1968, Fakten und Zusammenhänge* (Berlin, 1990); and *Die NVA und der Prager Frühling 1968: Die Rolle Ulbrichts unter der DDR-Streitkräfte bei der Niederschlagung der tschechoslowakischen Reformbewegung* (Berlin, 1995). See also the lively exchange prompted by the earlier of these publications: Walter Rehm, "Neue Erkenntnisse über die Rolle der NVA bei der Besetzung der ČSSR im August 1968," *Deutschland Archiv* 24, no. 2 (Feb. 1991): 173–85; and Rüdiger Wenzke, "Zur Beteiligung der NVA an der militärischen Operation von Warschauer-

Even if no such problems had arisen, confusion was bound to prevail among many of the East German and Polish units, who had been told they would be defending against American "imperialists" and West German "militarists" and "revanchists." Under those circumstances, it was not surprising that most of the Eastern European units were quickly pulled out. Nor was it surprising that Soviet leaders made no attempt to have any of the Eastern European forces included under the bilateral status-of-forces treaty.[174] Although the invasion did not impose stringent demands on Eastern European armies, their performance still fell short of the mark.

For the Soviet Union itself, the crisis also revealed notable shortcomings. Soviet leaders were unable to prevent the reforms in Czechoslovakia from spilling over into the USSR, especially into Ukraine.[175] Even after Soviet troops had crushed the Prague Spring, officials in Moscow were dismayed that "events in Czechoslovakia are still giving rise to illegal nationalist activities" in Ukraine.[176] Soviet leaders claimed that Ukrainian nationalists were "hoping to exploit the latest events in Czechoslovakia to disseminate vile sentiments and malicious fabrications" and to sow "bourgeois nationalist ideas about an 'independent Ukraine.'"[177] Shelest reported that "anti-Soviet" graffiti and thousands of leaflets condemning the invasion had turned up in Kiev and other Ukrainian cities.[178] The spillover ultimately was contained, but at the price of a stifling political clampdown. Whatever room there may have been before 1968 for discussion of political and economic reform in the Soviet Union, the invasion helped put an end to it. Brezhnev and his colleagues became increasingly unwilling to undertake reforms of any sort. Their aversion to change merely exacerbated the political and economic weaknesses of the Soviet Union that had been conducive to a spillover from the Prague Spring in the first place.

The invasion entailed further costs for the Soviet Union in terms of relations with certain Communist countries, not least Czechoslovakia. Shortly after the invasion, Soviet leaders privately acknowledged that "90 percent

Pakt-Streitkräften gegen die CSSR 1968: Einige Ergänzungen zu einem Beitrag von Walter Rehm," *Deutschland Archiv* 24, no. 11 (Nov. 1991): 1179–86. Wenzke returned to these points plus many others in his 1995 study.

174 "Stenografický záznam schůzky varšavské pětky v Moskvě z 27.9.1968 k situaci v Československu"; and "Stenografický záznam československo-sovětského jednání v Moskvě ve dnech 3.–4. řijna 1968," Oct. 3–4, 1968 (Top Secret), in ÚSD-SK, Z/S 14.

175 See the sources adduced in notes 98 and 99 to this chapter.

176 "Tsk KPSS: O nastroeniyakh dukhovenstva v svyazi s chekhoslovatskimi sobytiyami," Report No. 25583 (Secret), from V. Kuroedov, chairman of the Council on Religious Affairs of the USSR Council of Ministers, Sept. 11, 1968, in TsKhSD, F. 5, Op. 60, D. 24, Ll. 150, 153–6.

177 Ibid., L. 154.

178 Shelest, . . . *Da ne sudimy budete*, 404.

of the Czechoslovak population believe that the entry of Soviet troops was an act of occupation."[179] Reports from Soviet diplomats in late 1968 confirmed that even most members of the KSČ viewed the invasion in "highly negative" terms.[180] The anger and widespread resentment toward the Soviet Union had to be countered by sustained repression and "normalization," and even then, popular sentiments were only submerged, not eliminated. Moscow's goal of restoring cohesion to the Eastern bloc in 1968 permanently alienated the vast majority of Czechs and Slovaks. This price may have seemed worth paying at the time, but it guaranteed that the Czechoslovak regime would be unable to regain a semblance of popular legitimacy and would be forced instead to depend on Soviet military backing. If Soviet leaders had once hoped that "stability" in the Eastern bloc could be maintained by something other than coercion, the 1968 invasion put an end to those hopes.

Quite apart from this longer-term cost, the invasion had the immediate effect of deepening fissures elsewhere in the Warsaw Pact. Albania, which had been only a nominal member of the alliance since 1961, protested the intervention by severing its last remaining ties with the Pact and aligning itself ever more firmly with China. The invasion also led to acute tensions between Romania and the Soviet Union. Ceauşescu refused to let Bulgarian troops pass through Romania on their way to Czechoslovakia (they were airlifted to Ukraine instead), and he promptly condemned the invasion. Some observers at the time even thought that a complete rupture would ensue, but the actual effect was more mixed. On the one hand, Ceauşescu soon toned down his rhetoric and sought to mend relations with the other Warsaw Pact countries.[181] Over time, Romanian foreign policy

179 "Nekotorye zamechaniya po voprosu podgotovki voenno-politicheskoi aktsii 21 avgusta 1968 g.," L. 129.
180 "Informatsiya o druzheskikh svyazyakh oblastei i gorodov Ukrainskoi SSR s oblastyami, voevodstvami, okrugami, uezdami i gorodami sotsialisticheskikh stran v 1968 godu," Dec. 20, 1968 (Secret), in TsKhSD, F. 5, Op. 60, D. 2, Ll. 46, 64–5.
181 "Zapis' besedy s General'nym sekretarem TsK RKP Nikolae Chaushesku, 23 avgusta 1968 goda," cable no. 847 (Secret) from A. V. Basov, Soviet ambassador in Romania, to the CPSU Secretariat, Aug. 25, 1968, in TsKhSD, F. 5, Op. 6, D. 339, Ll. 47–53; "Zapis' besedy s poslom SFRYu v Bukhareste Ya. Petrichem, 2 sentyabrya 1968 goda," cable no. 917 (Secret) from A. V. Basov, Soviet ambassador to Romania, to the CPSU Secretariat, Sept. 5, 1968, in TsKhSD, F. 5, Op. 60, D. 339, Ll. 69–72; "Zapis' besedy s general'nym sekretarem TsK RKP N. Chaushesku, 3 sentyabrya 1968 goda," cable no. 915 (Secret) from A. V. Basov, Soviet ambassador in Romania, to the CPSU Politbiuro and Secretariat, Sept. 5, 1968, in TsKhSD, F. Op. 60, D. 339, Ll. 73–80; "O nekotorykh problemakh sovetsko-rumynskikh otnoshenii v svete pozitsii, zanyatoi rukovodstvom RKP v svyazi s sobytiyami v Chekhoslovakii," report no. 686 (Top Secret) from A. V. Basov, Soviet ambassador in Romania, to the CPSU Politbiuro, Sept. 23, 1968, in TsKhSD, F. 5, Op. 60, D. 339, Ll. 106–21; and "O pozitsii Rumynii v svyazi s sobytiyami v Chekhoslovakii," report no. MB-4809/GS (Top Secret) from B. Makashev, deputy secretary-general of the Soviet Foreign Ministry, to the CPSU Secretariat, Oct. 16, 1968, in TsKhSD, F. 5, Op. 60, D. 339, Ll. 188–94.

came further back into line with the rest of the bloc, and Soviet leaders were no longer so fearful that Ceauşescu would try to pull out of the Warsaw Pact.[182] On the other hand, the invasion dissipated any lingering chance that Romania would return to a meaningful role in the Pact. Ceauşescu was more determined than ever to pursue an independent military course. Romania not only continued eschewing joint military exercises, but also refused to submit to the unified wartime command structure that Soviet officials devised for the alliance in the late 1970s and early 1980s.[183]

As significant as these rifts within the Pact may have been, they were modest compared with the effects in other parts of the Communist world. The invasion lent further impetus to the bitter Sino-Soviet dispute, prompting China not only to denounce the Soviet action, but also to reinforce its own military units along the Sino-Soviet border. The events of August 1968, and the outbreak of two serious clashes between Soviet and Chinese forces on the Ussuri River in March 1969, were cited by Chinese Premier Zhou Enlai in mid-1969 when he declared the Soviet Union to be China's "main enemy." On that basis, Zhou and other Chinese leaders were soon willing to seek a rapprochement with the United States to present a common front against Soviet expansionism.[184] The Soviet invasion of Czechoslovakia was not the only factor that spurred this reorientation of Chinese policy, but it clearly had a far-reaching impact both in heightening diplomatic tensions and in stirring new fears among the Chinese leadership about Soviet military capabilities and intentions.

Even more striking was the schism that the 1968 crisis helped produce in the international Communist movement. The Communist parties in Western Europe, especially in Italy and Spain, had watched Dubček's reform program with great sympathy and hope. The violent suppression of the Prague Spring aroused open and vehement opposition to the Soviet Union within these parties and stimulated the rise of what later became known as "Eurocommunism."[185] The defection of most of the major West European

---

182 For earlier Soviet concerns about Romania's willingness to stay in the Pact, see "Rabochaya zapis' zasedaniya Politbyuro TsK KPSS ot 3 marta 1968," L. 92.

183 Romania's defiance on this score was first revealed by Colonel Ryszard Kukliński in "Wojna z narodem widziana od środkh," *Kultura* (Paris), 4/475 (Apr. 1987), 53. Kukliński, a senior officer on the Polish General Staff, was also a spy for the U.S. Central Intelligence Agency. He had to escape to the West in November 1981.

184 See the chapter in this book by Nancy Bernkopf Tucker. See also Kenneth Lieberthal, "The Background in Chinese Politics," in Herbert J. Ellison, ed., *The Sino-Soviet Conflict: A Global Perspective* (Seattle, 1982), 10–11.

185 See Jiří Valenta, "Eurocommunism and Czechoslovakia," in Vernon V. Aspaturian et al., eds., *Eurocommunism Between East and West* (Bloomington, Ind., 1980), 157–80. The disillusionment was equally important among non-Communist intellectuals, as discussed by Konrad Jarausch in his chapter in this book.

Communist parties from the Soviet orbit was nearly as important in its long-term consequences as the earlier splits with Yugoslavia and China, and far more important than the break with Albania. The emergence of Eurocommunism mitigated potential Soviet influence in Western Europe and significantly altered the complexion of West European politics. More important, the Eurocommunist alternative – an alternative which, unlike the Prague Spring, could not be subdued by Soviet tanks – became a potentially attractive, and thereby disruptive, element in Eastern Europe. The long-term costs of the invasion, in that respect, were considerable.

By contrast, the costs of the invasion vis-à-vis Western governments were only modest and transitory.[186] Although the political and economic benefits of détente with the United States had to be sacrificed for several weeks, Soviet officials accurately judged that almost all those benefits could be salvaged without undue delay.[187] In the meantime, the invasion redounded even more to the Soviet Union's advantage by reinforcing the West's implicit acceptance of a Soviet sphere of influence in Eastern Europe. Much as the 1956 invasion of Hungary had essentially ended talk of a Western-aided "rollback" of Communism and "liberation" of Eastern European countries, so the 1968 intervention in Czechoslovakia forced the United States to abandon even its far more cautious policy of "bridge-building."[188] In effect, U.S. officials concluded that any future "bridges" to Eastern Europe would have to go first through Moscow.

Similarly, the Czechoslovak invasion compelled West Germany to reorient its Ostpolitik in a way more palatable to the Soviet Union. Until 1968, the West German authorities had been reluctant to conclude any agreements that would imply formal recognition of the existing political configuration in Europe. Because the intervention in Czechoslovakia underscored Moscow's determination to prevent any change in the political and territorial status quo of Eastern Europe, the West German government recognized the necessity of acceding to this demand in its own policy toward the region.[189] From then on, leaders in Bonn emphasized East-West diplo-

---

186 "Depeše No. 378 čs tituláře z Washingtonu do Prahy z 21.8.1968," from Karel Duda, ČSSR ambassador in Washington, in ÚSD-SK, K – Archiv MZV, Dispatches Received, no. 7765/1968.

187 Memorandum no. 2588-Ts (Top Secret) from S. Tsvigun, deputy chairman of the KGB, to the CPSU Politburo, Nov. 15, 1968, in TsKhSD, F. 5, Op. 60, D. 311, Ll. 107–10.

188 For an overview of U.S. policy in the 1950s and 1960s, see Bennett Kovrig, *The Myth of Liberation: United States Policy in East-Central Europe* (Baltimore, 1974).

189 For further discussion of this point, see James H. Wolfe, "West Germany and Czechoslovakia: The Struggle for Reconciliation," *Orbis* 14, no. 1 (spring 1970): 170–2; Arnulf Baring, *Machtwechsel: Die Ära Brandt-Scheel* (Stuttgart, 1982), 178–360; and the chapter in this book by Niedhart.

matic "normalization," rather than territorial adjustments.[190] The new brand of Ostpolitik was in gear even before the formation of Willy Brandt's Social Democratic government in 1969, but it gained momentum thereafter. The status quo in Europe was explicitly codified not only in the series of interstate agreements on Germany in the early 1970s, but also in the Conference on Security and Cooperation in Europe (the Helsinki Accords) in 1975. Thus, in two respects, the Soviet Union's "rules of the game" in Eastern Europe gained further tacit acceptance from the West as a consequence of the 1968 invasion.

THE BREZHNEV DOCTRINE

The new framework for Soviet–Eastern European relations became even more explicit in the weeks following the invasion, when the Soviet Union proclaimed what became known in the West (although not in the USSR until 1989) as the "Brezhnev Doctrine." One of the clearest Soviet statements of the rationale behind the Doctrine actually came two months before the invasion, in a speech given by Foreign Minister Andrei Gromyko to the Supreme Soviet. For the Soviet Union, Gromyko declared,

there is nothing more sacred in the field of foreign policy than the consolidation of the commonwealth of socialist countries. The defense of the gains and the cohesion of states belonging to the socialist commonwealth is our sacred duty, to which our country will be loyal despite all trials. . . . Those who hope to break even a single link in the socialist commonwealth are planning in vain. The socialist commonwealth will never permit this.[191]

Gromyko's sentiments were echoed by lengthy editorials in *Pravda* on August 22 and September 26, which linked the fate of each socialist country with the fate of all others, stipulated that every socialist country must abide by the norms of Marxism-Leninism as interpreted in Moscow, and rejected "abstract sovereignty" in favor of the "laws of class struggle."[192] The Brezhnev Doctrine thus laid out even stricter "rules of the game" than in the past for the socialist commonwealth:

190 See Brandt's notes for the FRG Cabinet meeting on June 7, 1970, in Willy-Brandt-Archiv im Archiv der sozialen Demokratie der Friedrich-Ebert-Stiftung, Bonn, Bundeskanzler und Bundesregierung 91; cited by Niedhart in his chapter.
191 "O mezhdunarodnom polozhenii i vneshnei politike Sovetskogo Soyuza: Doklad Ministra inostrannykh del SSSR deputata A. A. Gromyko," *Pravda* (Moscow), June 28, 1968, 4.
192 "Zashchita sotsializma – vysshii internatsional'nyi dolg," *Pravda* (Moscow), Aug. 22, 1968, 2–3; and S. Kovalev, "Suverenitet i internatsional'nye obyazannosti sotsialisticheskikh stran," *Pravda* (Moscow), Sept. 26, 1968, 4.

Without question, the peoples of the socialist countries and the Communist parties have and must have freedom to determine their country's path of development. Any decision they make, however, must not be inimical either to socialism in their own country or to the fundamental interests of the other socialist countries. . . . A socialist state that is in a system of other states composing the socialist commonwealth cannot be free of the common interests of that commonwealth. The sovereignty of individual socialist countries cannot be set against the interests of world socialism and the world revolutionary movement. . . . Each Communist party is free to apply the principles of Marxism-Leninism and socialism in its own country, but it is not free to deviate from these principles if it is to remain a Communist party. . . . The weakening of any of the links in the world system of socialism directly affects all the socialist countries, and they cannot look indifferently upon this.[193]

Brezhnev himself reaffirmed the Doctrine three months after the invasion in a speech before the Fifth Congress of the Polish Communist Party. While acknowledging that the intervention had been "an extraordinary step, dictated by necessity," he warned that "when internal and external forces hostile to socialism are threatening to turn a socialist country back to capitalism, this becomes a common problem and a concern of all socialist countries."[194] Subsequently, that theme was enshrined as a "basic principle" of relations among socialist states.

The enunciation of the Brezhnev Doctrine codified Soviet attitudes toward Eastern Europe as they had developed over the previous two decades. The Doctrine owed as much to Stalin and Khrushchev as to Brezhnev, since the policies of these earlier leaders were merely reaffirmed in the Brezhnev era. Moreover, all the theoretical groundwork for the Doctrine had already been laid prior to the invasion by Gromyko's speech, the Warsaw Letter, the Bratislava Declaration, and numerous other Soviet statements.[195] To that extent, the Brezhnev Doctrine added nothing new. Nevertheless, the promulgation of the Doctrine was significant both in restoring a firmer tone to Soviet–Eastern European relations and in defining the limits of permissible deviations from the Soviet model of Communism. Among other things, the Doctrine suggested that, in the future, Soviet military intervention would not necessarily be in response to a specific development – as it had been to the revolution in Hungary in 1956 – but

---

193 Kovalev, "Suverenitet i internatsional'nye obyazannosti," 4.
194 "Rech' tovarishcha L. I. Brezhneva," *Pravda* (Moscow), Nov. 13, 1968, 2. According to bracketed comments in the text, the delegates at the Congress greeted this and several other passages of the speech with enthusiastic applause.
195 For a cogent review of the genesis of the Brezhnev Doctrine, see Karen Dawisha, "The 1968 Invasion of Czechoslovakia: Causes, Consequences, and Lessons for the Future," in Karen Dawisha and Philip Hanson, eds., *Soviet-East European Dilemmas: Coercion, Competition and Consent* (London, 1981), 9–25.

might also be *preemptive,* heading off undesired changes. Although a preemptive military option had always existed for the Soviet Union, the Brezhnev Doctrine made it explicit by suggesting that the Soviet government would never again risk "waiting until Communists are being shot and hanged," as in the autumn of 1956, before Soviet troops would be sent to "aid the champions of socialism."[196]

The Doctrine also confirmed that internal deviations from Communism, even if unaccompanied by external realignments, might be sufficient to provoke a Soviet invasion. Dubček and other Czechoslovak officials had concluded from the experience with Hungary in 1956 that the most important thing was to ensure that sweeping internal changes were not perceived as endangering Czechoslovakia's foreign orientation or its membership in the Warsaw Pact. The events of 1968 and the enunciation of the Brezhnev Doctrine made clear that Eastern European domestic as well as foreign policies would have to conform to the "common natural laws of socialist development, deviation from which could lead to a deviation from socialism as such."[197] If the internal policies of a given Communist party might "damage either socialism in its own country or the fundamental interests of the other socialist countries," the Soviet Union would have not only a right but a "sacred duty" to intervene on behalf of the "socialist commonwealth."[198]

In justifying such actions, the Brezhnev Doctrine imparted an explicitly ideological character to the Warsaw Pact. By its charter, the Warsaw alliance was originally "open to all states . . . irrespective of their social and political systems," and the charter pledged its signatories to "refrain from violence or the threat of violence in their international relations" and to "abide by the principles of mutual respect for their independence and sovereignty, and of noninterference in their internal affairs."[199] The intervention of allied forces in Czechoslovakia raised obvious questions about these principles. In a secret report a few months after the invasion, the CPSU Politburo acknowledged that "maintaining a line of noninterference" would be difficult because Soviet troops had committed "the most extreme act of interference possible in [Czechoslovakia's] internal affairs."[200] Rather than expressing regret about this development, the report emphasized that the

196 S. Kovalev, "O 'mirnoi' i nemirnoi kontrrevolyutsii," *Pravda* (Moscow), Sept. 11, 1968, 4.
197 "Rech' tovarishcha L. I. Brezhneva," 2.
198 Ibid.
199 "Dogovor o druzhbe, sotrudnichestve i vzaimnoi pomoshchi," *Pravda* (Moscow), May 15, 1955, 2, Articles 9, 1, and 8, respectively.
200 "Nekotorye zamechaniya po voprosu podgotovki voenno-politicheskoi aktsii 21 avgusta 1968 g.," Ll. 131–2.

Soviet Union must continue to "exert decisive interference in Czechoslovakia's affairs and to apply pressure through every available channel."[201]

For public consumption, however, Soviet officials had to come up with
some way of claiming that the invasion was consistent with the principles
laid out in the Warsaw Pact's charter. To that end, Soviet theorists began
distinguishing between "bourgeois" and "class-based" versions of state sovereignty and independence. They argued that the intervention, far from
overriding the principles of respect for sovereignty and noninterference,
had actually buttressed them by "defending Czechoslovakia's independence
and sovereignty *as a socialist state*" against "the counterrevolutionary forces
that would like to deprive it of this sovereignty."[202] The "bourgeois" concepts of independence and sovereignty, according to this argument, were
invalid because they lacked "class content."

By redefining the norms of international law within "the general context of class struggle," and by rendering paramount the interests of the
"socialist commonwealth," the Brezhnev Doctrine in effect transformed
the Warsaw Pact into a more formally ideological alliance than it had been
in the past. This further narrowed the prospects for individual alliance
members to deviate from Soviet policy, a point emphasized by Ceaușescu
in his protests over the invasion.[203]

EPILOGUE: THE INCEPTION OF "NORMALIZATION"

By the end of 1968, the Soviet Union had gone a long way toward consolidating the military and political gains of the invasion and toward overcoming most of the problems that had arisen. The conformity of the bloc had
been largely restored. Even so, the process of "normalization" in Czechoslovakia was far from over. Dubček was continuing to maneuver in a broadly
reformist direction, despite the enormous pressure he was coming under
from Moscow. It would take another four months before a new regime was
formed in Prague under Gustáv Husák and nearly a year more of intensive
"normalization" before the last remnants of the Prague Spring could be
eradicated.[204] In the meantime, Soviet leaders again had to undertake various forms of intimidation and persuasion to try to ensure that Dubček
would heed their wishes.

---

201 Ibid.
202 A. Sovetov, "Sovremennyi etap bor'by mezhdu sotsializmom i imperializmom," *Mezhdunarodnaya
     zhizn'* (Moscow), no. 11 (Nov. 1968), 7 (emphasis added).
203 "O pozitsii Rumynii v svyazi s sobytiyami v Chekhoslovakii," Ll. 188–94.
204 See Vladimír V. Kusin, *From Dubček to Charter 77: A Study of "Normalization" in Czechoslovakia
     1968–1978* (New York, 1978), 5–142.

At a meeting with Dubček and other KSČ officials in Kiev in early December, Soviet leaders emphasized their displeasure at the continued presence of reform-minded officials in the top party organs, the ČSSR security forces, and, above all, the Czechoslovak army.[205] Dubček acknowledged that "right-wing and even antisocialist forces" were still active in Czechoslovakia, but he defended his latest policies, arguing that the KSČ had largely isolated the unsavory elements. Brezhnev, Kosygin, and Podgornyi were far harsher in their assessments, and they demanded that Dubček move expeditiously to get rid of the "patently anti-Soviet . . . and irresponsible right-wingers" who were still acting in the name of the KSČ. Brezhnev and his colleagues also expressed dismay that the KSČ had still not reclaimed its "leading role" in Czechoslovak society, and they urged Dubček to "rebuff all these attacks" against the party.[206]

Although Dubček remained in power until April 1969, the tone of the Kiev meeting suggested that Soviet leaders had already concluded in early December that the situation would not fundamentally change unless Dubček himself were ousted. The KSČ first secretary had moved a considerable distance away from his earlier policies in a bid to accommodate Soviet demands, but it was increasingly evident that Dubček, unlike some of his colleagues such as Gustáv Husák, was unwilling to renounce the whole thrust of the Prague Spring. Earlier, when the basic problem was to gain credibility for the post-invasion regime in Czechoslovakia, the Soviet Union benefited by having Dubček back, but as of late 1968 and early 1969 this function had outlived its purpose. To the extent that Brezhnev and others sought a definitive return to orthodox Communism as well as a full-scale purge of the KSČ, the ČSSR government, and the Czechoslovak army and security forces, they sensed that their objectives could be met only by getting rid of the man who had long symbolized the Prague Spring.

It would be left to Husák and Lubomír Štrougal – both of whom accompanied Dubček, Černík, and Svoboda to the Kiev meeting – to extend "normalization" into its next, much harsher, phase. Joined by Bil'ak, Indra, and other members of the KSČ's revived "healthy forces" (who had suddenly become the dominant forces), they plunged Czechoslovakia into a "Prague Winter" that lasted more than twenty years.

---

205 "Záznam z československo-sovětského jednání v Kyjevě," Dec. 7–8, 1968 (Top Secret), in ÚSD-SK, Z/S 17.
206 Ibid., Ll. 518–30.

5

Ostpolitik

The Role of the Federal Republic of Germany in the Process of Détente

GOTTFRIED NIEDHART

THE MEANING OF OSTPOLITIK
IN A PERIOD OF TRANSITION

During the late 1960s and early 1970s, the Federal Republic of Germany (FRG) underwent considerable societal and political change. This change was a result of the willingness of elites to introduce reforms and the pressures exerted on the system by "sixty-eighters." Whereas the 1950s had been the first founding era in the country's history, the following period experienced a second "founding," one that included domestic reforms, changes in attitudes, and new approaches to foreign affairs. During this time, the Federal Republic also came to terms with the postwar order and accepted its identity as a separate West German state. Ostpolitik, or the official policy toward Eastern Europe, became the best-known symbol of this accommodation to the realities created by World War II. This policy not only belatedly recognized Soviet hegemony in Eastern Europe, but it also, as I argue in this chapter, signaled the moment when the FRG began to play a new role in international affairs. Because of the relative decline of the superpowers, West Germany acquired a new status and became one of the driving forces behind détente, an effort that the superpowers alone could not have sustained. Furthermore, it was very much in the Federal Republic's national interest to transform the existing Cold War pattern in East-West relations. Thus, this era marked the beginning of a new phase in West Germany's foreign relations, which culminated in the events of 1989–90.

The general concept of Ostpolitik – as a more flexible response to the realities of the postwar period – had already been developed during the

second half of Konrad Adenauer's chancellorship.[1] As a policy, it was reluctantly implemented in the mid-1960s and achieved its breakthrough after
the elections of September 28, 1969.[2] The Christian Democratic Union
(CDU/CSU), the dominant political party during the first two decades of
the Federal Republic, still held the largest number of seats in the Bundestag
in 1969 but no longer held a majority. Its coalition partner, the small Liberal Party (Freie Demokratische Partei or FDP), under Walter Scheel, had
switched allegiances in order to govern with the Social Democrats
(Sozialdemokratische Partei Dentschlands or SPD). As a result, the SPD
and the FDP formed a new coalition government under the chancellorship
of Willy Brandt (SPD).[3]

The new government, and especially its new foreign policy vis-à-vis the
East, encountered intense political opposition from the Christian Democrats and a substantial portion of the German public. Nevertheless, the
government's mandate was reaffirmed in early elections in November 1972.
Many contemporaries saw these elections as a referendum on Ostpolitik,
and consequently Brandt went on to shape German politics in the 1970s
much as Adenauer had done in the 1950s.[4] Whereas a majority of the electorate seemed to endorse Ostpolitik, a broad consensus formed only over
time. In 1975 the Christian Democrats opposed the Helsinki Conference
on Security and Cooperation in Europe; but when the Christian Democrat
Helmut Kohl became chancellor in 1982, he nonetheless continued
Ostpolitik.[5]

---

1 See Klaus Gotto, "Adenauers Deutschland- und Ostpolitik, 1954–1963," in Klaus Gotto et al., eds.,
   Konrad Adenauer: Seine Deutschland- und Aussenpolitik, 1945–1963 (Munich, 1975), 156–286; Hans-
   Peter Schwarz, *Adenauer: Der Staatsmann, 1952–1967* (Stuttgart, 1991), 840–53; Daniel Kosthorst,
   *Brentano und die deutsche Einheit: Die Deutschland- und Ostpolitik des Aussenministers im Kabinett Ade-
   nauer, 1955–1961* (Düsseldorf, 1993); Peter Siebenmorgen, *Gezeitenwechsel: Aufbruch zur Entspan-
   nungspolitik* (Bonn, 1990).
2 See Klaus Hildebrand, *Von Erhard zur Grossen Koalition, 1963–1969* (Stuttgart, 1984), 83–99,
   187–202, 327–39. Dirk Kroegel, *Einen Anfang finden! Kurt Georg Kiesinger in der Aussen- und Deutschlandpolitik der Grossen Koalition* (Munich, 1997). For a survey of recent research, see Günther
   Heydemann, "Deutschlandpolitische Neuansätze der 60er Jahre," *Historisch-Politische Mitteilungen* 1
   (1994): 15–32.
3 Arnulf Baring, *Machtwechsel: Die Ära Brandt-Scheel* (Munich, 1984), 169–76.
4 Defense Minister Helmut Schmidt gave expression to this when he tried to convince a member of
   his party that Ostpolitik was "a most important undertaking." Only time will tell whether it can be
   successful. "In case of success it will give Willy Brandt (and with him our party) the same status in
   German postwar history which Adenauer has already acquired" (Schmidt to Friedrich Beermann,
   member of the Bundestag, July 7, 1970. Copy in Willy-Brandt-Archiv im Archiv der sozialen
   Demokratie der Friedrich-Ebert-Stiftung, Bonn [hereafter WBA], Bundeskanzler und Bundesregierung [hereafter BK] 18).
5 On the attitude of the Christian Democrats, see Christian Hacke, *Die Ost- und Deutschlandpolitik der
   CDU/CSU:Wege und Irrwege der Opposition seit 1969* (Cologne, 1974); Clay Clemens, *Reluctant Real-
   ists:The Christian Democrats and West German Ostpolitik* (Durham, N.C., 1989).

The origins of Brandt's Ostpolitik can be traced back to 1961 when, as mayor of West Berlin, Brandt had to respond to the building of the Berlin Wall by the East German government.[6] The division of the city highlighted the failure of the old approach to the German question, as it became evident that the Western allies were prepared to accept the division of Germany. Some West German politicians, such as Wolfgang Schollwer (FDP),[7] as well as Brandt and his press secretary, Egon Bahr (SPD), understood these changes in international politics and thus were early proponents of Ostpolitik. Their concept for this policy was first presented at a conference in Tutzing, near Munich, which was attended by well-known politicians and foreign policy experts, including Adenauer himself. At Tutzing, Bahr used his well-known phrase "Wandel durch Annäherung" (change through rapprochement) for the first time.[8] The main arguments for Ostpolitik can be summarized as follows:

1. Politics should be based on two principles: realism and communication. The realities of the postwar settlement should be accepted. At the same time, there should be an increase in communication between East and West. Contact with the communist East might lead to its penetration by Western ideas, which would then engender gradual change.
2. Within the framework of President John F. Kennedy's "strategy of peace" and starting from the "common security interests" of the West, the "interests of the other side" should be acknowledged as legitimate. The realities of power politics could only be changed after they have been accepted first. The recognition of the status quo was the initial step to overcoming it.
3. The Soviet Union should be reassured of its predominance in Eastern Europe. Once Moscow had lost its fear of being pushed out of Germany and Eastern Europe, it could enter into a process of increasing communication with the West. A rapprochement between East and West might result in the "transformation of the other side." Communist rule was not to be abolished but changed.
4. The division of Germany would last as long as the division of Europe. The German question could only be solved through cooperation with the Soviet Union and not through antagonistic behavior.
5. The Federal Republic of Germany should be regarded as a "grown-up" member of the Western community. Having achieved integration into the

---

6 Diethelm Prowe, "Die Anfänge der Brandtschen Ostpolitik in Berlin 1961–1963," in Wolfgang Benz and Hermann Graml, eds., *Aspekte deutscher Aussenpolitik im 20. Jahrhundert* (Stuttgart, 1976), 249–86.
7 Wolfgang Schollwer, *FDP im Wandel: Aufzeichnungen, 1961–1966* (Munich, 1994). See also Gottfried Niedhart, "Friedens- und Interessenwahrung: Zur Ostpolitik der FDP in Opposition und sozialliberaler Regierung 1968–1970," *Jahrbuch zur Liberalismus-Forschung* 7 (1995): 105–26.
8 Andreas Vogtmeier, *Egon Bahr und die deutsche Frage: Zur Entwicklung der sozialdemokratischen Ost- und Deutschlandpolitik vom Kriegsende bis zur Vereinigung* (Bonn, 1996), 59–66.

West, the Federal Republic "should look after its interests with respect to the East in a more vigorous way."[9]

During the 1960s the question of Ostpolitik provoked an intense debate within Germany. Some wanted to retain the existing positions on the German question at any price, while others could even conceive of full diplomatic recognition of the German Democratic Republic (GDR). The majority of those arguing for progress in the FRG's relations with the East was prepared to recognize the existing borders in Europe but not the GDR as a "foreign country." In the late 1960s, a majority in the SPD and FDP supported this view, which was also held by some in the press, by the general public, and notably by the Protestant Church.[10]

Growing readiness to change the 1950s Cold War paradigm resulted from international developments, mainly that the Soviet Union had not retreated in the face of Western superiority, as many proponents of the strategy of "rollback" had hoped. Instead, it became a world power that reached strategic nuclear parity with the United States and had to be acknowledged as a hegemonial power in Eastern Europe, including the GDR. A clear indication of this new status was the adoption of the Brezhnev Doctrine in 1968, which in a certain sense could be regarded as equivalent to the Monroe Doctrine.[11]

Because of the changing international context, German diplomacy faced the task of redefining its perceptions of its main adversary, the Soviet Union, and of its chief ally, the United States. As President Lyndon B. Johnson made perfectly clear in October 1966, the United States was no longer willing to await the resolution of the German question as a precondition for progress in overall East-West relations.[12] In order to prevent the gap between Washington and Bonn from growing wider, the West German

9 Both speeches are printed in *Dokumente zur Deutschlandpolitik,* 4th series (Frankfurt am Main, 1978), 9:565–75. See also Willy Brandt, *Begegnungen und Einsichten: Die Jahre, 1960–1975* (Hamburg, 1976), 56–7; Willy Brandt, *Erinnerungen* (Frankfurt am Main, 1989), 73–6. For summaries of the main features of Ostpolitik, see also Helmut Schmidt, "Germany in the Era of Negotiations," *Foreign Affairs* 49 (1970–1): 40–50; Horst Ehmke, *Mittendrin: Von der Grossen Koalition zur deutschen Einheit* (Berlin, 1994), 125–42; and recently the memoirs of Egon Bahr, *Zu meiner Zeit* (Munich, 1996).
10 Peter Bender, *Die "Neue Ostpolitik" und ihre Folgen: Vom Mauerbau bis zur Vereinigung* (Munich, 1995), 121–4; Hartmut Rudolph, "Fragen der Ostpolitik im Raum der Evangelischen Kirche in Deutschland," in Wolfgang Huber and Johannes Schwertfeger, eds., *Kirche zwischen Krieg und Frieden: Studien zur Geschichte des deutschen Protestantismus* (Stuttgart, 1976), 460–540.
11 On the Brezhnev Doctrine, see Mark Kramer's chapter in this book.
12 Adrian W. Schertz, *Die Deutschlandpolitik Kennedys und Johnsons: Unterschiedliche Ansätze innerhalb der amerikanischen Regierung* (Cologne, 1992), 363; Frank Costigliola, "Lyndon B. Johnson, Germany, and 'the End of the Cold War,'" in Warren I. Cohen and Nancy Bernkopf Tucker, eds., *Lyndon Johnson Confronts the World: American Foreign Policy, 1963–1969* (Cambridge, 1994), 197.

government felt that implementing Ostpolitik was now urgent. Otherwise, the Federal Republic might become isolated within the Western alliance.

In November 1966 the so-called Grand Coalition led by Chancellor Kurt Georg Kiesinger (CDU), with Brandt as foreign minister and Brandt's close aide Bahr as the head of the foreign policy planning staff,[13] began to implement the first phase of Ostpolitik.[14] The CDU/SPD government established a new priority, namely, that détente in Europe was a precondition for improvements in the German question and not vice versa. However, its initial offer of an agreement on the renunciation of force did not lead to any real progress in German-Soviet relations. Substantive talks between Moscow and Bonn took place only a few months after the invasion of Czechoslovakia in August 1968.

At that time, the Grand Coalition was still intact. Chancellor Kiesinger agreed with Foreign Minister Brandt that the Soviet intervention in Czechoslovakia must not affect the Western approach to détente. West German ratification of the Nonproliferation Treaty was, however, postponed. Yet there was no return to the Cold War, since the NATO partners resolved to continue their policy toward the Soviet Union. In brutal fashion, the events of 1968 demonstrated that Western efforts to lessen East-West tensions had to go hand in hand with the de facto recognition of Soviet hegemony in Eastern Europe. Starting from this premise, a realistic Ostpolitik could continue or even be intensified. This view was encouraged when the Soviet leadership, having maintained its role in Eastern Europe in 1968, showed great interest in improving relations with the West in general and the Federal Republic in particular. Although the most dramatic steps in Ostpolitik had to wait until 1970, it must not be overlooked that the stage was set in 1968. Although the Soviet empire was a military giant, for economic reasons it had to rely on cooperation with the West. Similarly, the United States was interested in reducing tensions between the superpowers and scaling back on its global commitments.

The Federal Republic played a key role within this constellation. In January 1969, Moscow and Bonn initiated a diplomatic exchange. The establishment of the SPD-FDP coalition in October 1969 made possible a new departure in West German–Soviet relations. Ostpolitik was one of the most important links between the two governing parties, which otherwise rep-

13 Brandt, *Begegnungen,* 56; see also Brandt, *Erinnerungen,* 73–4.
14 Still a very useful survey is Richard Löwenthal, "Vom kalten Krieg zur Ostpolitik," in Richard Löwenthal and Hans-Peter Schwarz, eds., *Die zweite Republik: 25 Jahre Bundesrepublik Deutschland – eine Bilanz* (Stuttgart, 1974), 604–99. A summary of recent research is included in Bender, *Ostpolitik,* 316–34.

resented very different constituencies and held conflicting views on many issues.[15] Together, the two parties held only a slim majority in the Bundestag (the German parliament). Not only did the opposition Christian Democrats outrightly reject Ostpolitik but important minorities within the SPD and the FDP were also against it. The adoption of Ostpolitik was therefore not without political risks for the government. The policy was even endangered at one point when a few SPD and FDP deputies who objected to the treaties with Moscow and Warsaw defected to the opposition. The enormous international success of the Four-Power Agreement on Berlin in 1971 preserved the social-liberal coalition, which won a comfortable parliamentary majority in elections in 1972.[16]

At the end of the 1960s, Ostpolitik was part of the spirit of reform that animated the SPD, the FDP, and sections of the CDU. It had hardly anything to do with the student movement or the extraparliamentary opposition of these years. Among major international issues, only the Vietnam War was on the agenda of sixty-eighters. It is illuminating to read Ulrich Sahm's assessment of the situation. One of Bonn's top diplomats, Sahm commented that the student demonstrations worried him but that he could not devote "any time" to an examination of their agenda. He did not believe that the existing political order was in any case endangered and considered the student movement to be marginal.[17]

Ostpolitik was the result of climactic changes in international politics. From its founding in 1949, West Germany had always depended on its ability to adapt to international trends.[18] Whereas implementation of Ostpolitik had been predicated on a change in the political climate in the Federal Republic that made acknowledgment of the European status quo acceptable to the population, the prerequisite for the second aim of Ostpolitik, namely, the transformation of European politics, depended on the existence of sufficient room for maneuver for the semisovereign FRG. The United States had to acquiesce in German initiatives toward the East, and

15 For a summary of the views held by the SPD/FDP coalition, see A. James McAdams, *Germany Divided: From the Wall to Reunification* (Princeton, N.J., 1993), 79–84.
16 For the interplay of domestic and foreign affairs, see Reinhold Roth, *Innovation und politische Herrschaftssicherung: Eine Analyse von Struktur und Systemfunktion des aussenpolitischen Entscheidungsprozesses am Beispiel der sozialliberalen Koalition, 1969–1973* (Meisenheim, 1976). See also Günther Schmid, *Entscheidung in Bonn: Die Entstehung der Ost-und Deutschlandpolitik, 1969–1970* (Cologne, 1979).
17 Ulrich Sahm, *"Diplomaten taugen nichts": Aus dem Leben eines Staatsdieners* (Düsseldorf, 1994), 221–2. Sahm moved from the Auswärtiges Amt to the Bundeskanzleramt after Brandt had become chancellor in 1969. In 1972 he was appointed German ambassador in Moscow.
18 This argument runs right through Wolfram F. Hanrieder, *Germany, America, Europe: Forty Years of German Foreign Policy* (New Haven, Conn., 1989).

the Soviet Union had to give up its maximum goals. In the fall of 1969, conditions were favorable for Ostpolitik because the Soviet Union desired a relaxation of East-West tensions.[19] Similarly, the United States was willing to substitute confrontation for cooperation.[20] Looking back, Helmut Schmidt, the finance minister in 1973, spoke of a "changing world" in which the "traditional categories of East and West" had lost their significance.[21] Both superpowers were experiencing a crisis of hegemony and the conflict within international communism between the Soviet Union and the People's Republic of China indicated that the bipolar world order was dissolving.[22] Furthermore, in Western Europe and Japan "new centers of power" were emerging.[23]

Ostpolitik reflected both continuity and change within the international arena. It did not question the Federal Republic's membership in the Western alliance, but it called for improved European security and for confidence building between NATO and the Warsaw Pact. Although it continued the traditional Social Democratic and bourgeois anticommunist stance, Ostpolitik strove for pragmatic links between East and West in the areas of the economy, technology, and culture as a way to overcome the division of Europe. Regarding the German question, Ostpolitik pursued an all-German policy by different means and raised the issue of national interest not only with respect to the Federal Republic as a separate country but also with regard to the nation as a whole. At the same time, however, the existence of two separate German states was accepted and the existing frontiers were to be respected. Although this had already been the policy of earlier CDU governments, the formal recognition of postwar realities signaled an important change.

In what follows, Ostpolitik will be analyzed on three different, albeit intertwined levels: (1) European security issues, (2) East-West communication, and (3) German national interests.

---

19 Otto Winzer, foreign minister of the GDR, was informed that the time was over when both sides had exchanged documents only. Now Moscow wanted to start negotiations with the Federal Republic. Gromyko to Winzer, Sept. 1, 1969. Stiftung Archiv der Parteien und Massenorganisationen der DDR im Bundesarchiv, Berlin (hereafter SAPMO-BArch), Zentrales Parteiarchiv, Büro Ulbricht, J IV 2/202/81.

20 On U.S. politics, see the chapters by George C. Herring and Diane B. Kunz in this book. See also Raymond L. Garthoff, *Détente and Confrontation: American-Soviet Relations from Nixon to Reagan* (Washington, D.C., 1985); Warren I. Cohen, *America in the Age of Soviet Power, 1945–1991* (Cambridge, 1993).

21 Schmidt, in an after-dinner speech in October 1973 when U.S. Treasury Secretary George Shultz was in Bonn. Archiv der sozialen Demokratie der Friedrich-Ebert-Stiftung, Bonn (hereafter AdsD), Depositum Helmut Schmidt (hereafter HS) 5990.

22 On China, see Nancy Bernkopf Tucker's chapter in this book.

23 See also Schmidt's words as cited in note 21 to this chapter.

SECURITY: DEFENSE AND DÉTENTE

Three days after the elections of September 28, 1969, Egon Bahr drafted the foreign policy guidelines that would serve as a blueprint for the politics of the new SPD/FDP government.[24] Bahr stressed both continuity and change, and he ruled out any change with respect to the essentials of Germany's security; membership in NATO and the close alliance with the United States would continue to form the basis of German foreign policy. Accordingly, Bonn kept its allies, especially the United States, informed of every step in its evolving policy toward the Soviet Union. Even before Brandt was elected chancellor, he had asked the government of the United States to receive Bahr as his special envoy.

The first contact between the White House and the SPD leadership after the election happened on October 1, 1969, when Henry Kissinger spoke with Bahr on the telephone and both agreed to meet soon. The meeting that took place on October 13 initiated a series of talks and other communications.[25] According to Bahr's notes, three issues were dealt with in his conversation with Kissinger.[26] The first issue concerned bilateral relations: Bahr announced that the FRG would henceforth exercise a greater degree of self-confidence. Alluding to certain peculiarities in the relationship between the Federal Republic and the United States, Bahr added that Bonn did not intend to inquire every two months whether the Americans "still love us." Kissinger responded, "Thank God!" Second, Bahr discussed the issue of the Nonproliferation Treaty, which Bonn was willing to sign. Bahr attached only minor relevance to certain clarifications he expected from the Soviet government. Relevant and "absolutely central" for him was "the German–American relationship and the Alliance." Concluding this point, both Bahr and Kissinger complained about the Russians "in a moderate way." The third point was Ostpolitik. Bahr explained his ideas and concentrated on two aspects: the essential continuity of German foreign policy and the renunciation of the use of force in German-Soviet relations. Kissinger's advice was to start negotiations as soon as possible. He concluded by saying, "Your success will be our success."

24 Memorandum of Oct. 1, 1969. Werner Link, "Aussen- und Deutschlandpolitik in der Ära Brandt, 1969–1974," in Karl Dietrich Bracher, Wolfgang Jäger, and Werner Link, *Republik im Wandel, 1969–1974: Die Ära Brandt* (Stuttgart, 1986), 163–4; Werner Link, "Adenauer, Amerika und die deutsche Nachwelt," in Klaus Schwabe, ed., *Adenauer und die USA* (Bonn, 1994), 144; Brandt addressing the SPD members of the Bundestag, Oct. 3, 1969. AdsD, SPD-Fraktion, 5. Wahlperiode (hereafter WP) 137.
25 Note for Brandt by Bahr, Oct. 1, 1969. WBA, Loses Material.
26 AdsD, Depositum Egon Bahr (hereafter EB) 439/2.

Kissinger was no doubt more skeptical than Bahr as to whether Ostpolitik would be successful. Whatever his expectations might have been, Kissinger proposed to establish a "back channel" between the White House and the Chancellery in Bonn, enabling both politicians to communicate directly without the interference of the bureaucracies, particularly their respective foreign ministries.[27] Within a few days, this back channel can be seen in operation when Bahr was informed on October 23 that the Soviet government had proposed to begin the Strategic Arms Limitation Talks (SALT) on November 17, a proposal that Washington wanted to accept. For its part, Bonn kept the White House informed about a letter from Brandt to Soviet Prime Minister Kosygin dated November 19, in which he suggested bilateral talks on the basis of the existing commitments.[28] Secretary of State William P. Rogers expressed Washington's support for Bonn's negotiations when he visited Brandt in Bonn on December 6.[29] At the end of the month, Kissinger was informed of the imminent start of these talks in Moscow.[30]

The first two rounds of talks between Bahr and Gromyko had already been completed when Brandt traveled to Washington in April 1970. On that occasion, the White House gave no special advice for negotiations with the Soviet Union, nor did it voice specific objections to Ostpolitik.[31] Nonetheless, Kissinger had deeply felt reservations about the new government in Bonn and the direction of its foreign policy. In June, he told Paul Frank, the new undersecretary of state (*Staatssekretär*) in the German Foreign Office: "Let me tell you something! If anyone is going to pursue détente with the Soviet Union, it will be us."[32] Kissinger feared that the Soviet Union might succeed in achieving a "selective détente," by improving its relationship to some European countries, while "maintaining an intransigent position" toward the United States.[33] Despite the intense exchange of information between Bonn and Washington, Kissinger remained nervous about the resurgence of German nationalism and the implications of an Ostpolitik that could potentially undermine the coher-

27 Note by Bahr for Brandt, Oct. 14, 1969. AdsD, EB 439/2. See also Henry Kissinger, *White House Years* (Boston, 1979), 411.
28 AdsD, EB 439/2.
29 Ibid. 440/2. See also Ambassador Kenneth Rush to Brandt, Oct. 28, 1969. Ibid. Rush's predecessor had also endorsed Ostpolitik. George McGhee, *At the Creation of a New Germany: From Adenauer to Brandt: An Ambassador's Account* (New Haven, Conn., 1989), 243.
30 Bahr to Kissinger, Dec. 30, 1969. AdsD, EB 439/2.
31 Kissinger, *White House Years*, 423–4.
32 Paul Frank, *Entschlüsselte Botschaft: Ein Diplomat macht Inventur* (Munich, 1985), 287.
33 Kissinger, *White House Years*, 410, 528–9.

ence of the Western alliance.[34] Since Washington officially backed Ostpolitik, Bahr did not initially attach much importance to rumors that the Nixon
administration harbored doubts concerning the reliability of the West Germans. Therefore, in a letter to Kissinger, Bahr stressed their mutual trust
and added: "Whoever has a question or feels any cause for concern should
express it frankly."[35]

For Brandt and his aides, there was never any doubt that NATO would
remain the backbone of West German foreign policy.[36] The existence of
Germany's ties to the West was regarded as self-evident. Nevertheless, Herbert Wehner, a former Communist and the current party whip of the SPD,
pressed Brandt to underscore explicitly the continuity of Germany's commitment to the West in the chancellor's first policy declaration.[37] Although
Kissinger certainly did not assume that Brandt, Herbert Wehner, or Helmut Schmidt would pull the Federal Republic out of NATO or endanger
"Germany's Western association,"[38] he could not be sure about their successors. Since Moscow had never hidden its intentions to undermine
NATO through diplomatic and propagandistic means, Germany could be
tempted to abandon its Western orientation if the Russians offered unification in exchange for some form of neutrality. In Kissinger's view, Brandt
"possessed neither the stamina nor the intellectual apparatus to manage the
forces he had unleashed."[39]

Although Kissinger's now famous statement grossly underestimated
Brandt's abilities and intentions, it is also true that even members of the
chancellor's own cabinet differed in their enthusiasm for Ostpolitik. There
was general support for détente but skepticism about the ongoing negotiations in Moscow. Helmut Schmidt, who had traveled widely in the Soviet
Union in the 1960s and who had spoken to Gromyko in August 1969,
always refers to "Willy Brandt's Ostpolitik" in his memoirs.[40] Although
Schmidt, who was defense minister in 1970 and became chancellor in 1974,
generally endorsed Ostpolitik, he warned against "euphoria" and took every
opportunity to remind his colleagues that security matters should remain

---

34 Ibid., 409–11. See also Kissinger's memorandum for President Nixon, Feb. 16, 1970. Ibid., 529–30.
35 Bahr to Kissinger, July 24, 1970. AdsD, EB 439/2.
36 Brandt, *Erinnerungen,* 187.
37 Notes by Wehner (Einige Erinnerungsposten für die Regierungserklärung), Oct. 15, 1969. AdsD,
     SPD-Fraktion, 5. WP, Büro Wehner 2010; Wehner at a meeting of the executive of the parlia-
     mentary party, May 25, 1970. Ibid., 143.
38 Kissinger, *White House Years,* 408.
39 Henry Kissinger, *Years of Upheaval* (London, 1982), 144.
40 Helmut Schmidt, *Menschen und Mächte* (Berlin, 1991), 187.

their top priority.[41] Right after the signing ceremony in Moscow, Schmidt sent a remarkable handwritten letter to Brandt. For Schmidt the treaty was a "great step" forward and the beginning of a "new era" in East-West relations. However, this should not lead to any change in the Federal Republic's relations with its allies. Furthermore, Ostpolitik should not distract West German leaders away from domestic problems. Any "euphoric propaganda" would be counterproductive with respect to the GDR, the West, and the coming domestic debate within the Federal Republic on the treaty. Washington, London, and Paris should be informed immediately because it was Schmidt's impression that the White House was disconcerted by the pace with which the Brandt government had embarked on its Ostpolitik.[42]

The Federal Republic was certainly not trying to weaken NATO but rather hoped to increase the Western alliance's cohesion. Bonn was working toward an intensification of NATO's new approach to East-West relations that had been spelled out in the Harmel Report of 1967. This approach supposedly combined deterrence and détente.[43] Then Foreign Minister Brandt had therefore already urged his colleagues in April 1969 that NATO should not leave the issue of a European security conference to the East.[44] For him, security in Europe, or a "European alliance for peace," was not only a matter of military planning and strategy but also of common approaches to security through negotiations and confidence building measures between the blocs.[45] Using slightly different language, Schmidt wanted to supplement "security through deterrence" with "security through the lessening of tensions." A means to this end were Mutual Balanced Force Reductions (MBFR), which had been suggested by the NATO council in

41 Helmut Schmidt, *Strategie des Gleichgewichts: Deutsche Friedenspolitik und die Weltmächte* (Stuttgart, 1969).
42 Schmidt to Brandt, Aug. 13, 1970. WBA, BK 18. On August 18, Schmidt asked the planning staff of the Defense Ministry for an analysis of the Treaty of Moscow. In a memorandum of August 28, 1970, the main points, marked by Schmidt, were the following: The treaty did not remove the differences between both sides. It leaves room for maneuver with respect to peaceful change. It must not lead to an inappropriate feeling of security. The Federal Republic is in need of a solid safeguard in the West against any risks which might come up. AdsD, HS 1649 A.
43 On this, see Helga Haftendorn, *Sicherheit und Entspannung: Zur Aussenpolitik der Bundesrepublik Deuschland, 1955–1982* (Baden-Baden, 1983), 211–15; Helga Haftendorn, "Entstehung und Bedeutung des Harmel-Berichtes der NATO von 1967," *Vierteljahrshefte für Zeitgeschichte* 40 (1992): 169–221.
44 Brandt, *Erinnerungen,* 181. For Brandt there was an important side effect: Ostpolitik could be "Europeanized." Ibid.
45 Brandt to Brezhnev, Feb. 9, 1972: "Das von Ihnen angesprochene System zwischenstaatlicher Beziehungen zur Überwindung der Konfrontation in Europa – von mir einmal als Zielvorstellung ein europäischer Friedensbund genannt – soll auch meiner Meinung nach durch eine Konferenz für Sicherheit und Zusammenarbeit in Europa, an der die USA und Kanada teilnehmen, gefördert werden." WBA, BK 58.

May 1970. To achieve a new balance on a lower level would be "a contribution toward the evolution of more cooperative and less confrontational
patterns of relations in Europe."[46]

The main goal of Ostpolitik, namely, the strengthening of cooperation
within the existing framework of an "antagonistic cooperation" between
East and West, seemed to be realistic and necessary. Therefore, the Soviet
Union should be treated as a "legitimate" power that would accept the realities of the postwar order and that would be interested in stability and in a
common approach to European security.[47] Furthermore, détente seemed
to be in the vital interests of the Federal Republic because one could never
be sure about the American commitment to Germany: "It is not Holy
Writ that U.S. forces will have to remain in Europe at present strength forever and ever."[48] Although no short-term alternative to the role of the
United States in Europe existed and although Western Europe could not
"substitute the balance of Soviet Union/United States" in the foreseeable
future,[49] the fear of unilateral American action, or the resurgence of neo-
isolationism was fueled by the constant discussions in Washington about
the size of the U.S. military commitment.

Although President Richard M. Nixon's nervous question in August
1971 "Is the United States going to continue to be a great nation, number
one?" was not uttered in public,[50] and Brandt would certainly have answered
in the affirmative,[51] an adaptation to new circumstances seemed highly
probable and timely. This was particularly true against the background of
American involvement in Vietnam and the financial strain caused by American overreach.[52] That Washington was prepared to pursue its own interests
without consulting its European allies was particularly evident when the
dollar was taken off the gold standard in August 1971.[53] Faced with Soviet
military superiority, Europeans tried to shape a post–Cold War order while

---

46 Schmidt, "Germany," 46, 50.
47 On perceptions of the Soviet Union, see Reiner Albert, "Das Sowjetunion-Bild in der sozialli-
     beralen Ostpolitik 1969–1975," *Tel Aviver Jahrbuch für deutsche Geschichte* 24 (1995): 299–326. Occa-
     sionally Brandt was not really sure whether this realism on the Soviet side would last. He warned of
     illusions when he met President Nixon in December 1971. Brandt, *Begegnungen,* 395.
48 Schmidt, "Germany," 43. See the notes by Brandt in June 1970: "US bleiben, aber reduzieren."
     WBA, BK 91.
49 Undated notes by Brandt before meeting Brezhnev on Sept. 16, 1971 (Notizen für Krim Septem-
     ber 1971). WBA, BK 92. See also two years later Bahr to Brandt, July 12, 1973: "Unmöglichkeit,
     dass ein vereinigtes Europa in Fragen der Sicherheit Amerika ersetzen könnte." WBA, Loses Mate-
     rial.
50 H. R. Haldeman, *The Haldeman Diaries: Inside the Nixon White House* (New York, 1994), 344 (Aug.
     13, 1971).
51 Brandt, *Begegnungen,* 379.
52 See Kunz's chapter in this book.
53 For Brandt's resentment, see his *Begegnungen,* 379, 387, 395.

the United States was still fully able and willing to commit to Europe.[54] Because the United States was now perceived as an indispensable but somewhat uncertain ally and because it was confronted with an even less predictable adversary in the East, the Federal Republic had no reasonable alternative to a course of cooperation and détente.[55]

From the German point of view, the ultimate success would have been an early reduction of armaments in Europe. Brandt did not rule out the possibility that détente might result in a change in Soviet military thinking. Reassured of its predominance in Eastern Europe and released from West German "revanchism," Soviet leadership might respond to economic pressures and reduce its military expenditures. Brandt, however, was under no illusions that such a turn might already have taken place since his military advisors reminded him of the ongoing buildup of Soviet arms. Therefore, Ostpolitik did not have the expected immediate response, and the enduring Soviet military threat remained a constant irritation.[56]

The Western approach to making the Soviet Union "more manageable" needed extra time. In this period of transition, economic considerations were "in ascendance in Soviet policymaking," but Soviet foreign policy

54 There was a consensus on this issue shared by, e.g., Brandt, Bahr, and Schmidt. Link, "Aussen- und Deutschlandpolitik," 177.

55 Richard Löwenthal, professor of political science and close to the SPD leadership, addressing a group of foreign policy experts of the SPD, Feb. 2, 1972, depicted the United States in a way that was typical for the SPD: "Das Bild über die internationalen Bedingungen deutscher Aussenpolitik wäre unvollständig, wenn ich nicht noch über eine Veränderung sprechen würde, die uns allen Sorge macht, nämlich das, was mit der Währungskrise in der westlichen Welt, mit der . . . Nixon-Ankündigung von August vorigen Jahres und dem darauf folgenden zeitweiligen Chaos in den innerwestlichen Beziehungen sichtbar geworden ist. Ich erwähne es, nicht weil es zu einer entscheidenden Veränderung der Kräfteverhältnisse geführt hat – das hat es zum Glück nicht getan, das westliche Bündnis hat diese Krise für den Augenblick überstanden– , aber weil es zeigt, dass gewisse ernste Gefahren in diesem Bündnis auch weiterhin bestehen. Das Erbe von Vietnam sind wir nicht los und werden es auch nicht automatisch los sein, wenn der letzte amerikanische Soldat nach Hause zurückgekehrt ist; denn dieses Erbe besteht nicht nur in den zeitweisen Verlusten der Amerikaner, in der zeitweisen militärischen Lähmung und in diplomatischen Schwächen, dieses Erbe besteht in der Veränderung der öffentlichen Meinung in den Vereinigten Staaten, in der Entstehung einer Grundstimmung, die im besten Fall eine Konzentration auf die inneren Probleme und im schlechtesten Fall eine Konzentration auf den brutalen Egoismus verlangt und die daher die Funktionsfähigkeit der Vereinigten Staaten im Rahmen der westlichen Bündnisse auf längere Sicht verringert. Das ist eine Situation, mit der wir leben müssen. Wir haben, mit anderen Worten, auch in der Zukunft im westlichen Bündnis Faktoren der Instabilität, die nicht von hierher kommt, die nicht von der Ostpolitik herkommt, die insbesondere von der amerikanischen Situation herkommt." AdsD, Selbmann papers, 146.

56 See, e.g., Brandt in the Bundestag, Feb. 23, 1972, or Jan. 18, 1973. *Verhandlungen des Deutschen Bundestags: Stenographische Berichte* 79 (1972): 9791–2; 81 (1973): 123. See also Bahr in Jan. 1975: "Wir müssen erwarten, dass die Sowjetunion und ihre Verbündeten militärisch einen entsprechenden Kurs verfolgen. Der komplizierte Prozess der Entspannung könnte für Jahre angehalten werden, wenn man statt Truppenverringerung und Abrüstung Truppenverstärkung und Aufrüstung betreibt." Paper given at an SPD conference on international affairs, Jan. 17–19, 1975. AdsD, SPD-Parteivorstand, Internationale Abteilung, 11296.

"remained a unique combination of state, military, and party dimensions, inherited from the previous historic period and resistant to outside pressure for change."[57] Although the Soviet leaders wanted to import Western technology and to benefit from economic cooperation with the West, they also wished to block reform of the Soviet system itself. The lines of communication from West to East influenced Soviet attitudes only marginally. Nevertheless, the concept of communication was crucial.

COMMUNICATION: COOPERATION AND
IDEOLOGICAL ANTAGONISM

Communication was a key notion in the language of détente. In 1963 Brandt had urged his listeners at Tutzing that "we need as many forms of communication as possible."[58] In a divided world, divided Europe, and divided Germany only a dialogue would achieve any progress. As Helmut Schmidt put it in 1970, only by exchanging different viewpoints and by looking for possible fields of cooperation could the ultimate goal – "healing of the rift that has divided Europe" – be achieved.[59] Both sides should acquire a better knowledge of the other instead of sticking to their old fixations on the enemy. Until this point, firsthand knowledge of the Soviet Union and its leader had been scarce, and most diplomatic contacts had been confined to exchange of long statements with little open discussion. Accordingly, when Bahr embarked on his first mission to Moscow in January 1970, he was not sure he could even initiate dialogue.[60]

For Brandt, the breakthrough came in 1971 when he met Brezhnev in the Crimea. Both discussed world politics and bilateral relations without any formal agenda. After the meeting, Brandt was convinced that the Soviet Union and the Federal Republic had entered a phase of normal relations between two independent states that naturally included both conflict and cooperation, the very essence of Ostpolitik and détente: "Both sides know where they agree, where a rapprochement is conceivable, and where they have differences."[61] Roughly two years of Ostpolitik had produced the first results, although Brandt was certainly aware that it would be difficult to overcome the Soviet habit of suspicion and its ignorance of the Western

57 Vladislav M. Zubok, "Unwrapping the Enigma: What Was Behind the Soviet Challenge in the 1960s?" in Diane B. Kunz, ed., *The Diplomacy of the Crucial Decade: American Foreign Relations During the 1960s* (New York, 1994), 173.
58 Brandt in Tutzing in 1963 (see note 8 to this chapter). *Dokumente,* 567.
59 Schmidt, "Germany," 46.
60 Author's interview with Bahr, June 12, 1992.
61 Notes taken by Brandt, Sept. 18, 1971. WBA, BK 92.

world.[62] In 1974, before a visit to Moscow, Schmidt pointed out that the Soviet leadership had little knowledge of Western countries and Western thinking, which made frequent contacts indispensable to prevent misperceptions.[63] One of the most important achievements of Ostpolitik was therefore its success in changing Soviet perceptions of the Federal Republic and the West and in encouraging Soviet leaders to broaden the scope of East-West relations.[64]

East-West communication comprised many different areas, such as the exchange of viewpoints on matters of common interests as well as on conflicts, academic and cultural exchange, trade relations – everything that was listed in the Helsinki Final Act of August 1975.[65] Trade relations proved to be the field in which East-West relations developed best.[66] Apart from pure economic self-interest, it was thought that trade relations would also have an impact on politics. Although the issue of world peace could not be left to business, trade relations might help to stabilize détente.[67] One scholar has observed that trade exchange broadened the basis of détente because both sides believed in it.[68] West Germany perceived itself as a trading country, and this outlook corresponded with the possibility of a slow, gradual change toward a more consumer-orientated economy in the Soviet Union.

Ostpolitik was coupled with the far-reaching expectation that the new channels of communication would not only ease the division of Germany and Europe but help bring about structural change in the East. Although Soviet hegemony was recognized, in an age of modern technology and new means of communications Moscow would no longer be able to control the dynamics of the emerging East-West relationship. For Brandt, more communication and the increased "normalization" between the two Germanys would ultimately "change the Warsaw Pact."[69]

62 During a meeting of the party executive of the SPD Brandt called it the "Westfremdheit" of the Soviets. AdsD, Parteivorstandsprotokolle, Sept. 14, 1970.
63 Notes for a press conference, Oct. 22, 1974. AdsD, HS 131.
64 Author's interview with Valentin Falin, Nov. 11, 1993.
65 Wilfried von Bredow, *Der KSZE-Prozess: Von der Zähmung zur Auflösung des Ost-West-Konflikts* (Darmstadt, 1992).
66 This was Bahr's assessment when looking back in 1975. See note 61 to this chapter.
67 See, e.g., Foreign Minister Scheel, May 18, 1972, *Bulletin des Presse- und Informationsamts der Bundesregierung*, no. 74 (1972): 1061–5; Chancellor Schmidt after his trip to Moscow in 1974, *Verhandlungen des Deutschen Bundestags* 90 (1974): 8529. See also Manfred Knapp, "Analyzing East-West Economic Relations During the Period 1945–1989," in Gustav Schmidt, ed., *Ost-West-Beziehungen: Konfrontation und Détente, 1945–1989*, 3 vols. (Bochum, 1995), 3:45.
68 Karl Kaiser during a meeting of a study group on East-West relations, Apr. 21, 1975. Deutsche Gesellschaft für Auswärtige Politik, Bonn. Protokolle der Studiengruppe für Ost-West-Beziehungen.
69 "Normalisierung verändert WP." Notes by Brandt when he prepared carefully for the meeting of the cabinet on June 7, 1970. The cabinet had to decide whether it should enter the final stage of the negotiations with Moscow or still wait. WBA, BK 91.

In the long run, the policy of détente proved to be profitable to the West, especially to the Federal Republic. From the outset, Ostpolitik disputed the Soviet view that the frontiers in Europe were unalterable forever because Bonn accepted the status quo only as a modus vivendi. "The Soviet goal is to legalize the status quo. Our goal is to overcome it. It is a real conflict of interest," as Bahr succinctly stated it in 1968.[70] Although Bahr would not say so in public, there is persuasive evidence that the architects of Ostpolitik had not only reconciliation with the Soviet Union in mind but also the peaceful transformation of the postwar order. Contrary to Kissinger's temporary pessimism, namely, that the Soviet Union might be the only winner,[71] Brandt and Bahr did not rule out the chance that the Soviet Union might be the loser, and ultimately be forced to accept peaceful change. As Bahr wrote to Kissinger in 1973, the expansion of trade with the East would produce frictions within the communist countries and necessarily contribute to their evolution.[72]

What would the Soviet reaction be? Would the Soviet leadership tolerate the effects of détente within its own sphere of influence? For the time being, the Soviet government felt self-assured. When the East German government became increasingly alarmed about the impact of communications on East Germany and the dangers of "social democratism" (*Sozialdemokratismus*), Brezhnev advised East German leader Walter Ulbricht that the whole problem should be treated as a matter of relations between two sovereign states.[73] It seemed obvious that Brezhnev was unaware of the new dimensions of communication or he underestimated the implications when he tried to reduce those new elements in East-West relations to the level of government interactions.

The de-ideologization of East-West relations was critical to the process of détente, and both sides agreed to confine ideological questions to the domestic sphere. Only if the East-West conflict could be reduced to a "normal" power conflict was there chance for cooperation. For this goal, a price had to be paid by both sides. Moscow had to bury its hopes for the collapse of capitalism,[74] and the expansion of the socialist camp, not to mention world revolution. The West had to accept the Pax Sovietica in Eastern

---

70 Memorandum by Bahr, Oct. 1, 1968, Vogtmeier, *Bahr,* 129.
71 Kissinger, *White House Years,* 408–10, 533.
72 Bahr to Kissinger, Apr. 14, 1973: "Eine systematische, aber nicht wahllose Erweiterung der wirtschaftlichen Ost-West-Beziehungen wird die Widersprüche in den kommunistisch regierten Ländern steigern und zu weiteren Modifikationen des Systems beitragen." Quoted in Vogtmeier, *Bahr,* 177.
73 Meeting of the Warsaw Pact States, Dec. 2, 1970. SAPMO-BArch, Zentrales Parteiarchiv, Büro Ulbricht, J IV 2/202/270.
74 However, Soviet economists interpreted symptoms of crisis and change like the students' movement or the dissolution of the Bretton Woods system as a proof of the historical decline of capital-

Europe. Hence the concentration on interstate relations and not on support for the human rights movements in Eastern Europe.[75] Liberalization in the East could not be achieved by declarations or demands on behalf of high Western principles or by direct pressure on the Soviet government, but through gradual change within Eastern societies as a result of the dynamics of communication instigated by the policy of détente.

Détente in international affairs ran parallel to anticommunism in domestic affairs. Ostpolitik did not alter the strictly anticommunist stance of the SPD, and the leadership of the SPD did not ignore or underestimate possible communist initiatives for closer cooperation in Western Europe and tried to keep such contacts under tight control. The SPD was unwilling to participate in conferences or campaigns that were organized by communists.[76] When the Soviet ambassador to West Germany, for example, inquired in 1970 about the so-called Löwenthal paper, which stressed the differences between Social Democrats and Communists, he was told that Ostpolitik left the ideological conflict unchanged.[77] Whereas good relations between the Federal Republic and the Soviet Union were crucial, one had to be careful as far as relations with political parties, youth organizations, or trade unions were concerned. Soviet politicians would be welcomed as long as they represented the state. They were rejected, however, when they wanted to organize any unity of action on the nongovernmental level.[78]

NATIONAL INTERST: STATUS QUO AND PEACEFUL CHANGE

Ostpolitik was a highly controversial issue in West German politics, as had been Adenauer's "Westpolitik" in the 1950s. In both cases, the debate centered on the question of national unity and the self-determination of the

ism. Richard B. Day, *Cold War Capitalism: The View from Moscow, 1945–1975* (Armonk, N.Y., 1995), 248–76.

75 For a criticism of this consequence of Ostpolitik, and of its later stages in particular, see Timothy Garton Ash, *In Europe's Name: Germany and the Divided Continent* (London, 1993).

76 Brandt to Eugen Kogon, a well-known professor of political science, who was in favor of closer contacts with the communists, Sept. 28, 1970: "Ich habe nichts gegen Diskussionen, an denen in angemessener Form auch Kommunisten teilnehmen. Aber es ist wichtig, dass a) die Auseinandersetzungen über den Vertrag vom 12. August nicht unnötig belastet werden und b) eine aktive Friedenspolitik nicht als Verwischung der grundsätzlichen Positionen in Fragen der freiheitlichen Demokratie verstanden werden darf." WBA, Bk 11.

77 Meeting of Hans Jürgen Wischnewski and others with Ambassador Zarapkin, Oct. 31, 1970. WBA, Parteivorsitzender: Verbindungen mit Referaten in der SPD, 59.

78 Wehner to the Soviet journalist Naumow, Dec. 19, 1971, and to Hans Eberhard Dingels, head of the Abteilung für Internationale Beziehungen in der SPD, Dec. 19, 1971. AdsD, Selbmann papers 28. This was a reaction to the Soviet Committee for European Security, founded in 1971. Analogous committees were formed by Communist parties in West European countries. John van Oudenaren, *Détente in Europe: The Soviet Union and the West Since 1953* (Durham, N.C., 1991), 313.

German people. Adenauer's priority was clear. Since national unity could not be achieved, the security of the Federal Republic had to come first. The only way to accomplish this goal was through full integration into the West. Therefore, national unity had to wait.[79] Although West German politicians demanded reunification in almost every political statement they made, there was no active policy of unification. The SPD approved of this policy of integration with the West only in 1960 and accepted the fact that the German question, albeit still regarded as open, was not an operational goal. In the 1960s, a majority of West Germans started to identify with the Federal Republic, based on the success story of the "economic miracle" and the country's political stability. Earlier than the Christian Democrats, the SPD and the FDP decided to accept the existing situation and adapt their language to the political realities by differentiating between the interests of the nation, which was divided into two states, and the interests of the two separate states. Ostpolitik should serve both the interests of the Federal Republic and the interests of the German nation.

After 1969 the SPD/FDP government continued to define the interests of the Federal Republic as being identical with European and transatlantic ones. Security from the Soviet threat, economic growth, liberal access to world markets, political stability of the Western democracies – these were the common goals of all members of the Western community. Apart from the long-term goal of unification, there was no West German interest not shared by others. Ostpolitik never aimed at exclusive bilateral relations with the Soviet Union in order to pursue special interests. The one possible exception concerned trade relations, in which a normal competition among Western countries on the Soviet "market" ensued.[80] Whereas it remained to be seen whether the Soviet Union was actually a promising market, the enormous Soviet interest in economic and technological cooperation coincided with the smaller but sufficient interest of some West German industries.[81] The Federal Republic quickly became the USSR's largest Western

79 See the references in note 1 to this chapter.
80 For a comparison of West German and U.S. trade relations with the Soviet Union, see Hélène Seppain, *Contrasting U.S. and German Attitudes to Soviet Trade, 1917–91* (Houndsmills, 1992), 179–260.
81 Angela Stent, *From Embargo to Ostpolitik: The Political Economy of West German-Soviet Relations, 1955–1980* (Cambridge, 1981), 154–78; Volker R. Berghahn, "Lowering Soviet Expectations: West German Industry and Osthandel During the Brandt Era," in Volker R. Berghahn, ed., *Quest for Economic Empire: European Strategies of German Big Business in the Twentieth Century* (Providence, R.I., 1996), 145–57. Illuminating on different attitudes in the West German business community toward Ostpolitik and Osthandel are Volker R. Berghahn and Paul J. Friedrich, *Otto A. Friedrich, ein politischer Unternehmer: Sein Leben und seine Zeit, 1902–1975* (Frankfurt am Main, 1993), 351–8; Otto Wolff von Amerongen, *Der Weg nach Osten: Vierzig Jahre Brückenbau für die deutsche Wirtschaft* (Munich, 1992), 114–35. On the role of a German bank, see Lothar Gall et al., *Die Deutsche Bank, 1870–1995* (Munich, 1995), 662–6. See also F. Wilhelm Christians, *Wege nach Russland: Bankier im Spannungsfeld zwischen Ost und West* (Hamburg, 1990).

trading partner. Although trade with Eastern European countries formed only a small percentage of total West German trade, the Eastern bloc had potential, not only with respect to raw materials and energy supplies but also as a future market, which could help secure jobs in the Federal Republic.[82]

Although the interests of the Federal Republic and its Western allies were not identical, they were compatible. However, Ostpolitik brought about a change in style. Brandt maintained that he was the chancellor not of a defeated but of a liberated Germany. The Federal Republic was not yet a fully sovereign state and had to operate within the constraints derived from the rights of the Four Powers. But within these limits it wanted to take initiatives of its own.[83] The Federal Republic wished to be treated as an equal partner that could look after its interests independently.[84] Ostpolitik was an area where this ability was demonstrated, always in accordance with the general Western course of détente but, as Brandt underscored in his memoirs, more than just echoing American initiatives.[85] Although Brandt warned against overrating the role of the Federal Republic as an independent actor in East-West relations, he was convinced that Bonn should not underestimate itself "as a partner of the Soviet Union" either.[86]

A new style in its relationship with its allies, including the United States, was vital for the SPD/FDP government. Brandt wanted the Federal Republic to be "more equal,"[87] and Foreign Minister Scheel spoke of "maturity."[88] Defense Minister Schmidt proudly reminded his SPD colleagues in the Bundestag that the operational phase of Ostpolitik had started even before President Nixon had announced détente.[89]

Ostpolitik signaled a new self-confidence of the West German foreign policy establishment. Thanks to the success of Ostpolitik, the Federal Republic seemed to have reentered world politics.[90] Looking back in 1975,

82 This factor is mentioned by Brandt, *Begegnungen*, 223. Brandt's view was shared by others. See, e.g., Ernst Wolf Mommsen, chairman of the board of directors of Krupp in Essen, to Helmut Schmidt, Mar. 7, 1975. AdsD, HS 6193.
83 In retrospect Brandt and Kissinger agreed on this point; see Brandt, *Erinnerungen*, 189; Kissinger, *White House Years*, 411, 530.
84 Brandt, *Erinnerungen*, 170, 186–7.
85 Ibid., 190.
86 Brandt addressing the parliamentary party of the SPD, Mar. 4, 1969. AdsD, SPD-Fraktion, 5. WP, 119.
87 Brandt, *Erinnerungen*, 189.
88 At a meeting of the FDP Bundeshauptausschuss, Sept. 5, 1970. Archiv des Deutschen Liberalismus, Gummersbach (hereafter ADL), A12/92.
89 Schmidt at a meeting of the SPD-faction of the Bundestag, Dec. 14, 1971. AdsD, SPD-Fraktion, 6. WP, 81. Schmidt referred to Nixon's report on American foreign policy submitted to Congress in February 1970.
90 At least this was the view of Foreign Minister Scheel when addressing the party convention of the FDP, Oct. 23, 1972. ADL, A1/463.

Helmut Schmidt concluded that Ostpolitik had increased the worldwide
trust in West German politics and enhanced the capability of West Germans in international affairs.[91] Whereas the West German government was
hoping that the German part of "double containment" had become obsolete,[92] old fears of a resurgent German nationalism were much stronger
than the West German political elite was prepared to concede, because
many observers in the West worried about the course of German Ostpolitik.[93]

However, these apprehensions did not really have a grave impact on
Germany's relations with its Western allies. Governments in the East and
the West welcomed the acceptance of the European status quo by the Federal Government, because it turned out that the German question had not
become a matter of operational policy. At the same time, the SPD/FDP
government insisted on the principle of peaceful change. Frontiers were
declared "inviolable" but not "unalterable." As a result, the unification of
the two German states was left off the agenda, but it was not ruled out
altogether. Time and again, the government in Bonn stressed that unification by peaceful means must remain a possibility.[94] In the short term, Ostpolitik aimed at the improvement of security in Europe by respecting the
territorial status quo for the foreseeable future. But in the long run there
was an option for its revision. In 1973 Brandt did not hesitate to repeat
what he had said ten years earlier at Tutzing: "To accept the status quo
would ultimately provide the means that would lead to changes in the existing situation."[95]

91 Speech in the Bundestag, July 25, 1975. *Verhandlungen des Deutschen Bundestags* 94 (1975): 12827.
92 Wolfram F. Hanrieder, "Deutschland und die USA: Partner im transatlantischen Bündnis der
    Nachkriegsära," in Jürgen Elvert and Michael Salewski, eds., *Deutschland und der Westen im 19. und
    20. Jahrhundert*, pt. 1: *Transatlantische Beziehungen* (Stuttgart, 1993), 131. See also Hanrieder, *Deutsch-
    land*, 25–30.
93 On Kissinger's apprehension of a revival of German nationalism, see his *White House Years*, 409–11,
    529–30. On the whole, however, the positive image of the Federal Republic being a loyal and
    trustworthy partner of the West made progress in the United States. See Ernest May, "Das nationale
    Interesse der Vereinigten Staaten und die deutsche Frage, 1966–1972," in Gottfried Niedhart, Detlef
    Junker, and Michael W. Richter, eds., *Deutschland in Europa: Nationale Interessen und internationale
    Ordnung im 20. Jahrhundert* (Mannheim, 1997), 275. On the Johnson administration and its percep-
    tions of the Germans, see Costigliola, "Johnson," 173–9, 189–90; on France, see Georges Henri
    Soutou, "L'attitude de Georges Pompidou face à l'Allemagne," in Association Georges Pompidou,
    ed., *Georges Pompidou et l'Europe* (Brussels, 1995), 267–313; on Great Britain, see Brian White,
    Britain, Détente and Changing East-West Relations (London, 1992).
94 See, e.g., Brandt to Olof Palme, June 15, 1970; Brandt to Brezhnev, Apr. 24, 1973. WBA, BK 58.
95 In 1973, Günter Gaus, Staatssekretär in the Bundeskanzleramt, drafted a speech for Brandt with the
    following paragraph: "Die Anerkennung des Status quo, wie sie durch unsere vertraglich
    zugesicherte Respektierung der europäischen Grenzen erfolgt ist, schafft auf sehr lange Zeit gese-
    hen Möglichkeiten, den Status quo zu verändern. Europa wird sich Schritt um Schritt – aber wirk-
    lich nur Schritt um Schritt – verändern, weil in seinen zwischenstaatlichen Beziehungen zwischen
    West und Ost die ersten Ansätze einer Friedensordnung unter den Staaten geschaffen worden sind."
    Brandt sent it to Helmut Schmidt for approval, Sept. 7, 1973. AdsD, HS 5814.

6

China Under Siege

Escaping the Dangers of 1968

NANCY BERNKOPF TUCKER

For China, 1968 became a turning point – a year whose significance grew
as its legacy transformed both foreign and domestic affairs. Before the events
of that year, China endured international isolation and domestic turmoil.
To the north it faced mounting tensions with former allies in the Soviet
Union while to the south U.S. escalation of the war in Vietnam jeopardized security. At the United Nations, China remained a pariah, and across
the Taiwan Strait it continued to confront a rump regime that challenged
its legitimacy and sought to bring it down. Nevertheless, Mao Zedong had
believed that the international environment, though hostile, did not pose
any immediate danger to the survival of the People's Republic. Therefore,
he could take advantage of China's detachment from the world to deal
with pressing internal problems that tormented him. Abandoning his party
and his government to revolution, Mao sought to arrest the spread of subversive values and institutions.

But 1968 refocused the energies of the nation and most of its leaders.
The world, which Mao had shunned, intruded upon China's domestic
agenda. Not only did the chaos of the Great Proletarian Cultural Revolution need to be stemmed so that China would not be torn apart in civil
war, but some equilibrium had to be recovered so that Beijing could defend
itself against external enemies. Even though years of upheaval still lay ahead,
the choices made in 1968 served to sustain a unified nation and made possible the eventual re-creation of a functioning society.

Finally, during 1968, China's external enemies changed shape, modify-
ing the parameters of the Cold War. The United States, which had seemed

I thank Allen S. Whiting, Warren I. Cohen, Carole Fink, Detlef Junker, and Philipp Gassert, as well as
other members of the 1968 "team," for reading this chapter critically and providing thoughtful suggestions for improvement.

so formidable an antagonist, failed to vanquish a primitive foe during the Vietcong Tet Offensive and clearly would not seek to take the war across the Chinese frontier. On the other hand, the Soviet Union, with which frictions had been fierce but manageable, now became far more menacing. Moscow challenged the sovereignty of states in the communist bloc, forcing China's leaders to think the unthinkable and seek protection from their erstwhile adversary in Washington.

The event that spurred China's reevaluation of its place in the world occurred in Eastern Europe. On August 21, 1968, Soviet tanks rolled into Prague crushing a blossoming movement for the liberalization of Czechoslovakia's political and economic systems. The changes, having compromised the Czechoslovak communist leaders, threatened also to destabilize ruling parties elsewhere in Eastern Europe. Despite Prague's protestations of continued adherence to the Warsaw Pact, moreover, Czechoslovakia's new direction rendered its loyalty questionable, stirring anxieties about bloc security among Soviet military leaders.[1]

Finding the developments of the Prague Spring increasingly intolerable, Moscow ruthlessly put an end to the reform experiment. Soviet armed forces and political cadres swept away the new order, demonstrating that communist regimes could no more be toppled by internal sabotage than by external assault. Lest anyone miss the message, Leonid Brezhnev followed the invasion with a harsh pronouncement to the Polish United Workers' Congress in November that subsequently became known as the Brezhnev Doctrine. In it he made clear that the Soviet Union had the right, indeed the obligation, to use whatever means necessary to restore order and preserve socialism in communist countries.[2]

Chinese communist authorities, initially sympathetic to the ideological dilemma faced by Brezhnev, found Moscow's remedy for Czech experimentation unacceptable. Ironically China's ties to the states of Eastern Europe, with the exception of Albania, had been seriously attenuated for several years because of the Sino-Soviet split. Finding proximity to Soviet power more persuasive than Chinese denunciations of Moscow's revision-

1 Martin Malia, *The Soviet Tragedy: A History of Socialism in Russia, 1917–1991* (New York, 1994), 390–5. Malia argues that military loyalty was relatively unimportant to the Soviets, citing the example of Romania which essentially stopped participating in Warsaw Pact activities but avoided incurring Moscow's wrath by enforcing a strict communist system internally. In contrast Harry Gelman emphasizes the significance of the security issue. Harry Gelman, *The Brezhnev Politburo and the Decline of Détente* (Ithaca, N.Y., 1984), 99. See also Mark Kramer, "The Prague Spring and the Soviet Invasion of Czechoslovakia: New Interpretations," *Cold War International History Project Bulletin* 3 (fall 1993): 8–10, and Mark Kramer's chapter in this book.
2 "The Brezhnev Doctrine," *Problems of Communism* 17 (Nov.–Dec. 1968): 25.

ism and autocracy, governments in the area minimized contacts with Beijing.[3] China, therefore, had no particular liking for or relationship with the regime of Alexander Dubček that Brezhnev destroyed. In fact, Beijing had publicly decried Czech threats to the sanctity of communist party rule.[4] But for the Russians to crush a socialist government and declare that Moscow had the right to interfere militarily in the internal affairs of a communist state when the Soviet Union determined that socialist principles had been violated posed a grievous and acute threat to China. Beijing denounced Moscow's actions as "fascist banditry."[5]

Chinese condemnation arose directly from the conclusion that Brezhnev meant to threaten China as much as any state in Eastern Europe. And it was this realization that riveted Chinese attention to domestic and foreign policies, which had rendered China vulnerable enough in 1968 to fear Soviet invasion. Suddenly national survival demanded not just a stronger and better prepared military, but also a unified populace and powerful foreign friends.

The Sino-Soviet rift, which had developed in the 1950s and burst into public view early in the 1960s, had its roots in disputes over ideology, territory, history, and sovereignty. China challenged Soviet pursuit of détente with the West along with its alleged loss of interest in national liberation struggles. Rather than as a champion of the oppressed, the Chinese saw Moscow as attempting to compromise China's independence by insisting on the creation of a joint naval fleet based in Chinese ports and the establishment of radar facilities on Chinese soil. Moscow, in turn, not trusting in Chinese prudence, unilaterally rescinded promises to help Beijing develop a nuclear weapons capability.[6] Further, Moscow did not hide its contempt for Mao's very unorthodox economic innovations and withdrew its technical advisors abruptly in 1960, plunging Chinese modernization programs into disarray. Soviet leaders made absolutely clear their belief that

---

3 Vladimir Sobell, "The Reconciliation Between China and Eastern Europe," *Washington Quarterly* 10 (spring 1987): 100; Ming Chen, "Sino-East European Relations," in Hao Yufan and Huan Guocang, eds., *The Chinese View of the World* (New York, 1989), 263–5.

4 In 1956 China had similarly drawn a line between permissible internal experimentation carried out by the Communist Party, as in Poland, and change which undermined party control, as in Hungary. G. F. Hudson, Richard Lowenthal, and Roderick MacFarquhar, *The Sino-Soviet Dispute* (London, 1961), 2–4.

5 Thomas M. Gottlieb, *Chinese Foreign Policy Factionalism and the Origins of the Strategic Triangle*, Rand R-1902-NA, Nov. 1977, 115–18; Roger Glenn Brown, "Chinese Politics and American Policy: A New Look at the Triangle," *Foreign Policy* 23 (summer 1976): 3–23; O. B. Borisov and B. T. Koloskov, *Soviet-Chinese Relations, 1945–1970* (Bloomington, Ind., 1975), 219–25, 239–42, 322–8.

6 Zhang Shu Guang, *Deterrence and Strategic Culture: Chinese-American Confrontations, 1949–1958* (Ithaca, N.Y., 1992), 231–4; John W. Lewis and Xue Litai, *China Builds the Bomb* (Stanford, Calif., 1988), 60–5.

Maoist additions to the basic tenets of Marxism-Leninism, particularly claims that China would skip whole stages of development and soon overtake the Soviet Union, were ludicrous.[7]

Once the split had progressed to the point that party representatives began denouncing one another at communist bloc fora, compromises on issues such as border demarcation became progressively harder to reach. In 1962, for instance, Khrushchev embarrassed Mao by denouncing Chinese greed and cowardice in allowing foreign powers to retain control of Hong Kong and Macao. Mao's reply brushed aside the minor incursions by Britain and Portugal, focusing instead on Russia's far more flagrant imperialism in areas such as Mongolia and Xinjiang. A series of minor military incidents along the extended frontier between the Soviet Union and China, beginning in 1959, escalated tensions appreciably.[8] So too did Moscow's decision in 1966 to redeploy troops from Europe to the Far East where they could only be seen as a threat to China.

Thus the Sino-Soviet split by 1968 no longer could safely be dismissed as a rhetorical exercise. In the years since John F. Kennedy declared the dispute to be nothing more than a disagreement over how to bury the United States, the issues had become clearly defined and deeply entrenched. Efforts to resolve discord through negotiation in the wake of Khrushchev's ouster, on the assumption that personality had been a fundamental contributing force, failed in November 1964 and February 1965. Reportedly Marshal Rodion Malinovsky, the Soviet defense minister, suggested to Zhou Enlai that the Chinese ought to oust Mao just as the Russians had rid themselves of Khrushchev, which proved a less than auspicious way to facilitate a reconciliation. When Aleksei Kosygin later traveled to China at the behest of the Politburo "China Lobby" he found the gap unbridgeable.[9]

The failure had momentous implications both for the Sino-Soviet standoff and Soviet foreign and defense policies generally. Moscow's racist fears that hordes of yellow men would pour across the poorly defended far eastern border escalated with Chinese threats, such as Mao's declaration to a group of Japanese journalists in 1964, that China had "not yet presented the bill" for land seizures dating back to the Tsarist period. Consequently

---

7 Donald Zagoria, *The Sino-Soviet Conflict, 1956–61* (New York, 1966), 77–141; Steven M. Goldstein, "Nationalism and Internationalism: Sino-Soviet Relations," in Thomas W. Robinson and David Shambaugh, eds., *Chinese Foreign Policy: Theory and Practice* (Oxford, 1994), 224–48.

8 See, e.g., Dennis J. Doolin, *Territorial Claims in the Sino-Soviet Conflict* (Stanford, Calif., 1965).

9 Harvey W. Nelsen, *Power and Insecurity: Beijing, Moscow, and Washington, 1949–1988* (Boulder, Colo., 1989), 63; Vladislav M. Zubok, "Unwrapping the Enigma: What Was Behind the Soviet Challenge in the 1960s?" in Diane B. Kunz, ed., *The Diplomacy of the Crucial Decade: American Foreign Relations During the 1960s* (New York, 1994), 166.

Brezhnev initiated a significant expansion of military capabilities in Asia.[10] After 1965 defense against China consumed between one-seventh and one-ninth of all Soviet military resources. This decision, moreover, gave impetus to a more basic Soviet policy shift away from Khrushchev's concentration on strategic weaponry to a traditional more-is-better investment in conventional forces which Brezhnev found useful in his power rivalry with Kosygin and Nicholai Podgornyi and as insurance against the escalating American involvement in Vietnam. Soviet foreign policy generally grew more militarized, causing profound distress to the United States and its Western allies.[11]

For China, the expansion of Soviet coercive power in the Far East had the effect by 1968 of rendering an invasion plausible. Worried Chinese leaders had remarked upon the influx of Soviet soldiers and the multiplication of border incidents throughout the previous year. In July 1968 Soviet military exercises on the Sino-Mongolian border led to redeployment of troops from Fujian to the north.[12] Nevertheless, given China's limited intelligence-gathering capabilities, the dimensions of the Soviet military buildup along the Chinese border became clear only after Czechoslovakia when the Chinese focused their attention more directly upon assessing the threat.[13] In September 1968, for the first time, China publicly protested Soviet overflights of border territory, which had, in fact, been going on for some time.[14] Should the Soviets decide to attack, China's leaders knew, their success would be facilitated both by knowledge of large sectors of border terrain, from having fought there in the past against both Chinese and Japanese troops, as well as by their "detailed information on the performance of virtually all Chinese weapons systems."[15]

---

10 Arkady N. Shevchenko, *Breaking with Moscow* (New York, 1985), 164–5; Harrison E. Salisbury, *War Between Russia and China* (New York, 1969), 31–5; Edward E. Rice, *Mao's War* (Berkeley, Calif., 1972), 216.

11 Gelman, *Brezhnev Politburo*, 38–41, 80–1, 92–6; Seweryn Bialer, "The Soviet Union and the West: Security and Foreign Policy," in Bialer and Michael Mandelbaum, eds., *Gorbachev's Russia and American Foreign Policy* (Boulder, Colo., 1988), 461–2; Rajan Menon, *Soviet Power and the Third World* (New Haven, Conn., 1986), 99.

12 Melvin Gurtov and Hwang Byong-Moo, *China Under Threat: The Politics of Strategy and Diplomacy* (Baltimore, 1980), 212–13, 226.

13 Allen S. Whiting, *The Chinese Calculus of Deterrence* (Ann Arbor, Mich., 1975), 237–8. Gottlieb suggests there was also a political motive for the military to underemphasize the Soviet buildup, i.e., they wanted to focus on the U.S. threat. Gottlieb, *Chinese Foreign Policy Factionalism*, viii.

14 CIA #0360/69, Weekly Summary, Mar. 7, 1969, DDRS (Declassified Documents Reference Service) (1988), fiche 78 #1235.

15 Jonathan D. Pollack, "The Opening to America," in Roderick MacFarquhar and John K. Fairbank, eds., *The Cambridge History of China*, vol. 15: *The People's Republic of China*, pt. 2: *Revolutions Within the Chinese Revolution, 1966–1982* (New York, 1991), 408.

The possibility that Brezhnev meant his Czech adventure as a practice run for an effort to strip China of its antagonistic leadership, although small, seemed more credible in Beijing because of China's vulnerability in 1968.[16] The Great Proletarian Cultural Revolution had by then been under way for more than two years and had undermined China's political institutions, degraded its national defenses, and frayed the social fabric.[17] The chaos disrupted the major cities where national industry neared collapse and eroded control in rural areas creating food shortages that imperiled significant portions of the population.[18] Even in the sensitive domain of weapons manufacture, turmoil had disrupted production, leaving the armed forces short of guns and bullets.[19] But the political movement made China a target not just by weakening it. The Cultural Revolution also comprised a provocation to the Soviets since one of its main objectives was to root out Soviet-style revisionism in China.

Mao Zedong originally mounted the Cultural Revolution as a remedy for a series of challenges to his authority and the regime he had brought into being in 1949. Mao sought to triumph in a power struggle being waged around him, to rectify the thoughts and practices of a huge and increasingly unprincipled bureaucracy, and to expose the next generation to a revolutionary experience that would purify their thoughts and actions. The source of Mao's distress lay in the failure of his Great Leap Forward experiment, launched in 1958, in which he had departed from the Soviet model of development and tried through mass mobilization to expand the economy rapidly. Instead of accelerated growth the result proved to be a disastrous drop in industrial production and a famine so widespread and intense that 30 million people died, another 30 million projected births

16 Soviet "journalist" and probable agent of the KGB Victor Louis published a column in the *London Evening News* entitled "Will Russian Rockets Czech-mate China?" which argued that the Brezhnev Doctrine could easily be applied to China. Su Chi, "Soviet Image of and Policy Toward China, 1969–1979," Ph.D. diss., Columbia University, 1984, 115–16. Also Moscow Radio broadcast in Mandarin the Soviet conclusion that the GPCR had seriously undermined China's political, economic, and military systems. Foreign Broadcast Information Service (hereafter FBIS), June 28, 1968, A15–16.

17 CIA Intelligence Memorandum "The Spread of Lawlessness in Communist China," July 19, 1968, National Security File (hereafter NSF) Country Files, China vol. XII, Bx 242 and 243, Lyndon Baines Johnson Library Archives, Austin, Texas (hereafter LBJL).

18 CIA Intelligence Memorandum "Communist China: Foreign Trade 1967 and Prospects for 1968," May 1968, NSF Country Files, China vol. XII, Bx 242 and 243, LBJL; Memo Al Jenkins to Walt Rostow, July 22, 1968, NSF Country Files, China vol. XIII, Bx 243, LBJL; Memo Marshall Wright to Rostow, July 25, 1968, enclosing study by State Department "Political Implications of Communist China's Deteriorating Economy," NSF Country File China vol. XIII, Bx 243, LBJL; CIA Intelligence Memorandum, "Current Developments in Chinese Communist Agriculture," Aug. 1968, NSF Country Files, China vol. XIII, Bx 243, LBJL.

19 Gurtov and Hwang, *China Under Threat*, 187, 193, 197–8.

never occurred, while peasants in some areas resorted to cannibalism to survive. Reluctant to acknowledge responsibility, Mao objected when more pragmatic figures in the party leadership attempted to resuscitate the economy using mechanisms such as material incentives, technical expertise, and a measure of agricultural privatization.[20] As his biographer Stuart Schram has suggested, "Mao tended increasingly to make loyalty to himself the touchstone of authentically 'proletarian' ideas and policies; the more he encountered resistance the more extreme his stance became. He crippled economic recovery by persisting in policies he knew to be counterproductive, and savaged the ranks of the party that had put him in power on the pretext that it had become bureaucratic and revisionist."[21]

Further, Mao saw the turn to moderation as introducing trends he believed had undermined Soviet communism, causing Moscow's leaders to mouth the slogans of socialism but practice capitalism and imperialism. Therefore, Mao lashed out at his heir presumptive and on October 31, 1968, deposed Liu Shaoqi, whom he had come to see as "China's Khrushchev," for his alleged collusion with the Soviets and his dangerously revisionist policies. But the solution lay not just with changing the leadership. Mao felt he had to purge the entire nation of the corrosive effects of mounting inequality, self-interest, hierarchy, and dissent.

His chosen instrument, however, proved inadequate and unwieldy even for the great helmsman. Mao called upon the young people, primarily high school and college students, to become Red Guards and wage a campaign against resurgent capitalism. In so doing he hoped to give China's youth an inspirational experience comparable to that which he and his closest comrades had experienced on the Long March or in Yenan during World War II. Mao anticipated neither the factionalism, competition, nor terror that his Red Guards would evoke, but he also appeared little troubled by their violence and destructiveness. That they brutalized and humiliated their parents, ravaged China's ancient culture and traditions, and dismantled both the party and government served Mao's purposes in showing his opponents the error of their ways.[22]

---

20 Kenneth Lieberthal, *Governing China: From Revolution Through Reform* (New York, 1995), 102–11; Jasper Becker, *Hungry Ghosts: China's Secret Famine* (London, 1996).

21 Stuart Schram, "Mao Zedong a Hundred Years On: The Legacy of a Ruler," *China Quarterly* 137 (Mar. 1994): 134.

22 On the turbulence of the GPCR, there are many testimonials including Chang Jung, *Wild Swans* (New York, 1991); Nien Cheng, *Life and Death in Shanghai* (New York, 1987); and Li Zhisui, *The Private Life of Chairman Mao* (New York, 1994). In his controversial book, Dr. Li provides conflicting evidence regarding how much Mao knew about what actually was being done by the Red Guards. Lynn T. White has attempted to account for Mao's ability to engender so much violence in

Radicalism in foreign relations similarly did not dismay Mao. Cultural Revolution principles called upon the diplomatic corps to pursue China's revolutionary goals zealously, and so on two occasions in 1967 Red Guards seized the Foreign Ministry, rifling classified records and forcing Foreign Minister Chen Yi to deliver a self-criticism.[23] Beijing withdrew all but one of its ambassadors for political scrutiny and indoctrination, and in their absence, through much of 1968, Chinese embassies crudely attempted to foist Cultural Revolution propaganda on host countries.[24] At home and abroad demonstrations against, and sometimes attacks on, foreign representatives occurred, including those from fraternal communist governments.[25]

In the streets of Beijing and Moscow violence against the Soviet Union and China, respectively, became so intense that officials suspended diplomatic relations.[26] Those Chinese leaders who had continued to cling to the hope of resolving the Sino-Soviet dispute had little choice but gradually to give up that illusion. On the contrary, Moscow grew increasingly alarmed at Chinese irresponsibility. Rather than anticipating reconciliation, Moscow had to contend with the fact that in October 1966 Beijing had tested a nuclear device mounted on a missile, which for the first time gave China the capability of incinerating some Soviet cities.[27]

Policies of Chaos: The Organizational Causes of Violence in China's Cultural Revolution (Princeton, N.J., 1989).

23 Ishwer C. Ohja, *Chinese Foreign Policy in an Age of Transition* (Boston, 1969), 228–30; Melvin Gurtov, "The Foreign Ministry and Foreign Affairs During the Cultural Revolution," *China Quarterly* 40 (Oct.–Dec. 1969): 65–102; Xue Mouhong and Pei Jianzhang, eds., *Diplomacy of Contemporary China [Dangdai Zhongguo waijiao]* (Hong Kong, 1990), 258–61. Zhou Enlai worried about the negative image China was earning and insisted to Afro-Asian representatives in Beijing that the Chinese government had attempted to prevent the burning of the British Embassy in 1967 but unruly Red Guards had ignored orders. CIA Intelligence Information Cable, Jan. 15, 1968, NSF Country File, China vol. XII, Bx 242 and 243, LBJL

24 Peter Van Ness, *Revolution and Chinese Foreign Policy* (Berkeley, Calif., 1971), 216–17, 237. *Renmin Ribao* on May 27 praised Western demonstrators who "dared to look down on the law and bayonet of the reactionary ruling cliques, showed no fear of suppression, persisted in their heroic struggle, and demonstrated a lively, revolutionary spirit." Quoted in Robert V. Daniels, *Year of the Heroic Guerrilla: World Revolution and Counterrevolution in 1968* (New York, 1989), 184. In September 1968 a lengthy directive from the Foreign Minister attempted to correct the most egregious and embarrassing behavior of Chinese diplomats overseas. CIA Intelligence Information Cable, Sept. 19, 1968, NSF Country File, China vol. XIII, Bx 243, LBJL.

25 China also applauded French student-worker anti–Vietnam War demonstrations, taking credit for the supposed influence of Mao Zedong's thought upon the strikers. CIA Intelligence Memorandum #0588/68, "France's Student-Labor Crisis: Causes and Consequences," May 25, 1968, 12–13, DDRS (1987), fiche 120 #1813; Frank Costigliola, *France and the United States: The Cold Alliance Since World War II* (New York, 1992), 154–9.

26 Thomas W. Robinson, "Chou En-lai and the Cultural Revolution," in Robinson, ed., *The Cultural Revolution in China* (Berkeley, Calif., 1971), 266–7; Gurtov and Hwang, *China Under Threat*, 203–5, 216–17; Christopher Andrew and Oleg Gordievsky, *KGB: The Inside Story* (New York, 1990), 492.

27 Gordon H. Chang, *Friends and Enemies: The United States, China, and the Soviet Union, 1948–1972* (Stanford, Calif., 1990), 276–7, 279.

Brutality against foreigners, however, never reached the heights of savagery that the Chinese inflicted upon one another. During the spring of 1968, Red Guard factions raided military arms depots, even along the frontier in Xinjiang, and stole guns from supply trains en route to Vietnam in order to turn them upon other Red Guards. The carnage sent trussed and headless bodies floating down the Pearl River into Hong Kong, advertising to the world that near anarchy gripped China. Reports spoke of cities in flames and vicious battles raging on university campuses and in factories.[28] Mao was forced to divert more than half the PLA from national defense to curbing the excesses of the internal struggle.[29] But although he sought to use the PLA to help reconstitute governing authority in the provinces, he remained reluctant to throw his support exclusively to the army and thereby risk discrediting the entire Cultural Revolution. During the spring it became apparent, however, that the very coherence of the PLA was being undermined by conflicting directives to either render assistance to the radicals or suppress them.[30] Therefore, in July, Mao made it clear to his young Red Guards that the chaos had to stop. Responding to renewed fighting at Qinghua University in Beijing, which many saw as the unofficial Red Guard national headquarters, he dispatched "Worker-Peasant Thought of Mao Zedong Propaganda Teams" to curb the students, imposing the unity they had been too self-indulgent to maintain and ending the bloodshed.[31]

Mao had barely begun to enforce order when the Soviet invasion of Czechoslovakia followed by the Brezhnev declaration of limited sovereignty in the communist bloc suddenly made it imperative that the chaos of the Cultural Revolution be suppressed quickly. In October, Mao secretly convened the Twelfth Plenum of the Party Central Committee, which clarified the conservative direction policy would henceforth take. That autumn Mao also reinvigorated an old campaign designed to disperse sur-

---

28 Richard Baum, "China: Year of the Mangoes," in Richard Baum and Louise B. Bennett, eds., *China in Ferment: Perspectives on the Cultural Revolution* (Englewood Cliffs, N.J., 1971), 151. In contrast the student revolt on Italian university campuses at about the same time tended to beget a carnival atmosphere. An influential Italian paper chose, incongruously, to call the local revelry in Milan "The Nights of Mao." Robert Lumley, *States of Emergency: Cultures of Revolt in Italy from 1968 to 1978* (New York, 1990), 88.

29 Richard C. Thornton, *Soviet Asian Strategy in the Brezhnev Era and Beyond* (Washington, D.C., 1985), 9.

30 Hong Yung Lee, *The Politics of the Chinese Cultural Revolution* (Berkeley, Calif., 1978), 276–301.

31 Baum, "Year of the Mangoes," 151–2; Memo Al Jenkins to Walt Rostow, Aug. 21, 1968, NSF Country File, China vol. XIII, Bx 243, LBJL; Walt Rostow gave the president a summary of Jenkins memo, Aug. 26, 1968, NSF Country File, China vol. XIII, Bx 243, LBJL. Several accounts of the Cultural Revolution have been written from the viewpoint of Red Guards including Gordon Bennett and Ronald Montaperto, *Red Guard: The Political Biography of Dai Hsiao-ai* (Garden City, N.Y., 1972); Liang Heng and Judith Shapiro, *Son of the Revolution* (New York, 1983).

plus labor from urban areas and utilized it to dispose of the trouble-making "little revolutionary generals." Rather than leave them in the cities where they could rampage anew, Mao sent them to the countryside to learn from the peasants.[32]

Taking steps to end China's debilitating internal chaos was paralleled by efforts to find for China a powerful friend abroad in the ancient tradition of using barbarians to control barbarians. Beijing recognized that Moscow's assertion of a transcendent right to determine how communist states developed followed from its possession of superior military capabilities. China, therefore, needed both external support against the Soviet threat and assurance that, while preoccupied with trouble on the northern border, nothing untoward would occur in the south where American troops continued to battle the Vietnamese and Nationalist Chinese leaders on Taiwan sought an opportunity to launch an attack.[33] Thus on November 26, 1968, Zhou Enlai invited the United States to resume ambassadorial talks in Warsaw, which had been suspended since May, and reach agreement with China on observance of the mutually beneficial Five Principles of Peaceful Coexistence.[34] Washington replied positively on November 29, President-elect Richard M. Nixon having indicated his interest,[35] but two days before the Warsaw meeting was to have been held in February 1969 the defection of a Chinese diplomat gave anti-American voices in the Politburo an excuse to scuttle the meeting. Clearly, despite the growing Soviet menace, not everyone in positions of authority believed the time had come to talk to the United States.

32 Lowell Dittmer, *Sino-Soviet Normalization and Its International Implications, 1945–1990* (Seattle, 1992), 189. On the rustication of the Red Guards, see Thomas Bernstein, *Up to the Mountains and Down to the Villages: The Transfer of Youth from Urban to Rural China* (New Haven, Conn., 1977); Peter J. Seybolt, ed., *The Rustication of Urban Youth in China* (New York, 1975). By the end of 1970 some 5.4 million had been "sent down." Harry Harding, "The Chinese State in Crisis, 1966–9," in Roderick MacFarquhar, ed., *The Politics of China, 1949–1989* (New York, 1993), 220. The suppression of the student movement in China contributed to the disillusionment and splintering of the Maoist factions in the German student movement in the fall of 1968. Daniels, *Year of the Heroic Guerrilla,* 162.

33 Chiang Kai-shek repeatedly proposed to American presidents that Taiwan could help win the Vietnam War by landing troops in south China. Nancy Bernkopf Tucker, *Taiwan, Hong Kong, and the United States, 1945–1992: Uncertain Friendships* (New York, 1994), 96.

34 Zhang Baijia, "Zhou Enlai – the Shaper and Founder of China's Diplomacy," in Michael Hunt and Niu Jun, eds., *Chinese Communist Foreign Relations, 1920s–1960s* (Washington, D.C., 1995), 83–4; Gottlieb, *Chinese Foreign Policy Factionalism,* 99; Richard Wich, *Sino-Soviet Crisis Politics: A Study of Political Change and Communication* (Cambridge, Mass., 1980), 85.

35 The China specialist on the NSC, in a December 2 memo, expressed serious skepticism that the Chinese invitation meant any change in policy by Beijing. On the 5th, however, he suggested that the U.S. consider giving Beijing a signal that it "has policy alternatives in our regard." Memo Al Jenkins to Walt Rostow, Dec. 2, 1968, and Memo Jenkins to Rostow, Dec. 5, 1968, NSF Country File, China vol. XIII, Bx 243, LBJL.

Even without the American connection, however, the Chinese apparently felt they could not remain passive. In March 1969, the evidence suggests, Chinese troops provoked a serious exchange of gunfire with Soviet troops on Zhenbao (Damansky) Island in the Ussuri River.[36] Mao most probably acted to warn Moscow that China would not be a docile object of Soviet discipline.[37] But Mao got more than he bargained for when Soviet forces retaliated with a major show of force, and then the two countries embarked upon a series of bloody confrontations over the next several months.[38]

Analysts around the world began to speculate on the possibility of war between Moscow and Beijing. During the course of 1969 U.S. Secretary of State William Rogers told the press that in a concerted Soviet drive its troops could probably seize much of northern China including Beijing.[39] In Europe rumors circulated of Soviet plans to strike Chinese nuclear facilities, and Soviet Defense Minister Andrei Grechko reportedly advocated using nuclear bombs on China "once and for all [to] get rid of the Chinese threat."[40] That Chinese leaders took such menacing talk seriously became evident with initiation of a costly program of tunnel construction to serve as fallout shelters under China's major cities to protect the citizenry against the "handful of war maniacs" in the Kremlin.[41]

36 CIA "Sino-Soviet Border Remains Uneasy," June 30, 1969, DDRS (1988), fiche 78 #1240; Thomas W. Robinson, "The Sino-Soviet Border Dispute: Background, Development and the March 1969 Clashes," *American Political Science Review* 66 (Dec. 1972): 1188–9; Kenneth Lieberthal, *Sino-Soviet Conflict in the 1970s,* Rand R-2342-NA, July 1978, 5.

37 Roderick MacFarquhar, on the other hand, suggests that the attack might have been staged by Lin Biao who wanted to prove the centrality and justify the new political role of the PLA in national affairs. Roderick MacFarquhar, "The Succession to Mao and the End of Maoism, 1969–82," in MacFarquhar, ed., *Politics of China,* 263. Gurtov and Hwang rejected the idea that the attack had anything to do with domestic politics. Gurtov and Hwang, *China Under Threat,* 234, 238–41. The Chinese version appeared in Neville Maxwell, "The Chinese Account of the 1969 Fighting at Chenpao," *China Quarterly* 56 (Oct.–Dec. 1973): 730–9. Of course, still another possibility is that Mao may have seen actual fighting as the key to agreement on improving relations with the United States.

38 Based on the pattern of Chinese past deterrence behavior (see Allen S. Whiting, *Chinese Calculus of Deterrence,* 239–40 and passim), Moscow's vigorous response may have been designed to prevent a more significant Chinese blow to come if the USSR did not capitulate. Harold Hinton, *Bear at the Gate: Chinese Policymaking Under Soviet Pressure* (Stanford, Calif., 1971), 25. Moscow may also have hoped for a coup d'état against Mao yielding a more pro-Soviet leader. Nelsen, *Power and Insecurity,* 71.

39 Benjamin Welles, "Rogers Terms Czechoslovakia 'Grim Reminder,'" *New York Times,* Aug. 21, 1969; Paul F. Langer, "Soviet Military Power in Asia," in Donald Zagoria, ed., *Soviet Policy in East Asia* (New Haven, Conn., 1982), 272.

40 Bernard Gwertzman, "A Chinese Youth Writes to Soviet," *New York Times,* Aug. 28, 1969; Hedrick Smith, "U.S. Doubts Soviets Will Bomb China," *New York Times,* Aug. 29, 1969; Shevchenko, *Breaking with Moscow,* 164–6; Harry Gelman, *The Soviet Far East Buildup and Soviet Risk-Taking Against China,* Rand R-2943-AF, Aug. 1982, 29–48; Andrew and Gorievsky, *KGB,* 494.

41 FBIS, China, Oct. 8, 1969, A1–2; Allen S. Whiting, "Sino-Soviet Relations in the 1980s," in Richard A. Melanson, ed., *Neither Cold War Nor Détente?* (Charlottesville, Va., 1982), 92.

Caught in a war scare of their own making, Mao Zedong and Zhou Enlai sought immediately to reduce China's international isolation. Over the protests of more radical Cultural Revolution leaders they shifted Chinese policy away from support for leftist revolutionary insurgencies toward international reformism more acceptable to governments in the developing world.[42] They agreed to initiate talks with Canada in February 1969 designed to open diplomatic relations. Spurred by the Brezhnev Doctrine they also reached out to other potential victims of Soviet hegemonic intrabloc aggression. This meant a rapid reexamination of Chinese relations with Eastern Europe and efforts to heighten involvement there substantially, particularly with Romania and Yugoslavia. Perhaps above all, "the mending of the dispute with Yugoslavia . . . was a significant turning-point. It marked the elevation of strategy over ideology in the seeking of foreign confederates. Soviet 'social imperialism' had come to be seen by Mao as a greater threat to socialist China than Soviet (or Yugoslav) revisionism."[43] China courted the Eastern Europeans with local-language radio broadcasts, high-level visits, and trade agreements. On the more sensitive issue of assistance if the Russians marched, although China hinted at aid to the Romanians, more often Zhou pointed to the great distances involved and disclaimed the likelihood of useful support.[44]

At the same time, Europe, the Third World, and Canada could not do much to fortify China's national defenses, and so Mao and Zhou turned with increased conviction to the possibility of accommodation with the United States. The prognosis for reconciliation initially did not appear bright. The two countries had a considerable history of antagonism to overcome. Not only had they fought one another in Korea, there had also been two clashes over the offshore islands in the Taiwan Straits in 1954–55 and 1958. The United States had signed a Mutual Defense Treaty with the Nationalist Chinese regime on Taiwan in 1954, freezing the Chinese civil war. Moreover, Washington had supported covert attacks on the mainland and imposed a debilitating trade embargo. China after 1964 possessed a nuclear capability that frightened American policymakers, and in 1967 the

42 Harry Harding, "China's Changing Role in the Contemporary World," in Harry Harding, ed., *China's Foreign Relations in the 1980s* (New Haven, Conn., 1984), 191; Memo Al Jenkins to Walt Rostow, Sept. 23, 1968, NSF Country File, China vol. XIII, Bx 243, LBJL.
43 Michael B. Yahuda, "China and Europe: The Significance of a Secondary Relationship," in Robinson and Shambaugh, *Chinese Foreign Policy,* 278.
44 Morris Rothenberg, *Whither China: The View from the Kremlin* (Miami, Fla., 1977), 152; Ohja, *Chinese Foreign Policy,* 237–9; Charles Gati, "The Soviet Stake in Eastern Europe," in Seweryn Bialer and Thane Gustafson, eds., *Russia at the Crossroads* (Boston, 1981), 184; Elez Biberaj, *Albania and China: A Study of an Unequal Alliance* (Boulder, Colo., 1986), 76–7.

United States presented its antiballistic missile Sentinel program as a defense against the Chinese.[45] Moreover, in American eyes, China appeared to be the evil genius behind communist aggression in Vietnam.

Among the factors that complicated Sino-American reconciliation, Vietnam presented a particularly difficult problem. Although the original American commitment to Vietnam had been made more for the French than against the Chinese,[46] that balance shifted during the 1950s, and by the mid-1960s weighing China's role in the Indochina war consumed considerable time among U.S. analysts. When Defense Minister Lin Biao in 1965 pointed to the Vietnamese struggle against American imperialism as emblematic of national liberation struggles in which the rural peoples of the world, meaning the developing countries, would surround and ultimately defeat the cities, meaning the industrialized nations, he reinforced American determination to stop the falling dominoes in Vietnam.[47] At the same time, strategic decisions about how the war should be fought often hinged upon the likely Chinese reaction to American maneuvers. Some risks were taken, but the Johnson administration sincerely wanted to prevent a reprise of the Chinese intervention in Korea.[48]

From the Chinese perspective the Vietnam War constituted a potentially dire threat to national security, requiring efforts both to warn the Americans to keep their distance and to prepare for war should it come.[49] Zhou

---

45 Of course the ABM package actually was the result of American domestic political pressures. Gregg Herken, *Counsels of War* (New York, 1987), 196–8; Deborah Shapley, *Promise and Power: The Life and Times of Robert McNamara* (Boston, 1993), 390–4. U.S. analysts had just concluded that China lacked a "militarily useful nuclear capability." #CA 4864 "Recent Developments in Strategic Forces," 9–10, Dec. 31, 1966, National Security Files, Country File USSR, Box 231, F: ABM Negotiations, Jan. 1967–Sept. 1968, LBJL.

46 George C. Herring, "The Truman Administration and the Restoration of French Sovereignty in Indochina," *Diplomatic History* 1 (spring 1977): 97–117; Gary R. Hess, "United States Policy and the Origins of the French-Vietminh War, 1945–1946," *Peace and Change* 3 (summer–fall 1975): 21–33.

47 Robert S. McNamara, *In Retrospect: The Tragedy and Lessons of Vietnam* (New York, 1995), 215; Leonard A. Kusnitz, *Public Opinion and Foreign Policy: America's China Policy, 1949–1979* (Westport, Conn., 1984), 114. Zhai Qing reports that the article "Long Live the Victory of People's War," *Peking Review* 8 (Sept. 3, 1965): 9–30, was not, in fact, written by Lin but by a team of writers. Zhai Qiang, "China and Johnson's Escalation of the Vietnam War, 1964–65," 30–1, Conference on New Evidence on the Cold War in Asia, Hong Kong, 1996.

48 As Rusk reminded LBJ, "we must keep Communist China always in mind in our choice of military actions in Viet-Nam." Memo Rusk to LBJ, Feb. 22, 1968, DDRS (1993), fiche 114, #1335. Disputes occurred among high-level officials over where the line should be drawn. Shapley, *Promise and Power*, 302, 311, 341; George Ball, *The Past Has Another Pattern* (New York, 1982), 406; Dean Rusk, *As I Saw It* (New York, 1990), 456–7; Whiting, *Chinese Calculus of Deterrence*, 181–3; 194–5, 222. Regarding the likelihood of war, see "The Risks of the Present Course," Feb. 10, 1968, LBJL, DDRS (1992), fiche 264, #3207.

49 John Garver argues that American policymakers were right to fear Chinese entry into the war based on Chinese preparations. John W. Garver, "The Chinese Threat in the Vietnam War," *Parameters* 22 (spring 1992): 73–85.

Enlai told Ayub Khan, the president of Pakistan, in April 1964 to pass a message to Washington: "Should the United States impose a war on China, it can be said with certainty that, once in China, the United States will not be able to pull out, however many men it may send over and whatever weapons it may use. . . .When a war breaks out, it will have no boundaries."[50] Surprised by American ferocity in the Tonkin Gulf in August 1964, Mao responded not only by providing Ho Chi Minh assistance, but also by launching a costly effort to develop a Chinese industrial capacity deep in the hinterlands where it would be safe from an American attack.[51]

Although the U.S. government gave actual Chinese involvement little publicity lest the American people demand retribution, between 1965 and 1968 a total of some three hundred thousand soldiers of the PLA provided war support inside North Vietnam. This included the manning of anti-aircraft batteries as well as railway building and other construction, during which tasks the Chinese took casualties and inflicted losses. Chinese physical involvement and rhetorical belligerence signaled the United States regarding Beijing's determination to prevent the conquest of North Vietnam and to stop any direct challenge to Chinese security. In return, Washington attempted to let Beijing know that, despite massive American troop escalation in Vietnam, American forces would not provoke or endanger China.[52]

Nonetheless Sino-American confrontation over Vietnam might well have prevented China from making the decision to seek rapprochement with the United States had it not been for developments during 1968.[53] At the end of January the Vietcong staged its shocking Tet Offensive across South Vietnam, incurring heavy losses but winning a huge psychological and political victory. Regardless of the facts that the insurgents were driven back everywhere and that Vietcong units were decimated, they had demonstrated the vulnerability of South Vietnamese and American strong points, discredited U.S. government assessments of progress in the war, and demoralized the American public. As a result, Lyndon B. Johnson altered the

50 Xue and Pei, *Diplomacy of Contemporary China*, 198.
51 Barry Naughton, "The Third Front: Defense Industrialization in the Chinese Interior," *China Quarterly* 115 (Sept. 1988): 351–86.
52 Allen Whiting notes that the Chinese carried out their assistance in such a way that it could not be missed by American intelligence but would not receive public attention. Whiting, *Chinese Calculus of Deterrence*, 172, 186–8; Chen Jian, "China's Involvement in the Vietnam War, 1964–69," *China Quarterly* 142 (June 1995): 371–80; Zhai, "China and Johnson's Escalation," 16–22; Franz Schurmann, *The Logic of World Power* (New York, 1974), 515–16; Wang Jisi, "From Kennedy to Nixon: America's East Asia and China Policy," *Beijing Review* 31 (May 16–22, 1988): 41–4. The Chinese claim to have sent in a total of 320,000 troops between October 1965 and March 1968 and to have incurred 20,000 casualties. David Shambaugh, "Patterns of Interaction in Sino-American Relations," in Robinson and Shambaugh, *Chinese Foreign Policy*, 201.
53 For a more detailed discussion, see George C. Herring's chapter in this book.

direction of American policy by declaring that he would not run for reelection so that he could focus his attention on securing peace in Vietnam, and by announcing that future bombing of North Vietnam would be restricted to territory close to the demilitarized zone. Neither the Tet Offensive nor Johnson's decision served to end the war, but once Hanoi responded by going to Paris to negotiate despite Beijing's disapproval, the Chinese withdrew their forces from North Vietnam.

Thus, fortuitously, in the early months of 1968 the Vietnam War diminished as a source of Sino-American friction. The Chinese troop presence ceased to be of concern to the United States, and the prospect of an American lunge across China's border became less and less probable to the Chinese. Then, in October, Beijing dropped its opposition to Hanoi's engagement in peace negotiations. Shortly after Brezhnev made his doctrine public, moreover, President-elect Nixon let the North Vietnamese, and possibly the Chinese, know that the new administration planned to negotiate a withdrawal from Vietnam, further minimizing the Vietnam issue as a barrier to reconciliation between Washington and Beijing.[54]

Perhaps more disturbing for the Chinese than continuing American involvement in Vietnam was the mild American reaction to the Soviet invasion of Czechoslovakia. If Washington could look with equanimity at the repression of Europeans, what would be the reaction to Soviet aggression against Asians?[55] Or, what if Washington simply had been rendered so weak and dispirited that it would be unwilling to face down an expansionist Soviet Union?[56]

In fact, despite setbacks in Vietnam, the United States did share China's interest in and willingness to curb Soviet efforts to dominate Asia. Johnson's assessment of and response to the Czech crisis was complicated by his desire for a summit conference with Kosygin on disarmament that would end his presidency triumphantly, and by the positive benefits of the Soviet invasion upon lagging support for NATO in Europe and the U.S. Congress.[57] On China the advantages of rapprochement seemed clearer, particularly to Nixon and Kissinger when they assumed office. Determined to

---

54 Nixon, *RN*, 349; Dittmer, *Sino-Soviet Normalization*, 188. Regarding Chinese opposition to the talks, see Wich, *Sino-Soviet Crisis Politics*, 44, 81–2; Chen, "China in the Vietnam War," 384–5.

55 Even the Russians were surprised at the American reaction. Anatoly Dobrynin, *In Confidence* (New York, 1995), 178–86.

56 Although that fear did not dominate Chinese perceptions at the end of the 1960s, by the middle of the 1970s Beijing grew seriously concerned about declining U.S. power. Jonathan D. Pollack, "China and the Global Strategic Balance," in Harding, *China's Foreign Relations*, 156. The Nixon Doctrine announced in August 1969 would affirm the reduction of American troop levels in Asia.

57 Frank Costigliola, "Lyndon B. Johnson, Germany, and 'the End of the Cold War,'" in Warren I. Cohen and Nancy Bernkopf Tucker, eds., *Lyndon Johnson Confronts the World* (New York, 1994), 207–9.

extract more cooperative behavior from the Soviets than they had displayed in 1968, Nixon and Kissinger welcomed Moscow's anxiety regarding a Sino-American détente and its implications.[58]

Throughout 1968 uncertainty regarding motives and capabilities made the future of Sino-American relations a point of contention in and between China and the United States. Chinese ruling circles appear to have split over the direction that foreign policy should take.[59] Zhou Enlai and his supporters are thought to have urged better relations with the United States as problems with Moscow multiplied, rather than continuation of the risky strategy of opposition to both superpowers which the radicals like Jiang Qing favored. Lin Biao, it has been argued, led those who opposed approaching Washington and may have entertained hopes of reestablishing close connections to Moscow. Both the Zhou and Lin camps agreed that disarray in the United States brought about by its losses in Vietnam and the costs of the war, along with the concomitant domestic upheaval produced by the antiwar movement, provided an opportunity for changing policy.[60]

But Zhou and Lin seem to have reached contradictory conclusions regarding the significance of these developments. To Lin an America under pressure would be a more dangerous aggressor driven by irrational impulses to retain control everywhere. Moreover, as prescribed by Maoist doctrine, Lin and the radicals felt China should take the offensive against American imperialism while it remained in retreat so as to vanquish it once and for all. Happily this also would mean larger defense budgets for the People's Liberation Army under Lin's command. As for the Soviets, Lin may have propounded the view that Beijing had the capacity to confront both Moscow and Washington, as did the radicals, or he may have advocated reconciliation as Mao later claimed.[61]

Zhou, in contrast, argued that as a rising power the Soviet Union would be increasingly militant and expansionist. China would require assistance. Unexpectedly it could count on the United States for that aid because

---

58 William G. Hyland, *Mortal Rivals: Superpower Relations from Nixon to Reagan* (New York, 1987), 24; Kissinger, *White House Years*, 178–9, 186–7.

59 It remains unclear whether these groups functioned as factions or were momentary alliances which varied in relationship to different issues and changing times. Michael Hunt briefly discusses the pitfalls of factional analysis in Michael Hunt, *The Genesis of Chinese Communist Foreign Policy* (New York, 1996), 242.

60 John W. Garver, *China's Decision for Rapprochement with the United States, 1968–1971* (Boulder, Colo., 1982), 143–4n74; Gottlieb, *Chinese Foreign Policy Factionalism*, 11–28 and passim. Analysts who describe a two-line struggle include J. D. Armstrong, *Revolutionary Diplomacy: Chinese Foreign Policy and the United Front Doctrine* (Berkeley, Calif., 1977).

61 Lieberthal weighs the evidence regarding Lin's connections with the Soviet Union in Lieberthal, *Sino-Soviet Conflict*, 27–30. Jonathan Pollack rejects the likelihood of a connection. Pollack, "Opening to America," 414–16.

Washington, rather than remaining a voracious imperialist now sought to get out of Vietnam, cut its commitments in Asia, and, very possibly, relax its efforts to contain China.[62] In fact, during the year Johnson administration officials had, on several occasions, guardedly called for progress in U.S.-China relations. The government also stopped high-level reconnaissance flights over south China.[63] Nelson Rockefeller brought the China question into the presidential campaign with a July speech that advocated a dialogue with Beijing as did Nixon in a *U.S. News and World Report* interview in August.[64] Nixon's election rhetoric, calling for a reduction in America's presence in areas not vital to U.S. security, seemed to Zhou's group in Beijing as a declaration that his administration would concentrate on opposing Moscow in Europe and not the Chinese in Asia.[65]

Zhou also hoped that rapprochement with the United States would have the additional virtue of providing access to the world economy dominated, as Beijing saw it, by the United States. Given the disastrous economic situation in China, the prospect of trade and transfers of technology seemed irresistible. Moreover, if the United States no longer comprised a dangerous military challenger, defense budgets could be reduced and resources redirected to develop the economy.

There were, at the same time, troubling indications during 1968 and the early days of 1969 that Washington might be pursuing an anti-Chinese understanding with Moscow. Beijing strongly objected to the Nuclear Nonproliferation Treaty signed in July 1968, given its effective exclusion of China from obtaining a nuclear weapons capability while preserving American and Soviet bombs. Beijing railed at the signers, maintaining that "in concocting this treaty, the U.S. imperialists and Soviet revisionists aim at maintaining their nuclear monopoly and stepping up their preparations for nuclear warfare so as to carry out nuclear blackmail against other countries in a more unbridled way."[66] Washington and Moscow, in fact, seemed to be in agreement on the utility of implementing a general policy of containing China. Beijing reacted to heightened border tensions by declaring

---

62 John W. Garver, *Foreign Relations of the People's Republic of China* (Englewood Cliffs, N.J., 1993), 74–80; Garver, *China's Decision for Rapprochement,* 110–17, 124–30; Gottlieb, *Chinese Foreign Policy Factionalism,* 66–118.

63 Memo William P. Bundy (EA) and Anthony M. Solomon (E) to Rusk, 1968, LBJL, DDRS (1993), fiche 20, #143; #114300 Bundy to Ambassador, Taipei, Feb. 13, 1968, LBJL, DDRS (1994), fiche 61 #670; #167529 Rusk to Ambassador, Taipei, May 21, 1968, LBJL, DDRS (1994), fiche 61 #672; Kusnitz, *Public Opinion,* 118.

64 Kissinger, *White House Years,* 164–5.

65 Wich, *Sino-Soviet Crisis Politics,* 81–2.

66 *People's Daily Commentator,* June 13, 1968, "A Nuclear Fraud Jointly Hatched by the United States and the Soviet Union," *Peking Review* 11 (June 21, 1968): 17.

that "these crimes of the Soviet revisionist renegade clique are organized and planned actions in accordance with its policy of ganging up with U.S. imperialism against China."[67] The Soviets also facilitated the start of Vietnam peace negotiations and moved to improve their relations with Japan and Taiwan.

Early in 1969, Nixon further disappointed Beijing's moderates by failing to state publicly that the new administration would vigorously pursue better relations with China. On the day of his inauguration the Soviets proposed the start of Strategic Arms Limitation Talks (SALT), which Nixon quickly welcomed. And, almost at the same moment as Moscow fiercely retaliated for the Zhenbao incident, Nixon announced that Washington would deploy its Sentinel ABM system, which Beijing interpreted as evidence of "joint military opposition to China."[68]

Sober voices in Beijing, however, made the argument that the degree of collaboration between Washington and Moscow had been widely exaggerated and that in reality there remained fundamental contradictions between them. Based on a paper written by Chen Yi which argued this point of view, Zhou persuaded Mao to constitute a study group of top military figures whose reputations would leave them free to form independent opinions regarding the redirection of Chinese foreign policy. Over the following eight months the marshals prepared reports for Central Committee deliberation which presented three key arguments: (1) that continuing frictions between Washington and Moscow made it almost impossible for them to attack China jointly, (2) that, whereas the United States considered China a potential adversary, the Soviet Union identified China as its foremost enemy and therefore constituted a greater danger for Beijing, and (3) that this correlation of forces dictated negotiations with the United States without preconditions.[69] Although Mao himself had concluded in the early 1960s that China would inevitably have to fight a war against a U.S.-Soviet coalition, after Czechoslovakia he appeared to have modified his expectations and proved willing to accept the conclusions of Chen Yi's group.[70]

Washington contributed to the easing of Beijing's alarm over any possible conspiracy by its reaction to the continuing border crisis and Moscow's

---

67 Quoted in Gurtov and Hwang, *China Under Threat,* 226.
68 Wich, *Sino-Soviet Crisis Politics,* 89, 94; Gottlieb, *Chinese Foreign Policy Factionalism,* 111–13. Actually an announcement of strategic arms limitations talks should have occurred in the late summer but was derailed by the invasion of Czechoslovakia. Dittmer, *Sino-Soviet Normalization,* 196.
69 The original paper was delivered in December 1968. Chen Xiaolu, "Chen Yi and China's Diplomacy," in Hunt and Niu, *Chinese Communist Foreign Relations.*
70 He Di, "The Most Respected Enemy: Mao Zedong's Perception of the United States," *China Quarterly* 137 (Mar. 1994): 154.

talk of war. Instead of colluding with the Soviets or standing silently by, Washington delivered the message publicly and repeatedly that the United States would be deeply concerned were there to be a Soviet attack on China and, it hinted, might come to Beijing's assistance.[71] Beijing did enter into border talks directly with the Soviet Union to ameliorate the immediate crisis, but made no real effort to compromise with Moscow and moved with increasing conviction toward reconciliation with the United States.[72]

In the end, Zhou not only won the foreign policy contest with Lin,[73] but also proved able to bring about a compromise on the most difficult issue dividing the United States and the People's Republic. Prior to the invasion of Czechoslovakia and the Brezhnev Doctrine, the main barrier to better Chinese-American relations had invariably been the question of Taiwan. The Nationalist Chinese had taken refuge there after their defeat in the Chinese civil war and with United States protection had survived and prospered, remaining a challenge to the legitimacy of the communist government in Beijing. With the abrupt need for a mutually reinforcing anti-Soviet condominium, the Taiwan issue receded in immediacy. By 1972 Mao and Zhou proved willing to assert that, although their concession would in no way weaken their claim to the island, they would not expect an instant resolution of the problem of Taiwan in order to reach understanding on other matters. In turn, Nixon and Kissinger made clear that, although they would not abandon Taiwan completely, they could be persuaded to modify their commitments to the Chinese Nationalist regime. The formula that met the needs of both sides proved to be "one China, but not now."[74]

Once the Chinese had come to terms with the Americans, Moscow found the combination of China's numbers and U.S. weaponry deeply troubling. In response it launched a defense effort in the East that, over

71 Kissinger, *White House Years,* 184, 764–5; Thornton, *Soviet Asian Strategy,* 14. In fact, China initially asserted that the U.S. and USSR had been in collusion, giving East Europe to Moscow and Asia to Washington.
72 Lieberthal, *Sino-Soviet Conflict,* 8–22. John Garver considers the talks part of a pro-Soviet tilt, which, he suggests, means that China did not move toward normalization with the United States because of Czechoslovakia and the Brezhnev Doctrine, but his argument is not convincing. John Garver, "Chinese Foreign Policy in 1970: The Tilt Towards the Soviet Union," *China Quarterly* 82 (June 1980): 214–49.
73 The point at which Mao Zedong joined Zhou's camp remains in some dispute. Gottlieb believes he was quietly supportive already in November 1968, whereas Harold Hinton sees a more militant Mao. In fact, the evidence regarding Mao's position is scanty. Gottlieb, *Chinese Foreign Policy Factionalism,* 25, 97–104 (and direct refutation 102–3n198); Hinton, *Bear at the Gate,* 34–5.
74 Ironically, the paper prepared by the Policy Planning Council in the State Department for the new Nixon administration on "U.S. Policy Toward Communist China" by Ralph Clough recommended a long-term effort to separate Taiwan from the mainland and secure dual representation in the United Nations. Dec. 1968, DDRS (1993), fiche 269, #314.

time, would become so costly that it would contribute to the ultimate disintegration of the Soviet empire. Soviet leaders had already increased troop
deployments along the East Asian border from 15 to 33 divisions between
1965 and 1969, but with U.S.-Chinese rapprochement they felt compelled
to raise the commitment to 44 divisions in 1972 and to 50 divisions by
1982.[75] They supplemented ground force concentrations with emplace-
ments of intermediate range nuclear missiles, one-quarter of the Soviet air
force, and advanced naval craft for the Pacific fleet. Throughout the buildup
Soviet strategists worried about the prospects of having to fight a two-front
war while the United States no longer had to worry about its Asian flank.
Yet, at the same time, the leaders came to recognize that their militariza-
tion of the Soviet Far East both alienated Asian states Moscow had hoped
to befriend and placed a debilitating burden on limited Soviet resources.[76]

   Clearly, then, the 1968 Soviet invasion of Czechoslovakia and the enunciation of the Brezhnev Doctrine had fundamentally altered China's relations with the world. Interaction with the Soviet Union subsequently
became difficult and dangerous with Moscow assuming the role of China's
most likely adversary should war break out even as halting attempts continued to negotiate away border and other tensions.[77] At the same time, Beijing began a process of rapprochement with the United States which persisted despite disturbing developments such as the 1969 U.S.-Japanese
communiqué, which provided for the defense of Taiwan, and the 1970
American incursion into Cambodia. Normalization, although not con-
summated until 1979, furnished instant access for Beijing to political and
economic benefits from the free world. In 1971, for instance, after twenty-
two years of exclusion, Beijing assumed the Chinese seat in the United
Nations. Although Washington's ability to muster opposition had in any
case been declining, its shift to advocacy eliminated any possibility that
China's entry would continue to be blocked.[78]

   From Washington's perspective, of course, rapprochement with China
had as a central attraction the leverage it afforded against the Soviet Union.
Beijing might worry that the United States planned "to stand on China's
shoulders" to reach an accommodation with Moscow and then betray the

---

75 Banning N. Garrett and Bonnie S. Glaser, "From Nixon to Reagan: China's Changing Role in
   American Strategy," in Kenneth Oye, Robert J. Lieber, and Donald Rothchild, eds., *Eagle Resurgent? The Reagan Era in American Foreign Policy* (Boston, 1987), 257.
76 Nancy Bernkopf Tucker, "China as a Factor in the Collapse of the Soviet Empire," *Political Science
   Quarterly* 110 (winter 1995–6): 502–6.
77 Hinton, *Bear at the Gate,* 35–49.
78 The long-term prospect of excluding China had been diminishing, although between 1965 and
   1968 because of the violence of the Cultural Revolution support for Beijing in the General Assembly had lessened. Clough, "U.S. Policy Toward Communist China," 9, LBJL.

Chinese, but in fact Washington implemented a triangular strategy in which alignment with the Chinese forced Moscow to make concessions. Among top officials in the U.S. government, "the question [had quickly become] how, not whether, the Sino-American relationship should be used to improve the U.S. position vis-à-vis Moscow."[79]

For Moscow, whatever negative repercussions the Czech adventure had in Europe and with regard to the United States, among its most costly results was the exacerbation of Sino-Soviet antagonism. In prompting Beijing to seek normalization with the United States, the Soviet Union helped to generate conditions that ultimately contributed to the collapse of the entire Soviet empire.

Nineteen sixty-eight, then, could be said to have been a watershed in China's international history. Confronted by an external challenge, Beijing redirected both domestic and foreign policies to make the nation stronger, more unified and less isolated. At the same time, China, which had both shunned and been excluded from international organizations, the world economy, and cultural interaction before 1968, became party to the most compelling events of the year.

As protest movements across the globe challenged the political, social, and cultural roots of the dominant Cold War order, many people looked to China's cultural revolution for models through which to realize their own aspirations. Determined to jettison what they saw as repressive capitalist and bourgeois values, young people invoked the youthful Red Guards and Mao Zedong as symbols of struggle and success in renovating society. In June 1968, for instance, the organization at the heart of American activism, the Students for a Democratic Society, almost succumbed to the maneuverings of the pro-Chinese Progressive Labor Party, an offshoot of the Communist Party of the USA. The chaos bred by the Cultural Revolution appealed even more to Western guerrilla groups, such as the radical Weathermen in the United States, who in 1969 explicitly praised Mao and his heir apparent, Lin Biao, as heroes and celebrated the mass-based Red Guard revolutionaries for their "full willingness to participate in . . . violent and illegal struggle." What young people in the West failed to notice, however, was that the upheaval in China had not risen from the bottom to destabilize an entrenched system but had actually been initiated by the governing

79 Banning Garrett, "The United States and the Great Power Triangle," in Gerald Segal, ed., *The China Factor: Peking and the Superpowers* (New York, 1982), 96. In September 1969, for example, the president suggested that "a subtle move toward China" be made because Gromyko was in the U.S. Memo Nixon to Kissinger, Sept. 22, 1969, Nixon Presidential Materials, National Archives, College Park, Maryland.

authorities, and that, as Paul Berman, a veteran of the times, noted, the old Reds were manipulating the young Red Guards.[80]

The fact that their images of China did not reflect actual conditions made little difference. Young Italian intellectuals, for instance, yearned to learn from a mythologized China while few bothered to find out what had really happened there.[81] In fact, to most of the radicals in Europe, Latin America, and the United States, Chinese reality could not have been less relevant.

Some twenty years later much the same disjunction between myth and reality recurred as China again plunged into a domestic crisis while contending with external pressures that destabilized existing institutions.[82] The Beijing Spring of 1989, like the tumultuous events of 1968, witnessed students demonstrating in the heart of China at Tiananmen Square. But whereas in 1968 outsiders could only imagine what Chinese young people were doing, in 1989 television brought the actual events into the homes of viewers everywhere. To the world community their protests appeared to represent a yearning for democracy which, when brutally suppressed, energized antigovernment activity throughout the communist bloc. In 1968, Western radicals had waved copies of Mao's little red book at rallies to provoke the police and suggest a revolutionary consciousness. In 1989, communist bloc demonstrators waved pictures of a lone Chinese man facing down a tank, defying their own communist overlords to send tanks against them. Remarkably, in 1989, the Chinese example of excessive force turned against innocent citizens proved a powerful deterrent to massive repression in Eastern Europe and the Soviet Union itself.[83]

---

80 "You Don't Need a Weatherman to Know Which Way the Wind Blows," in William H. Chafe and Harvard Sitkoff, eds., *A History of Our Time* (New York, 1983), 235–8; Daniels, *Year of the Heroic Guerrilla,* 146. See also William L. O'Neill, *Coming Apart* (New York, 1971), 295; Milton Viorst, *Fire in the Streets: America in the Sixties* (New York, 1979), 488; Paul Berman, *A Tale of Two Utopias: The Political Journey of the Generation of 1968* (New York, 1996), 25, 98, 108. References to China could also be amusing. At a conference of child psychologists in May 1968, the chief of psychology at Mount Sinai Hospital tried to reassure American parents that the permissiveness toward young people in American society did not make them responsible for the fact that their children were now demonstrating in the streets. He reminded them that adolescents were in revolt all over the world, even in the rigid, traditionalistic, and authoritarian society of China. Whether anyone was reassured was not reported. See "Parents Excused in Youth Revolts," *New York Times,* May 12, 1968, 52.

81 Lumley, *States of Emergency,* 128; John Patrick Diggins, *The Rise and Fall of the American Left* (New York, 1992), 236. Sociologist Anthony Oberschall dismisses cross-cultural influences but does suggest other parallels between the movements of 1968 in China, Czechoslovakia, and France. See Anthony Oberschall, *Social Movements: Ideologies, Interests, and Identities* (New Brunswick, N.J., 1993), 312, 316, 321–3.

82 For a more general discussion of the relationship between 1968 and 1989, see the chapter by Konrad H. Jarausch in this book.

83 Tucker, "China as a Factor in the Collapse of the Soviet Empire," 514–17.

Ironically, as in 1968, the destruction of the Beijing Spring and of China's role as the vanguard for peaceful reform of the socialist system during 1989 became entangled in relations between China and the Soviet Union. This time the Soviet threat was not military but rather encapsulated in the popular concept of "glasnost." Mikhail Gorbachev had brought an era of reform to Moscow but had pursued political change more vigorously than economic reorganization in direct contrast to the path followed by the Chinese.

He had also set as a high priority the improvement of relations between Beijing and Moscow. To this end he had capitulated on all Deng Xiaoping's terms for reconciliation: removing troops from the Sino-Soviet border, withdrawing from Afghanistan, and dropping support for Vietnamese occupation of Cambodia. Gorbachev sought relief from Chinese military pressures on his eastern front, which had driven up defense budgets, helping to cripple Soviet growth and development. In celebration of the normalization of Sino-Soviet relations, which had deteriorated so steadily after August 1968, Gorbachev traveled to China where the world's media gathered to record the historic occasion.

What Gorbachev and the media found, once there, were protesters camped on Tiananmen Square. The young people welcomed Gorbachev to China with appeals for him to intervene in Chinese affairs and speak to China's leaders on behalf of the kind of reforms he had introduced in the Soviet Union. That alone angered the Chinese leadership, which would soon come to see Gorbachev's flexibility as weakness and his reforms as a counterrevolutionary betrayal of socialism. But, in addition, Deng Xiaoping and his associates were humiliated by the attention television and the press lavished upon their critics, robbing them of a triumphal moment and tarnishing their image as farsighted, imaginative, and productive. China's leaders doubtless would have turned on the student demonstrators even without this embarrassment, but it is also clear that the exposure heightened tension and made the continuing disarray intolerable.

Thus in 1989, as in 1968, developments in China preceded, paralleled, and interacted with events abroad in ways that modified political change and influenced the sounds and images of protest. And in 1989, as in 1968, China went its own way after the world took note of its turmoil and adapted what seemed useful elsewhere. Instead of joining in the new world order and joyfully embracing a more democratic system providing freer expression and broader popular participation, Beijing led China backwards to become a more repressive, defensive, and nationalistic society. The challenges of 1968 forced China to modify economic and military self-reliance and rethink its political view of the world, reaching out to the United States and joining the international community. The crises of 1989 and thereafter have, on the contrary, encouraged the Chinese to retreat politically and increasingly perceive their security to be endangered by the United States even as they draw prosperity from the international marketplace. The legacy of 1989, then, may prove as troublesome for Sino-American relations as the impact of 1968 was for Sino-Soviet relations.

PART TWO

From Chicago to Beijing

Challenges to the Domestic Order

7

1968 and the Unraveling of Liberal America

ALAN BRINKLEY

I

For more than twenty years after the end of World War II, a distinctive form of liberalism dominated American politics and much of American intellectual and cultural life. This liberalism had emerged out of the New Deal, but it bore only a partial resemblance to the rich, eclectic ideological world of the 1930s. Postwar liberalism was not concerned, as the New Deal had at times been, with the structure of economic power, the distribution of wealth, or the problem of monopoly. It was a consumerist liberalism, committed to "full employment" and high levels of purchasing power. It was a compensatory liberalism, designed to compensate for, not to remedy, the flaws of capitalism. Its tools were Keynesian fiscal policy, an expanded welfare state, and (by the 1960s) a vigorous effort by both the courts and the federal government to expand and protect the rights of individuals and groups. It did less to challenge than it did to confirm the character of modern industrial society.[1]

So powerful was this new regime, so ineffective the challenges to it, that many postwar liberals came to believe that it had established itself as the principal, even the only, important political tradition in American life. There had arrived, the historian Eric Goldman wrote in 1956, "a broad consensus in the thinking of Americans about the basic public issues of the day." The arrival of that consensus, he argued, "may well be considered one of the most important facts in all the American story."[2] Some scholars went farther and argued that liberalism was not just the dominant political tradition in the mid–twentieth century but the only serious political tradition throughout American history. Richard Hofstadter, for example, wrote of

---

1 A fuller account of this argument is in Alan Brinkley, *The End of Reform: New Deal Liberalism in Recession and War* (New York, 1995).
2 Eric Goldman, *The Crucial Decade: America, 1945–1955* (New York, 1956), 292–3.

the "common climate of American opinion" that had characterized the nation's past, the way in which all the "major political traditions" had "shared a belief in the rights of property, the philosophy of economic individualism, the value of competition." Louis Hartz, David Potter, and others made related arguments about the essential continuity of American history and the essential single-mindedness of American politics.[3]

Such beliefs in the uniformity and continuity of the American political tradition have few defenders today. And yet the postwar liberalism that produced those beliefs dominated the nation's public life for more than a generation, enjoyed a series of important victories, and left an extraordinary legacy of achievement. But no political movement lasts forever, and the reign of liberalism was no exception. Liberalism entered the 1960s near the height of its power; it departed the decade crippled, defensive, and widely reviled. It has never recovered.

No single set of events can explain so broad a political process as the unraveling of American liberalism. But events can illustrate that process, none so vividly as those of 1968. The traumas and upheavals of that turbulent year revealed some of the weaknesses within the liberal regime that made it vulnerable to external challenges. They also accelerated what was already a growing popular impatience with some of the principal liberal commitments of the time. Perhaps most of all, the events of 1968 sped the emergence of a powerful alternative to liberalism. It was not, as many Americans hoped or feared at the time, the Left. It was a resurgent and increasingly self-confident conservatism. However much radical politics seemed to dominate the public face of 1968, the most important political legacy of that critical year was the rise of the Right.[4]

II

A series of crises – crises of violence and dissent but also crises of confidence – cascaded across the American landscape in 1968 and made it perhaps the most traumatic year in the life of the nation since the end of World War II. Some of the events that made 1968 such an extraordinary moment in modern American history were random and unpredictable, to be sure,

---

3 Richard Hofstadter, *The American Political Tradition and the Men Who Made It* (New York, 1948), xxxvi–xxxvii. See also David M. Potter, *People of Plenty: Economic Abundance and the American Character* (Chicago, 1954); and Louis Hartz, *The Liberal Tradition in America* (New York, 1955).
4 The United States was not alone, of course, in experiencing a radical challenge that ultimately had the effect of strengthening the right. Koichi Hamada argues, for example, that in Japan, too, 1968 marked the beginning of a conservative resurgence. See his remarks at the conference "1968: The World Transformed," held at the Wissenschaftszentrum Berlin, May 24–6, 1996.

although no less important for that. Others were a result of problems and controversies peculiar to American society in the 1960s. But still others were the result of broad processes of change that had affected almost every modern industrial society and that produced upheavals all over the world at virtually the same time.

American involvement in the war in Vietnam was nearly a decade old, and unhappiness with the commitment – and with the foreign policy assumptions that had mandated and sustained it – had been growing steadily for several years. The formal antiwar movement had its origins in a "teach-in" at the University of Michigan in 1965, and it had grown to considerable proportions by the end of 1967. Even among those disposed to support American intervention abroad, the long and inconclusive war in Vietnam was producing considerable frustration. The year 1968 began with the issue of the war poised to explode.

Urban violence and racial discord had been an increasingly central fact of life since 1964, when disorders in Harlem began the long season of inner-city violence. The civil-rights movement, so confident and seemingly unified at its triumphant March on Washington in August 1963, began experiencing bitter public divisions in the summer of 1964, divisions that intensified and accelerated over the next two years. The relatively moderate leaders of the early years of the movement could no longer contain the growing restiveness of younger, more radical activists, who were losing patience with the strategy of nonviolence and interracial cooperation that Martin Luther King Jr. had established. Nor (as Manfred Berg makes clear elsewhere in this volume) could they absorb effectively the growing pressure from northern, urban African Americans for strategies that would address their deep economic grievances. Major riots in the Watts neighborhood of Los Angeles in 1965 and in Detroit in 1967 – riots sparked by altercations with police but that also revealed a festering rage about economic inequality – illustrated the potential for social turmoil that the effort to heal the nation's racial scars had unleashed. Black anger, and white anxiety, were already at a high level as 1968 began.[5]

But nothing so characterized the crises of 1968 as the rising tide of disenchantment and dissent among young people: the revolt of a generation.

---

5 See Manfred Berg's chapter in this book. See also James R. Ralph, *Northern Protest: Martin Luther King, Jr., Chicago, and the Civil Rights Movement* (Cambridge, Mass., 1993); Arnold R. Hirsch, "Massive Resistance in the Urban North: Trumbull Park Chicago, 1953–1966," *Journal of American History* 82 (1995): 522–50; and Thomas J. Sugrue, "Crabgrass-Roots Politics: Race, Rights, and the Reaction Against Liberalism in the Urban North, 1940–1964," *Journal of American History* 82 (1995): 551–78.

That revolt had roots in recent American history. Student unrest – inspired in part by the civil-rights movement – had begun on American campuses at Berkeley in 1964, and it had grown steadily over the next three years. But the broad discontents of the postwar generation were even more a result of a deeper, and more universal, series of changes. The men and women who were coming of age in advanced industrial societies in the late 1960s were part of a distinctive generation. Born in the aftermath of World War II, they were raised in the shadow of the Cold War. But they also grew up in the midst of unprecedented prosperity. The dramatic economic growth of the postwar era, and the expectations it produced, had much to do with the explosions in 1968. In the age of Cold War liberalism, according to both official and popular culture, those who lived in the capitalist world would be blessed with both prosperity and personal freedom. That was what distinguished the West from its communist adversaries: the opportunity of individuals to live their lives as they wished with reasonable comfort and security; the opportunity to pursue not just material success, but personal fulfillment. Never before in history had so many people come of age expecting so much of their world, and so much of themselves.

The upheavals among young people in 1968 – in the United States and throughout the industrial world – reflected, at least in part, the gap between these bright expectations and reality. For as members of the postwar generation moved toward adulthood, they discovered that conservative values and institutions still stood in their way. Colleges and universities remained wedded to patriarchal notions of learning. Communities and families still lived by rigid, Victorian notions of behavior and decorum. Both the state and society continued to sustain discriminatory structures that oppressed women and minorities and that perpetuated old patterns of entrenched privilege. American society, like most other industrial societies, was considerably less rigid and hierarchical in the 1960s than it had been a generation before, but neither was it fluid or tolerant enough to match the expansive expectations of its youth. And so a generation came of age unusually impatient with what to older men and women seemed ordinary restraints and conventions, and unusually outraged by evidence of injustices and inequalities that earlier generations had tolerated or endured. The particular events of 1968, as random and discrete as some of them were, occurred in the context of this rising determination of many young people to seize control of the future.

Nothing was new, then, to 1968 except the simultaneous eruption of so many long-held grievances – and a string of events that galvanized the discontent.

III

On January 31, 1968, the great Tet Offensive began in Vietnam. There has been much subsequent controversy over the real meaning of the Tet Offensive, and it now seems clear that, in military terms at least, it was a substantial victory for the United States and the South Vietnamese government. But at the time, for the vast majority of Americans watching it, it provided a stark illustration of the futility of the conflict in Vietnam, to which the United States ground troops had now been committed for almost three years.[6] It also provided graphic evidence of the savagery of the conflict – a savagery no worse, perhaps, than that of other twentieth-century wars, but a brutality that was now inescapable because of the ubiquity of televised images. It may be that nothing did more to undermine domestic support for the war in Vietnam than the image of a South Vietnamese officer pulling a pistol from his belt and shooting a captured NLF guerrilla in the head in the middle of a Saigon street; the young man sagged to the pavement, blood pouring from his skull, as American television cameras filmed the scene in color.[7]

Student opposition to the war was already strong even before Tet, but the events of that January pushed it rapidly to new levels. Only a little more than a month later, the growing unpopularity of the Vietnam War – and the energetic efforts of young volunteers opposed to the conflict – led to the surprisingly strong showing by Senator Eugene McCarthy of Minnesota, running for president as an antiwar candidate, against President Lyndon B. Johnson in the New Hampshire Democratic primary. Johnson withdrew from the presidential race shortly afterward.[8]

Whatever public consensus had existed behind the American role in Vietnam before 1968 crumbled quickly in the aftermath of Tet. Never again would a majority, or even a plurality, of the American people support the war. In the harsh light of post-Tet Vietnam, the once unchallenged commitment to the Cold War – a commitment central to American life, and to American liberalism, for at least twenty years – began to fray. To many critics, the Cold War now came to seem not a defense of liberty but a rationale for imperialism.[9]

---

6 Peter Braestrup, *Big Story: How the American Press and Television Reported and Interpreted the Crisis of Tet in Vietnam and Washington*, 2 vols. (Boulder, Colo., 1977), argues that reporters failed to understand the military results of the Tet Offensive, which were highly favorable to the American cause, and instead encouraged the public to believe that the war was being lost.
7 See Chester J. Pach Jr.'s chapter in this book; and Braestrup, *Big Story*, 2:266–81.
8 See Theodore H. White, *The Making of the President 1968* (New York, 1969), chap. 4.
9 Richard Scammon and Ben Wattenberg, *The Real Majority* (New York, 1970), 91.

On April 4, 1968, Martin Luther King Jr. was assassinated in Memphis, Tennessee, where he was working on behalf of a strike by African-American sanitation workers. In the aftermath of King's murder came the most widespread racial violence in American history: civil disorders in more than one hundred cities, which left forty people dead, three thousand injured, and billions of dollars of urban property destroyed.[10] The anger and violence helped shatter the already waning faith of any liberals in the possibility of peaceful, constructive solutions to the nation's racial problems – a faith that had been central to liberal ideology only a few years before. It also strengthened the already growing belief among many younger Americans (and especially among younger African Americans) that American society was irredeemably racist and that tolerant, interracial liberalism was inadequate to the task of liberation.

On April 23, 1968, students at Columbia University occupied the administration building and several other campus sites. New York City police finally cleared out the buildings, but the violence with which they did so radicalized many more students and paralyzed the university. The events at Columbia marked the real beginning of a sustained period of national campus unrest, in which the demands and grievances of students escalated quickly. Tom Hayden, who as a leader of Students for a Democratic Society had written the Port Huron Statement six years earlier, saw at Columbia a process of political engagement that pushed the student left far beyond the relatively tame concerns of the early 1960s. "The issues being considered by seventeen-year-old freshmen at Columbia University," he wrote at the time, "would not have been within the imagination of most 'veteran' student activists five years ago."[11] To many white, middle-class liberals – and to American intellectuals in particular – the university had long seemed a safe, reliable preserve of liberal values and ideas. But to many students at Columbia and elsewhere, the university had come to seem an agent of an oppressive state and an obstacle to personal freedom and fulfillment. At Harvard University, a year after the Columbia uprising, protesting architecture students produced a dramatic poster that expressed the diffuse grievances of many young men and women across the country against the universities, and the society they believed universities represented:

strike because you hate cops/strike because your roommate was clubbed/strike to stop expansion/strike to seize control of your life/strike to become more human

10 David J. Garrow, *Bearing the Cross: Martin Luther King, Jr., and the Southern Christian Leadership Conference* (New York, 1986), 616–24.
11 James Miller, *"Democracy Is in the Streets": From Port Huron to the Siege of Chicago* (New York, 1987), 290–2.

.../strike because there's no poetry in your lectures/strike because classes are a bore/strike for power/strike to smash the corporation/strike to make yourself free/strike to abolish ROTC/strike because they are trying to squeeze the life out of you.[12]

On June 6, 1968, Robert F. Kennedy – who had begun running for president three months earlier – was assassinated in a hotel in Los Angeles a few minutes after appearing before his supporters to claim victory in the California primary. This terrible event, so soon after the assassination of King, further weakened public confidence in the stability and unity of American society. It was particularly shattering to the many young men and women who had come to see in Kennedy (and, earlier, in his slain brother) a promise of enlightened, idealistic, and compassionate leadership. The contrast between popular reaction to John F. Kennedy's death in 1963 and the death of Robert Kennedy in 1968 suggests something of the change that was occurring in American life. Five years earlier, most (although never all) Americans rushed, rather too hastily many later came to believe, to embrace the idea that the president had been the victim of a single, crazed individual. The Warren Commission, appointed by President Johnson to investigate the assassination, endorsed that view, and for a time, few Americans were inclined to dispute the findings of so august a body. The death of President Kennedy, it seemed, was a terrible aberration, an event whose only explanation was the twisted psyche of a pathetic young man. In 1968, after an assassination that seems even more likely than the 1963 assassination to have been the work of a single individual, much of the public interpreted Robert Kennedy's death quite differently from the way they had earlier interpreted John Kennedy's. This was not an aberration. It was a result of a tendency toward violence and corruption deeply embedded in American life. Kennedy (and King) were not the victims of particular assassins; they were the victims of American society, of a sickness at the heart of the culture. Rather than appoint a new Warren Commission to investigate the assassination, President Johnson appointed a special commission to investigate society. Several years later, the President's Commission on Violence issued a powerful report endorsing the view that violence was endemic in American life and claiming that violence was a national illness that threatened the long-term health of the republic.[13]

---

12 *Atlantic Monthly,* Nov. 1986, 24.
13 National Commission on the Causes and Prevention of Violence, *To Establish Justice, To Insure Domestic Tranquility: The Final Report* (New York, 1970). Hugh Davis Graham and Ted Robert Gurr, eds., *Violence in America* (New York, 1969) is a significant scholarly expression of this view, prepared as a report to the National Commission. See also Christopher Lasch, "The Life of Kennedy's Death," *Harper's,* Oct. 1983, 32–40.

In August 1968, Democrats gathered in Chicago for their national convention, glumly prepared to nominate Vice President Hubert Humphrey, Johnson's handpicked successor and the choice of party regulars throughout the nation, as the party's nominee for president. Both inside and outside the convention hall, however, were scenes of terrible bitterness. There were sudden booms behind various alternative candidates: Eugene McCarthy, George McGovern, Edward Kennedy – anyone, it seemed, who might provide an alternative to the Johnson-anointed and thus discredited Humphrey. There was a bitter fight over the platform (and particularly over its Vietnam plank). There were physical confrontations on the convention floor between delegates and Chicago policemen. And there was an extraordinary demonstration of emotion and anger when, after the screening of a brief film tribute to Robert Kennedy, hundreds of delegates began singing the "Battle Hymn of the Republic" repeatedly, for more than twenty minutes, bringing the proceedings of the convention to a halt.[14]

Outside at almost the same time, several miles away in downtown Chicago, there was an open pitched battle between young antiwar demonstrators and the Chicago police. Radical groups from around the country had been planning for months for an enormous demonstration in Chicago to protest the Democratic Party's complicity in (and responsibility for) the Vietnam War. Although they had hoped for one hundred thousand protesters to arrive in the city, fewer than ten thousand actually came. (Tom Hayden, one of the founders of SDS, arrived in Chicago as the week began, looked around, and exclaimed: "My God, there's nobody here.")[15] The protests were rescued from failure by the insistence of Chicago officials and the Chicago police on treating this motley group of young people as a serious threat to public safety. On the night Humphrey was nominated, about four thousand demonstrators gathered on Michigan Avenue near Grant Park prepared to march to the convention hall; the police surrounded them, leaving them nowhere to advance and nowhere to retreat; and then the police charged (some of them chanting "Kill 'em").[16] Norman Mailer (watching from a hotel window across the street) described the scene, in his book on the conventions, *Miami and the Siege of Chicago:*

The police attacked with tear gas, with Mace, and with clubs, they attacked like a chain saw cutting into wood, the teeth of the saw the edge of their clubs, they attacked like a scythe through grass, lines of twenty and thirty policemen striking out in an arc, their clubs beating, demonstrators fleeing. Seen from overhead, from

14 *Newsweek,* Sept. 9, 1968, 334; *New York Times,* Aug. 30, 1968.
15 David Farber, *Chicago '68* (Chicago, 1988) is the fullest account of these events.
16 *New York Times,* Aug. 30, 1968; *Newsweek,* Sept. 9, 1968, 39.

the nineteenth floor, it was like a wind blowing dust, or the edge of waves riding foam on the shore.[17]

Mailer was not alone in watching from the nineteenth floor. He stood among a phalanx of television cameras, broadcasting the melee to an American audience estimated at 90 million people (and eventually to an even larger audience around the world). No one was more aware of that than the demonstrators themselves, who taunted the rampaging police (and, they knew, the television audience) with the chant "The whole world is watching."[18]

The national media reacted with undisguised horror to the events in Grant Park. "The assault from the Left was furious, fluky and bizarre," *Time* commented. "Yet the Chicago police department responded in a way that could only be characterized as sanctioned mayhem . . . and contravened every accepted code of professional police discipline."[19] The columnist Stewart Alsop claimed that "in Chicago, for the first time in my life, it began to seem to me possible that some form of American fascism may really happen here."[20]

The Chicago police were not unprovoked. The most radical of the demonstrators, the so-called Yippies, had been taunting and abusing the police for days: cursing them, calling them pigs, throwing plastic bags at them filled with human excrement. Some of the organizers of the march admitted later that the confrontation was exactly what they had wanted, what they had planned for. Jerry Rubin, one of the leaders of the Yippies, later said:

We wanted exactly what happened. . . . We wanted to create a situation in which the Chicago police and the Daley administration and the federal government and the United States would self-destruct. We wanted to show that America wasn't a democracy, that the convention wasn't politics. The message of the week was of an America ruled by force. This was a big victory.[21]

But whoever was to blame, there was an air of horror and unreality in Chicago, which (particularly when combined with the other traumatic events of the months preceding the convention) created a sense among

---

17 Norman Mailer, *Miami and the Siege of Chicago: An Informal History of the Republican and Democratic Conventions of 1968* (New York, 1969), 169.
18 See also Lewis Chester, Godfrey Hodgson, and Bruce Page, *An American Melodrama: The Presidential Campaign of 1968* (New York, 1969), 503–23; White, *The Making of the President, 1968,* 257–313; Farber, *Chicago '68,* 158.
19 *Time,* Sept. 6, 1968, 21.
20 Stewart Alsop, "Virus X and the Body Politic," *Newsweek,* Sept. 16, 1968, 108.
21 Allen J. Matusow, *The Unraveling of America: A History of Liberalism in the 1960s* (New York, 1984), 422.

many Americans that their society was in the throes of a major, perhaps irrevocable breakdown; that the crisis was so grave, the condition of the nation so precarious, that a genuine revolution might be impending. Out of that sense of crisis emerged several very different reassessments of American politics.

IV

From the end of World War II until at least 1966, mainstream politics in America had been essentially centrist. There were, of course, radicals on both the Left and the Right in those years, but their voices were seldom heard in the corridors of power or through the most powerful vehicles of the media. The two major parties (and the principal factions within each party) had kept their differences relatively muted. Except for the bitter fight between the white South and much of the rest of the country over the issue of race and civil rights, few fundamental disagreements had been visible within the mainstream. The one time in the postwar period when either party nominated a candidate who seemed to challenge some of the centrist, mildly liberal assumptions of the political center – in 1964, when the Republicans nominated the conservative Barry Goldwater – the result was the most crushing defeat in modern political history.

But by 1968, all the major pillars supporting this centrist liberalism had begun to crumble: the commitment to the Cold War, the faith in the possibility of peaceful social change, the belief in the essential health of American culture, even confidence in the American economy – which (as Diane B. Kunz shows elsewhere in this book) was itself showing the first, alarming signs of the decay that would blight American politics, and American society, through much of the 1970s and 1980s.[22] As the liberalism of the center decayed, other kinds of politics emerged to challenge it.

One was a politics born of the increasingly radical challenges to the center that had gained considerable strength during the great public crises of 1968. This new politics grew out of challenges to liberalism from African Americans, from the poor, from women, from gays and lesbians, Chicanos, from Native Americans (all of whose own liberation movements began or greatly expanded in the late 1960s), and from many others. And it drew as well from the restless, striving, angry movements of American youth – the antiwar movement, the New Left, and the counterculture. Even in combination, these movements still represented a small proportion of the popula-

22 See Diane B. Kunz's chapter in this book.

tion. But their visibility and their intensity gave them a disproportionate impact; and the social and political crises of 1968 made them seem more powerful than they were. Even many once moderate Americans now became convinced that the centrist, liberal assumptions they had uncritically accepted for twenty years were no longer adequate to the problems at hand and that some new political response would be necessary.

The result was a redefinition of liberalism by a growing number of centrist politicians, most of them in the Democratic Party. The most important figure in this redefinition – both before and after his death – was Robert Kennedy. By 1968, Kennedy had moved well beyond the relatively constricted, relatively cautious liberalism of the early 1960s, the liberalism of President Kennedy and his administration; and he had identified his own enormous political prestige (as well as the memory of his brother, whose legacy he was reinterpreting to fit his own new commitments) with a new, more expansive, at times more radical approach to social problems. Kennedy had become an outspoken critic of Johnson's policies in Vietnam in 1967. In the 1968 campaign, he became an outspoken critic of what he considered the inadequacy of Johnson's domestic policies as well. Kennedy became much more aggressive and assertive than Johnson in speaking out against urban poverty and was bitterly critical of the cutbacks in Great Society programs that had begun in 1967. He created a foundation in the Bedford-Stuyvesant district of Brooklyn, one of the poorest inner-city communities in the country, and had insisted that the work of the foundation be steered by the primarily African-American and Puerto Rican residents themselves. He visited the homes of sharecroppers in the Mississippi Delta and complained bitterly about malnutrition. He developed a highly visible alliance with Cesar Chavez, the Mexican-American labor organizer who was trying to unionize migrant farm workers in California and elsewhere, which made him the first major national politician to recognize Hispanics as a significant political force. He identified himself with an important movement emerging among Native Americans that called for rebuilding societies of the reservations and greater attention to the plight of Indians in America.[23]

In part, Kennedy was doing all this to improve his political prospects: to differentiate himself from Johnson and position himself as the principal liberal voice in the Democratic Party. He was also, apparently, acting to express

---

23 For a full account of Robert Kennedy's political transformation after 1965, see Arthur M. Schlesinger Jr., *Robert Kennedy and His Times* (Boston, 1978), chaps. 34–40; Richard N. Goodwin, *Remembering America: A Voice from the Sixties* (Boston, 1988), chaps. 23–25; and, for a slightly more skeptical view, Harris Wofford, *Of Kennedys and Kings: Making Sense of the Sixties* (New York, 1980), chap. 12.

genuine (if relatively newfound) conviction. But whatever his reasons, Robert Kennedy took the deep reverence Americans felt for the memory of his brother and identified it with a whole range of issues that John Kennedy had never embraced and probably had never even considered. When Robert Kennedy himself was killed, his own martyrdom became a powerful force pushing these issues onto the agenda of American liberals.

That, then, was one response to the turmoil of the 1960s, and to the crises of 1968: a significant expansion of the agenda of American liberalism; the identification of a powerful faction of the Democratic Party with the interests of the most dispossessed elements of the population; the intrusion into mainstream politics of some of the concerns, some of the language, and some of the style of the Left. "When we are told to forgo all dissent and division," Kennedy said in 1968, "we must ask – who is it that is truly dividing the country? It is not those who call for change, it is those who make present policy . . . who have removed themselves from the American tradition, from the enduring and generous impulses that are the soul of this nation." Or, on another occasion: "I am dissatisfied with our society. I am dissatisfied with our country." His cadence resembled that of his brother; but his words had a harsher, angrier, more radical tone.[24]

V

Many liberals, particularly those individuals who came to admire and even to love Robert Kennedy, believed that this was the direction in which American politics as a whole was moving. They were convinced that most of the public was, like them, horrified at the injustices and inequalities that the events of 1968 had revealed and were, like them, convinced that the only reasonable response was to take drastic action to confront the nation's social problems. But such liberals were wrong. Because the more common popular response to the turbulence of the late 1960s (and of 1968 in particular) was not a heightened concern for the dispossessed, not a commitment to progressive change, not a search for more effective social policies. The more common response was, rather, a search for order and stability, the effort to restore an imagined world of social harmony that the events of the 1960s seemed to have shattered. The most important political story of 1968 was, in the end, less the story of a revolution than of a powerful conservative reaction.[25]

24 Matusow, *The Unraveling of America*, 406.   25 *Time*, Sept. 13, 1969, 16–17.

On one issue after another, prevailing currents of public opinion ran sharply counter to the assumptions of the Left and of the newly militant liberalism uneasily allied with it. In turning against the war, many liberals believed, the public was embracing their own moral revulsion from the American commitment in Vietnam. In fact, the great majority of antiwar voters (70 percent of McCarthy's supporters in New Hampshire among them) turned against the war not because they had repudiated the value of the effort but because they had become convinced that the government was not willing to do what it would take to win. The very high level of American casualties during and after the Tet Offensive made the costs of the conflict seem incompatible with the limited nature of the American commitment to it.[26]

In responding with horror to the King assassination and the urban disorders it produced, the public was, many liberals assumed, embracing their own intensified commitment to working for racial equality. But among much of the public, the increasing violence of the struggle for racial equality – and the rise of more divisive economic demands among the leaders of that struggle – led to a growing disenchantment with the movement, as the posthumous history of King's last great project – the Poor People's Campaign – made clear.

In the aftermath of King's death, his protégés carried on his plans for a new march on Washington in the summer of 1968, which they hoped would pressure on Congress to pass new antipoverty programs in the same way that the March on Washington in 1963 had pressured Congress to pass civil rights legislation. According to Ralph Abernethy, King's successor as head of the Southern Christian Leadership Council and the principal spokesman for the new campaign, poor people would descend on Washington and "plague the Pharaohs of this nation with plague after plague until they agree to give us meaningful jobs and a guaranteed annual income."[27] But the Poor People's Campaign was never able to generate anything like the popular enthusiasm that earlier civil rights campaigns had produced. It attracted little attention from the media (most of it derisive or hostile) and relatively little support even from among African Americans. On June 19, Abernethy staged a Solidarity Day, modeled on the great 1963 demonstration. But while the 1963 march had attracted more than two

---

26 Philip E. Converse et al., "Continuity and Change in American Politics: Parties and Issues in the 1968 Election," *American Political Science Review* 63 (1969): 1,092; Scammon and Wattenberg, *The Real Majority*, chap. 7.
27 *New York Times*, May 14, 1968.

hundred thousand people, Solidarity Day attracted fewer than fifty thousand, and on June 23, only four days later, "Resurrection City" – the squalid campsite on the mall that the demonstrators had constructed – was closed down by the Washington police as a health hazard. The demonstrators dispersed. Congress proceeded with the process it had begun in 1967 of dismantling or defunding many of the War on Poverty programs of the Great Society.[28]

Another indication of the way many liberals misinterpreted public opinion was the Chicago convention. There was an almost unquestioned assumption among many liberal political figures, and much of the mainstream media, that the American people shared their anger about the police violence in Chicago. A substantial majority of the public was indeed angry, but not at the police. They were, rather, incensed at the behavior of the demonstrators and the apparent support the media had given them. A national poll conducted shortly after the convention showed that 71 percent of the public believed that the security measures imposed by the Chicago police had been justified; 57 percent believed that the police had not used excessive force. Senator Abraham Ribicoff of Connecticut, who had won the admiration of most liberals (and much of the media) for his speech to the convention berating Mayor Richard Daley of Chicago for engaging in "Gestapo tactics," found that what seemed to liberals an act of courage and honor appeared to his own constituents an intemperate blast at authority. For the first and only time in his political career, he faced a difficult reelection battle in Connecticut, fueled by popular anger at his behavior in Chicago.[29]

VI

Most of the American people, in short, did not see the events of 1968 as evidence of the injustice and repressiveness of American society and culture, or of the failures of a reactionary political establishment and a failed foreign policy. They saw those events, rather, as evidence of the unruliness and disruptiveness of the Left and of the descent of American society as a whole into an abyss of disorder and violence. And in responding to this perceived chaos, they turned in substantial numbers to two political figures who asked for support on the basis of their opposition to the "radical" turn in American politics.

One of those figures was Governor George C. Wallace of Alabama, who

28 *New York Times,* June 10, 20, 24, 1968.   29 *New York Times,* Aug. 31, 1968.

through the early 1960s had stood as a staunch defender of racial segregation and who had achieved renown for briefly resisting the federal government in 1963 when it ordered the integration of the University of Alabama.
In 1968 Wallace launched a campaign for the presidency that most national
Democrats dismissed at first as ludicrous. But he displayed remarkable
strength, not just in his native South but also in Michigan, Maryland, and
other northern and border states. In the fall, after he had failed to win the
Democratic nomination, he launched a third-party candidacy that at some
moments attracted the support of up to 22 percent of the electorate in public opinion polls (and up to 35 percent of American workers). His support
was widely distributed through every region of the country.

Most liberals at the time attributed Wallace's popularity to the racism of
his supporters, and to virtually nothing else. But Wallace's popularity in
1968 was not solely, perhaps not even primarily, a product of white racism.
It reflected a much deeper disillusionment with liberalism, a hatred of the
Left, and a profound fear of violence and disorder. It rested on the sense
among large numbers of working-class and lower-middle-class Americans
that the liberal mainstream of American politics had left them behind; that
the government and the elites associated with it – the media, the intelligentsia, the universities, even some of the major corporate organizations,
the people who had for many years largely determined the shape of public
discourse – had lost interest in them and had attached themselves to the
poor, to minorities, and to radicals; that the "little man," the "average American," was being squeezed out, ignored, abused, exploited.[30]

Wallace spoke clearly to that sense of alienation and anger. "Liberals,
intellectuals, and long hairs," he said, "have run this country for too long.
The average American is sick and tired of all those over-educated ivory
tower folks with pointed heads looking down their noses at us." His constituency, he said, was "this average man on the street, this man in the textile mill, this man in the steel mill, this barber, this beautician, the policeman on the beat . . . the little businessman." These were the people most
aware of the power of great institutions to control their lives. And the most
menacing such institution, the greatest and most ominous source of concentrated power, Wallace now told them, was a national government that
had become the instrument of the poor and blacks and radicals.[31]

Wallace's campaign faltered toward the end, and ultimately he received
not the 20 or 30 percent of the vote he had once predicted, but 13.5 per-

30 Dan T. Carter, *The Politics of Rage: George Wallace, The Origins of the New Conservatism, and the Trans-
    formation of American Politics* (New York, 1996), chaps. 10–11.
31 *New York Times*, Sept. 3, 1968; Chester et al., *An American Melodrama*, 280–1.

cent (still the best performance of any third-party candidate in 40 years). Wallace suffered because of his crudeness, his occasional clumsiness, and his inability to pierce the skepticism of a public unaccustomed to third-party candidacies. But he suffered most of all from the competition he faced from the Republican Party presidential candidate in 1968: Richard Nixon, who mounted a campaign that exploited many of the same resentments and grievances that Wallace was expressing, but who articulated them in a more conventionally acceptable way.

Nixon premised his campaign in 1968 on the assumption, very much like Wallace's assumption, that the average American was tired of the liberals and the radicals and the disorder they seemed to tolerate, that most voters wanted a return to stability, order, and traditional values. Wallace spoke of the "little man, this average American." Nixon spoke of what he called "Middle America" or, later, the "Silent Majority." Wallace denounced the "sissy-britches and the intellectual morons" who he claimed were dominating the Democratic Party and the federal government. Nixon talked about the "elite groups, the establishment." Both exploited what came to be known as the "social issue," what one of Nixon's campaign aides described as "a set of public attitudes concerning the more personally frightening aspects of disruptive change." And both talked about crime and promised to restore "law and order"; both drew analogies between the violence of the rising wave of street crime in American cities with the violence of antiwar demonstrators and student protesters. Violence "may masquerade as 'civil disobedience,' or 'freedom,'" Nixon said, "and it sometimes marches under the banner of legitimate dissent. . . . But when the slogans are stripped away, it still is violence plain and simple, cruel and evil as always, destructive of freedom, destructive of progress, destructive of peace."[32]

Nixon won the election, in the end, by a margin almost as small as the one by which he had lost in 1960: 500,000 votes, less than 1 percent. But it would be misleading to make too much of the closeness of his victory. What is most striking about the 1968 election is not the narrowness of the final vote, but the contrast it provides to the election four years before. In 1964, 61 percent of the American people had voted for a candidate, Lyndon Johnson, who was firmly identified with the optimistic liberal assumptions that had been gaining strength since the end of World War II. They had expressed their support for the promise of peaceful, progressive change through positive government. In 1968, 57 percent of the American people

32 Richard M. Nixon, Statement, May 5, 1968, in PPS 208 (1968). 26 (1), Speech Files, Nixon Library.

voted for two candidates – Richard Nixon and George Wallace – who were calling openly for a repudiation of much of what liberalism seemed now to have become, who were identifying it with radicalism and disorder.

VII

What did this striking reversal of the political fortunes of liberals mean? Some argued at the time that it was a fluke, a result of the traumas and crises of 1968 and of the fears they had spawned. And it is true, of course, that neither liberalism nor the Left vanished from American life in the aftermath of the 1968 election. The Nixon administration, carried forward by the momentum of nearly a decade of liberal initiatives, presided over – and at times actively encouraged – the creation of some of the most important expansions of federal power of the postwar era. Liberal voices, including the voices of people at least modestly radicalized by the events of the 1960s, continued for at least another decade to dominate the most powerful instruments of the media and continued for longer than that to dominate the world of the academy. The relativistic values, if not the politics, of the New Left and counterculture had a lasting effect on American popular culture through the 1970s and well beyond. The events of 1968 produced many legacies, and among them were lasting social and cultural changes that reflected some of the ideas and impulses of the Left.

But other, very different legacies of 1968 were at least as powerful – and in politics, at least, more enduring. Early in 1969, a conservative Republican congressional aide named Kevin Phillips published *The Emerging Republican Majority,* in which he tried to explain the meaning of the 1968 election. He argued that Nixon's victory was not an aberration but part of a lasting shift in voter loyalties. It was a result, he argued, of the growing self-consciousness of the American middle class, of its sense of its *own* interests, as opposed to the interests of minorities, of its belief that the middle class itself was now imperiled and in need of protection and that the preoccupation of liberal government with dissenters, minorities, and the poor was coming at the expense of the "average American."

Liberals, Phillips argued, were living in an illusory world. They believed they represented the wishes of the majority; but through their excesses, through their apparent alliance with radical groups and radical changes, they had lost touch with that majority. "The corporate welfarists, planners and academicians of the Liberal Establishment," he said, are a "privileged elite," with no constituency:

The great political upheaval of the 1960s is not that of Senator Eugene McCarthy's relatively small group of upper middle-class and intellectual supporters, but a populist revolt of the American masses who have been elevated by prosperity to middle-class status and conservatism. Their revolt is against the caste, policies and taxation of the mandarins of Establishment liberalism.[33]

Four years earlier, most liberals had believed (and many conservatives had feared) that Democratic liberalism, with its promise and confidence and hope, was so firmly entrenched as the dominant force in American politics that no conservative candidate could hope to overcome it in the foreseeable future. Now, Phillips was saying, liberalism had forfeited its mandate and a new politics had emerged: a politics that would reward candidates who defied the Left, repudiated the liberals, and tried to build a genuine conservative majority. This new politics demystified liberalism and put it on the defensive, where it has remained ever since.

The enduring realignment Phillips predicted did not occur in 1968. It may never occur. But it is clear that by the end of 1968 – because of the traumatic events of that turbulent year and because of the broad social problems and political resentments that produced those events – the powerful political consensus that American liberalism had worked so painstakingly to create for nearly twenty years – and that had dominated American politics for what was, in the end, only a very brief time in the mid-1960s – was shattered, perhaps irretrievably. American liberalism has been wandering in the political wilderness ever since.

33 Kevin Phillips, *The Emerging Republican Majority* (New Rochelle, N.Y., 1969), 469–70 and passim.

8

March 1968 in Poland

JERZY EISLER

Poland's important historical events are traditionally designated by the names of months. Thus, when Poles speak of "September" (written, despite the rules of Polish orthography, with a capital "S"), they mean the year 1939, the beginning of World War II, and their isolated struggle against German and Soviet aggression. When someone speaks of "October," this refers to the year 1956 and its tumultuous political events, including the threat of Soviet military intervention and the euphoria over Władysław Gomułka's return to power. Considered the "messenger of providence," Gomułka was able to democratize, liberalize, and humanize the system. When someone speaks of "December," this refers either to the workers' revolt on the Baltic coast in 1970 or to General Wojciech Jaruzelski's imposition of martial law in 1981.

When "March" is invoked, the year 1968 is undoubtedly recalled. Unlike the three earlier examples, however, there is still disagreement over the meaning of the tragic events of that year, which have been interpreted according to different perspectives and personal experiences. Those who were students in 1968 emphasize the meetings, demonstrations, and strikes at the universities. Members of the world of culture, science, and the arts have stressed the violent campaign against the intellectuals, as well as the ensuing purge of the mass media, publishing houses, and university faculties.

For Poland's small community of Jews, the events of March 1968 signified a brutal wave of official or semi-official anti-Semitism, which was clumsily masked as anti-Zionism. In the mid-1960s there were thirty thousand Jews and people of Jewish ancestry in Poland. In 1966, however, only seventy-five hundred belonged to the official Jewish social and cultural association (Towarzystwo Społeczno-Kulturalne Żydów w Polsce), including fifteen hundred elderly people. In the entire country, there were only fifteen hundred Jews between the ages of twenty-five and thirty-nine. Twenty-five percent of all Polish Jews were under eighteen years of age. Although there were five schools where Yiddish was still taught, one principal in Wrocław complained that his students spoke only Polish at home, which certainly indicates a highly advanced process of assimilation.[1]

March 1968 also witnessed a major struggle among the leaders of the Polish Communist Party, the essential features of which remain obscure even after thirty years. Although we are unable to achieve complete and definitive answers, we can pose useful and probing questions.

THE POLITICS OF ANTI-SEMITISM

By the early 1960s, there were rumors that General Mieczysław Moczar, the minister of the interior, had created an informal group of middle- and lower-level activists inside the Polish United Workers' Party (Polska Zjednoczona Partia Robotnicza or PZPR). The group was called "the partisans" because Moczar and his close collaborator, General Grzegorz Korczyński, had participated in the communist resistance movement during World War II. Moczar, with the support of the organization of the former guerrillas, the Association of Fighters for Freedom and Democracy, had gained considerable influence over many journalists, publicists, and writers as well as over some former soldiers of the Home Army who shared a common combatant past.

Moczar's main importance, however, derived from the increase of his authority within the politburo apparatus and his influence over the party's activists. Gossips alleged that he was Moscow's most highly esteemed national communist and that his aim was the "revival of the nation." The ideology of Moczar's group consisted of a form of jingoism (which was officially anti-German but unofficially anti-Soviet and anti-Russian) and anti-Semitism, as well as authoritarianism, anti-intellectualism, and the worship of strength.

According to their rivals, the guerrillas' main characteristic was their innate anti-Semitism, which they expressed in ruthless and instrumental ways. Allegedly, they intended to exploit the anti-Jewish prejudices and the view of the Jews as foreigners that existed in some social circles of Poland. But, according to the writer Artur Międzyrzecki, the essence of the guerrillas' anti-Semitism "was actually a form of hatred and a more general

---

1 Michael Checinski, *Poland: Communism, Nationalism, Anti-Semitism* (New York, 1982), 128–30, 239–41.

renunciation of the world. Neither racists nor anti-racists . . . they hated everybody, including Jews. Or, perhaps Jews above all. But not only them."[2]

To this day, the aims of Moczar and his guerrillas are not fully understood. There is still disagreement over whether Moczar planned to replace Gomułka as first secretary of the Central Committee or simply weaken him and become his first deputy. This much is known: the guerrillas used anti-Semitism in their campaign of urging older communist activists (and not just the Jewish ones) to retire and turn their posts over to the young, ambitious, and dynamic apparatchiks who had been politically formed in postwar Poland.

The Six-Day War of 1967, combined with the real and alleged reactions of Poland's Jews to Israel's military successes, had a strong impact on the power struggle within Poland's political elite. To be sure, Polish Jews were not the only group to applaud Israel's victories; the Israeli embassy in Warsaw received many telegrams and letters from Christians expressing sympathy and friendship. On June 6 the primate of Poland, Cardinal Stefan Wyszyński, in a mass in Warsaw, prayed for the Jewish nation and its right to its own state. This outpouring of pro-Jewish sentiment can be explained as follows. First, the average Pole had very little information about the actual situation in the Middle East. Second, some influential intellectuals from Jewish backgrounds were sympathetic to Israel and propagated the image of a tiny, beleaguered country of 2 million inhabitants surrounded by 100 million Arabs. And third, many Poles regarded the Arabs' defeat as a Soviet setback in a proxy war with the United States.

The Communist Party's directorate was fully aware of these sentiments. Moczar and his followers decided to use this occasion to eliminate their adversaries. Where real evidence was lacking, they used provocation, denunciation, and fabricated evidence. Gomułka's minister of defense and close collaborator, Marian Spychalski, became a target of the guerrillas, who spread rumors that his wife had been visiting her relatives in Israel when war erupted in the Middle East. "Moczar's men" were responsible for spreading this gossip as widely as possible. When the party called a meeting of an army unit, for example, some of the speakers directly attacked Spychalski, referring to his wife's stay in Israel and her alleged contacts with Defense Minister Moshe Dayan.

Two Jewish activists, Eugeniusz Szyr and Artur Starewicz, were also criticized by Moczar's minions. Prime Minister Józef Cyrankiewicz was

---

2 Artur Międzyrzecki, "1968: wspomnienia i dokumenty [1968: Memories and Documents]," *Więź* 7–8 (1988): 164.

accused of having hidden his Jewish ancestry and his real name, "Zimmerman." Colonel Zygmunt Ostrowski, who forewarned Spychalski's cabinet chief and contested all these accusations, was himself denounced as an Israeli agent. Ostrowski committed suicide on September 5, 1967.

There were also some ridiculous moments. Immediately after the Six-Day War, the head of the government information agency, Interpress, initiated his own "purge of Zionism" and dismissed all journalists with Jewish ancestry. When one of the targets of this dismissal asked for a definition of Zionism, the agency head replied weakly: although he did not have time to verify the details in an encyclopedia, generally speaking a Zionist was someone whose parents were Jewish.[3]

In the meantime, the authorities were compelled by the decision of the Warsaw Pact summit meeting in Moscow to sever all diplomatic ties to Israel. This occurred on June 12, 1967. Six days later, when the Israeli ambassador left Warsaw, he was bidden farewell by two hundred slightly inebriated men whose refreshment had been provided by Moczar's Ministry of the Interior and who, at the airport, expressed their "spontaneous" joy at the ambassador's departure.[4]

This incident probably marks the beginning of the official anti-Semitism campaign initiated by Moczar and his guerrillas. On June 19, 1967, Gomułka delivered a speech to the Sixth Trade Union Congress dealing mostly with the war in the Middle East and its effects on Poland. The first secretary announced:

Because Israel's aggression against the Arab countries has been welcomed by Zionist Jews and Polish citizens, I wish to announce that we shall not prevent Polish citizens of Jewish nationality from returning to Israel if they wish to do so. Our position is that every Polish citizen should have one country: the People's Poland. This opinion is shared by many Polish-Jewish citizens who have served our country faithfully. But we cannot remain indifferent to people who . . . support the aggressor and destroyer of peace and support its imperialism. Let all who believe they have been alluded to draw the appropriate conclusion.[5]

Over radio and television, millions of people heard Gomułka use the expression "fifth column" to refer to the Jews of Poland. The party's leaders were extremely displeased. Edward Ochab, a politburo member and the chief of the State Council, insisted on removing the offending expression from newspaper accounts of the address and also from the anthology of Gomułka's speeches. In 1981, Ochab said, "Yes, Gomułka shocked the

3 Paul Lendvai, *Anti-Semitism Without Jews: Communist Eastern Europe* (New York, 1971), 116–17, 146–9.
4 Peter Raina, *Political Opposition in Poland, 1954–1977* (London, 1978), 108–9.
5 *Trybuna Ludu* [People's Tribune], June 20, 1967.

members of the politburo with his ideas. Afterwards, I told him: 'You should not have expressed yourself in this way without the agreement of the politburo.' He began to apologize and explained that he had worked until late the night before, all by himself and without any help."[6]

This same expression was used by the guerrillas, who intensified their anti-Semitic campaign. They sent anonymous and insulting letters to citizens of Jewish ancestry and made threatening telephone calls. They also spread the idea of cutting off the hair of Polish women who had any relationship with Jews. Nevertheless, this propagandistic campaign against a fifth column at the time of the Six-Day War yielded only five hundred Jewish emigrants from Poland in 1967. The last big wave of Jewish emigration began nearly a year later.

THE POLITICAL STRUGGLE

The complex events of March 1968 cannot be viewed solely through the prism of an anti-Semitic campaign. Many diverse and even opposite currents coalesced at that time. It is important to remember that when Gomułka returned to power in 1956 he liberalized the system that had been created with the backing of the Red Army. By the end of the 1950s, however, political pressures along with restrictions on civil rights increased, and incidents of censorship mounted. In their struggles with political enemies, the authorities wielded police and administrative power, although less brutally than during the Stalinist era.

Frustration spread to every part of society. As a result of the increase in discontent, conflicts arose between the authorities and various social groups, ranging from the Catholic Church to the world of science, art, and culture. After 1958, church-state relations deteriorated rapidly. By the mid-1960s, the crisis came to a boil when Communists objected to the bishops' letter inviting German colleagues to participate in the celebration of the thousand-year anniversary of Christianity in 1966. The Polish leadership, and especially Gomułka, was infuriated by this letter, which, only twenty years after the end of World War II, contained such words as "we pardon" and "we beg of you." Superimposing their secular celebrations over the religious ones, the Communists barred Pope Paul VI from visiting Poland and withheld Cardinal Wyszyński's passport for three years.[7]

---

6 Teresa Torańska, *Oni* [Them] (London, 1990), 67.
7 For more details, see Piotr Madajczyk, *Na drodze do pojednania: Wokół oredzia biskupów polskich do biskupów niemieckich z 1965 rodu* [Way to Peace: Letter from Polish Bishops to the German Bishops in 1965](Warsaw, 1994). Cf. Antoni Dudek, *Państwo I Kosciol w Polsce, 1945–1970* [State and Church in Poland, 1945–1970] (Cracow, 1995) and Andrzej Micewski, *Kardynal Wyszyński: Prymas I Mąż Stanu* [Cardinal Wyszyński: Primate and Statesman] (Paris, 1982).

The government's attitude toward intellectuals was equally hostile, especially when they protested the party's rejection of liberalization during the
latter half of the 1950s. Poland's cultural and scientific elites observed political changes with considerable anxiety, mistrust, and impatience. They
rejected the official declarations of concern and understanding for their
position.

In February 1962 the government ordered the closing of the Crooked
Circle, a social, political, and artistic club in Warsaw. For seven years, the
club had been the site of meetings at which Poland's most acute problems
had been discussed. It had at least three hundred members and as many
sympathizers.[8]

Two years later, in March 1964, thirty-four writers and scientists wrote
a letter to Cyrankiewicz protesting the rationing of paper to publish books
and magazines and also against the increased censorship, which was threatening the development of the nation's culture. Some of the signers suffered
various forms of harassment and repression, but after Western Europe and
the United States protested loudly, the government saw fit to place only a
few of the intellectuals on trial.[9]

At the same time, the Polish economy began to deteriorate, afflicted by
stagnation of salaries and inflation. The younger generation, recognizing
the sharp decline in living standards that had taken place since the 1950s,
became disenchanted with the Communists. They increasingly lacked
motivation and interest in their future in Poland. At the same time, the
opening of the country to the outside world kindled the aspirations of tal-
ented young people who admired Western European and American societies, which they were beginning to know through books, magazines, films,
and popular music.

The two most important figures for Poland's youth were Jacek Kuroń
and Karol Modzelewski. These two young intellectuals, who for many
years had been associated with the Communist youth organization, jointly
prepared an "Open Letter to the Party" in which they criticized Poland's
postwar reality and maintained that the country's economy was in a state of
permanent crisis. They blamed the party elite, an unrestrained entity that
decided all important matters, for this dire situation. Kuroń and
Modzelewski called this elite "the central political bureaucracy."[10]

8 As far as we know, there is no scholarly study of this club but only a book by one of its members,
   Witold Jedlicki, *Klub Krzywego Koła* [Crooked Circle Club] (Paris, 1963).
9 For more details, see Jerzy Eisler, *List 34* [Letter of 34] (Warsaw, 1993).
10 "Open Letter to Members of the University of Warsaw Sections of the United Polish Workers'
   Party and the Union of Young Socialists," in *Revolutionary Marxist Students in Poland Speak Out
   (1964–1968),* trans. Gerald Paul (New York, 1972), 15–90.

When they tried to publish their text in March 1965, both men were arrested. In July they were sentenced to prison: Kuroń received three years; Modzelewski received three and a half years. Following their arrest, a new youth leader appeared at Warsaw University, Adam Michnik. His group soon came to be called "commandos" because these brilliant young people disrupted the routines of the party youth organization and disturbed their meetings with their radical and provocative speeches. Like typical commandos, they were bold and resolute. When they launched their left-wing critique of contemporary Poland, the authorities, who claimed to have a monopoly over leftist ideology, became enraged.[11]

Using their private connections, the commandos made contact with West European movements and circles, especially the French anarchist and Trotskyite organization *Jeunesse communiste révolutionnaire*. Through this group, Michnik published a French translation of Kuroń and Modzelewski's original letter. In May 1968 this became the most widely circulated text among the students occupying the Sorbonne.[12] During the trial of student leader Daniel Cohn-Bendit, when the judge kept demanding his name, he finally answered "Kuroń-Modzelewski," which indicated an important ideological tie.[13]

When Kuroń and Modzelewski were released from prison in the autumn of 1967, the commandos were revived. Already counting a few dozen members, their meetings were held in members' apartments, where political and social problems were discussed. A new issue suddenly emerged. Adam Mickiewicz's play *Dziady* was to be performed by the Warsaw National Theater. The play's director, Kazimierz Dejmek, wanted to celebrate the fiftieth anniversary of the October Revolution, which turned out to be a bad idea.

Shortly after *Dziady*'s first performance on November 25, 1967, the Communist Party discussed its anti-Soviet excesses. Indeed, the play's anti-Russian elements elicited tremendous applause from the public. The audience also noticed the numerous allusions to Poland's obeisance to the Soviet Union. By the end of the year, rumors began to circulate that the play was about to be closed because of the objections of the Soviet embassy in Warsaw. The last performance, which took place on January 30, 1968, provided the occasion for a demonstration against the government's assault on cul-

11 See the chapter, "Commandos," based on the recollections of its main representatives, in Jerzy Eisler, *Marzec 1968: Geneza-przebieg-konsekwencje* [March '68: Genesis, Development, and Results] (Warsaw, 1991), 87–115.

12 A. Paczkowski, "Marzec kontra Maj? [March Contra May?]," *Kwartalnik Polityczny "Krytyka"* 28–29 (1988): 58.

13 "Pewien polski ethos . . . Rozmowa Dany Cohn-Bendita z Adamem Michnikiem [Some Polish Ethos . . . Conversation of Danny Cohn-Bendit with Adam Michnik]," *Kontakt* 6 (1988): 40–7.

ture. After the play, about three hundred people marched to the Mickiewicz monument shouting "free play" and "free theater." The monument was decorated in the national colors of red and white. At the end of the demonstration, the police detained and heavily fined some of the participants.[14]

On January 31, 1968, two students from the commandos, Adam Michnik and Henryk Szlajfer, met with Bernard Margueritte, the French correspondent of *Le Monde* in Warsaw, and informed him of the general situation at the university. This news was then repeated over Radio Free Europe. When the authorities discovered the source of this information, both students were dismissed from the university.

In February, Irena Lasota, a member of the commandos, brought the following petition before the Polish parliament: "We, the youth of Warsaw, protest the decision to forbid performances of Mickiewicz's *Dziady* at the National Theater. We protest against the policy of eliminating the traditions of the Polish nation."[15]

Within two weeks, thirty-one hundred people in Warsaw had signed the petition. In Wrocław another thousand signed, but no support came from Poznań or cities in Silesia. To be sure, some signed lists had disappeared into the hands of the Security Services (Służba Bezpieczeństwa or SB). Signing the petition was a real act of civil courage because, at the time, anyone could become subject to prosecution.

At the same moment, Polish writers signed another petition that called for an extraordinary convocation of the Warsaw unit of the Polish Writers' Association. Despite the provisions of the group's charter, no such meeting had been organized since 1922. After 233 of its 600 members signed, a meeting took place on the afternoon of February 29, 1968, with 400 writers in attendance. It lasted until late in the night. A resolution that criticized the suspension of Mickiewicz's *Dziady* greatly disappointed the authorities.[16]

At the meeting most of the speakers referred to the suspension as a threat to cultural freedom that was typical of Communist behavior. But some went even further in their denunciations of the position of intellectuals in Poland. Among the speakers that night were Jerzy Andrzejewski, January Grzędziński, Paweł Jasienica, Mieczysław Jastrun, Stefan Kisielewski, Leszek

---

14 Detailed documentation concerning the *Dziady* affair was presented by Marta Fik in *Marcowa kultura* [March Culture] (Warsaw, 1995) in the chapter "About *Dziady*," 35–103. Cf. Zbigniew Raszewski, *Raptularz 1967/1968* [Diary, 1967–8] (Warsaw, 1993), and Eisler, *Marzec 1968*, 146–63.
15 Quoted in Eisler, *Marzec 1968*, 25.
16 On the writers' meeting, see Fik, *Marcowa kultura*, 107–86, and Eisler, *Marzec 1968*, 164–82.

Kołakowski, Artur Międzyrzecki, and Antoni Słonimski. The names of the speakers were taken down, and the party retaliated almost immediately. The authorities were especially furious over Kisielewski's depiction of state administration of the Polish culture as the "dictatorship of the dumb." Kisielewski paid dearly for this. On March 11 the writer, who was nearly sixty years old, was attacked and beaten by "unknown persons."

The turning point of the "March events" has generally been considered the students' meeting on March 8. The students gathered in the courtyard of Warsaw University to protest the dismissal of Michnik and Szlajfer, to express their solidarity with the writers' resolution, and to ask once more for the return of *Dziady* to the National Theater. Outsiders were also present to provoke the youths. After the meeting, armed police entered the university, dispersed the crowd, and beat up many youths. According to eyewitnesses, the police used excessive force against a peaceful, unarmed gathering.

In their analyses of this key event, some have accused the police of unjustified political intervention and the use of outside agitators to incite a riot. The guerrillas clearly wanted to use the students' meeting to achieve their aims and found it relatively easy to provoke the gathered crowd and then attack it brutally.

Some see the guerrillas' hand at work throughout the incident. It enabled them to accuse Gomułka of indecisiveness and criticize his tolerance of the intellectuals' complaints. The guerrillas now began their attacks against the Jews and against real and fabricated enemies. They alerted the Soviets to the strong "revisionist" currents in the Polish Communist Party that were particularly ominous in light of developments in neighboring Czechoslovakia. When the events of March 8, combined with the Czechoslovak example, created a political and social crisis in Poland and unleashed strikes, demonstrations, and riots beyond the university, a change in the party directorate appeared imminent. Gomułka seemed about to be replaced by the guerrillas or by Moczar himself.

Except for the authorities' intervention and brutality, the main parts of this thesis can never be proved. Undoubtedly, there was a covert political struggle taking place on the highest levels. And yet the students' anger over the censorship and their need to demonstrate solidarity with their persecuted friends was authentic. It is nevertheless possible that two different needs and goals converged on March 8, and that the meeting at Warsaw University may have been prepared by both the commandos and Moczar's faction.

THE STUDENT REVOLT

It should be underscored that the March events in Poland did not occur in a political vacuum but were parallel to what was happening in Czechoslovakia. As early as June 1967, Poland began to experience signs of the revival of politics beyond the party. In Czechoslovakia, liberalization and democratization accelerated in January 1968 with the replacement of the conservative Antonín Novotný with Alexander Dubček as first secretary of the Central Committee. Dubček had counted on the support of the wider "socialist community" and especially Gomułka's support. On February 7, 1968, the two held official and private talks in Morawska Ostrawa. But Gomułka, who had renounced his convictions of October 1956, responded to his Czech colleague's reformist plans with marked reserve.[17]

The Polish students' revolt, which used Czech slogans, tended to reinforce the authorities' conservatism. On Saturday, March 9, the mass media were silent over the events at the university. There were only brief reports on the back pages of two newspapers, both of which greatly distorted the course of events. At noon on March 9, students of the Warsaw Polytechnic protested against these lies and expressed solidarity with their friends at the university. But in their peaceful march to the editorial offices of *Życie Warszawy,* they were brutally set upon by the police and the voluntary reserves of the militia (Ochotnicza Rezerwa Milicji Obywatelskiej or ORMO). Again, many people were beaten or arrested. That morning, a roundup of commandos had begun, and within a few hours the majority of the group were in prison.

Perhaps the most significant event that followed this police action was the student riot of March 11. In the aftermath, violence spread throughout the country. Bloody demonstrations took place in Kraków, Poznań, Wrocław, Lublin, Szczecin, and Katowice. In other cities such as Białystok, Bydgoszcz, Gliwice, Olsztyn, Opole, and Toruń, the students organized meetings at the universities and voted on resolutions that condemned the policies of the government.

In cities without academic institutions, high schools, polytechnics, or universities, such as Legnica, Radom, and Tarnów, there were few conflicts with the armed forces. But everywhere else the student movement overwhelmed nearly all of Poland's public universities. According to the historian Andrzej Friszke, in the spring of 1968 the *Bulletin of the Ministry of*

---

17 The protocol of this meeting has been published in Poland: *Zaciskanie pętli: Tajne dokumenty dotycząca Czechosłowacji 1968 r* [The Tightening of the Rope: Secret Documents on Czechoslovakia '68], ed. A. Garlicki and A. Pączkowski (Warsaw, 1995), 15–48.

Foreign Affairs listed 140 Polish cities and towns where antigovernment handbills were being distributed in the streets and anti-Communist slogans displayed on the walls.[18]

Over time, the student opposition matured. On March 12 the students created a Committee of Delegates of the Faculties of Warsaw University, which was almost immediately abolished by the decision of Henryk Jabłoński, the minister of education. On March 20 the student movement regrouped and concentrated itself in Warsaw. Between March 21 and 23 several strikes were organized at Warsaw University and at Warsaw Polytechnic, where the situation grew particularly serious because the authorities decided to break up the student opposition at a meeting scheduled for 8 A.M. on March 23. A sizable armed force surrounded Warsaw Polytechnic and readied its attack. Both sides expected casualties because the students were also armed; this was confirmed in Col. Henryk Słabczyk's report to the departmental directors of the Ministry of Defense. In it he wrote:

If we need to take the building by force, it will not be easy. The Polytechnic building was well equipped for resistance. Its strong oak doors were barricaded, several fire extinguishers were prepared for use against the police, there were a few thousand bottles on the upper floors to throw at the invaders, and the building had many shelters in which to hide and find protection against chemical substances.[19]

It is difficult to explain the authorities' decision to crush the strike so quickly and decisively. One plausible explanation is the Warsaw Pact meeting being held in Dresden on March 23. It had been called to discuss the emergency situation in Czechoslovakia. Presumably, because the Polish delegates wanted to report that peace reigned in Warsaw, they needed to stop the strike as soon as possible. The strike at the university also ended on March 23. In Warsaw, as elsewhere in Poland, the students failed to achieve their goals not only because the authorities refused to talk to them but also because the party exploited their actions to attain its own goals.

The older generation of politicians cynically depicted the students' struggle for truth, freedom, democracy, and justice as an apolitical force. Perhaps this is why members of the March generation became so attached to the truth as a value in itself and also to the conviction that in some equivocal situations there should be no compromise and no fear of becoming the subject of any political game. On March 28, during the last meeting at

18 A. Friszke, "Ruch protestu w marcu 1968 (w świetle raportów MSW dla kierownitwa PZPR) [The Protest Movement in March 1968 on the Basis of Ministry of Foreign Affairs's Reports for the Party Directory]," *Więź* 3 (1994): 92.
19 Andrzej Garlicki, "Działania MO I SB w czasie wydarzeń marcowych 1968 r. w. Warszawie [The Actions of the Militia and Security Service During the March 1968 Events in Warsaw]," *Polityka* 10 (1992).

Warsaw University, the Declaration of the Students' Movement was ratified. It was the students' most mature and lasting contribution to the events
of March 1968.[20]

Going well beyond the narrow sphere of student concerns, the authors
of this document called for a new youth organization, for the abolition of
censorship, and for economic reforms leading to self-governing enterprises
and a market economy. They also supported the creation of independent
workers' unions, full independence of the judiciary, and the creation of a
constitutional court with jurisdiction for full judicial review. Not only was
this the most important document of the Polish student movement of 1968,
it also contained an ideological testimony used as a reference point for a
future generation of students.

The government responded promptly with a wave of arrests, which
included the members of the Committee of Delegates. Stanisław Turski,
the rector of Warsaw University, removed the names of thirty-four students from the Committee's list and suspended eleven of them. On March
30 there was an announcement of the dissolution of the faculties of Economics, Philosophy, and Pedagogy as well as the end of third-year instruction in Mathematics and Physics. As a result of this decision, 1,614 young
people were no longer considered students, and most of them were immediately drafted into the army. On April 10 Prime Minister Cyrankiewicz
announced to parliament that as of April 8 the police had detained 2,730
people throughout the country; 1,058 were freed within forty-eight
hours.[21]

The events of March 11, the key date of the student uprising, had mobilized the guerrilla opposition. As mentioned previously, there was considerable anti-Semitism in the press and the speeches of party leaders. Moczar's
faction targeted the Jewish students in particular. Even those who had not
participated in the demonstrations were placed under suspicion and their
parents were held responsible.

THE AFTERMATH

As a result of the government's reprisals, many people lost their jobs and
their party membership. At the meeting of the Polish United Workers'

---

20 *Wydarzenie marcowe 1968* [March 1968 Events] (Paris, 1968), 99–103.
21 *Sprawozdanie stenograficzne z 19 posiedzenia Sejmu Polskiej Rzeczypospolitej Ludowej w dniach 9, 10 i 11
    kwietnia 1968* [Proceedings of the Parliament of the Polish People's Republic, Apr. 9, 10, 11,
    1968], 79–81.

Party in October 1968, the first secretary of the Warsaw Committee, Józef Kepa, announced that there had been eight hundred dismissals from the top positions of some of the most important national enterprises and factories.[22] The newspapers, which continued to propound their anti-Semitic and anti-Zionist themes, also supplied details of the "hostile activities" and the "real goals of the meetings of the student organizers"; they accused the commandos and "protectors" of preparing a coup d'état.

The anti-Semitic campaign was closely associated with the purge of the intellectuals. Both campaigns in the mass media were reinforced by meetings organized in the largest industrial enterprises. The purpose of the meetings was to condemn the "enemies of order" and to vote on resolutions that supported Gomułka and the Communist Party. In the second half of March 1968 such meetings took place in several cities.

Although some Poles were undoubtedly opposed to the clubbing of students, few were brave enough to raise their voice in protest. Thus, one can appreciate the bold initiative of five Catholic deputies of *Znak* (Sign), Konstanty Lubinski, Tadeusz Mazowiecki, Stanisław Stomma, Janusz Zabłocki, and Jerzy Żawieyski, who, only three days after the militia and the ORMO had invaded Warsaw University, presented an interpellation to the prime minister criticizing the brutality. Some members of the party directorate also showed courage in protesting an action that discredited Poland in the eyes of world public opinion. The most significant actions were the resignations of Edward Ochab, a politburo member and president of the State Council, Adam Rapacki, the minister of foreign affairs, and Jerzy Albrecht, the minister of finance.

The Western European and American press condemned the anti-Zionist campaign and the purges in Poland. Once more, Poland's reputation abroad was tarnished, even if some of the criticism was not entirely justified. To accuse the Poles of a general attitude of anti-Semitism was as incorrect as to say there was no anti-Semitism in Poland at all.

By the summer of 1968 the political situation stabilized. The anti-Semitic campaign in the mass media was attenuated, and the wave of personal attacks ceased. Periodically, anti-Semitic statements reappeared in the newspapers, but now they were less venomous. Some dismissals continued, but in a far more limited manner than in the spring of 1968.

An important question still to be investigated is the impact of the March 1968 events on Gomułka's rule. Although historians continue to disagree over whether his authority was strengthened or weakened, it seems evident

---

22 *Warszawska Konferencja Przedzjazdowa* [Warsaw Conferences Congress] (Warsaw, 1968).

that Gomułka was hardly a loser that spring; although he suffered a temporary setback, he was able to hold on to power in Poland. To be sure, his
survival owed less to the disunity of his enemies than to the international
situation. At the time, the Poles joked that Moczar needed only one more
vote to get rid of Gomułka, that of Leonid Brezhnev, the general secretary
of the Soviet Communist Party.

We must also not forget the events that were occurring simultaneously
in Czechoslovakia, collectively known as the Prague Spring, and Gomułka's
role in fighting this movement. It is now clear that Gomułka was one of
the most ardent spokesmen in the Warsaw Pact urging Brezhnev to unleash
the military action in Czechoslovakia that crushed the experiment of
"socialism with a human face."[23]

The Warsaw Pact invasion took place on Tuesday, August 20, 1968, at
11 P.M., when sixteen Soviet, three Polish, one Bulgarian, and two Hungarian divisions crossed the Czechoslovak border at eighteen different locations. To be sure, Poland's participation shocked many of the country's
own citizens, but only a few were brave enough to speak out publicly.[24]

Nevertheless, the military aggression in Czechoslovakia and the participation of the Polish army reignited the students' opposition. Protests
appeared on walls, and leaflets were distributed in public places. Swiftly
retaliating, the government arrested and prosecuted 120 people. Beginning
in the autumn, legal proceedings, some lasting for several months, were
brought against the commandos. The leaders of the March movement,
who had already been brought to trial, now received far heavier sentences:
Jacek Kuroń and Karol Modzelewski each received three and a half years in
prison; Adam Michnik, three years; Józef Dajczgewand and Jan Lityński,
two and a half years; Seweryn Blumsztajn, Henryk Szlajfer, Barbara
Toruńczyk, and Antoni Zambrowski, two years.

The year 1968 was one of worldwide student protest. With the one
exception of Czechoslovakia, none of the movements can be compared to
Poland's, despite frequent references to the French case. The apparent parallels and similarities – the strikes at the universities, the meetings and street
manifestations, and the conflicts with the forces of public order – should
not obscure the fundamental differences. In Poland and Czechoslovakia,
students fought for elementary civil rights, rights already possessed by their
Western European counterparts.

---

23 See Alexander Dubček, *Hope Dies Last* (New York, 1993).
24 Lech Kowalski, *Kryptonim "Dunaj": Udział wojsk polskich w interwencji zbrojnej w Czechosłowacji w
    1968 roku* [Code Name "Danube": The Participation of the Polish Army in the Military Interven-
    tion in Czechoslovakia in 1968] (Warsaw, 1992).

There were two additional factors unique to Eastern Europe. In France, Germany, Britain, and the United States, students were confident that their protests would be widely discussed and disseminated by the mass media, whereas in Poland the news media were controlled by the government.[25] Polish students thus had to fight against a coordinated campaign of lies, misinformation, and defamation in the newspapers and on radio and television. Whereas student leaders in the West became heroes, their Polish counterparts were imprisoned by the state.

Another key difference derived from the nature of the two parallel student movements. Students in the West focused largely on their own problems, but in Poland the students represented a wide band of social groups and social concerns. Individually, Polish students were exposed to greater injury and loss. Their risks far exceeded those of student protesters in Western Europe, where institutionalized political pluralism made social protests possible. Finally, Polish students often risked their lives; Western European and American students did not.

The events of March 1968 created huge moral losses and widespread human tragedies. One direct result was that some fifteen to twenty thousand people emigrated from Poland. These events also made a significant political impact by exposing the collapse of the ideology of pure communism. Old communists were replaced by younger individuals who had had no opportunity to prove faithful to their convictions in Nazi or Soviet jails or in the antifascist underground. March 1968 can also be considered a key moment in the evolution of an independent opposition and in the relations between Catholics and atheist former communists. Differences over religion among Poland's citizens now seemed less important than their opposition to the Communist dictatorship and their desire to modify the system peacefully and gradually.

25 See the chapter by Stuart J. Hilwig in this book.

9

May 1968 in France

The Rise and Fall of a New Social Movement

INGRID GILCHER-HOLTEY

I

In France, the United States, and the Federal Republic of Germany, 1968 witnessed the greatest protest mobilization of the postwar period. The protest movements in each of these countries displayed a specific self-perception and constitution but were similar in values, forms of action, mobilization strategies, and accomplishments. These similarities go beyond national characteristics and illustrate features common to all social movements. Everywhere, the protesters challenged the established institutions of Western democracy. They questioned the exclusive right of representation by established parties and intermediary groups, confronted those parties and groups with an opposing power and public presence that negated traditional structures of institutional authority, and criticized the basic assumptions of the postwar order.[1] However one judges these phenomena historically, the spontaneous mobilization of protest movements within highly organized and affluent democratic societies requires explanation.

How, then, do we explain the events of May 1968 in France, for example, and the powerful effect they had? Different analysts have interpreted the May movement variously as a "new social conflict" (Touraine), a "generational revolt" (Morin), an "institutional crisis" (Crozier), and a "critical moment" in the development of society (Bourdieu). Just as divergent as these sociological constructions are the overall assessments of these events. They are judged as "revolts" (Touraine), quasi-revolution (Morin), "cultural

Sally E. Robertson of Arlington, Virginia, translated this chapter from the German.
1 For more on the radical changes within the political and societal institutional framework that the movements brought about, see Claus Offe, "Challenging the Boundaries of Institutional Politics: Social Movements Since the 1960s," in Charles S. Maier, ed., *Changing Boundaries of the Political: Essays on the Evolving Balance Between the State and Society, Public and Private in Europe* (New York, 1987), 63–106.

breakdown" (Crozier), or a crisis over control of the means of production
that became generalized (Bourdieu).[2] All of these interpretations have their
virtues. Insofar as they point toward long-term strains and problems, however, a link to the sudden mobilization is still missing and cannot be
deduced. The analytical foundation of this study is distinct from the aforementioned approaches.[3] I view the May events as an expression of a new
social movement.[4] Analytically defined, a social movement is an "organized
and sustained effort of a collectivity of interrelated individuals, groups, and
organizations to promote or to resist social change with the use of public
protest activities."[5]

In this chapter I argue that the program and course of action of protest
movements in the 1960s were aimed at mobilization, and that their forms
of action and objectives came together in this process. I examine the May
movement in France using theorems of research on social movements.[6] I
also discuss strategies of mobilization and forms of action and analyze their
dynamic effects within organizations as well as between the movement and
the institutions of authority.[7] In addition, I describe the self-generating
processes of action that occur within specific constellations of interrela-
tions[8] and explain the concepts of "critical event" and "critical moment."[9]
In section II, I reconstruct the cognitive constitution of the movement by
the intellectuals of the New Left. In section III, I develop seven theses in
order to explain the unique mobilization dynamics of the May movement
in France. Finally, in section IV, I attempt to determine the effects of the

2 Pierre Bourdieu, *Homo academicus* (Frankfurt am Main, 1988); Michel Crozier, *La Société bloquée*
   (Paris, 1970); Edgar Morin, Claude Lefort, and Cornelius Castoriadis, *La Brèche: Premières réflexions
   sur les évènements* (Paris, 1968; reprint, Paris, 1988); Alain Touraine, *Le Communisme utopique: Le
   mouvement de mai 1968* (Paris, 1968); Alain Touraine, *Die postindustrielle Gesellschaft* (Frankfurt am
   Main, 1972).
3 Ingrid Gilcher-Holtey, *"Die Phantasie an die Macht": Mai 68 in Frankreich* (Frankfurt am Main, 1995).
4 Alain Touraine also proceeds from this thesis. For the methodological differences between the structural analytical approach that he develops and the interactionist approach underlying this chapter, see
   Gilcher-Holtey, *Phantasie an die Macht*, 24–30.
5 Friedhelm Neidhardt and Dieter Rucht, "The Analysis of Social Movements: The State of the Art
   and Some Perspectives of Further Research," in Dieter Rucht, ed., *Research on Social Movements: The
   States of the Art in Western Europe and the USA* (Frankfurt am Main, 1991). See also Dieter Rucht,
   "Öffentlichkeit als Mobilisierungsfaktor für soziale Bewegungen," in Friedhelm Neidhardt, ed.,
   Öffentlichkeit, öffentliche Meinung, soziale Bewegungen, supplement to *Kölner Zeitschrift für Soziologie und
   Sozialpsychologie,* no. 34 (1994): 338–9.
6 Otto Rammstedt, *Soziale Bewegung* (Frankfurt am Main, 1978).
7 Jürgen Raschke, *Soziale Bewegungen: Ein historisch-systematischer Grundriss* (Frankfurt am Main, 1985);
   Patrice Mann, *L'Action collective: Mobilisation et organisation des minorités actives* (Paris, 1991).
8 Klaus-Peter Japp, "Selbsterzeugung oder Fremdverschulden: Thesen zum Rationalismus in den
   Theorien sozialer Bewegungen," *Soziale Welt: Zeitschrift für sozialwissenschaftliche Forschung und Praxis*
   3 (1984).
9 Bourdieu, *Homo academicus,* 254ff.

movement on the political system, on the New Left, on the structure of business and industry, and on lifestyles.

II

Social movements are categorized according to their goals. Whether they promote women, peace, or the environment, all gain their identity and distinction from their goals and specific viewpoints on social problems. The way in which problems are perceived and the strategic solutions that are then developed are the result of ideas and insights, explanatory hypotheses and interpretations, assumptions and attitudes. These in turn shape the self-concept of social movements. The movements are constituted in terms of ideas, or to use the new terminology, they are "cognitively" constituted.

In the case of 1968, the cognitive constitution of the movement cannot be deduced from its name alone. In fact, the movement had no universally recognized name, was not oriented toward a specific area of policy, but rather was directed toward the total structure of society. Its customary designation by a specific year lacks substance but indicates the peak of mobilization success and political effectiveness. In this respect, 1968 might be compared to 1848. Although university and high school students and young adults for the most part formed the core groups and adherents – in France, blue- and white-collar workers were also involved – it was not simply a student movement. Its cognitive constitution was not determined by problems of university reform or the educational system. Despite the fact that universities had the largest potential for mobilization, higher education was by no means the object or central topic of the movement.

Nineteen sixty-eight can be described in many terms. It was antiauthoritarian and individualistic, libertarian and socialistic, as well as democratic, anti-institutional, and antibureaucratic. Given the internal diversity of the core groups and the lack of organizational unity, many viewpoints can be found that different leaders promoted and transformed over time. The question is whether a core of ideas, moral concepts, patterns of explanation, and interpretations of reality constituted the movement cognitively. Did a perception of the present and objectives for the future give the movement its identity and distinguish it from others?

These questions must be answered before we can analyze the process that gave rise to this particular social movement. Such movements are the result of social action, not just ideas. Still, social action is mobilized only after it has been directed toward certain goals and points of reference, after at least the core groups of a movement have attained a cognitive identity. In their work, Ron Eyerman and Andrew Jamison have stressed this connection. They analyzed the process by which a movement forms its identity using what they call "cognitive praxis."[10] By this, they mean the development of an internal communication structure, a symbolic system of self-understanding and self-assurance that determines the direction of action and the intersubjective willingness to act. This "cognitive praxis" is determined by a framework of rules drafted by intellectuals and the transformation of those rules into relevant objectives. Over the course of the movement, this cognitive core is adapted and modified as a result of internal communication, continual grappling with the conditions under which actions are undertaken, and the internal and external interpretations of those events. The combination of the theoretical outlines, concepts, and projections of different intellectuals results in a syncretism that cannot be traced back to the theory of a single person. Nevertheless, the cognitive constitution of the movement, the formulation of the problem, the resulting perception of reality, and the objectives that are established cause the movement to develop according to specific dynamics that distinguish it.

The protest movements of 1968, which saw themselves as movements of the New Left, were preceded by the formation of an intellectual "Nouvelle Gauche" in France, the "New Left" in the United States, and "die Neue Linke" in Germany. Intellectual dissidents from traditional leftist parties were their founding members. By the end of the 1950s and the beginning of the 1960s, these New Left movements had emerged internationally in publications, discussion circles, journals, and actions. The cleaving off of the New Left from the Old Left resulted in part from contemporary occurrences, such as the events in Prague in 1948, the Twentieth Party Congress of the Communist Party of the Soviet Union, the suppression of the Hungarian Uprising, the Cold War, and the lack of public debate on nuclear arms in East and West. But it also had systemic causes that had unfolded during a critical debate on the development of socialism and communism since the 1920s. The New Left was convinced that the self-imposed restriction of democratic socialism to a welfare state model, as well as the perversion of communism under Stalin, had undermined the emancipatory content of the socialist and communist movement. This loss of the utopian perspective resulted in an incapacity of traditional left-wing parties to offer a real alternative to the status quo. They appeared to be imprisoned by realpolitik, unable to overcome the current political and social situation, and unwilling to address present problems or mold the future. They stag-

10 Ron Eyerman and A. Jamison, *Social Movements: A Cognitive Approach* (Cambridge, 1991).

nated materially, as measured by their numerical strength, and philosophi-
cally, as measured by their capacity to solve problems.

French developments best exemplify the systematic evolution of the
new cognitive orientation, or "cognitive praxis," of the New Left. The
intellectual New Left in France constituted itself around the journals *Socialisme ou Barbarie* (1949–66), *Arguments* (1956–62), and *International Situation-
niste* (1958–69). What was new about the New Left? The new cognitive
orientation with which the free-floating intellectuals of the New Left confronted the traditional Left consisted of the following five elements.[11]

1. A reinterpretation of Marxist theory: Referring to the early writings of Marx,
   the New Left accentuated the aspect of alienation rather than exploitation. It
   attempted to open up the theoretical interpretation by combining Marxism
   with existentialism and psychoanalysis in order to free the former from its scle-
   rotic paralysis and identification with institutionalized Marxism.
2. A new model of socialist society: The New Left was convinced that socialism
   must not be restricted to political and social revolution, seizure of power, and
   nationalization of the means of production. Rather, it must eliminate the
   alienation felt by the individual human being in everyday life, recreation, and
   family, as well as in sexual and societal relationships.
3. A new transformation strategy: The individual should be freed from subordi-
   nation to the collective. The premise was that changes in the cultural sphere
   must precede social and political transformation. New lifestyles and modes of
   communication had to be developed on an anticipatory and experimental
   basis by creating new cultural ideals, applying them in subcultures and testing
   them as alternatives within existing institutions.
4. A new organizational concept: The maxim was action, not organization. The
   New Left understood itself as a movement, not a party. As a movement, it
   used the full spectrum of direct action strategies, from the demonstrative-
   appellative to the direct-coercive action. It sought to generate awareness
   through action and agitate the public by provocation, while simultaneously
   using the action to change the individuals taking part in it.
5. A redefinition of the leaders of social change: The proletariat was no longer
   seen as the leader of social and cultural change. Instead, the New Left believed
   that the impetus for social transformation came from other groups: the new
   (skilled) working class, the young intelligentsia, and the social fringe groups.

The interrelationship of individual and collective emancipation, social
and cultural criticism, and cultural and social revolution inherent in the
thought of the New Left gave rise to the internal tension in the movement
of 1968. It also explains the plethora of categories with which researchers
label the movement as the expression of a generational conflict, as neo-

---

11 Gilcher-Holtey, *Phantasie an die Macht,* 44–104.

Marxist and antibureaucratic, or as a movement of cultural revolution or sexual emancipation. Its overarching social utopia combined the diverse threads and places the movement in the tradition of social utopias such as those espoused by Saint-Simon, Fourier, Proudhon, Marx, and Bakunin. However, its utopian content was not limited to the expectation of a collective emancipation of labor from outside control. It articulated themes and individualistic values that we now call "postmaterialistic," and it represented a transition between the "old" and "new" social movements.

The dazzling diversity that characterized the social movements in 1968 was magnified by the different trends in each country. By cutting the ties that bound the battle for emancipation to the proletariat, the "young intelligentsia" acquired a mandate to intervene in social conflicts as the new "revolutionary subject." Because of its loose form of organization and emphasis on external mobilization, the New Left attached itself to many causes, from the antinuclear and disarmament movements to civil rights and anticolonialism. In the United States, for example, the student movement, antiwar movement, and the civil rights movement acted together in 1968.[12] In Germany, the players included the *Ostermarsch* movement (campaign for nuclear disarmament), the opposition to the Emergency Laws, and the student movement.[13] Only in France did an interaction between students and workers take place that year. University protests spread to industry, producing the largest general strike in French history.[14] For a short time, it seemed possible that the New Left would become a broad social movement that would revolutionize the parties of the Old Left "from the bottom up." It was also thought that the student movement would gain political influence through the parallel actions of the student and worker movements.

12 On developments in the United States, see James Miller, *From Port Huron to the Siege of Chicago* (New York, 1987); Todd Gitlin, *The Sixties: Years of Hope, Days of Rage* (New York, 1989); Ronald Fraser et al., *1968: A Student Generation in Revolt: An International Oral History* (New York, 1988).
13 On developments in Germany, see Karl A. Otto, *Vom Ostermarsch zur APO: Geschichte der ausserparlamentarischen Opposition in der Bundesrepublik* (Frankfurt am Main, 1977); Karl A. Otto, *APO: Die ausserparlamentarische Opposition in Quellen und Dokumenten (1960–1970)* (Cologne, 1989); Lothar Rolke, *Protestbewegungen in der Bundesrepublik: Eine analytische Sozialgeschichte des politischen Widerspruchs* (Cologne, 1987); Heinz Bude and Martin Kohli, eds., *Radikalisierte Aufklärung: Studentenbewegung und Soziologie in Berlin 1965 bis 1970* (Weinheim, 1989).
14 On developments in France, see Touraine, *Le Communisme utopique;* Edgar Morin, Claude Lefort, and Jean-Marc Coudray, *Le Communisme utopique;* Laurent Joffrin, *Mai 68: Histoire des événements* (Paris, 1988); Geneviève Dreyfus-Armand and Laurent Gervereau, eds., *Mai 68: Les mouvements étudiants en France et dans le monde* (Nanterre, 1988); Alain Delale and Gilles Ragache, *La France de 68* (Paris, 1978); Adrien Dansette, *Mai 1968* (Paris, 1971). For an overview of the divergent interpretations of May 1968, see Michelle Zancarini, "Les Interpretations de mai 68," in IHTP, ed., *Les Années 68: Evénements, cultures politiques et modes de vie*, Lettre d'information no. 10 (Feb. 1996): 4–23.

III

In France, the formation of the 1968 movement began later than in other developed nations. One can observe a continual process of mobilization in the United States and the Federal Republic of Germany beginning in 1964 and 1965, respectively. In contrast, although there were scattered protests in France (for example, criticism of the universities in Paris in 1964 and in Strasbourg in 1966, as well as protests against the war in Vietnam), no direct link can be drawn between these smaller protests and the protest movement of 1968. The French movement did not start until international developments had reached their peak. Within a few weeks, however, it had caught up with the other movements in terms of mobilization and then surpassed the German and American protest movements in its political explosiveness.[15] What began as a revolt by a small minority of students in the Parisian suburb of Nanterre quickly developed into a general strike that paralyzed the entire country. It also caused a political crisis that threatened to topple the Gaullist system. How could this happen?

Thesis No. 1: The mobilization of the student movement in France happened spontaneously as the result of an essentially self-generating process of action.

To be sure, the French student movement emerged against the backdrop of a general crisis in the university system that directly affected the learning environment, career outlook, and life prospects of the students. But it was more than just a reaction to these deficiencies.[16] Since the mid-1960s, the student union (Union nationale des étudiants de France or UNEF) had been criticizing the structural weaknesses of the university and of government reform plans without garnering much support from the students. The student strike UNEF helped to organize in Nanterre at the beginning of the 1967–8 academic year faded away after a few weeks. The mobilization process which led to the May movement in France was not triggered until small core groups of students began undertaking limited unconventional actions in the spring of 1968 and noticeably "upset" university operations by breaking rules, violating taboos, and committing other provocations.

---

15 On the mobilization, see Gilcher-Holtey, *Phantasie an die Macht,* 105–269.
16 On the formation of the student movement and its cognitive orientation and politicization, see Jean-Pierre Duteuil, "Les Groupes d'extrême-gauche à Nanterre," in Dreyfus-Armand and Gervereau, eds., *Mai 68;* Daniel Cohn-Bendit and Gabrièl Cohn-Bendit, *Linksradikalismus: Gewaltkur gegen die Alterskrankheit des Kommunismus* (Hamburg, 1968); on the core political groups, see Hervé Hamon and Pierre Rotman, eds., *Génération,* vol. 1: Les *Années de rêve,* vol. 2: Les *Années de poudre* (Paris, 1987–8); Richard Gombin, *Le Projet révolutionnaire: Eléments d'une sociologie des événements de mai-juin* (Paris, 1969).

The student groups that initiated the protests, the "Enragés" and the "Movement of March 22," made explicit reference to the intellectual leaders of the New Left, or at least were influenced by their writings and viewpoints.[17] In particular, the writings of the "international situationists," that is, the group involved with *Socialisme ou Barbarie* and *Arguments,* played a large part in their thinking. Not only their strategies of action (direct, provocative, situative) but also their self-perception (antidogmatic, antibureaucratic, antiorganizational, and antiauthoritarian) fit into the philosophy of the New Left. Both groups focused on the university – the Enragés to abolish it, the Movement of March 22 to transform it into a "critical university" – as a means of action and a starting point for the radical transformation of society. They perceived themselves as the core movement of such a change. Their success in mobilizing large numbers of students was at first limited to the Nanterre campus. It might easily have subsided, as had the UNEF strike and other student protests before it, had the student protest not spilled over to the Sorbonne, which was responsible for disciplinary actions against eight students from Nanterre. Repressive measures were then used against the small core of student activists at the Sorbonne (in particular, the use of massive police force in the inner courtyard). These events caused the previously inactive student majority to demonstrate its solidarity with the active student minority. In a matter of days, the mobilization accelerated in a chain reaction of alternating student actions and government repression into a series of violent clashes between demonstrators and police around the Sorbonne and in the streets of the Latin Quarter. The dynamics of the actions brought more and more high school students and youths (and a few young workers) onto the side of the university students.

Within a week (from May 3 to 10), France had caught up with the developments in other Western nations. Within another twenty-four hours, the French student movement had surpassed the movements in the other countries. A large part of the organized working class showed solidarity with the students. What brought about the solidarity of French workers with the student movement?

Thesis No. 2: The student protest was conveyed to the workers by means of a "critical event" (Bourdieu).

In his book *Homo academicus,* Pierre Bourdieu develops a model that ascribes an innovative role and function to the "critical event" in the synchroniza-

---

17 For a history of "The Enraged," see René Viénet, *Wütende und Situationisten in der Bewegung der Besetzungen* (Hamburg, 1977).

tion of latent crises in different societal spheres. He thereby introduces a factor to the analysis of macrosociological structures and structural conflicts that "can definitely involve an element of chance." However, he also adheres to the theory of structural determination of events because events lead to the "critical moment" of general crisis only "if there exists a relationship of mutual, objective harmony between the agents experiencing crisis in one field that has reached the critical state and other agents endowed with similar dispositions produced by similar social conditions of existence (identity of condition)."[18] From his point of view, this independence within a larger dependence constitutes the "critical" historical event.

In France, the critical event that synchronized the perception of different social groups was the Night of Barricades (May 10–11) during which students and youths occupied an enclave in the Latin Quarter after a peaceful demonstration. In a spontaneous and playful manner, they started to build barricades within the occupied area. They were determined to leave this area only after the government had met the following demands: (1) the release of students arrested during a protest march, (2) reopening of the Sorbonne, which had been closed by order of the university president and was being guarded by police, and (3) withdrawal of police from the Latin Quarter. The barricading of Paris during the night of May 10–11 was a historic allusion to barricades of the Paris Commune in 1871 and the liberation of Paris from German occupation in 1944. Erected by high school and university students, they evoked memories of those earlier examples, without merely imitating them. They were expressive rather than instrumental in nature. Only later in the course of this provocative action and the subsequent police deployment was the student protest politicized by the media response, the public reaction, and the steps taken by the government and labor unions.

The activism of the students attracted the mass media. The effect of the movement on the outside world grew as a result of broadcasts from two radio transmitter vans that were driven into the occupied area immediately after the first barricades were erected. This spread the news not merely outside the Latin Quarter but far beyond the city limits of the capital itself. The media reports created an audience that attentively registered the events and formed its own opinion of them. Thus, the flames of student protest jumped from Paris to the provinces.

The government was in a tight spot, and a reaction was expected. It was faced with a loss of legitimacy, regardless of whether the authorities reacted in a lenient or in a repressive manner. Finding itself under increasing

18 Bourdieu, *Homo academicus,* 276.

pressure to act, it lacked a convincing plan of action and decision-making capabilities. In the prime minister's absence the cabinet ministers had difficulty coordinating their actions. After mediation attempts failed during the night, the ministers resorted to an interpretation of the situation that was strongly influenced by the president's opinion of how to deal with the situation. They started to see the demonstrating students as rebels and the demonstration for the three demands as an *émeute* (riot). After much hesitation, the minister of the interior had the barricades removed by police and security force troops in the early morning hours of May 11. The brutality of the police force (described by *Der Spiegel* magazine as a "battle without mercy") led to vociferous and immediate public protest. A critical event had occurred.

The Night of Barricades was neither determined by sociostructural factors nor planned by the groups or individuals involved. Rather, the critical event was a sequence or, more accurately, a coincidence of uncoordinated decisions by the government, situational decisions by individual groups within the movement, and repressive behavior on the part of the police. In other words, it resulted from contingent situations, creating an entirely new situation. This critical event disturbed the routine of everyday life and the normal unquestioned order of things. It synchronized the perception of different social groups and transformed a moment into a public event that was identical for everyone and measured by the same points of reference. It led the French labor unions to enter into solidarity with the student movement and its demands – not only in word but also in deed. To protest repression and emphasize the students' demands, the labor unions called for rallies and a 24-hour general strike. There was nothing more to it – at least at this point.

The situation changed, however, after a second political intervention. Returning from Afghanistan on the evening of May 11, Prime Minister Georges Pompidou granted all of the students' demands in a television address just fourteen hours after the brutal clearing of the Latin Quarter. The prime minister's decision contributed greatly to the transformation of this critical event into Bourdieu's critical moment.[19]

Thesis No. 3: The workers' mobilization process followed the same action strategy as the student movement. Common values united the parallel movements. The cognitive orientation of the New Left served as the integrative element of the socially heterogeneous movements.

---

19 On the model of the critical moment, see Ingrid Gilcher-Holtey, "Die Nacht der Barrikaden: Eine Fallstudie zur Dynamik sozialen Protests," in Neidhardt, *Öffentlichkeit,* 375–92.

Again, the movement began with a single action by a small, active minority. On May 14, after the 24-hour general strike organized by the unions, young workers in an airplane factory in the vicinity of Nantes refused to go back to work. Instead, they occupied the factory workshops, sealed off the plant, and took the plant manager into custody. With their actions, they were following the lead not only of the students in Paris, who had occupied the Sorbonne just after it reopened a day earlier, but also of agitation by the *Force Ouvrière* union in the Loire Atlantique region, with its anarchosyndicalist orientation. For some time, the representatives of that union had promoted direct action as a means of achieving worker demands – without success. Only under this specific sociopolitical constellation in the days between May 11 and 13 did this strategy succeed. The occupation of a provincial factory, barely noticed at first by the actors in the capital, triggered a chain reaction in the following days. The spontaneous strike spilled over to the Renault car factories and from there to other plants. Within just a few days, about 7.5 to 9 million workers were on strike – without a call from union headquarters.[20] What was their motivation?

There was no economic crisis on the eve of the May events, so the spontaneous process of mobilization cannot be explained by structural economic factors. There were conflicts over distribution and a rising unemployment rate, but the French economy had suffered far less from the recession of 1966 than had Germany's, and it was therefore less subject to economic fluctuation and breakdown. According to the Organization for Economic Cooperation and Development and the National Institute of Statistics and Economic Studies, France in 1968 was a stable and crisis-resistant country.[21]

This latent dissatisfaction cannot be traced solely to socioeconomic causes. Rather, it was the result of an increasing discontent with authoritarian structures in industry. In May 1968, this latent dissatisfaction turned into a collective willingness to act and a manifest attitude of protest that could not be controlled even by union leaders. The success of the students in getting the government to agree to their demands served as a model. The horizon of possibilities also expanded for other groups. New forms of action increased their willingness to act. In a statement that can be consid-

20 On the strike movement, see Pierre Dubois et al., *Grèves revendicatives ou grèves politiques: Acteurs, pratique, sens du mouvement de mai* (Paris, 1971).
21 OECD, "Prospects in France After the Strikes," *Oeconomic Outlook* 3 (1968): 52–69; I.N.S.E.E. (Institut National de la Statistique et des Etudes Economiques), "La Situation et les perspectives dans l'industrie d'après les enquêtes effectuées par l'I.N.S.E.E. en juillet 1968," *Etudes Conjoncture: Revue mensuelle de l'I.N.S.E.E.*, supp. 8 (1968).

ered a typical illustration of the mood of labor at the time, one worker said, "If the government submitted to the students, why shouldn't it submit to us?"[22] A situation was created wherein anything was possible, or at least seemed to be.

The workers in state-owned industries triggered the strike movement. Among them, the young workers in particular were the driving force and activated the rest of the workforce. Their goal was to force the *Etat patron* to submit by means of direct action. The direct action unleashed a dynamic force for mobilization. It was based on traditions within the labor movement and funneled a collective willingness to act without directing it toward a specific goal. For example, the occupation of factories could be (1) a means of exerting pressure on the government and industry in order to force them to negotiate or make concessions, (2) a way to demonstrate the independence of the local rank and file from the labor union apparatus dominated by the Old Left, or (3) the beginning of a comprehensive transformation in the structure of industry, business, and the economy based on either the anarchosyndicalist strategy or the concepts of the New Left. It all depended on the actors' intentions. The goals of the workers' strike movement evolved as a result of the dynamics of the process of societal interaction, as had the goals of the student movement.

The initial demands of the strike committees were not fundamentally different from the requests the unions had made prior to May. But a social movement is more than its printed words. The general assemblies inside the occupied plants expressed a certain "creative unrest" (*effervescence créatrice*), calling not only for an increase in wages and reduction of working hours but also for structural changes within industry and business. The noncommunist French Democratic Workers Union (Confédération française et démocratique du travail or CFDT), the orientation of which was closest to that of the New Left, created a new term expressing the expectations of so many workers: *autogestion.*[23] Just two days after the first spontaneous strike, the new slogan *autogestion* gave the strike a new dimension. With its demand for *autogestion,* the CFDT was calling for (1) reforms in the management and decision-making structures of business and industry, (2) reduction of hierarchies and the concentration of power, and (3)

22 Philippe Gavi, "Des ouvriers parlent," *Les Temps Modernes* 265 (1968): 82–3.
23 It was the first time that the national office of the CFDT mentioned the term *autogestion* in an official statement. The internal debates can be traced back to 1963. On the concept of *autogestion,* see Pierre Cours-Salies, *La CFDT: Un passé porteur d'avenir: Pratiques syndicales et débats stratégiques depuis 1946* (Paris, 1988); Pierre Rosanvallon, *L'Age de l'autogestion* (Paris, 1976); and Gesine Schwan, "Demokratischer Sozialismus zwischen Wohlfahrtsstaat und Selbstverwaltung," in Hannelore Horn et al., *Sozialismus in Theorie und Praxis: Festschrift für Richard Löwenthal* (Berlin, 1978).

opportunities for workers to release their creative potential through self-determination and self-administration. Although the institutional and legal details of how *autogestion* was to be developed and implemented remained unclear, the antihierarchical and antiauthoritarian component was sufficient to unite the student and worker movements in their goals. The democratization of the universities was to be followed by the democratization of industry: "A la monarchie industrielle et administrative, il faut substituer des structures démocratiques à base d'autogestion" (The industrial and administrative monarchy must be replaced with democratic structures based on autogestion). It was a "communauté d'aspiration" (A community united by common endeavors, hopes, and expectations) that united the worker and student movements.[24]

Thesis No. 4: The Old Left used its organizational power to crush the action strategies and goal orientation of the New Left. The conflict was channeled into the institutionalized mechanisms of the collective bargaining system.

The communist-oriented General Workers Union (Confédération générale du travail or CGT) did not support *autogestion* as a goal of fundamental social change. It dismissed as a *formule creuse* (empty formula) the concept of *autogestion,* which was oriented primarily toward changing power and decision-making structures rather than the distribution of wealth.[25] The CGT fought the alliance that had been formed between the student and worker movements. Wherever possible, it tried to prevent direct contact between students and workers at the plants and vehemently distanced itself from the figurehead of the student movement, Daniel Cohn-Bendit. Furthermore, it did everything within its organizational power to derail this social movement, which had already paralyzed economic life. Between 7.5 million and 9 million French citizens were on strike, and the crisis had the potential of turning into a revolutionary situation; but the CGT made every effort to direct the protest into the orderly channel of a mediated settlement. As the driving force behind a hasty collective bargaining agreement with representatives of government and industry (the Grenelle agreements of May 27), the CGT de-escalated the social crisis using traditional conflict resolution mechanisms. For the time being, however, the CGT was unable to enforce its strategy and goals effectively at the grassroots level.

24 Albert Detraz et les militants de la CFDT, "Positions et action de la CFDT en mai 1968," *Syndicalisme,* supplement (1969).
25 See also Peter Jansen et al., *Gewerkschaften in Frankreich: Geschichte, Organisation, Programmatik* (Frankfurt am Main, 1986), 36.

The general assemblies of workers in the plants protested against the wage settlements. Work did not resume, but the strike movement remained under the control of the union even after Grenelle, despite the fact that the workers had refused to agree to the wage settlements. On the plant level as well as industry-wide, the unions initiated new negotiations to restructure labor relations and wage scales, while continuing to try to suppress spontaneous protest and direct it into institutionalized channels. The strike movement turned into a labor dispute, the heterogeneous demands of which were distributed among various commissions and other bodies, which recommended economically acceptable compromise solutions. The power structures within businesses and the economic order of society were no longer subjects of discussion. However, the ensuing dialogue between employers and the unions was the result of pressure by the strike movement, which had forced employers to the table for collective bargaining and made them willing to compromise. The Grenelle agreements represented the first time that French businesses officially recognized the labor unions in their plants. They guaranteed the freedom of union locals to engage in union activities on plant property, the right of union members to assemble, the right to post union announcements on plant bulletin boards, and the right to distribute union newspapers.[26] Thus, the position of unions in the plants improved as a result of the spontaneous strike movement.

Still, this did not bring French workers anywhere near the level of participation in industrial relations enjoyed by German workers. To be sure, codetermination, in the sense of the German union tradition, had not been a goal of the French unions, which believed it would narrow the scope of their action. The unions also dismissed the idea of institutionalizing labor relations with an agreement that both sides were bound to honor for a specified contract period. The catchword *autogestion* expressed the sentiment of a minority, and it was never cast into a formal mold.

Only a few businesses tried to introduce self-governing structures. Most strikers supported a political solution to the social crisis. They considered their opponent to be not the *pouvoir patronat* but the Gaullist regime itself. They demanded a change in political power as a prerequisite for reforms of the social structure. This meant a shift in the goal orientation of the movement and in the means of conflict resolution. The unions paved the way for solutions but were at first unable to push them through. After the failure of the Grenelle agreements, they retreated from the stage, and the political parties took their place. The social movement entered a new arena

---

26 Raymond Aron, *Erkenntnis und Verantwortung: Lebenserinnerungen* (Munich, 1985), 335–6.

where, because of its spontaneous and antiparty character, it did not enjoy a firm structural foundation and for which its core groups were conceptually unprepared.

Thesis No. 5: The unintended consequences of the competing strategies of Prime Minister Pompidou and President de Gaulle led to a worsening of the political crisis. Pompidou's strategy was intended to pacify, depoliticize, and institutionalize the social conflicts, whereas de Gaulle's strategy was oriented toward mobilization, politicization, and plebiscitary preservation of power. As a result, the two strategies impeded each other.

The political establishment's options for reacting to such social movements can be said to have followed two alternative strategies: tolerance or repression. The strategy of tolerance implied recognition of the movement's interests and readiness to enter into a dialogue or negotiations, at least with the moderate factions of the movement. The strategy of repression, which rejected the movement as either unrealistic or illegitimate, defended the status quo by using police force to ban the organization and its activities. The two methods could be combined or applied alternately as they were by the government and president of France in May 1968. This strengthened the dynamics of the movement.

One reason that May 1968 in France became such a dramatic event was that the internal conflict between divergent strategies to cope with the conflict resulted in a power struggle between the holders of the two most important political offices – President de Gaulle and Prime Minister Pompidou. The bicephal political system of France, which was dependent on cooperation, was permanently damaged by their overt strategic differences and covert personal rivalry.

The policy of appeasement and accommodation followed by Pompidou immediately after his return from Kabul, Afghanistan, not only counteracted de Gaulle's position that "the state will not surrender" but also made it look ridiculous, as Raymond Aron has noted.[27] The power struggle between the two men escalated against the backdrop of the strike movement. Pompidou bet everything on the collective bargaining card, whereas de Gaulle dramatized the power struggle by announcing a referendum aimed at proving the public's confidence in him. Meanwhile, the whole political system started to shake.

The announcement of the referendum, and the inevitable politicization

---

27 Cited in Hamon and Rotman, eds., *Génération*, 555.

of the conflict that ensued, made it more difficult to achieve a socioeconomic solution to the crisis through the conflict-regulating channels of
collective bargaining. The protest was transferred into the political arena
and offered critics of the Gaullist regime the chance to turn their claim of
"Dix ans ça suffit" into a political decision. The failure of the Grenelle
agreements and the anticipated defeat of de Gaulle in the referendum created a situation in which the opposition parties in parliament stood a realistic chance of succeeding in their plan to form a "transitional government."

Thesis No. 6: The noncommunist New Left was unsuccessful in its attempt
to use the situation to define its own political standpoint.

The New Left could not bridge the gap between its self-perception as a
movement that mobilized by means of action and was committed to the
autonomy of the grass roots and the increasing pressure to coordinate
actions, organize divergent interests, and direct them toward a specific political goal. It developed no political plan of action and therefore disintegrated into two factions. One faction defended the grassroots mobilization
of action groups united in a network with nationwide coordination based
on a democratic model. The other supported the establishment of a new
left-wing party. Only a minority acknowledged – and then too late – the
option offered by Pierre Mendès-France and the United Socialist Party
(Parti socialiste unifié or PSU), a small party influenced by the ideas of the
New Left, to integrate representatives of the movement into a transitional
government and to organize new elections. Twenty years later, Daniel
Cohn-Bendit said that they had had only one chance and that was Mendès
France: "We ourselves should have proposed elections and put forward the
name of Mendès-France."[28]

   At the end of May 1968, however, the Communist Party (Parti communiste français or PCF) took a stand against precisely this opportunity.
Just as the CGT had mobilized against the concept of *autogestion,* the PCF
now used its organizational strength to prevent a transitional government
under Mendès-France. Even the united left under François Mitterrand, the
Federation of the Democratic and Socialist Left (Fédération de la Gauche
Démocratique Socialiste or FGDS), supported him only conditionally. Differences between the New and Old Left prevented the formation of uni-

---

28 See *L'Humanité,* June 24, 1968, 1.

fied left-wing opposition to the Gaullist regime. They missed the chance for a change in power provided by the dramatic political situation at the end of May. The great parallel action of student and worker movements, which had shaken French society and rocked the Gaullist regime, now dissolved. The unifying ideas of the New Left were too weak; the organized interests of the Old Left prevailed.

Thesis No. 7: By abandoning the referendum and deciding to hold new parliamentary elections, the government reestablished a strategy of action based on the institutions of the Fifth Republic.

The new elections transferred the sociopolitical conflict into the traditional channels of the competitive democratic party system. The political and social crisis quickly subsided. The old parties and established interest groups dominated the election campaign while the masses of mobilized youths were disenfranchised, since the voting age was twenty-one. The political factions in the bourgeois camp emerged from the crisis stronger than before. The transfer of power, which had seemed possible and very close at the height of the crisis, did not take place. In the view of the PCF, the election results supported their analysis that the social crisis of May 1968 was not a revolutionary situation. Responsibility for the defeat was assigned by *L'Humanité* even before the votes were counted. René Andrieu wrote in his editorial the day after the first ballot that it would be of great historical interest to know exactly who had taken the initiative to build the barricades in the streets of Paris. "Chaque barricade, chaque voiture incendiée apportait des dizaines de milliers de voix au parti Gaulliste, voilà la vérité" (Each barricade, each burning car brought tens of thousands of votes to the Gaullist party; that's the truth).[29] Only the statement by the PSU mentioned that all of the problems voiced by the social movement of May 1968 still existed and awaited solutions.

IV

The May movement in France was a spontaneous, unforeseen development. The success of the effort to mobilize large numbers of people was extraordinary, and the shock to the political system was considerable. Nonetheless, it is difficult to clearly identify its effects. In the following dis-

29 François-Georges Dreyfus, *Histoires des gauches en France, 1940–1974* (Paris, 1975), 308.

cussion, I examine four aspects that may be viewed as the results of the movement.

Effects on the Political System

Researchers on social movements assume that in order for a movement's central concerns to become part of the mainstream political agenda they have to be accepted and adopted by intermediary groups in the political decision-making process. Such a transfer did not occur in France, at least in the immediate aftermath of the events.

The immediate effects of the May movement on the political parties included the breakup of the tactical consensus between the FGDS and the Communist Party as well as the disintegration of the FGDS, which was the big loser in May 1968. The FGDS not only lost its votes and mandate but also its ability to maintain internal integration and form external coalitions. The Radical Party left the Fédération because it felt that the tactical liaison with the Communists sought by Mitterrand was no longer viable after the May events and the coup in Prague (August 1968).[30] The socialist party, the French Section of the Workers' International (Section française de l'in-ternational ouvrière or SFIO), also distanced itself from Mitterrand and his plans, criticizing in particular his high-handed decision of May 28, 1968.[31] The disintegration of the Fédération and the consequences thereof became especially obvious in the presidential elections of 1969. Unlike four years earlier, the Left no longer challenged with one candidate but with four competing candidates. Gaston Defferre ran for the FGDS, Jacques Duclos for the PC, Michel Rocard for the PSU, and Alain Krivine for the Trot-skyites. Together, the Left received only 30.3 percent of the votes on the first ballot. Of these, 21.5 percent voted for the Communist candidate and 3.7 percent for the PSU candidate. Gaston Deferre got just 5 percent and Alain Krivine slightly more than 1 percent. They were therefore unable to nominate a candidate for the second ballot. The race was decided between the Gaullist candidate, Georges Pompidou, and Alain Poher, who was nominated by the political center and supported by the Radical Party (Parti radical), which had separated from the united left. With 57.6 percent of

---

30 On the events of May 28, 1968, see Gilcher-Holtey, *Phantasie an die Macht,* chap. 5; on the critique of the SFIO, see Philippe Alexandre, *Le Duel de Gaulle-Pompidou* (Paris, 1970); and *L'Express,* no. 888, July 15–21, 1968, 8–9.
31 See Wolfgang Jäger, "Die sozialistische Partei und die kommunistische Partei Frankreichs," in Dieter Oberndörfer, ed., *Sozialistische und kommunistische Parteien,* vol. 1: *Südländer* (Opladen, 1978), 65ff.

the vote, Pompidou surpassed even the victory of de Gaulle in 1965 (54.5 percent), thus consolidating the political power of the Gaullists even after de Gaulle had left politics.

The debacle of the presidential election accelerated the internal transformation process within the SFIO, which reconstituted itself in July 1969 under new leadership as the Socialist Party (Parti socialiste or PS). In the following years, the PS was able to integrate the noncommunist Left. In 1971, the Convention des institutions républicaines under the leadership of Mitterrand joined the PS, as did a large part of the PSU in 1973–4 after the defection of Rocard. The concept of *autogestion* served as an integrative umbrella internally and as a distinguishing feature externally. The new Socialist Party, which had already come out in favor of cooperation with the Communists in 1969, drafted an election program together with the PCF in 1972. Setting aside ideological differences, it contained a list of reform measures and thus added a pragmatic political dimension to the tactical election coalition between the FGDS and the PCF (1965–8).[32] The formal rapprochement of socialists and communists following the divisions within the Left after the May events first proved effective in the presidential elections of 1974. Mitterrand received 49.2 percent of the vote on the second ballot, just barely losing to the candidate of the Independent Republicans and Gaullists, Giscard d'Estaing (50.6 percent). Compared to 1965, when Mitterrand garnered 43.7 percent of the vote against de Gaulle, the increase of 5 percent in nine years may seem minimal, but it signaled a trend that was to lead to a change in power in 1981. The resurgence in the socialists' strength after their relative and absolute defeat in 1968–9 was supported by a new generation of voters, those who were between seventeen and twenty years old in 1968. An opinion poll by the French Society of Public Opinion (Société française d'enquête par sondage or SOFRES) in 1974 showed that most of the young voters had a positive attitude toward the May events. They mostly supported the Socialist Party.[33] The public celebration that followed Mitterrand's election victory in 1981, buoyed by the feeling that a new France would now emerge, was reminiscent of the euphoria of May 1968 – a feeling of awakening and the projection of a new political perspective. Two years later, however, the socialist government had to change course again. Economic factors set limits on the hopes for a new society.

---

32 Jeröme Jaffré, "A Preliminary Note on French Political Generations," *European Journal of Political Research* 5, no. 2 (1977):151.

33 Niklas Luhmann, *Universität als Milieu: Kleine Schriften* (Bielefeld, 1992), 152–3.

Effects on the New Left

The May movement in France clearly demonstrated the dilemma of the New Left as a social movement. The uniquely dynamic mobilization it provoked was a challenge to the government, the political parties, and the unions, yet the New Left as a movement was unable to prevail against established parties and organizations. The New Left had been defeated by the institutions of the Old Left. The reasons for the failure of the New Left lay not in its values but in its refusal to give those values a permanent structure for action and an institutional base. Therefore, "power to the imagination" remained a vital program that fascinated and mobilized individuals but was unsuccessful in gaining power because power is based on entirely different organizational and decision-making premises than is the mobilization of the imagination. The internal tension and limited effectiveness of the New Left were due to the fact that it could not assume power without destroying itself.

With its strategy of self-organization through action, the New Left rocked the structures of authority, temporarily paralyzed the economy, and plunged the political system of France into what everyone involved perceived was a serious crisis. However, as successful as its strategy was in the initial phase, and as effortlessly as its actions managed to topple established structures, the New Left was unable to maintain the dynamics of its mobilization strategy. Mobilization by means of action is always a short-lived process. Permanent mobilization is impossible without a stabilization of the mobilized resources. Stabilization of the movement, however, required organization. Antiauthoritarian and antihierarchical in its values and practice, the New Left refused to establish permanent organizational structures.

It established no functional, democratically legitimated, and controlled leadership within the movement, because it believed that organizational structures would automatically lead to oligarchy. Therefore, it relied on the spontaneity and creativity of the grass roots to determine independently and autonomously the movement's goals, methods, and forms of action through a process of continual discussion and interaction. The volunteerism and activism of the movement released great energy and imagination. Individuals were changed by the actions, but the institutions of society were not. As Niklas Luhmann states laconically in his analysis of the movement of 1968, "Society does not have an address. Whatever one wants from it must be addressed to organizations."[34]

---

34 Rainer Paris, "Der kurze Atem der Provokation," *Kölner Zeitschrift für Soziologie und Sozialpsychologie* 41 (1989):33–52.

Focusing, internally and externally, on the autonomy and authenticity of the movement, the New Left as a social movement rejected political cooperation with intermediary organizations and developed no ability to build coalitions with potential partners in the political establishment. Without alliances, defined as the coordinated collaboration of autonomous but convergent political powers, no movement can successfully accomplish its goals. By failing to establish a network of potential allies, the New Left blocked its chances for mediation and sacrificed political influence.

Despite its success at mobilization, the New Left, as a collective agent for mobilization, lost its initiative. Within the movement, antiauthoritarian elements were infiltrated by authoritarian left-wing cadre groups. Foremost among these were the Maoists, who shared the New Left's opposition to Gaullism and the Communist Party, but not its rejection of the orthodox model of democratic centralism. The "short breath of provocation," that is, the structural weakness of the New Left as a movement that mobilized by means of action campaigns, left the door wide open for the hierarchically organized cadre groups.[35] Their influence increased in proportion to the decline in mobilizing power of the New Left. After May 1968, they took the place of the New Left movement without carrying on its legacy. To the extent that they became militarized and used terrorist methods, they destroyed the "charisma of ideas."

The self-exclusion of the New Left from the process of political coordination of interests led to an isolation of the movement and a renunciation of the opportunity to influence the political process. The opportunity to share in the power along with Mendès France was discussed but not pursued. They did not even consider cooperating with a left-wing alliance led by Mitterrand. The imagination and energy of the New Left's core groups were directed not toward participation in making politically feasible changes but toward the ideal of forming an autonomous left-wing movement. This movement would gain strength by weakening the Old Left, breaking down its organizational power, and causing its members to reaffiliate by means of spontaneous actions.

Effects on the Structure of Business and Industry

Being anticapitalistic and at the same time believing in economic growth, the New Left still perceived the problems of society primarily as problems

---

35 Gesine Schwan, "Demokratischer Sozialismus zwischen Wohlfahrtsstaat und Selbstverwaltung," in Horn et al., *Sozialismus in Theorie und Praxis,* 584.

of distribution, that is, material equalization of disadvantages and abolition
of personal inequality and the asymmetry in human relations. It sought to
achieve equal opportunity by expanding participation rights and chances
for economic partnership. It concentrated on the control of management
power through worker councils but did not develop a new model for industrial organizations. Anti-institutional in its orientation, it advocated development of the power to counter existing institutions. Yet the action-
oriented power it created did not produce a stable counter-system.

The possibility of encroachment onto the Old Left's organizational and
recruiting territory was seen at the beginning of the spontaneous plant
occupations, but the New Left did not succeed in holding the workers permanently with its actions. The plant occupations did not mean a change in
industrial structures, or in the ownership or authority structures of the
plants. In the end, the unions' strategy of material claims and equalization
of disadvantages prevailed over the concept of redistributing leadership and
decision-making powers advanced in the *autogestion* model but not given
institutional form in 1968.

By the time the election campaign began, if not before, the New Left
had succumbed in the political arena to the organizational power of the
parties of the Old Left. After the collective bargaining of Grenelle failed,
the Old Left had been unchallenged in formulating alternative action strategies in the environment of political crisis exacerbated by the continuing
strike. Its willingness to participate in the new parliamentary elections
pulled the rug out from under all hopes of a political opposition constituted by direct democratic methods, strengthened the power of unions as
intermediary negotiating partners, and contributed to demobilization of
the strike movement and stabilization of the political order. That the intermediary mechanisms continued to function, even under the exceptional
conditions created by the general strike, was an important reason for the
resolution of the grave crisis of May 1968.

None of the parties adopted the central idea of *autogestion* during the
election campaign. It took time to accomplish the programmatic implementation and dissemination of the idea, which conveyed the hope "of
eliminating alienation and exploitation, as well as hierarchy and power in
general, wage labor, and the division of labor, in short, the realization of
true democracy."[36] It did not begin to take root until the 1970s, after the
concept had been discursively and theoretically developed within the

36 See Rosanvallon, *L'Age de l'autogestion.*

CFDT.[37] After the Socialist Party united with the Convention des institutions républicains in 1972, it included *autogestion* in its platform, entitled "Changer la vie." Two wings developed within the party, a radical and a moderate faction, each of which had its own interpretation of the *autogestion* concept.[38] Finally, even the party that had dismissed the concept as a *formule creuse* in May 1968, namely, the Communist Party, implicitly adopted it in 1977–8. However, this did not lead to a change in their concept of socialism.

Effects on New Lifestyles

The stability of the institutional system steered the impulses of the New Left toward subculture experimentation with new lifestyles and cultural forms that dealt with the institutional problems by withdrawing from them.

Being both individualistic and socialistic, the New Left rebelled against the alienation in the realm of production and in everyday life. In the struggle against alienation, they broke taboos, norms, and traditional values. They violated rules in order to provoke and to delegitimize the institutions of authority. Most activists felt a subjective emancipation in violating rules and disregarding established structures of organization and power. They perceived their experiences as progress toward individual self-determination and self-actualization. Subcultures developed that preserved the atmosphere of awakening, present in the origins of the New Left, but the political program gave way increasingly to a cult of individual affliction. Thus, the awakening of 1968 ended up for many people as the shaping of alternative lifestyles, as the individualization of life's opportunities and risks, but also as political retreat into the private realm.

Individual emancipation based on eliminating the alienation in everyday life and in personal relationships was inherent in the strategy of the New Left. However, its concept of transformation did not end with individual self-actualization but included, as a sine qua non, political and social emancipation through collective self-determination and self-administration. The essential goal was to escape from the "stahlharten Gehäuse der Hörigkeit" (iron cage of bondage) that blocked individual actions by means of the power wielded over human beings by the need for consumer goods and the

---

37 See party congress of Paris in 1975, cited in Jäger, "Die sozialistische Partei und die kommunistische Partei Frankreichs," in Oberndörfer, ed., *Sozialistische und kommunistische Parteien,* 93–100.
38 See Wolfgang Jäger, "Gewerkschaften und Linksparteien in Frankreich," in Hans Rühle and Hans-Joachim Veen, eds., *Gewerkschaften in den Demokratien Westeuropas,* vol. 1: *Frankreich, Italien, Spanien, Portugal, Griechenland* (Paderborn, 1983), 63–7.

dependence on hierarchically organized bureaucracies that governs all aspects of an individual's life in modern society. It was a program that questioned not only the secular tendencies of the drive for efficiency in Western society but also the modern way of life and the political, economic, social, and cultural structures that produced it. This is the source of the fascination that surrounds the events of May 1968 in France.

A Laboratory of Postindustrial Society

Reassessing the 1960s in Germany

CLAUS LEGGEWIE

THE PROTEST MOVEMENT BETWEEN
HISTORY AND THE PRESENT

Today, 1968 is an almost magical date – and still a very controversial one.[1] For some, "1968" represents a lost battle in a culture war, whereas for others it denotes victory in a cultural revolution. Self-satisfied gloating after the fact would be just as inappropriate as the spirit of revenge that inspires many conservative politicians and neoconservative intellectuals in Europe and, particularly, in the United States. This attempt to reverse the moral, intellectual, and political climate is reflected in an exemplary evaluation of the 1960s by German editorial writer Ludolf Herrmann: "We have coped with Hitler, even if not yet definitely. However, what we have not coped with yet is our coping with Hitler, as it led to the student rebellions of 1968 and to fundamental value shifts during the subsequent years. . . . In terms of history, we have been alienated from ourselves, and we must now attempt to reverse that alienation." Newt Gingrich recently echoed this blunt statement after being sworn in as speaker of the U.S. House of Representatives in 1994. He described the 1960s as a watershed era and added, "From 1965 to 1994, we did strange and weird things as a country. Now we're done with that and we have to recover."[2]

Barbara A. Reeves of Berlin, Germany, translated this chapter from the German.

1 This chapter is a revised version of "1968: Ein Laboratorium der postindustriellen Gesellschaft: Über die Tradition der antiautoritären Revolte seit den 60er Jahren," *Aus Politik und Zeitgeschichte* B 20/88 (May 13, 1988): 3–15. Reprinted here with the permission of the Bundeszentrale für politische Bildung, Bonn.

2 Ludolf Herrmann, "Hitler, Bonn und die Wende: Wie die Bundesrepublik ihre Lebenskraft zurück gewinnen kann," *Die Politische Meinung*, no. 204 (1983): 13ff.; Newt Gingrich is quoted in Todd Gitlin, "Afterword," in Stephen Macedo, ed., *Reassessing the '60s: Debating the Political and Cultural Legacy* (New York, 1997), 283.

The 1990s are still haunted by the 1960s. In contrast to both of these partisan statements, this chapter focuses on the unintended consequences and longer-term effects of 1968. More than merely bringing student rebellion, it signaled an overdue cultural and political transformation of Western societies and symbolized a lasting process of accelerated social change that affected not only advanced capitalist societies but also the societies of "actually existing socialism" in Eastern Europe and the Third World. After three decades, it is necessary and timely to attempt a sober explanation of the causes and effects of this extraordinary historical experience that so powerfully affected an entire generation. From the perspective of events, 1968 initially marked a convergence of processes in all three worlds that, without having been a revolution in the strictest sense, may be called revolutionary. In January 1968, the Vietcong Tet Offensive reached Saigon, portending victory in a "people's war" and anticipating the eventual defeat of American imperialism in Southeast Asia and the end of Western political hegemony in former colonies. Then, the Prague Spring demonstrated that the posttotalitarian Soviet order could be reversed from within. Finally, Paris May was the tumultuous echo of a silent revolution that brought up postindustrial and postsocialist conditions.[3] In all three processes, the unintended consequences overwhelmed original intentions and signaled the success of "socialism at the periphery" in the Third World, "socialism with a human face" in Eastern Europe, and "advanced socialism" in the West. The "mobilization cycle" started in the United States and proceeded everywhere, like an eruption varying in intensity and duration.[4] Yet the cycle did not end until 1989, when the next quasi-revolutionary wave, again bringing many unintended consequences, started. The 1960s really became history only in their aftermath. Against ubiquitous revisionist and some current partisan efforts, we must historicize 1968 and subject the ideas and impulses behind this remarkable year to critical analysis.

THE *KAIRÓS* OF THE ANTIAUTHORITARIAN PROTEST MOVEMENT

Allowing the fairly long wave of national and international protests to be reduced to a single date is consistent with the perception of the "breach"

3 Alain Touraine developed this thesis in *Le Communisme utopique: Le mouvement de mai 68* (Paris, 1968); *L'après socialisme* (Paris, 1980); see also Ronald Inglehart, *Kultureller Umbruch* (Frankfurt am Main, 1989), and Helmut Klagges et al., *Werte und Wandel* (Frankfurt am Main, 1992).
4 Herbert Kitschelt, "Zur Dynamik neuer sozialer Bewegungen in den USA," in Karl-Werner Brandt, ed., *Neue soziale Bewegungen in Westeuropa und den USA: Ein internationaler Vergleich* (Frankfurt am Main, 1985), 248–305; Doug McAdam and Dieter Rucht, "The Cross-national Diffusion of Movement Ideas," *Annals of the American Academy of Political and Social Science* 258 (1993): 56–74.

(Edgar Morin), which the protagonists of revolt hammered into the historical normality and continuity of the times. In the chronological stream of history, they marked a caesura in the right place at the right time (*kairós*), in a way that was not historically possible either before or since.[5] Nineteen sixty-eight thus focused on, in a manner specific to time and place, motives for outrage prevailing at the "end of the postwar era" (Ludwig Erhard). These motives, which were synchronized by the international mass media around the universalized perception of a catalytic event (the Vietnam War), had a mutually reinforcing effect.[6] In that process, the protest movement of the 1960s, which was largely but not exclusively sustained by university and younger students and articulated by intellectuals, followed an older protest history, from the perspectives both of action typologies and of the history of ideas. It culminated in the continued history of opposition of the "new social movements."[7] Caesura and the flow of time, the moment of crisis and the continuity of 1968, must therefore be accorded equal attention if we are to examine more closely the causes of the protest movement. I shall begin with several different social scientific explanatory models.

The Generational Paradigm

The common reference to the "typical sixty-eighter," whom the mass media and younger generations purport to be able to identify almost by type, points to possible collective and stable patterns of attitudes and behavioral orientations on the part of those born between approximately 1940 and 1950. This type of generational paradigm would be consistent if a sociodemographic generational type had endured: Among today's 40- to 50-year-olds, we would find generation-specific values, attitudes, and options (that is, in voting behavior), and, projected into the future, we could expect to find specific patterns of aging among retirees in the next millennium.

Hypotheses regarding historical-political patterns of socialization among generations have not been sufficiently tested empirically. Nonetheless, we may note at least two characteristics that distinguish the generation of 1968: They were the first "true" postwar and postfascist generation free from personal involvement in the catastrophe of National Socialism (and also Stalin-

---

5 See Edgar Morin, Claude Lefort, and Cornelius Castoriadis, *La Brèche: Premières réflexions sur les évènements* (Paris, 1968).

6 On the constitutive character of the Third World protest, see Ingo Juchler, *Die Studentenbewegungen in den Vereinigten Staaten und der Bundesrepublik Deutchland der sechsziger Jahre* (Berlin, 1996); Paul Berman, *A Tale of Two Utopias: The Political Journey of the Generation of 1968* (New York, 1996).

7 See Lothar Rolke, *Protestbewegungen in der Bundesrepublik: Eine analytische Sozialgeschichte sozialen Widerspruchs* (Opladen, 1987); Wolfgang Krausshaar, *Protestgeschichte der Bundesrepublik Deutschland* (Munich, 1996).

ism) and World War II. They were nevertheless affected all the more intensely by the psychopolitical processing of these events. First, the generation of 1968 experienced the "good fortune of being born later" (according to Helmut Kohl) to a particularly great degree. Second, they experienced an unusually long period of peace and relative material prosperity, historically speaking, during their early political socialization; this, however, took place under the constant threat of nuclear destruction and was accompanied by long-term unrest on the global periphery. Before that of the current new university-educated entrants to the labor force, this generation was the last to enjoy a relatively smooth integration into the protected branches of the labor market, and it continues to climb the career ladder relatively quickly into the contemporary "establishment."[8]

Both of these generational experiences also resulted in an attitude that placed greater demands on politics, as distinguished from the political "skepticism" and instrumental orientation toward economic reconstruction ascribed to previous generations. This development, which may be characterized as a "re-ideologicalization" and a "shift to the left," took up and merged varying elements: (1) those of a radical, subculture-based modernism and hedonism, (2) those of a civil rights movement seeking to realize Western ideals of democracy and freedom, and (3) those striving for a "completion of the democratization process," sometimes along socialist or communist lines.

Internationally, the protest movement bore the label of a New Left. In terms of its intellectual background and relationship to the present, the New Left's forms of argumentation still had an "old European" quality, and the perspective of its argumentation was still rooted in industrial society. But the inner dynamics of the questioning of existing power and societal structures transcended these limitations.[9]

Because some evidence exists in support of a conclusion that participants (especially those who shaped opinion) formed a generation, and because the family has not been forgotten as the central arena of conflict for antiauthoritarian protest, we could support the thesis that generational conflict triggered the revolts: the "eternal" rebellion of young people against

---

8 On the "political generation," see Helmut Fend, *Sozialgeschichte des Aufwachsens* (Frankfurt am Main, 1988); Heinz Bude, *Das Altern einer Generation: Die Jahrgänge 1938–1948* (Frankfurt am Main, 1996); Helmut Fogt, *Politische Generationen: Empirische Bedeutung und theoretisches Modell* (Opladen, 1982); see also Alexander Mitscherlich, *Die vaterlose Generation* (Munich, 1964). "1968" in the context of generations is also discussed in Lewis S. Feuer, *The Conflict of Generations: The Character and Significance of Student Movements* (London, 1969).

9 Donatella delle Porta and Dieter Rucht, *Left-Libertarian Movements in Context: A Comparison of Italy and Germany, 1965–1990* (Berlin, 1991); see also Herbert Kitschelt, *The Transformation of European Social Democracy* (New York, 1994).

their parents struck out toward the left, "supercharging" the otherwise rather apolitical, private forms of protest (the unconventional fashion, music, and manners of the youth subcultures of the 1950s) by means of a social-critical total commitment. Such an assumption is fostered by the (often vivid) life stories of individual representatives of the student movement.[10] Such stylized scenarios begin with impressive proof of familial, usually paternal, repression and end with diagnoses of long-term alienation. This theme of the violent release in liberating acts of anger at the denial of "question time" (Christian Geissler) by Nazi fathers plays an important role in the self-descriptions of later Red Army Faction (RAF) members.

Representative studies of the social background and development of actors in 1968, as well as the opposing hypothesis, from socialization theory, of the "fatherless society" (Alexander Mitscherlich), however, contradict this exaggerated interpretation.[11] The late oedipal scenario, as portrayed in the (by no means completely fictitious) fairy tale about the "generation who set out to learn fear," offers only limited illustrative material for the "deviant behavior" of countless thousands (whereas in international comparative studies, this typically German generational constellation had to take a back seat anyway). Such studies tend to prove that generational tensions were less a cause than a consequence of political activism that, for its part, was largely consistent with liberal-to-left dispositions "at home" and further radicalized them. Opposition, protest, and political-cultural nonconformity were the results of "totally normal" upbringings that, only a few years earlier, most likely would have led to rather "conventional" convictions and behavioral dispositions.

Authoritarian or permissive parenting styles, in and of themselves, were in no way the trigger or aggravator of radical protest behavior – regardless of whether one proceeds from the image of the lasting dominance of "strong" parental figures or, probably more accurately, from a largely fatherless (and motherless) society, in which the family has lost its traditional function, including that of protecting the individual from totalitarian control or late capitalist manipulation. As such, the protest movement also reflects a transformation, identifiable in terms of family sociology. It was no coincidence that in 1968 the public not only devoted considerable atten-

---

10 See, e.g., Bernward Vesper, *Die Reise: Romanessay* (Frankfurt am Main, 1977); see also Tobias Mündemann, *Die 68er . . . und was aus ihnen geworden ist* (Munich, 1988), and Margaret M. Braungart and Richard G. Braungart, "The Life-Course of Left- and Right-Wing Activist Leaders from the 1960s," *Political Psychology* 11, no. 2 (1990): 243–82.

11 Klaus Allerbeck, *Soziologie radikaler Studentenbewegungen* (Munich, 1973); Seymour M. Lipset and Philip G. Altbach, eds., *Students in Revolt* (Boston, 1969).

tion to matters of socialization, child rearing, and education but also demonstrated its willingness to make positive changes.

The Student Paradigm

The pioneers of the protest movement were constantly defending themselves against the restrictive label of "student movement."[12] Of course, it is undisputed that the colleges and universities were centers of activity, and that students, more than pupils or apprentices, set the tone in all activities that made a public impression, and especially in the realm of theory. Outside of the universities, intellectuals played a prominent "pioneering thinker" role, many of them members of the nontenured faculty and nonprofessional staff, largely from the humanities and social sciences departments. The milieu of the already overcrowded university was, without doubt, the meeting place where individuals with an inclination toward protest encountered broad social issues. Universities and campuses also played an important role in crystallizing the generational context of homogenous peer groups.

However, references to certain subjective or objective features of that milieu form an insufficient explanation for the young students' particular willingness to protest. Pointing in a similar direction are criticisms of worsening conditions for students, anticipation of future unemployment for graduates, status anxiety, rejection of the co-optation of the scientific-technological intelligentsia for capitalist purposes, and the thesis of the "treason of the intellectuals," which can be found in a particular type of neoconservative critique. But all of those issues could have been resolved by means of a reform of higher education. The increasing "overshooting" of education-based occasions for protest beyond the campuses shows, however, that the universities were a sort of parade ground for already well-developed social critiques, and they were the symbolic goal of larger-scale protest. Students, nontenured faculty, and intellectuals simply refused to commit themselves to and be limited by the reform of higher education and cultural policy, even if this would later become their primary field of activity.

In the Federal Republic of Germany, protesting students were often caricatured as the grave diggers of the venerable German university; in reality they were, ironically enough, in some senses the defenders of the classic collegiate ideal, which admitted only gradual differences between students and professors and committed both to a search for truth, free of state influ-

---

12 See, e.g., Rudi Dutschke in *Geschichte ist machbar* (Berlin, 1980), 129ff.; and Jürgen Habermas, *Protestbewegung und Hochschulreform* (Frankfurt am Main, 1969), 137ff.

ence and utilitarian aims. Every day, they were reminded how little this Humboldtian ideal corresponded to reality. Their demands for the autonomy of higher education and the democratization of the university were intended as an attempt to save the university as a forum for a critical public and for reflection.[13] This attempt was represented by the battle on two fronts: (1) against "professorial despotism" and technocratic "state surveillance" and (2) for "freedom from manipulation by special interests" (Sozialistische Deutsche Studentenbund memorandum, 1965) and experiments in the "critical university" or the "active strike." Today, at a time when the universities threaten to waste all of their energies on self-administration, this (often impetuous) attempt must be seen in a completely different light than the corporate bodies supposedly serving "scholarly freedom" would seem to suggest. Following a (sometimes vandalistic) "hot phase" of student protest in 1968–9, the critical students bid farewell to their alma mater – a "long goodbye," as it turned out.

The protest movement was a student movement to the extent that, in the university milieu, it could sharpen and make relevant latent motives for political protest in a process of secondary political socialization, thanks to the special social position of the new generation of academics, the homogeneity of the student role, and the high degree of reflexivity of certain academic departments. Still, the protest movement was more than that: It was a broader social and political movement, activated by students and "intellectuals of the masses" that soon expanded beyond the universities and sought to forge coalitions with the scientific-technical professionals and the liberal middle class as well as with labor movement organizations and activists.

The protest movement of the 1960s thus should not be interpreted solely in terms of individual or group psychology as a "youth protest" or "student revolt." Rather, it should be viewed as the nucleus of a political and social movement whose "strategic" groups lent subject character to a still diffuse, directionless structural break and shift in values within late capitalist society and attempted to give them some direction.

The Crisis Paradigm

"The antiauthoritarian movement . . . was, of course, not a movement against authoritarian repression, but rather a movement of shaking off the

13 On this point, see *Hochschule in der Demokratie, SDS Memoranda, 1961–1965;* and *Universität und Widerstand: Versuch einer Politischen Universität in Frankfurt* (Frankfurt am Main, 1968); and Stephan Leibfried, *Wider die Untertanenfabrik: Handbuch zur Demokratisierung der Hochschule,* 3d ed. (Cologne, 1967).

remnants of an authority that was no longer sure of itself."[14] Hermann
Lübbe's interpretation, of course, turned cause and effect on their heads. In
fact, trust was not the only thing that had disappeared (deliberately and out
of nowhere); so had the capacity of the growth economies and their political institutions to function. Together these developments could then be
interpreted as a legitimation crisis of late capitalism. This interpretation
was possible because of the palpable interruption (in both Germany and
France) of the "thirty glorious years" (Jean Fourastié) between 1945 and
1975. As early as the mid-1960s, in an atmosphere of a seemingly unabated
increases in wealth, slowing growth rates, signs of stagnation, growing labor
problems, and fiscal budgetary deficits heralded the impending end of the
"short dream of never-ending prosperity" (Burkart Lutz). Intellectual
killjoys had not simply invented it. The credibility deficit arose not because
young "provocateurs" made fun of authority figures, institutions, and common sense but because the monomaniacal obsession with growth, consumption, and waste set the normative tone for "postconventional" industrialized societies. Incidentally, this anticipated, albeit in a half-formed
manner, "questions of meaning" that came to be raised after the dawning
of a new ecological consciousness.

In the 1960s, three phenomena contributed to the sense of crisis: economic growth began to stagnate, the political-institutional foundations of
Western liberal democracies were subjected to a "process of involution"
(Johannes Agnoli), and, following the satisfaction of many basic needs for
material security, value hierarchies began to shift in the direction of a "postmaterialism." Within this context, traditional patterns of how to organize
one's life appeared as undesirable restrictions on opportunities for personal
development, and "society" reported a growing need for autonomy vis-à-
vis the state and the political class, as did the "individual" vis-à-vis collective control institutions.

In some ways, the legitimation crisis of the 1960s was a reaction to the
divergence of technocratic supermodernization (all large-scale technological projects realized against significant opposition were conceived and prepared at that time) and conservative life experiences – in Adenauer's "CDU
state," just as in "Grandpa's France" during the era of Charles de Gaulle.
The disquiet articulated by student protest groups, journalists, writers, and
other "leading minds" overlapped with a willingness to change on the part

14 Lübbe, *Endstation Terror*, 42; see also Daniel Bell, *Die Zukunft der westlichen Welt: Kultur und Technolo-
gie im Widerstreit* (Frankfurt am Main, 1976). On the legitimacy crisis at the time, see also Claus
Offe, *Strukturprobleme des kapitalistischen Staates* (Frankfurt am Main, 1972); on the following,
Burkhart Lutz, *Der kurze Traum immerwährender Prosperität* (Frankfurt am Main, 1984), and Jean
Fourastié, *Les trente glorieuses: ou, La revolution invisible de 1946 à 1975* (Paris, 1979).

of increasingly large segments of the population, who locked horns with the model of a "chancellor democracy," which was characterized by weak participation and a secretive political style (or also with the neo-Bonapartist style of the French Fifth Republic, which was seen as a "republican monarchy").

Technocratic and also leftist technocratic interpretations took this "disquiet" as the impetus for a project of readjustment and reform; that is, they interpreted the refusals and seeds of revolt as signs of an insufficiently acknowledged need for modernization.[15] Where modern societies are politically and socially "blocked," in extreme cases they require sudden correction by outsiders in order to initiate a process of "unblocking." The diagnosed deficits in modernization were then described in such a way that the technological and capital structures and everyday culture were no longer compatible. Democratization and industrialization no longer functioned in a synchronized fashion. And it seemed that political democracy must be accompanied by economic democracy, or by a democratization of "all areas of life." Such an approach, which objectifies protest and functionalizes it for the adaptive capacity of modern systems, benefits from hindsight, that is, knowledge of events subsequent to 1968. In the Federal Republic, the Social Democratic–Liberal coalition transformed antiauthoritarian impulses into "structural reforms"; in France, the wage-scale achievement of the Grenelle Agreement abolished the anachronistic remnants of social and industrial relations, providing an impetus for social-liberal reforms.

According to this interpretation, then, 1968 is accorded the function of having freed the energies of the "life-world" from the prison of conservative institutions and norms. One could say that this is surely one of the truths of that process that occurred "behind the backs" of the *enragés,* but also that this systemic self-modernization has not borne fruit. The system-theoretical objectification of the protest movement does not do justice to the specific motives for outrage on the part of the protest movement.

AUSCHWITZ–VIETNAM:
THE SCANDAL OF THE PROTEST MOVEMENT

Motives for Outrage from the Past

The vehement exposure of "helpless antifascism" (Wolfgang F. Haug), as the level of "dealing" with the National Socialist past was referred to in the

---

15 See, e.g., Michel Crozier, *La société bloqué* (Paris, 1964), or Regis Debray, *Modeste contribution aux discours et cérémonies officielles du dixiéme anniversaire [de mai 68]* (Paris, 1978).

1960s, has been accurately described as one of the major motivations behind the development of the West German protest movement. In his lecture at the Reichstag building in 1983, Hermann Lübbe condemned this motive for outrage as "initially a theoretical, but then also a political-moral delegitimation of the attempts, which had been part of the early history of the Federal Republic, to bring the National Socialist past into current political consciousness." Yet Lübbe, born in 1926, defends the process by which his own generation had "dealt with" National Socialism following 1945, which he accurately describes with the term "communicative silence," before the revolt, in "relationships of nonsymmetrical discretion" (between victims and perpetrators), until the revolts began, "where someone came from [was] less important than where he was willing to go."[16]

In this sentence, which is basically unobjectionable, we can hear the pain of a post– and indisputably anti–National Socialist generation, which was later known as the "flak helpers." In the 1960s and in the years since, members of the younger APO ("Ausserparlamentarische Opposition" or extraparliamentary opposition) generation have, with growing intransigence, accused this generation, first, of never having confronted National Socialism adequately, and, second, of having deliberately incorporated "brown" (Nazi) elements, both in terms of personnel and ideology, into West German public life – an accusation that can be hurtful to any older person who experienced and helped shape the early history of the Federal Republic. Nonetheless, the underlying aspiration, which was, in a manner of speaking, to re-create the Federal Republic by breaking the discreet "silence" with antifascist intentions, was hardly an attack aimed at its "delegitimation." When, as early as 1959, a mentor of the protest movement (in the face of reemerging anti-Semitism) stated that he viewed "the persistence of National Socialism within democracy as potentially more threatening than the persistence of fascist tendencies against democracy,"[17] and when a prominent student leader condemned the "fascism inside the structure" (Rudi Dutschke) of West German society even more than the breathtaking electoral successes of the NPD in the second half of the 1960s, both did so more out of concern for the republic than out of destructive antidemocratic tendencies.

Today, it is generally agreed that the theories of fascism (especially of a Soviet-style Marxist ilk) that were revived at the time had many weaknesses

---

16 Hermann Lübbe, "Es ist nichts vergessen, aber einiges ausgeheilt: Der Nationalsozialismus im Bewusstsein der deutschen Gegenwart," *Frankfurter Allgemeine Zeitung,* Jan. 24, 1983, 9; Lübbe refers to Wolfgang Fritz Haug, *Der hilflose Antifaschismus* (Frankfurt am Main, 1967).
17 Theodor W. Adorno, "Was bedeutet: Aufarbeitung der Vergangenheit?" in *Eingriffe* (Frankfurt am Main, 1963), 126.

and blind spots and that the ubiquitous and sweeping accusations of fascism were weighed down by tactical elements, meaning that 1968-style antifascism had quite a few problematic aspects of its own. But the benefits of addressing the issue of the National Socialist past anew – especially from socioanalytical perspectives – would be hard to deny. There is no rational reason why keeping alive the memory of Auschwitz and the connection between National Socialism and a crisis of capitalism should be classified as a "violation" of the "rump nation" that was the old Federal Republic.

The protest movement opposed the "molded society" (Rüdiger Altmann) out of concern for the persistence of totalitarian tendencies; they sought out political coalitions to oppose the passing of the Emergency Laws, organized the campaign against the highly manipulative Springer press, and took possession of "the streets," that is, of public space. If they occasionally underestimated the relative stability of the second German republic and resorted to acts of defensive overdramatization, it was hardly avoidable under the circumstances. What seems more important is that this republican substitutionalism was necessary to promote democracy as a process and to counter inherently antidemocratic regressive tendencies. On June 2, 1967, following the fatal shooting of the student Benno Ohnesorg, the "long-term, perhaps successful attempt to found a republican and democratic Federal Republic began after many years in which it had been, and still is, only, or primarily, the product of the military defeat of the German Reich and the control from outside of the victorious powers" (Ekkehart Krippendorf). This summary expresses the republican aspirations of the protest movement as well as the unresolved ambivalence surrounding postwar Germany's political-cultural and political-institutional "Western integration."[18]

Motives for Outrage in the Present Day

Certainly, "antifascist" activism contributed to the lasting alienation of the protest generation from the political mainstream, including, incidentally, the by no means casual dissociation of these SDS cadres from the Social Democrats, who were developing all too easily into a broad-based majority party. These processes of mutual distancing (and animosity) are often viewed as German idiosyncrasies, but one could point to analogous, equally "silenced" events from the past that also became present-day scandal material elsewhere. This is illustrated by the French example of the "shield-and-

18 Ekkehart Krippendorff, "Die Deutschen sind nicht mehr, was sie waren," *Der Spiegel*, no. 23 (1987): 34.

sword-theory," born of a no less precarious ideological-political act, which had placed collaborators and members of the resistance in a comparable relationship of discretion after the fact. This construct became untenable in the 1960s following political, literary, and cinematic critiques, especially because the civil war fronts that had existed from 1940 onward (Marshal Pétain versus General de Gaulle) were revived. The participation of the French in the extermination of Jews and in maintaining the continuity of the extreme Right now became an issue (initially raised by foreigners).

For the sixty-eighters in France, the "lesson" (Pierre Vidal-Naquet) of activist support for the Algerian independence movement between 1954 and 1962 was particularly relevant. Both in terms of personnel and program, this forged a direct path to the central motive for the politicization of the 1960s, particularly opposition to the Vietnam War. The protest movement was not merely "antifascist," it was also perforce "anti-imperialist."[19]

More successful in the Federal Republic than the leftist "Algeria Project," which had remained marginal, were the writings of Algerian activist Frantz Fanon. The reading of his works created the "abstract presence of the Third World in the metropolis" (Oskar Negt). It was no coincidence that the first demonstrations in West Germany's major cities, and especially in West Berlin, concerned Algeria and triggered demonstrations, including the anti-Shah protest on June 2, 1967, with the aforementioned consequences. The APO had not only turned its back on the "German question," which was at an impasse, but it also extended the political debate beyond parochial issues involving the East-West conflict. In doing so, the APO justified their claims to be a New Left. The postfascist Federal Republic had imposed on itself an abstract taboo on violence; but the Vietnam War and the theoretical analyses of the type engaged in by Fanon now illustrated sharply that a global context of violence was present and that the country faced new political and moral challenges.

Having directed attention to this structural and acute violence as a global social issue and having helped to bring about the American debacle in Vietnam by means of organizing worldwide protest is another of the indisputable contributions of the protest movement of 1968. As it happens, one of the broadest new social movements was created out of the remnants of anti-imperialist committees, circles, and groups (many church groups

19 See Frantz Fanon, *Die Verdammten der Erde* (Frankfurt am Main, 1966), and the first few years of *Kursbuch* and *Argument,* and Werner Balssen and Karl Rössel, "Hoch die internationale Solidarität," in *Zur Geschichte der Dritte-Welt-Bewegung in der Bundesrepublik* (Cologne, 1986); on the relationship between the Social Democratic Party of Germany (SPD) and the SDS, see the study by Tilman Fichter, *SPD und SDS: Parteilichkeit jenseits der Partei* (Opladen, 1988).

among them). Although the activism often degenerated into sectarian pos-
turing, and even today remains surrounded by an intolerable, completely
self-perpetuating mystification of violence, "internationalism" is still one of
the messages to emerge from the 1960s that is worth maintaining in the
face of the unabated use of violence and force in North-South relations.
This type of "anti-imperialism" should not be confused with the crude
anti-Americanism and anti-Semitism of the "urban guerillas," whose paranoid "victim" attitude and desperate militancy is more reminiscent of the
competitive imperialism, for example, of the German right wing.[20]

Antifascism and anti-imperialism, the two central motives for outrage
on the part of the generation of 1968, were conveyed in a third "anti."
According to the theoretical analysis, both evils emerged, after all, from the
contradictory dynamics and crisis tendencies of the capitalist mode of production. Consequently, a legion of theoretical analyses were dedicated to
the study and critique of the political economy of capitalism, which followed the various schools and traditional strains of socialism and Marxism,
respectively. The fact that capitalism, the market economy, and profit max-
imization are currently being unabashedly celebrated once again, and that
they are also enjoying significantly more acceptance among the sixty-
eighters, is perhaps less of a challenge to the basic legitimacy of the critique of capitalism than an indication of a central flaw in the political style
of 1968. That style remained largely incapable of producing alternative
economic and social concepts to forge a middle or third way between "wild
capitalism" and a "planned economy."[21]

"The Private Is Political"

The "ideas of 1968" do not constitute any coherent (revolutionary or
reformist) program for societal change. They encompassed too many goals,
and too many of the goals and rationales were too unclear; much of the
discussion never moved beyond the stage of obsessions and *Traumtänzerei*
(dream dancing) (Fritz Teufel). The social utopias of a postcapitalist, nonau-

20 For a general background, see Dan Diner, "Imperialismus, Universalismus, Hegemonie: Zum Verhältnis von Politik und Ökonomie in der Weltgesellschaft," in Iring Fetscher and Herfried Münkler,
eds., *Politikwissenschaft* (Reinbek bei Hamburg, 1985), 326ff.
21 Various approaches to this question can be found in the publications of Thomas Schmid, ed., *Die
Linke neu denken: Acht Lockerungen* (Berlin, 1984); *Das pfeifende Schwein: Über weitergehende Interessen
der Linken* (Berlin, 1985); *Das Ende der starren Zeit* (Berlin, 1985); *Befreiung von falscher Arbeit: Thesen
zum garantierten Mindesteinkommen,* 2d ed. (Berlin, 1987). On the libertarian-ecosocialist approach
coming from the New Left, see also André Gorz, *Wege ins Paradies* (Berlin, 1983).

thoritarian society were always part of actions and campaigns because the "new human being" and the "new history" (Rudi Dutschke) could only be crystallized out of refusal and rebellion. The idea was that voluntarist and exemplary actions would bring movement into old and rigid structures. Another reason why a firm program was never set down is that the protest movement, as a relatively diffuse creation when compared to earlier social movements, did not possess an organized center. Yet the extraparliamentary opposition movements of the 1960s were more centralized and institutionalized, like political parties, than the later amorphous "new social movements" of the 1970s.

In the Federal Republic, the most noteworthy contributors of ideas included, above all, the Socialist German Student Union (Sozialistische Deutsche Studentenbund or SDS) alongside other political student associations and the Republican Clubs (Republikanische Clubs or RC), joined by other political organizations. In addition, paperback book series, journals (*Das Argument, Kursbuch, neue kritik, diskus, alternative*), theory reading groups, autonomous projects of the "critical university," and so forth, played a significant role that was strongly shaped by generally unorthodox, lively references to older theoreticians of "Western Marxism" (Jean-Paul Sartre, the Frankfurt School, Herbert Marcuse, and André Gorz) and socialist or communist traditions ranging from the early socialists to the Third and Fourth Internationals.[22]

An extremely important trait in the self-definition of the protest movement was its antiauthoritarian thrust. Here as well, the antithought mode seems to dominate, but still the attempt to break with the "authoritarian personality" by practicing new relationships between the generations and the genders contains that very potential for sociocultural and political modernization that makes "1968" so influential and interesting even today. It is here that the "positive" approaches to transformation lie, which go beyond the defensive "down with . . ." without falling into the authoritarian trap of creating yet another set of rules.

When it comes to the social and cultural dimension, the experiments in "new living" concentrated on, above all, the collective living and educational projects of the 1960s, whose models were borrowed from subcultures in the United States. They were geared toward individuals effecting self-change and were supposed to act as models for "society as a whole." The playful and alienating violations of the rules provoked both a high

---

22 The relationship of the student movement to theory is dealt with by Jörg Bopp, "Geliebt und doch gehasst," *Kursbush,* no. 78 (1984): 121ff., and Otto Kallscheuer, "Das 'System des Marxismus' ist ein Phantom: Für den theoretischen Pluralismus der Linken," *Kursbuch,* no. 48 (1977): 59ff.

degree of defensiveness and resistance and an intricate practice of limitation, so that in the long run, the consequence actually was a change in consciousness that transcended marginal groups ("communards," "freaks," "hippies," "provos"). This was made that much easier since, twenty years after the end of the war, with unprecedented material wealth and decreasing working hours, a latent willingness to "transform values" was present in broad segments of the population. Society adopted neither the "flipped-out" subcultures' (more proclaimed than practiced) sexual libertinism nor their explicit claim that communes were the "suitable unit for waging class warfare" (Bernd Rabehl). Since then, however, the utopias of the "hedonistic left" have to some extent become a modest reality, both in the still-dominant educational institutions (family, kindergarten, school) and in the soon widely established alternative projects (communal living arrangements, parent-run child care centers, free schools), so that one can speak of the absorption of minority "pilot projects" – presented by relevant minorities – into the majority culture, and of a clear recentering of common sense. Nowadays, these are by no means limited to the wealthy middle class any longer but, rather, have long since reached those living in proletarian contexts (and have contributed to their dissolution!).

The desire for self-change not only polarized mainstream society but also led to an exemplary conflict among the leftist "avant-garde": in contrast to the traditional left, which was dominated by middle-aged professional men and which actually respected the division of "private" and "public," antiauthoritarian activists made the private sphere, which had been "betrayed" in the context of late capitalism, into an antifunctional effect, into a political issue and battlefield itself. All imaginable power relationships between generations and genders were turned into a field of experimentation for nonauthoritarian practices. Left-wing critics ironically spoke of that goal as "socialism in one house" – what was liberated social and sexual communication in synthetic large families when compared to a liberation process encompassing the peoples of the entire globe? The opposing question then became: What was this without the prerevolutionizing of the revolutionaries?[23]

Meanwhile, the fact that the actors of 1968 have bid farewell to the "beloved revolution" (Daniel Cohn-Bendit) has led many of them to ignore

---

23 Among the antiauthoritarian "sources," in addition to the already-cited literature, see Frank Böckelmann and Herbert Nagel, eds., *Subversive Aktion: Der Sinn der Organisation ist ihr Scheitern* (Frankfurt am Main, 1978); Reimut Reiche, *Sexualität und Klassenkampf* (Frankfurt am Main, 1988); *Kommune Zwei: Versuch der Revolutionierung des bürgerlichen Individuums* (Berlin, 1969); Rainer Langhans and Fritz Teufel, *Klau mich* (Berlin, 1968); and Heide Berndt, "Kommune und Familie," *Kursbuch* 17 (1969): 129–45.

the victory within this defeat. As already stated, it lies in the fact that societies have adopted many of the antiauthoritarian impulses of the revolt, and in Germany, for example, the "authoritarian personality" as a social character has faded in importance. Defending this success means more than merely protecting more liberal styles of education on the various levels against educational counterreforms undertaken in the course of the political drift to the right and neoconservative "rollback"; it also means submitting the overly simplistic notion of "self-realization" to a more precise dialectic of authority and autonomy. "Authority," when confronted with individuals capable of autonomy, is as transitory as it is unavoidable.[24]

New Politics: The Left-Libertarian Approach

The cultural revolutionary character of the protest movement was clearly stronger and more far-reaching than its political-institutional potential for innovation. The perspective of societal self-realization and self-administration was more pronounced among antiauthoritarian protesters than their political creative capabilities were.

This thesis may come as a surprise, considering the spurt of innovation that the protest movement unleashed for the benefit of democratic reform of the welfare state, or the long-term effects in the form of the divisions of "new politics." We must also not overlook the emergence of green or alternative party constellations. On this point, Jürgen Habermas has spoken of a "process of fundamental liberalization" triggered by the cultural revolts.[25] However, this "increase" in democracy, in the liberality of the political culture, and in citizen participation in planning decisions was far more filtered by the state than was consistent with the antiauthoritarian, that is, libertarian, self-perception. The current blurring of political attributions – most clearly visible in the figure of the "intelligent independent voter" – points squarely to the lack of clear political-institutional alternatives.

As to the political-institutional dimension of 1968, the protest movement at the time vacillated between a defensive republican–civil rights strategy and an offensive radical left-wing strategy. It presented extremely critical diagnoses of the state of the liberal democracies, parliamentary

---

24 In support, see Richard Sennett, *Autorität* (Frankfurt am Main, 1986), and Wilfried Gottschalch, "Das Autoritäre im Antiautoritären," *Freibeuter* 29 (1986): 48ff. On the discussion regarding the persistence and obsolescence, respectively, of authoritarian structures of character and personality, see Schmid, *Die Linke neu denken,* as well as the essays by Wolfgang Kraushaar and Micha Brumlik in Helmut Dubiel, ed., *Populismus* (Frankfurt am Main, 1987).
25 Jürgen Habermas, "Der Marsch durch die Institutionen hat auch die CDU erreicht," *Frankfurter Rundschau,* Mar. 11, 1988, 1.

representation, and the suspension of control functions by means of press concentration, large corporate interests, and the monism of the major parties – without necessarily being antiparliamentarian in the process. It would probably be more accurate to say that the New Left, in its rather melancholy aparliamentarianism, insisted on the realization of constitutionally based civil rights and democratic principles before going forward, in the face of the existing constitutional reality, to develop far-reaching socialist-communist concepts of transformation. The soviet republic espoused by many APO representatives (also introduced into French discussions after May 1968 by the *deuxième gauche,* that is, the PSU, the left-wing socialist party, and the CFDT trade union under the catchword *autogestion*) illustrates the ambivalence of the "fundamental opposition" at the time. Understood from a postmodern perspective, this self-administrative socialism contained a wealth of participatory impulses that withdrew responsibilities from the authoritarian administrative state and the political technocracy and returned political matters to the hands of mature citizens. The left-libertarian impetus of 1968 is certainly current and implicitly present in demands for decentralization, participation in decision making, and self-administration, and in discussions about citizen participation, referenda, and the communalization of politics. But the protest movement, which was in the midst of "proletarianizing" itself, increasingly appealed to authoritarian, state-socialist models that disregarded the dialectical unity between socialism and democracy. The enthusiasm of many antiauthoritarian protesters for the Chinese Cultural Revolution, which emerged from their critique of the division of manual and intellectual labor, and thus for a hypertotalitarian political regime, confirms this relapse into political traditionalism, for which they have only themselves to blame.

The New Left, in its own avant-garde fashion, had too little confidence in society's capacity to (re)create itself and in the developmental possibilities of postliberal forms; this influenced their latent tendency toward authoritarian, and even didactically dictatorial, solutions that, owing only to their political weakness, never had a chance for practical realization. The outmoded avant-gardism of the late protest movement reveals a flaw that was present from the start: social, aesthetic, and, incidentally, technical modernism was accompanied by a political-institutional traditionalism that, in the end, was responsible for the New Left's lack of political success.[26] The liberal-conservative representatives of the political "center," allied

---

26 One illustration among many is the "Gespräch über die Zukunft," with Rudi Dutschke, Bernd Rabehl, and Christoph Semler in *Kursbuch* 14 (1968): 146ff.

with a rabid, Anglo-Saxon-type of neoliberalism, were the primary beneficiaries of the aforementioned "intermixture" of political milieus and attitudes. Neoliberal social theory, disguised as possessive individualism and achievement-oriented ideology, took up the human desires for liberation. The best example of this distortion is the common critique of the contemporary social welfare state, which can only be reconciled with libertarian antistatism and a leftist critique of the bureaucracy when viewed from the most superficial perspective.

Since even aging leftists (still) lack an alternative concept attractive to the masses in the current period of increasing risks in all areas of life and social insecurity, however, as voters, citizens take refuge in the *juste milieu* of the "turnaround" regimes, which awaken an impression of political initiative and leadership. What is mainly expected of them is competence in economic policy, which also includes holding on to the property accumulated during the "golden years" and, awkwardly enough, the guarantee of liberties and newly won opportunities for democratic participation, which often represent a "legacy of 1968." In the course of the last two decades, this process of displacement has resulted in the seemingly contradictory coexistence of "red-green" with "black" sentiments, attitudes, and expectations, which are probably already creating value struggles in late-capitalistic societies, leaving the impression of an ever increasing "confusion."[27]

Thus, the "critical test" of the tradition of 1968 would be to define "individualism" as a hegemonic concept in ways different from current practice, particularly in the midst of an insidious and nonetheless forced social atomization and accelerating fragmentation of the public sphere. That is to say, it would be important to define the concept in opposition to the social Darwinist rules of battle and the unchecked and increasing concentration of power in "private" hands in the Western postindustrial societies.

27 On this topic, see Harry Hanolka, *Schwarzrotgrün: Die Bundesrepublik auf der Suche nach ihrer Identität* (Munich, 1987).

II

The Third World

ARIF DIRLIK

The ambiguity built into the title of this chapter is intentional. A Third World perspective on 1968 requires a double vision. First, it demands recognition that as idea and reality the Third World was conspicuously present in the events of 1968, not only in the many different areas encompassed by the term "Third World" but also and more importantly in the First (and Second) Worlds; it is reasonable to suggest that the emergence of the Third World both as a challenge to the First but also as a substitute for the Second World of Soviet and Eastern European communism was a crucial aspect of 1968. Second, it enjoins us to recognize the many contexts that shaped the participation of people in the Third World in the events of 1968. This raises the question of whether or not 1968 can serve as a marker in Third World histories in the same sense that it has come to mark a watershed in First and Second World histories and, for that very reason, of the dialectic between the general and the particular in the construction of 1968 as a historical marker.

It is this latter aspect that has priority in the subsequent discussion. Given the immense territory, and even more immense differences, of societies covered by the term "Third World," which do not lend themselves to comprehensive coverage and certainly defy any one historian's expertise, the discussion is illustrative rather than comprehensive. My selection of those cases where there were significant events in 1968 does not, I hope, produce the misleading impression that 1968 was equally important everywhere in the Third World. Conversely, I have relied for my choices on the expertise of others, and it is possible that there were other cases equally important that did not find their way into the discussion either because there is little scholarship on them or because I was unable to identify such scholarship. I have sought to select at least one case from each continental region and, in doing so, I tried to be attentive to difference as much as to commonality.

The cases I discuss in this chapter are those of China, India, and Turkey in Asia, Egypt and Ethiopia in Africa, and Mexico in Latin America.

Nineteen sixty-eight as I understand it was not the temporal location for some universal spirit or tendency that manifested itself differently in different places. Nor did it carry the same significance everywhere as a historical "turning point." From a European and United States perspective, the intensification of student activity in the immediate years leading up to 1968, and its seemingly irreversible decline thereafter, yields an impression of 1968 as a distinct historical marker. This is not so in the Third World. The prior history of intellectuals' involvement in national liberation struggles blurs the distinctiveness of 1968, as does the intensification of radical activity in many places *after* 1968. Among the Third World nations that experienced major student activism in the 1970s were Brazil, the Central African Republic, Chile, Ecuador, El Salvador, Ethiopia, Ghana, India, Indonesia, Malaysia, Morocco, Nicaragua, South Africa, South Korea, Sri Lanka, Sudan, Tanzania, Thailand, and Zambia.[1]

From a global perspective, 1968 derives its significance from the conjuncture in that year of many movements around the world that had been burgeoning for some time, whose coincidence in time constituted the year as a historical marker. This coincidence makes 1968 appear as the culmination of previous years, or the point of departure for the years to come; it does not follow that the individual movements that went into the making of 1968 necessarily reached their culmination in that year, or even that 1968 appears equally significant when viewed from within these different movements. It is as if a multiplicity of temporalities crossed paths at that moment of history, pulled together by global forces that momentarily overcame their many differences, only to sharpen those differences and propel them once again over their individual trajectories. That momentary conjuncture would leave a lasting mark on their futures, but if we are to grasp 1968 with all its contradictions, their differences are no less significant than the more readily discernible commonalties that came to the foreground that year.

Commonalties there were, to be sure. In 1968 movement seemed to follow movement in one country after another. Everywhere, student movements held center stage, yielding the impression of the politicization of education on a global scale. The predominance of students in these movements almost inevitably guaranteed the enunciation in many different con-

---

1 Y. G.-M. Lulat, "Determinants of Third World Student Political Activism in the Seventies: The Case of Zambia," in Philip G. Altbach, ed., *Student Politics: Perspectives for the Eighties* (Metuchen, N.J., 1981), 234.

texts of common questions related to education, educational institutions, and their role in society. In every instance, the relationship between education and politics seemed to be a burning issue. Communications between widely different societies, compounded in many cases with organizational ties among students, suggested not just disparate movements with common concerns, but gave the appearance of an organized movement that transcended national and even continental boundaries. As a contemporary observer put it,

Many people believe that there is an organised conspiracy behind student protests in different parts of the world, especially in the United States and Western Europe. We have found no evidence of this. At the same time it is no pure coincidence that students in different places often protest about the same things in the same way. First, many students are affected by the same issues – the war in Vietnam, racial discrimination, consensus politics and over-strained educational systems. The ideas of Herbert Marcuse and Che Guevara can be attractive in many different countries. National frontiers mean less than generation frontiers nowadays. Secondly, there is a great deal of cross-pollination, some of it organised and some not. . . . In each place the grievances were rooted in native soil but the confidence and the techniques to express them were passed down the line.[2]

The commonalties, however, may be exaggerated. Not only were the grievances "rooted in native soil"; in many cases, the movements of 1968 had their own histories, which made for significant differences in their configuration and called for significantly different resolution of the grievances that gave rise to them. In the words of a historian (himself a participant) of the 1960s political movements in Turkey, "It is not quite right to establish connections between the events in Europe and those in Turkey. Doubtless, the psychological effects created by communications media created some measure of conformity with the events there [that is, in Europe]. But events unfolding in Turkey, with their own integral appearance, were in no way carbon copies of the events in Europe."[3]

Before I go on to sketch out several Third World cases that illustrate these commonalties and differences, it is important to note two general differences that distinguish the Third World contexts. First, 1968 being most conspicuously a year of student political upheaval, it is essential to bear in mind the differences in student political participation between the First and the Third Worlds. Whereas in the former case the emergence of students

2 Richard Davy, "Students in Revolt," *The Statesman,* June 1968. Quoted in S. K. Ghosh, *The Student Challenge Round the World* (Calcutta, 1968), 113–14.
3 Suleyman Genc, *Oniki Mart'a Nasil Gelindi: Bir Devrin Perde Arkisi, 1960–1971* [The Road to March 12: Backstage to a Period, 1960–71] (Ankara, 1971), 109–10.

participating in politics was a phenomenon of the 1960s, in most Third World cases students long had been participants in politics, and their activities had played an important part in national liberation struggles against colonialism. In their case, therefore, the novelty of 1968 as a discrete marker was attenuated significantly by this prior history.

Second, although it is possible to argue that a global circulation of ideas played an important part everywhere in the events of 1968, it is also necessary to bear in mind that significant differences existed in the intensity and reach of communications between the First and the Third Worlds, if only because the media, especially television, were far less accessible in Third World societies. Whereas students in First World societies could already literally watch worldwide events in the 1960s, for students in Third World societies, radio, newspapers, and organizational networks played the most important part in communication. The differential impact of different media must be factored into the analysis of 1968 in the Third World and, within it, the impact of worldwide events in different national situations. The question is technical, dependent on the level of technological development, but not just technical, since political controls over the media were also quite significant in determining access to worldwide events. In any case, as with the previous qualification, limited access to information on global events enhanced the part local developments played in shaping the events of 1968 in the Third World.

1968 IN THE THIRD WORLD

People's Republic of China

The worldwide upheavals of 1968 were arguably the least relevant to the People's Republic of China, which was as cut off from the world as it is possible for a major social formation to be in the modern age. To be sure, there were significant upheavals in China that year. In the most closely documented case, Qinghua University in Beijing, one of China's most prestigious universities, was the scene of pitched battles between different factions of students between April and July 1968 that ultimately involved workers, the People's Liberation Army, and the highest levels of party and government leadership.[4] There were comparable events all over China in 1968. But these events owed little to developments elsewhere during the year.

4 William Hinton, *Hundred Day War: The Cultural Revolution at Tsinghua University* (New York, 1972).

My reason for beginning with China is not because of the relevance of 1968 to China, but because of the relevance of China to 1968. *Because* China was cut off from worldwide events in the 1960s, especially after 1966, it is exemplary of a Third World situation in which 1968 was a product of internally generated conflicts. Yet the events in China during these years would have a worldwide impact, as first the Sino-Soviet split and then the Cultural Revolution (officially, 1966–9), brought the People's Republic to the center of world radicalism and turned the Chinese revolutionary experience into a paradigm not only in the Third but also in the First World. From the Philippines to Peru, from Japan to North America, Mao Zedong's Marxism and the practices of the Cultural Revolution were to play a significant part in the making of 1968.[5] The attraction of Maoism, Ronald Fraser writes, "arose not only for its 'organizational model' but because it seemed to provide a ready revolutionary answer to the deformations of Russian-style communism and Western communist parties. Since the Sino-Soviet split of the early 1960s, China came to provide an alternative revolutionary model that, for many students, was given additional weight by the Cultural Revolution of 1965–69."[6] In 1968 China was in the throes of the Cultural Revolution, which was already past its radical high point. The "revolution in the revolution" that Mao Zedong had initiated in 1966 quickly had gone beyond what seemed permissible to the radical leadership and by 1968 had degenerated into factional struggles. The student battles at Qinghua University and elsewhere continued to raise revolutionary slogans in legitimation of factional power struggles and would shortly culminate in a wholesale purge of radical students in an effort to restore the power of the Communist Party. But in 1968 the slogans still carried to many inside and outside of China the prestige of the revolutionary dreams that had inspired them, which were themselves rooted in the history of the Chinese revolution. And those dreams were very much part of the making of 1968.

Central to the Chinese revolutionary paradigm was a model of development that promised an alternative to the uncontrolled consumerism of advanced capitalist societies and the bureaucratism of Soviet-style socialism, which, for all their differences, seemed to share a developmentalist ideology that generated not a democratically distributed happiness but

---

5 For Maoism in Asia and Latin America, see the essays in Arif Dirlik, Paul Healy, and Nick Knight, eds., *Critical Perspectives on Mao Zedong Thought* (Atlantic Heights, N.J., 1997). For France and the United States, the most thorough analysis is Belden Fields, *Trotskyism and Maoism: Theory and Practice in France and the United States* (New York, 1988).
6 Ronald Fraser, ed., *1968: A Student Generation in Revolt* (New York, 1988), 322–3.

social and political hierarchies that fed on oppression, exploitation, and alienation. The assertion of priority to the people while undergoing development was a major source of Maoist Marxism's attractiveness, as was the premise that social and political solidarity more than compensated for an equally shared poverty. That prominent slogan of the Cultural Revolution years "self-reliance" reasserted the possibility of social and national dignity in poverty, as it promised control over everyday economic and social life against subjection to the abstract forces of the market and bureaucracy.[7] The condition for self-reliance, needless to say, was national autonomy against the forces of material and cultural imperialism. Self-reliance was key not only to the material premises of Maoist socialism but, more important, also to the creation of a new culture, without which socialism could not become a reality. Distancing the Chinese population from the corrupting influence of a global culture dominated by capitalism (or its bureaucratic counterpart in Soviet-style socialism) was to become a condition in Maoist radical thinking for reducing the class, gender, ethnic, and generational divisions in Chinese society – a prominent goal of the Cultural Revolution in the mid-1960s.

In historical hindsight, the Cultural Revolution represents an undertaking where the commitment to the creation of such a new culture was to assume the dimensions not just of a moral but also of a religious imperative. Rather than help overcome social divisions, however, the reification of ideology was to render them into insuperable antagonisms that could be resolved only by the annihilation of those consigned to enemy status. This is exactly what the students on the Qinghua campus set out to do in 1968. But this is seen only in hindsight. While the Cultural Revolution lasted, and under the conditions of the 1960s, what was most striking about the Cultural Revolution was the moral fervor with which Maoists addressed problems of social division and alienation. China was also exemplary because, in contrast to other societies, it was the political leadership that initiated the attempt to revolutionize society. Religious worship of a leader, which often reached comical proportions, seemed a small price to pay for radicals who sought democracy politically but seem to have been concerned primarily with the alienating forces at work in shaping their societies.

---

7 For a reading of Mao along these lines by an African intellectual (also director, International Institute for Labour Studies, and deputy director-general, International Labour Office), see Albert Tevoedjre, *Poverty: Wealth of Mankind* (Oxford, 1979), 66. I am grateful to Roxann Prazniak for bringing this work to my attention.

The Maoist paradigm drew further appeal from its conflation with other Third World struggles in the 1960s, which together served as harbingers of a new kind of socialism and a new society. Especially important in this regard were the struggles in Vietnam and Cuba. In 1968, Vietnam was the most immediate example of a people-based revolution, which also brought to the foreground the global conflict between the First and the Third Worlds. If China offered a paradigm of alternative development, Vietnam in the 1960s was an example of a society striving to achieve that paradigm against the immediacy of imperialism. The blow to the U.S. war effort by the Tet Offensive in January 1968 was testimony to the power of the people against the mightiest war machine created by advanced capitalism. The people-based anti-imperialist struggle in Vietnam would give additional weight to a people-based developmental model, since both were products of Third World national liberation struggles against imperialism, of which the Chinese Revolution had been the first instance. Guerrilla warfare, which presupposed close integration of the people and the military, came to symbolize such struggles. This was the "organizational model."

Guerrilla warfare, as exemplified in the Tet Offensive, needs to be distinguished, however, from another example of guerrilla warfare personified at the time by Che Guevara's undertaking in Bolivia, which had resulted in his death at the hands of the CIA and the Bolivian military just a few months earlier. This confusion, which was inspirational in 1968, was fatal to the radical movement it inspired. There is a major difference between a military operation such as Tet, which was carefully designed in its use of guerrilla tactics, and a guerrilla operation conceived as a venture in largely unknown territory, hoping to result in a military operation of national liberation. Fidel Castro was to decree 1968 "The Year of the Heroic Guerrilla." During the year, in the Third World and the First, pictures of Guevara often accompanied those of Mao, creating the impression of a global guerrilla. But Mao and Che were worlds apart. They did share some common concerns, chief among them anti-imperialism, a concern for a people-based socialism, and a faith in the ability of revolutionary struggle to create a new revolutionary culture.[8] But what united them in 1968 were First World images of the Third World and Third World notions that what worked against imperialism in one place would work equally well in another. The latter, needless to say, contravened the basic premises of guerrilla warfare; but in the heady days of 1968, such subtle distinctions did not carry much weight.

8 Che Guevara, *Socialism and Man* (New York, 1978).

These images can be summarized in the words of a Maoist Indian intellectual in 1970 (who, I should note, was opposed to "Guevarism" as a contemporary form of "Bakuninism"):

American imperialism has been struck a massive blow by the heroic people of Vietnam and is now facing final defeat. As a result the American people too is revolting. Asia, Africa, Latin America – nowhere can American imperialism keep the masses subdued and world revolution is moving step by step towards final victory. Just as day by day imperialism is being trapped by the deepening crisis, China, the centre of world revolution, has strengthened the basis of socialism and proletarian dictatorship and has internally moved toward rapid progress. Workers' Cultural Revolution in China and its 9th Party Congress are the guarantee for Marxism-Leninism, national liberation struggles and socialist movements not just in China but all over the world.[9]

India

Nineteen sixty-eight was ushered in in New Delhi by a "riot" in Connaught Place of "mostly educated young men." According to a report in *The Times of India* on January 2, 1968,

The hooligans began throwing stones and empty bottles at passing vehicles without any provocation. The wife of an ambassador was among those molested by the mob. . . . A Sub-divisional Magistrate was the victim of mob fury. . . . The location of a police station 100 yards away did not deter the rowdies. The policemen on duty were helpless spectators. One of the victims of the unprecedented mob behavior was Mrs. Mona Albuquerque. . . . The car of a senior surgeon of the Willingdon Hospital was stopped in Connaught Place. The hooligans tore off the clothes of a woman member of the party. A Medical Officer of the New Delhi Municipal Committee and his wife were molested near Madras Hotel. The car of a Sub-divisional Magistrate was attacked on Parliament Street.[10]

"Hooligans" the rioters may have been, but the prominence of officials and foreigners among their targets suggests that the attacks may not have been as indiscriminate as the *Times* report and Ghosh's commentary make them out to be.

The "riot" was but one instance of the "repeated student holocausts" that marked the Indian educational scene throughout the 1960s.[11] In 1968, there were "fifty-nine student agitations that obstructed the normal functioning of academic institutions." In terms of number and scope, however,

---

9 Promode Sengupta, *Naxalbari and Indian Revolution* (Calcutta, 1983), 109. Originally published in Bengali in 1970.
10 Quoted in Ghosh, *Student Challenge,* 167.
11 The term is from Ghosh, *Student Challenge,* 77.

student agitation in 1968 is dwarfed by the events of 1966, when there were "approximately 2,206 student demonstrations, of which 480 were violent,"[12] and 1970, when "organized attacks on [education institutions] began in full swing."[13] At Calcutta University in 1970, Banerjee writes, "As files and records, question papers and answer scripts, chairs and tables went up in flames, stenciled portraits of Mao Tsetung gazed down approvingly from the school and college walls which shrieked out in loud letters: 'political power grows out of the barrel of a gun.'"[14] In the ensuing months, students engaged in a "cultural revolution," when they attacked the busts of "comprador capitalists" (including Gandhi) and engaged the police in armed struggles; by November, there were ten thousand to twenty thousand revolutionary cadres operating in West Bengal, about half of them in the Calcutta area. The fighting left thirty-six policemen dead and four hundred injured.[15]

The Vishwa Yuvak Kendra study of "student agitations" offers a detailed account of student activity in 1968. Student activity took place all over the country and, according to the categories used, ranged from agitation over specific student issues to protest with significant social and political consequences, such as the anti-English agitation in Rajasthan, the anti-Hindi agitation among Tamil students in Mysore and Andhra Pradesh, and partisan political movements to protest the visit of World Bank President Robert McNamara. Some of this agitation continued throughout the year; other instances, over more trivial issues, such as the "soccer game agitation" or the "Roadside Romeo agitation," involved specific incidents and were limited in scope and duration. The latter, too, however, may be taken as evidence of widespread student unrest.[16]

In 1968, it was not students but peasant insurgents that held center stage in Indian radicalism. Peasant uprisings in Naxalbari between May and July 1967 were followed by struggles of tribal Girijans against landlord oppression in Srikakulam, which by the end of 1968 had given rise to a guerrilla movement. Communist intellectuals had been involved in peasant mobilization since the early 1960s. They were joined in 1966 by Marxist student

12 N. Jayaram, "India," in Philip G. Altbach, ed., *Student Political Activism: An International Reference Handbook* (Westport, Conn., 1989), 96.
13 Sumanta Banerjee, *India's Simmering Revolution: The Naxalite Uprising* (London, 1984), 178. For the student movements before 1968, see Lloyd I. Rudolph, Susanne H. Rudolph, and Karuna Ahmed, "Student Politics and National Politics in India," *Economic and Political Weekly* (July 1971): 1655–68.
14 Ibid.
15 Ibid., 178–86. See also Sanjay Seth, "Indian Maoism: The Significance of Naxalbari," in Dirlik, Healy, and Knight, eds., *Critical Perspectives on Mao*.
16 Vishwa Yuvak Kendra, *The Dynamics of Student Agitations* (Bombay, 1973), 59–98, for a detailed overview of the student agitation in 1968.

leaders who had been expelled from the Presidency College in Calcutta after student protests in October. Agrarian insurgency after 1967 created dissension among Indian Marxists that led in the spring of 1969 to the formation of the Maoist Communist Party of India (Marxist-Leninist), the Naxalites headed by Charu Mazumdar.

"Throughout 1968 and up to the birth of the CPI (M-L) in May 1969, the urban movement of the Communist revolutionary students and youth was marked by demonstrations in Calcutta and other towns in defense of the peasants' armed struggle, and often on economic issues like rise in food prices."[17] Nevertheless, student agitation after 1966 and involvement in the revolutionary events in the countryside stimulated more coherent organization of the youth movement in India than had been the case earlier. It also prompted a turn to the left under the Maoist banner of the Naxalites that would culminate in the radicalism of 1970 and after.

While the Naxalites adopted the Maoist banner, and Charu Mazumdar declared that "China's Chairman is Our Chairman," Chinese leaders, outwardly supportive, privately expressed some wariness of the Naxalites. Banerjee notes that the Naxalites were very much part of the "contemporary, worldwide impulse among radicals to return to the roots of revolutionary idealism," adding however that the "Naxalbari movement drew inspiration from the Indian jacqueries of the 18th and 19th centuries as well as from the organized armed peasants' struggles led by the Communists in Telengana in the 1940s."[18] From another perspective, Sengupta, himself a Maoist, in 1970 charged Mazumdar with distorting the Chairman's views by the "petit-bourgeois revolutionism of . . . Che Guevara's theory of guerrilla war."[19]

Turkey

Nineteen sixty-eight was an eventful year in Turkey.[20] Beginning in April, a "boycott and occupation" movement began at Turkish universities and quickly spread from Ankara to Istanbul, and on to provincial universities in every major city. By June, higher education in Turkey had been immobilized.

17 Banerjee, *India's Simmering Revolution*, 177.
18 Ibid., iii. For Chinese responses to the Naxalites, see ibid., 201–4.
19 Sengupta, *Naxalbari and Indian Revolution*, 112.
20 Unless noted otherwise, the account of the events in 1968 below is based on Genc, *Oniki Mart'a Nasil Gelindi*, esp. 102–86.

The educational concerns that had led to the "boycott and occupation" movement, in which many students participated, were shortly overshadowed by factional struggles among students. These would turn universities into battlegrounds, where armed groups faced one another in ongoing battles much the same as at Qinghua University in Beijing. Configured by the political divisions that had rocked the country since 1965, student movements in 1968 became the vehicles through which deep-rooted social and political divisions were articulated. Not surprisingly, the movement spilled out of the universities into the streets in city after city in a "low-intensity" civil war that would last well into the 1970s.

As in the cases of China and India, the participation of groups other than students was responsible for this impression of civil war. Beginning in February 1968, worker unrest accompanied student agitation, resulting in a highly visible worker takeover of a rubber plant in Istanbul in July. Class conflict (exacerbated by tribal and ethnic confrontations) had been endemic in the rural areas throughout the decade, especially in eastern Turkey. Large numbers of residents in urban areas took part in conflicts among students. These conflicts were fueled, and further deepened, by divisions within the political system.

The student movement in Turkey also expressed itself in the language of contemporary radicalism. Anti-imperialism and the quest for national political and economic autonomy were central to the grammar of this language, nourished in the years after the Cuban Missile Crisis but especially with the conflict in Cyprus in 1965. Many were growing apprehensive that Turkey was little more than a pawn in a global American strategy; violent response to the provocations of the U.S. Sixth Fleet marked at least two instances of radical activity in 1968. The desire for a new autonomous national culture as well as concern for people-based and place-based revolution were evident most conspicuously in the emerging concern for the Kurdish peoples of eastern Turkey. The major left-wing radical student organization, Dev-Genc (Union of Revolutionary Youth), which came into existence in April 1968, was to serve as a recruiting ground for Maoism. As in India, Maoism would come to inspire the revolutionaries of 1968. Although they drew inspiration from Mao and Lenin, in the fashion Sengupta ascribed to Guevaraism, radicals of the extreme Left viewed themselves as "professional revolutionaries," whose business it was to make revolution. Out of revolution would emerge a new revolutionary society and culture.

What distinguished the Turkish case in 1968 (and lent it some similarities to the case of India), however, was the ideological division in radical ranks, which in this case was not restricted to leftists. The Left in Turkey, whatever its resemblance to the contemporary worldwide resurgence in leftist movements, was on the defensive for most of the 1960s. As elsewhere, it was internally divided, but the significant divisions were those between leftist intellectuals, right-wing Islamic fundamentalists (including the later prime minister, Necmettin Erbakan), and right-wing nationalists led by Alparslan Turkes, whose fascist ideology was dynamized by yearnings for a Greater Turkey ("Turan"), stretching from Central Asia to present-day Turkey. Organizing around mosques, in the case of the fundamentalists, and populist organizations with their commando camps, in the case of the nationalists, right-wing political groups and their activities played an important part in shaping the radical movement in 1968 and thereafter. By August, some of the Islamic groups had declared a "jihad" against the Left, promising that Turkey's future would not be Vietnam or Cuba but Indonesia.[21] It was Turkes's guerrillas who seem to have turned political into armed conflicts in August 1968, stimulating guerrilla formations that in the subsequent years would shape radical activity.

The liberal journalist Metin Toker, who, like a good liberal, condemned all radicalisms for their very radicalism, has nevertheless astutely pointed to the structural contradictions that shaped the radical movements of the 1960s: "A constitution, open to the left, that gives priority to reforms in that direction. A regime in power since 1965, when everything started: totally closed to the Left but open to the Right. . . . And a worldwide ultra-leftism in student movements in 1967–8."[22] Following the military coup on May 27, 1960, a new constitution had been proclaimed that, while fundamentally reaffirming Kemalist ideology (especially secularism and statism), had opened the way to political freedoms that permitted the growth of leftist parties and ideologies. It also fostered an unprecedented open inquiry into the meaning of the Kemalist republic.[23] The new regime, however, was unable to contain the growth of Islamic political movements. Even before 1965, these movements were on the resurgence.[24] With the

21 Ibid., 157.
22 Metin Toker, "Solda ve Sagda Vurusanlar: Turkiye'de Iki Yonlu Ihtilal Ortaminin Anatomisi" [Fighters on the Left and the Right: Anatomy of the Two-Directional Revolutionary Circumstances in Turkey] (Ankara, 1971), 160–1.
23 For a comprehensive discussion of the political consequences of the constitution from 1961, see Yildiz Sertel, *Turkiye'de Ilerici Akimlar* [Progressive Movements in Turkey] (Istanbul, 1967).
24 In 1963 the author wrote of the resurgence of Islam in politics. See Arif Dirlik, Preface, in Nusret Kurosman, ed., *Cesitli Cepheleriyle Ataturk* [Ataturk in His Various Aspects] (Istanbul, 1963). This volume was the product of a yearlong conference at Robert College (presently, Bosporus University), intended to inquire into the meaning of Kemalism from a variety of social and political perspectives, something that would have been impossible before the 1960s.

electoral victory of the Justice Party in 1965, the regime in power put its weight behind these movements, encouraging their growth against the threat of communism. The Associations for Battling Communism (founded in 1963), and the Commandos of Turkes, himself a leader of the military coup in 1960, were to play an important part in the events of 1968. As Genc notes, whereas in most societies leftists initiated the events of 1968, in Turkey, a female student in the Faculty of Theology at Ankara University initiated the "boycott and occupation" movement. She had insisted on wearing a headdress to classes, an act that challenged not only the legality but also the very legitimacy of Kemalist secularism.[25]

Egypt and Ethiopia

There was student ferment all over Africa in the course of the 1960s. In most cases, especially in sub-Saharan Africa, this student ferment culminated in the radical movements of the 1970s referred to earlier. The immediate consequence of student ferment in the 1960s was to produce more coherent organization of the students.[26] In the two cases of Egypt and Ethiopia, however, 1968 witnessed significant student activity. These cases are also interesting because they reveal still other factors in the making of Third World student movements in 1968.

On February 21, 1968, students in Cairo and Alexandria took to the streets in support of a workers' strike, ending fourteen years of student quietude. Over the next week, "the uprising in Cairo alone resulted in two workers being killed, 77 civilians and 146 policemen being injured, and 635 people being arrested, in addition to damage to vehicles and buildings in the capital."[27]

Frustrations born out of the defeat in the war with Israel in 1967 played an important part in both the strike and subsequent student activity. Nevertheless, these frustrations provided the occasion for voicing dissatisfaction with the Nasser regime. Demands for democracy in the university and society at large were prominent among student demands. Slogans such as "Down with the military state" and "Down with the intelligence state"

---

25 Genc, 113.
26 The many volumes edited by Altbach cited in this chapter contain discussions of movements in sub-Saharan Africa. See also William J. Hanna, ed., *University Students and African Politics* (New York, 1975).
27 Ahmed Abdalla, *The Student Movement and National Politics in Egypt* (London, 1985), 149. February 21 was Students' Day, celebrated every year in memory of Bloody Thursday in 1946. On that day in 1946, twenty-three anti-British demonstrators were killed and more than a hundred wounded by British troops in Cairo. See ibid., chap. 4, for details.

were audible in the student demonstrations. The February demonstrations, moreover, seem to have been relatively free of factionalism. As one student observed, "The 1968 movement was the only one that encompassed students of all tendencies . . . and was not affected by conflicting ideological tendencies."[28]

Whereas some members of the government made feeble efforts to blame student demonstrations on outside forces or reactionaries who had been overthrown by the revolution of 1952, on the whole the authorities took a conciliatory stance toward the students as "our sons and brothers." The concessions of the government toward greater freedom in the university, accompanied by the promise of greater political freedoms, defused the situation. But the calm that had been restored was broken in November, when students took to the streets once more, this time in response to the New Education Act, which sought to bring greater rigor to university entrance examinations. Demonstrations that began in the city of al-Mansoura on November 21 spread quickly to other cities, resulting in considerable bloodshed and destruction. Although the issue seemed to be more strictly about higher education, participants in the demonstrations and strikes also included nonstudents. This second round of violence in 1968 came to an end with "practical" problems presented by the month of Ramadan.[29] This time the government's response was less lenient, as the strikes resulted in the curtailing of freedoms that had been extended to students earlier. The contradictions brought to the surface by the events of 1968 were not resolved and would culminate in more militant student activity in the 1970s.

The student movement in Egypt in 1968 followed a long period of calm and was triggered by the national crisis created by defeat in war. By contrast, the student movement in Ethiopia in 1968 was one in a series of events that had gotten under way in the early part of the decade, drew on a multiplicity of sources that contributed to increasing student militancy, and would culminate in the revolution of 1974.

The student uprising in Ethiopia began over a seemingly trivial issue and outwardly appeared to be regressive. The issue was a fashion show to be held at the University College of Addis Ababa, an institution dominated by foreigners. On March 30, students began to gather in the vicinity of Ras Makonnen Hall where the fashion show was to be held. As the guests began to arrive,

---

28 Ibid., 151–8; quotation on 158.   29 Ibid., 159–65.

some of the students began to engage in physical acts of violence; women were struck and slapped, rotten eggs were thrown indiscriminately at guests and participants; some guests were dragged from their cars and molested. Students spat upon women, staff members and other university officials. . . . At this point, and only at this point, it became abundantly clear that unless the police were immediately summoned, acts of outrageous terrorism would continue.[30]

The police were called in, thirty-eight students were arrested, the student union was shut down, and the university was closed the following week. The university remained closed until early April, but when it was reopened a considerable number of students continued their boycott of classes. When the new academic year began in November, students were powerful enough to reinstate their union. Marxists were prominent in the reinstated student union, which would help escalate student radicalism after 1968.

The focus on the fashion show as an occasion for protest lent the student movement of 1968 a misogynistic character. "Female students were harshly rebuked for their 'shameful' participation in the fashion show," and a student pamphlet asserted that "History will remember them as accomplices of neocolonialists . . . responsible for the introduction of miniskirts to this country and its repercussions on the morality of the society."[31] Yet, as in contemporary China, the movement of 1968 articulated a sharp consciousness of the cultural dimensions of colonialism. Another pamphlet stated that the "fashion show is nothing but one such agency for neocolonialism . . . an instrument for the creation of favourable market for luxury goods. The origin of such goods being the developed nation, the cash from the sale of such textile goods does not at all contribute to the growth of our local revenue."[32]

As it took shape in the early 1960s, the student movement in Ethiopia was initially concerned with student freedoms. Students, who had learned about the necessity of freedom in the classroom, were increasingly conscious of their own lack of freedom to conduct their own affairs. This raised consciousness was nourished over the decade by other concerns. The intensified involvement of the United States in Ethiopian affairs after 1960 also fed a growing awareness of the neocolonialization of Ethiopian society. Opposition to the United States was to intensify with the war in Vietnam,

---

30 Quoted in Randi R. Balsvik, *Haile Sellasie's Students: The Intellectual and Social Background to Revolution, 1952–1977* (East Lansing, Mich., 1985), 218. The use of this hall for the fashion show was an additional cause of resentment, as Ras Makonnen Hall was deemed to be a location for the preservation and development of the national culture.
31 Ibid., 215.   32 Ibid., 214.

which seemed to be clear evidence of American imperialism in the Third World. Decolonization movements in other African societies, especially after 1958 when students from other African states began to arrive in Ethiopia to attend the university, also affected the students. They would contribute significantly to the growth among Ethiopian students of a consciousness of "Africanity," especially in the cultural realm. This coincided with changes in the class composition of students at Ethiopian institutions of higher learning. Tiruneh writes that "the proletarianization of the student body paralleled the intensification of student political opposition to the government."[33] Students were intensely aware of the gap that separated them as students from their origins in urban and rural poverty; after 1965, concern for rural poverty, the government's obliviousness to it, and the need for its resolution were to become integral to student consciousness.

The Crocodile Society, established in 1964, introduced Marxism-Leninism into the Ethiopian student movement. By the time of the Sixth Congress of the National Union of Ethiopian Students in March 1967, Marxism in its Maoist variant had emerged as an important current in the student movement. The resolutions of the congress "virtually" ignored the Soviet Union, while they

in no uncertain terms proclaimed support and admiration for Mao's China and Castro's Cuba; U.S. imperialism was denounced throughout. The congress recognized the "immense achievement" of the Chinese revolution and demanded the "rightful place" of the People's Republic of China in the United Nations. It supported "wholeheartedly" the cause and struggle of the Cuban revolution, which was stated to have "heralded a new era in the revolutionary movement in Latin America."[34]

In the case of the Ethiopian student movement, organizational networks played a significant role, since the Ethiopian Students' Union in Europe and the Ethiopian Students' Union in North America were linked to the movement in Ethiopia. Nevertheless, a consciousness of Africanness was central to the way in which the movement's ideology was expressed. Especially important was the contradiction between the social, political, and economic consequences of neocolonialism and the neocolonialist culture that dominated university education. The response to the fashion show in 1968, trivial on the surface, was triggered by this deep-seated contradiction.

---

33 Fentahun Tiruneh, *The Ethiopian Students: Their Struggle to Articulate the Ethiopian Revolution* (Chicago, 1990), 65.
34 Balsvik, *Haile Sellasie's Students*, 176–7.

Mexico

The Ethiopian student movement was rooted in the deepest contradictions of Third World political economy and culture in the 1960s but found expression in 1968 in a farcical protest against miniskirts. The student movement in Mexico City that year, beginning with a trivial conflict between students from two schools, would bring the year to a tragic culmination. The Tlatelolco Massacre on October 2, 1968, which ended the student uprising in Mexico, claimed approximately three hundred lives. The massacre made no sense, Donald Mabry writes, "except that it stopped the movement a few days before the Olympic Games opened." No other event of that year is more emblematic of the conflict between the idealistic aspirations of a generation of Third World students and the cupidity of Third World governments, aspiring through symbolic achievements to be included in the ranks of the leading nations.[35]

The movement in Mexico got under way in late July 1968. In the previous months there had been no major student activity, although sporadic student violence and vandalism against one another and the public had become almost a daily routine. The government's decision on July 23 to send in the hated *granaderos* to stop student fighting, and the brutality with which the *granaderos* performed their task, was to turn student infighting into a confrontation between students and the government. A student demonstration on July 26 to protest the July 23 event coincided with a pro-Cuba march (the date was the anniversary of the Cuban revolution) organized by the procommunist Central National of Democratic Students. Whereas the two demonstrations seem to have been independent of one another, protests against police brutality inevitably merged with calls for urban guerrilla revolution. The day ended with another battle between students and *granaderos*.[36]

The student demands that emerged from these confrontations had little to do with strictly educational questions but insisted that the government respect student rights, punish responsible officials, abolish the *granaderos,* and, most important, abolish article 145 of the penal code, that is, the antisubversion law.

A turning point in the confrontation occurred on July 29–30. The police attacked on several campuses that night, including one case in which the police used a bazooka to blast open a historic school door. For the students,

35 Donald J. Mabry, *The Mexican University and the State: Student Conflicts, 1910–1971* (College Station, Tex., 1982), 265.

36 Unless otherwise noted, the account of events here is based on ibid., 236–66.

the *bazukazo* became symbolic of the government's readiness to use extreme violence. In the following days, student strikes, which had been spreading from campus to campus, assumed a more centralized form. Although August 1968 saw efforts to negotiate, massive demonstrations that month in Mexico City indicated popular support for the students: 100,000 on August 5, 300,000 on August 13, and 400,000 on August 27. Protesters repeated their demands for reform. Handbills in the demonstrations "became more critical of the inequities both in Mexico and in the world but . . . few demanded revolution. Left-wing German journalists visiting the student leadership were astonished that the Mexicans were considered revolutionary because they were demanding the enforcement of a democratic constitution."[37]

Signs of possible conciliation in early September were extinguished by a silent demonstration of 250,000 on September 13, which showed that the movement was still vital, and by the decision of the government to respond by taking over the campus of the National Autonomous University of Mexico (Universidad Nacional Autonoma de Mexico or UNAM) on September 18. The invasion by the army sparked renewed violence in the streets, leading to a major battle at the Santo Tomas Vocational School in northern Mexico City. An eyewitness account gives a sense of the many confrontations during these months:

The attack . . . didn't catch us completely unprepared, as the students at UNAM had been, because we had long since taken certain precautions. We'd stored up Molotov cocktails, zip guns, sticks and stones, fire-crackers, skyrockets . . . like a sort of bazooka. They didn't hurt anybody; they were quite harmless – but they *did* explode with a loud bang and really disconcerted the *granaderos*. . . . The confrontation with the *granaderos* began around 6 P.M. and lasted till nightfall when the Army troops appeared on the scene. The mounted police arrived, equipped with firearms, and shortly afterward we heard them shooting at the buildings. They threw tear-gas grenades at the buildings of the housing unit nearby, and men, women and children began pouring out of them, scared half to death. . . .The most dramatic thing that happened, and the thing that shocked us the most, was when the *granaderos* occupied the medical school, shortly after we'd brought our wounded there.[38]

37 Ibid., 255–6. Elena Poniatowska reported a student chant in demonstrations, "We don't want Olympic Games! We want a revolution!" It would be silly, I think, to take such a chant literally (as with many of the chants and slogans of 1968), but beleaguered authorities were no doubt capable of that. See Elena Poniatowska, *Massacre in Mexico*, trans. Helen R. Lane (Columbia, Mo., 1992), 12.
38 Poniatowska, *Massacre in Mexico*, 77–8.

On September 30, feeling that it had won, the government evacuated the UNAM campus. Students immediately planned for a rally for October 2. By 6 P.M. a crowd of nearly five thousand had gathered in the Plaza of Three Cultures. Shortly thereafter, the massacre began.

Perhaps more closely than in the cases described above, the student movement in Mexico expressed its protest in the language of contemporary student movements. A member of the Consejo Nacional de Huelga, the central strike committee, remembered that during the meetings of the Council, the delegates "explained certain philosophical tendencies, revolutionary tactics, and methods of persuasion. They did not discuss the next demonstration, they talked about Lenin, Marcuse, the Sino-Soviet quarrel, imperialism, and other subjects that tried the patience of the majority of the delegates, who were on the verge of downright rebellion."[39]

Not surprisingly, the Cuban revolution and its leaders held an especially prominent place in Mexican revolutionary lore. Another student recalled, "I never really thought of Zapata as a student symbol, an emblem. Zapata had become part of the bourgeois ideology; the PRI [Revolutionary Institutional Party (Partido Revolucionario Institucional)] has appropriated him. Maybe that's why we chose Che as our symbol at demonstrations from the very first. Che was our link with student movements all over the world! We never thought of Pancho Villa either."[40] Yet students had, or constructed in the course of activity, a sense of their connection to the legacy of earlier movements in Mexico. One student observed,

The 1968 Student Movement was not suddenly born that same year; it did not come about by spontaneous generation. . . . In many parts of the country, students had previously led the entire nation in protest movements whose general tenor was very much like that of the 1968 Movement. The most important movements of this sort were those in Puebla in 1964, Morelia in 1966, and Sonora and Tabasco in 1967. Moreover, the demonstrations in support of Cuba, Vietnam, and the Dominican Republic mobilized large groups of students. . . . The Teachers' Movement in 1958, the Railway Workers' Movement in 1958–1959, and the demonstrations in support of the Cuban revolution all contributed to this process, which reached its peak in 1968.[41]

"By marching through the streets," another student recalled, "we were more or less avenging all of the students in the provinces who had been victims of repression before our turn came: the students of Puebla, Tabasco, Chihuahua, Sinaloa, Guerrero, Sonora, and in a certain sense, the victims of oppression in Morelia, Hermosillo, and Monterrey."[42]

39 Ibid., 30.   40 Ibid., 32.   41 Ibid., 9–10.   42 Ibid., 8.

THE THIRD WORLD AND 1968

A Third World perspective on 1968 suggests that in order to appreciate the complexities of radical movements during that year, it is necessary to retain a "double vision" that is both global and local. The events of 1968 were played out on many national terrains and were informed by a conceptualization of the globe in terms of the Three Worlds, which may have reached their sharpest delineation at this time. But 1968 also represented an unprecedented globalization of radical consciousness, which questioned national boundaries and the boundaries implied by the metaphor of three "worlds." Acute awareness of relations of oppression and exploitation between the Three Worlds, which did much to produce 1968, was accompanied by an equally acute awareness that these relations, and the problems to which they gave rise, rather than distance these worlds from one another, brought them closer together within a global structure of oppression and exploitation that merely took different forms in different contexts. Hence the solutions to these problems in one context were found to be relevant in others.

At the same time, however, there was an emerging awareness of the necessity of place-based solutions to these problems. If American imperialism, dramatized by Vietnam, loomed large in worldwide radicalism, discrediting American solutions to the problems of the world, another casualty of 1968 was the earlier radical solutions represented by Soviet communism, especially after the invasion of Czechoslovakia in 1968. In the 1960s, paradigms of alternative development increasingly represented by Third World national liberation movements came to replace earlier models of development, capitalist or communist. Crucial to these paradigms, at least in theory, was sensitivity to people- and place-based development. Place-based paradigms of development are also subversive of the idea of national liberation, but this was little noted at the time, except perhaps in the occasional distinction drawn between Mao Zedong's Marxism and Che Guevara's "anarchism" or between modern agrarian movements and native traditions of agrarian uprising. It would take further developments before Zapata once again acquired prestige in the eyes of Mexican, and world, radicals.

Instead, in 1968 there was a tendency to globalize the new paradigms of development that had emerged from many local contexts. As Third World radicals were inspired by radical movements in Europe and the United States, First World radicals adopted as their own Third World solutions to societal problems. Ronald Fraser gives an account of Maoists in France who "in one small town . . . unfurled their red flags in the marketplace, displayed a picture of Mao and distributed leaflets. . . . Peasants gathered with apparent interest round their lorry. A woman comrade took the loud-speaker and began: 'Comrade peasants!' Hardly had she uttered the words when 'the masses' began running in all directions, some of them shouting, 'I'm going for my gun!'"[43] Charu Mazumdar in India was gently chided by Chinese leaders for indiscriminately applying Chinese solutions to India. Students in Third World societies were inspired not only by the ideas but also by the styles of First World radicals, which were not always welcomed in their immediate environments. "A hundred and fifty pesos for a skirt like that!" muttered a Mexican mother, "and it's not even twenty inches long!"[44]

Whereas globalization was the order of the day in 1968, and overshad-owed the implicitly place-based orientation of the new radical paradigms, we need to resist the temptation to ascribe a common identity to the radi-cal movements of the year, especially in the Third World contexts, where prior history was quite important in shaping each movement, its concerns, and configurations. In the Third World, the 1960s were years of both stu-dent empowerment and student frustration. University students were unquestionably members of the elite, or at least on their way to becoming members, which gave them a sense of their own importance and a desire to assert themselves politically. At the same time, in most Third World soci-eties facing problems of neocolonial development, students faced not only authoritarian political and university regimes but also limited prospects. The entry into higher education of students from nonelite, especially rural, backgrounds further exacerbated the contradictions between education, social status, and political power. Third World students shared some of these concerns with their First World counterparts, although to different degrees, which is responsible for the strong appearance of commonality among students worldwide.

In their search for the causes of student "delinquency" (Edward Shils), analysts of student movements in the 1960s and 1970s have focused on these contradictions almost to the exclusion of other considerations.[45] In addition to problems internal to education, and the relationship between education and society, however, it is important to note that government corruption and lawlessness often played an important part in instigating student activity. The United States's undeclared war in Vietnam may be

---

43 Fraser, *1968*, 228.   44 Poniatowska, *Massacre in Mexico*, 14.
45 This disdainful attitude pervades discussions about students in the volumes edited by Altbach referred to previously. See also Seymour M. Lipset and Philip G. Altbach, eds., *Students in Revolt* (Boston, 1969), which was reprinted from a special issue of *Daedalus*. The introductory theoretical essay is by Shils.

Arif Dirlik

emblematic of such lawlessness, as may events during the Chinese Cultural Revolution. In the cases discussed here, government lawlessness played a part in almost every instance of student mobilization and conflict, possibly the most egregious case being that in Turkey, where the government actively instigated right-wing attacks on all those deemed to be of the Left. Corruption, especially amid conditions of general social misery, would also emerge as a central concern of students, exacerbating and further politicizing the already heightened consciousness of social problems.

Nevertheless, these common concerns assumed different configurations in different locations, depending on national or social context and the available traditions of radicalism. Specific political events were responsible for triggering radical movements, and, once under way, these movements drew on earlier radical precedents in methods of organization, as well as for the form and content of the demands they made on the political system. In certain cases there were direct links between the movements of 1968 and their "prehistories." In other cases, such links may have been constructed in the course of radical activity, "inventing" traditions of radicalism. In any event, whereas 1968 witnessed important events in Third World societies, different languages of radicalism arose in different contexts that shared a common vocabulary but derived their grammar from their concrete historicity.

Whether or not 1968 served as a marker in different Third World contexts, the year holds significance at least as a metaphorical marker, when the circumstances and concerns that gave rise to the movements of the 1960s began to be replaced by other circumstances and concerns that in hindsight articulated a reconfiguration of global relations. In some ways, the movements were discredited by their own historical unfolding. Government repression, as in the United States, Germany, and Italy, and internal dissension in Third World countries such as Turkey and India would produce guerrilla movements after 1968 that quickly degenerated into terrorism. Fidel Castro's refusal to condemn the Soviet invasion of Czechoslovakia in the very "Year of the Heroic Guerrilla" would create doubts about Cuba. The Chinese leadership's increasingly explicit renunciation of the Cultural Revolution in the 1970s, and its partial reconciliation with the United States, would gradually extinguish the appeals of the Chinese paradigm. Colonialism itself gradually dissipated as an issue as American and European corporations moved toward "multicultural" employment policies that accommodated Third World elites and students. "Miracle economies" fueled by export-oriented development policies, the origins of which predated 1968, gradually came to replace earlier aspirations toward autonomous national development. The idea of national political, economic, and cultural liberation, which had done so much to inspire the radicalisms of 1968, would become a casualty of the aftermath of 1968.

National boundaries, and those of the three worlds, which had been put into question by the globalizing ideological forces of 1968, were to be rendered even more porous in ensuing years by the very material developments within capitalism and the new communication technologies that made possible those developments, which have rendered the radicalisms of 1968 a distant memory. Many graduates of 1968 have had little difficulty in accommodating themselves to this new form of globalism. Yet the decline of the national idea, and the status of the nation-state, has brought to the surface the ideal of the place-based movement, which had also been at the core of those radicalisms, even if it had been disguised by the ideology of national liberation. Other graduates of 1968, from China to India to Mexico, are at work in many places, keeping alive the possibilities of alternatives to an apparently victorious capitalism. "El Sup" may be only the most audible among them.

PART THREE

"Ask the Impossible!"

Protest Movements of 1968

12

The Revolt Against the Establishment

Students Versus the Press in West Germany and Italy

STUART J. HILWIG

Thirty years after the student rebellions rocked the world's universities in 1968, scholars still line up on various sides of the barricades. Despite three decades of debate, we remain far from a consensus on the causes and meaning of the student revolts. I seek to broaden the field of discussion by introducing an important element neglected by most previous studies of the student movement. This element was the establishment. Previous works assumed the revolutionary potential of the student movements and their threat to the established order, but few scholars investigated the establishment's response to the students. Since 1968, when Jürgen Habermas, Raymond Aron, and Alain Touraine fired the first salvos in the academic debate on the significance of the student upheavals, scholars have focused on the students' positions during the late 1960s but have neglected the targets of their revolts. My study looks at one key target, the popular press, which in 1968 served as a mouthpiece for the established political and social order in West Germany and Italy. This chapter focuses on the unique cultural and historical factors that informed and shaped the students' battle with the popular press, and it examines the effects this battle between kiosk and campus had on the politics and power structures of these two young republics. In particular, I investigate the battle by students in West Berlin with the Springer press and that of students in Turin against the local daily *La Stampa*. These two cases are indicative of larger national dimensions because both presses commanded wide and influential audiences and both cities became major sites of student demonstrations in 1967–8.

This chapter benefited greatly from insightful and inspiring suggestions provided by Carole Fink, Alan Beyerchen, Claudio Fogu, and Michael Seidman.

Theories on the causes and goals of student activism in 1968 fall into three conceptual categories. The first, that of the delusion theorists, characterizes the protesters as spoiled children of the bourgeoisie ensnared in a web of utopian rhetoric.[1] Another group, who have taken a more objective, less emotional approach, are the generational theorists. They employ cohort analysis to understand the conflict between the "baby boomers" born after 1945 and their parents who had lived through the war and achieved a measure of affluence in the 1960s.[2] A third group, who have focused on ideology, view the unrest of 1968 in more conceptual terms as a symptom of deeper problems in Western society, such as the failure of democratic mechanisms or the continuance of class conflict.[3]

From their observations of American and Western European student demonstrations, members of all three groups project their theories onto a broad international plane. However, these global interpretations prove less useful at explaining the deeper causes of specific local and national movements. Paul Piccone, the author of a study of modern Marxism in Italy, has recently contended that scholars must begin to "unmask" the international mythology surrounding 1968 and discover the uniquely national problems that contributed to the European student protests. Political scientist Sidney Tarrow's meticulous study of protest and democracy in Italy argues that "unless we place the movements of the late 1960s within their national and historic contexts, we shall not be able to judge either their newness, their breadth, or their impact on democracy."[4]

The student movements in West Germany and Italy provide striking examples of the importance of national and historical context. The Federal Republic of Germany and the Republic of Italy make fascinating cases for

1   See Raymond Aron, *The Elusive Revolution: Anatomy of a Student Revolt,* translation of *Revolution introuvable* by Gordon Clough (New York, 1969). Alain Schnapp and Pierre Vidal-Naquet, *The French Student Uprising, November 1967–June 1968: An Analytical Record,* translation of *Journal de la commune étudiante* by Maria Jolas (Boston, 1971).

2   Lewis S. Feuer, *The Conflict of Generations: The Character and Significance of Student Movements* (New York, 1969); Feuer's argument also reminds one of Freud's band of tribal sons who seek to destroy the father in *Totem and Taboo.* Ronald Fraser, *1968: A Student Generation in Revolt* (London, 1988).

3   Alain Touraine, *Le Mouvement de mai ou le Communisme utopique* (Paris, 1968). Jürgen Habermas, *Protestbewegung und Hochschulreform* (Frankfurt am Main, 1969). See also Marxist writer Rossana Rossanda who argued that the poor job prospects for Italian and French university graduates resulted in a massive rejection of the capitalist system by the student movement; for a short summary of her views, see Aldo Marchetti, "Alla ricerca della rivoluzione introvabile: Prolegomeni a futuri studi sulle rivolte studentesche del 1968," *Classe* 2, no. 3 (1988): 69–111.

4   See Paul Piccone, "Reinterpreting 1968: Mythology on the Make," *Telos* 77 (1988): 7–43. For his work on Marxism, see *Italian Marxism* (Berkeley, Calif., 1983). Seymour M. Lipset and Philip G. Altbach, eds., *Students in Revolt* (Boston, 1969). Sidney Tarrow, *Democracy and Disorder: Protest and Politics in Italy, 1965–75* (Oxford, 1989), 3.

comparison because both societies had experienced periods of fascism, foreign invasion, defeat, and destruction followed by major postwar political transitions, rapid economic development, and integration into the NATO alliance. For these young republics, the unrest of 1968 challenged the bases of postwar stability. Both the students and the press reached backward to the years of fascism and even earlier times, one to battle against the establishment, the other to defend the status quo. In 1968 the popular press defended middle-class values, the democratic state, university officials, and political leaders from the onslaught of student parades and polemics.

The historiography of the Italian and West German student movements has emphasized the students' struggle against an authoritarianism rooted in the historic trajectories of their respective national cultures.[5] Scholars of postwar Italy and West Germany note that the students attacked the establishment because they felt democracy had been compromised by a manipulative press that supported politically myopic regimes in the two nations. By comparing the press coverage of the student movement in Turin with the coverage of the movement in West Berlin, we can see how the popular press and student protesters grappled with issues of the past and the stability of their untested democracies. By analyzing the press's response to these two movements, we shall see how the establishment in Turin and West Berlin developed similar strategies to defend the status quo from the challenge posed by student rebels. Such a comparison will also reveal important historical and cultural differences between the Italian and West German experiences of 1968.

Between 1949 and 1963, when Konrad Adenauer led the center-right coalition governments of the Christian Democratic Union (CDU) and the Christian Socialist Union (CSU), an older generation of Germans, weary of war and politics, turned to the business of economic reconstruction. This distancing from politics, characterized by Fritz Stern as the "unpoliti-

---

5 For West Germany, see Geoff Eley, "Germany Since '68: From the APO to the Greens," *Socialist Review* 18 (1988): 93–157. Mary Fulbrook, *The Divided Nation: A History of Germany, 1918–1990* (New York, 1992), 283. Kurt Sontheimer, *The Government and Politics of West Germany,* trans. Fleur Donecker (New York, 1973), 132. Gordon Smith, *Democracy in Western Germany: Parties and Politics in the Federal Republic,* 3d ed. (London, 1986), 79–80. For Italy in general, see Paul Ginsborg, *A History of Contemporary Italy: Society and Politics, 1943–1988* (London, 1990). Peppino Ortoleva, "Le Culture del '68," in Aldo Agosti, Luisa Passerini, and Nicola Tranfaglia, eds., *La cultura e i luoghi del '68* (Milan, 1991). Robert Lumley, *States of Emergency: Cultures of Revolt in Italy from 1968 to 1978* (London, 1990). Tarrow, *Democracy and Disorder,* 5–11 and 151–3. For Turin, in particular, see Luisa Passerini, "Le Mouvement de 1968 comme prise de parole et comme explosion de la subjectivité: Le cas de Turin," *Le Mouvement social* 143 (avril–juin 1988): 39–74; and Marco Revelli, "Il '68 a Torino. Gli esordi: La comunità studentesca di Palazzo Campana," in Agosti, Passerini, and Tranfaglia, eds., *La Cultura e i luoghi del '68.*

cal German" and by Ralf Dahrendorf as the "apolitical German," led to the concentration of power in the hands of a small political and cultural elite.[6] By the first half of the 1960s, however, several developments eroded the culture of consensus that had persisted during the Adenauer years. In 1961 the ideological division between East and West Germany became a physical reality with the construction of the Berlin Wall. In 1963 the *Spiegel* Affair led to Defense Minister Franz Josef Strauss's resignation and contributed to Adenauer's decision to step down as chancellor that year.[7] Leading intellectuals such as Karl Jaspers, Günther Grass, and Heinrich Böll viewed the *Spiegel* Affair as an indication of authoritarian tendencies in the Federal Republic.[8] A year later, the émigré sociologist and disciple of the Frankfurt School Herbert Marcuse published *The One-Dimensional Man,* which became the handbook of many European student leaders. It stated that mass consumerism had allowed a few powerful leaders to "manipulate" the masses through control of politics, the media, and commerce.[9]

A climate of rebelliousness prevailed in the West German universities. Throughout the spring of 1966, students protested overcrowding, outdated teaching styles, and the federal government's attempts to impose *numerus clausus,* which would have restricted enrollment in a number of disciplines. Members of the Socialist German Student Union (Sozialistischer Deutscher Studentenbund or SDS) and other left-leaning groups opposed the decision of the Social Democratic Party's (Sozialdemokratische Partei Deutschlands or SPD) to join a "Grand Coalition" with the Christian Democrats, thereby threatening democracy by ensuring that the governing parties would have almost 90 percent of the votes in the Bundestag. Leaders of the West German Left called on students and all those opposed to the Grand Coalition to form an extraparliamentary opposition (ausserparlamentarische Opposition or APO) to the government.

6 Fritz Stern, "The Political Consequences of the Unpolitical German," *The Failure of Illiberalism: Essays on the Political Culture of Modern Germany* (New York, 1972), 3–25; originally delivered as an address to the Pacific Branch meeting of the American Historical Association in 1957. Ralf Dahrendorf, *Society and Democracy in Germany* (New York, 1979); this first appeared in German in 1966.

7 The *Spiegel* Affair revealed Defense Minister Strauss's willingness to take unconstitutional measures against the West German press that were chillingly reminiscent of the Nazi years. For a concise account of the Spiegel Affair, see Dietrich Orlow, *A History of Modern Germany 1871 to Present* (Englewood Cliffs, N.J., 1987), 286–7.

8 Dennis L. Bark and David R. Gress, *A History of West Germany, Volume II: Democracy and Its Discontents 1963–1988* (Cambridge, Mass., 1989), 693–5.

9 Marcuse argued that the neocapitalism of the postwar era had given rise to a consumer culture that diverted the masses from the real issues of political pluralism, social welfare, and civil and sexual freedoms. His work is an interesting blend of Freudian theories of sexual repression and Marxism's critique of late capitalist society; see Herbert Marcuse, *The One-Dimensional Man* (Boston, 1964). Feminist Betty Friedan argued a similar theory on women's enslavement to goods in *The Feminine Mystique* (New York, 1963).

The growing student movement united on several issues: opposition to the U.S. war in Vietnam and to West German aid to Israel in 1967, as well as to the proposed Emergency Laws in the Bundestag. These laws would enable a small commission composed of members from the Bundestag and cabinet to run the government of the Federal Republic in the event of a foreign invasion or acute internal unrest.[10] By 1967, West German student groups, led by radical SDS ideologues at the Free University in West Berlin, directed their protests against one major figure of the West German cultural establishment, the media mogul Axel Springer, who enjoyed practically a monopoly of the press in West Berlin. Between 1967 and 1968, the students' conflict with the Springer press became the forum for a larger debate over the stability of postwar democracy that reached the highest levels of political authority.

The enemies immediately recognized each other and prepared for combat. Springer answered the marching, charging feet of student demonstrators with blaring headlines that could be read from every corner newsstand in the Federal Republic. When students surrounded the Springer press offices in West Berlin during the turbulent Easter riots of 1968, delivery men drove through a police gauntlet of barbed wire and braved a barrage of stones and Molotov cocktails to make their daily runs. The battle between Springer's press and the SDS, which unfolded in the streets of West Berlin, created the rhetoric and symbols that framed much of the political debate in 1968. The conflict between the students and Springer should not be viewed within a binary "charge and counter-charge" framework but as a dialectical unfolding in which the students and the Springer press fed off each other's rhetoric. Between June 1967 and May 1968, the conflict between the students and the press escalated until the violence and civil disorder forced the federal government to respond, but only after the two sides had already seized control of the public debate in the Federal Republic. The government was forced to respond on three key issues: the anticommunism associated with the Cold War, the role of the German past in the postwar era, and the stability of democracy in West Germany.

10 The Emergency Laws were ratified in May 1968. They governed internal emergencies, natural disasters, and rioting (not strikes) as well as external emergencies, such as a military invasion. During internal emergencies, the federal government could call on police, army personnel, and the border guards if states governments were unable to deal with the emergency. In this case, the freedom of individual movement could be restricted. In external emergencies, an emergency parliament, comprised of 33 members (22 from the Bundestag [lower chamber] and 11 from the Bundesrat [upper chamber]), would meet; the federal president would have no special powers. Everyone was subject to the draft. Surveillance of phone calls and mail as well as expropriation of goods without immediate compensation would also go into effect in such an emergency. Federal elections would be suspended until six months after the end of the state of emergency. This information comes from David Childs and Jeffrey Johnson, *West Germany, Politics, and Society* (New York, 1981), 38.

Springer's biography may help us understand his views on youth and politics. Born in Hamburg in 1912, Axel Springer was the son of a local newspaper publisher. After receiving a medical deferment in World War II, he helped his father run the newspaper until the Nazis shut it down in the early 1940s. Springer detested the Nazi regime, which, like many of his generation, he subsumed under the rubric of totalitarianism, which also included communism. After the war, Springer succeeded in gaining a controlling interest in *Die Welt,* which was sold as a respectable daily along the lines of the London *Times.* In sharp contrast, Springer also published a racy tabloid called *Das Bild* that featured sensational stories alongside provocative photographs and targeted a lowbrow audience. Thus, the Springer press reached a wide spectrum of West German society in the late 1960s. Like many Germans who prospered after the war, Springer was a firm supporter of Adenauer and demonstrated that support in *Die Welt* and *Das Bild.* By 1966, Springer's firm controlled 40 percent of the West German press, including 80 percent of all regional dailies and 90 percent of all Sunday editions. *Das Bild,* with a daily circulation of four million copies, had name recognition second only to Volkswagen.[11] Springer himself listed the four main principles of his editorial policy at a meeting of European publishers: "(1) Unconditional support for attempts to restore German unity, (2) reconciliation between the German and Jewish peoples, (3) rejection of any kind of political totalitarianism, and (4) acceptance of and support for the social market economy."[12] Consequently, even if one disregarded the salacious articles in *Das Bild* and turned to the sober reporting of *Die Welt,* the basic editorial guidelines were essentially the same.

Several events involving protest action pitted West Berlin students against the Springer press between June 1967 and April 1968. On June 2, 1967, West Berlin police shot and killed Benno Ohnesorg, an architecture student, who had been peacefully observing a student demonstration. Ohnesorg's senseless death convinced the activists that their grievances extended beyond the campus into broader political issues in West German society. In November 1967 the protesters ran an "Expropriate Springer" campaign that identified the newspaper mogul as the standard-bearer of the conser-

11 Biographical sketch and statistics are from Hans Dieter Müller, *Press Power,* trans. J. A. Cole (London, 1969), 6 and 78. Müller further noted that the Springer press "campaigned against Left intellectuals in radio and television, Berlin students, the philosopher Jaspers, and cabaret. It campaigned for the Federal Government's Emergency Laws, a new Fatherland Christianity associated with Pastor Evertz, the august figure of the President of the Federal Republic, and the war in Vietnam," 182–3.
12 Axel Springer's personal views and editorial policies are printed in Axel Springer, "Much Ado About a Newspaper Publishing House," *Address to the Übersee Club,* Oct. 26, 1967 (Berlin), 19–20.

vative establishment and raised the issue of press monopolies. In January 1968 student activists in West Berlin held an "Anti-fascist Springer Tribunal" that "convicted" Springer of attempting to revive old German nationalism and authoritarianism. A month later, in February, students and left-wing activists held a Vietnam Congress in West Berlin. Predictably they condemned the war as an act of American imperialist aggression, but they also compared American atrocities in Vietnam to Nazi war crimes. Many West German activists identified with the Vietnamese, because they too lived in a nation divided by the Cold War. In April 1968 riots erupted in all major West German cities after one of the leaders of the student movement, Rudi Dutschke, was shot by a right-wing fanatic who had been an avid reader of Springer's papers. The riots included a concerted national attack on Springer press offices, the climax of the students' battle with the popular press. The last major demonstrations occurred in May 1968 when the extraparliamentary opposition, composed of student activists, left-wing radicals, and trade unionists, marched on Bonn to protest the ratification of the Emergency Laws. Less violent than the Easter demonstrations, this was the final and most broadly supported student attempt to halt West Germany's alleged return to fascism.

As noted by Ulrich K. Preuss, the student protesters forced West Germans to take a new look at the Nazi era and angrily responded to their parents' silence, which had descended on the "new" Germany after 1945.[13] The war in Vietnam provided the stimulus for student protesters in the Federal Republic to resurrect painful memories of the Nazi years. West German youth protested against the atrocities in Southeast Asia by likening them to the destruction of their own country in World War II. A student at the Free University told journalist Anne Armstrong: "For years I'd had nightmares about the terrible bombing of Dresden at the end of World War II. I could see the houses burning still. And that's why I identified with the Vietnamese – the campaign against the war was a kind of working through my personal history."[14]

Student activists equated Springer's conservative media with the Hugenberg press, whose radical nationalism helped destroy the Weimar Republic and which had courted Hitler. In a commentary on the Easter riots, Karl and Frank Wolff, two leading members of the SDS, wrote that the proposed Emergency Laws were not unlike the Enabling Law used by Hitler to gain absolute power in 1933. Furthermore, the Grand Coalition was

13 Ulrich K. Preuss's remarks at the conference, "1968: The World Transformed," held at the Wissenschaftszentrum Berlin, May 24–6, 1996.
14 Anne Armstrong, *Berliners: Both Sides of the Wall* (New Brunswick, N.J., 1973), 88.

compared to the partnership between the Nazis and the nationalists.[15] By
protesting against Springer, a major mouthpiece for policies of the Grand
Coalition, the students felt they could discredit a government that they
equated with the Hitler regime. After Dutschke was shot, Bernd Rabehl, a
leading member of the SDS, said that "the events made us realize we had
an historic role to play."[16]

During the Easter riots of 1968, the violence and rhetoric of the Weimar
era was revived. Students gathering outside the Springer offices in Hamburg called the press magnate and the police "Nazis" and "SS"; the police
returned these taunts with "communist swine!"[17] According to Theodor
Adorno, the students had adopted the role of the Jews as objects of persecution by the state.[18] The Berlin Evangelical Student Community linked
Springer directly with the Third Reich, noting that "Springer journalism
= pogrom journalism" and "the crooked Jewish nose in *Stürmer* = *Bild's*
bearded caricatures of students."[19] Figure 12.1 shows a typical caricature of
students in *Die Welt,* Springer's respectable daily.

The second issue tackled by the student movement was the rabid anticommunism of West German society. The students considered Springer's
media monopoly to be proof that Ludwig Erhard's "social market economy" was a sham cover for a plutocracy of wealthy business leaders tied to
the ruling Christian Democrats. The Cold War had enabled politicians and
businessmen like Springer to divert attention away from domestic problems
like educational reform and onto the foreign bogeyman of world communism. Many left-wing intellectuals and university students saw the Berlin
Wall as the price of Adenauer's dogma of anticommunism. The students
believed Springer's hard-line stance toward East Germany had exacerbated
tensions between East and West. In 1968 radical students initiated a public
debate on Ostpolitik by demanding Western recognition of the GDR in
an effort to improve relations among all Germans.[20] Members of the German Campaign for Disarmament also supported the students' anti-Springer
crusade because they felt that Springer had "heated-up the Cold War, [and]

---

15 From an APO magazine, *Neue Kritik* 47 (Apr. 1968): 3–6, cited in Karl A. Otto, *APO: Ausserparlamentarische Opposition in Quellen und Dokumenten 1960–1970* (Cologne, 1989), document no. 141,
278. For an excellent account of Alfred Hugenburg and his press empire, see John A. Leopold,
Alfred Hugenburg: The Radical Nationalist Campaign Against the Weimar Republic (New Haven, Conn.,
1977).
16 Bernd Rabehl quoted in Fraser, *1968,* 166.
17 *Der Spiegel* 18 (1968): 48.
18 Adorno's comment is ironic when one considers that the SDS and other New Left students protested
against the U.S.'s and FRG's aid to Israel's "imperialist aggression" against the Arabs in the Six-Day
War. See Adorno in *Der Spiegel* 26 (1968): 44.
19 *Der Spiegel* 19 (1968): 42.
20 Wilhelm Bleek, "From Cold War to Ostpolitik: Two Germanies in Search of Separate Identities,"
World Politics 29 (1976): 117.

„Halt, Ihr Idioten! Ihr Habt Meinen Wagen Erwischt!"

Figure 12.1. Caption: "Stop! You idiots! You've got my car!" Banner reads: "Down with capitalists!" (March 16, 1968). Reproduced by permission of *Die Welt*.

made Berlin the front-line city. [He] has connected the possession of atomic weapons with national dignity and promoted Strauss's comeback."[21] Although a majority of West Germans supported the West's position in the Cold War, the students' attack on Springer was the first public split in the anticommunist consensus of the Adenauer years and paved the way for Willy Brandt and the implementation of Ostpolitik.

The third issue was the persistence of authoritarianism and the threat to democracy. Since the founding of the Federal Republic in 1949, many of its citizens feared that Germans might not be ready for, or capable of, democracy. This was expressed in the phrase "Bonn is not Weimar but . . . ," first articulated by Fritz René Allemann in 1956.[22] The students considered the authoritarian nature of the universities symptomatic of lingering antidemocratic attitudes. They viewed the restrictive *numerus clausus*

21 Andreas Buro: "Überlegungen zur Springer-Aktion der Kampagne"; excerpt from a speech given on Nov. 4–5, 1967. Buro was the Speaker of the Campaign for Disarmament; in Otto, *APO*, document no. 124, 258.

22 The original phrase came from Fritz René Allemann, *Bonn ist nicht Weimar* (Cologne, 1956). See also David Childs, *From Schumacher to Brandt: The Story of German Socialism 1945–1965* (New York, 1966) in the chapter entitled "Bonn Is Not Weimar but," 45–66.

330 Stuart J. Hilwig

as proof of authoritarianism in the academic establishment.[23] Foreshadowing Alain Touraine's analysis of the European student revolt, Siegward Lönnendonker, coauthor of *A Short History of the SDS*, wrote that "the students rebelled because they felt like alienated cogs in the academic process, which in turn was part of a gigantic and confusing industrial or state machine."[24]

Springer was the students' prime adversary because of his ability to turn public opinion against them. Intellectuals such as Heinrich Böll, Golo Mann, Walter Jens, Eugen Kogon, Theodor Adorno, and Alexander Mitscherlich joined the students in linking Springer's press with the dangers of authoritarianism. After the shooting of Dutschke in April 1968, they signed a manifesto equating "the alliance of unscrupulous consumer journalism with a revived nationalistic ideology [that] for years has systematically defamed the democratically committed students and intellectuals and fostered a climate of violence."[25]

Of the many West European student movements that attacked authoritarianism in the academy and in politics in 1968, only the West German movement drew so heavily on the past, linking Dresden and Vietnam, the fall of Weimar and the perceived weaknesses of Bonn. Only in the Federal Republic did a conservative newspaper publisher have the will and power to counter the students' rhetoric with his own interpretations of the German past, the Cold War, and the nature of postwar democracy.

Springer's response to the West Berlin student rebellion reflected his past and his entrepreneurial ambitions. For Springer, as for many middle-aged Germans, Adenauer's government represented the first stable democracy in their lifetime. Consequently, the students' rude antigovernment banners and street demonstrations appeared to threaten structures carefully constructed by their elders.[26] Springer contested the students' views of Weimar and the Third Reich. He believed that it was the instability of pluralist democracy during the Weimar years that had led to Hitler's seizure of power, and thus he felt that the outbreak of public disorder in 1968 constituted a similar threat. The democratic state was in danger of collapsing under pressure from "young rowdies," just as Weimar democracy had collapsed under the pressure of the Brown Shirts.

Springer rebutted the charges of "Springer-Nazi" with his own incessant references to the German past, particularly the Weimar years. The editori-

23 In an early protest against conditions in the universities, three thousand West Berlin students occupied rooms and held teach-ins at the Free University in June 1966. See Fraser, *1968*, 104.
24 Siegward Lönnendonker, quoted in ibid., 323.
25 "Solidarity Statement of Renowned Intellectuals" from Apr. 13, 1968, in *Die andere Zeitung*, Hamburg, Apr. 25, 1968, 9; reprinted in Otto, *APO*, document no. 130, 264–5.
26 Bark and Gress, *A History of West Germany*, 73–4.

als in his media repeatedly linked the early Nazi mobs with the student protesters of 1967–8. Following the SDS's "Springer Tribunal" in February 1968, an edition of *Das Bild* announced "End of the Twenties, Now Begins the Start of the Thirties," noting that because Weimar Germany had not dealt effectively with disorder, the battles between the extreme Left and Right had produced Hitler and the subsequent destruction of Germany and much of Europe.[27] Springer likened 1960s Berlin to the early 1930s, judging "Berlin more licentious in the past few years than during Weimar."[28] Other aging Germans shared this Spenglerian view, disapproving of the young people's sexual freedoms and counterculture and perceiving the emerging drug scene as a return to the decadence of Weimar.[29] The Springer press equated the SDS's demonstrations with the rallies of Hitler's storm troopers. An article in *Das Bild* in June 1967 proclaimed that "The Germans want no brown and no red SA, no columns of toughs, but peace."[30] The Springer press depicted SDS leader Dutschke as a psychopathic demagogue, like the one who had seized power in the 1930s. Figure 12.2, "Difficult Diagnosis," shows doctors examining Dutschke's brain with the additional caption "It is different than 1932," which subtly links Dutschke and recent events with those of 1932.[31] Hurried readers glancing through the columns of *Die Welt* undoubtedly linked the disturbing picture with the highly provocative reference to the presidential campaign of 1932 during which the Nazi Party featured a picture of Hitler's disembodied head on campaign posters.[32] Springer and the students engaged in a histrionic war of words and symbols that falsely transposed 1930s Berlin with its grinding poverty and violent street fighting to the prosperous and peaceful West Berlin of the 1960s. However, these anachronistic references to the 1930s struck a deep emotional chord among West Berliners of all age groups, reminding them of a past that continued to haunt German society.

Springer's press came to the defense of vigorous anticommunism by conveniently equating Soviet communism with Nazi fascism as two similar

27 Kommentar in *Das Bild*, Feb. 5, 1968 (Berlin ed.), cited in Otto, *APO*, document no. 125, 259–61.
28 Axel Springer quoted in Anne Armstrong, *Berliners: Both Sides of the Wall* (New Brunswick, N.J., 1973), 207.
29 An article from Springer's *Welt am Sonntag* (Feb. 26, 1967) was entitled "Is the Emancipation of Women to Know No Bounds: Repercussions of the Sex Wave." The article argues that women's liberation and the contraceptive pill have led to sexual promiscuity in modern society. Cited in Eckart Kuhlwein, ed., *The German Tribune*, no. 296 (1967): 5.
30 Report from *Das Bild* (June 3, 1967) on the incidents at the anti-Shah demonstration in Berlin, in Otto, *APO*, document no. 110, 236.
31 *Die Welt*, Feb. 21, 1968: 2.
32 An excellent example of the "disembodied head" campaign poster can be found in Otis C. Mitchell, *Hitler over Germany: The Establishment of the Nazi Dictatorship, 1918–1934* (Philadelphia, 1983): plates between 152–3.

Figure 12.2. Caption: "Difficult Diagnosis" (February 21, 1968). Reproduced by permission of *Die Welt*.

varieties of totalitarianism. He thus waged a broad struggle against the communists and attacked left-wing students and intellectuals who endangered the democracy of the Federal Republic: "If you ask me, there are more genuine communists in West Berlin than in the whole of East Germany."[33] Springer conjured up a communist conspiracy to subvert West German democracy from within and stressed this theme in his newspapers and political cartoons. The headlines between 1967 and 1968 imparted a sense of urgency and played on Germans' fears and insecurity. In April 1967, radical left-wing students allegedly threatened to assassinate U.S. Vice President Hubert Humphrey with a bomb. Although the whole incident was a hoax, the *Berliner Morgenpost* ran the headline "Free University Students Complete Bombs with Explosive Material from Peking."[34] Even Springer's more respectable daily, *Die Welt*, fostered an atmosphere of conspiracy. An article appearing on the front page of the daily, on January 10, 1968, ominously warned, "Communists Intensify Activity: Increasing Infiltration in the Federal Republic Expected."[35]

The rhetoric and political cartoons of the Springer press also fostered a fear that the student movement was the vanguard of a worldwide commu-

33 Springer quoted in Armstrong, *Berliners,* 202.
34 *Berliner Morgenpost* in *Der Spiegel* 19 (1968): 38.
35 *Die Welt,* Jan. 10, 1968: 1.

nist revolt against capitalism. It was Springer's *Die Welt* that first gave Rudi
Dutschke his nickname "Red Rudi" and that noted on February 16, 1968,
that "In the SDS, revolutionaries now set the tone."[36] The more inflammatory *Das Bild* heightened the German populace's fears of communism with
its frequent exhortations to "Stop the Terror of the Young Reds!" Figure
12.3, "We demand more freedom!" is an excellent example of the kind of
political cartoons found in *Die Welt*. This cartoon contrasts foolhardy West
German students demonstrating against capitalist society with caged students in Warsaw. Not only does the cartoon warn young West Berliners
that it is easy to take one's freedom for granted in the democratic part of
Germany, but the image of the cheese underscores the prosperity of Western societies in comparison to the poverty found in the Soviet bloc. Unlike
the violent, destructive image of students in Figure 12.1, this cartoon used
the nonthreatening image of mice, which further underscored the naïveté
that Springer associated with student ideals. This inconsistency of representation demonstrated how Springer selected from a variety of images
ranging from pathological to innocent according to the dictates of his
intended message.

Springer's rhetorical and pictorial characterizations of the students
shaped the consciousness of many West Germans in regard to an internal
communist threat to their young democracy. There was a deluge of readers' letters to Springer publications after the attempted assassination of
Dutschke, in which the majority expressed satisfaction "that Dutschke had
been put out of action" or asked, "When will this communist pig Dutschke
finally croak?"[37] A Berlin cab driver gave this opinion: "[Springer's] a big
man, our students and radicals don't like him, but he knows what's what.
Over there [he gestured with his thumb in the direction of the Wall], they
hate him, and that says a lot."[38]

Springer defended the democracy of the Grand Coalition. If the students saw the Social Democratic alliance with the Christian Democrats and
the proposed Emergency Laws as a return to authoritarian forms, Springer
regarded these same political developments as sound measures. Having
grown up in the chaos of the Weimar era, he favored a strong state and
considered authority a positive quality of democratic government. In an
interview with the center-left *Spiegel,* Springer explained his newspapers'
relationship with the government: "The pages of the Springer House are

36 *Die Welt*, Feb. 16, 1968: 3.
37 See Merritt, "The Student Protest Movement in West Berlin," *Comparative Politics* 1 (1968–9): 531.
38 Quoted in Armstrong, *Berliners,* 198.

Figure 12.3. Caption: "Student Demonstrations in Berlin (left) and Warsaw." Banner reads: "We demand more freedom!" (March 16, 1968). Reproduced by permission of *Die Welt*.

not loyal to the government, rather loyal to the state, a difference that is often overlooked today."[39] Actually, Springer favored a state that was strong against students or left-wing elements but not strong against big business. According to Hans Dieter Müller, the federal government winked at Springer's press monopoly, and in return, his media became a silent partner to the state in the 1960s.[40] Springer's headlines were particularly inflammatory in their portrayal of the "antidemocratic" actions of the students emphasizing the violence of West Berlin radicals. After the shooting of

39 Springer in *Der Spiegel* 23 (1967): 34.   40 Müller, *Press Power*, 134.

Benno Ohnesorg, *Das Bild* announced, "These people have left the grounds of democracy" and "Their terror must be broken!"[41] After the shooting of Dutschke, *Das Bild* appealed "to the politicians and judges of this country: Stop the terror before it's too late. Bring to court those who take advantage of our democracy to commit criminal acts of violence."[42]

Aside from provocative words such as "terror" and "left-wing radicals," the Springer press transmitted visual messages of authority and democracy. A striking example of Springer's progovernment stance is evident in Figure 12.4, "No Eros at the Foot of the Barricades," which shows the benevolent authority of the West German police. Not only has the officer emerged unscathed from the tumult of the barricades, but he is also the central figure who has "saved" West German youth from the violence of the student movement. Such heroic portrayals of the police helped reinforce Springer's positive view of government authority and negative image of the student movement.

Springer was even able to turn the students' demands for freedom of the press and freedom of opinion against them, terming their attacks on his buildings as an attack on democratic rights. An article on the front page of *Die Welt* declared, "Freedom of opinion: Yes – Terror: No."[43] To Springer, the wide circulation of his periodicals reflected a market plebiscite for his editorial policies.[44] Springer denied the danger of press concentration threatening freedom of opinion in West Germany and later even hindered a federal investigation into press monopolies.[45]

The debate between Springer's press and the West Berlin student movement between the autumn of 1967 and spring of 1968 had political repercussions. Student rebels in West Germany questioned their historical inheritance. The campaign between the students and the press magnate questioned the Bonn government's ability to safeguard freedom of opinion and tested the boundaries of dissent in the nineteen-year-old republic. The myriad images, words, and fears dating from the Weimar period and Hitler era that pervaded the student-Springer exchange suggest that 1968 marked the first stirring of a public debate over Germany's troubled past.

Having investigated the West Berlin students' conflict with the Springer media, we will notice many familiar landmarks in the case of Turin. However, underneath these superficial signposts lie issues that are unique to

41 Quoted in *Der Spiegel* 19 (1967): 41.   42 *Das Bild* quoted in Müller, *Press Power,* 12.
43 *Die Welt,* Apr. 18, 1968: 1.
44 Springer, "Much Ado About a Newspaper Publishing House," 5–6.
45 Springer claimed the Günther Commission's investigation of press concentration was a politically motivated attack against him; see *Der Spiegel* 21 (1968): 33.

Figure 12.4. Appeared with caption: "No Eros at the foot of the barricades!" (February 3, 1968). Reproduced by permission of *Die Welt*.

Italy's cultural and historical development. In its battle with the press, the Italian student movement shared with its West German counterpart concern over the country's troubled past and its untested democracy. The Italian press often linked the student demonstrations to the Fascist period and defended the policies of its center-left government in Rome. Italian students also raised serious questions about the past and the stability of democracy. Differences in cultural and political development meant, however, that the Turin students' battle with the popular press would unfold in ways much different from the West German case. An investigation of their struggle against the daily *La Stampa* will help us understand the issues of the Italian *Sessantotto* (1968).

Postwar Italy underwent a period of rapid economic development similar to that of the Federal Republic of Germany. In fact, the Italian "economic miracle" was more transformative than the German *Wirtschaftswunder,* as the predominantly agrarian nation of Italy became an industrial leader in the 1950s. Throughout the 1950s the Catholic centrist party, the Christian Democrats, maintained coalition governments supported by conservatives and liberals. Like their German counterpart, the Italian Christian Democrats tied their nation tightly to NATO, developed a social market economy fueled by several semipublic corporations, and became a member of the emerging united Europe. Yet unlike the FRG, Italy was forced to confront the crushing poverty in the Mezzogiorno caused by years of political neglect and reactionary social conditions.[46] Although the Communist and Socialist parties had a wide following in Italy because of their links to wartime resistance against the Germans, neither adopted a revolutionary platform, opting to work within the system.[47] Unlike the docile West German trade unions, the resistance legacy also bequeathed a militant trade unionism to Italian labor.

During the 1960s, several developments gave rise to a radical student movement in Italy. In the 1962 elections, the Italian Socialists and Social Democrats joined with Christian Democrats in Amintore Fanfani's famous "opening to the left," while the Italian Communist Party (Partito Communisti Italiani or PCI) and the Liberals remained in tacit, if nonthreatening, opposition. The Socialist move toward the center and PCI's inertia drew many students and disaffected socialists to New Left conceptions of socialism. One of these was *operaismo,* or "workerism," which was developed by Raniero Panzieri in the early 1960s. Panzieri sought to return Italian socialism to its Gramscian roots and proposed a trade unionism that relied on methods of direct democracy. Panzieri's work formed the ideological basis for many of the Italian university protests.[48] Italian students also imbibed the anticonsumer, anticapitalist ideas found in Herbert Marcuse's *One-Dimensional Man,* which was a best-seller in 1968.[49]

The Catholic Church was another important factor that pushed many to join the New Left in the early 1960s. Unlike in West Germany, where Catholic student organizations competed with Protestant student groups, in Italy the student body was overwhelmingly Catholic and was therefore heavily influenced by the Church. Vatican II initiated a gradual loosening of doctrinal taboos, and John XXIII overturned years of fervent anticommunism when he refused to endorse the Christian Democrats publicly in the 1963 elections. He also called for a dialogue between Catholics and Communists,[50] and he thus allowed members of the Catholic student union,

---

46 Giorgio Galli, "The Student Movement in Italy," 498.
47 For a concise history of the Italian Left since World War II, see Tito Perlini, "Left-Wing Culture in Italy Since the Last War," trans. Geoffrey Nowell-Smith, *20th Century Studies* 5 (Sept. 1971): 6–17. See also Alexander J. De Grand, *The Italian Left in the Twentieth Century: A History of the Socialist and Communist Parties* (Bloomington, Ind., 1989).
48 Panzieri left the Italian Socialist Party (Partito Socialisti Italiani or PSI) in 1960 and has been called the "father of the Extraparliamentary Left in Italy"; his ideas of *operaismo* were published in the *Quaderni Rossi*. See Stephen Hellman, "The 'New Left' in Italy," in Martin Kolinsky and William E. Patterson, eds., *Social and Political Movements in Western Europe* (London, 1976), 243–73.
49 Richard Boston, "The Italian Chaos," *New Society* 347 (May 22, 1969): 788–91.
50 Frank P. Belloni, "Dislocation in the Italian Political System: An Analysis of the 1968 Parliamentary Elections," *Western Political Quarterly* 24 (Mar. 1971): 114–35. A priest later published *Letter to*

Intesa, to form an alliance with the Communist Student Union (Union Goliardica Italiana) in its struggle for university reform.

Similar to West German students, Italian students began to mobilize in 1965 against conservative proposals for reform. One of these proposals, the Christian Democrats' Gui Bill, offered only half measures to overhaul Italian universities, including *numerus clausus* to thin enrollments. But students demanded a radical reorganization of their universities to solve the problems of overcrowding, inadequate funding, outdated teaching styles, and the authoritarian, almost "feudal" bearing of the professorate. In particular, the students blamed the high attrition rate in Italy on the archaic university system, which they believed placed too much control of a student's curriculum in the hands of professors.[51]

In these early phases of protest, a number of other issues served to radicalize the student movement. Similar to the students at the Free University of Berlin, the Italian students interpreted the center-left government as proof of the ideological bankruptcy of the official left-wing parties. By 1968, such slogans as "We are against reformism" and "We are not with Dubček. We are with Mao" became common currency among the Italian New Left.[52] Much like their counterparts in West Germany, Italian students turned to Third World Marxists, such as Mao and Guevara, as models of a new revolutionary Marxism. Italy's support for NATO, the colonels' regime in Greece, and the Vietnam War galvanized left-wing students against the policies of the Moro government.[53]

Although regional differences make any discussion of a prototypical Italian case difficult, Turin provides a good example of the ways in which the Italian student revolt unfolded in 1967–8. Most of the protest activity of

---

a Teacher, which drew attention to the incredible poverty in the Mezzogiorno and the inadequacy of the public schools in Italy. This work served to bridge the gap between Catholic doctrine and Socialist theory by advocating a vigorous policy of social reforms within a Christian context; see *Letter to a Teacher by the Schoolboys of Barbiana,* trans. Nora Rossi and Tom Cole (New York, 1970).

51 See Preuss's remarks at the Berlin conference. He notes that "1968" really began in 1965 with student demonstrations for radical university reforms, 13. Although Italy's percentage of university students was comparable to the rest of Europe, only 44 percent ever received their degree. See Boston, "The Italian Chaos," 788; and Galli, "The Student Movement in Italy," 497–9.

52 Valdo Spini, "The New Left in Italy," *Journal of Contemporary History* 7 (Jan.–Apr. 1972): 55–6.

53 Seventy thousand people attended Paolo Rossi's funeral, including PSI leader Pietro Nenni. For parliamentary discussion of Rossi's death, see *Atti Parlamentari: Discussioni* (Camera dei Deputati), vol. 23 (Apr. 27–8, May 17–18, and June 1, 1966; hereafter *AP*). These discussions provide a classic debate between the PCI, MSI, PSU, and the DC on the legacy of fascism, with socialist and communist deputies invoking the heroic legacy of the resistance and the MSI claiming fascism is dead but law and order is still necessary. A short synopsis of the Rossi events can be found in Boston, "The Italian Chaos," 788–9. On Third World revolutionary movements and their influence on the West, see the chapters by Nancy Bernkopf Tucker and Arif Dirlik in this book.

the Italian student movement occurred in the cities of the northern industrial triangle, and the University of Turin often set the pace for student activities throughout the peninsula.[54] Turinese activists published a *Carta Revendicativa,* or "Charter of Grievances," that many other university activists adopted, and they became the first protesters to systematically interrupt lectures in a process called the "white occupation."[55] Turin was also the headquarters of the second largest circulation Italian daily, *La Stampa,* which upheld the views of middle-class residents and university officials and supported the policies of the center-left government.[56] The students also targeted *La Stampa* as a symbol of Italian capitalism because the newspaper was owned by FIAT, the automobile manufacturer. During the autumn of 1967 and spring of 1968, *La Stampa* rebuffed student attacks by continuously criticizing their activities and defending the leaders and policies of the establishment.

The student movement in Turin can be divided into two phases, each progressively more threatening to the local establishment. The first was generally peaceful and was distinguished by the students' use of nonviolent protests within the boundaries of the campus. The death of Paolo Rossi, an architecture student at the University of Rome, in April 1966, allegedly caused by fascist violence, motivated many Turin students to step up their protests against the Gui Bill. On November 27, 1967, students occupied the Palazzo Campana, which housed the law, education, and humanities departments, in response to rector Mario Allara's decision to move the science faculty to suburban La Mandria.[57] The occupation in 1967 was unique because the students managed to occupy the Palazzo Campana for an entire month between November 27 and December 27, and sporadically through January.[58] During the first phase of the movement, the generally peaceful student occupations contrasted sharply with the violent evacuation proce-

---

54 Lumley, *States of Emergency,* 6.
55 Carlo Oliva and Aloisio Rendi also noted that unlike other university occupations of 1967–8, Turin students kept up the occupation of campus buildings through the Christmas break. Carlo Oliva and Aloisio Rendi, *Il Movimento studentesco e le sue lotte* (Milan, 1969), 21–2.
56 *La Stampa,* an independent daily, had a circulation of 400,000 copies. Although owned by FIAT, scholars have noted that the paper does not have a conspicuously pro-FIAT editorial policy. For more information on the Italian press, see "The Press: Opinions Are Sacred," *The Economist* 222 (Mar. 18, 1967): special section on Italy, xxix–xxx, and Kenneth E. Olson, *The History Makers: The Press of Europe from Its Beginnings Through 1965* (Baton Rouge, La., 1966), 231–52.
57 The students demonstrated against the rector's decision because they saw it as an attempt to remove part of the university from the center of city life and because the move would make it difficult for commuter students to get to class. Some students also noted that important ecological habitats would be threatened by the construction at La Mandria; see Revelli, "Il '68 a Torino," 213–15.
58 Ibid.

dures ordered by the rector. These forced evacuations prompted a series of "white occupations" in which coordinated groups of students disrupted lectures between January and February 1968.[59]

In the second phase of the movement, university protesters began to leave the campus for the city streets. Between March and May 1968, students protested sporadically in the city center and, like students in West Berlin, concerned themselves with larger social issues. The spring months witnessed an increase in violence, as students willingly clashed with police and disrupted downtown traffic. Many left-wing students assisted the nascent workers' movement at FIAT and protested against *La Stampa*. On March 7, Turin students marched down the Via Roma to protest the arrest of student leaders, smashed the windows of the main offices of *La Stampa*, and battled with police throughout the afternoon.[60] This demonstration signaled an important turning point in the movement. After March 7, student activists increasingly turned to violence in their battle with the establishment and, like their West Berlin counterparts, identified the press as a key target of their protests. The final event in this heated phase of the Turin student movement occurred on June 1, when a second, more violent demonstration pitted students against the police. Students gathered to support the workers and students on strike in France and marched through the center of Turin. Again, the demonstration ended with an attack on the headquarters of *La Stampa*. This time, however, many students wore motorcycle helmets similar to Japanese students and chanted, "No to social peace in the factories!" and "Only violence helps where violence reigns!"[61]

Although student demonstrations continued in Italy into the 1970s, the massive demonstrations began to diminish after the school year ended in June 1968.[62] Many students left the movement when it failed to elicit political reforms at the national level. For the more committed student activists, the growing worker unrest offered an opportunity to extend their opposition to the capitalist state outside the university campus, and the giant FIAT plants in Turin offered fertile ground for activists and their brand of *operaismo*.[63]

---

59 Overall, the rector called police to evacuate students five times between the beginning of January and the end of February; a review of events appears in "Cronaca Cittadina," *La Stampa*, Mar. 1, 1968: 2.

60 Twenty-three protesters were arrested after the March 7 riots.

61 *La Stampa*, June 2, 1968: 2. For a synopsis of the 1968 election results, see Ginsborg, *A History of Contemporary Italy*, 326–7.

62 Minister of Education Luigi Gui failed in his attempt to use the student upheavals as an impetus to pass his reform bill before the end of the fourth legislature, and university reform became a dead letter. *AP,* vol. 43 (Mar. 1, 1968): 44573–44601.

63 See Lumley, *States of Emergency,* 63–7; and Gerd-Rainer Horn's chapter in this book.

To understand why Turinese students vented their rage against *La Stampa* in ways similar to their compatriots' attacks against the Springer media in West Berlin, we must look closely at *La Stampa's* coverage of the students from November 1967 to June 1968. Similar to Springer's press, *La Stampa* supported the establishment's position toward the students and helped to foster a climate of tension between the students and residents of Turin. From the beginning of the occupations in November, the paper attempted to paint student activists as an extremist minority. The day after the first occupation, residents of Turin read: "The occupation [was] decided by an assembly of 500 people and [was] disapproved by the mass of youths."[64] Later in December, when it became clear that the occupation would not be a short-lived phenomenon, the newspaper suggested that school officials take action: "Evacuating the building by force could be a favor to the occupants or those tired and divided by internal polemics."[65] During December and January, *La Stampa's* tone was reproachful toward the students but without the harsh rhetoric of Springer's *Die Welt*. The daily's local section often ran small headlines above the lead article announcing "Still Profound Crisis at the University" or "Still No End to Disorders at the University."[66] The protests were described as "disorders" or "grave episodes" during which "brawls" or "uproar" occurred through December and January.[67] The newspaper also featured several antistudent letters from local residents, one protesting the discovery of a crucifix in a university trash can.[68] Another irate reader wrote, "I am a father who works ten hours a day so that my son may study at the university. . . .I do not believe that there is a big difference between the March on Rome and the occupation of the university. The weapons remain the same: intimidation and contempt for democratic laws."[69] Similar to Springer's political cartoon that linked SDS leader Rudi Dutschke to the events of 1932, this reader's letter to *La Stampa* anachronistically linked the student movement to Mussolini's grasp for political power in the early 1920s and hinted that the students posed a similar threat to Italian democracy.

After a bomb threat in the Faculty of Law on February 16, *La Stampa* adopted a tone closer to Springer's media, branding the students as real threats to civil order. It described the activists as *filocinesi* (sympathizers of

---

64 *La Stampa* quoted in Revelli, "Il '68 a Torino," 216.   65 *La Stampa* quoted in ibid., 218.
66 *La Stampa*, Jan. 3, 1968: 2, and Jan. 27, 1968: 2.
67 "Cronaca Cittadina," *La Stampa*, Jan. 11, 17, 18, 1968.
68 "Specchio dei tempi," *La Stampa*, Jan. 17, 1968: 2.
69 Quoted in Giovanni De Luna, "Aspetti del movimento del '68 a Torino," in Aldo Agosti, Luisa Passerini, and Nicola Tranfugalia, eds., *La Cultura e i luoghi del '68* (Milan 1991), 198.

Communist China) and supporters of Chairman Mao, characterizations that, according to Robert Lumley, "conjured up the red menace and the yellow peril all in one."[70] And for the first time, in February 1968, the newspaper portrayed Turin students as "left-wing fascists" by showing photos of student demonstrators raising their arms in a fascist salute and shouting "Mao-Mao."[71] On March 3, 1968, *La Stampa* described how agitators, breaking into a meeting of students who wanted to return to school, had raised their arms in Roman salutes and shouted, "Viva Ho Chi Minh! Viva Guevara!"[72] (Figure 12.5). As defender of the center-left government and of the local authorities in Turin, *La Stampa* labeled the activists a dangerous, left-wing, and fascist threat to civil order. The Communist Party deputy from Turin, Giorgina Levi Arian, complained to the parliament that only *La Stampa* provided news in Turin and that it had termed the occupants of the Palazzo Campana "subversive elements, lazy people, loafers without values, . . . truly revolutionary." Other PCI deputies sympathized with students, and Deputy Levi Arian urged all her fellow deputies to read their charter of grievances, which she distributed to the parliament.[73] Despite Levi Arian's warning, the Turin press concocted a persuasive tale of communist conspiracy much as Springer had done in West Berlin. In Italy, however, the left-wing students had to be branded Maoists in order to disassociate them from the more acceptable and nonthreatening version of Italian communism.

La Stampa depicted the school administration, police, and government officials as defenders of democracy and order. It also emphasized the activities of the "silent majority" of students who objected to the occupations and wanted to return to their studies and begin their exams.[74] In photographs, the Turin press's coverage of the police was similar to Springer's. In Figure 12.5, we see police gently carrying a student out of the Palazzo Campana. Despite Levi Arian's and other politicians' denunciations of police violence, *La Stampa* always portrayed the police as nonthreatening.[75] Minister Taviani and Minister Gui, both Christian Democrats, consistently upheld university administrators' decisions to use police force against student occupations at universities throughout Italy in 1967–8. The opposi-

70 Lumley, *States of Emergency,* 73.   71 *La Stampa,* Feb. 21, 1968: 2.
72 *La Stampa,* Mar. 3, 1968: 2.   73 *AP,* vol. 42, Feb. 8, 1968: 43309–310.
74 Passerini, "Le mouvement de 1968 comme prise de parole et comme explosion de la subjectivité: le cas de Turin," 43. For example, "Students Against Agitation Ask When They Can Begin Exams," *La Stampa,* Feb. 7, 1968: 2.
75 Parliamentary inquiries were made to the Minister of the Interior and Minister of Public Instruction concerning police repression at the University of Turin and the University of Padua: *AP* vol. 41, Jan. 12, 1968: 42274, and Jan. 17, 1968: 42469.

Figure 12.5. Police removing a student from the Palazzo Campana, Turin (January 11, 1968). Reproduced by permission of *La Stampa*.

tion parties, the PCI and the Italian Liberal Party (Partito Liberale Italiane or PLI), repeatedly denounced what they felt was state support for the violation of university autonomy and the right to peaceful assembly. In another parallel to the West Berlin press, *La Stampa* placed the student movement outside of the boundaries of democratic society so that it could portray members of the Moro government as defenders of the state. In casting politicians as united defenders of democracy, *La Stampa* and the Springer press masked the deep divisions that plagued Moro's government and the Grand Coalition.

In contrast to its sober, sensible depiction of members of the establishment, *La Stampa* portrayed the protest leaders as brooding, sinister individuals. Demonstrations were portrayed as confused, chaotic outbursts (see Figure 12.6, which depicts students at the March 7 protest in Turin). That many of the protesters were carrying open umbrellas in this picture from *La Stampa* leads one to wonder how so many of the protesters managed to

Figure 12.6. Demonstrations in Turin (March 7, 1968). Reproduced by permission of *La Stampa*.

engage in *tafferugli* (brawls) and *violenza* (violence) without losing their umbrellas.[76]

One of the most striking differences between the Springer media's visual presentation of the West Berlin student movement and *La Stampa*'s pictorial record is the place of women in the two movements. In the West German case, militant women were not prominent in *Die Welt*'s pictures of protesters, but in the Italian case, women appear often in the Turin demonstrations. Figure 12.7 shows student leaders Laura DeRossi and her fiancé, Luigi Bobbio, meeting with DeRossi's parents after she was released from prison on bail. The DeRossis are portrayed as concerned, bourgeois parents, and daughter Laura is depicted as a "daddy's girl" rather than an "extremist" student leader. In this picture, *La Stampa* hinted that many of the activists, like DeRossi, were simply middle-class kids who had gone astray. In comparison to Figure 12.7, in Figure 12.8 women are seen as members of a frenzied mob. The women in this image are demonstrating in solidarity for their friends who have been jailed following the March

76 See "Parade of Students in the Streets of the City Concludes with Brawls and Violence," *La Stampa*, Mar. 8, 1968: 2.

Figure 12.7. Student leaders Luigi Bobbio and Laura DeRossi meeting DeRossi's parents after being released from prison (March 26, 1968). Reproduced by permission of *La Stampa*.

Figure 12.8. Women demonstrators in Turin (April 25, 1968). Reproduced by permission of *La Stampa*.

demonstrations. The article notes that a group of *belle ragazze* (beautiful girls) at the head of the demonstration was shouting, "The university is ours!"[77] For a predominantly Catholic nation with circumscribed roles for women, the image of women leading demonstrations undoubtedly shocked Turin's bourgeois society. Natalie Zemon Davis has written on the visual power of sex-role reversal in the depictions of revolutionary crowds. Seeing women in leadership roles greatly upset Western society, which generally defined protest and revolution as activities led by men. French historian Dominique Godineau noted that during the first days of the 1789 Revolution, "Women sounded the tocsin, beat drums in the streets of the city, mocked the authorities and the military. . . . They played the role of 'firebrands.' "[78]

In conclusion, a comparison of the press's response to the Italian and West German student movements of 1968 offers a number of interesting similarities and differences. The student movements articulated similar concerns over the German and Italian past and the legitimacy of democracy in the two republics. The popular press in West Berlin and Turin adopted similar strategies in responding to the students and defending the position of the government; but national, historic, and cultural differences produced different approaches to the unrest.

Axel Springer's *Die Welt* and FIAT's *La Stampa* each found that branding the students as "left-wing fascists" proved highly effective in turning public opinion against the demonstrators. By linking leftist students with the fascist era, the press played on the older generation's fear of disorder, fascism, and communism. Correspondingly, student leaders invoked the terms "Fascista" and "Nazi" in an effort to mobilize the students and society against a repressive establishment. Such rhetoric opened a debate that had remained closed during the immediate postwar years. The two newspapers also heightened public fears by repeating words such as "violence" and "hooliganism" in their headlines. Subliminally, these words conveyed a sense of urgency that supported the idea of a communist conspiracy within the student movement. Springer's papers and *La Stampa* pointed to the property damage caused by student demonstrations as evidence that these

---

77 *La Stampa,* Apr. 25, 1968: 2.
78 See Natalie Zemon Davis, "Women on Top," in her collection of essays, *Society and Culture in Early Modern France: Eight Essays* (Stanford, Calif., 1975). Dominique Godineau, "Daughters of Liberty and Revolutionary Citizens," in Georges Duby and Michelle Perrot, eds., *A History of Women,* trans. Arthur Goldhammer (Cambridge, Mass., 1993), vol. 4. See also Arlette Farge, who wrote that during the early-modern period, the bourgeoisie feared male ideologues would prey on impressionable young women, in "Protesters Plain to See," in Natalie Zemon Davis and Arlette Farge, eds., *A History of Women,* trans. Arthur Goldhammer (Cambridge, Mass., 1993), vol. 3.

student "vandals" sought to undo the sacrifices of postwar reconstruction. Significantly, both presses alternated between condemning the students as violent, Marxist radicals and as naive, middle-class kids who had drifted away from bourgeois values.

The press coverage of the two movements portrayed the police and university officials as benevolent public servants. Springer's policeman at the foot of the barricades and *La Stampa's* carabinieri carrying occupants from the Palazzo Campana projected an image of the gentle law officer preserving social peace. Government officials in Bonn and Rome supported the press version. For example, Deputy Lothar Haase, a conservative Christian Democrat, adopted Springer's tone when he inquired about the government's plans to deal with "international left-wing extremist groups who intended to disrupt peace and order."[79] Likewise, Interior Minister Paolo Emilio Taviani (Democrati Christiani or DC) declared that the government of Italy intended to defend the "democratic state" and "the Constitution" after the rioting at the University of Rome in March 1968.[80] Taken together, the students and the establishment mirrored one another in their fears that democracy was in danger.

The Italian and West German student-press controversies, however, revealed several important differences arising from their different histories and culture. In West Germany, the frequent use of terms associated with the Weimar and Hitler eras suggests that the students and the establishment of the postwar republic feared that instability might lead to dictatorship. In Italy, the use of "Fascista" by Italian students and the press was an assault on ancient hierarchies reinforced by Mussolini. Another important difference is the portrayal of women in the two newspapers. Although women were well represented in the SDS and the Turin student movements, Springer did not focus on them as often as the Italian press did because his press was able to prey upon West Germans' greater fear of communism. Most likely, the greater role ascribed to women in *La Stampa's* depiction of the student movement stems from the editors' desire to shock middle-class readers by placing the "women on top," a reversal of gender roles that violated the patrifocal values of Italian society. Although *Die Welt* and *La Stampa* used similar rhetoric in their condemnation of student attacks on their offices, the two newspapers adopted different tones in regard to the students. The Italian press took a less embattled, less sarcastic tone than Springer's toward left-wing activism. In a besieged West Berlin, with his offices right next to

---

79 *Verhandlungen des Deutschen Bundestages (5.Wahlperiode): Stenographische Berichte,* vol. 67 (173. Sitzung, 10. Mai 1968): 9257.
80 *AP,* vol. 43 (Mar. 1, 1968): 44576.

the Berlin Wall, Springer interpreted the students' protests as personal attacks not only on himself but also on the city's freedom. The Italian establishment had a less negative view of communism because of its association with wartime resistance and the PCI's reformist posture. Moreover, the tactic of the occupation was a traditional form of protest in the industrial cities of the north.[81] Thus, although West Berlin and Turin students hurled a similar onslaught of Marxist polemics against their respective societies and singled out the popular press as targets of their violence, important historical and cultural factors accounted for the distinct responses of the press in these two nations.

There is irony in both cases. The Italian student protesters gradually allied with militant factory workers in the northern industrial regions. These workers, having imbibed the ideas of *operaismo* from the student movement, took massive strike actions outside of the regular union and PCI channels. Later that autumn, however, the General Federation of Italian Labor Unions (Confederazione Generale Italiana del Lavoro or CGIL) and other unions regained control of the workers' movement and won substantial concessions from factory owners. In the meantime, the Italian students, having opted to leave the campus for the factory gates, saw their movement for university reforms wither and die, with a substantial restoration of previous academic authority and university administration by 1970. Despite its impact on the workers and its concrete demands, the Italian student movement failed to change the universities substantially.

In contrast, the West German student movement failed to mobilize the workers because labor unions secured higher wages and shorter work hours for West German workers amid a return to rapid growth and prosperity following the minor recession of 1967. More consensual relations between labor and management in West Germany, and the general state of prosperity in the Federal Republic, all worked to nip any militancy among West German workers in the bud. Furthermore, West Germans had feared communism as a residue of the Nazi years and on behalf of their captive "brothers and sisters" behind the Wall. The students' Marxist chants and slogans horrified citizens and workers in isolated West Berlin. Nevertheless, the Easter riots of 1968 prompted real political action in the Federal Republic. Springer's powerful press monopoly was reined in by the efforts of Eberhard Gunther's parliamentary commission on press monopolies, substantial university reforms were enacted, and the ungainly Grand Coalition

---

81 During the "red years" before Mussolini came to power, radical Marxists and anarchists occupied many factories in northern Italy. In 1943, socialist workers occupied factories in Turin to protest the Fascist war effort.

was replaced in 1969 by a Social Democratic government under Willy Brandt.

The students' battles with the press and the political establishment in West Berlin and Turin opened a debate over the stability of democracy and the role of the past in postwar culture and political life. The student activists' adoption of Marxist rhetoric proved to be self-limiting as Preuss argued, for the students in the SDS claimed they were "no more than just appendages of the true and genuine historical agent, the working class."[82] When the West German workers refused to heed the call of the SDS and Italian workers later discarded *operaismo* for old-fashioned union solidarity in the Hot Autumn of strikes in 1969, student activists on both sides of the Alps concluded that they had failed to mobilize the workers. The students' failure stemmed from their misunderstanding of the world outside the campus gates. Although the fortunes of university students and recent graduates were declining due to burgeoning college enrollments, the fortunes of blue-collar workers actually rose in 1968. The students, however, did draw attention to the problems of postwar culture: the failure of the "new" republics of Italy and West Germany to address lingering issues of the past, the rising danger of a consumer society that quietly fostered political apathy in the wake of growing material comfort, and the dangers of a powerful mass media that pervaded public and private consciousnesses.

Oddly enough, it was the growing power of the media, with its headlines and flashy pictorials found at every kiosk, every bus stop, and on millions of kitchen tables, that enabled the students' voices to be heard. *La Stampa's* "City Chronicle" did more to publicize the demands of the occupants of the Palazzo Campana than any bullhorn or campus rally ever could. *Die Welt's* caustic headlines and ominous cartoons assured the SDS of an audience and helped perpetuate a cultural movement that did, in fact, force West Germans to reflect on the Nazi years. As the student activists and popular press fought for a public audience in 1968, words and images from the early twentieth century again haunted West Germans and Italians. In the two young republics, the students and their opponents kindled fears that democracy might fail, and they gave different panaceas for its survival.

---

82 See Preuss's remarks at the Berlin conference.

13

The Changing Nature of the European Working Class

The Rise and Fall of the "New Working Class" (France, Italy, Spain, Czechoslovakia)

GERD-RAINER HORN

Most analysts of global "1968" identify that turbulent year as the moment when new social movements emerged as powerful actors on the international political stage. Nineteen sixty-eight therefore stands as a metaphor for the eruption of the student movement reaching from Berkeley to Berlin. The associations that initially come to mind when 1968 is mentioned more closely approximate notions of cultural revolution or even sexual revolution than they do the traditional idea of a workers' revolution.[1] Although I do not wish to detract from the ubiquitous student protests of that fateful year, in this chapter I focus attention on the proletarian dimension of 1968.

I begin this survey of working-class involvement in the battles of 1968 with a depiction of the contribution of the labor movement to the turbulent events in France, Italy, Spain, and Czechoslovakia. Here I argue for the centrality of trade union and Old Left struggles in any serious analysis of 1968 in these four countries. I then furnish a more in-depth look at the working class, which, on closer observation and despite its militancy, was perhaps more heterogeneous than at any other time in the twentieth century. Next I highlight the changing composition of the European working class in the second half of the century. Finally, I examine the internal reconfiguration of Europe's oldest ongoing social movement by focusing on the contribution of a new technical and administrative intelligentsia, called the "new working class" or "new middle classes," to the process and the outcome of global 1968.

A brief note on the temporal and geographic limits of this study: I chose

---

1 Exemplifying this understanding of "global 1968" is Ronald Fraser, *A Student Generation in Revolt: An International Oral History* (New York, 1988). The lively discussions at the Berlin conference on "Global 1968" similarly reflected this assessment of events.

France and Italy as the most obvious examples of the social impact of working-class unrest generated by the spirit of 1968. I include Spain and Czechoslovakia because these two states, though governed by different kinds of regimes, witnessed a similarly central role of the proletarian Left in the events of 1968. Spain was still in the throes of the military dictatorship of Francisco Franco. Czechoslovakia, except for a brief period prior to August 1968, was ruled by a Stalinist *nomenklatura,* and its social and economic system was of a totally different kind compared to those of France, Italy, and Spain. Yet as far as the internal recomposition of the working class as a social actor was concerned, it is precisely the similarity of circumstances that attracted my attention to this seemingly anomalous set of countries as ideal cases to test the thesis of the transnational nature of these forces.

In all four Central and Western European states, the new working class played a prominent role in shaping 1968 globally. In each of these countries, the new working class was in the vanguard of the proletarian Left. To be sure, in all four cases the "proletarian May" failed to alter qualitatively the respective social systems they had set out to reform or replace. But despite these ultimate failures, the proletarian dimension of 1968 powerfully underscored the importance of working-class forces in any frontal challenges to the political, economic, or social status quo, no matter if the last came cloaked in state socialist or market capitalist garb. Last but not least, the working-class dimension of 1968 also underscores that viable social movements, whether "new" or "old," operate on a transnational scale, ignoring all political, social, and economic boundaries.

Nevertheless, it is impossible to restrict one's analytical gaze only to that year. In the same way that the "spirit of the 1960s" continued to manifest itself in the first half of the 1970s, the working-class unrest spawned during 1968 did not end with the New Year's Eve celebration. Even in Czechoslovakia, where proletarian resistance was halted by the Warsaw Pact armies, the upheaval extended into 1969. France and Italy witnessed unusual amounts of activism at the point of production and elsewhere in society through 1974–5. In Spain, the cycle of revolt lasted until the late 1970s and became part of the prodemocracy movement.

WHAT DID THE WORKING CLASS DO IN 1968?

The French May

France constitutes the exception to the popular identification of 1968 with the forces of the nonproletarian Left. It would be difficult to ignore the sudden, massive intervention of France's powerful leftist working class into the political and economic battles of 1968. Prior to May 1968 there were few indications of this sudden surge. Yet careful analysts have noted that for more than a year prior to the "French May" an explosive mixture of working-class militancy, employer unwillingness to budge, and government stonewalling had created the preconditions for social unrest.[2]

These factors made a workers' rebellion possible; they were necessary – although not sufficient – elements to foment unrest. The all-important catalyst for setting French labor into motion was the eruption of violent student struggles in early May, setting an example for the discontented elements of the working-class Left. This link was most tangible in the city of Nantes, specifically among the workers at Sud-Aviation, long known for their radical proclivities. A forceful, although minority, union led by a charismatic duo with close ties to the student Left – one an anarchosyndicalist, the other a Trotskyist – suddenly gained a larger hearing when students at Nantes University copied their Parisian colleagues and opted for a militant course. On May 14, 1968, the workers of Sud-Aviation occupied their aircraft factory.[3]

News of this unexpected and unusual move spread throughout France. The next day, inspired by the actions at Sud-Aviation, the workforce at Renault-Cléon began an open-ended strike, occupied the factory, and refused to let the company director out of his office. A telephone call to militant union members at Renault-Flins led to similar action there. By the evening of May 16, seventy thousand French workers were out on strike, fifty thousand of them members of the vast if geographically dispersed Renault workforce. On May 17 the strike affected the textile industry. On May 18 the sole trains rolling in all of France were two leaving Paris, one destined for Strasbourg and another filled with pilgrims headed for Lourdes. That same day, telephone and telegraph service was interrupted throughout the country. On May 19, all airplanes were grounded. On May 21, according to union estimates, 5 million workers were on strike, far surpassing the previous high-water mark for French strike activity, the 2 million strikers of May–June 1936, and the strike continued to spread.

On May 27, government officials, employer representatives, and union

---

2 See, e.g., some concise and pertinent statements in Peter Lange, George Ross, and Maurizio Vannicelli, *Unions, Change and Crisis: French and Italian Union Strategy and the Political Economy, 1945–1980* (London, 1982), 28.

3 The description of the strike wave in France follows the concise narrative in Ingrid Gilcher-Holthey, *"Die Phantasie an die Macht": Mai 68 in Frankreich* (Frankfurt am Main, 1995), 285–97. A brief English-language survey can be found in David Caute, *The Year of the Barricades: A Journey Through 1968* (New York, 1988), 232–6.

negotiators reached an agreement at Grenelle that eventually led to the end of this largely elementary and spontaneous movement. The agreement raised the minimum wage in industry by 35 percent, called for a 10 percent across-the-board wage increase, and ordered a significant reduction in the length of the average workweek. Striking workers' initial opposition to the Grenelle accords could not be sustained, and the wave of strikes receded during the first week of June.[4] Yet 6 to 8 million workers had participated in an unprecedented series of strikes that frequently assumed the characteristics of a festival of the oppressed.[5] And, crucially, the strikes of late May 1968 paved the way for accelerated strike action over the next half-dozen years.[6]

Italy's "Creeping May"

Whereas the involvement of the French working class in 1968 was essentially limited to a relatively brief, although powerful, outburst in the second half of May, Italian workers had been slowly increasing their strike activity since 1966. Its high point was reached in the "hot autumn" of 1969. Whereas the sudden emergence of the French movement lent it a spontaneous and open-ended character, which made the government appear helpless and ready to fall, the Italian "creeping May" never frontally disarmed the government in the same way. Yet the societal crisis it produced in Italy was every bit as intense as May 1968 in France. Indeed, the short- and medium-term effects of the events in Italy were more powerful than the brief two-week flash north of the Alps. For more than a half-dozen years, class relations in Italy were in a constant state of flux, and the challenges to the social order were more profound there than in any other European country.

In 1967 there was a slight augmentation of industrial action over the previous year, with a total of 2.24 million workers laying down their tools.

---

4 For the initially hostile reactions by strikers to the Grenelle agreement, see Gilcher-Holthey, *Phantasie,* 331–8. On the reflux of the French strike movement, see Jacques Kergoat, "Sous la plage, la grève," in Antoine Artous, ed., *Retours sur mai* (Paris, 1988), 60–1.
5 This estimate is given by Kergoat, "Sous la plage," 62, on the basis of careful calculations strongly suggesting that the most commonly cited estimate of 9–10 million strikers is somewhat inflated. Given a contemporary French workforce of 15 million, the slightly lowered estimate detracts little from the overall impact of the proletarian French May.
6 A table indicating heightened strike activity after 1968, compared to the years since 1950, can be found in Lange, Ross, and Vannicelli, *Unions, Change and Crisis,* 62, although one should note that, whereas the number of strikes after 1968 shows a qualitative leap, the same does not hold true for the total number of "striker days" and the number of workers involved.

The number more than doubled in 1968. Yet it was 1969 that witnessed the zenith of industrial unrest, when in the fall 5.5 million workers walked off their jobs in a rash of local, regional, and national strikes. On November 19, 1969, almost the entire Italian labor force participated in a one-day general strike. During the rest of the year, more than 7 million workers challenged management's control, a figure equal to the French participation rate in May 1968.[7] In the first half of the 1970s, class struggles in Italy continued, albeit at a diminished rate.

Yet what made the unrest in Italy more threatening than that in France was not the total number of work stoppages or strikers involved. Rather, it was the degree to which it went beyond narrow economic concerns and challenged the prerogatives of management and the state in a sustained fashion. Heading the list of suprafactory and supraindustry concerns were two demands that spearheaded the movement in the course of 1968 and in effect prepared the landscape for the escalation of the following year. In November 1968 all three trade union federations called for a general strike to demand a significant increase in pension payments for retired workers. The strike was the culmination of a yearlong campaign against the government, which controlled pension schemes, and resulted in partial victory.[8] The second issue involved regional salary variations, which allowed Italian employers to benefit from north-south differences, a powerful tool for divide and rule. Efforts to nullify this provision began in early 1968 and culminated in an across-the-board termination of such schemes in March 1969.[9] Both actions were to some extent successful because Italy's three main labor federations were united in their approach, unlike in France, where the General Workers Union (Confédération générale du travail or CGT), with its narrow economic orientation, had little in common with the French Democratic Workers Union (Confédération française et démocratique du travail or CFDT), with its increasing radical and self-management orientation.

Openly political demands, geared toward the state and largely bypassing the level of factory management, were thus crucial to Italian developments from the start. This did not mean, of course, that management was spared

---

7   The figure of 5.5 million strikers during the "Hot Autumn" and the information on the November 19 general strike is culled from Joanne Barkan, *Visions of Emancipation: The Italian Workers' Movement Since 1945* (New York, 1984), 75–6. A table showing the total number of striking Italian workers per annum from 1955 to 1970 can be found in Dominique Grisoni and Hugues Portelli, *Les luttes ouvrières en Italie (1960–1976)* (Paris, 1976), 74.

8   On the significance of the pension struggle, see Barkan, *Visions of Emancipation*, 69–70, and Grisoni and Portelli, *Les luttes ouvrières,* 98–102.

9   See, above all, Grisoni and Portelli, *Les luttes ouvrières,* 100–2, on this particular issue.

its share of grief. The workers' desire for influence and autonomy was translated into concrete demands at the point of production just as much as, if not more than, these challenges to the authority of the state. Except for the second half of May, it was in Italy, not France, where factories and neighborhoods, labor struggles and concerns of the new social movements collaborated for present and future purposes. One such issue, tangential to most unions elsewhere in Europe at the time and thereafter, was the struggle for decent and affordable housing conducted by Italian trade unions in the first half of the 1970s.[10] In Italy, according to two French observers, the "politicization of the workers' struggles" could be described "as a movement *from the factory to the state.*"[11]

Spain and Czechoslovakia

Spain and Czechoslovakia witnessed no such gigantic labor actions as did Italy and France, although for different reasons. In Spain the labor movement was still operating semiclandestinely under the Franco regime. Not until the mid-1970s did Spanish labor operate under anything resembling "normal" conditions. Strike activity in 1976, following Franco's death in November 1975, therefore far exceeded labor actions in preceding years. Yet similar to the situation in Italy and France, from 1967 onward a distinct trend toward militancy and politicization characterized the Spanish working class.[12] A national day of protest against political repression and the loss of purchasing power held on October 27, 1967, constituted the decisive turning point in Spain. In Madrid, Barcelona, and elsewhere, large numbers of workers demonstrated in the streets, battling police forces and suffering numerous arrests.[13] Subsequent repression largely accounts for a slight downturn in strike activity for 1968, but then the movement resumed. More important, 1967 constitutes a watershed year for the nature of demands raised by Spanish strikers. That year, solidarity strikes and work stoppages for openly political claims began to dominate Spanish labor

---

10 On union involvement in tenant struggles, see Robert Lumley, *States of Emergency: Cultures of Revolt in Italy from 1968 to 1978* (London, 1990), 262–4.
11 Grisoni and Portelli, *Les luttes ouvrières,* 140; emphasis in the original.
12 Strike statistics from 1963 through 1976 can be studied by combining the two tables presented in Walther L. Bernecker, "Die Arbeiterbewegung unter dem Franquismus," in Peter Waldmann et al., eds., *Die geheime Dynamik autoritärer Diktaturen* (Munich, 1982), 130, and in Sebastian Balfour, *Dictatorship, Workers and the City: Labour in Greater Barcelona Since 1939* (Oxford, 1989), 143.
13 Brief descriptions of the October 27 action can be gleaned in Balfour, *Dictatorship, Workers and the City,* 94–5, and in Max Gallo, *Spain Under Franco: A History* (London, 1973), 352.

activism at the expense of claims related to collective bargaining and similar economic concerns.[14]

Czechoslovak workers almost never went on strike in this period. Prior to the Soviet invasion of August 1968, only isolated wildcat strikes occurred, although the threat of strikes was sometimes used as tool to bargain for higher wages.[15] During the Prague Spring, workers were reluctant to confront the regime that had permitted trade unions to exist for the first time in twenty years. After the Soviet invasion, however, when strike action or the threat of strikes were riskier, workers resorted only occasionally to the latter.[16] After August 1968, trade unions demanded free elections, adherence to elementary civil rights, and the removal of particularly outspoken "conservatives," that is, opponents of reform, from the leadership ranks of the Communist Party.[17] More visibly yet, a wide network of workers' councils arose in the months after the beginning of the Warsaw Pact occupation. In January 1969, council members representing eight hundred thousand workers, one-sixth of the entire workforce, gathered in Plzeň to deliberate.[18] Ultimately, though, as is well known, the Czech workers' councils disappeared in the wake of the repression in the course of the year.

WHERE WAS THE VANGUARD?

The Unskilled as Motor Force of Change

Most social scientists regard the unskilled or semiskilled proletariat as the vanguard of social change in 1968 and the following years. This interpretation is probably most pronounced in the case of Italy, although analysts differ over the chronology of events. Robert Lumley, for example, simply highlights "the emergence of the semi-skilled workers of the large factories of the manufacturing sector as a leading protagonist of industrial action."[19]

---

14 See the relevant table in Bernecker, "Die Arbeiterbewegung," 138, and the graph in José Maravall, *Dictatorship and Political Dissent: Workers and Students in Franco's Spain* (New York, 1978), 37.

15 H. Gordon Skilling, *Czechoslovakia's Interrupted Revolution* (Princeton, N.J., 1976), 583.

16 Galia Golan, *Reform Rule in Czechoslovakia: The Dubček Era 1968–1969* (Cambridge, 1973), 287.

17 Golan, *Reform Rule*, 286.

18 Figures are taken from Milos Bárta, "Les conseils ouvriers en tant que mouvement social," *Autogestion et socialisme* 9–10 (Sept.–Dec. 1969), 17. Barta, on 19, also reports that such councils were noticeably absent in the Slovak portion of the state. Although comprising 20 percent of the Czechoslovak workforce, Slovak places of employment represented a mere 4.2 percent of all existing workers' councils.

19 Lumley, *States of Emergency*, 181.

According to Joanne Barkan, following a brief period when "skilled workers and activists who had some previous strike or union experience" were
the most active social forces, by the fall of 1968 "the semiskilled and
unskilled workers took over the leading role."[20] For Ida Regalia, Marino
Regini, and Emilio Reyneri, "the young, mostly immigrant, semi-skilled
workers, who had been almost excluded from the industrial relations system until 1968, did not begin to establish themselves as autonomous protagonists in important conflicts until the autumn of 1968 and the spring of
1969, finally dominating the scene in the 'hot autumn' of 1969."[21] John
Low-Beer, whose work focuses on the contributions of the new working
class to the proletarian 1968, suggests that by "the early seventies technicians were displaced from the political limelight by young, semiskilled
workers, often immigrants from rural areas."[22] Despite differences over the
precise moment when the unskilled or semiskilled began to take center
stage in Italian working-class struggles, there seems to be widespread agreement that they did indeed play a prominent role.

There is a similar consensus on the French experience. For Patrick
Fridenson "alliances between the various groups and networks of semiskilled workers in the French auto factories"[23] hold the key to working-
class activism in the late 1960s, and Gérard Noiriel states, "For several years
the unskilled worker was king, and manifold sociological works were
devoted to this new figure."[24] Even Alain Touraine, one of the key proponents of the centrality of the new working class in global 1968, highlights
the catalytic role of the unskilled in France:

> Just as the skilled workers toward the end of the nineteenth century and the begin-
> ning of the twentieth became the agents of a revolutionary movement by means of
> the alliance with the unskilled . . . this new aristocracy of producers, that is, the
> technical intelligentsia could not push the workers movement in the direction of
> qualitatively new demands unless itself pushed by the revolt of the least privileged
> categories of workers, the least integrated into the factory, the most directly threat-
> ened.[25]

One difficulty in this focus on the unskilled or semiskilled is the neglect
of sociological detail that characterizes virtually every single one of these

20 Barkan, *Visions of Emancipation,* 69, 70.
21 Ida Regalia, Marino Regini, and Emilio Reyneri, "Labour Conflicts and Industrial Relations in
   Italy," in Colin Crouch and Alessandro Pizzorno, eds., *The Resurgence of Class Conflict in Western
   Europe Since 1968,* 2 vols. (New York, 1978), 1:109.
22 John R. Low-Beer, *Protest and Participation: The New Working Class in Italy* (Cambridge, 1978), 21.
23 Patrick Fridenson, "Automobile Workers in France and Their Work, 1914–83," in Steven L. Kaplan
   and Cynthia J. Koepp, eds., *Work in France* (Ithaca, N.Y., 1986), 539.
24 Gérard Noiriel, *Workers in French Society in the 19th and 20th Centuries* (New York, 1990), 219.
25 Alain Touraine, *Le mouvement de mai ou le communisme utopique* (Paris, 1968), 162.

studies. There is insufficient definition of the unskilled and the semiskilled, which are rarely distinguished from each other. Workers regarded by one observer as semiskilled are seen by others as unskilled, and some use the terms almost interchangeably. And the available literature on Spain provides virtually no sociological differentiation of the rebellious workforce. Strike statistics for Spain merely point to the iron and metal industries, mining, construction, textiles, and the chemical industry as the most conflict-prone branches, which may suggest an equal participation of the skilled and unskilled or semiskilled.[26] In general, advocates of the unskilled Taylorean workforce as social vanguard echo the analysts of labor struggles in the 1930s when the unskilled or semiskilled first entered national politics in a decisive way on both sides of the Atlantic. They have drawn attention to first-generation proletarians, who had undergone significant internal or foreign migration and had few ties to the more traditional bastions of working-class activism.

The "New Working Class" Thesis

Other observers highlight new departures rather than continuities in working-class struggles of the late 1960s and the early 1970s. The Slovak economist Eugen Löbl, for example, suggests that the events of 1968 in Czechoslovakia were the first manifestation of a future trend in social evolution, a revolution instigated and led by the intelligentsia. "If, two or three centuries ago, the intelligentsia was still a small group of educated individuals, today it has grown into a broad social stratum that is characterized not only by its subjective characteristics, that is, its level of education, but has also taken over a completely new role in society. In the past, the manual worker was the sole creator of material values. Today the entire intelligentsia participates in this process; and, without the intelligentsia, this incredible economic boom of the postwar decades could not have taken place."[27]

Löbl points to the diminution of the relative numerical weight of blue-collar workers in modern economies. In addition, he continues, its "relative prosperity leads to bourgeoisification, to the depoliticization of the working class." Whereas the blue-collar working class increasingly restricts its social vision to the improvement of its material status, the intelligentsia has moved into the front ranks of progress and adamantly demands improvements in the quality of social life. "Therefore, the intelligentsia

---

26 Table 5 in Bernecker, "Die Arbeiterbewegung," 132.
27 Eugen Löbl, "Die intellektuelle Revolution," in Eugen Löbl and Leopold Grünwald, *Die intellektuelle Revolution* (Düsseldorf, 1969), 41.

represents not merely its own social interest, but the interest of the entire people."[28]

Löbl's thesis, namely, that the Prague Spring was the start of a new era in which the scientific and intellectual elite would act as the liberator of humanity, is closely linked to the most significant contribution of the literature on 1968: a recognition of the contributions of technicians and middle-level managers to emancipatory struggles in industrial societies. Starting in the second half of the 1950s, French industrial sociologists in particular had begun to analyze this new phenomenon in a series of research projects carried out in a number of major French manufacturing concerns.[29] These sociological inquiries had been the direct result of a sudden wave of activism centered on this new working class, first in France and somewhat later in Italy.[30] The theory of the new working class is most closely associated with three eminent French sociologists, André Gorz, Alain Touraine, and Serge Mallet.

Underlying the assessment of all three social scientists is the recognition of a profound sense of alienation deeply affecting this rapidly growing stratum of the dependent workforce precisely in the most dynamic sectors of the world capitalist economy. Technicians, engineers, and other highly educated members of the late capitalist workforce suffer in particular from an inability to apply their natural and learned creativity at the point of production in the service of a larger cause. Gorz compares this sense of frustration to the malaise of manual workers in the nineteenth century:

The impossibility of living which appeared to the proletarians of the last century as the impossibility of reproducing their labor power becomes for the workers of scientific or cultural industries the impossibility of putting their creative abilities to work. Industry in the last century took from the countryside men who were muscles, lungs, stomachs: their muscles missed the open spaces, their lungs the fresh air, their stomachs fresh food; their health declined, and the acuteness of their need was but the empty functioning of their organs in a hostile surrounding world. The industry of the second half of the twentieth century increasingly tends to take men from the universities and colleges, men who have been able to acquire the ability to do creative or independent work; who have curiosity, the ability to synthesize, to analyze, to invent, and to assimilate, an ability which spins in a vacuum and runs the risk of perishing for lack of an opportunity to be usefully put to work.[31]

Together with this greater capacity for innovation and creative expression in the workplace, the new working class also demonstrates a greater

28 Löbl, "Die intellektuelle Revolution," 95.
29 A brief survey of these early ventures can be found in the introduction to the 1963 edition of Serge Mallet, *La nouvelle classe ouvrière* (Paris, 1963), 21–5.
30 Low-Beer, *Protest and Participation*, 20–1.
31 André Gorz, *Strategy for Labor* (Boston, 1967), 105–6.

interest in larger societal and cultural concerns. Their demands far outstrip the reach of the factory and place of employment. "The demand for self-management which arises out of productive praxis cannot be contained within the factory walls, the laboratories and research bureaus. Men who cannot be ordered around in their work cannot indefinitely be ordered around in their life as citizens, nor can they submit to the rigid decisions of central administrations."[32] These "new proletarians of culture"[33] fight "on all levels, in the name of an overall alternative. . . .The cultural battle for a new conception of man, of life, education, work, and civilization, is the precondition for the success of all other battles for socialism because it establishes their meaning."[34]

Gorz developed his interpretation of the changing social forces in late capitalist society several years before the social explosion of 1968 focused general attention on this phenomenon. Perhaps the most famous analysis of 1968 from the point of view of French industrial sociology, Touraine's *Le mouvement de mai ou le communisme utopique,* written and published toward the end of that year, picks up several of Gorz's key themes, such as the new working class's greater proclivity toward taking up qualitative demands addressing noneconomic issues, or the tendency of higher education to produce no longer a privileged intellectual elite but, instead, a subordinate, although highly skilled, proletarian workforce. Most important, Touraine postulates the uncontested vanguard role of this new working class in the struggles of that turbulent year: "The principal agent of the May movement was not the [blue-collar] working class, but the entirety of those individuals whom one could term professionals . . . and among them the most active were those who exert the greatest independence vis-à-vis the large organizations for which they work directly or indirectly: students, journalists of the state-run radio and television network (Office du radiodiffusion-télévision française or ORTF), technicians employed by research centers, researchers in the public or private sectors, teachers, etc."[35]

The individual most closely associated with the theory of the new working class was Serge Mallet. He was also the one to ask most directly the question under investigation in this chapter: "In the end, we do not need to know whether there continues to exist a working class; instead we need to know who precisely within this working class constitutes the force of the vanguard, who has the possibility to envision most clearly the future of working people, and, on the other hand, we need to know who cannot

32 Gorz, *Strategy for Labor,* 126.   33 Ibid., 108.   34 Ibid., 132.
35 Touraine, *Le mouvement de mai,* 25–6.

psychologically overcome their actual social conditions on the basis of their objective situation."[36]

Again, like Gorz and Touraine, Mallet recognizes the privileged position of this new working class and draws attention to its new role as the central human agent in the process of obtaining social liberation. "Only the active population strata that are integrated into the most advanced production processes will be able to give expression to the corresponding alienation and will thus be able to envisage superior forms of development. In the same manner that the small peasantry, which was a revolutionary factor in 1789, was unable to comprehend the [1871] Paris Commune, the working class of the declining industries will be unable to formulate in a positive manner an alternative to neocapitalist society. Its struggle will of necessity revert to the reactionary, corporatist, Malthusian aspects as did the English handloom weavers in 1840."[37]

The New Working Class in the Heat of Battle

Gorz and Mallet developed the theory of the new working class as the new vanguard in the decade since 1958. The realities of 1968 initially enhanced the stature of their bold and imaginative proposition. France in particular saw a multiplicity of workers' struggles in which the new working class was most heatedly engaged. Less pronounced in branches of industry where skilled white-collar workers played more the role of supervisors than the role of technical support staff, the new white-collar proletariat displayed an unusual amount of energy and imagination that propelled it to center stage. Technicians and, in several instances, even middle-level managers at Berliet, Peugeot, Thomson, and other leading French industrial establishments constituted solid blocs of supporters to the activities of company-wide strike committees and factory councils that were the lifeblood of the working-class dimension of 1968 in France. The vanguard role of the new working class was most visible at places of employment dominated by this social stratum, such as the ORTF, the National Center for Scientific Research (Centre nationale de la recherche scientifique or CNRS), or the nuclear energy research lab (Commissariat à l'énergie atomique or CEA) at Saclay. In these and other locations almost exclusively staffed by the new

---

36 Serge Mallet, *La nouvelle classe ouvrière* (Paris, 1968), 23; all subsequent citations from this book refer to this 1968 paperback edition.
37 Ibid.

working class, thousands of participants repeatedly gathered for protracted and engaged discussions, literally at a moment's notice.[38]

Virtually identical observations were reported in Italy. "Technicians were prominent in all the white-collar strikes. The most notable of these struggles occurred in the advanced sectors that employed predominantly technically trained labor."[39] Francoist Spain saw a similar entry of white-collar activists onto the front pages of newspapers beginning in 1968. Perhaps the most remarkable development here was the politicization of the civil service. The lower grades of the Spanish civil service in particular began to organize into illegal unions with an active presence at the very center of the state, namely, the ministries. Sit-down strikes and illegal assemblies were significant forms of activism by the clandestine Association of Public Employees, founded in the course of 1969.[40] Bank workers were perhaps the best-organized group of white-collar employees in Spain under Franco. In the mid-1960s, they developed close ties to the underground Left. By 1970, 65 percent of bank employees supported the nationalization of banks, and 69 percent believed that Spain's legal system was essentially a means to perpetuate an exploitative system of class domination.[41]

By the early 1970s, the militant example of Spanish bank workers began to have ripple effects among other white-collar workers, including teachers and journalists.[42] Yet, at the same time, the Spanish example of white-collar activism pointed in the direction of enlarging the definition of the new working class to include less privileged sectors of the white-collar workforce, compared to the technical and administrative intelligentsia favored by French industrial sociologists. According to Raymond Carr and Juan Pablo Fusi Aizpurna, the new working class should encompass a much wider array of white-collar employment, including "bank clerks, typists, secretaries, laboratory technicians, school teachers."[43] Yet even for observers who may insist on the narrower definition of the new working class, Spain fits nicely into the trend openly displayed in democratic Italy and France. Walther Bernecker, perhaps the most careful observer of Spanish industrial sociology outside Spain, observes: "The shifting of the strike intensity from

---

38 Claude Durand, "Ouvriers et techniciens en mai 1968," in Pierre Dubois et al., *Grèves reventicatives ou grèves politiques?* (Paris, 1971), 36–9, provides a useful brief introduction to the high visibility of the new working class in French workers' struggles of 1968.

39 Low-Beer, *Protest and Participation*, 39, is one of many researchers reporting on this state of affairs.

40 Raymond Carr and Juan Pablo Fusi Aizpurna, *Spain: Dictatorship to Democracy* (London, 1979), 84.

41 Maravall, *Dictatorship and Political Dissent*, 61–2 and 176. On the exceptional militancy of Spanish bank workers, see also José Félix Tezanos, *Estructura de clases en la España actual* (Madrid, 1975), 80–3.

42 Balfour, *Dictatorship, Workers and the City*, 154.   43 Carr and Fusi, *Spain*, 83.

one economic sector to another mirrors the socioeconomic change of
Spain in the 1960s and 1970s: if initially the mining, metalworking, and
construction sectors saw the most conflicts, the 1970s added to this the
occupational fields of the 'new' middle classes (education, medical doctors,
banking, and postal clerks)."[44] Educators and physicians, at the very least,
squarely fit the qualification for admission to the new working class, as postulated by Gorz and others.

The most astounding parallels to France and Italy, however, occurred
not in Spain but in noncapitalist Czechoslovakia, once again suggesting
that the changing face of Europe's working class was the result of a process
that transcended political boundaries and, simultaneously, the reach of
entire socioeconomic systems. Starting in the summer of 1968, the
Czechoslovak state witnessed the rapid emergence of workers' councils as
decisive agents for social and political change, particularly in the Czech
provinces. The data unequivocally suggest that the technical and administrative intelligentsia played by far the most dynamic role in the construction
and consolidation of these organs of workers' control. Examining the minutes of a general meeting of workers' council representatives in January
1969, one finds frequent reference to the relative passivity of manual workers and the corresponding overrepresentation of the "socialist" new working class in the structures of the council system. A Prague factory representative, for example, reported that their "council includes one foreman,
while the rest are white-collar staff, including six people with higher education qualifications, several technicians and economists, a lawyer, etc."[45] A
more representative survey of 114 enterprise councils likewise reported
that "71.5 percent of the council members are technicians, of whom 55
percent are from what are called the higher technical staff,"[46] and Valdimir
Fisera, commenting on the overall national picture, suggests that "seventy
percent of those elected were managerial staff or technicians,"[47] an elo-
quent testimony to the social and political presence of the new working
class east as well as west of the Iron Curtain. H. Gordon Skilling points to
an intimately related feature of the Czech council system: "The councils
were significantly not called 'workers' councils' but 'councils of the work-

44 Bernecker, "Die Arbeiterbewegung," 133.
45 Vladimir Fisera, ed., *Workers' Councils in Czechoslovakia 1968–9* (London, 1978), 66.
46 Fisera, ed., *Workers' Councils,* 155.
47 Vladimir Fisera, "Introduction," in Fisera, ed., *Workers' Councils,* 15. Elsewhere Fisera notes that
   even among the council representation originating in the blue-collar workforce, skilled workers
   were overrepresented compared to their overall numerical strength; see Joseph and Vladimir Fisera,
   "Cogestion des entreprises et économie socialiste – l'expérience tchécoslovaque, 1967–1970,"
   Revue de l'Est 2 (Jan. 1971): 54–5.

ing people,' a broader term including all employed persons, whether white-
or blue-collar."[48]

Society, Quality of Life, and Culture

One of the contentions put forth by the advocates of the new working
class thesis is this group's greater proclivity to address issues that go beyond
salary questions or other concerns closely related to the point of production. Especially in France, this new working class raised political demands,
and sectors of employment dominated by these social strata exhibited the
most dynamic and imaginative forms of activism. In France, according to
Claude Durand, "it was in the technical sectors where new demands regarding the hierarchical structures, the control over the organization of labor,
the control and management of personnel and, in certain cases (Thomson,
CEA, CNRS) the demand for co-determination or self-management of
laboratories were born."[49] In a few cases (ORTF, CNRS), a more frontal
attack on the functioning of the enterprise was carried out by means of
workforce demands for co-determination of the overall objectives of the
entire organization.[50] The sector dominated by the new working class also
witnessed far more instances of spontaneous actions than did traditional
blue-collar industries, where workers were consulted "but where, for all
practical purposes, the decisions were reached in [backroom] gatherings of
factory union representatives."[51] In general, blue-collar industries saw a
plethora of informational meetings, but with relatively few opportunities
for meaningful expression of opinion by the rank and file. Conversely, new
industries witnessed a minimum of organizational restraints and a maximum of creative expression.[52] Touraine, Wieviorka, and Dubet propose
that "it may be in order to speculate whether the desire for unanimism is
specific to the sociability of unskilled workers, by contrast with the 'democratism' of skilled workers and, more especially, the 'elective sociability' of
technicians."[53]

Analyzing the role of the new working class roughly fifteen years after
1968, the same team of authors gave the new working class thesis a novel
twist by suggesting that workplace democracy may have been less important than is generally assumed and that technicians in the modern sector

48 Skilling, *Interrupted Revolution,* 436–7.   49 Durand, "Ouvriers et techniciens," 64.
50 Ibid., 68.   51 Ibid., 134.   52 Ibid., 153–4.
53 Alain Touraine, Michel Wieviorka, and François Dubet, *The Workers' Movement* (Cambridge, 1987),
    119.

"were more interested in life outside work than in democratizing the firms they worked for." Further: "They saw that their colleagues were increasingly interested in problems outside their work, especially those which called into question the overall orientation of society and thus also involved the management of their personal life."[54] Moreover: "The technicians described their colleagues as being oriented toward leisure activities and their personal lives, or involved in movements outside work, mostly of a cultural nature."[55]

As previously noted, in Italy demands "directly concerned with labor relations within the enterprise but with the position of the working class in the overall political, economic and social system"[56] were not uncommon. And what sets Italy even farther apart from France is that, in Italy, many of the qualitative demands were directly addressed to governmental authorities rather than the individual company management. Yet, significantly, it is far more difficult to trace the quality of trade union demands to the pioneering role of the Italian new working class compared to their French colleagues. A similar ambivalence regarding the vanguard role of the new working class in the formulation of demands characterizes the situation in Spain and Czechoslovakia. Under conditions of dictatorial rule, simple economic demands may almost automatically take on immediate political and social relevance. Therefore, the focus on the character of demands, as an indicator of the political imagination of their advocates, holds far less credibility here than in countries under formal democratic rule. Spain and Czechoslovakia fit into this particular mold.

The French case, then, appears to be the sole example of a social movement during 1968 wherein the new working class appears to have definitely fulfilled its role of political vanguard as measured by their active engagement in the formulation of qualitative and noneconomic demands. Were there perhaps sound reasons why this new approach to the question of the agent of progressive social change disappeared from academic sight with equal speed in the course of the early 1970s compared to its meteoric ascent in the decade of the 1960s?

Critique of the New Working Class Thesis

Despite its popularity in certain influential circles, the new working class thesis has elicited few serious academic rejoinders. Perhaps the most interesting critique has come from Low-Beer, who carried out his own in-

---

54 Touraine, Wieviorka, and Dubet, *Workers' Movement,* 74.   55 Ibid., 169.
56 Regalia, Regini, and Reyneri, "Labour Conflicts," 132.

depth sociological study of the Italian technical intelligentsia. He came to the conclusion that Gorz, Touraine, and others have placed far too much emphasis on the point of production as the key factor determining the new working class's political orientation and proclivity toward activism. Low-Beer strongly suggests that the social background of the new working class, and its groundedness in the left-wing working-class tradition through its upbringing in militant blue-collar households, in short, their "individual or collective histories . . . their political attitudes and their prior orientation to work" influence their behavior at the production site and not the reverse. Whereas French industrial sociologists have postulated a one-way causal link from production relations to all other walks of life, Low-Beer finds "strong causal relationships only in the opposite direction: from attitudes acquired outside the work situation to militancy in the work situation."[57]

An even more persuasive corrective came from a more careful sifting of the empirical evidence of 1968. For example, as previously mentioned, the data on Spain strongly suggest that although white-collar workers were central to working-class militancy, the core groupings within this social category were by no means restricted to the technical and administrative intelligentsia. And, in general, the new working class thesis lost much of its luster in the wake of the realization that, despite its bouts of militancy in the heat of the battle, the new intelligentsia deradicalized as quickly as they had mobilized in the first place. Although his observation is perhaps somewhat overdrawn, Jacques Kergoat notes in the French context: "Once class conflicts go beyond the context of the enterprise and the stakes become clear . . . the vast majority of the administrative intelligentsia returns in a more or less discreet fashion to its original camp."[58] Renaud Dulong adds, "Increasingly, the institutional link with top-level management, the latter wishing to reestablish the entirety of all traditional social relations, reconsolidates itself."[59] "At the conclusion of the strike wave the end result is the return to ground zero: the administrative intelligentsia, born of the crisis, disappears with it."[60]

---

57 Low-Beer, *Protest and Participation,* 41. André Gorz makes a similar observation in a 1971 article in which he begins to distance himself from the new working class thesis as motor force for progressive social change: "Their attitude in confrontational moments depends primarily on their prior political and ideological convictions"; see André Gorz, "Techniques, techniciens et lutte des classes," *Les Temps Modernes* 301–2 (Aug.–Sept. 1971): 169–70.

58 Kergoat, "Sous la plage," 78.

59 Renaud Dulong, "Les cadres et le mouvement ouvrier," in Dubois et al., *Grèves revendicative,* 222.

60 Dulong, "Les cadres," 241. However, Donald M. Reid, in a recent article on French workplace inspectors after 1968, suggests a more nuanced summary of the personal/political itinerary of the new working class. Reid points out that this post-1968 generation of labor inspectors remains neither mired in "their most radical aspirations" nor completely disillusioned. Instead, they have "pio-

The ambivalent consciousness of the new working class, exposed by its erratic behavior during its activist phase, was also revealed in its diverse political, social, and cultural commitments. In France, where the new working class was prominently engaged on the Left, "right-wing support among technicians and supervisors was considerably higher than among manual workers."[61] Likewise, a Czech sociologist reported: "There was a higher percentage for the councils among the technically orientated intelligentsia, but also a higher percentage of opponents."[62] The multilayered nature of new working-class consciousness is perhaps best exemplified by survey results of Spanish bank workers' social attitudes. According to Carr and Fusi, "In the mid-seventies, 41 percent of bank employees favored 'Socialism' but at the same time supported compulsory religious education." And, "While a majority of bank clerks favor the nationalization of the private banks, only a minority favor birth control." "Yet since the birthrate of their class is the lowest in Spain," these white-collar radicals had to "practice in private what they condemn in public."[63]

The most effective refutation of the new working class thesis, however, originates yet again from a team of French sociologists, including Touraine, an erstwhile advocate of this approach. Reporting in the mid-1980s on field work carried out among the entire spectrum of the wage-dependent labor force in many regions of France, the authors assault one of the key elements of the new working class thesis, namely, the supposed fact of the class's growing alienation at the point of production as a result of its constantly stifled creativity and imagination:

The idea of a "new working class" implies the establishment of a new positive relationship to work on which a desire for collective control of the technology can be based. No such orientation was discernible among the technicians in any of our different groups. They hardly ever spoke about their technical work, their craft; their militancy was not based on their knowledge or their practical abilities nor on their strategic position within production. Technicians in the chemical, iron-and-

---

neered efforts to break with the hierarchical norms of the state civil service while rethinking – rather than rejecting – the state's right and duty to intervene in the workings of private enterprise. In both realms, the former *jeunes inspecteurs* have retained their contestatory ways in changing historical circumstances." See Donald Reid, "'Les jeunes inspecteurs': Ideology and Activism Among Labour Inspectors in France After May 1968," *French History* 8, no. 3 (1994): 315.

61 Richard Hyman, "Occupational Structure, Collective Organisation and Industrial Militancy," in Crouch and Pizzorno, eds., *Resurgence of Class Conflict*, 2:62. In a similar fashion Renaud Sainsaulieu points out that the French new working class's overall unionization rate was lower than the blue-collar rate, yet among this minority the rate of activists compared to passive, dues-paying members was higher than among blue-collar trade unionists; see Renaud Sainsaulieu, *Les relations de travail à l'usine* (Paris, 1972), 244.

62 Reported in Fisera, ed., *Workers' Councils*, 67–8.   63 Carr and Fusi, *Spain*, 84–5.

steel, and data processing industries showed no sign at all of being the distant heirs of craft workers. The majority of them made no reference at all to the pride in their skill which was a major component in working-class consciousness. . . . The technicians seemed even further removed than the manual workers from the qualities of labor on which industrial society was founded, and which Serge Mallet retained at the very center of his thesis.[64]

Given the apparent limitations of the new working class thesis, what, then, are the consequences of this selective survey of working-class attitudes and behaviors in 1968 and its aftermath? Should one draw the ultimate conclusion and second the evolution of Gorz, who was another early proponent of the new working class thesis and who in 1980 announced his *Adieux au prolétariat?*

CONCLUSION

In many ways, Gorz in 1980, and others since then, merely replicated similar thought processes that had first affected Western social scientists in the 1950s, although the most recent wave of disillusioned radicals prefers to circumscribe this evolution with talk of "the end of history" rather than use the comparatively moderate slogan of "the end of ideology" prevalent in discussions before 1968. Both sets of discussions were a reflection of the reflux of workers' struggles in the wake of the social upheavals affecting Western societies between 1943 and 1948 in the earlier case, and following the cycle of turbulence between 1967 and 1975 in the most recent manifestation of ideological moderation.

The proletarian dimension of 1968 proved to be the temporary undoing of the former debate. To begin with, not all observers had become passive following the downturn of social struggles after 1948. Among the most militant social thinkers and activists, however, only a few had retained their belief in the emancipatory potential of the working class. Some replaced "workers" with "Third World peoples" as the most promising agent of social change; others focused on marginalized racial minorities or students as the harbingers of progress.[65] The working-class dimension of 1968 profoundly altered these intellectuals' debates. As a topic of conversation, the working class suddenly became fashionable for more than just veterans of an aging Old Left.

64 Touraine, Wieviorka, and Dubet, *Workers' Movement,* 168–9.
65 For one important reflection on this evolution, written under the influence of 1968, see Lucio Magri, "Réflexions sur les événements de Mai," *Les Temps Modernes,* nos. 278–80 (Aug.–Nov. 1969), particularly 710.

In one sense, the pre-1968 debate regarding the importance of the new working class can be seen as closely related to the general de-emphasis of traditional working-class struggles after 1948. Theorists of the new working class, directly or indirectly, reflected a similar deep-seated pessimism regarding the potential of blue-collar workers compared to their more openly scornful colleagues.[66] But the concrete processes of 1968 permitted some new working class theorists to incorporate their findings in an elegant and persuasive fashion into a more general revaluation of the working class *tout court*.

This is most patently visible in a study by Roger Garaudy that includes many of the themes prominent in the works of Löbl, Gorz, Touraine, and Mallet but goes beyond them in one crucial sense. Garaudy first draws attention to the ongoing "scientific and technological revolution," which he regards as "the most radical revolution in human history."[67] He then describes the French May as the "first great strike of the cybernetic age" that "was not directed solely against the exploitation of labour but also against its alienation."[68] He firmly asserts that a "primary role" in the desired and impending radical societal changes "will be played by the engineers, the technologists, and the cadres, as also by a great many intellectuals."[69] Garaudy concludes with an assessment of the prospects for advanced industrial societies. Using the example of the United States, he writes: "The only force that could be a majority force in existing American social conditions is the working class in the broadest sense of the term, namely, the class that is playing the decisive role in the present state of the productive forces and is jointly constituted by the white-collar workers and the blue-collar workers. This new 'historic bloc' is the only factor capable of involving even wider social strata in a vast movement for the renewal of American society."[70] Rather than placing all hope on *one* working-class fraction, Garaudy suggests that it is the potential for unity that should elicit enthusiasm from critics of contemporary social reality.

I regard this as the most important lesson of the proletarian dimension of 1968. The combative spirit of this "moment of madness" rekindled the awareness of the continued relevance of the working class as potential agent for progressive change, but with two important provisos. First, it was recognized that the working class was a fundamentally reconstituted and con-

---

66 This is pointed out most clearly by Pierre Cours-Saliès in his *La CFDT: Un passé porteur d'avenir* (Paris, [1989]), 155.

67 Roger Garaudy, *The Crisis in Communism: The Turning-Point of Socialism* (New York, 1970), 43.

68 Ibid., 201.   69 Ibid., 66.   70 Ibid., 63.

stantly reconstituting social class, qualitatively different from its composition in earlier instances of sociopolitical militancy. Second, it soon became equally obvious that attempts to isolate one particular fraction of this class as *the* agent of social change were bound to be empirically wrong and counterproductive.[71] The rapid waning of the new working class thesis after 1968 was in large part due to the continued pervasiveness of the variant espoused by Gorz, Touraine, and Mallet, in contrast to Garaudy's more open-ended and inclusive version.[72] In sum, perhaps the most subversive lesson of the struggles between 1967 and 1975 may therefore be the seemingly simplistic realization that the working class today, as in earlier times, is multilayered yet at the same time capable of unified and system-challenging action.

As a critical aspect of global 1968, working-class issues were at the center of developments in only a few countries. Why this was so remains to be explained. Nevertheless, in assessing 1968 globally, elements of cultural revolution far outweigh instances of a genuine workers' revolution. But the overall relegation of the proletarian May to second-class status came at a price. In the words of Ulrich K. Preuss, the ubiquity of the student insurgency guaranteed that "the rules of the game [would change]" in the wake of 1968.[73] Yet the confinement of the worker revolt to a few countries equally ensured that the game would remain the same.

71 One such warning can be found in Jean Lojkine, "The Decomposition and Recomposition of the Working Class," in Mark Kesselbaum and Guy Groux, eds., *The French Workers' Movement: Economic Crisis and Political Change* (London, 1984), 119–31.
72 There existed, of course, additional mutations of the "new working class" thesis. For one influential version, regarding these new strata as key components of extra-factory auxiliary forces performing a crucial role in forming an "external vanguard," see Sergio Bologna and Francesco Ciafaloni, "I tecnici come produttori e come prodotto," *Quaderni Piacentini* 8 (Mar. 1969): 52–71.
73 Comments made by Ulrich K. Preuss during discussions at the conference, "1968: The World Transformed," Wissenschaftszentrum Berlin, May 24–6, 1996.

14

The Women's Movement in East and West Germany

EVA MALECK-LEWY AND BERNHARD MALECK

Parallel to international developments, both postwar German states underwent a process of modernization and adjustment from the mid-1960s to the late 1980s. The reform of societal and political structures failed in the former German Democratic Republic (GDR), and the East German state left the international political stage with reunification in 1990. In contrast, the modernization of the Federal Republic of Germany (FRG) was accomplished within the context of a parliamentary system and was symbolized by the "transfer of power" from a conservative government to a social-liberal coalition in the fall of 1969.[1] This change can be attributed in no small measure to the evolution of extraparliamentary opposition and the student movement of 1968.

Nineteen sixty-eight, the high point of the student movement, also witnessed the birth of the West German women's movement. At the same time, the GDR supported the military intervention in Czechoslovakia in 1968 and suppressed any domestic attempt to allow diversity of opinion or elements of democratic socialism. These developments meant that East German women had no political latitude for independently expressing their concerns in the form of an autonomous women's movement. Only art and literature, as substitutes for public discussion, were available as means to articulate experiences with sex discrimination in everyday life and to establish a modern woman's consciousness.[2]

Sally E. Robertson of Arlington, Virginia, translated this chapter from the German.

1 See, e.g., Arnulf Baring, *Machtwechsel: Die Ära Brandt-Scheel* (Stuttgart, 1984); Mary Fulbrook, *The Divided Nation: A History of Germany, 1918–1990* (New York, 1992), 207; Christoph Klessmann, *Zwei Staaten, eine Nation: Deutsche Geschichte 1945–1970* (Bonn, 1988); Dietrich Thränhardt, *Geschichte der Bundesrepublik Deutschland 1949–1990* (Frankfurt am Main, 1996). See also the chapter by Claus Leggewie in this book.
2 Dietrich Staritz, *Geschichte der DDR* (Frankfurt am Main, 1996); Hermann Weber, *DDR: Grundriss der Geschichte 1945–1990* (Hannover, 1991); Klessmann, *Zwei Staaten, eine Nation,* 279.

THE FEDERAL REPUBLIC OF GERMANY

Since the early 1960s, women in the FRG had increasingly been taking advantage of opportunities for greater equality through occupational training and certification. The number of female apprentices and university students continuously climbed.[3] Benefiting from a labor shortage and a prosperous economy, more and more women entered the paid workforce in a full- or part-time capacity.[4]

Official policy on women's issues and the image of women in West German society thus became growing problems. Reform of the marriage and abortion laws by the social-liberal coalition permitted the necessary processes of adaptation to social and cultural changes, although this process was laborious and was not resolved until 1977, when the new marriage law was passed. The extraparliamentary women's movement contributed significantly to the generation of the political pressure necessary to bring this about.

By the time they took office in 1969, the Social Democrats (Sozialdemokratische Partei Deutschlands or SPD) and the Liberals (Freie Demokratische Partei or FDP) had endorsed rapid reform of criminal laws, including liberalization of the abortion law. The battle for liberalization of abortion laws not only brought together existing women's groups in the Federal Republic, but it became the "actual crucible" for the emergence of the new women's movement, as it was in the other Western European nations and the United States.[5]

The Emergence of a New Women's Movement

The extraparliamentary opposition and antiauthoritarian student movement shaped the common cultural and political horizons of the 1960s generation in the Federal Republic. This generation has been a defining influence and cultural anchor for democratic developments in West Germany over the last thirty years. It was the cultural and philosophical origin of the new women's movement in the Federal Republic and of the environmental and peace movements. The identity of the West German women's

---

3 The percentage of female students at West German universities grew from 25 percent in 1965 to 33.7 percent in 1975.

4 In 1968, 49.7 percent of women between the ages of fifteen and sixty-five in the FRG were employed, representing 36.2 percent of the total workforce.

5 Alice Schwarzer, *So fing es an! Zehn Jahre Frauenbewegung* (Cologne, 1981); Herrad Schenk, *Die feministische Herausforderung: 150 Jahre Frauenbewegung in Deutschland* (Munich, 1992). On the United States, see Alice Echols, "Women's Liberation and Sixties Radicalism," in David Farber, ed., *The Sixties: From Memory to History* (Chapel Hill, N.C., 1994), 153–4.

movement, its organizational structures and forms of institutionalization, was significantly shaped by the philosophy and political practices of the extraparliamentary opposition and the student movement.[6]

The West German women's movement was part of an international development that can be observed in the late 1960s and early 1970s in nearly every Western European nation and the United States. These movements were unified by their goal of eliminating inequality and disadvantages through partisan actions in the interest of women. The concrete forms and themes of each movement, however, had specific national characteristics determined by the political culture of each country and its socioeconomic and legal peculiarities. "Nonetheless, the meaning feminism has and the nature of its impact in individual nations will reflect very specific historical developments and political cultures. Despite some common concerns, the way the women's movement organizes and the issues it makes central vary from country to country depending on the political tools and opportunities available in each setting."[7]

The student movement in the Federal Republic was shaped by the protest against the Vietnam War, the debate over the Emergency Laws, the problem of wealth in the First World and poverty in the Third, and the dissociation from the basic ideological patterns of the East-West conflict in the form of "realist" socialism and "imperialism."[8] Students created a new protest culture and took as their theme the question of individual responsibility with respect to national and community structures.[9] In the universities, the movement called for reform of authoritarian structures and self-determination of curricula. On the political level, it criticized traditional partisan politics and advocated issue-oriented lobbying by independent voters. The student movement garnered much public attention by questioning the continuities between the history of the Federal Republic and

6 Karl-Werner Brandt, *Neue soziale Bewegungen: Entstehung, Funktion und Perspektive neuer Protestpotentiale: Eine Zwischenbilanz* (Opladen, 1982); Karl-Werner Brandt, Dieter Büsser, and Dieter Rucht, eds., *Aufbruch in eine andere Gesellschaft: Neue soziale Bewegungen in der Bundesrepublik* (Frankfurt am Main, 1986); Bernhard Maleck and Stefan Bollinger, *Denken zwischen Utopie und Realität* (Berlin, 1987); Joachim Raschke, *Soziale Bewegungen: Ein historisch-systematischer Grundriss* (Frankfurt am Main, 1985); Roland Roth and Dieter Rucht, eds., *Neue soziale Bewegungen in der Bundesrepublik Deutschland* (Bonn, 1987); see the chapter by Ingrid Gilcher-Holtey in this book.
7 Myra Marx Ferree, "Political Strategies and Feminist Concerns in the United States and Federal Republic of Germany," *Research in Social Movements: Conflicts and Change* 13 (1991) : 221–40.
8 Jürgen Habermas, *Protestbewegung und Hochschulreform* (Frankfurt am Main, 1969); Geoff Eley, "Germany Since '68: From APO to the Greens," *Socialist Review* 1 (1988) : 93–157; Kurt Sontheimer, *The Government and Politics of West Germany* (New York, 1973); see also the chapters by Arif Dirlik, Stuart J. Hilwig, and Konrad H. Jarausch in this book.
9 Rudi Dutschke, *Mein langer Marsch: Reden, Schriften und Tagebücher aus 20 Jahren,* ed. Gretchen Dutschke-Klotz, Helmut Gollwitzer, and Jürgen Miermeister (Reinbek bei Hamburg, 1980), 43.

that of National Socialist Germany and the role their parents' generation had played in the Third Reich and the attempted annihilation of the Jews.[10] The new women's movement shared the student movement's call for a critical distance from the state, rejection of traditional organizational forms, and a philosophy of self-determining, nonalienated individuals. These movements believed that politics should derive primarily from the interests of the people affected by it and that individuals should move toward "democratic self-administration," thus setting in motion the process of social transformation.[11]

The new women's movement in West Germany, as in the United States and other countries, thus had its intellectual foundation in the student movement, while at the same time arising from a conflict within the Socialist German Student League (Sozialistische Dentsche Studentenbund or SDS), the engine behind the German student movement. Some of the female students participating in the student movement felt discriminated against by their male colleagues. Although they were industriously doing grassroots work, making coffee and typing and distributing leaflets, their male comrades, the "theorists and leaders" of the student movement, had no ear for women's problems. The girlfriends and wives of the movement's leaders were regarded simply as "brides of the revolution" by the public and by the leaders themselves. One of the first female students' leaflets read: "We were envious because equal rights always came somewhat harder to us than to our male comrades, because we always fell short of the desired 'lofty flights' of genius, because our individual attempts to integrate studies, love, and children only dissipated our energies or simply caused us to become hard-hearted."[12] Whereas the women were continually confronted with "antiauthoritarian" developments within the student movement, ironically, those who presented themselves as antiauthoritarian never thought of "allowing their own actions to be examined."[13]

Therefore, at the end of 1967, some women decided to begin meeting in separate working groups that would exclude men. These personal expe-

10 See the chapter by Harold Marcuse in this book.

11 Particularly important for the intellectual foundation of the West German student movement was Herbert Marcuse. See especially his *Vernunft und Revolution* (Darmstadt, 1972), *Das Ende der Utopie: Vorträge und Diskussionen in Berlin 1976* (Frankfurt am Main, 1980), and *Triebstruktur und Gesellschaft* (Frankfurt am Main, 1982). The writings of Theodor W. Adorno and Max Horkheimer, the founders of "critical theory," were also important. See Max Horkheimer and Theodor W. Adorno, *Dialektik der Aufklärung* (Frankfurt am Main, 1969). See also Jürgen Habermas, *Stichworte zur "Geistigen Situation der Zeit,"* 2 vols. (Frankfurt am Main, 1982), and Maleck and Bollinger, *Denken zwischen Utopie und Realität,* 224.

12 Schwarzer, *So fing es an!* 14.

13 Ingrid Schmidt-Harzbach, "'Frauen erhebt euch': Als Frau im SDS und im Aktionsrat," in Hilke Schlaeger, ed., *Mein Kopf gehört mir: 20 Jahre Frauenbewegung* (Munich, 1988), 51–3.

riences with the men in the SDS, and the resulting personal problems, triggered a call for the formation of a "women's working group." In Berlin, one of the strongholds of the student movement, the women's working group was established not only by students but also by other women with no direct connection to the university, including working women, housewives, and the wives or girlfriends of leftist men, about half of whom were mothers. What united these women was their desire to take active part in the extraparliamentary movement and to confront the women's problems that existed but were being suppressed. The women's working group included some women who had already done their homework on women's issues and were discussing Simone de Beauvoir's *Second Sex* and Betty Friedan's *Feminine Mystique.*[14]

The fact that there already was a women's movement in America – and women in other European countries were joining together for action campaigns – had an encouraging and inspiring effect. "Every little newspaper report about the so-called women's lib in America and the 'Dollen Minnas' in Holland" was eagerly consumed.[15] Despite these influences and stimuli from the United States, however, the new German women's movement was by no means a mere offshoot of the North American movement, as Alice Schwartzer has determined in retrospect. "Entirely independent of what was going on across the Atlantic, women's discontent grew here in various countries almost simultaneously – and just as independently from one another – until it reached a glorious point of offensive protest. The time was ripe."[16]

Since January 1968, the women had been meeting regularly once a week outside the university at the "Berlin Republican Club." The level of enthusiasm was high. "Hundreds of women came and went. This delight in talking, exchanging ideas! We were inseparable; we sat around together till late at night."[17] In May 1968 the women's working group was renamed the

14 Simone de Beauvoir, *Das andere Geschlecht: Sitte und Sexus der Frau* (Hamburg, 1951); Betty Friedan, *Der Weiblichkeitswahn oder die Selbstbefreiung der Frau* (Reinbek bei Hamburg, 1963); see the bibliography in Jutta Menschik, ed., *Grundlagentexte zur Emanzipation der Frau* (Cologne, 1976).

15 Schmidt-Harzbach, an activist in the student movement, describes this process in an autobiographical essay. She stresses that many women read classic texts of Marxism, e.g., by Alexandra Kollontai, Rosa Luxemburg, Clara Zetkin, August Bebel, Karl Marx, and Friedrich Engels, in addition to the contemporary New Left literature. Schmidt-Harzbach, "Frauen erhebt euch!" 50–7. Frigga Haug, *Frauen-Politiken* (Berlin, 1996). According to Herrad Schenk, the feminist literature and women's movement of the United States began to exert its indisputably significant influence on the German women's movement in the early 1970s. Schenk, *Die feministische Herausforderung,* 89.

16 Schwarzer, *So fing es an!* 15.

17 Helke Sander was one of the most important figures in the Berlin women's movement, as well as a feminist author and filmmaker. The conversations with Sander were recorded and interpreted by Schwarzer. See Schwarzer, *So fing es an!* 13–15.

"Action Council for Women's Liberation" to clarify the relationship to the student movement and the extraparliamentary opposition. The discussions soon crystallized around certain focal points.[18] One important point was discrimination against mothers. Since even the "leftist comrades" left the responsibility for child care, education, and the household to their wives, these women were unable to participate in delegate conferences and other actions of the student movement. At the same time, their work was not valued in any practical sense, nor was it even included in the theoretical plans for social liberation.[19] At first, the women took a practical approach to solving their problems. By taking it upon themselves to set up *Kinderläden* (day-care centers), they created child-care options that put to a practical test the student movement's ideas about antiauthoritarian education. The focus of the substantive discussion became the desire to talk about the relationship between the sexes as a power relationship. The relationship of production to reproduction, of wage labor to domestic and reproductive labor, thus became a central theoretical problem in the coming years. What were the structural causes of discrimination against women and the mechanisms that continually regenerated the power discrepancy between the sexes?[20]

By posing these questions, the women left the context of the theoretical discussion of the student movement. Silva Kontos described the debate in the new women's movement as a simultaneous departure from two dominant traditions of middle-class society: liberalism and the labor movement. Both traditions had developed political programs for women's emancipation that set the tone for the discourse on women's issues up to the end of the 1960s.[21] This process of departure was associated with an attempt to appropriate and "retake" the history of the earlier German women's movement. A generation of women began laboriously to uncover the archives

18 Topics for the eight subject-specific working groups (WG) included: WG 1: the image of women in the press; WG 2: the role of women in the revolution; WG 6: the role of kindergartens and establishment of a kindergarten at the Free University of Berlin; WG 7: antiauthoritarian education, including psychoanalysis of children and government policy toward women and the family; WG 8: emancipation theory. The stated goal of this working group was "to develop a new theory of emancipation to be understood not only as women's emancipation. This theory should explain why a change in the position of women must simultaneously bring a change in society as well."
19 Haug, *Frauen-Politiken,* 179; Schmidt-Harzbach, "Frauen erhebt euch," 52; Ulrike Maria Meinhof, "Die Frauen im SDS," in Elefanten Press and Kristine von Soden, eds., *Hart und zart: Frauenleben 1920–1970* (Berlin, 1968; reprint, Berlin, 1990).
20 Hazel E. Hazel, "Unwissenschaftliche Betrachtungen eines weiblichen Monsters,"*Kursbach* 17 (June 1969): 47–51; Petra von Morstein, "Der Begriff 'Frau,'" *Kursbuch* 17 (June 1969): 52–68; Karin Schrader-Klebert, "Die kulturelle Revolution der Frau," *Kursbuch* 17 (June 1969): 1–46; Giesela Brandt, Johanna Kootz, and Giesela Steppke, *Zur Frauenfrage im Kapitalismus* (Frankfurt am Main, 1973).
21 Silvia Kontos, "Zum Verhältnis von Autonomie und Partizipation," in Barbara Schaeffer-Hegel, ed., *Vater Staat und seine Frauen* (Pfaffenweiler, 1990), 50–63.

and search for the buried and silenced history of the German women's movement, which had been thoroughly expunged from the German social consciousness during the period of National Socialism. In 1968 women had to rediscover completely the history of their own movement. What female historians excavated from archives in the form of texts and arguments was amazing in its variety and persuasiveness.[22] They discovered that a democratic women's movement had existed in Germany for over 120 years and had achieved considerable success by the late 1920s in its battle for women's education, social reforms, and women's suffrage.[23] Although there was an official rejection of Nazi ideology in the Federal Republic of Germany in 1945, and the principle of equal rights for both sexes was adopted in the Basic Law, a conservative view of gender roles remained decisive well into the 1960s.[24] The particular difficulties that this raised for the German women's movement of 1968 in its attempt to discover its own roots have been described in retrospect by many of the women who were involved at the time:

In other words, while we were making history, the others were writing it. And if we didn't know before that they had better archives, we learned it as soon as we went looking for the buried history of the first women's movement, of which they passed on to us only the lie about the so-called "proletarian" and "middle-class" factions of the movement, along with an image of the "suffragettes" that was a scarecrow-like distortion. History is not only the past; it is the future, too. Without history, we are without roots or identity. Without history, we must always start over again from the very beginning, from square one. Which is what we did in 1968 – again.[25]

The two tasks of these women – studying women's history and discovering new issues – soon bore fruit. In September 1968 delegates to the SDS conference in Frankfurt am Main gathered amid considerable media attention. At the conference Helke Sander, the spokeswoman for the Berlin Action Council for Women's Liberation, astonished the predominantly

---

22 The first bibliography on the German women's movement was published by Elisabeth Boedeker, *Marksteine der deutschen Frauenbewegung von ihren Anfängen im 19. Jahrhundert bis zum Neuanfang nach 1945* (Selbstverlag, 1968). See Renate Bookhagen's preface to a reprint of Hedwig Dohm, *Die wissenschaftliche Emanzipation der Frau* (Berlin, 1874; reprint, Berlin, 1976), vii–ix.

23 Ute Gerhard, *Unerhört: Die Geschichte der deutschen Frauenbewegung* (Reinbek bei Hamburg, 1990). For a discussion of sexual reform in the 1920s, see Verena Krieger, *Entscheiden: Was Frauen (und Männer) über den Paragraphen 218 wissen sollten* (Hamburg, 1987); and Rosamarie Nave-Herz, *Die Geschichte der Frauenbewegung in Deutschland* (Hannover, 1989), 55.

24 At first, it was the exception rather than the rule for a woman to enter the workforce, although working was acceptable for women without children or to supplement insufficient household income. Later, it became a more generally important component in the life planning of women. Overall, fewer women worked in the FRG than in the GDR. Friederike Maier, "Zwischen Arbeitsmarkt und Familie: Frauenarbeit in den alten Bundesländern," in Gisela Helwig and Hildegard Maria Nickel, eds., *Frauen in Deutschland 1945–1992* (Bonn, 1993), 262.

25 Schwarzer, *So fing es an!* 8.

male audience with a speech on the problems and experiences that had
been discussed by women in Berlin:

Women are searching for their identity. They cannot find it by participating in campaigns that do not directly address their conflicts. They can only find it when the social conflicts that have been displaced into women's individual private lives are articulated so that women become organized and politicized. Most women are apolitical because politics have always been defined unilaterally and their needs have never been addressed. . . .We cannot solve the societal suppression of women on an individual basis. Thus, we cannot wait until after the revolution because a purely political-economic revolution does not eliminate repression in private life.[26]

The women relatively naively assumed that the Congress would be a forum
"well-disposed toward us" and that this speech would win over the SDS to
the women's cause.[27] The women saw their theoretical task as expanding
the societal concept of the student movement and, thus, as an important
chance for actual, "revolutionary" modernization. They were firmly convinced that the inclusion of women could tap unused potential for political
and social change. Therefore, Helke Sander attempted with her speech at
the Congress to win support for their plan from male SDS comrades. At
the same time, however, she made it unmistakably clear that, if the men in
SDS were unwilling to respond substantively to the women's ideas, they
were no more than an "overinflated counterrevolutionary yeast dough" and
the women would be forced to go their own way. The male executive
committee of the Congress, and the overwhelming majority of the delegates in the hall, failed to understand the women's call and continued with
the agenda. The press interpreted the resulting conflict, which culminated
when one of the male delegates from Berlin threw a tomato, as the women's
protest against their male SDS comrades.[28] The women's issues therefore
appeared in the media primarily as a "battle between the sexes" within the
SDS. The immediate consequence of this conflict was the formation of a
number of new women's groups. The focus of discussion in these groups,
called *Weiberräte* (women's councils), was the discrepancy between the
emancipatory claims of the men and their actual behavior. At the following SDS Congress in Hannover, representatives from eight women's groups
were in attendance.[29]

26 Speech by Helke Sander before the gathering of SDS delegates in Hamburg on September 13, 1968. Speech reprinted in *Frauenjahrbuch,* ed. Frankfurter Frauen, 1 (Frankfurt am Main, 1975), 11–12.
27 See interview with Helke Sander in Schlaeger, ed., *Mein Kopf gehört mir,* 23–36.
28 Meinhof, "Die Frauen im SDS," in Elefanten Press and von Soden, eds., *Hart und zart,* 484.
29 Schenk, *Die feministische Herausforderung,* 87. See also "Geschichte des Frankfurter Weiberrates," *Frauenjahrbuch* 1 (1975): 19–48.

The New Women's Movement

In 1968, the first clear "declaration" of a new women's movement in the Federal Republic took place. The first published texts were on the role of "feminine ideology," the function of marriage, and "love" as the sexual exploitation of women.[30] At first, students set the tone in the emerging women's groups. However, when the student movement ended and the extraparliamentary opposition fell apart after the social-liberal coalition took control of the government in 1969, these groups retreated into theoretical discussion circles or resignation. The new women's movement strode onto the political stage of the Federal Republic demanding elimination of Paragraph 218 and consciously rejecting and violating regulations regarding abortion.

The new women's movement distanced itself from the existing religious, professional, and cultural women's organizations in the Federal Republic. These groups had formed in 1949 a coalition that, since 1969, went by the name of the Deutscher Frauenrat (German Women's Council). Its major member organizations, the rural women, Catholic women's clubs, housewives, attorneys, and others, worked within the existing political parties for "improvement of the position of women" in family, career, workplace, politics, and society.[31] Because the new women's movement criticized the "existing system," there was almost no personal contact between the women's groups formed in the early 1970s and the traditional women's organizations.

The common theme of the new women's groups was the fight for a new abortion law. Inspired by the actions of French women, in June 1971, 374 German women publicly acknowledged in *Stern* magazine having had illegal abortions, and they demanded that the ban on abortions be lifted. This action was spectacular and attracted an enormous amount of attention from the West German public. This "self-incrimination campaign" developed into a coalition of women and women's groups, "Campaign 218," which collected signatures, distributed flyers, and organized a variety of actions. In the spring of 1972, about four hundred women from thirty-five groups in twenty different cities met for the first Federal Women's Congress. The major topics of discussion were self-organization by women, work and

30 See Schrader-Klebert, "Die kulturelle Revolution der Frau"; Heide Berndt, "Kommune und Familie," *Kursbuch* 17 (1969): 1–46. In her essay on the history of the Frankfurter Weiberrat, the author quotes texts by Kate Millett (*Sexus und Herrschaft*), Germaine Greer (*Der weibliche Eunuch*), Juliette Mitchell (*Frauenemanzipation*) in *Frauenjahrbuch* 1 (1975): 40. See also FFBIZ, "Dokumentation zur neuen Frauengeschichte," Loseblattsammlung, Berlin, 1989.
31 Deutscher Frauenrat, *Handbuch deutscher Frauenorganisationen* (Bonn-Bad Godesberg, 1989), 3.

careers, the role of the family in society, and "Campaign 218."[32] Of particular significance for subsequent developments was the discussion of the
reasons and necessity for self-organization of women outside the male-
dominated organizations. "Self-determination through autonomy" became
a key concept of the fresh self-awareness in the new West German women's
movement. It was a focus for experiences with both the men in the "New
Left" and the established parties and women's organizations.[33] Inherent in
the concept was the idea that only through independent organization and
pressure from outside could parties and parliaments be moved to address
and meet women's demands.

Autonomy, the word and the concept, as a form of institutional independence became an important feature of the self-concept of the new
women's movement. How different women and groups put it into practice
varied. While some radicalized the idea over time and fundamentally
rejected any form of cooperation with institutions, parties, or government
organizations, others relativized the principle of autonomy by agreeing on
a case-by-case basis to certain cooperative actions with mixed-gender organizations in order to achieve concrete goals. The situation was more complicated for women who were active within certain institutions such as
labor unions, political parties, or government.[34] Because the new women's
movement declared "autonomy" to be synonymous with feminism, women
within traditional institutions who shared the ideological positions of the
feminist movement were seen as "not really feminist."[35] This caused irritation among some women, as well as verbal exclusion and restriction of

32 Schwarzer, *So fing es an!* 21–31; *Frauenjahrbuch* 1 (1975): 50–75. The women left the Federal
   Women's Congress of March 12–13, 1972, in Frankfurt am Main knowing with certainty that a
   new women's movement existed: "All in all, there is one thing about which there can no longer be
   any doubt after this Congress: we have a German women's movement." Reprinted in *Frauenjahrbuch*
   1 (1975): 37ff.
33 Myra Marx Ferree, "Equality and Autonomy: Feminist Politics in the United States and West Germany," in Mary Fainsod-Katzenstein and Carol McClurg-Mueller, eds., *The Women's Movement of
   the United States and Western Europe* (Philadelphia, 1987), 183; Silvia Kontos, "'Von heute an gibt's
   mein Programm': Zum Verhältnis von Partizipation und Autonomie in der Politik der neuen
   Frauenbewegung," *Forschungsjournal Neue Soziale Bewegungen,* no. 2 (1989): 56–9; Ursula Nienhaus,
   "Autonomie und Frauenprojektbewegung," in Renate Rieger, ed., *Der Widerspenstigen Lähmung?*
   (Frankfurt am Main, 1993), 41–2; Schmidt-Harzbach, "Wer sind wir – woher kommen wir? Zur
   Situation der Frauenbewegung in Berlin (West)," in Arbeitskreis Autonomer Frauenprojekte Berlin,
   ed., *20 Jahre und kein bisschen weiser?* (Bonn, 1992), 132–4.
34 Myra Marx Ferree, "Was heisst Feminismus? Frauenfragen, Frauenbewegungen und feministische
   Identität von Frauen in den neuen Bundesländern," in Christiane Lemke, Virginia Penrose, and Uta
   Ruppert, eds., *Frauenbewegung und Frauenpolitik in Osteuropa* (Frankfurt am Main, 1996), 115.
35 This was perceived as a paradox by American feminists. Ibid. At the same time, it leads to the overarching issue of which women belong to the women's movement. Does the concept of the women's
   movement include only those women who consider themselves autonomous, or does it include all
   women dedicated to feminist thinking, even those who are active in established political institutions? See also Nienhaus, "Autonomie und Frauenprojektbewegung," 45–7.

many women in the established parties, government institutions, and labor unions.[36]

For the time being, however, the program of autonomy inspired the women's movement, as seen in the incipient battle for a new abortion law. It gave birth to institutions such as information and counseling centers for women on issues of contraception, sex education, and abortion, as well as the women's health centers. Over time, these centers came to address a broader spectrum of issues, from the fight against the control of women's bodies by traditional medicine, including psychology, to the conflict over modern genetic and reproductive technologies. These institutions also included the women's centers from which the so-called women's project culture developed.

The autonomous women's groups based their fight against Paragraph 218 on the right of the individual woman to self-determination with regard to her body. They rejected the idea that government authorities had the right to intervene in a woman's personal, individual lifestyle choices. They differed in this respect from the social-liberal coalition government, which was prepared to liberalize abortion law, but based primarily on paternalistic arguments. The law passed by the Bundestag in 1974 contained social aid programs for women aimed at making it easier for them to decide to carry a pregnancy to term, and it permitted abortion in the first trimester in exceptional cases.[37] In 1975, however, the Federal Constitutional Court declared this law unconstitutional.[38] This placed the issue of abortion back on the agenda of the parliament, and in 1976 a new law was passed that was to remain in effect until 1993 in the territory comprising the old Federal Republic. This law required as a precondition for abortion that there be a compelling reason (indication) as well as prior compulsory consultation with a physician.[39] In particular, the rationale of a "general emergency" that this law provided for, often described as a "social" reason, gave the affected women greater latitude in their decision making. Eighty percent of the legal abortions performed in the following years were approved by way of the emergency rationale. But the women in question still had no

---

36 Arbeitskreis Autonomer Frauenprojekte Berlin, ed., *20 Jahre und kein bisschen weiser?;* Renate Rieger, "Frauenprojekte in Ostberlin," in Rieger, ed., *Der Widerspenstigen Lähmung?,* 54–68; Brigitte Runge, "Frauen-Selbsthilfe und Frauen-Projekte," in Christel Farber and Traute Meyer, eds., *Unterm neuen Kleid der Freiheit das Korsett der Einheit* (Berlin, 1992), 173–84; see also Schenk, *Feministische Herausforderung.*

37 The concept on which this law was based was also referred to as a policy of "help, don't penalize."

38 "Urteil des Bundesverfassungsgerichts vom 25.2.1975," *Neue Juristische Wochenschrift,* no. 13 (1975): 576; see also Krieger, *Entscheiden,* 58.

39 The indication ruling did not lift the ban on abortion but instead formulated indications (compelling reasons) that permitted penalty-free abortion.

real right to free choice. In this respect, the new law still did not address the actual intent of the women's movement.[40] This reinforced the conviction of autonomous women's groups that parliamentary work and cooperation with political parties did not ultimately produce the desired results.[41]

The program of autonomy thus comprised not only institutional independence (rejection of affiliation with political parties, critical distance from institutions, and independence from male-dominated standards and organizational and behavioral forms and from men themselves as the actors and conveyors of patriarchal ideology) but also the idea of women's individual self-determination. Therefore, the original experiences of women in 1968 became a theoretical concept and a specific way of life: "Feminism is not just a political conviction. It is a new way of life that we must win for ourselves, step by step. Therefore, we have no finished package to offer. Nothing shall be imposed on women from outside, neither political knowledge nor commitments to other people. Rather, they shall put themselves first, name their own dissatisfactions and work together with other women in similar positions."[42] Most of the new women's groups were therefore constituted as "self-discovery groups," often on the model of American "consciousness-raising groups."[43] In the ideal case, they led to new projects and to a change in the individual and social environment.

In this way, the original idea behind the student movement (social transformation by having the involved parties identify their own interests) was transformed into feminist strategy and politics. The goal of these politics, as Mechthild Cordes recently contended, was a society in which gender differences no longer served as a means of unequally distributing societal opportunities.[44] These organizational forms, which developed from the concept of autonomy, were to reject the authoritarian and hierarchical and be, instead, vertical, egalitarian, and self-determining. Their symbol became the "vertical network," which was contrasted with traditional hierarchical institutions.[45] The new women's movement was particularly successful in three areas: (1) the *Frauenhausbewegung* (women's housing cooperatives), (2) the focus on the issue of sexual violence, and (3) the development

---

40 Eva Maleck-Lewy, *Und wenn ich nun schwanger bin? Frauen zwischen Selbstbestimmung und Bevormundung* (Berlin, 1994), 109.
41 Kontos believes that frustration resulting from the reform of para. 218 led to the radicalization of the German women's movement. Kontos, "Von heute an gibt's mein Programm," 57; see also Claudia Pinl and Marianne Weg, "Institutionelle Folgen der Frauenbewegung: Autonomie oder Institution?" *Forschungsjournal Neue Soziale Bewegungen*, nos. 3–4 (1989): 36–7.
42 Ingrid Schmidt-Harzbach, quoted in Nave-Herz, *Die Geschichte der Frauenbewegung*, 71.
43 Schenk, *Die feministische Herausforderung*, 93.
44 Mechthild Cordes, *Frauenpolitik: Gleichstellung oder Gesellschaftsveränderung?* (Opladen, 1996), 108.
45 Arbeitskreis Autonomer Frauenprojekte Berlin, ed., *20 Jahre und kein bisschen weiser?* 16; Cordes, *Frauenpolitik*, 113.

of an independent women's cultural scene (for example, women's publishing houses and bookstores, women's art, communications and cultural centers, vacation houses, and educational facilities). The movement thereby changed the public discussion in the Federal Republic.

By the end of the 1970s, the limits of the new women's movement started to become more apparent. The absence of an interregional network and reliable structures for influencing the parliamentary process, political parties, and government institutions was being perceived increasingly as a shortcoming. More and more people felt that autonomous structures were inadequate to produce greater gender equality and eliminate discrimination against women.[46] Within the women's movement, this led to a broad discussion of the relationship between autonomy and institution, autonomy and equality. Therefore, in the early 1980s, the women's movement began to expand its arsenal of political forms by exerting increased influence in the political and governmental arena. This was evidenced, for example, by the fact that first the Greens, then the SPD, and finally in October 1996 even the CDU adopted women's quotas to varying degrees.[47] "State feminism" in the form of antidiscrimination legislation, state and local institutionalization of policies of equality, quotas, and the like became a second important element in the fight for equal rights,[48] while the concept of autonomous politics continued to exist, though in modified form.[49]

THE GERMAN DEMOCRATIC REPUBLIC

The year 1968 was of great symbolic and practical political significance for the East German women's movement. It became a key year for identifying the possibility or impossibility of forming and developing social movements in the GDR.

The Political System

The GDR had no autonomous political women's movement comparable to that in the old Federal Republic. This was due primarily to the political

---

46 Cordes, *Frauenpolitik,* 29; Marx Ferree, "Equality and Autonomy" and "Was heisst Feminismus?";
   Pinl and Weg, "Institutionelle Folgen der Frauenbewegung," 43.
47 On the Greens, see Regina Lang, *Frauenquoten: Der einen Freud, der andern Leid* (Bonn, 1989), 76.
   On the SPD, Petra Weis, "Hürdenlauf an die Macht? Politische Partizipation von Frauen in der
   SPD und die Quote," in Eva Maleck-Lewy and Virginia Penrose, eds., *Gefährtinnen der Macht: Politische Partizipation von Frauen im vereinigten Deutschland – eine Zwischenbilanz* (Berlin, 1995), 75. On
   the CDU, see "Bundesparteitag der CDU," *Berliner Zeitung,* Oct. 22, 1996.
48 Cordes, *Frauenpolitik.*
49 Rieger, "Frauenprojekt in Ostberlin"; Maleck-Lewy and Penrose, eds., *Gefährtinnen der Macht;*
   Marx Ferree, "Was heisst Feminismus?"

situation in the GDR. The extensive exclusion of women from political responsibility followed traditional patterns but was modified by the Stalinist influence on the GDR. Although traditional patriarchal conditions became solidified on the political level, there were some considerable socioeconomic and legal changes that benefited women.[50] Political power in the GDR was in the hands of a small group of leaders, the "Politburo of the Central Committee of the German Socialist Unity Party" (Sozialistische Einheitspartei Deutschlands or SED), which had never been legitimated in free elections. No women were full members of the Politbu001o; a few participated in an advisory capacity (only two in 1989). The forty-five government ministers included only one woman, and she was the wife of East German leader Erich Honecker.[51]

This does not adequately describe the position of women in the GDR, however. Over the course of its existence, the GDR undertook a number of reforms that led to improvements in the legal and societal position of women. The first constitution of the GDR in 1949, like the Basic Law of the Federal Republic, established the equality of men and women as a constitutional principle. In contrast to the Federal Republic, however, all laws and regulations that violated this constitutional principle were abolished. The Federal Republic did not take this step until 1957 when it passed the Equal Rights Law. Even then it continued its legal discrimination against women by establishing the *Hausfrauenehe* (a legal state of being in a domestic union) and by its unequal treatment of illegitimate children. The GDR then passed a "Law Governing Women's Rights and the Protection of Mothers and Children" in 1950. The idea behind this law was that equal rights for women required not just formal equal rights but also specific provisions guaranteeing a series of social protections. The new constitution of 1968 made "advancement of women" a binding task for government and society.[52] Beginning in the late 1960s, vocational training and certification was viewed as the key to achieving equal rights and equal opportunities for women.

However, none of this fundamentally changed the political order of the GDR. The central political focus after the building of the wall was modernization of the East German economy. There was a desire to make better use of the existing potential workforce and to place more emphasis on

50 Christina Schenk and Christiane Schindler, "Frauenbewegung in Ostdeutschland – Innenansichten," in Maleck-Lewy and Penrose, eds., *Gefährtinnen der Macht,* 183–201.
51 Gerd Meyer, "Frauen und Parteielite nach dem XI. Parteitag der SED: Gründe und Hypothesen zur Kontinuität der Unterrepräsentation," *Deutschland-Archiv,* no. 12 (1986): 1296–1300.
52 Constitution of the GDR of 1968 and 1974, Article 20.

certification, science, and research. This brought women, in particular, into the field of vision of political leaders, and the government concentrated on integrating them into the labor process. In 1950, they represented 39.8 percent of the workforce, compared to 45 percent in 1960 and 48.3 percent in 1970.[53] This process was based on solid economic, demographic, and social conditions. The GDR's plans for building up an extensive, growing economy could not succeed without including the labor potential of women in the workforce.

Ideologically, policy toward women in the GDR was drawn from the "tradition of the labor movement" and was based on the idea that integrating women into the workforce essentially solved the problem of equal rights.

The program and concrete examples had a patriarchal structure in the sense that the role of women in them was never more than functional, always in relation to some other, higher purpose. They were co-creators of socialism, workers, bearers of children. Their autonomous claims as women to subjectivity, self-actualization and the option of choosing between different lifestyles – independent of the functional requirements of the state – did not fit into this picture.[54]

A public discourse on gender relations was not carried out in the GDR.

Against this backdrop, GDR policy toward women after the 1960s was remarkable in various respects. Although there was an undiminished focus on creating conditions for full employment for women, the unequal distribution of power and resources in favor of men remained unchanged. This created a dilemma that was ultimately unresolvable. The inclusion of women in (certified) vocations created new prospects for individual women. Yet women's options were restricted because they were bound to social tasks and obligations by bearing the sole responsibility for the family and reproductive work imposed on them by society.[55]

In the original plan for women's policy in the GDR, women were to be relieved of "unproductive housework" and family duties by establishment of a comprehensive system of social services. However, due to economic pressures and inadequate political will, this plan was never implemented. A different path was followed. The GDR pushed through the certification, advancement, and integration of women in vocational life and, in 1971, declared that equal rights between the genders had been achieved. This

---

53 Staritz, *Geschichte der DDR*, 231.
54 Irena Dölling, "Gespaltenes Bewusstsein: Frauen- und Männerbilder in der DDR," in Helwig and Nickel, eds., *Frauen in Deutschland*, 29.
55 Jutta Gysi and Dagmar Meyer, "Leitbild: Berufstätige Mutter – DDR-Frauen in Familie, Partnerschaft und Ehe," in Helwig and Nickel, eds., *Frauen in Deutschland*, 140.

officially blocked any further debate over equal rights for women. Further-more, by linking all sociopolitical measures to the woman as mother, tradi-tional gender roles were solidified and the responsibility of women for chil-dren and family was firmly established. At the same time, the legal and social reforms, and the integration of women into the workforce, pro-duced emancipatory effects and gave women a certain external indepen-dence, the manifestation of which is reflected in the high divorce rate and the growing number of single mothers.[56]

Despite the repeated conflicts between the ideological pronouncement of equal rights and the actual living conditions of men and women, the new developments did not lead to revision of the official image of women. The only exception was deletion of Paragraph 218 from the new Criminal Code of the GDR, which took effect on July 1, 1968, and the so-called *Fristenlösung* (a ruling in 1972 that all women would be allowed to abort until the fetus was viable). In doing this, the GDR fulfilled one of the old-est demands of the women's movement. On the issue of abortion, the gov-ernment refused to intervene in the private lives of women, who were per-mitted to choose abortion freely within the first twelve weeks of pregnancy. Abortion was provided free of charge, as were contraceptives. This liberal abortion legislation and the sociopolitical measures to ensure women's place in the workforce contributed to some degree to the "identification of the female citizens of the GDR (especially the youth) with their government."[57] A large majority of the women in the GDR not only accepted the abor-tion law but also considered it a good solution. One of the most important reasons for the development of the women's movement in the FRG there-fore did not exist in the GDR.[58]

Prague 1968 and the East German Public

The "Prague Spring" was an important event in the development of oppo-sition in the GDR and could have been the starting point for an indepen-dent women's movement. In the minds of many people in the GDR, the attempt at democratization in Czechoslovakia and the establishment of

56 Barbara Bertram, Walter Friedrich, and Otmar Kabat vel Job, *Adam & Eva heute* (Leipzig, 1988), 157; Gysi and Meyer, "Leitbild," 147–9.
57 Uta Schlegel, *Politische Einstellungen Ostdeutscher Frauen im Wandel,* Texte zur politischen Bildung, no. 5 (Leipzig, 1993), 11.
58 Maleck-Lewy, *Und wenn ich nun schwanger bin?* 101; Myra Marx Ferree and Eva Maleck-Lewy, "Talking About Women and Wombs: Discourse About Abortion and Reproductive Rights in the GDR During and After the 'Wende,'" paper presented at the conference "Gender and Reproduc-tive Politics in Eastern Europe," Ciocco, Italy, June 1996.

"socialism with a human face" was associated with the hope that a democratization process could be set in motion in their country as well. Based on access to East German archives, it is now evident that there was far more protest and unrest in the GDR than was previously assumed. There was considerable sympathy and support in the GDR for the reform socialists in Prague, not only among intellectuals and artists, but in all strata of GDR society, particularly among youth between the ages of eighteen and twenty-five.[59]

The hope that reform socialism would catch on in other Warsaw Pact countries was shattered by the military intervention in Czechoslovakia and the role played by the GDR leadership. Chairman of the State Council Walter Ulbricht, like his Polish counterpart Gomułka, feared that the reform movement would spill over into the GDR. In his foreign policy, therefore, he supported violent termination of the Czechoslovakian experiment.[60] In its domestic policy, the GDR took severe measures against those who sympathized with the Prague Spring and democratic reform socialists.

It was bitter times for anyone who had flirted with the ideas of the Prague Spring, or who appeared to have done so. Of course, this wave of discipline and intimidation did not assume the same proportions as in Czechoslovakia, where around a third of party members were thrown out of the party and thus lost their career positions. . . . The SED regime had demonstrated that it was capable of nipping any resistance in the bud. In doing so, however, it necessarily destroyed the critical potential that it needed to make the system more flexible and efficient.[61]

Intellectuals and artists in particular criticized and protested the policies of the GDR leadership. After the invasion of Czechoslovakia, thousands of SED members were reprimanded, lost their positions, or were suppressed in other ways.[62]

Under such conditions, no independent political movement for democratization and no autonomous women's movement could develop in the GDR. More and more people, both men and women, began to withdraw

---

59 On the reaction of East Germans to the Prague Spring, see Stefan Wolle, "Die DDR-Bevölkerung und der Prager Frühling," *Aus Politik und Zeitgeschichte* 36 (Aug. 28, 1992): 35–45; Mary Fulbrook, "Popular Discontent and Political Activism in the GDR," *Contemporary European History* 2 (1993): 273; Armin Mitter and Stefan Wolle, *Untergang auf Raten: Unbekannte Kapitel der DDR-Geschichte* (Munich, 1993).

60 On the military invasion and the role of the GDR and other Warsaw Pact states, see Mark Kramer's chapter in this book.

61 Mitter and Wolle, *Untergang auf Raten*, 467, 480.

62 An internal report of the SED refers to 3,358 members who did not support the invasion of Czechoslovakia and were punished. See ibid., 463.

into "niches,"[63] either resigning themselves to the situation or trying out individual solutions to their problems. Under the political conditions of the time in the GDR, it was no longer possible to articulate the idea of democratizing gender relations as a component of democratic development and a prerequisite for a modern interpretation of women's emancipation. That idea did not surface again in the political dialogue until the fall of 1989 with the women's awakening.[64]

Literary Feminism in the GDR

Among the most prominent forerunners and sources of the East German women's movement was the creation of a "literary feminism" associated especially with the work of Christa Wolf, Maxie Wander, Irmtraud Morgner, Brigitte Reimann, and others.[65] Wolf's book *Nachdenken über Christa T.,* which appeared in 1968, and Brigitte Reimann's *Franziska Linkerhand* were the first in a series of works with a feminist orientation which soon came to be known as the women's literature of the GDR.[66] This literature focused on individual women's experiences, viewpoints, and strategies for coping with life.[67] Demands were also articulated in this way. In her book *Guten Morgen, Du Schöne,* which contains interviews with women, Maxie Wander writes:

We should not really be surprised when conflicts in socialist society arise that have stewed in the dark for decades, poisoning human life. We do not become aware of conflicts until we are capable of coping with them. We are all on uncharted territory and are left largely to ourselves. We are looking for new ways of life, in the

63 This term was coined by Günter Gaus to characterize social conditions in the GDR. See Günter Gaus, *Wo Deutschland liegt: Eine Ortsbestimmung* (Hamburg, 1983). In the 1970s, Gaus was the permanent representative of the FRG to the GDR and led a number of treaty negotiations between the two states.
64 UFV and Argument-Frauenredaktion, eds., *Ohne Frauen ist kein Staat zu machen,* 1990, 5–56.
65 See Sonja Hilzinger, *"Als ganzer Mensch zu leben . . .": Emanzipatorische Tendenzen in der neueren Frauenliteratur der DDR* (Frankfurt am Main, 1985). See also Ulrike Enders's detailed review in *Deutschland-Archiv,* 1987, 867–9.
66 Literary scholar Hannelore Scholz sees in Christa Wolf's book the "beginning of a literary and aesthetic women's movement in the GDR." On the utopian dimension of women's demands on life in the literary texts of women writers in the GDR in the 1970s and 1980s, see Hannelore Scholz, "Wir sind auf den ganzen Menschen aus und können ihn nicht finden," in Hanna Behrend and Eva Maleck-Lewy, eds., *Entmännlichung der Utopie: Beiträge zu Utopiediskussion in feministischer Theorie und Praxis* (Berlin, 1991), 74; see also Ilse Nagelschmidt, "Konzeptionelle Überlegungen zur Aufarbeitung von Frauenliteratur der DDR," *Zentrum für Interdisziplinäre Frauenforschung Bulletin* 8 (1994): 56 (special issue entitled *Feministische Annährungen an Literatur und Kunst*).
67 This literature also provides additional impetus for cultural criticism and theory, a sociology of everyday life and education, research on youths, as well as for the questioning of traditional gender images. See Christiane Lemke, *Die Ursachen des Umbruchs 1989: Politische Sozialisation in der ehemaligen DDR* (Opladen, 1991), 252.

private sphere and in society. We cannot emancipate ourselves independent of men, only in interaction with them. Indeed, what we are trying to do is to release ourselves from the old sex roles and achieve human emancipation in general.[68]

In the GDR, literature often served as a substitute for public discussion. In many cases, it addressed issues otherwise subject to a strict taboo.[69] East German women writers followed Western developments in the women's movement with great interest. Christa Wolf said of the West German women's movement that

their paths to self-discovery often involve a retreat into their own gender; it must be difficult for them to encompass all of society in their plans. And yet, how much solidarity they have amongst themselves, how much effort they exert to acknowledge their own situation, how much spontaneity and inventiveness they show in their self-help businesses, how much imagination, how much variety! I cannot believe that we in the GDR have nothing to learn from that.[70]

In this way, Wolf made it clear that, in her opinion, women's policy in the GDR was inadequate. She gave notice that there was an overriding question that needed to be answered, namely, what a humane society should look like.

Women, who have matured through coping with real and significant experiences, are signaling a radical demand: to live as complete human beings, to be allowed to make use of all their senses and capabilities. This demand is a great challenge for a society that, like all communities in this day and age, places myriad constraints on its members, in some cases necessary constraints. At any rate, knowingly or not, society itself has awakened this demand and can no longer satisfy it with plans for the advancement of women, with daycare and child subsidies alone, not even, in my opinion, by appointing more women to those bodies in which the important questions are decided by men, as they are everywhere in this man's world, including in our country.[71]

With these statements, Wolf also gained an audience in West Germany. Her position was adopted there as a programmatic statement and embraced by feminists internationally as well.[72] In the GDR, the thoughts and predictions of Wolf, Maxie Wander, and others found many readers, both

---

68 Maxi Wander, *Guten Morgen, Du Schöne: Protokolle nach Tonband* (1977; reprint, Berlin, 1980), 7.
69 See Meyer, "Frauen und Parteielite," 1318–19.
70 Christa Wolf, "Berührung: Ein Vorwort" to a new edition of Maxi Wander, *Guten Morgen, Du Schöne* (Munich, 1990), 18.
71 Ibid., 20.
72 Ute Gerhard, "Die staatlich institutionalisierte 'Lösung' der Frauenfrage: Zur Geschichte der Geschlechterverhältnisse in der DDR," in Hartmut Kaelble, Jürgen Kocka, and Hartmut Zwahr, eds., *Sozialgeschichte der DDR* (Stuttgart, 1994), 399.

male and female. This literature functioned as a "catalyst for a new critical public discussion."[73]

An independent women's movement came into being in the fall and winter of 1989–90. Literary feminism quite clearly paved the way for it. In the late 1970s and early 1980s, the first nongovernmental women's groups were formed in the GDR as a sign of growing opposition to the ruling power structures. They were formed initially in the context of the East German peace movement, mostly under the auspices of the Protestant Church, the only institution in the GDR that offered shelter to opposition groups and consciously took advantage of the latitude they enjoyed after the suppression of the Prague Spring.[74]

Change and Awakening

Mikhail Gorbachev's assumption of power in the Soviet Union in 1985 also encouraged opposition groups in the GDR. Large portions of the population began to demand changes. However, the "starting point for involvement of women's and lesbian groups – unlike in the old FRG – was not the power struggles of individual women but the disappointing discovery that there was no place in the GDR for critical public discussion of societal realities and that it was not possible or permissible to debate and formulate in public any demands for democratization of society or fundamental reform of the political system."[75] Only about two hundred to three hundred women were involved in women's groups in the 1980s, but the "initiatives and groups were in communication with one another for years and organized meetings and actions; as socializing groups, they could raise sensitivity and stimulate discussion beyond their own memberships."[76]

When Erich Honecker was ousted in the fall of 1989 as party chief and president of the GDR, the significance of these existing groups became evident. In a very short time, a women's movement sprang up throughout

---

73 Christiane Lemke feels that women's literature flowered in the GDR because there was no women's movement there and, therefore, "existing potential conflicts were coped with, and a distinct female identity was articulated, primarily in literature." Lemke, *Die Ursachen des Umbruchs,* 252.

74 Samirah Kenawi, *Frauengruppen in der DDR der 80er Jahren* (Berlin, 1995), 22, 27. Kenawi documents the history of East German women's groups in the most comprehensive collection published to date. On the peace movement in the GDR and on the role of the church, see John Sandford, "The Peace Movement and the Church in the Honecker Years," in G.-J. Glaessner and I. Wallace, eds., *The German Revolution of 1989* (Oxford 1992); Fulbrook, "Popular discontent," 278ff.

75 Schenk and Schindler, "Frauenbewegung in Ostdeutschland," 185.

76 Anne Hampele, "'Arbeite mit, plane mit, regiere mit': Zur politischen Partizipation von Frauen in der DDR," in Helwig and Nickel, eds., *Frauen in Deutschland,* 302. Hampele argues that therefore the groups can be called a "movement." Schenk and Schindler characterize the women's groups as being only the rudiments of a women's movement.

the GDR. Along with other groups, it became one of the driving forces of the new democratization process. Up to that point, developments in the GDR had led right up to the threshold of developing a women's movement, but the movement had not been awakened before due to the repressive political conditions. Like men, women in the GDR wanted fundamental social transformation. For the first time, there was the "possibility of active participation within political organizations or in the form of demonstrations" as well as "the certainty . . . that entrenched structures could be dissolved and the road to far-reaching changes could be opened."[77] The women's declared intention was to propose a feminist reform project both as a corrective influence on male-dominated ideas for democratizing the socialist society and as a statement of the women's own demands, and to implement this reform project by means of independent action and intervention in the political debate.[78]

Of central importance was to voice publicly the view that, despite claims of equality, women in the GDR had largely been mere objects of politics and that the GDR's paternalistic policies on women had never given them the opportunity to represent their own interests as independent political actors. The culmination of this development was the establishment of the Independent Association of Women (Unabhängiger Frauenverband or UFV) on December 3, 1989.[79] Equal participation of women's representatives at the "roundtables," consideration of demands concerning women's equality in the draft constitution developed at the central roundtable, appointment of a UFV representative to a position in the Modrow government, and rejection of an attempt to reconsider existing GDR legislation on abortion demonstrated the political influence and effectiveness of the East German women's movement. Particularly effective was the fight for affirmative action positions at every level of government, for the development of a women's culture (women's projects, bookstores, cafés, etc.), and for the entry into parliament of independent candidates from the women's movement. An important phase in the East German women's movement

---

77 Schenk and Schindler, "Frauenbewegung in Ostdeutschland," 185.
78 See the manifesto of the UFV from Dec. 3, 1989: "Ohne Frauen ist kein Staat zu machen," and the program of the UFV from Feb. 17, 1990, both reprinted in Cordula Kahlau, ed., *Aufbruch: Frauenbewegung in der DDR: Dokumentation* (Munich, 1990), 28–38, 67–72, respectively; see also Bernhard Maleck, *Wolfgang Ullmann: "Ich werde nicht schweigen"* (Berlin, 1991).
79 On December 3, 1989, twelve hundred women from all over the GDR gathered in East Berlin and decided to create a political organization, which was then officially established in February 1990. Anne Hampele characterizes the UFV as a "movement organization." Anne Hampele, "Überlegungen zum Unabhängigen Frauenverband," *Berliner Debatte – Initial: Zeitschrift für sozialwissenschaftlichen Diskurs*, no. 4 (1994): 71–82. In this awakening phase, the UFV was synonymous with the women's movement in the GDR.

ended with the free elections in March 1990. Afterward, the movement broke up into a variety of smaller groups with specific interests, and its political influence rapidly declined.

A key issue in the reunification process of the two German states was the danger that East Germany would be pressured by West German politicians to adopt West German abortion laws. However, this attempt by the government of the old FRG was unsuccessful. They ultimately had to accept the facts that the old GDR law would remain in effect for a transitional period after reunification and that a new law for reunified Germany would have to be worked out. The parliamentary debates on this issue dragged out until 1994 (when the Bundestag passed the current law) and have still not entirely subsided. The focus was on the fight against repression of women's interests by reunification politics, as seen in the displacement of women from the labor market, and the defense of the GDR's more favorable sociopolitical laws.[80]

CONCLUSIONS

The year 1968 was important in the history of both the East and West German women's movements. For the West German women's movement, the process of becoming independent grew out of the 1968 movement. There was great resonance from the public in the ensuing debates regarding Paragraph 218, without much political impact. The debate in the FRG centered on themes of autonomy and equality but not equal rights.

For the East German women's movement, the impossibility of developing as a movement became clear in 1968 with the passage of the new GDR constitution, the introduction of a new criminal code, and the crushing of the Prague Spring. At the same time, however, the emergence of women's literature raised the claim for a feminist redesign of politics and society. The focus of their involvement was on political participation, self-determination, and changing male and female stereotypes. In 1989 the East German women's movement developed the innovative idea of creating an umbrella organization of independent groups whose purpose would be to generate publicity for the situation of women and to coordinate activities of the various women's groups, factions, and projects, thus helping them to increase their political effectiveness.

The East and West German women's movements were born and developed under different social conditions, political situations, and cultural

---

80 Myra Marx Ferree, "'The Time of Chaos Was the Best': Feminist Mobilization and Demobilization in East Germany," *Gender and Society* 8, no. 4 (1994): 614.

environments. Their activists underwent fundamentally different political socialization processes. Prior to German reunification, although there were points of overlap and interaction, the two movements developed largely independently of each other. That includes overlapping issues, which led to joint actions after government unification, such as the fight against Paragraph 218 and joint actions to maintain jobs for women and government-subsidized daycare.

In Germany today, the women's movement is therefore composed of two streams coming from different sources that have difficulties reaching a common vision and perspective for action.[81] Despite numerous, recurrent attempts at collaboration and unification, there is therefore still not (or, better, not yet) a common German women's movement.

81 Ulrike Helwert and Gieslinde Schwarz, *Von Muttis und Emanzen: Feministinnen in Ost- und West-deutschland* (Frankfurt am Main, 1995).

15

1968: A Turning Point in American Race Relations?

MANFRED BERG

I

In pondering the historical significance of a particular year, historians must resist the temptation to consider everything that happened during that year as crucial simply because they have chosen it as the object of their interest. Given this caveat, does the year 1968 qualify as a turning point in American race relations, that is to say, as a particular point in time when certain developments or trends distinctively changed course?

Obviously race relations – a term that then was still universally associated with the relations between white and black Americans – had been in crisis for quite a while before 1968. Since the mid-1950s the African-American civil rights movement had challenged the southern system of white supremacy by legal, political, and nonviolent direct action.[1] The black freedom struggle triggered a countermovement of "massive resistance" among white southerners ranging from obstruction in the U.S. Congress to brutal mob violence against peaceful protesters and murderous terrorism. The violence in the South had compelled the Eisenhower and Kennedy administrations, however reluctantly, to acknowledge at least some federal responsibility for the protection of black civil rights. Despite bitter opposition from southern lawmakers, Congress passed a succession of federal civil

---

1 The literature on the civil rights movement has been burgeoning for many years. For an introduction to the scholarship, see Adam Fairclough, "Historians and the Civil Rights Movement," *Journal of American Studies* 24 (1990): 387–98; Steven F. Lawson, "Freedom Then, Freedom Now: The Historiography of the Civil Rights Movement," *American Historical Review* 96 (1991): 456–71. The most important overviews are Harvard Sitkoff, *The Struggle for Black Equality, 1954–1992*, 2d ed. (New York, 1992); Manning Marable, *Race, Reform, and Rebellion: The Second Reconstruction in Black America, 1945–1990*, 2d ed. (Jackson, Miss., 1991); Robert Weisbrot, *Freedom Bound: A History of America's Civil Rights Movement* (New York, 1990). In addition, see two useful edited collections, Charles W. Eagles, ed., *The Civil Rights Movement in America* (Jackson, Miss., 1986); Armstead L. Robinson and Patricia Sullivan, eds., *New Directions in Civil Rights Studies* (Charlottesville, Va., 1991).

rights bills from the fairly limited Civil Rights Act of 1957 to the sweeping laws of 1964 and 1965, which prohibited racial segregation and discrimination in public facilities and employment and, for all practical purposes, placed the administration of southern elections under federal supervision.[2] The sense of crisis in American race relations was gravely exacerbated and, most important, elevated to the national level by the violent eruption of the black inner-city ghettos in the North, beginning with the Harlem riots of July 1964.[3]

But even if Americans had become used to violent racial conflict during the "long hot summers" of the mid-1960s, few could have failed to realize that the assassination of Martin Luther King Jr. on April 4, 1968, in Memphis, Tennessee, was an event of truly historic proportions. The violent death of America's most prominent proponent of nonviolent social change seemed to have pushed race relations to the very crossroads that many had predicted for some time, including King himself when he had asked in his last book, published in 1967, *Where Do We Go from Here?: Chaos or Community?*[4] President Lyndon B. Johnson and Robert F. Kennedy, brother of the slain president and soon to be victim of political murder himself, pleaded with blacks to heed the martyred leader's commitment to nonviolence despite their understandable anger.[5] But in the eyes of black radicals it was too late. Stokely Carmichael, former director of the Student Nonviolent Coordinating Committee (SNCC) and a leading radical, told "white America" that it had made a serious mistake in killing King because he had been "the one man of our race that this country's older generations, the militants and the revolutionaries and the masses of black people would still listen to."[6] Almost instantly, Carmichael seemed to have been proved right

2 On the "massive resistance" in the white South, see Numan V. Bartley, *The Rise of Massive Resistance: Race and Politics in the South During the 1950s* (Baton Rouge, La., 1969); Neil R. McMillen, *The Citizens' Council: Organized Resistance to the Second Reconstruction, 1954–64,* 2d ed. (Urbana, Ill., 1994). On the civil rights policies of the Eisenhower and Kennedy administrations, see Robert F. Burk, *The Eisenhower Administration and Black Civil Rights* (Knoxville, Tenn., 1984); Mark Stern, *Calculating Visions: Kennedy, Johnson, and Civil Rights* (New Brunswick, N.J., 1992); Hugh Davis Graham, *The Civil Rights Era: Origins and Development of National Policy 1960–1972* (New York, 1990), esp. 27–121, 125–76. On the struggle for black voting rights, see Steven F. Lawson, *Black Ballots: Voting Rights in the South, 1944–1969* (New York, 1976); Steven F. Lawson, *In Pursuit of Power: Southern Blacks and Electoral Politics, 1965–1982* (New York, 1985).
3 William L. O'Neill, *Coming Apart: An Informal History of America in the 1960s* (New York, 1971), 170–8, passim; John Morton Blum, *Years of Discord: American Politics and Society, 1961–1974* (New York, 1991), 252–64; Joe R. Feagin and Harlan Hahn, *Ghetto Revolts: The Politics of Violence in American Cities* (New York, 1973).
4 Martin Luther King Jr., *Where Do We Go from Here?: Chaos or Community?* (New York, 1967).
5 On Kennedy, see Weisbrot, *Freedom Bound,* 268. For Johnson's televised speech, see *The Public Papers of the Presidents: Lyndon B. Johnson, 1963–1968/69* vols (Washington, D.C., 1965–70), 1968–9, book 1: Jan. 1 to June 30, 1968, 493.
6 Quoted in Clayborne Carson, *In Struggle: SNCC and the Black Awakening of the 1960s,* 2d ed. (Cambridge, Mass., 1995), 288.

when riots, especially ferocious in the nation's capital, broke out in 170 cities, leaving forty-three people dead and thousands injured. Even after the unrest had died down, the specter of racial civil war continued to loom. The United States, one political analyst commented, stood "on the threshold of the most critical period in its history since the first shot was fired on Fort Sumter in 1861."[7]

For all the gloomy predictions, King's assassination did not precipitate a race war. Although urban unrest continued on a lower level well into the early 1970s, improved "riot control" by the authorities and a sense of exhaustion among ghetto militants prevented the repetition of disorders comparable to those in the spring of 1968.[8] Nevertheless, in retrospect Martin Luther King's death stands out not only as the premature end of an exceptional individual but also as the convergence of the three principal forces that shaped American race relations during the 1960s. First, it marks the end of the civil rights struggle as a distinctive, activist social movement. Second, the outburst of anger and violence in the wake of the assassination highlights the increasing radicalization of African Americans, which had found its political expression in the rallying cry of "Black Power." Third, the murder of America's foremost civil rights leader, although its exact circumstances have remained controversial, must be seen as an extreme manifestation of a "white backlash" against black demands for equality and opportunity. In order to assess how American race relations changed in the late 1960s, we must discuss the interplay and legacies of these three forces.

Viewed from an international perspective, the violent racial conflicts in America contributed to the sense of worldwide upheaval that made 1968 such a momentous year. Black radicals, in particular, tried to make the international connection by linking their fight to the "worldwide struggle being waged by the poor and oppressed against imperialism and the world's chief imperialist, the United States of America." Beyond the exchange of solidarity addresses and the granting of exile, however, there is no evidence for actual systematic cooperation between black revolutionaries and their comrades in the Third World.[9] To be sure, racism, along with capitalism, imperialism, fascism, and colonialism, became an ideological key target of

7 Chuck Stone, *Black Political Power in America* (Indianapolis, 1968), 247. On the riots, see Feagin and Hahn, *Ghetto Revolts*, 105.
8 Feagin and Hahn, *Ghetto Revolts*, 105–8.
9 "The Black Panther Party Stands for Revolutionary Solidarity," in Philip S. Foner, ed., *The Black Panthers Speak*, 2d ed. (New York, 1995), quotation on 220; "To the Courageous Vietnamese People, Commemorating the Death of Ho Chi Minh," ibid., 32. In 1970 the Black Panthers offered the Vietcong black volunteers, but the offer was politely turned down. See letter of Aug. 29, 1970, by Huey P. Newton to the National Liberation Front of South Vietnam and the reply of Oct. 31, 1970,

leftist protest all over the world during the late 1960s, but nowhere else did the race issue play such a prominent role as it did in the United States. Neither the internationalist rhetoric of the Left nor the paranoid conspiracy theories of the Right should obscure the basically indigenous character and origins of the racial violence that shattered America during this period. Rather than resulting from or being influenced by international developments, it reflected the legacy of centuries of slavery, segregation, and racial discrimination.

II

Since the early 1950s the struggle for African-American civil rights had been carried out on two levels. On the local level, indigenous movements began challenging racial segregation and discrimination by civil disobedience and nonviolent mass protests. On the national level, a coalition of black organizations, foremost among them the National Association for the Advancement of Colored People (NAACP), and white liberal supporters lobbied for civil rights legislation and sought to induce the federal government to assume an active role in fighting racism.[10] Most historians agree that the civil rights movement as both a local and a national movement had run its course by the end of the 1960s and that the death of Martin Luther King marks a clear and visible break.[11] Although the civil rights coalition scored its last major legislative victory in the aftermath of King's death with the Civil Rights Act of 1968, which prohibited racial discrimination in housing and made interference with other persons' civil rights a federal crime, enforcement of the bill remained weak, and it was obvious that Congress considered the issue of civil rights legislation settled.[12]

The movement's decline began when it had achieved its basic goals of doing away with legally mandated segregation and disfranchisement in the

by Nguyen Thi Dinh, in Clyde Taylor, ed., *Vietnam and Black America: An Anthology of Protest and Resistance* (Garden City, N.Y., 1973), 290–5.

10 There is no scholarly history of the NAACP and its strategies available at this time. See my own forthcoming book *"The Ticket to Freedom": The National Association for the Advancement of Colored People and the Struggle for African-American Voting Rights, 1909–1970.*

11 On King, see the most recent biographies by David J. Garrow, *Bearing the Cross: Martin Luther King, Jr., and the Southern Christian Leadership Conference* (New York, 1986); Taylor Branch, *Parting the Waters: America in the King Years 1954–63* (New York, 1988); and Adam Fairclough, *To Redeem the Soul of America: The Southern Christian Leadership Conference and Martin Luther King, Jr.* (Athens, Ga., 1987).

12 On the Civil Rights Act of 1968, see Graham, *Civil Rights Era*, 255–77; see also Johnson's memoirs, *The Vantage Point: Perspectives of the Presidency, 1963–1969* (New York, 1971), 176–8.

South and turned to tackling broader issues of de facto segregation and economic inequality in the nation at large. The ideological and tactical consensus unraveled and the moral drama surrounding earlier campaigns waned. A mutually reinforcing process of black radicalization and white backlash alienated support from both the public and the federal government. The failure of the "Poor People's March on Washington" in the wake of King's death, led by his successors in the Southern Christian Leadership Conference (SCLC), testified to the loss of momentum.[13]

Interpretations of this process and of the movement's historical record vary widely, however. Historian J. Mills Thornton has argued that the civil rights movement ended because its enemies had been defeated, and that it simply lost the support of the American people when it subsequently embraced "the collectivist ideals of egalitarian socialism."[14] At the other end of the argument, Marxist historian Manning Marable has deplored the movement's inability to transform the struggle for civil rights into a struggle against racism and capitalism that went beyond limited gains for a small black elite.[15]

Historians who emphasize progress concede that the liberal reforms of the 1960s did not fulfill many hopes for a better life but point to the dramatic legal and social change that occurred in American race relations, especially in the South, during this period – "a stunning achievement of liberation," as Hugh Graham has called it.[16] The blame for the diminishing of goodwill between the races is equally assigned to both white racism and the demagoguery of black militants. In contrast, historians focusing on the lack of progress have primarily indicted the unwillingness of the white majority to consider any meaningful redistribution of wealth and power beyond granting mere formal equality of opportunity. Black radicals are criticized not for confronting mainstream values but for indulging in self-serving sectarianism that only weakened a struggle already under heavy attack from the forces of backlash.[17]

If economic demands had replaced civil rights as the key factor in American race relations during the second half of the 1960s, the protagonists of

---

13 Fairclough, *To Redeem the Soul of America,* 386–9. On the decline of the movement, see Doug McAdam, *Political Process and the Development of Black Insurgency, 1930–1970* (Chicago, 1982), 181–229.

14 J. Mills Thornton, "Commentary," in Charles W. Eagles, ed., *The Civil Rights Movement in America* (Jackson, Miss., 1986), 151.

15 Marable, *Race, Reform, and Rebellion,* 149–54, 226–30.

16 Graham, *Civil Rights Era,* 452; see also Weisbrot, *Freedom Bound,* 288–317.

17 Sitkoff, *The Struggle for Black Equality,* 210–35; Carson, "Civil Rights Movement," 229–31; William H. Chafe, "One Struggle Ends, Another Begins," in Charles W. Eagles, ed., *The Civil Rights Movement in America* (Jackson, Miss., 1986), 126–48; Jack M. Bloom, *Class, Race, and the Civil Rights Movement* (Bloomington, Ind., 1987), 222–4.

liberal reform could claim that they had indeed made a determined effort to address the problem of poverty on which President Johnson had declared "unconditional war" in January 1964. Trying to create what LBJ dubbed the "Great Society," the Johnson administration proposed and enacted the most comprehensive social reforms since the New Deal, including job training for disadvantaged youth, federal assistance to education, medical insurance for the poor and the elderly, and housing subsidies and urban renewal.[18] In combination with a large tax cut and a stunning overall prosperity of the American economy, the "War on Poverty" seemed to yield impressive results. Between 1963 and 1969 the proportion of blacks and whites below the poverty level declined by roughly 40 percent, while unemployment for both races decreased by the same margin. The median income of black men rose by 30 percent, twice as fast as that of white men, and black women almost closed the racial income gap by advancing to more than 90 percent of the median income of white women. Such gains, however, must not eclipse the fact that in comparative perspective African Americans remained heavily disadvantaged in both absolute and relative terms. Despite a drop from a staggering 51 percent in 1963, about 32 percent of all blacks continued to live below the poverty level in 1969. Their unemployment rate was still more than twice as high as that for whites.[19]

Even though the Great Society was based on overall growth rather than redistribution of wealth, progress appeared to be on its way for African Americans as well. For traditional civil rights organizations like the NAACP and the National Urban League (NUL), which had lived through decades of tokenism and compromise with racism from a succession of presidents, LBJ and the Great Society seemed a godsend. In the 1964 presidential campaign the NAACP, for all intents and purposes, had abandoned its long-standing policy of nonpartisanship and helped bring about a record registration and turnout of black voters. Although Johnson received 61 percent of the total popular vote, his share in predominantly black districts exceeded 90 percent. NAACP Executive Director Roy Wilkins enthusiastically cabled to the president: "The People have not spoken; they have shouted."[20]

---

18 Johnson's declaration of "unconditional war on poverty," in his State of the Union Message of Jan. 8, 1964, *The Public Papers of the Presidents: Lyndon B. Johnson,* 1964, 1:114; "Great Society" speech at the University of Michigan, Ann Arbor, May 22, 1964, ibid., 704–7. For an overview and discussion of the War on Poverty programs, see Allen J. Matusow, *The Unraveling of America: A History of Liberalism in the 1960s* (New York, 1984), 217–71. See also Diane B. Kunz's chapter in this book.

19 For the development of unemployment rates and poverty, see Jessie Carney Smith and Carrell Peterson Horton, eds., *Historical Statistics of Black America,* 2 vols. (New York, 1995), 1:992–3, 1101–2. On the development and comparison of income trends, see Reynolds Farley and Walter R. Allen, *The Color Line and the Quality of Life in America* (New York, 1987), 283–315, esp. 293–300.

20 Wilkins's telegram of Nov. 5, 1964, Records of the National Association for the Advancement of Colored People, Library of Congress, Manuscript Division, Washington, D.C., group III, series A,

Wilkins and NUL Director Whitney Young subsequently became Johnson's closest black allies, whom the Texan courted and prodded with his inimitable rustic charm. To ensure the administration's commitment to civil rights and social reforms, the leaders of the NAACP and the NUL were prepared even to support its policy on Vietnam, echoing the president's assurance that the United States could afford both "guns and butter," and otherwise claiming that the war in Southeast Asia and the civil rights struggle in America were "separate issues."[21]

Neither assertion proved correct. The Vietnam War depleted the War on Poverty of its financial resources and gravely exacerbated the widening chasm between the moderate and the radical wings of the civil rights movement. As early as 1965, SNCC had called upon young blacks to resist fighting "other colored people in Vietnam, so that the white American can get richer." While established civil rights leaders like Wilkins reasoned that black Americans could not afford "to tinker with patriotism," young militants came to see Vietnam in the context of a worldwide anticolonialist revolution of which the black struggle in America was part and parcel.[22] Martin Luther King had also registered his concerns early on, but for some time had avoided breaking openly with the administration, hoping it might come to a peaceful solution. In April 1967, however, America's best-known civil rights leader came out with a forceful indictment of American involvement in Vietnam, accusing his government of being "the greatest purveyor of violence in the world today."[23] King's attacks, predictably, infuriated the White House, which took it as final proof that he had come under communist influence, and drew sharp rebuttals from black leaders eager to reassure their standing with the administration.[24]

box 175 (hereafter NAACP III A 175). For the NAACP strategy during the 1964 campaign and the election results, see Henry Lee Moon, "How We Voted and Why," *The Crisis,* 72, Jan. 1965, 27–31.

21 See, e.g., LBJ's state of the union address of Jan. 12, 1966, and Wilkins's congratulatory telegram of Jan. 13, 1966: *The Public Papers of the Presidents: Lyndon B. Johnson,* 1966, 1:3; NAACP IV A 35. On the NAACP's policy toward the Vietnam War, see Manfred Berg, "Guns, Butter, and Civil Rights: The National Association for the Advancement of Colored People and the Vietnam War, 1964–1968," in David K. Adams and Cornelis van Minnen, eds., *Aspects of War in American History* (Keele, 1997), 213–38.

22 "Mississippi Negroes Being Urged to Dodge Draft," *New York Times,* July 31, 1965, copy in NAACP III A 232; Roy Wilkins, "Negroes and the Draft," Roy Wilkins Column (RWC) of Aug. 29, 1965, Roy Wilkins papers, Library of Congress, Manuscript Division, Washington, D.C., box 39.

23 King's speech of Apr. 4, 1967, at New York City's Riverside Church is printed in James Melvin Washington, ed., *A Testament of Hope: The Essential Writings and Speeches of Martin Luther King, Jr.* (San Francisco, 1991), 233. On the evolution of King's position on Vietnam, see Garrow, *Bearing the Cross,* 540–77, passim; Fairclough, *To Redeem the Soul of America,* 333–55.

24 For the reaction to King's speech, see Garrow, *Bearing the Cross,* 553–55; Resolution of the NAACP Board of Directors, Apr. 10, 1967, NAACP IV A 10; RWC of Apr. 15, 1967, "Dr. King's New Role," Wilkins papers, box 39.

Early in 1968, however, it became evident that there were not enough
guns or butter available to win either the war in Indochina or the war on
poverty. In January the Vietcong's Tet Offensive led to a dramatic loss of
public confidence in the war effort. The next month the National Advisory Commission on Civil Disorders, established by Johnson in July 1967
to study the causes of the racial riots and to make recommendations to prevent their recurrence, published its report. The commission, named after
its chairman, Illinois Governor Otto Kerner, included, among others, New
York's liberal Republican mayor, John V. Lindsay, the police chief of
Atlanta, representatives of big business and labor, Massachusetts Senator
Edward Brooke, the only African-American member of the Senate, and
NAACP leader Wilkins. Criticized as the "responsible" establishment by
both black and white radicals upon its appointment, the commission issued
a scathing indictment of "white racism," which it held "essentially responsible for the explosive mixture which has been accumulating in our cities
since the end of World War II." The American nation was "moving toward
two societies, one black, one white – separate and unequal."[25] Yet for all its
drastic language, the 600-page report in essence epitomized the spirit and
approach of 1960s liberalism. It was based on the vision of a unified and
integrated nation, and it proposed a social contract according to which
mainstream society had to pay for peace, while black insurgents had to
repudiate violence if they wanted change: "The vital needs of the nation
must be met; hard choices must be made, and, if necessary, new taxes
enacted. Violence cannot build a better society. . . . The community cannot – and will not – tolerate coercion and mob rule." Calling for "unprecedented levels of funding and performance" in new social programs, the
commission specifically asked the federal government to create two million
new jobs both in the private and public sectors within three years, to establish a national standard of public assistance above the poverty level, and to
build six million new housing units for low-income families within five
years. Warning against "indiscriminate and excessive use of force" to quell
unrest, the commission recommended the reform of local law enforcement
in order to deter and punish rioting effectively.[26]

The Kerner Report amplified the prevailing impression that American
race relations were headed toward a crossroads. A month before his death,
Martin Luther King predicted that to ignore its recommendations would
be to permit the country to sink into a "nightmarish racial doomsday."[27]

25 National Advisory Commission on Civil Disorders, *Report* (New York, 1968), esp. the summary,
   1–29, quotations 1 and 10.
26 Ibid., 2, 17–19, 24, 26, 28.
27 King's congratulatory telegram to Roy Wilkins, Mar. 4, 1968, NAACP IV A 35.

But the political and economic support for a reform effort of the kind and magnitude that the report demanded had long since eroded. President Johnson acknowledged the "extremely close agreement between the commission's proposals and the administration's program," but considered it totally unrealistic that Congress, which was demanding deep cuts in social spending, would ever appropriate the estimated costs of $30 billion for its implementation. LBJ remembered vividly how House conservatives had ridiculed his Rat Extermination and Control Act of 1967 as the "civil rats bill."[28] In putting the blame on Congress, Johnson, of course, conveniently glossed over the pivotal role that his war policy had played in destroying his dream of a Great Society.

The inconclusive fate of the Kerner Report testified to the exhaustion of liberalism in the late 1960s. The Great Society, long denounced by conservatives as "federal extremism" threatening liberty, had also come under massive attack from the Left, which rejected its "bureaucratic welfarism" that primarily served corporate interests and made the poor even more dependent.[29] The notion that money could buy racial peace and integration had become particularly questionable. Neither the explosion of the ghettos nor the rise of black nationalism could be explained as simple functions of socioeconomic conditions. Although the Kerner Commission rightly deplored the disproportionate unemployment and horrendous housing problems of the black ghetto, these predicaments had existed for a long time. Actually, as some observers pointed out, the white flight to the suburbs had somewhat improved housing choices for urban blacks. Moreover, African Americans living in rural areas were even more severely affected by poverty than were black residents in the central cities.[30]

III

If the American public was no stranger to racial violence and its social collaterals, the way it got the message in the 1960s was new and unsettling. Just as war had never been so close before the "television war" in Vietnam,

---

28 See Johnson, *Vantage Point,* 172–3, on his reaction to the Kerner Report, and 84–5, on the Rat Control Act.

29 See the Republican platform for the 1964 presidential election, Arthur M. Schlesinger Jr., ed., *History of American Presidential Elections,* 10 vols. (New York, 1985), 9:3634–5. For a New Left critique, see the 1966 article by Tom Hayden, "Welfare Liberalism and Social Change," in Allan M. Winkler, ed., *The Recent Past: Readings on America Since World War II* (New York, 1989), 162–8.

30 Charles Abrams, "The Housing Problem and the Negro," in Talcott Parsons and Kenneth B. Clark, eds., *The Negro American* (Boston, 1965), 512–24. In 1968, 54.6 percent of rural blacks were living below the poverty level, compared to 26 percent in central cities and 28.3 percent in suburban areas; see *Historical Statistics of Black America,* 1:1009.

the images of "civil war" in American inner cities conveyed a sense of national crisis that had never before been associated with the race issue. When southern segregationists unleashed brutal terror against peaceful civil rights marchers earlier in the decade, Americans watched in horror but could persuade themselves that this was a problem of backward "rednecks" in Dixie. When the national capital was burning in 1968 and the marines had to defend the White House against black rioters, nobody could deny that this affected the nation as a whole. However, television images do not create uniform and unambiguous reactions among viewers. What specific remedies were to be employed – more social reform or tougher law enforcement – remained a volatile and contested political issue.

Not surprisingly, the causes and consequences of the ghetto riots were extremely controversial. The Congress of Racial Equality (CORE), a civil rights group that had recently repudiated integration and nonviolence, greeted the "hot summer" of 1967 as the "beginning of the Black Revolution." The Black Panthers, the most famous of the militant fringe groups, also welcomed the rebellion of the masses, but, in the typical vein of the self-styled revolutionary vanguard, chided them for "handling the resistance incorrectly." Instead of the "sporadic, short-lived, and costly" riots, it hoped to educate blacks in proper "guerrilla warfare."[31] White conservatives eagerly echoed these spurious claims, blaming the unrest on agitators. If evidence for a "conspiracy" could not be found, as the Kerner Commission had stated, the lack of respect for law and order seemed a sufficient explanation and uncompromising repression the proper solution for the race riots.[32]

Liberals interpreted the ghetto disorders as outbursts of frustration rooted in socioeconomic deprivation. The Detroit riots of 1967, the nation's worst in terms of casualties and damage, were characterized by "a spirit of carefree nihilism," according to the Kerner Report.[33] However, the political implications of the riots should not be overlooked. Not only did they have an immediate impact on city and state authorities, and on the federal government, they were also less random and "blind" than they appeared. As the Kerner Report acknowledged, violence and looting were primarily

---

31 "A Black Manifesto – CORE," July 31, 1967, copy in NAACP IV A 43; on CORE, see August Meier and Elliott Rudwick, *CORE: A Study in the Civil Rights Movement, 1942–1968* (Urbana, Ill., 1975); Huey P. Newton, "The Correct Handling of a Revolution," in Foner, *Black Panthers Speak,* 41.

32 American Independent Party platform for the 1968 presidential elections, in Schlesinger, ed., *History of American Presidential Elections,* 9:3800; National Advisory Commission on Civil Disorders, *Report,* 9.

33 National Advisory Commission on Civil Disorders, *Report,* 4.

directed "against local symbols of white American society, authority and property" – especially the police and the businesses of absentee merchants.[34] The dichotomy between "constructive" civil disobedience and "destructive" riots, on which representatives of the civil rights movement understandably insisted, tended to obscure that both were manifestations of protest aimed at creating political disruption to highlight grievances and to force authorities to negotiate.[35] However, both also emanated from different social and political environments that were not exchangeable. As Martin Luther King and the SCLC had experienced during their 1966 open housing campaign in Chicago, the nonviolent ethics and tactics, so successful in the South, could not easily be transplanted to the ghetto where collective violence was part and parcel of youth culture.[36] In its riot profiles the Kerner Commission aptly described the peculiar political attitude formed in the ghetto:

The typical rioter was a teenager or young adult, a lifelong resident of the city where he rioted . . . somewhat better educated than his nonrioting Negro neighbor . . . usually underemployed or employed in a menial job. He was proud of his race, extremely hostile to both whites and middle-class Negroes and, although informed about politics, highly distrustful of the political system.[37]

This sounded like good news for black radicals who had gradually renounced both nonviolence and the goal of integration and replaced it with the demand for Black Power. Although not new, the phrase immediately caught on with both young black activists and the American public at large when SNCC leader Carmichael popularized it during a civil rights march in Mississippi in June of 1966.[38] The media were quick to equate Black Power with violence, revolution, and "reverse racism," charges echoed by moderate civil rights leaders who feared that the slogan would alienate white supporters and fuel the racist backlash. At the NAACP convention in 1966, Roy Wilkins denounced it as "antiwhite power . . . a reverse Mississippi, a reverse Hitler, a reverse Ku Klux Klan."[39] Under Wilkins's firm

---

34 Ibid., 6.
35 For an interpretation of the riots that emphasizes their political dimension, see Feagin and Hahn, *Ghetto Revolts*, 31–55.
36 On the SCLC's 1966 Chicago campaign, see James R. Ralph, *Northern Protest: Martin Luther King, Jr., Chicago and the Civil Rights Movement* (Cambridge, Mass., 1993), esp. 93–5, on the issue of gangs and nonviolence; Fairclough, *To Redeem the Soul of America*, 279–307, esp. 288–9.
37 National Advisory Commission on Civil Disorders, *Report*, 7.
38 On the Meredith march and the emergence of the "Black Power" slogan, see Carson, *In Struggle*, 207–11.
39 "Roy Wilkins Warns NAACP of Extremists," unidentified newspaper clipping, NAACP IV A 16. For the preceding debates over SNCC's adoption of black nationalism, see also "Racist Label Rejected by SNCC Head," *Washington Post*, May 30, 1966, NAACP IV A 50; RWC of June 4, 1966, "SNCC's New Road," Wilkins papers, box 39.

leadership the NAACP remained steadfast in its commitment to integration, while SNCC and CORE eventually embraced separatist programs
and excluded white members. King and the SCLC were also not happy
with Black Power because the term implied a departure from integration
and nonviolence. However, King realized that it was more than just a fanciful slogan and reflected a genuine and mounting anger within the black
community.[40]

Black Power never represented a clear political or philosophical meaning. In its "pluralist" version, it espoused "community control" of businesses, schools, and law enforcement, as well as the building of independent black political organizations. Because "pluralists" continued to
acknowledge the framework of American society, they were considered
moderate in comparison to black nationalists. "Nationalists" again were
subdivided among territorial separatists, anticapitalist revolutionaries, and
Afrocentrist culturalists.[41] Although many of its advocates borrowed heavily from Marxist terminology, the reception of Marxism proper was limited
because Black Power clearly assigned theoretical and political priority to
race rather than class.[42]

For all the ideological and strategic differences within the Black Power
movement, its proponents basically agreed that African Americans had to
fight for their own political, economic, and cultural empowerment regardless of the approval of whites. In their view, the main enemies were no
longer southern segregationists who denied blacks an equal place in the
American system, but the system itself, its white liberal protagonists and
their black allies. The cause of civil rights was gratuitously pronounced
irrelevant, and the threat of violent race war became a standard line in
every interview of H. "Rap" Brown, Carmichael's successor as chairman of
SNCC and the media's favorite black bogeyman.[43] The Black Panthers'

---

40 On the adoption of separatism by SNCC and CORE, see Carson, *In Struggle*, 236–43, passim;
    Meier and Rudwick, *CORE*, 409–31. On King's position toward "Black Power," see his 1967
    "Black Power Defined," in Washington, *A Testament of Hope*, 303–13; Fairclough, *To Redeem the
    Soul of America*, 309–31.
41 For the ideological distinctions between pluralists and nationalists, see William L. Van Deburg, *New
    Day in Babylon: The Black Power Movement and American Culture, 1965–1975* (Chicago, 1992), 112–91.
    The most important programmatic text on "Black Power," albeit in the "pluralist" fashion, is Stokely
    Carmichael and Charles V. Hamilton, *Black Power: The Politics of Liberation in America* (New York,
    1967).
42 For a Marxist critique of "Black Power," see Marable, *Race, Reform, and Rebellion*, 96–9.
43 See the *New York Times Magazine*, Sept. 28, 1969, reprinted as Martin Arnold, "There Is No Rest
    for Roy Wilkins," in August Meier, John Bracey, and Elliott Rudwick, eds., *Black Protest in the Six-
    ties*, 2d ed. (New York, 1991), 325–38, 328–9; Weiss, *Whitney Young*, 175. For the repudiation of
    the civil rights cause, see "A Black Manifesto – CORE," July 31, 1967, NAACP IV A 43. On
    "Rap" Brown, see Carson, *In Struggle*, 252–7.

paramilitary outfit and boisterous talk of guerrilla warfare were rarely vindicated by action but attracted the clandestine and sometimes deadly attention of the FBI's "Counterintelligence Program," which aimed to destroy radical civil rights leaders and militant "Black Powerites" alike.[44]

The conflict between black demands for "community control" and white liberals was played out dramatically in 1968 during the New York City teachers' strike over the dismissal of several white teachers in the Ocean Hill–Brownsville school district, an impoverished and virtually all-black and Puerto Rican neighborhood in Brooklyn. The complicated story of the yearlong confrontation between a white, well-organized, and heavily Jewish teachers' union and a predominantly black school board of ghetto residents cannot be told here at length.[45] The Ocean Hill school district was part of an experiment, started in the fall of 1967, to decentralize New York's absurdly bureaucratic school system and to give more power to parents and teachers – a widely accepted objective that did not even touch on the explosive issue of school desegregation. Before long, however, the project evolved into a prolonged and disastrous tug-of-war between the newly elected local school board and the United Federation of Teachers (UFT) over the right to appoint, transfer, and dismiss teachers and principals from the district. In its exercise of community control, the school board frequently ignored legal and administrative rules, and teachers were intimidated and sometimes assaulted by students and radical activists. The teachers' union, for its part, showed little regard for the special needs and interests of the Ocean Hill community and single-mindedly insisted on the enforcement of labor rights. In October 1968 the confrontation culminated in a citywide teachers' strike, which lasted for five weeks and ended with an almost complete victory of the union. The Ocean Hill school board was suspended and the decentralization experiment effectively ended.

The Ocean Hill affair is noteworthy for several reasons. First, the legitimate concerns of poor blacks and Puerto Ricans to improve their schools and to have a say in the education of their children was, to some extent, instrumentalized by militants who equated community control with the imposition of their own views and aims, regardless of legal considerations or established procedures and, if necessary, by threat of force. The demand

---

44 On the – often illegal – FBI policy toward the civil rights movement and black radicalism, see the well-documented study by Kenneth O'Reilly, *"Racial Matters": The FBI's Secret File on Black America, 1960–1972* (New York, 1989), esp. 261–324. For the Panthers' rhetoric on violence, see Foner, *Black Panthers Speak*, 19–20, passim.

45 For the following, see Martin Mayer, "The Full and Sometimes Surprising Story of Ocean Hill, the Teachers' Union and the Teacher Strikes of 1968," in Meier, Bracey, and Rudwick, *Black Protest in the Sixties*, 169–229; O'Neill, *Coming Apart*, 183–7.

that community control had to mean the establishment of black enclaves where "white" laws and authority were effectively suspended, however, was totally unacceptable even to the most sympathetic liberals. At the same time, the outcome of the Ocean Hill standoff also showed the limits of radical influence in the ghetto. Despite widespread fears, the dissolution of the local school board did not trigger a riot.

Second, the conflict pitted black interests against labor interests that had been considered basically congenial since the mid-1930s when the American labor movement had rid itself of its traditional racism. Ironically, the New York UFT had been particularly supportive of black civil rights, its leader had marched with King in Selma and worked for the desegregation of New York City schools.[46] But when professional interests and the power of the union were at stake, black demands for community control were perceived as hostile and fought off with determination. The enormous public support that the teachers' strike enjoyed underscored the notion that whites increasingly saw black demands for power as a direct attack on their own interests.

Third, the high proportion of Jewish teachers in the UFT and among those dismissed by the Ocean Hill school board provoked ugly overtones of anti-Semitism on the part of some blacks.[47] Whether these incidents were deliberately exaggerated or not, they further shattered the notion that African Americans and Jews were natural allies in the struggle against bigotry, an idea cherished since the early days of the NAACP. Anti-Semitic rhetoric, to be sure, had been a staple tenet of Black Muslim ideology, and Malcolm X had not refrained from casual indulgence in anti-Semitic slurs. In the public view, however, this had been overshadowed by the close cooperation between blacks and Jews in the civil rights movement.[48] With the rise of Black Power, anti-Semitic rantings became a way for black militants to express their contempt for and to break with white liberals and the civil rights establishment.

By 1968 it was obvious that Black Power had struck a strong chord among many mainstream African Americans. At its annual convention, even the NAACP passed a resolution that endorsed Black Power and defined it as the "control of economic, educational, and political institu-

---

46 Mayer, "The Full and Sometimes Surprising Story of Ocean Hill," 227–8.
47 On this aspect of the Ocean Hill conflict, see Jonathan Kaufman, *Broken Alliance: The Turbulent Times Between Blacks and Jews in America,* 2d ed. (New York, 1995), 139–64.
48 See, e.g., Peter Goldman, *The Death and Life of Malcolm X,* 2d ed. (Urbana, Ill., 1979), 14–5. To Malcolm X the NAACP was a "Jewish organization" because it had a Jewish president. See Gertrude Samuels, "Two Ways: Black Muslim and NAACP," in Meier, Bracey, and Rudwick, *Black Protest in the Sixties* (New York, 1991), 40.

tions within the black community." NAACP leader Wilkins and his NUL colleague, Whitney Young, both spoke at the CORE convention, held under the banner of "Black Nationalism – CORE's philosophy for survival." Whereas Wilkins made it perfectly clear that the NAACP would never support racial separatism, Young paid his respects to "those who choose segregated living."[49] If established civil rights leaders wanted to demonstrate that they were not out of touch with the times, they had a point. Surveys among middle-class African Americans showed that 59 percent approved of the idea of Black Power, and 18 percent even supported a separate black nation. Fifty percent thought the riots had been useful, whereas 33 percent believed violence would also be necessary in the future.[50] These data, however, reflected disillusionment with white America's commitment to racial change more than genuine political radicalization. The civil rights groups that had embraced separatist programs and renounced nonviolence, most important among them being SNCC and CORE, were already in steep decline, while the NAACP and the NUL managed to preserve their organizational base. In fact, the NAACP gained a net of twenty thousand members between 1965 and 1969.[51]

IV

Black and white liberals alike were increasingly haunted by the specter of a backlash. Historian C. Vann Woodward worried if the Second Reconstruction, as he had coined the civil rights struggle, could suffer the same fate as the First Reconstruction, which gradually unraveled after the North abandoned black civil rights for the sake of national reconciliation.[52] The term "backlash," as it was used in the second half of the 1960s, referred to a growing resentment against black demands for equality and opportunity outside the South where racism was not legally sanctioned, but in many informal ways no less firmly entrenched than below the Mason-Dixon Line. Whereas the "massive resistance" of southern segregationists slowly

49 *Washington Post,* "The New Orthodoxy," July 10, 1968; "Wilkins Opposes Black Separatism," *Washington Post,* July 6, 1968; speech by Whitney Young before CORE convention, NAACP resolution quoted in July 6, 1968, all in NAACP IV A 43.
50 See the opinion polls in *Historical Statistics of Black America,* 2:1259.
51 On the decline of SNCC and CORE, see Carson, *In Struggle,* 287–98; Meier and Rudwick, *CORE,* 409–31. The NAACP membership grew from roughly 440,000 to 460,000, before plummeting by 100,000 in 1970 because of doubling of membership fees. See Martin N. Marger, "Social Movement Organizations and the Response to Environmental Change: The NAACP, 1960–1973," *Social Problems* 32 (1984): 23–4.
52 See his 1967 essay, "What Happened to the Civil Rights Movement," reprinted in C. Vann Woodward, *The Burden of Southern History* (Baton Rouge, La., 1993), 167–86.

gave way after 1965 to a grudging compliance with the civil rights laws and various Supreme Court decisions, opposition to the desegregation of schools and residential areas mounted in the North.

Northern hostility toward blacks was hardly new. Cities like Chicago and Detroit had a long history of racial violence incited by competition for jobs and decent housing. During the open housing marches through Chicago's white working-class neighborhoods in 1966, King and the SCLC encountered violent hatred not unlike that experienced in Selma, Alabama, the preceding year.[53] The infamous white backlash of the 1960s, however, was primarily political in nature. The dramatic confrontations between nonviolent blacks and brutal white supremacists during the first half of the decade had convinced a majority of Americans that the racial caste system of the South was a national embarrassment that had to end. With the implementation of civil rights and social welfare legislation in 1964–5, however, many whites began to view black protests with rising impatience. Disenchantment ran especially high among ethnic blue-collar whites in the urban north who feared that black gains would come at their expense. The congressional elections of 1966 saw a massive defection of this group from the Democratic Party, which lost over forty seats in the House and three in the Senate.[54]

The political champion of white backlash was Alabama Governor George C. Wallace, one of the most ardent antagonists of the civil rights movement, who in 1963 had vowed to uphold "segregation forever."[55] The following year he made a surprisingly strong showing in the Democratic presidential primaries winning 34 percent of the vote in Wisconsin, 30 percent in Indiana, and 43 percent in Maryland before dropping out of the race he had only tentatively entered.[56] In 1968, a well-organized Wallace launched the most successful third-party presidential bid since 1924, transforming race into a potentially decisive election issue. His American Inde-

---

53 Arnold R. Hirsch, "Massive Resistance in the Urban North: Trumbull Park, Chicago, 1953–1966," *Journal of American History* 82 (1995): 522–50; Thomas J. Sugrue, "Crabgrass-Roots Politics: Race, Rights, and the Reaction Against Liberalism in the Urban North, 1940–1964," *Journal of American History* 82 (1995): 551–78; Ralph, *Northern Protest,* 114–30; Fairclough, *To Redeem the Soul of America,* 279–309.

54 For the political implications of the backlash, see McAdam, *Political Process,* 192–5, 214–16; Blum, *Years of Discord,* 267–70.

55 On George Wallace, see the recent biography by Dan T. Carter, *The Politics of Rage: George Wallace, the Origins of the New Conservatism, and the Transformation of American Politics* (New York: 1995); see also his assessment of Wallace's impact on the political history of the United States: Dan T. Carter, "Legacy of Rage: George Wallace and the Transformation of American Politics," *Journal of Southern History* 62 (1996): 3–26.

56 All election results are given according to Robert A. Diamond, ed., *Congressional Quarterly's Guide to U.S. Elections* (Washington, D.C., 1985), 414–15.

pendent Party qualified for the ballot in all fifty states, and his aggressive "law and order" rhetoric resonated strongly among many Americans frightened by racial and political violence. Two months before the elections, polls reported Wallace's approval rating at more than 20 percent.[57] The Alabamian owed his appeal largely to his skillful adaptation of traditional southern populism to a national audience. Combining racism, albeit in a slightly coded language, and concern for the common (white) people, he posed as the mouthpiece of all hard-working, patriotic Americans whose values were mocked by unkempt protesters and whose freedom was encroached on by liberal eggheads trying to mandate social change.

Although Wallace never stood a chance of winning the presidency, his campaign had an important, perhaps even a decisive, impact on the 1968 elections. The American Independent ticket carried five states of the Deep South and polled 13.5 percent of the popular vote nationwide. Wallace's strong showing among the northern and midwestern white ethnic working class chipped away at a cornerstone of the Democratic electoral coalition and gave slim pluralities to Republican nominee Richard M. Nixon in Illinois, Missouri, New Jersey, Ohio, and Wisconsin – all of which Johnson had swept in 1964. Nixon beat Vice President Hubert Humphrey by a razor-thin plurality of the popular vote but had a comfortable lead in the electoral college. The Republican candidate had also catered to the "forgotten Americans" and to the resentment of white southerners against federal meddling in "states' rights," so the combined 57 percent of the total vote that he and Wallace received seemed to indicate the magnitude of the white backlash. Indeed, voters were sharply divided along racial lines. Whereas nine out of ten blacks cast their ballot for the Democratic candidate, less than 40 percent of whites had picked Humphrey.[58]

The importance of the backlash factor for both the outcome and the consequences of the 1968 elections must not be overestimated, however. Wallace supporters were indeed primarily motivated by racism and the perceived threat from black radicalism. The core of the Wallace constituency outside the South consisted of white working-class men between the ages of eighteen and thirty-five – a mirror image of the Black Power movement in terms of age, class, and gender.[59] But the outcome of the elections can hardly be attributed to backlash voters focused on race. Rather, it reflected

57 Blum, *Years of Discord*, 310–11.
58 *Congressional Quarterly's Guide to U.S. Elections*, 461–2. For an overview of the campaign and an analysis of the elections, see David S. Broder, "Election of 1968," in Schlesinger, ed., *History of American Presidential Elections*, 9:3705–52.
59 See Carter, "Legacy of Rage," 11.

overall disappointment with the liberal agenda of the Johnson administration. As Allen Matusow has observed, by 1968 the promises to manage the economy, solve the nagging problems of race and poverty, and keep America at peace had been broken.[60] Moreover, LBJ's landslide victory four years earlier, which had given him a mandate for civil rights and social reform, had taken place under highly exceptional circumstances. Johnson had been able to sell his vision in reverence for his martyred predecessor, the economy was surging, American involvement in Vietnam was still invisible, and the moral urgency of the civil rights issue was undeniable. Moreover, the Republicans nominated an archconservative candidate who frightened the public with irresponsible talk concerning the use of nuclear weapons. In comparison to Nixon's narrow defeat to John F. Kennedy in 1960, Barry Goldwater lost about seven million Republican votes.[61] Even without Vietnam, the race riots, and white backlash, it is likely that many of these voters would have returned to the Republican fold. Rather than representing a dramatic reversal of ideological and political loyalties, the outcome of the 1968 elections suggests that the backlash basically occurred among those voters who had never been staunch supporters of civil rights legislation in the first place but had merely accepted it as a temporary necessity. As soon as they perceived it as a threat to their own interests, they turned to conservatives or demagogues like Wallace.

But the racist appeal always remained limited. When the AFL-CIO and other major unions launched a vigorous pro-Humphrey campaign in the fall of 1968 to educate workers about Wallace's alleged hostility to organized labor, this did much to shore up traditional loyalties, albeit not enough to secure Humphrey's election.[62] Perhaps even more important, the Democrats did not try to placate potential Wallace voters in their own ranks by abandoning the cause of civil rights. Their nominee, Hubert Humphrey, was a veteran hero of the civil rights coalition since his bold pro–civil rights speech at the 1948 Democratic national convention. The convention seated an interracial delegation from Mississippi, making good on a promise given four years earlier when the regular segregationist state party had prevailed over the interracial Mississippi Freedom Democratic Party. The party's platform proudly cited the civil rights laws passed during the Johnson administration, including the open housing bill, and endorsed

60 Matusow, *Unraveling of America,* 395; see also Alan Brinkley's chapter in this book.
61 *Congressional Quarterly's Guide of U.S. Elections,* 460–1; John Bartlow Martin, "Election of 1964," in Schlesinger, ed., *History of American Presidential Elections,* 9:3565–94. In contrast to Brinkley's chapter in this book, I think that the 1960 election, rather than the one in 1964, provides the more appropriate comparative reference for the outcome of the 1968 elections.
62 Broder, "Election of 1968," 3745–6.

the recommendations of the Kerner Report.[63] If advocacy of black rights had become a liability, Democratic Party leaders were willing to accept it. Although vilified by black radicals, liberals by and large did not turn their backs on civil rights. The major foundations and other large donors dramatically increased their contributions to the NAACP and the NUL during the late 1960s in order to strengthen the moderate wing of the movement.[64]

Moreover, the civil rights coalition in Congress also held firm after Richard Nixon became president. His nominations of conservative southerners to the Supreme Court twice failed, as did his administration's attempts to dilute the stipulations of the Voting Rights Act when it came up for extension in 1970.[65] From the perspective of the civil rights movement, the new administration looked like a far cry from the happy days of Lyndon Johnson. The NAACP was extremely critical of both Nixon's intentions and his performance, accusing him of openly joining "with the enemies of black people."[66] The president's courtship of the white South, however, could easily obscure the fact that his administration's civil rights policies were highly ambivalent and in some respects astounding. While it actively opposed the busing of schoolchildren for the purpose of educational desegregation, the proportion of black children attending segregated schools in the South plummeted from 68 percent to 8 percent between 1968 and 1972, a lower figure than for the rest of the nation. Even more surprising, it was the Nixon administration that first enacted federally mandated racial quotas in employment.[67]

Whether Nixon's civil rights record outweighs those of his predecessors, as historian Joan Hoff recently argued, or whether these changes occurred

63 Humphrey's 1948 speech in Schlesinger, ed., *History of American Presidential Elections,* 8:3184–6; on the seating of Mississippi delegation, see Broder, "Election of 1968," 3734; on the Democratic Platform of 1968, see Schlesinger, ed., *History of American Presidential Elections,* 9:3770–1.

64 Herbert H. Haines, "Black Radicalization and the Funding of Civil Rights: 1957–1970," *Social Problems* 32 (1984): 31–43.

65 On the legislative struggle for the Voting Rights Act in 1970, see Steven F. Lawson, *In Pursuit of Power: Southern Blacks and Electoral Politics, 1962–1982* (New York, 1985), 121–57; Graham, *Civil Rights Era,* 346–65.

66 On the clashes between the NAACP and the Nixon administration that culminated during the 1972 annual convention, see "Civil Rights During the Nixon Administration, 1969–1974," Library of Congress, Manuscript Division, pt. 1: the White House Files, reel 4, frames 215–46, esp. the speeches by NAACP Chairman Bishop Spottswood, 234–46, and Labor Director Herbert Hill, 222 (quotation). See also numerous attacks on the Nixon administration by Roy Wilkins in his weekly column. See, e.g., RWC of Nov. 29, 1969, "A Haynesworth Parallel," Wilkins papers, box 40; RWC of Mar. 4, 1970, "Not So Benign," ibid.; RWC of Nov. 20, 1971, untitled, ibid., box 8.

67 For a detailed account of the civil rights policies of the Nixon administration, see Graham, *Civil Rights Era,* 301–449; John Robert Greene, *The Limits of Power: The Nixon and Ford Administrations* (Bloomington, Ind., 1992), 36–47, on busing and school desegregation.

largely as a result of forces beyond his control and contrary to his intentions cannot be discussed here in detail.[68] Clearly, Nixon's personal and political affinities lay with those whites, in the North and in the South, who opposed "forced" integration of schools, neighborhoods, and the workplace. But facing a Democratic majority in Congress, the liberal wing of the Republican Party, a federal judiciary unwilling to turn back the clock, and the growing strength of the black vote, the Nixon administration was hardly in a position to wage an all-out fight against the gains African Americans had made during the 1960s, even if it had wanted to do so. In his reelection bid, Nixon predictably focused on the Wallace voters who again gave the Alabamian their support in the 1972 Democratic primaries, but an assassination attempt by a mentally disturbed maverick in May left Wallace paralyzed. As it turned out, the backlash vote hardly mattered, since Nixon trounced Democrat George McGovern, his "radical" opponent, carrying every state except Massachusetts and the District of Columbia. Given the near eclipse of all other political issues by the Watergate scandal after 1972, it makes little sense to speculate how Nixon would have used his electoral mandate in the field of civil rights. But by the end of his first term, despite the president's cool attitude toward blacks and constant fears about white backlash, the Second Reconstruction had undoubtedly been consolidated.[69]

V

In his famous last sermon on April 3, 1968, the eve of his death, Martin Luther King told a mesmerized audience that he was not concerned about his personal fate because God had allowed him to go to the mountaintop and see the promised land: "I may not get there with you. But I want you to know tonight, that we, as a people, will get to the promised land."[70] The biblical allegory of the Israelites' escape from Egypt, a familiar theme of black religious rhetoric, conveyed the image of African Americans as a common people, following a common trajectory to a common goal. As we have seen, by 1968 this notion had become increasingly tenuous. During slavery the promised land had meant freedom from bondage; under the oppressive caste system of segregation and white supremacy it had been

---

68 Joan Hoff, *Nixon Reconsidered* (New York, 1994), 77–114, 113. For a view that stresses Nixon's "southern strategy," see Weisbrot, *Freedom Bound*, 278–87; Blum, *Years of Discord*, 332–41.
69 Marable, *Race, Reform, and Rebellion*, 131, assumes that without Watergate, repression against black radicals would have been stepped up. For the consolidation argument, see Graham, *Civil Rights Era*, 445–9.
70 "I see the Promised Land," in Washington, *A Testament of Hope*, 279–86, 286.

"first-class citizenship" in a society in which people, in King's famous dream, are "not judged by the color of their skin but by the content of their character."[71] At the time of his death, however, African Americans no longer held a common vision of where the promised land lay and how to get there.

Although it had lost its momentum as a mass movement, the civil rights movement did not disappear after 1968. The Urban League, the NAACP, and other moderate groups continued to work for black interests within the framework of the American legal and political system. Many civil rights activists made the transition from protest to politics, most prominent among them King's SCLC co-worker Jesse Jackson who twice ran for the Democratic presidential nomination in the 1980s.[72] Black voter registration soared in former hard-core racist states such as Mississippi, where in 1964 a mere 7 percent of eligible blacks had been registered, compared to more than 75 percent in 1982. Between 1970 and 1982 the number of black elected officials increased from 1,469 to 5,160 nationwide, with 3,140 of them holding office in the South. In 1968 the Congressional Black Caucus had five members in the House and one in the Senate; in 1994 it counted forty representatives and one senator.[73]

The right to vote did not, however, bring about the far-reaching empowerment that civil rights activists had expected. Instead, the electoral constellation of 1968 has basically been perpetuated in national politics. African-American voters are the single most loyal and ideologically liberal Democratic constituency, whereas the Republican Party has followed Nixon's "southern strategy" and reestablished itself in the South as the party of white conservatives.[74] In the conservative political environment of the mid-1990s with its "Republican Revolution," widely perceived as hostile to their interests, black voters have little to bargain for in supporting moderate Democrats.

Political inclusion also has not translated into economic equality and integration. The statistics of misery that document the significant disadvantages of many blacks in income, housing, health care, job opportunities, and the devastating impact of drugs and violence on the social fabric

71 "I Have a Dream," ibid., 219.
72 See Katherine Tate, *From Protest to Politics: The New Black Voters in American Elections,* 2d ed. (Cambridge, Mass., 1994), 137–48.
73 Cf. Lawson, *In Pursuit of Power,* 297 (registration); for the numbers of black elected officials, see Chandler Davidson, ed., *Minority Vote Dilution* (Washington, D.C., 1984), 278–81; Juan Williams, "Blacked Out in the Newt Congress," *Washington Post,* Nov. 20, 1994, C1 and 4.
74 On the political loyalties and ideological orientation of black voters, see Tate, *From Protest to Politics,* 50–74. On the revival of the two-party system in the South, see Earl Black and Merle Black, *Politics and Society in the South* (Cambridge, 1987), 259–316.

of much of black America need not be repeated here. The dismal living conditions of the so-called black underclass have even fanned suspicions of a deliberate genocidal "plan" against African Americans, while conservative critics view these conditions as the result of cultural pathologies within the black community itself.[75] Black liberals decry the persistence of racism, but they also emphasize that change has to come from within. At any rate, a return to 1960s-style solutions appears completely unrealistic. Much of the Kerner Report may still read as a basically accurate description of the black ghetto in the 1990s, but its proposal of wealth redistribution through increased taxation is inconceivable today when "tax breaks for the middle class" is the mantra of American politics. Yet riots also remain a possibility, as the city of Los Angeles experienced in 1992.

Certainly, not everything went from bad to worse. The removal of racial barriers has fostered the development of a viable black middle class.[76] Ironically, its success is often taken as proof that African Americans have overcome past discrimination and that special remedies are no longer needed. Affirmative action is seen as a violation of the American individualist creed that the civil rights movement itself had heeded in its quest for a "color-blind" society. This goal can only be achieved, as conservative political scientist Abigail Thernstrom has emphatically argued, by delivering "the message that, black or white, rich or poor, with effort and discipline the chances are good you can make it. America is a land of opportunity. It's a message of hope and it is even true."[77]

Whether America really has become a color-blind society is, of course, highly debatable. There is also no consensus that it should be. In contrast to the abortive political movement, black cultural nationalism, espoused by the Black Power movement, has flourished in the African-American community and has exerted an important influence on the rise of today's multiculturalism, which stresses diversity and group consciousness.[78] Claims for the recognition of a distinct African-American culture, something considered radical and separatist in the 1960s, are now fairly mainstream. School

---

75 For a recent overview of relevant statistics, see the National Urban League, *The State of Black America*, ed. Billy J. Tidwell (New York, 1994), 213–36. Marable, *Race, Reform, and Rebellion*, 192–7, 206–13. Marable appears to consider the existence of a "Plan" thinkable. In *The End of Racism: Principles for a Multiracial Society* (New York, 1995), Dinesh D'Souza argues that indigenous cultural deficiencies, not external racism, account for the plight of the black underclass.

76 See Graham, *Civil Rights Era*, 452–4.

77 Abigail Thernstrom, "A Class Backwards Idea: Why Affirmative Action for the Needy Won't Work," *Washington Post*, June 11, 1995, C1–2. For a defense of affirmative action, see Roger Wilkins, "Racism Has Its Privileges: The Case for Affirmative Action," *The Nation*, Mar. 27, 1995, 409–16.

78 Van Deburg, *New Day in Babylon*, 40–62, 306–9.

integration, the most controversial issue of the entire civil rights era, is no longer a priority for African Americans who are more concerned with the quality of education than with the racial balance within schools.[79]

The legacy of Black Power is perhaps most visible today in the idealized memory of Malcolm X, who has become the hero of young blacks trying to express racial pride. The Black Muslim spokesman had undoubtedly been the most articulate critic of the integrationist thrust of the civil rights movement in the early 1960s and became a powerful intellectual influence on Black Powerites after he was murdered in 1965, allegedly by other Black Muslims.[80] Ironically, the Nation of Islam, which Malcolm X left in 1964 because of its authoritarianism and lack of political vision, has now become the strongest voice of radical black nationalism. The Nation of Islam and its enigmatic leader, Louis Farrakhan, stunned white America with their enormously successful "Million Man March" in October 1995. Few commentators have failed to point out the sharp contrast between the inclusive message of the March on Washington in 1963 and the Million Man March, which excluded not only whites but also women. The highly esoteric religious teachings of the Nation of Islam preach the superiority of the black race over "the white devil," and its rabid anti-Semitism has acquired considerable notoriety. However, its social message of self-improvement, discipline, and black capitalism is basically a conservative one, and Muslim vigilantes have gained much respect among blacks for fighting drugs in the ghetto. Rather than as a wholesale endorsement of the Nation of Islam and its doctrines, the Million Man March should be seen as a manifestation of racial pride and solidarity among a minority that continues to view itself, with good reason, as the prime target of racism and discrimination in the United States.

Although it is strongly denounced in public discourse, racism remains a potent social and political force. Hate crimes against African Americans are much more common than usually assumed, and the rise of militant fringe groups carries with it strong antiblack overtones. In political discourses about crime and welfare, race is an omnipresent subtext. George Wallace himself has repudiated his past and apologized to blacks, but his legacy lingers on. In the early 1990s, David Duke, a former leader of the Ku Klux Klan, came close to winning races for U.S. senator and governor in Louisiana on a fairly open racist message. Duke received a majority of

79 Sitkoff, *The Struggle for Black Equality,* 224; Nat Henthoff, "Segregation Forever?" *Washington Post,* Dec. 23, 1995, A17.
80 Malcom X, with the assistance of Alex Hailey, *The Autobiography of Malcolm X* (New York, 1965); Van Deburg, *New Day in Babylon,* 1–10.

white votes and was defeated only by a record turnout of blacks, united with upper-class whites.[81] In a less racially pronounced way, right-wing politicians, such as Oliver North and Patrick Buchanan, have tried to mobilize the "angry white males" – men who feel victimized by "reverse discrimination."

To argue, as historian Dan T. Carter has recently, that Wallace set the tone for a "continuing subliminal manipulation of racial issues" that reflects a "general debasement of the culture of American politics," however, seems a little overblown.[82] American conservatives certainly make no secret of their favoring the interests of the white middle class over those of the black underclass, but they are very different from the race baiters of the past, and old-style racial bigotry is no longer a winning electoral strategy. Moreover, Bill Clinton's 1992 revival of the traditional Democratic coalition has shown that it is always possible to appeal successfully to African Americans and the much-vilified white working class at the same time.[83]

Since 1968, the legacy of the African-American civil rights struggle has been firmly incorporated into American culture and politics. Of course, symbolic recognition like Black History Month and the commemoration of Martin Luther King Jr.'s birthday as a national holiday can always be dismissed as tokenism. What is more important, perhaps, is that the civil rights movement has become the model for numerous other groups and causes, including women, Hispanic Americans, Native Americans, and gays and lesbians. This so-called Rights Revolution has, as Hugh Graham has demonstrated, thoroughly transformed the American regulatory state, creating networks of bureaucracies and clienteles that have become integral parts of the legal and political system.[84] Neither the egalitarian and "colorblind" society that liberals had hoped for in the 1960s nor the far-reaching visions of black liberation and self-determination harbored by radicals have been achieved during the past thirty years, but both concepts have contributed to the fundamental changes in the history of American race relations. At the inevitable risk of oversimplification, we may conclude that the year 1968 marks the threshold when the seemingly clear-cut civil rights issues of the 1960s began to evolve into the infinitely more complex world of today's multiculturalism.

81 On the Duke campaigns, see Adam Fairclough, *Race and Democracy: The Civil Rights Struggle in Louisiana, 1915–1972* (Athens, Ga., 1995), 463–77.
82 See Carter, "Legacy of Rage," 24.
83 Tate, *From Protest to Politics,* 181–209.
84 Graham, *Civil Rights Era,* esp. 454–76.

16

The Revival of Holocaust Awareness in West Germany, Israel, and the United States

HAROLD MARCUSE

All the protest movements of 1968 shared a concern with legitimacy. When legitimacy cannot be based on metaphysical arguments, it is commonly derived from interpretations of history. In 1968 two major historical experiences, Nazism and the Holocaust, were wielded as symbolic weapons. Both contributed to, and were shaped by, the events of that watershed year.

This chapter discusses the role of Holocaust consciousness in 1968 in West Germany and compares it with that in two other countries, Israel and the United States. West Germany was the only successor state identified with the crimes of the Third Reich;[1] its rebellious youth demanded a clear accounting for the past. Israel, whose legitimacy derived in part from its identification with the victims of the Holocaust, was suddenly transformed into a conqueror after the 1967 Six-Day War. And the United States was the country that had liberated Europe in 1944–5 but during the Vietnam War suddenly found itself accused of Nazi-like atrocities. Only in West Germany did rising awareness of the Holocaust help to precipitate the conflicts of 1968; that recovery of knowledge began to take place in the late 1950s.

THE WEST GERMAN BACKGROUND

By the mid-1950s, the horrors of the Third Reich were almost completely excluded from public discussion in West Germany.[2] Within the next ten

---

1 By identifying themselves as resisters and victims of Hitler, East Germany and Austria had succeeded in dissociating themselves from the crimes of the Third Reich.
2 See Robert G. Moeller, "War Stories: The Search for a Usable Past in the Federal Republic of Germany," *American Historical Review* 101, no. 4 (Oct. 1996): 108–48; and pt. 2 of Harold Marcuse, *Remembering Dachau: Forgetting Genocide* (Cambridge, 1998).

years, however, the situation was transformed. Several important incidents coincided with the adolescence of the generation of 1968.

The first was the "Anne Frank wave," which began with the republication of her diary in 1955. Within five years, seven hundred thousand copies were sold, making it the best-selling paperback in West German history. By February 1960, a theater adaptation had been performed 2,150 times for 1.75 million viewers, and the 1959 film version had already been seen by almost 4.5 million people.[3] In 1958, a collection of testimonies relating Anne's deportation to Auschwitz and her death from typhus at Bergen-Belsen also became a best-seller and was adapted as a radio play that reached a large audience.[4]

In 1957 Alain Resnais's short, stark documentary *Night and Fog* brought scenes from the concentration camps back into the movie houses of West Germany. Discussed on television and used for instructional purposes in schools, *Night and Fog* presented the first graphic depiction of the workings of the camps and of the techniques of mass murder used by the Nazis since the end of the first Nuremberg Trial, in 1946.[5]

An event of longer-term significance occurred in 1958 with the establishment of the Ludwigsburg Central Office for the Pursuit of National Socialist Crimes of Violence, a national clearing house dedicated to bringing Nazi perpetrators to justice.[6] The first major trial in 1958–9, in which two exceptionally sadistic SS sergeants were convicted of sixty-seven and forty-six individual murders and on many counts of manslaughter, respectively, was made into a film and distributed to school suppliers in some parts of Germany.[7]

A fourth episode linked the Holocaust even more directly with West Germany's present. Between Christmas 1959 and the end of January 1960, a

---

3 Ulrich Brochhagen, *Nach Nürnberg: Vergangenheitsbewältigung und Westintegration in der Ära Adenauer* (Hamburg, 1994), 434, n. 70; also Alvin Rosenfeld, "Popularization and Memory: The Case of Anne Frank," in Peter Hayes, ed., *Lessons and Legacies* (Evanston, Ill., 1991), 243–78.

4 Ernst Schnabel, *Anne Frank: Spur eines Kindes* (Frankfurt am Main, 1958), translated as *Anne Frank: A Portrait in Courage* by R. and C. Winston (New York, 1958).

5 Karl Korn, "Nacht und Nebel," *Frankfurter Allgemeine Zeitung*, Apr. 13, 1956. See also *Die Zeit*, Mar. 7, 1957, and the teacher's guide by Günter Moltmann, *Der Dokumentarfilm Nacht und Nebel* (Hamburg, 1957; reprint, Düsseldorf, 1960). For a general discussion of the film, see Walter Euchner, "Unterdrückte Vergangenheitsbewältigung: Motive der Filmpolitik in der Ära Adenauer," in Rainer Eisfeld and Ingo Müller, eds., *Gegen Barbarei: Essays Robert Kempner zu Ehren* (Frankfurt am Main, 1989), 346–59, 347–8.

6 The office was created after a former mass murderer attempted to sue for his reinstatement as a police officer. See Reinhard Henkys, *Die nationalsozialistischen Gewaltverbrechen: Geschichte und Gericht* (Stuttgart, 1964), 196–7, and Peter Steinbach, *Nationalsozialistische Gewaltverbrechen: Die Diskussion in der deutschen Öffentlichkeit nach 1945* (Berlin, 1981), 46ff.

7 Ralph Giordano, *Hier fliegen keine Schmetterlinge: Zwei Dokumentarfilme* (Hamburg, 1961). The trial proceedings were published in Hendrik George Van Dam and Ralph Giordano, eds., *KZ-Verbrechen vor deutschen Gerichten: Dokumente aus den Prozessen,* 2 vols. (Frankfurt am Main, 1961; reprint, Frankfurt am Main, 1966), 1: 151–510.

wave of anti-Semitic vandalism, partially supported by East German agitators, tarnished Bonn's carefully established distancing from the Nazi past.[8]
The vandalism prompted official investigations of history textbooks and curricula, the publication of new textbooks, and increased pedagogical attention to the process of "mastering the past" (*Bewältigung der Vergangenheit*).[9]

In addition to formal history instruction and the recollections of their
parents, young West Germans learned about the Nazi period from the mass
media, which now included television. In the 1950s, magazines such as
Stern and *Quick* had found praiseworthy elements in some Nazi leaders,
had downplayed Nazi atrocities, and had discredited attempts to draw
lessons from the past. But that changed dramatically by circa 1960.[10]

In the early 1960s an accusatory literature by Germans too young to
have been complicit in the Nazi regime emerged. It included Christian
Geissler's *Sins of the Fathers* (1960) and Gudrun Tempel's *Germany: An Indictment of My People* (1963). Hermann Eich, although a member of the generation that had supported the Nazi regime, recognized the anger of the
younger generation. He admitted, "It is no use quoting the Allied bombing of Dresden [to them]. Dresden is the end of a chain whose links we
ourselves forged."[11]

The trial of Adolf Eichmann in Jerusalem in 1961 electrified West Germany.[12] The Israeli prosecutor, in order to avert the danger of exonerating

8 See the government's "White Book" on the incidents: Germany, Federal Government, ed., *The Antisemitic and Nazi Incidents from 25 December 1959 Until 28 January 1960* (Bonn, 1960). For a less tendentious contemporary portrayal, see Peter Schönbach, *Reaktionen auf die Antisemitische Welle im Winter 1959–1960* (Frankfurt am Main, 1961). On the East German agitators, whose exact role remains unclear, see Michael Wolffsohn, *Die Deutschland-Akte: Juden und Deutsche in Ost und West: Tatsachen und Legenden* (Munich, 1995), 18–27; and Werner Bergmann, *Antisemitismus in öffentlichen Konflikten* (Frankfurt am Main, 1997), 245–6.

9 See, e.g., the publication of Theodor Adorno's famous essay "Was bedeutet: Aufarbeitung der Ver-gangenheit," in the educators' journal *Staat, Erziehung, Gesellschaft* 5, no. 1 (1960): 3ff. For later analyses, see Klaus Köhle, "Die Vergangenheitsbewältigung – Geschichte eines Problems," in Raimund Baumgärtner, Helmut Beilner, and Klaus Köhle, *Das Dritte Reich* (Munich, 1971), 9–30; Karl Borcherding, *Wege und Ziele politischer Bildung in Deutschland: Eine Materialsammlung zur Entwick-lung der politischen Bildung in den Schulen 1871–1965* (Munich, 1965); and Karl Mielcke, *1917–1945 in den Geschichtsbüchern der Bundesrepublik* (Hannover, 1961), 58–68. Hannah Vogt, *Schuld oder Ver-hängnis: 12 Fragen an Deutschlands jüngste Vergangenheit* (Frankfurt am Main, 1961), the first textbook since the late 1940s to deal openly and comprehensively with the Nazi period, was directly inspired by the wave of vandalism. See Gordon Craig's introduction to the English edition, *The Burden of Guilt*, trans. Herbert Strauss (Oxford, 1964).

10 George Feil, *Zeitgeschichte im Deutschen Fernsehen: Analyse von Fernsehsendungen mit historischen The-men 1957–1967* (Osnabrück, 1974); Michael Schornstheimer, *Bombenstimmung und Katzenjammer: Vergangenheitsbewältigung: Quick und Stern in den 50er Jahren* (Cologne, 1989), 20–1.

11 Hermann Eich, *The Germans*, trans. Michael Glenny (New York, 1965), 217. The original German edition, *Die unheimlichen Deutschen*, was published in 1963.

12 Hans Lamm, ed., *Der Eichmann-Prozess in der deutschen öffentlichen Meinung* (Frankfurt am Main, 1961); Gerhard Schoenberner, "Der Prozess Eichmann und die Folgen," *Frankfurter Hefte* 16 (July 1961): 433ff.

the tens of thousands of cogs in the machine of mass extermination by pinpointing responsibility on the chief architect of the Holocaust, focused his case on Eichmann's role in the huge, complicated Nazi state system. He thereby turned the trial into what one historian called a powerful "lesson in contemporary history."[13]

During the next five years, the public sphere in West Germany became increasingly absorbed with the past. The Central Prosecutor's Office initiated four major trials of members of execution squads, including the sensational Frankfurt trial of Auschwitz personnel, which ran from December 1963 to August 1965.[14] In the years that followed, the German intellectual world produced a series of important works examining the links between West Germany's past, present, and future.[15] Of particular importance for the emerging protest generation was the discussion of fascism sparked by Ernst Nolte's historical study of the phenomenon in France, Italy, and Germany. The discussion unfolded primarily on the pages of *Das Argument,* a Berlin journal devoted to issues of concern to the 1968 generation.[16]

In its last years, the Adenauer government became increasingly sensitive to charges of continuity with the past. Revelations about officials' ties with the Nazis, once brushed aside as East German subversion, now elicited formal responses and explanations.[17] The so-called *Spiegel* affair of 1962, in

13 Steinbach, *Nationalsozialistische Gewaltverbrechen,* 53. For a listing of important contemporary publications see Randolf Braham, *The Eichmann Case: A Source Book* (New York, 1969).

14 Henkys, *Nationalsozialistische Gewaltverbrechen,* 197; Hermann Langbein, ed., *Der Auschwitz-Prozess: Eine Dokumentation in zwei Bänden* (Frankfurt am Main, 1965). See also Eugen Kogon, "'Auschwitz und eine menschliche Zukunft:' Eröffnungsrede zur Ausstellung von Dokumenten von und über Auschwitz in der Frankfurter Paulskirche, Busstag, 1964," in *Frankfurter Hefte* 19 (1964): 830–8; Martin Walser, "Unser Auschwitz," *Kursbuch* 1 (1965) and *Stuttgarter Zeitung,* Mar. 20, 1965; and Peter Weiss, *Die Ermittlung* (Frankfurt am Main, 1965).

15 See, for instance, Ulrich Sonnemann, *Das Land der unbegrenzten Zumutbarkeiten: Deutsche Reflexionen* (Hamburg, 1963); Kurt Sontheimer, "Der Antihistorismus des gegenwärtigen Zeitalters," *Neue Rundschau* (1964): 611–31; Karl Jaspers, *Wohin treibt die Bundesrepublik? Tatsachen – Chancen – Gefahren* (Munich, 1966); Hans Buchheim, *Aktuelle Krisenpunkte des deutschen Nationalbewusstseins* (Mainz, 1967); Gert Kalow, *Hitler: Das gesamtdeutsche Trauma* (Munich, 1967); Alexander and Margarete Mitscherlich, *Die Unfähigkeit zu trauern: Grundlagen kollektiven Verhaltens* (Munich, 1967); and Armin Mohler, *Vergangenheitsbewältigung: Von der Läuterung zur Manipulation* (Stuttgart, 1968).

16 Ernst Nolte, *Der Faschismus in seiner Epoche* (Munich 1963). On the significance of the fascism discussion, see the preface to the fourth edition of Wolfgang Fritz Haug, *Der hilflose Antifaschismus* (Cologne, 1977), 2, and Ronald Fraser et al., *1968: A Student Generation in Revolt* (London, 1988), 50.

17 T. H. Tetens, *The New Germany and the Old Nazis* (New York, 1961). See the documentation in Vereinigung der Verfolgten des Naziregimes, ed., *Die unbewältigte Gegenwart: Eine Dokumentation über die Rolle und Einfluss ehemals führender Nationalsozialisten in der Bundesrepublik Deutschland* (Frankfurt am Main, 1961), as well as Lewis Edinger, "Continuity and Change in the Background of German Decision-Makers," *Western Political Quarterly* 14 (Mar. 1961): 17–36. From the GDR perspective, see Nationale Front des demokratischen Deutschlands, ed., *Braunbuch: Kriegs- und Naziverbrechen in der Bundesrepublik: Staat, Wirtschaft, Armee, Justiz, Verwaltung, Wissenschaft* ([East] Berlin, 1960, 1965, 1968).

which the government applied measures reminiscent of Nazi censorship against the popular news magazine and its journalists, led to the resignation of Minister of Defense Franz-Josef Strauss and hastened the retirement of Adenauer himself.[18]

Other institutions were also placed on the defensive. Rolf Hochhuth's play *The Deputy* (1963) charged the papacy with inaction in the face of detailed knowledge about the extermination of European Jews.[19] Several West German universities offered public lecture series on the role of the academy during the Nazi era; the lectures were promptly criticized for their apologetic tendencies and unconscious linguistic links to National Socialist diction.[20]

The formation of the Grand Coalition government in 1966 caused a blossoming of activism at the political extremes. On the far right, a nationalist neo-Nazi party, the National Democratic Party (Nationaldemokratische Partei Deutschlands or NPD) gained a substantial number of votes in state elections between 1966 and 1968, while on the far left, the extraparliamentary opposition (ausserparlamentarische Opposition or APO) was formed.[21] The intensification of American involvement in Vietnam contributed to the radicalization of Germany's youth. By 1966 the Socialist German Student League (Sozialistische Deutsche Studentenbund or SDS) protested its own government's complicity with slogans such as "Murder by poison gas!" and "genocide."[22] The term "genocide" (*Völkermord*) had been firmly linked to the Holocaust in the 1965 parliamentary debate about extending the statute of limitations for mass murder committed during the Nazi era.[23] Already in 1966 young radicals were applying the epi-

---

18 The best summary is in David Schoenbaum, *The Spiegel Affair* (New York, 1968). See also Joachim Schoeps, *Die Spiegel-Affäre des F.-J. Strauss* (Hamburg, 1983), and Ronald Bunn, *German Politics and the Spiegel Affair: A Case Study of the Bonn System* (Baton Rouge, La., 1968).

19 Rolf Hochhuth, *Der Stellvertreter* (Hamburg, 1963). The play went through numerous editions in a matter of months; by November 1967 more than 350,000 copies of the German edition had been printed. On public discussion, see Fritz Raddatz, ed., *Summa iniuria oder durfte der Papst schweigen? Hochhuths "Stellvertreter" in der öffentlichen Kritik* (Hamburg, 1963), and Dolores and Earl Schmidt, *The Deputy Reader: Studies in Moral Responsibility* (Chicago, 1965); and Andreas Huyssen, "The Politics of Identification," *New German Critique*, no. 19 (winter 1980): 128ff.

20 Wolfgang Fritz Haug, *Der hilflose Antifaschismus: Zur Kritik der Vorlesungsreihen über Wissenschaft und Nationalsozialismus an deutschen Universitäten* (Frankfurt am Main, 1967, 1968, 1970; Cologne, 1977). Haug was the editor of *Das Argument*.

21 Lutz Niethammer, *Angepasster Faschismus: Politische Praxis der NPD* (Frankfurt am Main, 1969), 98–229 gives a state-by-state examination of the election results of the NPD.

22 The terms are taken from posters secretly put up in the name of the SDS in Berlin by Rudi Dutschke and Bernd Rabehl in February 1966. Quoted in Karl A. Otto, *APO: Ausserparlamentarische Opposition in Quellen und Dokumenten (1960–1970)* (Cologne, 1989), 209–10.

23 See Karl Jaspers, "Für Völkermord gibt es keine Verjährung," *Der Spiegel*, no. 19 (Mar. 10, 1965): 49ff., and reprinted in several of his later works.

thet to Southeast Asia: the slogan "Vietnam is the Auschwitz of America" appeared on the walls of Dachau.[24]

A slightly older, intermediate generation, born in the 1920s and 1930s, viewed left-wing radicalism as an echo of the right-wing violence that had brought Hitler to power. Its mass-media spokesman, press magnate Axel Springer, called the radicals "gangs of thugs" and decried their "SA methods."[25] After the demonstrations against the visit of the Shah of Iran in 1967, the student government of Berlin's Free University received a host of threatening letters drenched in Nazi invectives: "Starting now my colleagues and relatives are prepared with dog whips and night sticks," and "Vermin should be doused with gasoline and set on fire. Death to the red student plague!"[26]

1968 IN WEST GERMANY

During three major incidents in 1968, West Germany was forced to confront the Nazi past. In May, after more than ten years of discussion, parliament prepared to adopt the so-called Emergency Laws. The Grand Coalition now had sufficient votes to pass laws that would establish an important prerequisite to West Germany's full autonomy, ending the Western allies' right to intervene in emergency situations. At a huge protest march on the eve of the passage of those laws, opponents recalled the emergency laws of the 1920s that had been used to undermine democracy during the Weimar Republic and that had eased Hitler's path to power.[27]

A few months later a group of protesters appeared at Dachau where survivors had organized an elaborate ceremony to celebrate the completion of a permanent memorial site.[28] Many of the foreign survivors of Dachau had made careers as military men in NATO countries, and they gave the ceremony a decidedly military flavor with marches and music by honorary for-

24 "Anti-U.S. Posters at Dachau," *New York Times,* Nov. 8, 1966, 18.

25 "Demonstrieren – Ja! Randalieren – Nein!" *Bild,* June 3, 1967, quoted in Otto, *APO,* 236. Stuart J. Hilwig's chapter in this book offers many examples of the use of Nazi-era images in the escalating student battle between Springer and the student protesters.

26 Wilhelm Backhaus, *Sind die Deutschen verrückt? Ein Psychogramm der Nation und ihrer Katastrophen* (Bergisch Gladbach, 1968), 253–4. The Nazi flavor is more obvious in the original German: "Bei meinen Kollegen und Verwandten liegen ab sofort Hundepeitschen und Weichmacher bereit," and "Ungeziefer muss man mit Benzin begiessen und anzünden. Tod der roten Studentenpest!"

27 Michael Schneider, *Demokratie in Gefahr? Der Konflikt um die Notstandsgesetze: Sozialdemokratie, Gewerkschaften und intellektueller Protest (1958–1968)* (Bonn, 1986), 182–8, 230–1, 239–40. Excerpts from the protest speeches are printed in *Blätter für deutsche und internationale Politik* 11 (1966), 1053–64.

28 Detailed documentation of the ceremony can be found in the Dachau Memorial Site Archive, binder "Mahnmal 1968."

mations of the Belgian, French, and American armies. Not only the military aura of the occasion raised the ire of young Germans, who felt the anti-imperialist lesson of Nazi aggression was being ignored. They also objected to the participation of NATO forces, which were supporting the military junta in the Greek civil war, and especially to the presence of Klaus Schütz, the mayor of West Berlin. Schütz, who as head of the Parliamentary Council represented the West German president at Dachau, had defended the police riot in 1967 in which the Berlin student Benno Ohnesorg was killed. More recently, in April 1968, he had ordered the brutal dispersal of mass demonstrations after an attempt was made on student leader Rudi Dutschke's life. During Schütz's keynote speech a few dozen young demonstrators unfurled banners and chanted slogans such as "Today pogrom and propaganda, tomorrow the Final Solution, Herr Schütz"; "They commemorate today and exterminate tomorrow"; "We fight against fascism, NATO, and imperialism"; and "Dachau greets Hitler's successors."

Although the protesters identified themselves with the anti-Nazi resistance, the primarily francophone Dachau survivors did not understand their slogans. When someone called out "C'est les fascistes!" a physical struggle ensued between old antifascists and young radicals. One protester described his experience that day: "Five cops grabbed my Vietnam flag, but I didn't let go. . . . When we went past the VIP bleachers an old antifascist jumped down and punched me in the face. I lost my flag. A half hour later the old man came running up to me, hugged me, stroked my cheek again and again, and repeated, probably about ten times, 'Pardon, mon camarade.'"[29] Although the older generation of survivors found the protest out of place, they harbored no sympathies for the West German political establishment.

The third climactic event took place in Berlin on November 7, 1968, coincidentally the eve of the thirtieth anniversary of the *Kristallnacht* pogrom. On the last day of the CDU party congress, Beate Klarsfeld walked up to Chancellor Kurt Georg Kiesinger, called him a "Nazi," and slapped him. She was immediately arrested. The twenty-nine-year-old wife of the French Nazi hunter Serge Klarsfeld, who had long condemned Kiesinger's past as a top-ranked propaganda official in the Nazi Foreign Office, read a prepared statement expressing the "rage" of German youth over the leadership roles of former Nazis.[30]

29 Louis Köckert, *Dachau . . . und das Gras wächst . . .: Ein Report für die Nachgeborenen* (Munich, 1980), 108.
30 Beate Klarsfeld, *Die Geschichte des PG 2633930 Kiesinger: Dokumentation mit einem Vorwort von Heinrich Böll* (Darmstadt, 1969), 75; and Beate Klarsfeld, *Wherever They May Be!* (New York, 1975), 50–63.

How widespread was the awareness of the Nazi past among young activists in 1968? Anecdotal evidence suggests that it was substantial.[31] Miriam Hansen (b. 1949), whose parents had given her a copy of Anne Frank's diary in the early 1960s and who had followed the Frankfurt Auschwitz trial very closely before enrolling at Frankfurt University in 1967, later recalled that "a whole generation stood accused."[32] Detlef Hoffmann (b. 1940), who had seen *Night and Fog* and heard the Anne Frank radio documentary in the 1950s and who followed Holocaust-related events closely, identified strongly with the protest movement.[33]

This consciousness of the Holocaust does not necessarily imply, however, that these historical events had deep emotional roots in all members of the 1968 generation. Prior to the summer of 1968, the use of analogies was rooted more in political instrumentalism than in a detailed knowledge of these events. Several studies conducted in the second half of the 1960s confirm this finding. For example, a study in 1965 characterized the attitudes of young people who evinced interest in the Nazi era as "cool, rational, upstanding . . . and without historical imagination."[34] Another study, prompted by the political violence following the Easter 1968 assassination attempt on Rudi Dutschke, found that students recited their knowledge of the National Socialist period by rote, as if it were ancient history, and that they described "the horrors of the concentration camps . . . in a disconcertingly sober and detached way."[35] Even after the climactic events of 1968, change was slow in coming. For instance, when a 1964 study of historical consciousness among young Germans was republished in 1970, its authors wrote, "Although the younger generation's political sensibilities and readiness to become politically involved have remarkably expanded, its ahistorical relationship to the past has not changed."[36]

31 There is considerable evidence that the Holocaust was very present in the minds of activists: see Dörte von Westernhagen, *Die Kinder der Täter: Das Dritte Reich und die Generation danach* (Munich, 1987); Peter Sichrovsky, *Born Guilty: Children of Nazi Families* (New York, 1988); Sabine Reichel, *What Did You Do in the War, Daddy? Growing Up German* (New York, 1989); Dan Bar On, *Legacy of Silence* (Cambridge, Mass., 1989); and Fraser et al., *1968,* 19, 32. For reflections by members of a slightly older generation, see Ludwig Marcuse, ed., *War ich ein Nazi? Politik-Anfechtung des Gewissens* (Munich, 1968).

32 Michael Geyer and Miriam Hansen, "German-Jewish Memory and National Consciousness," in Geoffrey Hartmann, ed., *Holocaust Remembrance: The Shapes of Memory* (Oxford, 1994), 175–90, 180–1. The quotation is from p. 175.

33 Detlef Hoffmann, interview with the author, Apr. 28, 1991, and his "Erinnerungsarbeit der 'zweiten und dritten' Generation und 'Spurensuche' in der zeitgenössischen Kunst," *Kritische Berichte* 16, no. 1 (1988): 31–46.

34 Walter Jaide, "Die Jugend und der Nationalsozialismus," in *Die neue Gesellschaft* 12, no. 3 (1965): 723–31, 730.

35 Fritz Vilmar, "Der Nationalsozialismus als didaktisches Problem," *Frankfurter Hefte* 21, no. 10 (Oct. 1968): 683.

36 Ludwig Friedeburg and Peter Hübner, *Das Geschichtsbild der Jugend,* 2d ed. (Munich, 1964; reprint, Munich, 1970), 5.

Since 1967, some influential members of the intermediate generation, those born in the late 1920s and early 1930s who had been schooled by Nazism but not active in it, had been trying to steer the protest movement toward a more moderate course. Generally sympathetic to the political concerns of the young protesters, they rejected their radical methods and attempted to find a following among the moderates. Many of them were among the 120 West German intellectuals who in March 1968 signed a public appeal to demonstrators and police to respect legality.[37]

A few prominent individuals were openly critical of student radicalism. The social philosopher Jürgen Habermas, an early protagonist of the politicization of students, coined the term "left-wing fascism" (*Linksfaschismus*) to characterize the violent tactics of the most radical protesters.[38] The political scientist Richard Löwenthal openly linked the youthful protesters with Nazi ideology as the "unconscious continuation of some of the intellectual currents that helped to make those [Nazi] horrors possible."[39] The historian Hans-Joachim Winker, an astute critic of romanticized images of the Third Reich, also reproached the APO in 1968 for its overblown attacks on the Bonn government.[40]

It is, of course, difficult to gauge the effects of such rebukes on West German youth. Anecdotes such as the following suggest that even with the passage of time some radicals did not gain a deeper, self-critical understanding of the implications of the Nazi past for the present. In the 1980s a high-school student recalled:

We once had a history teacher. Long beard, ski sweater, jeans – the works. Boy, did he carry on about everything. For hours, he'd talk about the Jews, the Communists, the Gypsies, the Russians – victims, nothing but victims. . . . Once, someone asked him in class: "Tell us, where was the madness? Why did all those people shout hurrah and Heil? . . . There must have been something to it." He just looked stupid, our dear teacher. He called the boy who'd asked the question a neo-Nazi, asked him whether he had no respect for the victims, and so on. . . . Then he let loose. He screamed at us. Gone was that left-wing softy of the sixties. All hell broke

---

37 "Aufruf zur Wahrung der Rechtsstaatlichkeit," *Die Zeit,* Mar. 8, 1968. Some prominent examples of this generation are Walter Jens (b. 1923), Siegfried Lenz (b. 1926), Günter Grass (b. 1927), Jakov Lind (b. 1927), Martin Walser (b. 1927), Jürgen Habermas (b. 1928), Walter Kempowski (b. 1929), Hans Magnus Enzensberger (b. 1930), and Rolf Hochhuth (b. 1931).
38 See Jürgen Habermas, "Kongress 'Hochschule und Demokratie,' " in Jürgen Habermas, *Protestbewegung und Hochschulreform* (Frankfurt am Main, 1969), 137–49. Further excerpts from that original debate are published in Otto, *APO,* 239–48. Although Habermas quickly distanced himself from the term, a controversy surrounded it. Ibid., 1949–52. See Wolfgang Abendroth et al., *Die Linke antwortet Jürgen Habermas* (Frankfurt am Main, 1968); Jürgen Habermas, "Scheinrevolution unter Handlungszwang," *Der Spiegel* 22, no. 24 (June 10, 1968): 57–8; and Karl-Dietrich Bracher, *Zeitgeschichtliche Kontroversen um Faschismus, Totalitarismus, Demokratie* (Munich, 1976).
39 Richard Löwenthal, *Romantischer Rückfall* (Stuttgart, 1970), 13.
40 Hans-Joachim Winkler, *Das Establishment antwortet der APO* (Opladen, 1968).

loose. At last we had broken through the facade of this all-understanding, all-knowing, all-explaining puppet.[41]

However, a preponderance of evidence suggests that many members of the 1960s generation did indeed develop a more self-reflective, less instrumental understanding of the causes of the Holocaust in the wake of 1968. The Jusos, the official youth organization of the Social Democratic Party, for instance, steered a course between the middle generation's general defense of the establishment and the APO's use of violent tactics.[42]

Two subsequent events at Dachau illustrate the transformation of Holocaust awareness among the politically active youth. In January 1969 the satirical magazine *Pardon* staged a symbolic reopening of the Dachau concentration camp to draw attention to the parallels between a proposed new "protective custody" law and its Nazi-era predecessor.[43] In contrast to the September 1968 incident, Dachau survivors were informed beforehand and were present to lend their support.

In the fall of 1969 the annual commemorative ceremony for young people in Dachau was given a radically different format. Instead of speeches, three parallel working groups were organized to discuss three topics: "The goals and tactics of nonviolent resistance," "The roots of National Socialism and right-wing extremism today," and "Democracy and industrial society." Led by experts such as Gerhard Schoenberner, these workshops offered serious historical discussion instead of superficial historical analogies.[44]

Afterward, a large proportion of the radicals of 1968 entered the mainstream through what was called "the long march through the institutions." For example, as high school teachers they took their classes to concentration camp memorial sites in unprecedented numbers.[45] By the early 1970s, the Jusos began working within the Social Democratic Party to create a more informed awareness of the Nazi past. In March 1970, the Dachau chapter of the Jusos developed an elaborate program of local research, sem-

---

41 Quoted in Sichrovsky, *Born Guilty*, 30–1. For similar anecdotes, see Reichel (b. 1946), *What Did You Do in the War, Daddy?* 8–9, and Ian Buruma, *Wages of Guilt: Memories of War in Germany and Japan* (New York, 1994), 140–1.
42 "Entschliessung des Bundeskongresses der Jungsozialisten zur Ausserparlamentarischen Opposition, 11–12 Mai 1968," *Sozialistische Hefte* 5 (1968): 309–10; reprinted in Otto, *APO*, 275.
43 Peter Knorr, "Warum nicht gleich KZs? Auf Wiedersehen in Dachau," *Pardon* 8, no. 2 (Feb. 1969): 36–9.
44 "Gedenken durch Diskussion: Veranstaltung des Bayerischen Jugendrings im ehemaligen KZ Dachau," *Süddeutsche Zeitung*, Oct. 30, 1969; A.Z., "Dachau – nicht nur zum Gedenken: Bayerische Jugend im ehemaligen KZ Dachau," *Tat*, Nov. 15, 1969.
45 In 1969, the number of school groups visiting the Dachau museum nearly doubled, from 471 to 911. In the early 1970s, that number climbed to over a thousand groups per year, and by the end of the decade it had surpassed five thousand. See Harold Marcuse, "Nazi Crimes and Identity in West Germany: Collective Memories of the Dachau Concentration Camp, 1945–1990," Ph.D. diss., University of Michigan, 1992, 399.

inars, films, and in-depth discussions that prefigured the development of Holocaust consciousness in West Germany during the next two decades.[46]

With the end of the Grand Coalition and the accession of Willy Brandt to the chancellorship in 1969, the new relationship to the past of the younger generation was reflected at the highest level of politics. When Brandt, a political exile between 1933 and 1945, kneeled before the Warsaw ghetto monument in December 1970, he expressed an openness to and a remorse for the Nazi past that would have been unthinkable just a few years earlier.[47] His Ostpolitik, bringing rapprochement with some of the Third Reich's victims, was another outcome of the new consciousness forged by the late 1960s.[48]

The unreflective use of the Holocaust, however, did not completely disappear from West Germany after 1968. In the 1970s a small minority of extremist radicals heightened the violent tactics of the late 1960s to a terrorist campaign against the "establishment." Although putatively fighting against fascist structures, their methods reproduced fascist behavior. The crassest example of this occurred during the hijacking of a French aircraft en route from Tel Aviv in June 1976.[49] When the plane landed in Entebbe, Uganda, all of the hostages, except the Jewish passengers, who included some concentration camp survivors, were released. One of them showed his Auschwitz tattoo to the German hijackers, who responded that their goals were different from those of the Nazis. Although that may have been true, these young radicals' tactics certainly were not. In spite of this violent legacy, 1968 marked a watershed in the broader public awareness of Nazi criminality.

ISRAEL

As in West Germany, the subject of the Nazi extermination of the Jews was almost absent from Israeli public discourse until the 1950s. Holocaust survivors, whose horrendous experiences were difficult to comprehend by a militantly pioneering society, bore the stigma of not having resisted. Israel's public recollections of the Nazi era focused on ghetto uprisings, not on mass degradation and extermination. According to Tom Segev, the

---

46 "Jungsozialisten zum Theme KZ," *Dachauer Volksbote,* Mar. 18, 1970, and Kurt Göttler, "Jusos kurbeln das Gespräch an: Dachau und das KZ im Kreuzverhör/Diskussionsabend der Jungsozialisten bringt zahlreiche Vorschläge," *Münchner Merkur/Dachauer Nachrichten,* Apr. 24, 1970.
47 See *Der Spiegel* 24 (14 Dec. 1970), cover story.
48 See the chapter on Ostpolitik by Gottfried Niedhart in this book.
49 See Jillian Becker, *Hitler's Children: The Story of the Baader-Meinhof Terrorist Gang* (Philadelphia, 1977), 17–18; see also Stefan Aust, *The Baader-Meinhof Group* (London, 1987).

Holocaust served mainly as a political bargaining tool to obtain reparation payments from West Germany and to strengthen Israel's position in the international community.[50]

Israel's relationship with West Germany was part of the uneven process of social recovery of memory that began in the late 1950s. Adenauer's meeting with Prime Minister David Ben Gurion in New York on March 14, 1960, paved the way for economic and military cooperation and for the establishment of full diplomatic relations in May 1965.[51] The protests that accompanied the arrival of the new West German ambassador gave witness to the persistence of Nazi stereotypes. In Israeli perceptions, West Germany remained a disconcerting amalgam of the old and the new.[52]

For Israel, as for West Germany, the Eichmann trial marked a turning point in the collective process of recovering knowledge of the Holocaust.[53] In contrast to West Germany, the politicization of the Holocaust was sparked neither by domestic unrest nor by debates over foreign policy, but by an external threat in the spring of 1967. Whereas West Germans produced analogies with the political chaos of the Weimar years, in Israel the primary comparison was between Hitler and Egypt's president, Gamal Abdel Nasser.

In May 1967, Nasser expelled the United Nations force that was patrolling the Gaza Strip and placed an embargo on goods passing through the Red Sea bound for Israel. Using a vocabulary reminiscent of Hitler, he promised to "exterminate" Jewish capitalists and create a "Greater Arabian Empire."[54] On the eve of the Six-Day War, Israelis were terrified. As a soldier recalled, "People believed we would be exterminated if we lost the war. We got this idea – or inherited it – from the concentration camps. It's

---

50 Tom Segev, *The Seventh Million: The Israelis and the Holocaust*, trans. Haim Watzmann (New York, 1993), esp. 153–252; see also Chaim Schatzker, "Die Bedeutung des Holocaust für das Selbstverständnis der israelischen Gesellschaft," in Doron Kiesel and Ernst Karpf, eds., *Identität und Erinnerung* (Frankfurt am Main, 1990), 154–62; and Yael Zerubavel, "The Death of Memory and the Memory of Death: Masada and the Holocaust as Historical Metaphors," *Representations* 45 (winter 1994): 72–100, esp. 85–6. For background, see Monty Noam Penkower, *The Holocaust and Israel Reborn: From Catastrophe to Sovereignty* (Urbana, Ill., 1994).

51 Inge Deutschkron, *Bonn and Jerusalem: The Strange Coalition* (New York, 1970); Rolf Vogel, ed., *The German Path to Israel: A Documentation* (London, 1969), 115–21, 159–76; Lily Gardner Feldman, *The Special Relationship Between West Germany and Israel* (Boston, 1984); and Segev, *Seventh Million*, 318–20.

52 See, e.g., Vera Elyashiv, *Deutschland, kein Wintermärchen: Eine Israeli sieht die Bundesrepublik* (Düsseldorf, 1964) and Amos Elon, *In einem heimgesuchten Land: Reise eines israelischen Journalisten in beiden deutschen Staaten* (Munich, 1966); English edition, *Journey Through a Haunted Land: The New Germany* (New York, 1967).

53 Segev, *Seventh Million*, 323–4; Akiva Deutsch, *The Eichmann Trial in the Eyes of Israeli Youngsters: Opinions, Attitudes and Impact* (Ramat-Gan, 1974).

54 *Der Spiegel* 21, no. 23 (May 29, 1967), 121, 125.

a concrete idea for anyone who has grown up in Israel, even if he personally didn't experience Hitler's persecution."[55] Another soldier, who two days before the war had visited the Israeli museum that commemorated the ghetto fighters, recalled, "I felt that our war began there, in the crematoriums, in the camps, in the ghettos, and in the forests."[56]

These associations with the Holocaust undermined the government's attempt to steer a less confrontational course with Israel's Arab neighbors. Prime Minister Levi Eshkol, the main proponent of a moderate course, was compared to Neville Chamberlain. Before the outbreak of war, Israelis satirized his efforts by joking that umbrellas were sold out in Tel Aviv.[57]

After Israel's spectacular victory in the Six-Day War, however, some soldiers drew on the Holocaust to express their discomfort in the role of military occupiers:

If I had any clear awareness of the world war years and the fate of European Jewry it was once when I was going up the Jericho road and the refugees were going down it. I identified directly with them. When I saw parents dragging their children along by the hand, I actually almost saw myself being dragged along by my own father. . . . It wasn't so noticeable in times of action, but just at those moments when we felt the suffering of others, of the Arabs, against whom we fought.[58]

International support for Israel was especially pronounced in West Germany and the United States. After press warnings that Israel was under a "threat of extermination," thousands of West Germans participated in pro-Israel demonstrations, made generous donations to aid-Israel societies, and volunteered to undertake reconstruction work after the war.[59] In *Der Spiegel,* the one-eyed Israeli defense minister Moshe Dayan was compared to the anti-Nazi resistance fighter Claus von Stauffenburg, who had also worn an eye patch.[60]

In the United States there was a similar outpouring of moral and material support.[61] Only on the Left, which linked American intervention in Vietnam to Israel's lightning victory and conquest, was the reaction split. One of the few critics of Israeli policy, the Polish-Jewish Marxist Isaac Deutscher, argued that the legacy of the Holocaust in no way justified

---

55 Quoted in Kibbutz Siach Lochamim, ed., *The Seventh Day* (London, 1970), 164.
56 Uri Ramon, "The Consciousness of the Holocaust During the Six-Day War" (1969), quoted in Segev, *Seventh Million,* 392.
57 "Die Regenschirme sind ausverkauft," *Der Spiegel* 21, no. 24 (July 5, 1967): 112.
58 Kibbutz Siach Lochamim, *Seventh Day,* 163–4. See also the entire discussion, entitled "I Knew That We Must Not Forget," 163–75.
59 Vogel, *German Path,* 304–15.
60 *Der Spiegel* 21, no. 27 (July 26, 1967): 69.
61 Lucy Dawidowicz, "American Public Opinion," *American Jewish Yearbook* 69 (1968): 198–229.

Israeli belligerence toward the Arabs, and that the consequences might be similar to those of Germany's extreme nationalism in the 1930s.[62] This critique, disconcertingly close to Arab and Soviet charges that Zionism was a racist ideology, did not attract a large following in the West.

Israel's new role as an occupying power initiated a brief process of introspection about the role of the Holocaust in contemporary Israeli politics, but such reflections were neither widespread nor long lasting. The terrorist murders of eleven Israeli athletes at the Olympics in Munich in 1972 and the Arab surprise attack on Israel in October 1973 rekindled the powerful imagery of annihilation. The hardliner Menachem Begin, a Holocaust survivor who had joined Eshkol's cabinet in 1967, first spearheaded and then, as prime minister after 1977, presided over the public use of the Holocaust as a legitimizing factor in Israeli politics.[63]

Begin's election victory, ending three decades of Labor control and producing the first peace treaty with a major Arab state, stirred a new debate over Israel's relationship to the European past. In the wake of the shock of 1973, the divisive war in Lebanon, and the prolonged Palestinian uprising (Intifada), large numbers of Israeli youth, joined by some members of the middle and older generations, not only challenged the automatic connection between Hitler and Arab leaders but also began to question their own behavior toward the Arab people. A serious revision of the causes and results of the Six-Day War began, however, only with the end of the Cold War. Israel's debate over the past and the present continues to this day.[64]

THE UNITED STATES

In the twentieth century, the United States departed from its traditional isolationism to assert itself as an international role model, as the "honest broker" in World War I, liberator in World War II, and vanguard of freedom and democracy during the Cold War.[65] In the 1960s, this self-image, which underlay the United States' massive involvement in Vietnam, provided the components for a major public debate about America's own past.

---

62 Isaac Deutscher, "On the Arab-Israeli War," *New Left Review*, no. 44 (July–Aug. 1967): 30–45, reprinted in Isaac Deutscher, *The Non-Jewish Jew and Other Essays*, ed. Tamara Deutscher (London, 1968), 126–52, esp. 137, 141–2, 147–8.

63 Segev, *Seventh Million*, 225–6, 396–404.

64 See Richard B. Parker, *The Six-Day War: A Retrospective* (Gainesville, Fla., 1996) based on discussions among Israeli, Arab, American and Russian policymakers and historians held between June 3–5, 1992 in Rosslyn, Virginia.

65 See Tony Smith, *America's Mission: The United States and the Worldwide Struggle for Democracy in the Twentieth Century* (Princeton, N.J., 1994).

At the beginning of that decade, most young Americans perceived no connection between their elders and the period of the Holocaust. What had occurred in Europe during World War II was firmly and comfortingly linked to specifically German traits, whether as described in William Shirer's best-seller *The Rise and Fall of the Third Reich* (1960) or as analyzed in Hans Kohn's treatise *The Mind of Germany: The Education of a Nation* (1960).[66] In addition to reading Anne Frank's diary, with its sequel, and Elie Wiesel's memoir *Night* (1960), Americans first learned the grim details of the Holocaust through the Eichmann trial.[67] Raul Hilberg's massive study *The Destruction of the European Jews* (1961), although not widely read at the time, set a new standard for scholarly research on the subject.[68]

At first the escalation of U.S. military activities in Vietnam in 1965 was accompanied by an outpouring of public support. The Johnson administration inverted the analogy of British appeasement in the 1930s to justify its policy of supporting a beleaguered ally in Southeast Asia as part of America's Cold War commitment to freedom.[69]

At the same time, America's own record in World War II came into question. Gar Alperovitz's *Atomic Diplomacy: Hiroshima and Potsdam* (1965) argued that the use of atomic weapons against Japan had been an unnecessary slaughter of human life.[70] In 1968 Arthur Morse, Sheldon Spear, and David Wyman published works chronicling America's apathy and inactivity during the Holocaust.[71]

---

66 For the role of the Holocaust in contemporary American images of Germany, see Henry Cord Meyer, *Five Images of Germany: Half a Century of American Views on German History* (Washington, D.C., 1960); Klaus Epstein, "Das Deutschlandbild der Amerikaner," in Hermann Ziock, ed., *Sind die Deutschen wirklich so? Meinungen aus Europa, Asien, Afrika und Amerika* (Herrenalb/Schwarzwald, 1965), 181–211; Norbert Muhlen, "The U.S. Image of Germany, 1962, as Reflected in American Books," *Modern Age* 6 (1961–2): 418–27; Gavriel Rosenfeld, "The Reception of William Shirer's *Rise and Fall of the Third Reich* in the United States and West Germany, 1960–1962," *Journal of Contemporary History* 29 (1994): 95–128.

67 See American Jewish Committee, ed., *The Eichmann Case in the American Press* (New York, 1962), and Pierre Papadatos, *The Eichmann Trial* (New York, 1964). Contrary to prevailing opinion, the Holocaust was a subject of popular TV shows in the 1950s. See Jeffrey Shandler, "This Is Your Life, Hanna Bloch-Kohner: Die Geschichte einer Auschwitz-Überlebenden im frühen amerikanischen Fernsehen," in Fritz Bauer Institut, ed., *Auschwitz: Geschichte, Rezeption, Wirkung* (Frankfurt am Main, 1996), 371–405.

68 Earlier works on the Holocaust, such as Léon Poliakov, *Harvest of Hate* (Syracuse, N.Y., 1954) and Gerald Reitlinger, *The Final Solution: The Attempt to Exterminate the Jews of Europe, 1939–1945* (New York, 1953), lacked the archival detail of Hilberg's book.

69 Yuen Foong Khong, *Analogies at War: Korea, Munich, Dien Bien Phu, and the Vietnam Decisions of 1965* (Princeton, N.J., 1992), 176–90.

70 Gar Alperovitz, *Atomic Diplomacy* (New York, 1965, 1967).

71 Arthur Morse, *While Six Million Died* (New York, 1968); David Wyman, *Paper Walls and the Refugee Crisis, 1939–1941* (Amherst, Mass., 1968); and Sheldon Spear, "The U.S. and the Persecution of the Jews in Germany, 1933–1939," *Jewish Social Studies* 30 (Oct. 1968). U.S. President Jimmy Carter was influenced by Morse's book. See Edward Linenthal, *Preserving Memory: The Struggle to Create America's Holocaust Museum* (New York, 1995), 19.

By the mid-1960s, meanwhile, a more positive image of West Germany was beginning to emerge in the United States. The dissemination of the experiments of the psychologist Stanley Milgram, which underscored a general human ability to inflict harm on others, diminished the sense of a specifically German responsibility, as well as of the complete innocence of others for the Holocaust.[72]

Nevertheless, the predominance of America's self-perception as the unsullied hero of World War II persisted. That changed drastically in January 1968, however, after North Vietnamese forces launched the massive Tet Offensive, especially after photographs of the shooting of a suspected Vietcong infiltrator brought the war's brutality home to millions of Americans.[73] As two journalists later wrote, "By early 1968 [favorable] comparisons with the war against the Nazis disappeared altogether from American television."[74]

Another event, perpetrated by U.S. troops after the Tet Offensive, turned the Holocaust analogy completely around, namely, the March 1968 massacre of hundreds of defenseless civilians in the South Vietnamese village of My Lai. A helicopter reconnaissance pilot who rescued some of the civilians recalled the massacre in terms of "what the Nazis had done in the last war – marching people to a ditch and blowing them away."[75] The French magazine *Express* editorialized in late November: "The Americans have learned that they have become the equals of the French in Indochina, Madagascar, and Algeria, and of the Germans at Oradour."[76]

The Six-Day War had already revived Holocaust images in the United States. Historian Edward Linenthal considers the Six-Day War "by far the most important event in the resurrection of Holocaust imagery in American life."[77] One year later, the first two textbooks designed for college courses on the Holocaust – the term itself was applied to the Nazi geno-

---

72 Stanley Milgram, *Obedience* (film: New York University, 1965; videotape: Pennsylvania State University, 1969); Stanley Milgram, *Obedience to Authority* (New York, 1974). On the new image of West Germany's governing elites compare Lewis Edinger's more positive assessment in "Post-totalitarian Leadership Elites in the German Federal Republic," *American Political Science Review* 22 (Mar. 1969): 58–82, with his 1961 article cited in note 17.

73 In a widely used textbook, Alan Brinkley wrote, "No single event did more to undermine support in the United States for the war," in Richard N. Current et al., *American History: A Survey*, 7th ed., vol. 2 (New York, 1987), 880.

74 Michael Bilton and Kevin Sim, *Four Hours in My Lai* (New York, 1992), 28.

75 Michael Terry in a Nov. 20, 1969, interview with Seymour Hersh, quoted in Bilton and Sim, *Four Hours*, 254.

76 Quoted in Bilton and Sim, *Four Hours*, 364. An article in *Time*, Dec. 5, 1969, 30, citing the Soviet paper *Trud*, made the same comparison. The inhabitants of the village of Oradour were massacred and the village destroyed by a retreating SS Division in June 1944.

77 Linenthal, *Preserving Memory*, 9; see also Dawidowicz, "American Public Opinion," 225–9.

cide for the first time – were published.[78] Soon there was a proliferation of Holocaust studies, workshops, monuments, and museums as well as serious historical and philosophical analyses of the subject.

In 1968 the American antiwar movement, like its West German counterpart, employed extensive Holocaust imagery to challenge the morality and legitimacy of its government's Cold War policies. The instrumental use of this analogy startled and angered the middle and older generations. The German-Jewish émigré scholar Peter Gay chided the "under 20s [for their] casual use of the name Auschwitz [and] of the ominous word 'genocide.'"[79]

CONCLUSION

In 1968, there were heated disputes between the protest movements and ruling elites over continuities with the past. Two historical analogies, Nazism and the Holocaust, were repeatedly applied to the moral and political debates that year in West Germany, Israel, and the United States.

We can discern three different generations interacting within the public spheres of three robust democracies. The youngest generation, whose consciousness was formed in the 1950s in the aftermath of a vicariously experienced world war, viewed the establishment as rigid and repressive. The eldest group, born before the mid-1920s and holding political views shaped by experiences during the 1920s, 1930s, and 1940s, supported rigid structures within the system and held reactionary values. The intermediate group, born roughly in the late 1920s, defended the system but recognized a need for evolutionary change.

In West Germany, all three groups used historical rhetoric to gain ground in the public sphere with epithets such as "genocide," "fascism," and "stormtroopers," while the mass media generally supported the forces of order. In the United States, the elders deployed Cold War and Vietnam-era stereotypes such as "commies" and "fags," the youthful protesters responded with "Nazis" and "pigs," while the media propagated the invective of both

---

78 Nora Levin, *The Holocaust: The Destruction of European Jewry, 1933–1945* (New York, 1968) and Judah Pilch, ed., *The Jewish Catastrophe in Europe* (New York, 1968). Also compare Emil Fackheim's collection of essays, *Quest for Past and Future: Essays in Jewish Theology* (Bloomington, Ind., 1968), which contains only one brief reference to the Holocaust, with his next major publication, *To Mend the World: Foundations of Future Jewish Thought* (New York, 1982), in which the Holocaust plays the central role.

79 Peter Gay, "Introduction," to Karl Dietrich Bracher, *The German Dictatorship: The Origins, Structure, and Effects of National Socialism,* trans. Jean Steinberg (New York, 1982), vii.

sides. In Israel, where a younger protest generation had not yet emerged, the division ran between hawkish promoters of war against a reincarnated Hitler and dovish advocates of accommodation with its Arab neighbors. Afterward, new and disquieting parallels were raised by members of all generations, from youthful soldiers to Holocaust survivors, between Israeli and Nazi conquerors.[80] In all three countries, however, 1968 represented a moment of transformation. As the Cold War reignited that year in Asia and Europe and began moving in a new direction, there was an effusion of political rhetoric based on historical analogy. Even if that rhetoric remained detached from the emerging body of serious scholarship seeking to broaden and deepen our understanding of the horrors of the Hitler era, internationally a public awareness of the history of the Holocaust returned in 1968 and has not yet abated.

80 Segev, *Seventh Million,* 397, mentions the use of Holocaust imagery by recent immigrants to Israel as well.

17

The Nuclear Threat Ignored

How and Why the Campaign Against the Bomb Disintegrated in the Late 1960s

LAWRENCE S. WITTNER

Beginning with the Bikini hydrogen-bomb tests of 1954, and cresting in the late 1950s and early 1960s, a powerful campaign against nuclear-weapons testing – and, more broadly, nuclear annihilation – swept around the globe. Sparked by prominent intellectuals such as Bertrand Russell, Albert Schweitzer, and Linus Pauling, it was led by mass protest organizations in the West and in Japan.[1] Although organizational activity was far more limited in the nations of the Communist bloc and the Third World, important antinuclear efforts emerged there as well.[2] In the spring of 1962, an estimated two hundred thousand people took part in forty-four antinuclear (Easter) marches in thirteen countries; by 1964, the number of marchers had reached half a million, in twenty nations.[3] Asked in early 1963 about the abolition of nuclear weapons, the public backed it by 96 to 1 in Italy, 48 to 1 in France, 21 to 1 in West Germany, and 9 to 1 in Britain.

---

1 These included the Campaign for Nuclear Disarmament and the Committee of 100 in Great Britain; the Campaign for Nuclear Disarmament in Australia, New Zealand, and Ghana; the National Committee for a Sane Nuclear Policy (SANE), Women Strike for Peace, and the Student Peace Union in the United States; the Campaign for Nuclear Disarmament and the Voice of Women in Canada; the Movement Against Atomic Armament in France; the Struggle Against Atomic Death, the Easter March Movement, and their successors in West Germany; Gensuikin in Japan; the Campaign Against Atomic Weapons in Denmark; Protest Against Nuclear Weapons in Norway; the Action Group Against a Swedish Atomic Bomb; and similar movements in Austria, Belgium, Finland, Greece, Ireland, Italy, the Netherlands, Switzerland, and numerous other nations.
2 The full story of this movement is told in my recent book, *Resisting the Bomb: A History of the World Nuclear Disarmament Movement, 1954–1970* (Stanford, Calif., 1998). For a briefer account, see April Carter, *Peace Movements* (London, 1992), 40–84. The activities of the Communist-led peace movement were far less significant, and, given space limitations, I shall not discuss them here.
3 *International Bulletin*, Aug. 1962; *Sanity*, Easter Sunday, 1962, May 1962, Apr. 1964.

Similar attitudes prevailed elsewhere.[4] And yet, within a few years, the antinuclear campaign had run its course.

On the surface, it is difficult to account for this. Protest against the Bomb helped set the tone for the ferment of the late 1960s by discrediting the political Establishment, spawning revolts by key constituencies (that is, intellectuals, students, and women), and developing more dynamic, extra-parliamentary forms of political action, including mass demonstrations and civil disobedience. Furthermore, under the impact of the nuclear disarmament movement, not only the culture of politics but also the politics of culture was transformed until, ultimately, there remained little connection between the music, slogans, and iconography of the late 1950s and those that triumphed a decade later. Even so, if the struggle against the Bomb helped generate the tumult of later years, the latter did not return the favor. Indeed, the politics and cultural developments of the late 1960s were hard on antinuclear protest – so hard that it almost vanished.

THE DECLINE OF THE MOVEMENT

The powerful British movement waned rapidly. Although the Committee of 100, whose program of mass civil disobedience had terrified the British government, continued for a time to stage small demonstrations at military bases and around other political issues, it formally dissolved in 1968.[5] By contrast, the Campaign for Nuclear Disarmament (CND) remained active in the struggle, organizing new demonstrations, statements, and fundraising appeals. But even this flagship of antinuclear activity – which had claimed a turnout of 150,000 people for the culminating rally of its 1962 Aldermaston (Easter) march – underwent a sharp decline. In 1964, CND abandoned the Aldermaston march and, facing serious financial problems, cut the staff, services, and activities of the national office. Most of the CND's prominent leaders dropped away, as did most of the membership. By 1971 the CND – only recently the largest citizens' movement in modern Britain – had debts that exceeded its annual income and only 2,047 members. Wearers of the famous nuclear-disarmament pin were greeted with the comment "CND? I thought that died long ago."[6]

4 "Some Worldwide Attitudes Toward Disarmament and Nuclear Issues" (July 1963), 2, box 16, "R" reports, 1960–3, Office of Research, United States Information Agency records, Washington National Records Center, Suitland, Md.
5 Michael Randle, "Non-violent Direct Action in the 1950s and 1960s," in Richard Taylor and Nigel Young, eds., *Campaigns for Peace: British Peace Movements in the Twentieth Century* (Manchester, 1987), 142.
6 Minutes of the CND Executive Committee meeting of Sept. 5, 1970, reel 1, Campaign for Nuclear

In Canada, where the British CND model had been widely emulated, events followed a similar course. Beginning in late 1963, the antinuclear movement rapidly lost momentum. Prominent figures withdrew from the Canadian CND, and by early 1965 most of the local branches were weak or defunct. After wrestling with the issue of the group's continued existence for several months, the national executive committee finally decided to wind up Canadian CND's operations on June 1.[7] Meanwhile, the main student nuclear-disarmament group, the Combined Universities CND (CUCND), also took stock and concluded that their movement was on the wane. At the end of 1964, CUCND stalwarts helped form a new group, the Student Union for Peace Action, and CUCND ceased to exist. Its magazine, *Our Generation Against Nuclear War,* became simply *Our Generation.* Although the Voice of Women (VOW) proved more durable, for the most part it dropped nuclear issues as it plunged ahead with new ventures. Furthermore, by the mid-1970s, even VOW had dwindled to what two of its leaders called "a hard core."[8]

In West Germany the once promising movement began to break up during the late 1960s. For a time the antinuclear campaign continued its remarkable growth, prospering from the tension between an increasingly radical student culture and the frozen politics of the Federal Republic. In 1968 it burgeoned still further thanks to a groundswell of opposition to emergency powers legislation considered by the Bundestag. Accordingly, it changed its name to the Campaign for Democracy and Disarmament and that spring – shortly after the attempted assassination of the popular student leader Rudi Dutschke – staged the largest Easter march yet. Nevertheless, the movement grew so large and all-encompassing that it lost its antinuclear focus. Indeed, the Campaign for Democracy and Disarmament soon suffered from bitter factionalism and other internal disputes over its goals and strategy. Consequently, by 1970 the West German movement was disintegrating.[9]

Disarmament Records (Harvester microfilm; hereafter British CND Records); Richard Taylor, *Against the Bomb: The British Peace Movement, 1958–1965* (Oxford, 1988), 102–3, 108–12; *Peace News,* July 10, 1964; John Minnion and Philip Bolsover, eds., *The CND Story* (London, 1983), 150; John Cox, *Overkill: The Story of Modern Weapons* (Harmondsworth, 1981), 220–1.
7 Minutes of the Canadian CND Executive Committee meetings of Jan. 26, Feb. 20, and Apr. 13, 1965, box 1, Canadian CND Records, Mills Memorial Library, McMaster University, Hamilton; Gary Moffatt, *History of the Canadian Peace Movement Until 1969* (St. Catherine's, Ont., 1969), 93, 97.
8 Minutes of the Combined Universities CND meeting of Jan. 28, 1964, box 1, Combined Universities CND–Student Union for Peace Action Records, McMaster University; "Editorial Statement," *Our Generation* 3:4 and 4:1 (n.d.): 3–5; Kay Macpherson and Meg Sears, "The Voice of Women: A History," in Gwen Matheson, ed., *Women in the Canadian Mosaic* (Toronto, 1976), 89.
9 Karl A. Otto, *Vom Ostermarsch zur APO: Geschichte der ausserparlamentarischen Opposition in der Bun-*

Antinuclear movements elsewhere also underwent a sharp decline. In
Denmark nuclear-disarmament marches and other activities ebbed after
1963. Voting in December 1966 to terminate its campaign, the Campaign
Against Atomic Weapons closed its office in Copenhagen and stopped
publication of its journal.[10] Much the same thing happened in Norway,
Sweden, and Belgium, where antinuclear campaigns disappeared in the
mid-1960s.[11] In the Netherlands and France, Easter marches and other
antinuclear agitation persisted into the latter part of the decade, only to
come to an abrupt end – as did much of the antinuclear movement – by
1970.[12] The Swiss Movement Against Atomic Armaments existed formally until 1969. In fact, however, it ceased its activities in 1967, when it
held its last Easter march.[13] In Australia, CND groups expired during 1965.
By that time, branches of the New Zealand CND were also becoming
inactive. Several years later, the New Zealand CND itself collapsed, with
its Auckland branch lingering on as the only survivor of the nationwide
organization.[14]

Although the nuclear disarmament campaign held up better in the
United States, it was also in trouble. After late 1963, student protest against
the Bomb faded rapidly. When, in the spring of 1964, only twenty-five
delegates turned out for the convention of the Student Peace Union, the
organization disbanded. A few years later, the small Committee for Nonviolent Action, close to collapse, was absorbed by the War Resisters' League.

desrepublik, 1960–1970 (Frankfurt am Main, 1977), 145–77; Peter H. Merkl, "Pacifism in West Germany," *School of Advanced International Studies Review*, no. 4 (summer 1982): 87; Joyce Marie Mushaben, "Cycles of Peace Protest in West Germany: Experiences from Three Decades," *West European Politics* 8 (Jan. 1985): 29–30.

10 Erling Bjol, *Hvem bestemmer: Studier i den udenrigspolitiske beslutningsproces* (Copenhagen, 1983), 216–17; Klaus Jorgensen, *Atomvåbnenes rolle i dansk politik med saerligt henblik på Kampagnen mod Atomvåben 1960–68* (Odense, 1973), 90–1.
11 Sten Sparre Nilson, "The Peace Movement in Norway," in Werner Kaltefleiter and Robert Pfaltz-graff, eds., *The Peace Movements in Europe and the United States* (London, 1985), 37; Kent Lindkvist, "Mobilization Peaks and Declines of the Swedish Peace Movement," in Katsuya Kodama and Unto Vesa, eds., *Toward a Comparative Analysis of Peace Movements* (Hants, 1990), 159; Nadine Lubelski-Bernard, "Les mouvements de la paix en Belgique (1945–1960)," in Maurice Vaïsse, ed., *Le Pacifisme en Europe des années 1920 aux années 1950* (Brussels, 1993), 384.
12 I. D. Verkuil, *De grote illuse: De Nederlandse vredesbeweging na 1945* (Utrecht, 1988), 49–50; Claude Bourdet to Madame, Monsieur, Feb. 1968, Bourdet correspondence, Pierre Mendès-France papers, Institute Pierre Mendès-France, Ecole Polytechnique, Paris.
13 Brassel and Tanner, "Zur Geschichte der Friedensbewegung in der Schweiz," in Thomas Bein et al., eds., *Handbuch Frieden Schweiz* (Basel, 1986), 70; Markus Heiniger, "Die schweizerische Antiatombewegung 1958–1963," Lizentiatsarbeit, University of Zurich, 1980, 160–72.
14 Ralph Summy and Malcolm Saunders, "Disarmament and the Australian Peace Movement," *World Review* 26 (Dec. 1987): 32; report from the New Zealand CND National Committee to the annual conference, Aug. 21–2, 1965, folder 356, War Resisters International Records, International Insti-tute for Social History, Amsterdam (hereafter WRI Records, Amsterdam); Elsie Locke, *Peace Peo-ple: A History of Peace Activities in New Zealand* (Christchurch, 1992), 186.

Both the National Committee for a Sane Nuclear Policy (SANE) and Women Strike for Peace survived intact and continued to function as peace groups but lost momentum and support. Symptomatically, Norman Cousins, who had founded SANE and chaired it for its first six years, withdrew from the organization in 1967. Furthermore, both groups departed increasingly from nuclear issues. In 1969, to reflect its change of focus, SANE dropped the word "Nuclear" from its name.[15]

In the Soviet Union, where the problem of the Bomb continued for a time to preoccupy prominent intellectuals,[16] nuclear disarmament gradually ceased to be their central concern. In early 1966, leading peace-oriented physicists, joining with a group of liberal artists, denounced the Communist Party's plans for the rehabilitation of Stalin. Andrei Sakharov, the most prominent antinuclear activist, became increasingly involved with domestic political issues, particularly supporting Soviet dissidents and other victims of the regime. As he later noted, he "turned from worldwide problems to the defense of individual people." Even Sakharov's famous antiwar essay, *Progress, Coexistence, and Intellectual Freedom* (1968), although stressing the need to avert a nuclear holocaust, placed a higher priority on freedom of thought, arguing that it provided "the only guarantee of the feasibility of a scientific-democratic approach to politics, economy, and culture." In November 1970 Sakharov joined with two other physicists to form a Committee for Human Rights. He and other Soviet dissidents continued to call for disarmament, but without making the issue a top priority.[17]

In Japan the movement persisted, although on a much reduced scale. Condemning Chinese and French atmospheric nuclear tests, Gensuikin also demanded the conclusion of comprehensive test-ban, nonproliferation, and nuclear-disarmament treaties, as well as a pledge of nonuse of nuclear weapons by the nuclear powers. To block Japan's nuclearization, Gensuikin staged demonstrations in front of the Diet building in 1967, 1968, and 1969. Meanwhile, organizations of atomic bomb survivors remained active, publishing antinuclear literature and demanding relief legislation. In Hiroshima, memorial services recurred annually on August 6,

15 Charles Chatfield, *The American Peace Movement: Ideals and Activism* (New York, 1992), 114; Lawrence S. Wittner, *Rebels Against War: The American Peace Movement, 1933–1983* (Philadelphia, 1984), 280; Paul Boyer, "From Activism to Apathy: The American People and Nuclear Weapons, 1963–1980," *Journal of American History* 70 (Mar. 1984): 825–6, 837.
16 See, e.g., Andrei Sakharov, *Sakharov Speaks* (New York, 1974), 15–16, 36–8, 55–114; Andrei Sakharov, *Memoirs* (New York, 1990), 281; Fedor Burlatsky, *Khrushchev and the First Russian Spring: The Era of Khrushchev Through the Eyes of His Advisor* (New York, 1991), 257–8, 260, 262.
17 *New York Times,* July 22, 1968, Dec. 16, 1989; Zhores A. Medvedev, *Soviet Science* (New York, 1978), 107; Kevin Klose, *Russia and the Russians: Inside the Closed Society* (New York, 1984), 156; Sakharov, *Memoirs,* 267–80; Sakharov, *Sakharov Speaks,* 24–5, 44.

stressing strongly antinuclear themes. Yet even in Japan, fewer people heeded the message. The movement, at least, appeared factionalized, demoralized, and lacking in central direction. In 1972, a foreign observer contended that Japan's "public allergy to nuclear weapons" had come to an end.[18] He was wrong, but his mistake was understandable.

With national organizations on the wane, the international movement also faded. Despite the potential of the International Confederation for Disarmament and Peace (ICDP), founded in early 1964, this nuclear disarmament international failed to establish itself as a powerful organization. Instead, it remained poorly funded, thinly staffed, and – given the decline of its constituent groups just as it began operations – never able to develop much of an international campaign.[19] The Pugwash movement fared better in the late 1960s, continuing to attract an impressive array of arms control and disarmament specialists to international conferences. Nevertheless, it also experienced a loss of momentum. In 1972, Eugene Rabinowitch commented that the Pugwash movement seemed to be "standing still." To some extent, he maintained, "it has become an 'establishment,' rather than a pioneering . . . effort."[20]

Meanwhile, nuclear weapons ceased to provide a subject of much concern to the mass media or to the general public. Between 1964 and 1970, magazines and newspapers in the United States sharply reduced their coverage of nuclear issues, while the number of books dealing with nuclear war also declined substantially. "Writers rarely write about this subject anymore, and people hardly ever talk about it," observed the columnist Stewart Alsop in the late 1960s. "There has been something like a conspiracy of silence about the threat of nuclear war." According to pollsters, between 1959 and 1965, the percentage of Americans viewing nuclear war as the nation's most urgent problem fell from 64 to 16 percent. Soon the issue

---

18 "A Summing Up of the Movement and Organization of the Japan Congress Against Atomic and Hydrogen Bombs" (Apr. 3, 1970), 7–8, Japan Congress Against A & H Bombs Records, Swarthmore College Peace Collection (hereafter SCPC), Swarthmore; Committee for the Compilation of Materials, *Hiroshima and Nagasaki* (New York, 1981), 582; *The Meaning of Survival* (Hiroshima, 1983), 176–83; Setsuo Yamada, "Peace Declaration" (Aug. 6, 1970), folder 333, WRI Records, Amsterdam; Herbert Passin, "Nuclear Arms and Japan," in William H. Overholt, ed., *Asia's Nuclear Future* (Boulder, Colo., 1977), 67.
19 Carter, *Peace Movements,* 77; Claude Bourdet to the author, June 25, 1993; minutes of the ICDP Council meeting of June 24–7, 1964, International Confederation for Disarmament and Peace Records, SCPC (hereafter ICDP Records); Peggy Duff to Dear Friend, Oct. 1967, reel 3, British CND Records.
20 Joseph Rotblat, "Movements of Scientists Against the Arms Race," in Joseph Rotblat, ed., *Scientists, the Arms Race and Disarmament: A UNESCO/Pugwash Symposium* (London, 1982), 137; Rabinowitch to Edwin D. Fowle, June 7, 1972, box 1, Eugene Rabinowitch papers, University Library, State University of New York, Albany.

vanished entirely from the surveys. Opinion polls had similar findings in Canada. In 1963, a Gallup survey had reported that 18 percent of Canadians identified nuclear weapons as "Canada's chief worry." But, after surveying the worries of Canadians in late 1965, the Gallup organization remarked that "no one even mentions nuclear weapons." In the early 1970s, an American sociologist contended that the atom bomb was "no longer an editorial topic for local newspapers or a conversation piece at dinner tables." It had become "a dead issue."[21]

Other societies also showed a newfound complacency about the nuclear arms race. In Denmark concern about the nuclear issue declined during the late 1960s, and the number of newspaper and magazine articles about it fell off substantially. Between March 1964 and April 1966, the French public's opposition to their nation's *force de frappe* declined from 49 to 42 percent, while support rose from 39 to 46 percent. In Japan one poll in 1969 found that the Japanese people opposed their country's acquisition of nuclear weapons by 62 to 16 percent and another by 72 to 14 percent. But peace movement leaders were horrified by the rising number of respondents – reaching a majority by 1972 – who declared that Japan would eventually possess nuclear arms, a fatalism they viewed as encouraging this development. Writing in the mid-1970s, Alva Myrdal expressed her astonishment that "people all over the world have become conditioned to live on unconcerned about the steadily increasing risk" of nuclear war.[22]

A variety of factors account for the crumbling of the nuclear disarmament movement and of its popular support. Some of these, like exhaustion and frustration, are hardly surprising. Indeed, they appear endemic to this kind of campaign, for they reflect the natural tendency of mass social movements to lose momentum and support. Resigning from the Committee of 100, Vanessa Redgrave remarked that she could no longer spend her time preparing for demonstration after demonstration.[23] In addition, activists

21 Rob Paarlberg, "Forgetting About the Unthinkable," *Foreign Policy* 10 (1973): 136; Boyer, "From Activism to Apathy," 825–6; Mary P. Lowther, "The Decline of Public Concern over the Atom Bomb," *Kansas Journal of Sociology* 9 (spring 1973): 77, 79; Peyton V. Lyon, *Canada in World Affairs, 1961–1963* (Toronto, 1968), 78.
22 Erik Boel, *Socialdemokratiets Atomvåbenpolitik: Denmarks atomvåbenfri status* (Aarhus, 1986), 15; George H. Gallup, ed., *The Gallup International Public Opinion Polls: France 1939, 1944–1975* (New York, 1976), 417, 521; Sadao Asada, "Japanese Perceptions of the A-Bomb Decision, 1945–1980," in Joe C. Dixon, ed., *The American Military in the Far East* (Washington, D.C., 1980), 213–14; Alva Myrdal, *The Game of Disarmament: How the United States and Russia Run the Arms Race* (New York, 1976), 318–19.
23 Brandon, *The Burning Question: The Anti-nuclear Movement Since 1945* (London, 1987), 52. For other illustrations of exhaustion, see Homer Jack to Norman Thomas, Mar. 8, 1963, reel 62, Norman Thomas papers (New York Public Library microfilm); Jorgensen, *Atomvåbnenes rolle*, 85; L. John Collins, *Faith Under Fire* (London, 1966), 344. For an analysis, see Nigel Young, "Why Peace Movements Fail: A Historical and Social Overview," *Social Alternatives* 4 (Mar. 1984): 13–14.

faced the psychologically difficult task of a sustaining a long-term confrontation with the prospect of nuclear annihilation.[24] Beyond these items,
however, lurk others rooted more specifically in the public policy, politics,
and intellectual assumptions of the 1960s. And it is to these factors that we
should turn for a fuller understanding of why the antinuclear movement
faltered in the latter half of the decade.

CO-OPTATION

Plagued by feelings of exhaustion, many campaigners for nuclear disarmament, like broad sections of the general public, were ripe for co-optation.
Reasons for consolation did exist – often sufficient to convince weary
activists that they could relax their guard against the world's slide toward
nuclear catastrophe. The Cuban missile crisis, although shocking in itself,
convinced many people that the great powers, despite their terrifying
nuclear arsenals, would not proceed to nuclear war. Indeed, a period of
Soviet-American rapprochement followed, punctuated by arms control
and other agreements that lowered Cold War tensions. Meanwhile, in Great
Britain, the 1964 election victory of the Labour Party raised hopes for that
nation's adoption of a more dovish foreign and defense policy. Later in the
decade, in West Germany, the advent to power of the Social Democrats
defused central European enmities and drew many young activists into
mainstream politics.[25] Not even the election to the American presidency of
a veteran Cold Warrior like Richard Nixon stopped the trend toward
accommodation among nuclear-armed nations. Consequently, much of
the world was swept by a new mood of détente, in which a nuclear war
seemed increasingly unlikely.[26]

The most important development along these lines was the atmospheric
test-ban treaty of 1963. Like most of the public, peace groups around the
world welcomed it. At the same time, they made clear that it constituted
only the first item on their agenda. In Canada, noted Combined Universi-

24 See, e.g., Locke, *Peace People,* 186; Spencer Weart, *Nuclear Fear: A History of Images* (Cambridge,
    1988), 264, 266–7; Robert J. Lifton, *Death in Life: Survivors of Hiroshima* (New York, 1967), 500–10.
25 Eugene Rabinowitch, "New Year's Thoughts 1964," *Bulletin of the Atomic Scientists* 20 (Jan. 1964):
    2; April Carter to the author, Mar. 7, 1994; Sheila Jones to the author, Aug. 25, 1995; "Minority
    Report of the Executive Committee" (Nov. 1964), reel 1, British CND Records; Merkl, "Paci-
    fism," 87–8.
26 David S. Meyer, "Peace Protest and Policy: Explaining the Rise and Decline (and Rise and Decline)
    of Antinuclear Movements in Post-War America," paper presented at the American Political Sci-
    ence Association convention, Washington, D.C., Aug. 1991, 14; Malvern Lumsden, "Nuclear
    Weapons and the New Peace Movement," *World Armaments and Disarmament: SIPRI Yearbook 1983*
    (New York, 1982), 119.

ties CND, members viewed the treaty as "an important first step, a step which the insistent activities of the peace movement had helped prepare the way for," but "only a small first step" toward nuclear disarmament. In Great Britain, the CND's *Sanity* proclaimed a "Test Ban Victory" and went on to argue that it was "well worth celebrating." Even so, "we know very well that this is only a first step. . . . We want . . . *all* forms of nuclear testing . . . covered by the treaty. Then we want Britain to give a lead that will take the world . . . to celebrating actual disarmament." In Ireland, CND's newspaper praised the treaty as reflecting "the determination of ordinary people everywhere" and urged the movement to press on "to the final abandonment and destruction of all nuclear arms."[27] Much the same outlook prevailed in the United States. Writing to SANE's new chair, Benjamin Spock, Cousins warned that "in kicking up our heels we want to be careful that the resultant dust doesn't obscure the main and remaining dangers."[28]

Yet despite these precautions, much of the public and part of the movement soon believed – as SANE's Homer Jack later complained – "that peace broke out with the test ban!" In response to the signing of the treaty, support for nuclear disarmament agitation melted away rapidly in Sweden, Denmark, Austria, Holland, Belgium, Great Britain, Canada, New Zealand, Australia, the Soviet Union, the United States, and numerous other nations.[29] In part, the dwindling support for the movement reflected the decline of the immediate danger of radioactive contamination through nuclear fallout. As Sakharov recalled, "When nuclear tests were driven underground in 1963, the biological effects of nuclear radiation ceased to alarm people. I was no exception."[30] Furthermore, the treaty seemed to herald a sharp turn toward peace and disarmament. The Toronto CND reported that "after the signing of the test-ban treaty, many people began to

27 Combined Universities CND National Secretariat to All CUCND Executive Committees, Aug. 6, 1963, box 1, Combined Universities CND-Student Union for Peace Action Records; *Sanity,* Aug. 1963; *Banner,* ca. Aug. 1963.
28 Cousins to Spock, Sept. 26, 1963, box 14, 1971 series, Benjamin Spock papers, George Arents Research Library, Syracuse University, Syracuse. See also "FAS: For Further Arms Control," *Bulletin of the Atomic Scientists* 19 (Nov. 1963): 46; *Sane World,* Oct. 15, 1963.
29 Personal interview with Homer Jack, June 12, 1988; Jan Andersson and Kent Lindkvist, "The Peace Movement in Sweden," in Kaltefleiter and Pfaltzgraff, eds., *The Peace Movements,* 12; *END Journal* (Feb.–Mar. 1984), 14; George Breuer, "Limits to Unilateralism," *END Journal* (Apr.–May 1983), 26; Philip P. Everts and G. Walraven, *Vredesbeweging* (Utrecht, 1984), 43; Lubelski-Bernard, "Les mouvements de la paix," 384–5; Peggy Duff, *Left, Left, Left* (London, 1971), 224; Summy and Saunders, "Disarmament," 31–2; Dimitri Roussopoulos, "The Politics of the Peace Movement," *Our Generation* 15 (fall 1982): 4; Moffatt, *History,* 95; Carter, *Peace Movements,* 41.
30 Sakharov, *Memoirs,* 204.

feel that it was no longer necessary to campaign for nuclear disarmament, but that the great powers would soon settle their differences and agree to disarm." With the arrival of the test ban, recalled Dr. Bernard Lown, a founder of Physicians for Social Responsibility, "it was clear to me that the nuclear war issue would fade into history, because humanity was finally understanding the dangers." Although disarmament groups continued to hammer away at the nuclear arms race, the mass media largely abandoned the issue as no longer newsworthy.[31]

The antinuclear movement also lost ground because it could not cut itself off from other foreign and defense policy issues. "Ban the British Bomb was adequate in 1958," noted an internal British CND paper, "but in 1964 it has developed into an argument about the future of . . . the Nassau Agreement, of the Polaris submarines and bases, and about MLF." The CND would "have to say no to this and yes to that, often in great detail." That same year, antinuclear physicist Hideki Yukawa complained about the Japanese peace movement's "exclusively anti-Bomb approach," leading to "silence about small wars, conventional arms, and violence in general." In fact, however, as such comments indicate, during these years the movement was finding it impossible to ignore related issues. Repression in Greece, the admission of China to the United Nations, and Third World economic development all became important sources of concern to peace activists and their organizations.[32] Dutch, Swedish, and American peace groups turned increasingly to addressing the problems of Third World nations,[33] as did the Pugwash movement, which devoted three of the six conferences it held between 1965 and 1970 to economic development issues. By 1970, even Rabinowitch – long a mainstay of the antinuclear movement – was arguing that "confrontation between rapidly advancing 'developed' world and stagnant 'undeveloped' world . . . is as much a threat

31 "T.C.N.D. Bulletin" (June 12, 1965), box 7, Radical Organizations Archive, McMaster University; Gale Warner and Michael Shuman, *Citizen Diplomats* (New York, 1987), 36; Locke, *Peace People,* 185–6.
32 "Majority Report of the Executive Committee" (Nov. 1964), reel 1, British CND Records; *Peace News,* Aug. 21, 1964; Taylor, *Against the Bomb,* 266–9; Macpherson and Sears, "Voice of Women," 81.
33 Everts and Walraven, *Vredesbeweging,* 46; Lindkvist, "Mobilization peaks," 159; Student Peace Union, "Statement on Foreign Policy" (1964), box 1, Student Peace Union Records, State Historical Society, Madison.

for the peaceful future of mankind as is the confrontation of nuclear super-powers."[34]

Naturally, the movement was deeply disturbed by the August 1968 War-saw Pact invasion of Czechoslovakia. Irate at the military crushing of the "Prague Spring," peace groups led protest demonstrations around the world. Meeting two days after the invasion began for the ICDP's biannual confer-ence, delegates immediately condemned it and pressed ahead with protest activities. On behalf of the War Resisters' International, Hugh Brock, April Carter, and Michael Randle organized simultaneous leafletting and protests in Warsaw, Sofia, Budapest, and Moscow.[35] Opposition to the inva-sion was widespread in the Soviet Union, particularly among the intelli-gentsia. Long discussions about the event occurred in private homes, and, as Sakharov later revealed, "many persons" refused "to attend the innumer-able official meetings held in support of the intervention." On August 25, Pavel Litvinov and Larisa Bogoraz led a small group of dissidents to Red Square for a public protest. Bearing signs reading "Hands Off Czechoslova-kia," they sat briefly by a traditional execution site in prerevolutionary Rus-sia before KGB agents beat them up, destroyed their posters, and arrested them.[36]

By far the greatest international preoccupation, however, was the Viet-nam War. Commenting on the movement's decline, Jack recalled that, with the war's escalation in 1965, "the attention of American and European activists soon was transferred from next steps in disarmament to massive efforts to end the war in Southeast Asia." The CND's Peggy Duff, too, concluded that, around the world, "the war in Vietnam superseded the Bomb in public interest and concern." For many participants in the antinu-clear campaign, as for the general public, the war in Southeast Asia "seemed a more immediate danger" than did nuclear war. It also drew on the same feelings of "moral revulsion," triggered this time by the spectacle of a great power using the latest technology to destroy a small peasant nation. Thomas Merton, a Trappist monk and theologian, while utterly rejecting nuclear war, had clung to the Catholic Church's traditional "just war" theory. Nev-ertheless, shocked by the brutality of the Vietnam conflict, he eventually

---

34 Joseph Rotblat to Bertrand Russell, Feb. 23, 1966, Class 625, Russell Archives 1, McMaster Uni-versity; Rotblat, "Movements of Scientists," 137; Rabinowitch to Hans Thirring, Sept. 30, 1970, box 3, Rabinowitch papers.

35 Duff, *Left, Left, Left,* 244; Dimitrios Roussopoulos, *From Protest to Resistance* (Montreal, 1986), 62; Brock to Vera Brittain, Sept. 25, 1968, "Brock, Hugh" folder, Vera Brittain papers, McMaster Uni-versity; Randle to the author, Oct. 4, 1994.

36 Roald Z. Sagdeev, *The Making of a Soviet Scientist* (New York, 1994), 131–2; Sakharov, *Memoirs,* 290–1.

concluded that it had become impossible to distinguish morally between nuclear holocaust and this kind of "conventional" war. "The war in Vietnam," he wrote, "is a bell tolling for the whole world."[37] Millions of people reached a similar conclusion.

In Great Britain, as Randle noted, activism shifted "away from the Bomb and toward the issue of the Vietnam War." As early as August 5, 1964, CND issued "an urgent call" to political, union, church, youth, and other organizations "to take immediate action in demanding an end to the war in Vietnam." With the Johnson administration's escalation of the war in 1965, CND and the Committee of 100 organized and supported a variety of protest activities. In addition, the CND staged large demonstrations against the war in 1966 and 1967.[38] Nevertheless, the momentum in the antiwar struggle shifted for a time to the Vietnam Solidarity Campaign, an organization that identified with Vietnam's Communist revolutionaries and dismissed CND, now merely one of many groups opposing the war, as "passé and irrelevant." CND gravitated toward the more moderate British Campaign for Peace in Vietnam – which favored British dissociation from U.S. policy and the right of the Vietnamese to settle their own affairs – and provided the group with officers and office space. In this fashion, as a number of CND leaders remarked, the Vietnam War diverted the attention of the antinuclear movement and, ultimately, weakened it.[39]

Much the same pattern developed in Japan. Appalled by the Vietnam War, especially the American use of "napalm bombs and other weapons of mass destruction," Gensuikin declared in the spring of 1965 that it felt compelled to address the issue. The war, it argued, was "interlaced significantly with other problems of the world," including the nuclear arms race; indeed, the Vietnam conflict threatened "to explode into a worldwide nuclear war." Accordingly, that year, Gensuikin made the war the centerpiece of its World Conference Against A and H Bombs. It also joined with unions, women's organizations, the Zengakuren, the left-wing parties, and other citizens' groups to form the Japan Peace for Vietnam Committee,

37 Homer Jack, *Nuclear Politics After Hiroshima/Nagasaki* (Swarthmore, 1987), 45; Duff, *Left, Left, Left,* 268; Peggy Duff, "What You Don't Know About the Arms Race," *Our Generation* 13, no. 1 (1979): 8; Patricia McNeal, *The American Catholic Peace Movement, 1928–1972* (New York, 1978), 141–2.
38 Michael Randle to the author, Oct. 4, 1994; "CND Statement on Vietnam Crisis" (Aug. 5, 1964), folder 273, WRI Records, Amsterdam; minutes of the CND Executive Committee meetings of May 15, Sept. 11, and Oct. 16, 1965, reel 1, British CND Records; Andrew Papworth to Vera Brittain, Oct. 28, 1965, "Committee of 100" folder, Brittain papers; "Easter '67," Class 630, Russell Archives 2; Cox, *Overkill,* 217–18.
39 Cox, *Overkill,* 215, 218–19; Richard Taylor, "The Marxist Left and the Peace Movement in Britain Since 1945," in Taylor and Young, eds., *Campaigns,* 168–9; Duff, *Left, Left, Left,* 207; personal interview with Sheila Jones, July 10, 1990.

better known as Beheiran. Growing rapidly, Beheiran organized enormous antiwar demonstrations. In 1970 it rallied almost eight hundred thousand people against the war and in defense of Japan's "peace constitution." Although this represented an unprecedented outpouring of the Japanese peace constituency, Beheiran's exclusive focus on the Vietnam War had the effect of marginalizing the nuclear issue.[40]

In Canada the Vietnam War quickly supplanted nuclear war as the movement's top concern. Even as it tottered toward collapse in 1965, the Canadian CND petitioned and protested against the conflict. It also produced a new leaflet with the nuclear arms issue downgraded to point number two; point one was "Vietnam." Later that year, the final issue of CND's newsletter reported that its plans for creating "a broader organization" had been stalled, for "the Vietnam crisis monopolizes all efforts at the moment."[41] Combined Universities CND sponsored a December 1964 demonstration calling for withdrawal of all foreign troops from Vietnam and for a Canadian initiative to bring the war to an end. Thereafter, its successor, the Student Union for Peace Action, threw itself into teach-ins and other antiwar ventures.[42] Meanwhile, the Voice of Women made ending the Vietnam War its major priority. It exposed the American use of nerve gas, defoliants, pellet bombs, and napalm in the war, aided civilians in Vietnam and American draft resisters in Canada, and implored the Canadian government to adopt a "peacemaker role." It also sponsored an exchange of visits with Vietnamese women, taking the latter on an antiwar speaking tour of Canada.[43]

Naturally, the Vietnam War had particular resonance in the United States. Even before President Lyndon B. Johnson began dispatching a million U.S. personnel, American peace groups sharply criticized U.S. policy. In September 1963, rejecting U.S. support for the Diem dictatorship, SANE

40 "Invitation to the Twentieth Anniversary World Conference Against A- & H-Bombs" (May 20, 1965), Japan Congress Against A & H Bomb Records, SCPC; Nobuya Bamba, "Peace Movement at a Standstill: Roots of the Crisis," *Bulletin of Peace Proposals* 13 (1982): 41; Yoshiyuki Tsurumi, "Beheiran," *Japan Quarterly* 16 (Oct.–Dec. 1969): 444–8; Nobuya Bamba and John Howes, "Conclusion: Japanese Society and the Pacifist," in Nobuya Bamba and John Howes, eds., *Pacifism in Japan: The Christian and Socialist Tradition* (Vancouver, B.C., 1978), 270–1.

41 Minutes of the Canadian CND Executive Committee meeting of Apr. 13, 1965, box 1, Canadian CND Records; Canadian CND Newsletter, no. 3 (Sept. 22, 1965) and 4 (Dec. 15, 1965), folder 188, WRI Records, Amsterdam.

42 Lana Lockyer to War Resisters' League, Dec. 15, 1964, box 2, Combined Universities CND–Student Union for Peace Action Records; Myrna Kostash, *Long Way from Home* (Toronto, 1980), 45–54.

43 Kay Macpherson, *When in Doubt, Do Both: The Times of My Life* (Toronto, 1994), 118–28; Macpherson and Sears, "Voice of Women," 79–80, 84–6; "Vietnamese Women Visit Canada" (July 1969), Voice of Women Records, SCPC.

argued that, unless a democratic regime was established, the government of the United States should abandon its military and economic role in Vietnam. Later that fall, SPU and SDS organized antiwar picketing, charging that the American government was sacrificing "the needs of the Vietnamese people to America's Cold War interests." The following year, pacifist groups and the Socialist Party sponsored the first substantial antiwar demonstration in New York City.[44] With the escalation of the war in 1965, peace organizations began the whirlwind of protests against the Vietnam War that ultimately convulsed the nation. Women Strike for Peace (WSP) organized a Mothers' March on Capitol Hill to Stop the Killing and numerous other antiwar activities. Even the antinuclear Federation of American Scientists came out strongly against the war, contending that it was "damaging to the interests of our nation, of the people of Vietnam, and of mankind."[45] Naturally, the obsession of these groups with the war undermined their antinuclear programs, which in most cases virtually disappeared. Furthermore, in this context, groups like WSP and SANE lost ground to the broad coalitions that, increasingly, directed antiwar protests, or to newer, more youthful, and sometimes more militant organizations.[46]

In other nations that sent troops to Vietnam, the war also became a source of enormous controversy, with the same debilitating effects on antinuclear activism. In Australia, the Victorian CND dissolved into the Vietnam Day Committee and the Sydney CND became the Vietnam Action Committee. Australia's revulsion against the war led to startlingly vigorous and widespread peace protests, including a turnout of 120,000 people for an antiwar demonstration in May 1970. It also broke the momentum of the antinuclear struggle, which slowly dissipated.[47] In New Zealand, the CND

44 *Sane World* (Nov. 1, 1963), 1; Philip Altbach to Advisory Council Members, Oct. 5, 1963, Class 640, Russell Archives 1; Gail Paradise to Charlie Walker, Oct. 7, 1963, box 6, Student Peace Union Records; David McReynolds to Dear Friend, Dec. 5, 1964, box 35, War Resisters' League Records, SCPC; Nancy Zaroulis and Gerald Sullivan, *Who Spoke Up? American Protest Against the War in Vietnam, 1963–1975* (Garden City, N.Y., 1984), 26.
45 Donald Keys to Norman Thomas, July 7, 1965, box 70, "March on Washington for Peace in Vietnam," box 68, series B, National Committee for a Sane Nuclear Policy Records, SCPC (hereafter SANE Records); Amy Swerdlow, *Women Strike for Peace: Traditional Motherhood and Radical Politics in the 1960s* (Chicago, 1993), 129–42, 159–86; Federation of American Scientists, "On the War in Vietnam" (Mar. 5, 1967), box 49, 1972 series, Federation of American Scientists' Records, Joseph Regenstein Library, University of Chicago.
46 Personal interview with Homer Jack, June 12, 1988; Swerdlow, *Women Strike for Peace,* 129–30, 164; "Preliminary Mobilization Memorandum," National Mobilization Committee to End the War in Vietnam Records, SCPC; Charles DeBenedetti and Charles Chatfield, *An American Ordeal: The Antiwar Movement of the Vietnam Era* (Syracuse, N.Y., 1990), 114–274, 350.
47 Summy and Saunders, "Disarmament," 32; Alan D. Gilbert and Ann-Mari Jordan, "Traditions of Dissent," in M. McKernan and M. Browne, eds., *Australia: Two Centuries of War and Peace* (Canberra, 1988), 355–7; Richard Gordon and Warren Osmond, "An Overview of the Australian New Left," in Richard Gordon, ed., *The Australian New Left: Critical Essays and Strategy* (Melbourne, 1970), 23.

issued an antiwar statement in August 1964. At the same time, however, it warned members that "we are a Campaign for NUCLEAR Disarmament, and must not lose punch by spreading ourselves too wide." But, in fact, the CND proved unable to resist the challenge of the war's escalation. At its 1965 Easter march, noted the group's *Bulletin,* "Vietnam was inevitably the issue in everyone's mind." The CND held marches, vigils, and other protests against the war and formally affiliated with the Joint Council on Vietnam, which coordinated strategy for New Zealand's emerging antiwar movement. That August, the CND reported that "the continuing crisis in Vietnam has overshadowed . . . the [antinuclear] work of the Campaign." Within a short time, the Vietnam crisis swallowed it almost completely.[48]

Even in nations not directly involved in the conflict, the trend was much the same. Some of Denmark's leading nuclear disarmament activists played key roles in protests against the Vietnam War. In Finland, the Committee of 100 organized its country's first antiwar teach-ins. In Italy, the CND staged a demonstration against the war as part of the October 1965 "International Days of Protest" and also waged an antiwar petition campaign.[49] Peace and disarmament groups in Austria, Ireland, and the Netherlands moved quickly to condemn the Vietnam War, as did the West German Campaign for Disarmament, which as early as its 1965 Easter march called Vietnam "the most dangerous focus of crisis in the world."[50] In Sweden, Bertil Svahnström, chair of the Campaign Against Atomic Weapons, announced the formation in August 1965 of a Committee for Peace in Vietnam, on which he served as international secretary. The new group brought together most Swedish peace organizations, as well as political parties and other citizens' groups, in a massive antiwar campaign.[51] In France, all the major elements of the antinuclear movement threw their energies into the struggle against the war in Vietnam. The French Movement Against Atomic Armament (MCAA) sponsored antiwar marches and helped form the Indochina Solidarity Front. To reflect its broadened concerns, in 1968 it renamed

48 *Bulletin,* Sept. 1964, May 1965; Locke, *Peace People,* 192–3; Kevin Clements, *Back from the Brink: The Creation of a Nuclear-Free New Zealand* (Wellington, 1988), 102–6; "Report from New Zealand Campaign for Nuclear Disarmament" (Aug. 21–2, 1965), folder 356, WRI Records, Amsterdam.
49 Bjol, *Hvem bestemmer,* 217; Ilkka Taipale, "The Peace Movement in Finland," in Kimmo Kiljunen et al., eds., *Finnish Peace Making* (Helsinki, 1987), 27; Giovanni Maciocia to Eric Weinburger, Oct. 23, Dec. 2, 1965, box 7, Committee for Nonviolent Action Records, SCPC.
50 Breuer, "Limits to Unilateralism," 26; News Release no. 34 (Dec. 29, 1964), box 5, WRI Records, SCPC; Everts and Walraven, *Vredesbeweging,* 44; "Frieden für Vietnam" (1965), folder 247, WRI Records, Amsterdam.
51 Bertil Svahnström, "Swedish Vietnam Committee Formed" (Aug. 23, 1965), folder 388, "Vietnam Peace Project" (1966), folder 387, WRI Records, Amsterdam; Andersson and Lindkvist, "The Peace Movement," 12.

itself the Movement for Disarmament, Peace, and Liberty. Meanwhile, abandoned by activists, antinuclear protest declined precipitously.[52]

The movement's international organizations followed a roughly similar trajectory. Turmoil over the war spilled over into the Pugwash conferences during 1965 and 1966. Pressed for action by Russell and other stalwarts, Rotblat drew on contacts with the French, Ho Chi Minh, and others to arrange a secret meeting in Paris in an unsuccessful attempt by Pugwashers to bring the conflict to an end.[53] Meanwhile, the ICDP swung into action, coordinating worldwide protests against the war. It mobilized well-known intellectuals and other prominent figures, sent a religious delegation to Hanoi, and played a key role in organizing the 1967 Stockholm conference on Vietnam. Although the ICDP, like other peace internationals, survived as an organization, it left the nuclear issue behind as it single-mindedly devoted itself to halting the Vietnam conflict.[54]

MISUNDERSTANDING THE PROBLEM

The ruthless military interventionism of the great powers, coupled with their intractable commitment to nuclear weapons, led many antinuclear activists to conclude that they faced a deeply rooted, systemic problem. This, in turn, suggested that championing nuclear disarmament was too shallow, that something more fundamental was necessary before the Bomb could be banned. Typically, Duff concluded that "the simple moral issue to which the campaigns clung as the source of all evil was a symptom rather than a cause. The invention and development of nuclear weapons coincided with and was fed by a similar escalation in the cold war." In Duff's view, an effective movement had to come to grips with the fact that "the bombs were the children of the blocs, that the blocs were the offspring of the cold war, and that the cold war was sustained and nourished by political systems" in East and West.[55] But what were the systems?

In the Soviet Union, peace activists decided that the system was the one that regularly harassed them: dictatorship.

---

52 Jolyon Howorth, *France: The Politics of Peace* (London, 1984), 29; "Pourquoi cette Marche?" (1966), folder 209, WRI Records, Amsterdam; Claude Bourdet, "Désarmement nucléaire en France," unpublished manuscript in author's possession, 1990, 8.

53 Joseph Rotblat, *Scientists in the Quest for Peace: A History of the Pugwash Conferences* (Cambridge, 1972), 64, 68–9; Rotblat to Russell, Aug. 5, 1965, Class 625, Russell Archives 1; personal interview with Joseph Rotblat, July 11, 1994.

54 Peggy Duff to Dear Friend, Oct. 1967, reel 3, British CND Records; "Vietnam: A Call for Action Now" (May 5, 1965), minutes of the ICDP Executive meeting, Jan. 27, 1966, ICDP Records; Kenneth Lee to Devi Prasad, Dec. 6, 1968, folder 151, WRI Records, Amsterdam.

55 Duff, *Left, Left, Left*, 267.

Arms control discussions [Sakharov concluded] can produce decisive results only when they are joined to the resolution of broader and more complicated problems of military-political and ideological confrontation, including questions of human rights. . . . As long as a country has no civil liberty, no freedom of information, and no independent press, then there exists no effective body of public opinion to control the conduct of the government and its functionaries. Such a situation is not just a misfortune for citizens unprotected against tyranny and lawlessness; it is a menace to international security.

Not surprisingly, Sakharov and other Soviet peace proponents increasingly championed the defense of human rights for, as he said, "in the final analysis it is impossible to achieve international security and trust without first overcoming the closed nature of Soviet society."[56] Litvinov, too, soon viewed overcoming state repression as the key to progress. All Soviet human rights activists regarded nuclear weapons with dismay, he later remarked. But they emphasized human rights because they came to believe that a victory in this realm was essential if war and nuclear weapons were to be curbed.[57]

In Western democracies, a portion of the antinuclear constituency also developed a systemic analysis and, like Soviet activists, condemned a system close at hand – in this case, capitalism. Confronted by a savage war on a poor peasant nation, accompanied by long-term racism and endemic poverty, many of America's student activists responded by turning sharply leftward. Increasingly, SDS and other youthful peace groups argued that these ills reflected a vicious American imperialism, driven by the greed of U.S. corporations. For the first time, many activists began to identify with Third World revolutionaries.[58] The same process of radicalization occurred in Canada, where the Student Union for Peace Action emerged along roughly the same lines as SDS. One Canadian New Leftist recalled, with satisfaction: "The war in Vietnam . . . shocked the peace movement out of its woolly aspirations for 'international peace' and forced it to come to terms with the operations of American corporate capitalism."[59] Indeed, in Canada, Great Britain, West Germany, Switzerland, Sweden, New Zealand, and other Western nations, a youthful New Left burst onto the scene in the

56 Andrei Sakharov, *Alarm and Hope* (New York, 1978), 117, 172–3. See also ibid., 4–5, 11, 104–5; Andrei Sakharov, *My Country and the World* (New York, 1975), 63–4.
57 Telephone interview with Pavel Litvinov, Oct. 7, 1990. See also Yuri Orlov, *Dangerous Thoughts: Memoirs of a Russian Life* (New York, 1991), 195.
58 Todd Gitlin, *The Sixties: Years of Hope, Days of Rage* (New York, 1987), 261–408; Kirkpatrick Sale, *SDS* (New York, 1974), 344–657; Nigel Young, *An Infantile Disorder? The Crisis and Decline of the New Left* (London, 1977), 174–9.
59 "Student Union for Peace Action," Student Union for Peace Action Records, SCPC; Roussopoulos, *From Protest to Resistance*, 129–30; Kostash, *Long Way*, xxiv–xxv, 3–6, 28.

late 1960s with a militantly anticapitalist, antiimperialist, and occasionally violent message.[60] Moreover, although this swing to the left developed largely among the restless young, it affected others too. In the context of the Vietnam War, even Russell dropped his calls for Soviet-American détente and promoted a sharply anticapitalist analysis, championing Third World revolution and excoriating the machinations of "U.S. imperialism."[61]

This "revolutionary" emphasis seriously undermined the movement. In Great Britain, the growing sectarianism of the British New Left and of the campaign against the Vietnam War – which disintegrated repeatedly into violent confrontations with the police – repelled numerous peace activists. American pacifists found themselves whipsawed between partisans of revolutionary solidarity and defenders of their traditional nonviolence.[62] In West Germany, the Easter marches became infused with such a revolutionary flavor that more moderate elements withdrew from them in disgust, leading to their collapse. Much the same thing happened in Austria, where radicals seized control of the 1968 Easter march and, thereby, ensured that it would be the nation's last. At the same time, the excitement and romantic appeal of revolution pulled youthful idealists away from the difficult, more humdrum, tasks of the antinuclear movement. As an historian of the British nuclear disarmament campaign has observed, with talk of revolution in the air, "CND and the whole edifice of established Labour Movement politics seemed somewhat dull, unadventurous and *passé*." In France, as Claude Bourdet has noted, MCAA branches became "greenhouses" of the near revolution of May 1968. After the student rebellion collapsed, many of them never revived.[63]

Other kinds of radical thinking also crowded the struggle against the Bomb from center stage or left it disoriented. In Great Britain, Committee of 100 activists turned toward empowering the poor through the develop-

60 Young, *An Infantile Disorder?* 158–9; Otto, *Vom Ostermarsch zur APO,* 158, 173–6; Mushaben, "Cycles," 29–30; Brassel and Tanner, "Zur Geschichte," 71; Lindkvist, "Mobilization Peaks," 159; Clements, *Back from the Brink,* 103–4.
61 Ronald W. Clark, *The Life of Bertrand Russell* (London, 1975), 602–3, 614–15; Ralph Schoenman, "Bertrand Russell and the Peace Movement," in George Nakhnikian, ed., *Bertrand Russell's Philosophy* (London, 1974), 243–5.
62 Michael Bess, *Realism, Utopia, and the Mushroom Cloud: Four Activist Intellectuals and Their Strategies for Peace, 1945–1989* (Chicago, 1993), 116–18; Howard Clark, "Nonviolent Resistance and Social Defense," in Gail Chester and Andrew Rigby, eds., *Articles of Peace* (Bridgeport, Conn., 1986), 58; Margaret Hope Bacon, *One Woman's Passion for Peace and Freedom: The Life of Mildred Scott Olmsted* (Syracuse, N.Y., 1993), 318–19.
63 Karl A. Otto, "'Ostermarsch der Atomwaffengegner': Die Friedensbewegung in der 60er Jahre," *Geschichtsdidaktik* 7, no. 2 (1982): 172–3; Gerhard Jordan, "Peace Activities in Austria Since 1945," unpublished paper in author's possession, 1; Richard Taylor, "The Labour Party and CND: 1957 to 1984," in Taylor and Young, eds., *Campaigns,* 121; Bourdet, "Désarmement nucléaire," 7–8.

ment of squatters' movements. In France, MCAA branches popularized new ideas of social transformation: ecology, *autogestion,* and feminism.[64] Moreover, as the emerging women's movement turned into a worldwide liberation struggle, it began to redefine the issue of violence, replacing the antinuclear movement's emphasis on global militarism with a focus on domestic and sexual violence. Activists in the women's movement also condemned the maternalist emphasis of women's antinuclear groups and showed little interest in joining them. Two former leaders of the Voice of Women recalled plaintively: "With . . . the emphasis on the liberation of women in the late 1960s, the young intellectuals were effectively occupied in discovering themselves and the facts of their oppression. To raise one's consciousness as a woman became to them more urgent than . . . disarmament." Even if this judgment is too harsh, the women's liberation movement certainly raised new and difficult issues for the antinuclear campaign to confront, notably by insisting that another deeply rooted system – patriarchy – was responsible for the arms race.[65]

Consequently, in the West, as in the East, many activists moved beyond emphasizing the dangers of the Bomb to developing systemic analyses. Proceeding down these lines, they became the major radicals and social critics of their time. But their systemic critiques, although laying the groundwork for an attack on an array of other important problems, failed to contribute much to the campaign for nuclear disarmament. Quite the contrary, when it came to the nuclear menace, their systemic analyses often proved either futile or debilitating. Nor, in retrospect, should this surprise us. In their desperate efforts to cope with the multiple crises of the 1960s, many activists had either lost sight of or failed to comprehend the driving force of the nuclear arms race – the pathology of the international system. And, inevitably, this misreading of the problem weakened attempts to generate a solution.

CONCLUSION

Consequently, in the mid- to late 1960s, just as the antinuclear movement was achieving its first important victories – including an atmospheric test ban treaty, a nonproliferation treaty, and other nuclear arms control mea-

64 Young, *An Infantile Disorder?* 158; Howorth, *France,* 29–30.
65 Jill Liddington, *The Long Road to Greenham: Feminism and Anti-militarism in Britain Since 1820* (London, 1989), 198–203; Macpherson and Sears, "Voice of Women," 83–4; Swerdlow, *Women Strike for Peace,* 227–31, 238–9.

sures it had demanded – it underwent a time of troubles. In part, its difficulties were endemic to a mass movement, particularly to one with this
kind of focus. In part, its troubles reflected its very success. But the movement's disarray also resulted from new international developments in the
late 1960s, from the new concerns of peace activists, and from the new
approaches they adopted to address them. In this sense, the preoccupations
of "1968" had a devastating impact on the struggle against the Bomb. Only
in the late 1970s and early 1980s, as the world seemed to lurch toward
nuclear catastrophe, did the peace movement and the public return to their
earlier concern with freeing humanity from the threat of global annihilation.

Epilogue

18

1968 and 1989

Caesuras, Comparisons, and Connections

KONRAD H. JARAUSCH

Taken as such, one-nine-six-eight and one-nine-eight-nine are merely four-digit numbers without any particular significance. But when considered as years, they can stop conversations by provoking unexpectedly emotional responses because they evoke extraordinary memories: The word "sixty-eight" conjures up images of student protests, occupied buildings, confrontations with the police, or flower children making love not war. References to "eighty-nine" produce associations of harried refugees, courageous dissidents, and powerless Stasi, as well as the overwhelming joy of the fall of the Berlin Wall. The vividness of such pictures implies that these moments possess an emotional charge that has etched them into collective memory beyond the pale recollections of normal existence. But what do these two dates have in common, other than that the number "68" stood on its head makes "89"?[1]

One answer might be that both years signify key caesuras of development after World War II that are especially pronounced in Central Europe. In private conversation, many people date developments in their own lives in reference to these startling events, whether they approve of their consequences or not. In the grand narrative of postwar history, both sixty-eight and eighty-nine mark significant interruptions, places where the story line ruptured, the plot intensified, and the direction altered. As the cliché of "turning points" indicates, such dates are used as shorthand for important and lasting changes that propel events onto a previously unlikely course. In twentieth-century Germany most historical periodization has focused on

---

1 See the cover of Timothy Garton Ash, *The Magic Lantern: The Revolutions of '89 Witnessed in Warsaw, Budapest, Berlin, and Prague* (New York, 1990).

461

the world wars and regime collapses of 1918, 1933, and 1945.[2] Despite their profound impact, 1968 and 1989 feel somehow out of place in this enumeration, suggesting that they might possess a different quality.

Perhaps a systematic comparison between these postwar caesuras can help illuminate their peculiar character by highlighting their commonalities and differences. However, hermeneutic historians might object to such an approach by arguing that differences in spatial and temporal context as well as in fundamental character make contrasting sixty-eight with eighty-nine intellectually hazardous. Although undeniable, such risks can nonetheless be minimized by clarifying what precisely is to be compared, which criteria are to be used, and how the changes are to be evaluated.[3] One of the founders of historicism, Johann Gustav Droysen, already knew that comparisons need not obliterate uniqueness but are rather essential in discovering the particular nature of a given set of events.

Comparing 1968 with 1989 is unfortunately complicated by the fierce polarization of the public discourses that surround these events. Since many adults have lived through the student revolt and the collapse of communism, personal memories are bound to color their reactions for or against. Moreover, in the construction of "history" contending ideological camps have produced contradictory narratives, with the Left celebrating the youth rebellion but deploring the failure of socialism and the Right blaming intellectuals for the outbreak of anarchy but welcoming German unification. Sometimes these antagonists seem not to be speaking of the same subject at all but of entirely different developments. To escape such rhetorical traps, historians must therefore distance themselves and reflect on their own stake in these debates.[4]

The following remarks attempt a selective comparison of 1968 and 1989 as historical caesuras in postwar development. They largely center on Germany, since it is the only place that participated both in the Western youth revolt and in the Eastern collapse of communism, major upheavals that dwarf in importance other potential watersheds.[5] As frequent references to

2 Karl Dietrich Bracher, "Zeitgeschichtliche Anmerkungen zum 'Zeitenbruch' von 1989/90," *Neue Züricher Zeitung*, Jan. 20, 1991; and Klaus Tenfelde, "1914 bis 1990 – Einheit der Epoche," *Aus Politik und Zeitgeschichte* B 40 (1991): 3–11; and Werner Müller, "Doppelte Zeitgeschichte: Periodisierungsprobleme der Geschichte von Bundesrepublik und DDR," *Deutschland Archiv* 29 (1996): 552–9.
3 Konrad H. Jarausch and Hannes Siegrist, "Amerikanisierung und Sowjetisierung – Eine vergleichende Fragestellung zur deutschen Nachkriegsgeschichte," in Konrad H. Jarausch and Hannes Siegrist, eds., *Amerikanisierung und Sowjetisierung in Deutschland 1945–1970* (Frankfurt am Main, 1997), 11–46.
4 Konrad H. Jarausch, *Die unverhoffte Einheit 1989–1990* (Frankfurt am Main, 1995), 12ff.
5 A somewhat comparable case would be Czechoslovakia where the 1968 effort to humanize socialism played a pivotal role in preparing the "velvet revolution" of 1989. See Mark Kramer's chapter in this book; for the related, but less widespread, Polish protest, see also Jerzy Eisler's chapter in this book.

sixty-eight indicate, the former has come to be accepted as the most significant turning point in the evolution of the Federal Republic of Germany (FRG), while the latter, in evasive allusions before or after the *Wende* (turnaround), demarcates the end of the German Democratic Republic (GDR) as an independent state as well as the return of national unity. The German case provides particularly suggestive contrasts since the two competing states were part of the opposing Cold War camps, therefore illuminating some of the wider trends of both sides in one contested space.

1968 AS CULTURAL REVOLUTION

From a historian's point of view, much of the literature on 1968 is rather disappointing. The further the occasion recedes in the past, the more nostalgic and inconclusive reminiscences of sixty-eighters as well as media restagings during various anniversaries become.[6] Suggesting irony and ambiguity, literary attempts at portraying the social and personal upheavals mainly help to dramatize the events.[7] In contrast, social scientists tend to ponder the causes of generational rebellion and educational analysts probe the institutional background of student revolt in comparative terms.[8] But in spite of some suggestive studies of radical organizations and evocative oral-history collages, there are hardly any comprehensive histories of sixty-eight so far, perhaps because the subject is so controversial and diffuse.[9]

In contrast to the momentous changes of other caesuras, the actual events of the year 1968 appear rather minor in retrospect. Conventional accounts of the German student revolt highlight only a handful of dramatic incidents: (1) the death of Benno Ohnesorg on June 2, 1967, during the anti-Shah demonstration in Berlin; (2) the activists' anti-Springer campaign and show trial at the end of that year; (3) the leftist anti–Vietnam War congress in February 1968; (4) the shooting of student leader Rudi Dutschke in April by a right-winger; and (5) the extraparliamentary opposition (ausserparlamentarische Opposition or APO) march on Bonn in May to protest

6 Oskar Negt, *Achtundsechzig: Politische Intellektuelle und die Macht* (Göttingen, 1995), 21ff.
7 Michael Lützeler, "Von der Intelligenz zur Arbeiterschaft: Zur Darstellung sozialer Wandlungsprozesse in den Romanen und Reportagen der Studentenbewegung," in Michael Lützeler and Egon Schwarz, eds., *Deutsche Literatur in der Bundesrepublik seit 1965* (Königsstein, 1980), 115–34.
8 Klaus Allerbeck, *Soziologie radikaler Studentenbewegungen: Eine vergleichende Untersuchung in der Bundesrepublik Deutschland und den Vereinigten Staaten* (Munich, 1973); and Philip G. Altbach and Seymour Martin Lipset, *Students in Revolt* (Boston, 1969).
9 Tilman Fichter, *SDS und SPD: Parteilichkeit jenseits der Partei* (Opladen, 1988); James F. Tent, *The Free University: A Political History* (Bloomington, Ind., 1988); and Bernd Rabehl, *Am Ende der Utopie: Eine politische Geschichte der Freien Universität Berlin* (Berlin, 1988).

the proposed Emergency Laws.[10] Even allowing for the rapid spread of mass protests to other campuses and emotional confrontations with the police, by themselves these are rather paltry affairs with few casualties, hardly the stuff of which demarcations between historical eras are usually made.

The importance of sixty-eight in public memory therefore has to rest on something else, namely, the mythologization of the struggle in the media. Protesters themselves excelled in dramatizing their agenda and picturing their movement as the heroic uprising of a critical vanguard for the oppressed within Germany and without. With witty posters, peppery handbills, rousing chants, mass marches, ingenious sit-ins or teach-ins, and other provocations, they spread their message among the student clientele. At the same time, the conservative press, led by the tycoon Axel Springer, painted the protesters in alarmist colors as ingrates and misguided children of the bourgeoisie or as dangerous revolutionaries and anarchists threatening property, order, and morality. This media contest for generational solidarity or public disapproval was largely an exercise in symbolic politics, seeking to mobilize support by means of emotion and persuasion.[11]

Beyond its symbolic power the significance of sixty-eight also derives from its ideological innovation. Breaking out of the Cold War confrontation, the New Left program contributed significantly to the revival of self-criticism within the Western camp. Today, some of its overblown texts read like a curious mixture of antifascist critiques of the elders, neo-Marxist attacks on capitalism, and participatory pleas for grassroots democracy. Some of this intoxicating cocktail derived from a desire to democratize institutions in practice; other ingredients represented a strange blend of Freudianism and the Frankfurt School; yet others were a delayed confrontation with the suppressed Nazi past. At the same time, an antiauthoritarian lifestyle sought to undermine "bourgeois" behavior through experiments with drugs, free love, communal living, and so forth.[12] One of the most fascinating aspects of 1968 is the speed with which this rhetoric and practice spread from a hard core to a broader group of youthful sympathizers.

10 Slightly modified list from Stuart J. Hilwig's chapter in this book. Cf. also Tent, *Free University*, 331ff.
11 Elizabeth Peifer argues in her dissertation, "From Event to Experience: The Myth of 1968 in German Political Culture," Ph.D. diss., University of North Carolina at Chapel Hill, 1997, that 1968 must be understood less as a series of real events than as the result of discursive contests that created a larger-than-life myth.
12 See the countless documents in Siegward Lönnendonker, Tilman Fichter, and Jochen Staadt, eds., *Hochschule im Umbruch*, vol. 5: *Gewalt und Gegengewalt 1967–1969* (Berlin, 1983); and Konrad H. Jarausch, *Deutsche Studenten 1800–1970* (Frankfurt am Main, 1983), 226–41.

Outliving the dramatic mobilization of youth, this generational revolt also triggered a series of new social movements. As forms of critique of Adenauer Germany, pacifism, feminism, and environmentalism had already begun to formulate their programs in the late 1950s and early 1960s. But the student revolt combined these separate causes into a systemic critique and spread their message to the educated segment of an entire generation where it shed its outsider status and became normative to a degree. In order to combat the bourgeois mainstream, these movements adopted many of the protest forms of the students, absorbed some of their unorthodox Marxist ideology, and endorsed much of the countercultural lifestyle. Although some of its elements were quickly commercialized, this shared protest/experience helped to produce a shift toward "postmaterialism" in the younger generation that rejected the consumerism of their parents.[13]

In a more conventional sense, the generational rebellion in 1968 accelerated a series of political reforms that ironically helped to stabilize the Federal Republic. In institutional terms, student protest initiated a gradual move toward greater participation in different institutions such as university governance. On the national level, pressure by the extraparliamentary opposition reinforced the switch from a CDU-led government to a social-liberal coalition under Willy Brandt that sought to expand the scope of the welfare state. On the international plane, the antiwar agitation also reinforced the shift toward a Central European détente in the form of the well-known Ostpolitik, which sought reconciliation with Germany's eastern neighbors.[14] Resulting from a contested interplay of New and Old Left, these departures softened some of the most objectionable features of Adenauer Germany and thereby helped save the system from more drastic challenges.

The activists' ubiquitous assault on tradition eventually produced a massive backlash that sought to undo some of its changes. Inflamed by the Springer press, the older generation, religious circles, and even much of the working class remained skeptical of the student rhetoric. Some of the ideological dogmatism inherent in the K-groups, the violence of the Baader-Meinhof terrorists, or self-destructive behavior of the communes' anarchical lifestyle seemed to bear out the critics' worst fears. Through the exaggeration of its intent, sixty-eight gradually turned into a negative sig-

13 Robert Ingelhart, *The Silent Revolution: Changing Values and Political Styles Among Western Publics* (Princeton, N.J., 1977); Sylvia and Martin Greiffenhagen, *Ein schwieriges Vaterland: Zur politischen Kultur im vereinigten Deutschland* (Munich, 1993). See also Claus Leggewie's chapter in this book.
14 Christoph Oehler, *Hochschulentwicklung in der Bundesrepublik Deutschland seit 1945* (Frankfurt am Main, 1989); Arnulf Baring, *Machtwechsel: Die Ära Brandt-Scheel* (Munich, 1984); and Gottfried Niedhart's chapter in this book.

nifier, a generalized reference point for all the changes that threatened the order, stability, and decency of the middle class. Trying to capitalize on this resentment, the center-right parties began to campaign against this symbol, demanding a *Wende* of their own so as to return to older values and safer practices.

Because of such paradoxical features, sixty-eight might best be understood as a transformational experience, a kind of "cultural revolution." Since the political system was not overthrown and economic structures remained in place, skeptics might deprecate it as a mere "epiphenomenon," a delayed modernization crisis. But such minimizing fails to explain the symbolic force of the date, which suggests that one look for other, less tangible indicators instead. What actually changed were individual consciousness, social style, and cultural temper, a whole wealth of ideas and attitudes, of personal and interpersonal relationships. Sixty-eight was a rupture of the statist tradition that opened new space for antiauthoritarianism, egalitarianism, individualism, or universalism and obliterated the distinction between high and popular culture.[15] Whereas the precise processes of change remain elusive, it is indisputable that German values and behavior did become more open and democratic after that year. This transformation is part of a wider cultural shift, also evident in other Western countries such as France and the United States.

1989 AS CIVIC REVOLUTION

Although it has had less time to develop, the debate about the fall of communism is similarly polarized between celebratory and catastrophic discourses. The German media are full of sensationalist disclosures of corruption within the Socialist Unity Party (Sozialistische Einheitspartei Deutschlands or SED) or allegations of complicity with the security police or Stasi. The public hearings of the Bundestag commission of inquiry have produced interesting testimony and lengthy expert opinions, but they ultimately became bogged down in electioneering. Surprised by the end of the GDR, social scientists theorize more about the collapse of the SED and the subsequent system transformation than they offer contextual analyses of the democratic awakening. Bothered by a lack of perspective and uncertain documentation, historians are just beginning to propose tentative

---

15 Lothar Baier et al., *Die Früchte der Revolte: Über die Veränderung der politischen Kultur durch die Studentenbewegung* (Berlin, 1988).

explanations.[16] The shock of 1989–90 is still so profound that myths of "liberation" or "colonization" dominate over sober analysis.

In causal terms, there might be several unexpected connections between the events of 1968 and 1989. The Soviet repression of democratic socialism during the unforgettable Prague Spring disillusioned Eastern intellectuals with the project of building a better Germany. Although the SED managed to repress overt unrest, artists like Wolf Biermann and Stefan Heym lost faith in communism's antifascist claims to moral superiority.[17] At the same time the Brezhnev Doctrine squelched economic reforms such as the New Economic System and launched the COMECON on the road to bankruptcy. In spite of the sealed border, some of the concerns of Western advocates of nuclear disarmament, sexual equality, and ecological consciousness eventually seeped across into the GDR. In a way, the small and embattled human rights movement of dissidents in the 1980s was a delayed response to the Eastern repression and Western reform associated with 1968.[18]

The context in which the democratic awakening unfolded was, however, quite different from the matrix of generational rebellion. In spite of its considerable authoritarian shortcomings, the FRG was at least nominally a democracy that provided formal rights that could be claimed and enlarged through protest and provocation. In contrast, the GDR was at best a *Fürsorgediktatur,* a welfare dictatorship, that took care of the basic needs of its citizens in exchange for their unquestioned political loyalty.[19] When the GDR leadership refused to follow the Soviet lead toward *perestroika,* ordinary East Germans began to find their accustomed modesty and retreat into privacy unbearable, while dissidents felt emboldened by Gorbachev. In contrast to the Western possibility of replacing the government by election, the SED was locked into Honecker's post-Stalinist dictatorship that allowed no real possibility for reform.

16 Laurence H. McFalls, *Communism's Collapse, Democracy's Demise?* (New York, 1995); Charles S. Maier, *Dissolution: The Crisis of Communism and the End of East Germany* (Princeton, N.J., 1997); and Konrad H. Jarausch, "The GDR as History: Reflections on Public Debate and Academic Controversy," *German Politics and Society* 15 (1997): 33–48.

17 Stefan Heym, *Nachruf* (Frankfurt am Main, 1990), 737ff.; Armin Mitter and Stefan Wolle, *Untergang auf Raten: Unbekannte Kapitel der DDR-Geschichte* (Munich, 1993), 367ff.

18 See Kramer's chapter in this book. Cf. also Ulrike Poppe, Rainer Eckert, and Ilko-Sascha Kowalczuk, *Zwischen Selbstbehauptung und Anpassung: Formen des Widerstandes und der Opposition in der DDR* (Berlin, 1995).

19 This term comes from Jarausch, "The GDR as History," 44. Cf. also Sigrid Meuschel, *Legitimation und Parteiherrschaft in der DDR: Zum Paradox von Stabilität und Reform in der DDR* (Frankfurt am Main, 1992), and Christiane Lemke, *Die Ursachen des Umbruchs: Politische Sozialisation in der ehemaligen DDR* (Opladen, 1991).

The actual events of the fall of 1989, while amplified by the media, were also more momentous than those of the student revolt. In human terms the mass exodus with its embassy occupations in Budapest, Prague, and Warsaw as well as its border crossings was much more compelling. It took greater courage to stand up to ruthless *Vopos* (police) or Stasi thugs in protesting for human rights than to provoke the FRG *Bullen* (cops). Through the mobilization of the Monday demonstrations in Leipzig, the civic movement accomplished what the sixty-eighters failed to do, namely, to link dissident leaders with working-class followers so as to succeed in overthrowing first a government and then a regime. Some of the programmatics of the New Forum and the hopes for a third way, cultivated by the Round Table, may have contained echoes of the student revolt, but the fall of the Wall passed all earlier efforts in symbolic and substantive significance.[20]

In contrast to the increasing radicalization of sixty-eight, the national turn during the winter of 1990 surprised participants and observers alike. When the protesters succeeded in liberating the public sphere for free expression, the timid and silent majority of East Germans articulated its own desires and repudiated the leadership of the dissidents.[21] Fed up with further attempts to reform moribund socialism and enticed by exaggerated images of Western affluence, ordinary GDR citizens chose the apparently successful system of the Federal Republic. Decades of frustration with the lack of "the thousand little things" under state planning had pent up a consumer demand that exploded with elemental force in favor of a social market economy. Even if there was little overt nationalism, the semantic shift from "we are *the* people" to "we are *one* people" was the inevitable result.

Unlike the gradual reforms triggered by the student revolt, the transformation of East Germany after unification was abrupt and thorough. Not only did the accession of the five new states to the old FRG introduce a Western parliamentary system with human rights and an elaborate social safety net in eastern Germany, but the collapse of the GDR also initiated a massive reconstruction from above and from the outside, in which the Trust Agency (*Treuhandanstalt*) dissolved the large-scale state monopolies and converted them into smaller private companies, owned mostly by Western firms. Although ample transfer payments from Bonn cushioned the shock,

20 Elisabeth Pond, *Beyond the Wall: Germany's Road to Unification* (Washington, D.C., 1993); Jarausch, *Unverhoffte Einheit,* passim; and Maier, *Dissolution,* 108ff.
21 Jens Reich, *Rückkehr nach Europa: Zur neuen Lage der deutschen Nation* (Munich, 1991), 204ff., and Dirk Philipsen, *We Were the People: Voices from East Germany's Revolutionary Autumn of 1989* (Durham, N.C., 1993).

the social result of this deindustrialization was devastating unemployment, especially for women. As if these changes were not brutal enough, the switch to the Western system also purged academic institutions and instilled a competitive, pluralistic culture that devalued Eastern competence and spurred extensive disorientation.[22]

Dissatisfied with the lack of ideological innovation, some former sympathizers of sixty-eight have labeled eighty-nine a *nachholende Revolution,* a mere attempt to catch up with the advanced West. No doubt the recovery of human rights and parliamentary politics as well as the restoration of a welfare capitalism were efforts to restore what had been propagated in 1848 or 1918 and lost after 1945. The return of a reduced form of unity in a German national state also fits this pattern.[23] But echoes of sixty-eight in the dissident agenda regarding peace, gender equality, ecology, and human rights also went beyond older democratic aims. Although illusory, the hopes for a third way did not reject socialism in order to restore capitalism but rather intended to make a qualitative leap into a postsocialist and post-capitalist world.[24] While ordinary people looked to the West, intellectuals possessed a utopian vision that sought to transcend both German pasts.

Although the meaning of 1989 remains contested, it might be considered a new type of "civic revolution," aiming at a rebirth of civil society. Interpreting the overthrow of the SED as a collapse of communism begs the question of agency, but explaining it through the mobilization of the masses links 1989 to earlier popular upheavals such as 1918 or 1848. No doubt the stagnation of the planned economies and the erosion of Soviet control were essential preconditions, but the Charter 77 movement in Czechoslovakia, the Polish Solidarnošc (Solidarity) union, and the German peace movement fought not just for the recovery of civil rights but also for the construction of a new form of civic self-organization. Although the postunification blues has made many dissidents repudiate the term, the democratic awakening in East Central Europe seems to herald a different kind of bloodless revolution, seeking to free civil society from a totalitarian state.[25]

22 Helga Welsh, Andreas Pickel, and Dorothy Rosenberg, "East and West: United and Divided?" in Konrad H. Jarausch, ed., *After Unity: Reconfiguring German Identities* (Providence, R.I., 1997), 103–36.
23 Jürgen Habermas, *Die nachholende Revolution* (Frankfurt am Main, 1990); and Ralf Dahrendorf, *Reflections on the Revolution in Europe* (New York, 1990).
24 See, e.g., Helga Köningsdorf, *1989 oder ein Moment der Schönheit* (Berlin, 1990); and Stefan Heym, *Die sanfte Revolution: Prosa, Lyrik, Protokolle, Erlebnisberichte, Reden* (Leipzig, 1990).
25 Manfred Hettling, ed., *Revolution in Deutschland? 1789–1989* (Göttingen, 1991). Jarausch, *Unverhoffte Einheit,* 112ff., 205ff., 303ff.; and the specious critique of Hartmut Zwahr, "Die Revolution in der DDR im Demonstrationsvergleich: Leipzig und Berlin im Oktober und November 1989," in

COMPARING 1968 AND 1989

Due to this mixture of resemblances and differences, comparisons between 1968 and 1989 are at once intriguing and frustrating. The temporal and spatial distance, the incommensurability of the contexts, the particularity of their respective actors and agendas, and the distinctiveness of their events and results complicate systematic contrasts between these events. Nonetheless, East German dissidents and West German observers acted in 1989 on the basis of their memories of 1968 and frequently invoked comparisons between the two sets of developments. When a leading GDR dissident tried to explain the need for reform to a Western sixty-eighter, he argued tellingly, "You had your sixty-eight and we didn't."[26] Such a comparison is legitimate because it is not just a mind game of historians but a part of the record itself.

On a certain level of abstraction, a systematic comparison can uncover a number of striking similarities between the caesuras of 1968 and 1989. For the sake of clarity, it might help to look at such criteria as the international context, the process of mobilization, the techniques or aims of the protesters, and the achievements or results of their protests.[27] Because the detailed discussion of these dimensions would exceed the bounds of this chapter, a few suggestions have to suffice as an indication of some of the potential resemblances.

Both upheavals were part of wider international changes that also engulfed neighboring countries and only assumed a particular intensity in Germany due to its terrible past and divided present. Each rupture required certain enabling conditions that were the result of transnational developments such as the American defeat in the Vietnam War in the 1960s and the waning of Soviet control in Eastern Europe in the 1980s. In both cases wider trends, such as the spread of the peace movement and the example of *perestroika*, emboldened internal protesters to take to the streets. In a way, the two revolts were a challenge against the respective hegemonial power, namely, the United States in 1968 and the Soviet Union in 1989.[28] Whereas the Nazi legacy reinforced the generational rebellion but delayed the break

---

Manfred Hettling and Paul Nolte, eds., *Nation und Gesellschaft in Deutschland* (Munich, 1996), 335ff.

26 Quoted in the introduction to Peifer's dissertation on the mythologization of 1968.

27 For a different kind of comparison, focusing on the role of the intellectuals, see Rüdiger Bubner, "How Philosophy Failed to Grasp Its Time in Thought," paper presented at the conference "1968: The World Transformed," Wissenschaftszentrum Berlin, May 23–5, 1996.

28 See George C. Herring's and Lawrence S. Wittner's chapters in this book.

with the antifascist SED, the division limited the student revolt to West Germany and the democratic awakening to East Germany.

In both cases participants experienced a sense of palpable excitement, a feeling of a historic confrontation, a perception that something major was about to change. Although difficult to explain, this shift in perception played an essential role in mobilizing protesters by suggesting that their actions might actually have some positive effect. The half-heartedness of repression led to a great increase in actionism such as demonstrations and resolutions, in which people who had been mute suddenly dared to voice their own demands. In both social movements students or intellectuals also played a vanguard role in articulating popular disagreement with the system and in providing the initial spark that eventually started a wider conflagration. Within this unparalleled politicization, a tension remained between the neo- or post-Marxist aims of the leaders and the more practical participatory hopes of their followers.[29]

Both movements successfully used civil rights techniques of nonviolence, borrowed from Mahatma Gandhi and Martin Luther King Jr., in order to dramatize their demands. This strategy of peaceful protest, which made clever use of the new medium of television, was predicated on an enemy who behaved repressively but nonetheless observed some limitations on the use of force.[30] Both challenges to their respective systems pursued a democratic agenda of expanding popular participation and their aims of postmaterialism and a third way sought to carve out a space between communism and capitalism. In their rhetoric these movements were a peculiar blend of modest reformism, directed toward remedying concrete abuses, and visionary utopianism, demanding an entirely new world. Each started in the social and extraparliamentary realm but eventually sought a transformation of politics.

Both revolts produced major changes in their countries, revitalizing public discourse and initiating changes that overthrew repressive structures and expanded citizens' rights. The generational rebellion of 1968 reinforced the domestic and international reform agenda of the social-liberal coalition in West Germany, whereas the civic rising of 1989 liberalized the post-Stalinist SED so fundamentally that it ceded power in East Germany almost

---

29 Negt, *Achtundsechzig*, 60ff.; Steven Pfaff, "Collective Identity and Informal Groups in Revolutionary Mobilization: East Germany in 1989," *Social Forces* 75 (1996): 91–118. See also Gilcher-Holtey's chapter in this book.
30 The methods of the protesters are underanalyzed for 1968. For 1989, see Gerhard Rein, *Die protestantische Revolution* (Berlin, 1990).

without a fight.[31] But each upheaval also had largely unintended consequences that limited the achievement of their original aims and deflected
their impetus into different directions. One consequence of the student
revolt was the terrorist violence of the Red Army Faction (RAF), whereas
the democratization of the GDR unexpectedly led to national unification.[32] If one abstracts a pattern of democratic renewal from both sixty-
eight and eighty-nine, these otherwise disparate events begin to exhibit
some remarkable similarities.

A closer look at 1968 and 1989, reveals, however, many differences that
are so fundamental as to undermine some of the surface similarities. Especially when one descends from generalizations into the peculiarities of each
situation and examines the actual sequence of events, the distinctions loom
larger. Here somewhat different criteria of the character of the system,
composition of the movements, specific ideological aims, and ultimate
impact of changes may be more enlightening. Their cursory application to
each respective upheaval serves to highlight some of the following distinctions.

In spite of the perceived repressiveness of each government, the difference in the nature of the respective system, such as the FRG of the 1960s
and the GDR of the 1980s, was rather considerable. West Germany was,
after all, a capitalistic democracy with irritating authoritarian features,
whereas East Germany was essentially a Communist dictatorship, only softened by extensive social provisions.[33] Symbolically represented by the
impenetrability of the German-German border, the international context
also produced different results in the divided country. As part of the West,
the FRG became caught up in its transnational youth revolt while East
Berlin remained quiet. But as member of the Eastern bloc, the GDR was
involved in the repudiation of communism while Bonn cheered from the
sidelines. The constant comparison with the other side, resulting from
being on the front line between hostile ideological blocs, initially favored
repression but eventually hastened revolt.[34]

Although there was a generational aspect to both protests, it operated
differently in both situations. The sixty-eighters were largely students,

---

31 Gale Stokes, *The Walls Came Tumbling Down: The Collapse of Communism in Europe* (New York,
    1993). Maier, *Dissolution,* 108ff., does not explicitly mention 1968 in his discussion of the Central
    European pattern of revolution. Cf. Jarausch, *Unverhoffte Einheit,* 309ff.
32 Jillian Becker, *Hitler's Children* (Philadelphia, 1977), and Peter Merkl, *German Unification in the Euro-
    pean Context* (University Park, Pa., 1993).
33 This difference is sometimes forgotten, which leads to a simplistic equation of both systems. Cf.
    Jürgen Kocka, *Die Vereinigungskrise: Zur Geschichte der Gegenwart* (Göttingen, 1995), 9ff.
34 Peter Bender, *Episode oder Epoche? Zur Geschichte des geteilten Deutschland* (Munich, 1996).

reacting also against the overcrowding of the universities, but this group was demonstratively absent in 1989, since it was highly ideologized by the SED. In contrast to the quiescence of thirty-five to forty-five-year-olds in the 1960s, white-collar workers, intellectuals, or artists of this age group, who resented the mendacity of the system, were the initial dissidents of 1989.[35] To the chagrin of the activists, the working people remained generally disinterested in the 1960s, but their mobilization provided the crucial mass base for the success of the Leipzig demonstrations during the fall of 1989. In consequence, sixty-eight became essentially an academic affair, whereas mass participation eventually turned the democratic awakening into a direction quite different from the wishes of its dissident mentors, organized in the New Forum.

Scrutiny of the evidence also demonstrates that the ideological programmatics differed rather fundamentally between both movements. Whereas the generational revolt was motivated by an antifascist revulsion against the unacknowledged complicity of their elders with the Third Reich, the democratic awakening eventually turned this critique on the GDR itself and developed a leftist form of anticommunism that revived the totalitarian model.[36] In contrast to the self-professed Third World internationalism of the student rebels evident in the Che Guevara cult, the majority of the East German citizens in the winter of 1989 rediscovered national solidarity as the quickest way toward a freer and better life. Whereas anti-Vietnam protests turned the sixty-eighters toward an anticapitalist form of anti-Americanism, GDR citizens overcame their propaganda clichés and embraced the blandishments of Western consumer society, ignoring all postmaterialist warnings of leftist intellectuals.[37]

In spite of their common role as caesuras, both ruptures had fundamentally different consequences. By dramatizing the authoritarianism of the university system, cultural institutions, gender relations, and individual lifestyles, the student revolt undoubtedly triggered important reforms in West German culture and society. Gained through a patient institutional struggle of the new social movements, such as pacifism, feminism, and environmentalism, this change of consciousness took years to achieve.[38] In

---

35 Klaus R. Allerbeck, *Soziologie radikaler Studentenbewegungen* (Munich, 1973), and Klaus-Dieter Opp and others, *Die Volkseigene Revolution* (Stuttgart, 1993).

36 Alf Lüdtke, "'Coming to Terms with the Past': Illusions of Remembering, Ways of Forgetting Nazism in West Germany," *Journal of Modern History* 65 (1993): 542–72; and Konrad H. Jarausch, "The Failure of East German Anti-Fascism: Some Ironies of History as Politics," *German Studies Review* 14 (1991): 84–102.

37 Hubertus Knabe, ed., *Aufbruch in eine andere DDR: Reformer und Oppositionelle zur Zukunft ihres Landes* (Hamburg, 1989); and Reich, *Rückkehr nach Europa,* 204ff.

38 Gerd Langguth, *Suche nach Sicherheiten: Ein Psychogramm der Deutschen* (Stuttgart, 1995), 21ff.

contrast, the overthrow of the post-Stalinist dictatorship had more immediate and drastic effects, since it did not stop with a reform of the GDR but
led to the complete dissolution of the second German state. The unexpected unification with West Germany introduced the successful FRG patterns into eastern Germany, thereby totally transforming the political, economic, social, and cultural pattern of East German lives.[39]

Such fundamental differences caution against any facile conflation of the
two sets of events. Viewed at a high level of generality, sixty-eight and
eighty-nine might have been somewhat equivalent attempts at democratizing seemingly oppressive regimes, but their contexts, origins, and out-
comes radically differed. Although they appeared dramatic at the time, difficulties in the FRG, such as the overcrowding of universities and the
revulsion against the Vietnam War, turned out to be less deep-seated than
did problems in the GDR, such as economic stagnation and political repression by a one-party dictatorship. In spite of much initial bumbling, the
democratic system of the Federal Republic proved flexible enough to be
reluctantly transformed, whereas the Communist GDR, after an initial
attempt to remake itself, ceased to exist.[40]

RELATIONSHIPS BETWEEN 1968 AND 1989

Perhaps more illuminating than a comparison between student revolt and
democratic awakening might be an exploration of their potential relationships.[41] Since both sets of events took place within one short generation,
there are likely to be substantive connections between them, and their
understanding might be mutually refracted in popular parlance and academic analysis. In terms of causation, one key question is whether there
were any actual influences, learning processes, or programmatic echoes
between 1968 and 1989. In terms of perception, an important issue might
be how images of the generational rebellion continue to define the German Left and how interpretations of the fall of communism tend to legit-
imize the rise of a New Right.[42] Perhaps some answers to these queries can

---

39 Konrad H. Jarausch and Volker Gransow, eds., *Uniting Germany: Documents and Debates, 1944–1993*
     (Providence, R.I., 1994). See also Michael Thomas, ed., *Abbruch und Aufbruch* (Berlin, 1992).
40 Ronald Fraser, *1968: A Student Generation in Revolt* (New York, 1988). For the eighteenth-century
     historian Robert Darnton, the key reference point was instead the French Revolution of 1789; see
     Berlin Journal, 1989–1990 (New York, 1991).
41 Christoph Klessmann argues in favor of such a relational analysis of postwar history in the intro-
     duction to Christoph Klessmann and Georg Wichert, eds., *Das gespaltene Land: Leben in Deutschland
     1945–1990: Texte und Dokumente zur Sozialgeschichte* (Munich, 1993).
42 See the article series in the *Frankfurter Allgemeine Zeitung* on "What's Left" in 1992 and the subse-
     quent discussion on "What's Right" in 1994.

be found in a look at the process of learning from the events and at the construction of their memories.

In most respects, the lessons of 1968 for 1989 appear to have been positive. The internal democratization in West Germany that was accelerated by the student revolt helped refute Communist accusations of neo-Nazism and made the Federal Republic more attractive to the East Germans. At the same time, the brutal repression of democratic socialism in Czechoslovakia broke the loyalty of many intellectuals to the GDR and limited the ideological appeal of Marxism in the FRG. Moreover, the example of a largely peaceful mass movement that demanded the democratization of an authoritarian system proved instructive, even if the SED did everything in its power to discredit it as anarchistic. Finally, some of the agenda of the subsequent new social movements trickled across the Wall because it addressed pressing problems that were largely ignored in the GDR.[43]

As a source of ideological identity, the relationship of eighty-nine to sixty-eight seems more problematic and contested. Because they still define themselves in reference to 1968, many West German leftists have misunderstood eastern dissent as a reprise of their own protests, hoped that it would achieve some of the things that they had failed to reach, and been disappointed in the result.[44] Because the Right always considered the cultural revolution of the 1960s deleterious, it sought to use the opportunity of unification to undo its effects on the larger Germany. In a well-orchestrated campaign, this self-styled "generation of eighty-nine" called for greater international assertiveness, the revival of German nationalism, the restoration of male authority, and the like. New Right resentment transformed sixty-eight from a shining example into a caricature of everything that seemed wrong in society and polity.[45] Both years therefore continue to hold magic power in defining group membership, ideological stance, and cultural style.

The most important connection between these dates lies in their symbolic meaning as reference points for important changes in postwar Germany. Popular opinion and academic analysis have accepted 1968 and 1989

43 Mary Fulbrook, *Anatomy of a Dictatorship: Inside the GDR, 1949–1989* (Oxford, 1995), 193ff., 201ff.

44 Fritz Haug, *Versuch beim täglichen Verlieren des Bodens unter den Füßen neuen Grund zu gewinnen: Das Perestroika-Journal* (Hamburg, 1990); and Konrad H. Jarausch, "The Double Disappointment: Revolution, Unification, and the German Intellectuals," in Michael Geyer, ed., *The Power of Intellectuals in Germany* (Chicago, 1997).

45 Ulrich Greiner, "Die Neunundachtziger," *Die Zeit,* Sept. 16, 1994; and Wolfgang Engler, "Der aufgeschobene Streit," *Die Zeit,* Nov. 4, 1994. Cf. also Konrad H. Jarausch, "Normalisierung oder Re-Nationalisierung? Zur Umdeutung der deutschen Vergangenheit," *Geschichte und Gesellschaft* 21 (1995): 571–84.

as the two overriding caesuras since the end of World War II that fundamentally transformed the character of the successor states and thereby prepared the return of national unity. In contrast to earlier turning points such
as 1918, 1933, or 1945, these ruptures involved neither lost wars nor the
establishment of a dictatorship, but rather peaceful efforts to gain greater
participation. As part of transnational currents of youth revolt and communist collapse, these later caesuras did not pit Germans against their neighbors but reinforced their place in the general pattern of Western development. For these reasons, both mark different contributions to the gradual
emergence of a democratic political culture in Germany.[46]

The challenge of this dual legacy is the construction of a democratic
tradition for a united Germany. Unlike earlier catastrophes, these two efforts
to enlarge the space of individual self-determination represent, in spite of
some exaggerations and unfortunate consequences, aspirations that might
serve as the foundations for a more liberal self-image. As a sometimes confused but exuberant attempt to break with authoritarian traditions, the student revolt exudes a subterranean fascination that still continues to inspire
some youth today. Similarly, the self-dissolution of the post-Stalinist dictatorship through courageous dissidents, reform communists, and mobilized
masses has created a model of what a docile people can achieve when sufficiently aroused. Even if they remain contested, the memories of these
democratic moments can serve as positive examples for the building of a
new, postnational Germany.[47]

Ultimately, the symbolic dates sixty-eight and eight-nine possess a wider
significance that transcends Central European concerns. The cultural revolution of 1968 was "a departure which in its contradictions moved the
entire Western world" and yielded "a gain in liberality for all." Despite its
misguided Marxist theorizing, the youth rebellion succeeded in strengthening antiauthoritarian tendencies, participatory desires, and postmaterialist values in the West. In contrast, the Eastern bloc repression of the con-
current attempt to create a "socialism with a human face" in Prague stripped
the socialist project of creating an egalitarian alternative to capitalism of its
moral credibility. Unwilling to reform until Gorbachev's halfhearted steps,
the communist system therefore became a casualty of the "velvet revolu-

---

46 Konrad H. Jarausch, "Die postnationale Nation: Zum Identitätswandel der Deutschen 1945–1995,"
     Historicum (spring 1995): 30–5. Cf. also Peter Merkl, *The Federal Republic of Germany at Forty-five:
     Union Without Unity* (New York, 1995).
47 Heinrich August Winkler, "Rebuilding of a Nation: The Germans Before and After Unification,"
     Daedalus 123 (1994): 107–27; and Kocka, *Vereinigungskrise,* 133ff.

tion" of 1989.[48] Ironically, the youth rebellion helped save the Western system against which it protested, whereas the democratic awakening two decades later ended up dissolving socialism in Eastern Europe rather than revitalizing it. For all their differences, these pivotal dates therefore suggest a continuity across the blocs in the struggle to enlarge the domain of human dignity.

48 Robert Leicht, comparing 1968 with 1989 in *Die Zeit,* Oct. 7, 1994, and Hartmut Zwahr, "Auch die DDR hatte ihr 68-er Erlebnis: Der Prager Frühling weckte die Hoffnung auf Wandel," *Die Zeit,* June 11, 1993.

Index

Turkey in 1968, 304–7; student protests in, 304–5

UFT, 409–10
UFV, 393
Ulbricht, Walter, 115–16, 121, 127–9, 142, 159, 188, 389
UNEF, 259–60
Union nationale des étudiants de France (UNEF), 259–60
United Federation of Teachers (UFT), 409–10
United Socialist Party of Poland (PSU), 268
United States: centrist politics in, 228–30; and China, 52; civil rights movement in, 397–403, 411–20; economic consequences of 1968 in, 83–110; federal budget deficit in, 90; foreign assets vs. liabilities in, 99; gold stocks in, 101; Holocaust awareness in, 434–8; liberalism in, 219–36; national-defense outlays in, 89; race relations in, 397–420; as televisual society, 10; violence in, 221, 225, working class in, 370, 413
Ustinov, Dmitrii, 159
Utley, Garrick, 75
utopias, social, 258

Vester, Michael, 18
Vietcong, *see* Tet Offensive
Vietnam syndrome, 52
Vietnam War: atrocities in, 421; Chinese perspective on, 205–6; and détente, 31–3; and domestic consequences for United States, 35; and economic consequences in United States, 88–91; effect of, on nuclear-disarmament campaign, 450–4; financial expenditures for, 35; My Lai massacre during, 436; and NATO, 34–5, 42, 49–51; opposition to, 16, 17, 25–6, 221, 288, 375, 403–4, 425–6, 437, 463; on television, 55–81, 405; U.S. involvement in, 221, 231; and U.S.-Japanese relations, 17
Vietnamization, 36, 48, 53
violence: in China, 201; in civil rights movement, 399–400, 406–7; racial, 412, 418; in United States, 221, 225
Voice of Women (VOW), 441
voting rights, 417
Voting Rights Act, 93
VOW, 441

Wallace, George C., 232–5, 412–13, 420
Wander, Maxie, 390–2; *Guten Morgen, Du Schöne,* 390
War on Poverty, 86, 232, 402–3
Warren Commission, 225
Warsaw Letter, 147–8, 168
Warsaw Pact, 4–5, 13, 20, 22–3, 111; Albania excluded from, 118; and Brezhnev Doctrine,

169–70; and coercive diplomacy, 145–51; and cohesion among states, 112; collapse of, 137; Czechoslovakia's membership in, 135–6, 138, 161, 169; East Germany's role in, 116; effect of, on student revolt, 247, 250; and interoperability and standardization of armaments, 113; media on, 135; and Middle East relations, 120; and NATO, 179; and normalization between two Germanys, 187; and nuclear sharing, 114, 140; and political reforms and military actions, 123, 139, 141, 146, 149–50; and Prague Spring, 127–9, 132, 141–2; and real vs. paper alliance, 113–14; severs ties to Israel, 240; Soviet hegemony in, 114
Webster, Don, 71, 74
Wehner, Herbert, 182
Welt, Die (newspaper), 328, 329, 332, 334, 336
West Germany, *see* Federal Republic of Germany
Western Group of Forces, 160–1
Westmoreland, William C., and Tet Offensive, 39–40, 43, 47, 56, 60–3, 68–70, 72–3, 76–7, 80, 90
Westpolitik, 189
Wheeler, Earle G., 38–40, 46, 50, 56–7, 71–2, 80
Whiting, Allen, 206n52
Wiesel, Elie, *Night,* 435
Wilkins, Roy, 402–3, 407–8, 411
Wolf, Christa, 390–2; *Nachdenken über Christa T.,* 390
Wolff, Frank, 327
Wolff, Karl, 327
women: equal rights of, in East Germany, 386–8, 392–4; exclusion of, from East German politics, 386, 392; Polish, and ties to Jews, 241
women's movements, 16, 25; on autonomy, 382–4; in East Germany, 373, 385–95; emergence of, in East and West Germany, 374–80, 392–4; after German reunification, 395; and literary feminism in East Germany, 390–2; new, in West Germany, 376, 381–5; success of, West German, 384–5; in West Germany, 373–85, 394–5
Woodward, C. Vann, 411
workers' movements: in Czechoslovakia, 356–7, 364; European, 351; in France, 260, 262–5, 351–4, 362–4; in Italy, 348, 351–2, 354–6, 363–4; in Spain, 356–7, 363–4, 367
working class: alienation in, 360; European, 351–71, Italian, 358; men of, in George Wallace's constituency, 413; and point of production emphasis, 367; and unskilled as force of change, 357–9; *see also* new working class
World Bank, 61, 85